How to access the supplemental web study guide

We are pleased to provide access to a web study guide that supplements your textbook, *Sport Marketing, Fourth Edition.* This web study guide features exclusive video interviews with leaders in the sport industry, offering insight into how they incorporate marketing strategies into their daily work. Activities built around these clips guide you in using core concepts from the text to answer questions about the applied situations in the interviews. Web search activities also provide opportunities for you to compare strategies found on sport organization websites, YouTube, and other online locations.

Accessing the web study guide is easy!
Follow these steps if you purchased a new book:

1. Visit **www.HumanKinetics.com/SportMarketing**.

2. Click the <u>fourth edition</u> link next to the corresponding fourth edition book cover.

3. Click the Sign In link on the left or top of the page. If you do not have an account with Human Kinetics, you will be prompted to create one.

4. If the online product you purchased does not appear in the Ancillary Items box on the left of the page, click the Enter Key Code option in that box. Enter the key code that is printed at the right, including all hyphens. Click the Submit button to unlock your online product.

5. After you have entered your key code the first time, you will never have to enter it again to access this product. Once unlocked, a link to your product will permanently appear in the menu on the left. For future visits, all you need to do is sign in to the textbook's website and follow the link that appears in the left menu!

→ Click the Need Help? button on the textbook's website if you need assistance along the way.

How to access the web study guide if you purchased a used book:

You may purchase access to the web study guide by visiting the text's website, **www.HumanKinetics.com/SportMarketing**, or by calling the following:

800-747-4457 . . . . .U.S. customers
800-465-7301 . . . . .Canadian customers
+44 (0) 113 255 5665 . . . . European customers
08 8372 0999 . . . . Australian customers
0800 222 062 . . . . .New Zealand customers
217-351-5076 . . . . .International customers

For technical support, send an e-mail to:
support@hkusa.com . . . . U.S. and international customers
info@hkcanada.com . . . . Canadian customers
academic@hkeurope.com . . . . European customers
keycodesupport@hkaustralia.com . . . . . Australian and New Zealand customers

HUMAN KINETICS
The Information Leader in Physical Activity & Health

04-2014

Product: Sport Marketing, Fourth Edition, web study guide

Key code: MULLIN-QE2AL4-OSG

This unique code allows you access to the web study guide.

Access is provided if you have purchased a new book. Once submitted, the code may not be entered for any other user.

Sport Marketing

FOURTH EDITION

Sport Marketing

FOURTH EDITION

Bernard J. Mullin, PhD
Aspire Group

Stephen Hardy, PhD
University of New Hampshire

William A. Sutton, EdD
University of South Florida

Human
Kinetics

Library of Congress Cataloging-in-Publication Data

Mullin, Bernard James.
  Sport marketing / Bernard J. Mullin, Stephen Hardy, William A. Sutton. -- Fourth edition.
     pages cm
  Includes bibliographical references and index.
  1. Sports--Marketing. I. Hardy, Stephen, 1948- II. Sutton, William Anthony, 1951- III. Title.
  GV716.M85 2014
  338.4'3796--dc23

                              2013031098

ISBN-10: 1-4504-2498-8 (print)
ISBN-13: 978-1-4504-2498-1 (print)

The web addresses cited in this text were current as of December 2013, unless otherwise noted.

Acquisitions Editor: Myles Schrag; **Developmental Editor:** Amanda S. Ewing; **Assistant Editor:** Casey A. Gentis; **Copyeditor:** Bob Replinger; **Indexer:** Andrea J. Hepner; **Permissions Manager:** Dalene Reeder; **Graphic Designer:** Nancy Rasmus; **Graphic Artist:** Dawn Sills; **Cover Designer:** Keith Blomberg; **Photograph (cover):** Layne Murdoch/NBAE via Getty Images; **Photo Asset Manager:** Laura Fitch; **Photo Production Manager:** Jason Allen; **Art Manager:** Kelly Hendren; **Associate Art Manager:** Alan L. Wilborn; **Illustrations:** © Human Kinetics, unless otherwise noted; **Printer:** Courier Companies, Inc.

Printed in the United States of America   10 9 8 7 6 5 4 3 2 1

The paper in this book was manufactured using responsible forestry methods.

Human Kinetics
Website: www.HumanKinetics.com

United States: Human Kinetics
P.O. Box 5076
Champaign, IL 61825-5076
800-747-4457
e-mail: humank@hkusa.com

Canada: Human Kinetics
475 Devonshire Road Unit 100
Windsor, ON N8Y 2L5
800-465-7301 (in Canada only)
e-mail: info@hkcanada.com

Europe: Human Kinetics
107 Bradford Road
Stanningley
Leeds LS28 6AT, United Kingdom
+44 (0) 113 255 5665
e-mail: hk@hkeurope.com

Australia: Human Kinetics
57A Price Avenue
Lower Mitcham, South Australia 5062
08 8372 0999
e-mail: info@hkaustralia.com

New Zealand: Human Kinetics
P.O. Box 80
Torrens Park, South Australia 5062
0800 222 062
e-mail: info@hknewzealand.com

E5690

Guy Maxton Lewis, 1926-2013

We dedicate this book to the memory and legacy of Professor Guy M. Lewis, a true genius and visionary. Guy was a key founder and builder of undergraduate and graduate programs in sport studies and sport management at both the University of Massachusetts and the University of South Carolina. Throughout his long and active career, he constantly searched for ways to integrate the theoretical with the practical, scholars with practitioners. His professional contributions include the North American Society for Sport History, the Sport Management Arts and Sciences Conferences at UMass, and the International Sports Business Conferences at South Carolina. We happily consider ourselves among the many students, colleagues, and professional associates who have benefitted from his wisdom and counsel. He will be missed. His contributions will endure.

Contents

Chapter 1   ## The Special Nature of Sport Marketing   **1**

Chapter 2   ## Strategic Marketing Management   **27**

Chapter 3   ## Understanding the Sport Consumer   **57**

Chapter 4   ## Market Research in the Sport Industry   **87**

Contributors

Leigh Buwen
Manager of Consumer Research
Turnkey Intelligence

Kathy Connors
Principal and Founder
KMC Consulting, LLC

Kirsten Corio
Vice President, Team Marketing and Business
  Operations
NBA

Jaclyn Cranston
Senior Manager of Sales and Service
Turnkey Intelligence

Evelyn Dwyer
Manager of Consumer Research
Turnkey Intelligence

Jay Gladden
Dean and Professor
School of Physical Education and Tourism
  Management
Indiana University–Purdue University
Indianapolis

John Grady
Associate Professor
University of South Carolina

Haynes Hendrickson
President
Turnkey Intelligence

Steve McKelvey, JD
Associate Professor
University of Massachusetts Amherst

Nikolay Panchev
Vice President of Consumer Research
Turnkey Intelligence

Steve Seiferheld
Senior Vice President of Consumer Research
Turnkey Intelligence

Foreword

As my 30 years as NBA commissioner comes to an end, I can't help but reminisce about just how far the sport industry has come during this period. Perhaps nowhere is this growth more evident than in sport marketing. It is hard to believe that just 30 years ago when the authors of *Sport Marketing, Fourth Edition,* wrote their original manuscript, the term sport marketing was rarely used. Now, the term is common and regularly used to encompass all of the activities in this book—activities that accurately depict the evolution of the sport industry as I have experienced it during my tenure at the NBA. I have had the good fortune of working with many of the most talented executives in the industry. As the industry has evolved, so have the leadership and business capabilities of the teams. Now, most of our teams have more than 100 employees who sell tickets and sponsorships; provide great customer service; develop marketing, advertising, and branding strategies; activate platforms for marketing partners and sponsors to drive their businesses; produce TV and radio broadcasts locally; service the media and place proactive messages; develop and produce the shows; and do meaningful work in the community through innovative and socially responsible programs. This latest edition continues to place those activities in a comprehensive framework, showing how the moving parts work together to develop the sport business locally, nationally, and globally; and it refreshingly illustrates where the use of new technologies now play their essential part. Particularly insightful are the data collection, aggregation, delivery, and targeting technologies used in ticket marketing and sales and for increasing fan engagement using content delivered predominantly via mobile devices.

The principal authors have a combination of academic and professional experience that is extraordinary. Their education and experience as university professors provide them with unique perspectives. Their research and analytical skills lead to objectivity and an ability to identify key industry needs. The theoretical framework they have created into which every marketing strategy is set—the marketing planning process—leads to a consistency in all branding, sales, and marketing strategies. Better yet, the authors have practical experience in the field in senior executive capacities covering several segments of the sport industry, which has given them a wealth of knowledge on best practices and the understanding of what actually works and what doesn't. Collectively, they have implemented just about all of the best practices firsthand for leagues, sport conferences, and the most challenging of all situations, start-up teams and turnarounds.

I have observed the work of the authors for almost fifteen years as they contributed to the way NBA teams conduct their business. Clearly the most significant contributions were the substantial increase in the sharing of best practices and real data, increased adoption of direct marketing techniques, focus on the customer "driveway to driveway" experience, and the basis of teams' business strategies on the authors' landmark work—the attendance frequency escalator. As a result, most NBA teams today have much more sophisticated database-building and customer relationship management (CRM) capabilities. The teams more effectively use proactive outbound fan relationship management centers or telemarketing sales and intelligently targeted e-marketing programs that are designed to increase trial, improve retention, and drive attendance. These successful teams focus on the stepping-stone approach to fan development: Encourage more people (particularly youth) to play the game, connect players and coaches more favorably with the community, get more fans to watch or listen to broadcasts, progressively encourage fans to get off the couch or off the computer or mobile device and sample the NBA game in person, and offer a full menu of full- and partial-season ticket plans designed to move fans up the attendance frequency escalator. The greatest benefit of this approach has been a significant increase in the lifetime value (LTV) of fans in the respective team markets, and ultimately, the league itself.

Mixing in their unique intellect and personalities, the authors use their vast academic and practical experience to make this book a must-read for future generations of sport marketers, managers, and perhaps even commissioners in their "retirement."

David J. Stern
Commissioner, National Basketball Association

Preface

There is only one way to describe the massive changes in the sport world since the first edition of *Sport Marketing* came out in 1993: "Holy cow!" as the late Harry Caray always put it. In 1993 most people would have thought that the Internet was a spy ring and that a web page was something in a newsletter of Ducks Unlimited. When our second edition appeared in 2000, the Internet was old hat, but it was still the most innovative medium of the age. File sharing was just beginning in 2000. And what of the concept of social media? In 2000 Internet nerds would have thought that YouTube was a phrase deriding old media. Hardly. By 2007 YouTube.com had become the hottest site on the Internet. More than a million video clips were viewed each day, many of them sporting events. In 2014 we can add Facebook, Twitter, Instagram, and other social media as both products and experiences that have transformed the way that consumers engage sport. And just about everything has gone wireless, especially with the explosive growth of smartphones. Marketers have adapted. Executives throughout the sport world get their industry news and data through online services such as SportsBusinessDaily.com and SBRnet.com, and trade publications, such as *Street & Smith's SportsBusiness Journal* and *Athletic Business,* have online versions. But they all employ social media and wireless technologies to gather and dispense information. We have incorporated many of the latest marketing ideas in this edition, but new products and services are emerging daily.

Some things haven't changed much. The competition for the sport and entertainment dollar is as heavy as ever. Sport marketing is a competitive business involving as much front-office strategy, risk, discipline, and energy as that shown by the players and coaches who figure so prominently in the public's imagination. The fourth edition of *Sport Marketing* offers abundant examples of the latest issues in the competitive marketplace.

As academics, we have been studying changes in the sport industry for over 40 years, long before *Forbes* and *Fortune* began to take sport seriously with regular coverage. When we started out as graduate students in the early 1970s, few scholars were willing to accept sport as a serious topic of study. Now leading academics in marketing, management, law, and economics (to name only a few disciplines) are rushing headlong for book contracts on sport. We have both followed and helped build this growing body of literature. More important, each of us has also worked *inside* the industry, trying to make sense of the ways that fans, players, coaches, the media, equipment companies, and others interact to make the game tick. We have planned, administered, or consulted on literally thousands of events across just about every sport considered mainstream and at just about every level. This book emanates from our own fusion of experience as academics and practitioners. We have written a survey that we hope is as useful for the classroom student as it is for the athletics director of a college or high school or the marketer of a professional franchise.

We have tried to balance theoretical models with case studies from the rinks, fields, courts, slopes, gyms, tracks, and other venues that make up the sport marketplace. If theory is the skeleton that gives structure to thinking, then case studies put meat on the bones. Although most of our examples are from the United States, we have added considerable material from sports in other countries and cultures.

Readers of past editions will find both continuity and change in this book. Chapters 1 through 3 provide an overview of the sport market and sport marketing as an area of study and as a process. Chapters 4 (by Haynes Hendrickson, Steve Seiferheld, Nikolay Panchev, Jaclyn Cranston, Leigh Buwen, and Evelyn Dwyer of Turnkey) and 5 consider conceptual tools and steps of preliminary market research and market segmentation, which are critical to overcoming a tendency to equate promotions with marketing. Chapters 6 through 13 explore the nuts and bolts of marketing plans—the five Ps of sport marketing: product, price, promotion, place, and public relations. But these Ps are conceptually robust, so readers will note special chapters or chapter sections on branding (Jay Gladden), sales and service, engagement and activation, community relations (Kathy Connors), and social media (Kirsten Corio). The last three chapters

eBook

available at
your campus bookstore
or HumanKinetics.com

offer some important elements on legal issues (Steve McKelvey and John Grady), control, evaluation, and projecting the future. The book is filled with sidebars written by other industry and academic leaders. We thank them all for their contributions.

The world of sport marketing continues to challenge and excite us. We only hope that this edition is as enjoyable to read as it was to write.

Web Study Guide

A new and exciting addition to the fourth edition is the web study guide (WSG), which gives students the opportunity to listen to sport industry leaders talk about how they incorporate marketing strategies into their daily work through exclusive video clips produced by David Perricone, who has experience as an academic and practitioner. Activities are built around these video clips, asking students to do what these industry experts already do: integrate core concepts and strategies from the textbook into applied situations.

Besides the video-based exercises, the web study guide has web search activities in which students will assess and compare strategies that can be found on sport organization websites, YouTube, and other online locations. These two activity types ensure that students will have even more opportunity to engage in the material found in these pages. Throughout the book, students are directed to the web study guide with cross-references like this:

ACTIVITY 1.2 The Global Marketing Strategy

College sport marketing has traditionally been centered in the United States. In this WSG activity, you will learn how a globalized marketplace is changing college sports.

The web study guide is available at www. HumanKinetics.com/SportMarketing.

Instructor Resources

A full array of instructor resources are available:

- **Presentation package plus image bank**: The presentation package includes more than 400 slides that cover the key points from the text, including 30 select figures and tables. Instructors can easily add new slides to the presentation package to suit their needs. The image bank includes all the figures and tables from the book, separated by chapter. These items can be added to the presentation package, student handouts, and so on.

- **Instructor guide**: The instructor guide includes a sample syllabus and ideas for semester-long activities and case studies. Individual chapter-by-chapter files include a chapter summary, chapter objectives, chapter outline, and classroom ideas, which include the suggestion of case studies from the online journal *Case Studies in Sport Management.*

- **Test package**: The test package includes more than 200 questions in true–false, multiple-choice, fill-in-the-blank, and short-answer formats. These questions are available in multiple formats for a variety of instructor uses and can be used to create tests and quizzes to measure student understanding.

- **Chapter quizzes**: New to the fourth edition are chapter quizzes. These LMS-compatible, ready-made quizzes can be used to measure student learning of the most important concepts for each chapter. More than 150 questions (8 to 10 questions per chapter) are included in true–false, multiple-choice, fill-in-the-blank, and short-answer formats.

Instructors can access these ancillaries by visiting www.HumanKinetics.com/SportMarketing.

Acknowledgments

Our chapter notes acknowledge the sources that we have used. In addition, we offer special acknowledgments to a number of people. The first is David Stern, one of the premier sport marketing minds in the world. We thank David for giving two of us the opportunity to work in the NBA as well as for sharing his insights and providing daily inspiration through his strategic marketing initiatives. We also recognize the contributions and value of the late Bill Veeck, whose writings and innovations continually remind us of the importance of the fans and sport consumer behavior. Likewise, we appreciate Mike Veeck because he has done the same and has forced us to examine our own practices and approaches when we forget about the fans. On the academic side, we are indebted to Philip Kotler for his numerous contributions to the field of marketing, which have influenced our thinking in terms of sport marketing. We have dedicated this edition to Dr. Guy Lewis, who has been instrumental in shaping the academic coursework and program content for many of the undergraduate and graduate programs in sport management. Matt Levine of SourceUSA, one of the original and leading sport marketing consultants who helped shape the study of sport consumer behavior, has also continued to inspire our thinking. We acknowledge the many academics who contribute to *Sport Marketing Quarterly* and are members of the Sport Marketing Association (SMA). The research of our academic colleagues and their tireless preparation of the sport marketers of tomorrow provide constant inspiration and motivation to us.

We also offer special thanks to our chapter and sidebar contributors: Melissa Rosenthal Brenner, Leigh Buwen, Ward Bullard, William Carafello, Catherine Carlson, Leigh Castergine, Kathy Connors, Kirsten Corio, Jaclyn Cranston, Lou DePaoli, Ari de Wilde, Evelyn Dwyer, Jay Gladden, John Grady, Shane Harmon, Adam Haukap, Chris Heck, Haynes Hendrickson, Jeff Ianello, Dae Hee Kwak, Amber Lilyestrom, Jordan Maleh, Amy Jo Martin, Steve McKelvey, Brian Norman, Nikolay Panchev, Dave Perricone, Sarah Sceery, Jared Schoenfeld, Susan Schroeder, Steve Seiferheld, Chad Seifried, Dr. Alan Seymour, Peter Stringer, Jennifer Tobias, and Eric Woolworth.

Many other people helped us obtain, organize, and develop materials for the book. Mia Ramer, Madison Southerlin, and Ben Holmes at the Aspire Group did research work to update data on participation, demographics, and other sidebar facts. University of South Florida graduate students Kristine Carcione, Kayla Chesanek, Katie Hatch and Amanda Puccinell also contributed their expertise. Abe Madkour and the staff at *SportsBusiness Daily* (now an essential resource for anyone trying to make sense of the sport industry) have been ever gracious with their help and permissions. Abe also contributed his views on the future in our last chapter. Others who have given constant support and inspiration include Dot Sheehan, Steve Metcalf, and Marty Scarano of the University of New Hampshire and Roger Godin of the Minnesota Wild. Thanks also to Kirstin Kay and Tanya Downey at the University of Massachusetts, Amherst for providing us with the picture of Guy Lewis on the dedication page.

This book could not have been done without the help and dedication of our editors from Human Kinetics—Myles Schrag and Amanda Ewing. They whipped us, encouraged us, and coddled us as the time and case required. They are outstanding professionals.

In our capacities as sport administrators and consultants, we have worked with hundreds of dedicated executives, marketers, coaches, salespersons, customer service professionals, public and community relations personnel, and sports information directors who have inspired us with their energy, dedication, and passion. As academics, we thank and salute our colleagues and students over the years at the University of Washington, Robert Morris University, Ohio State University, the University of Massachusetts, the University of New Hampshire, the University of Central Florida, and the University of South Florida. These colleagues and students have challenged, stretched, reshaped, and indulged our thinking on all the topics in this book. We hope that we can convey to our readers their wisdom, their enthusiasm, their wonder for learning, and their passion for moving the field forward.

Photo Credits

Chapter 1

The Special Nature of Sport Marketing

OBJECTIVES

- To understand the market forces that create the need for enlightened marketing strategies in the sport industry
- To understand marketing myopia and other obstacles to successful marketing strategy
- To recognize the components of the sport product and the sport industry
- To recognize the factors that demand a different approach to the marketing of sport

Sports Illustrated was clear in its assessment: "Nothing, anywhere, has ever resembled the ascendance of Jeremy Shu-How Lin, a legend seemingly pulled from the imagination of a goose-fleshed David Stern, if not Disney's most hyperbolic global marketing exec." And this was only five games into Linsanity or Linmania or . . . Linmarketing. Overlooked out of Palo Alto High School, taunted with racial slurs while playing at Harvard, undrafted and twice cast off by NBA teams, Lin made the most of his February 2012 chance with the New York Knicks. He was an early Valentine gift for his team, for Madison Square Garden, for the NBA, for the world of basketball, and for sports fans everywhere. Oh, and don't forget marketers. Nine games into the drama, Lin had led the Knicks to an 8-1 record as he threw up all-star numbers by averaging 25 points, 9.2 assists, and 3.8 rebounds per game. Both Lin and the Knicks cooled off a tad by the All-Star break at month's end. By mid-March they had suffered a losing streak that mirrored the earlier run of wins. The team changed coaches. And then Lin went down with a season-ending injury, fueling an equally strong conversation with a long lineage in sport. Would he last in the league, or would he flame out? In July 2012 the Houston Rockets ensured the story's extension when they signed free agent Lin to a three-year, $25.1 million deal.[1]

Time would tell whether Jeremy Lin endured in the NBA. But action on the court was only half the story. Linsanity, regardless of how long or short the run, offered a miniseries on the world of sport marketing in the early 21st century. Jeremy Lin was both a player and a product to be branded, monetized, and distributed in a global system. He embodied key ingredients of the successful sport brands of the era.[2]

Stickiness

Jeremy Lin and his performance held the public's imagination because they contained all the elements that Chip and Dan Heath claimed were crucial to the "stickiness" of any product or idea:

- Simplicity—Basketball statistics are simple. Unlike the economy or the political landscape, basketball did not require observers to unravel or parse complicated formulas or polls in considering Lin's performance.

- Unexpectedness—Few basketball experts predicted that Lin would even play in the NBA, let alone be a phenomenon.

- Concreteness—No conceptual fuzziness was involved in watching a YouTube clip of Lin highlights.

- Credibility—This question would loom large over time, as it does with every player in every sport, at every level. Jeremy Lin was the real deal in February 2012. Would he hold up?

- Emotion—One look at the way Lin played or the way that fans responded in Madison Square Garden revealed great depth of emotion.

- Narrativity—Lin's background, his struggle to succeed, and his triumph (however brief) were the fodder for endless stories.

International Reach

As with David Beckham in world football and Alex Ovechkin in ice hockey, stories about Jeremy Lin played up his following across continents, in this case to China. One mid-February report from China noted that "The clearest sign that Jeremy Lin's appeal has spanned the Pacific to mainland China may lie not in the 1.4 million Chinese microblog [Twitter-like] messages mentioning him in recent days, but in a rare failure to meet demand here in the heart of one of the world's largest centers of pirated garment manufacturing." As one store clerk near Shanghai noted tellingly, "His jerseys have sold out, even including the counterfeit ones." A Chinese friend of Lin reported that Lin highlights were streaming out of mounted video monitors along the Beijing subway. "Everyone thinks it's crazy in the U.S.," said Cheng Ho, "but it's a much bigger storm here in China." For two decades, sport properties (players, teams, leagues, events, venues) had expanded their market horizons from the national to the global. China was on everyone's mind, especially in basketball. After all, 65 million Chinese viewers had watched their national team play a preliminary match against Greece in the 2010 FIBA World Championships held in Istanbul. That figure far exceeded the 24 million who watched Butler versus Duke in the 2010 NCAA Men's Basketball Championship. Jeremy Lin might not solve America's trade imbalance with China, but he was surely contributing.[3]

Link to Social Identity

Lin was a symbol of many things to many people. He was hope to underdogs of any nationality, especially those of Chinese heritage, and especially on the Chinese mainland, where a Communist party chief posted a microblog focusing on Jiaxing—the home of Lin's maternal grandmother. Xi Jinping, vice president of the People's Republic, happened to be visiting Barack Obama when Linsanity was at an apex. He told the *Washington Post*, "I do watch NBA games on television when I have time." Only four months earlier, party leaders had announced a new initiative to promote "spiritual affluence" and "creativity" so that Chinese culture—with "core socialist values"—might match other Chinese products on the export market. With the great Yao Ming in retirement, apparently the capitalist NBA's Jeremy Lin would do in the short run. But if Chinese Communists wanted to claim him, so did Chinese Christians, who emphasized his great grandfather's conversion and hoped that young Jeremy's success and faith would help their cause. So did Taiwanese, because Jeremy's family had fled the mainland. Like most popular players and teams, Jeremy Lin could symbolize many things to many people.[4]

Media Squabbles

For many in the New York metro area, Linsanity was the condition caused by an inability to watch the Knicks on television. At the height of the mania in mid-February, some 2.5 million New York state Time Warner cable customers could not watch the Knicks because of a squabble over carriage costs demanded by the MSG network, which televised Knicks games. One Chinatown resident summed up the frustration. "It doesn't make sense," he complained, "for a New Yorker to not be able to watch their home teams." Welcome to the dollars and cents world of sport product distribution, where teams and leagues have formed television networks (e.g., Big Ten, Pac 12, University of Texas) that require carriage on a cable system, preferably on a standard platform that reaches all customers, and returns a hefty per-customer fee. In other words, every new sports network wants the deal that ESPN has. Negotiations in New York turned bitter and led to a 48-day blackout. In this case Linsanity won the day. Governor Andrew Cuomo and public pressure corralled the two firms to reach a deal, in time to watch Lin and the Knicks cool off. Given the ever-rising rights fees that networks have paid to teams and leagues, however, we may expect more squabbles and more blackouts for sports fans.[5]

Valuation, Monetization, and Marketing Metrics

Just a few decades ago, a meteor like Jeremy Lin would have been measured solely by playing stats and salary. Although Lin's numbers were closely followed, the media circulated an equal amount of information on his value as a commodity. As *Sports Illustrated*'s Pablo

> continued

Torre reported, three weeks of Linsanity had spiked stock in the MSG Corporation (owner of the Knicks) by 11 percent. The Knicks online store had seen traffic and sales skyrocket by over 4,000 percent. The MSG cable channel had seen its metro ratings rise 70 percent. An area sporting goods chain had sold over 50,000 items of Lin merchandise. Over the first week of the run, Lin got more social media buzz than President Barack Obama. Even after the cool-down, fan interest kept rising. Two late February games drew ratings over 7.3 for the MSG Network, both higher than the regular-season record set in 1995 for a game that featured Michael Jordan redux. On the other hand, when Lin injured his knee, sales of Lin merchandise suffered. The Modell's sporting goods chain was stuck with 40,000 items to sell. His July free-agent departure to Houston cut T-shirt prices from $20 to $5; replica jerseys sank from $60 to $20, and that was the day after the Knicks announced that they would not match the Houston offer. [6]

In 2012 Jeremy Lin was a product that captured attention, emotion, and sales on an international stage. Despite sport scandals of all stripes—racism in the English Premier League, endless doping sagas in cycling, match fixing in cricket, a cover-up of pedophilia at Penn State—fans around the world remained eager to embrace someone like Jeremy Lin, who combined hard work with inherent talent and made the most out of his chance, no matter how long it lasted. In many respects, he was simply repeating a fundamental sports story, only he was living and playing in a rapidly changing marketplace.

Although entrepreneurs have been selling sport for centuries, rational systems of marketing sport are relatively new. In this chapter, we discuss the need to employ modern marketing principles in the sport domain. We examine sport industry trends in growth and competition that heighten the need for scientific, professional approaches to sport marketing. We consider examples of lingering marketing myopia in sport, as well as significant progress. Next, we consider the components of the sport product and the sport industry. Finally, we outline the numerous features that in combination make sport marketing unique.

ACTIVITY 1.1 Recent History of Sport Marketing

In this WSG activity, you will consider how sport marketing has changed in the past 30 years, why sport is unique to marketing compared to traditional products, and how sport marketing professionals can be more successful in their work.

The NBA and Global Marketing Strategy

Jeremy Lin is a marketing parable, but so is the NBA. Over the last three decades, David Stern emerged as lord of a far-flung, international empire inappropriately called the National Basketball Association. When Stern became commissioner in 1984 (he had been NBA general counsel since 1978), the NBA was a struggling enterprise, despite having stars such as Magic Johnson and Larry Bird. Teams were playing in arenas filled to less than two-thirds capacity, NBA merchandise sales were only about $15 million, and network television coverage was limited—the finals were shown on tape delay. Worse yet, corporate sponsors were scared off, in large part because of a poor public image resulting from drug scandals and labor strife. As one NBA executive recalled in a 1991 profile of Stern, "If you had 30 minutes with a prospective sponsor, your first 20 minutes were spent trying to convince him that the players weren't all on drugs."[7]

Even before his elevation to the commissionership, Stern had laid the foundation for the NBA to become one of the most successful brand names in sport. He did it by recognizing and using standard tools of marketing. He knew, among other things, that product recognition required a more expansive television package. In turn, the broadcast networks demanded a more stable product with a cleaner image. That meant getting owners and players to agree on several fundamental issues, including revenue sharing, salary caps, and tougher drug testing. As a Spalding executive concluded, "A good marketing guy knows that he has to get the product right before marketing it. That's what Stern did with basketball."[8]

If Stern spent the 1980s getting his product right, he focused the next decades on worldwide product distribution. More than anything, Stern believed in going global. The NBA could create an empire along the lines of British mercantilism—with fine, finished products moving from North America to distant centers of exchange like Moscow, Buenos Aires, Cape Town, and Beijing—especially Beijing. Some surveys conducted in 2003 suggested that among China's more than 1 billion people, basketball had supplanted soccer in popularity. In the first four years of the new millennium, the Chinese edition of the NBA's *Time and Space* magazine had boomed to a circulation of over 200,000. NBA games were a regular Sunday feature on China Central Television. NBA logos adorned the apparel worn by the coolest kids on China's hoop courts, which now drew the crowds once reserved for Ping-Pong tables.[9]

By 2004 the NBA finals were broadcasted to 205 countries in 42 languages. The international traffic on NBA.com was well over 40 percent of the total; the league had nine foreign-language websites. Yao Ming was only the tallest of the internationals on NBA rosters; the total number had expanded from 65 in 2002–2003 to 84. The synergy was obvious. For instance, Dirk Nowitzki's success with the Dallas Mavericks translated into five television outlets in Germany. And every new foreign star meant more foreign exposure. By October 2004 the NBA had 212 international television deals.[10]

Much of the NBA's success stemmed from what might be called an open-architecture strategy in its global expansion. That is, the focus of

effort was as much to promote basketball as it was to promote the NBA brand of basketball. The NBA did not initially look to enter markets with total product control. In 1987 David Stern visited Beijing with the simple notion that Chinese national television, CCTV, might be interested in showing weekly NBA highlights for a share of advertising revenues. That arrangement slowly grew to include live games broadcast on provincial and local television stations during Michael Jordan's heyday. When Yao Ming joined the NBA in 2002, the stream of distribution and revenues turned into a torrent. Run-of-the-mill games drew up to 15 million viewers for morning broadcasts and triple that number for a game with Yao. Stern was hardly alone in his China strategy. In 2009 alone foreign enterprises invested $572 million on 34 sport projects. From 2000 through 20009, total foreign sport investment increased 12-fold. The NBA learned by hard experience that the Chinese wanted partners to build their own talent and their own league, the CBA, and Chinese Central Television could be a hard-nosed negotiator. Stern and his associates have suspended their notions of an NBA China, instead planning for exchanges for Chinese referees and coaches to obtain advanced training in the United States and for a player's academy in southern China. Working with China as a partner fits with David Stern's long view that what is good for the global game will be good for the NBA.[11]

Stern's "soft power" approach to global presence has paid off in many ways, not least of which is a good working relationship with FIBA, the game's international governing body. In early 2011 FIBA secretary general Patrick Baumann, a Swiss, told the international *SportsPro Magazine* that David Stern ranked among the three most influential people in the history of basketball. "The NBA is probably the very best at marketing its league," he emphasized. Although not conceding on the level of organization or growing the game, he noted that on "the exploitation of the rights and making this property a valuable property from a commercial standpoint, I think there is no other league than the NBA."[12]

The global economy also boosted prospects for other sport leagues. The National Hockey League and Major League Baseball, for instance, both attracted top talent from overseas, such as

David Stern (center, holding trophy) has helped to turn the NBA into a global empire.

Europeans to the NHL and Asians to MLB. But the flows of commerce worked along multiple currents. Russia's Kontinental Hockey League and Japan's Nippon Professional Baseball have attracted top players and coaches from North America. Expanding sports networks deliver televised events across countries and continents. Americans have ESPN, Canadians have TSN, and Europeans have Eurosport. The Middle East has Al Jazeera Sport; Australians have TVN. And this is only a short list. The most pronounced consequences of such circulation occurred in world football, the globe's number one game. FIFA, the international governing body, reported that television coverage of the 2010 World Cup in South Africa "reached over 3.2 billion people 'in-home' around the world, or 46.4 per cent of the global population, based on viewers watching a minimum of over one minute of coverage." Every country and territory on the globe had viewers. Staggering though the number is, it did not even

include "people watching out-of-home at the FIFA Fan Fests and other public viewing venues, as well as in pubs, bars, restaurants, clubs, hotels, or even online and via mobile handsets."[13]

In football's global market, the world's talent moved to European leagues, especially England's Premiership, Italy's Serie A, and Spain's La Liga. If the NBA looked to Europe and China for expansion markets, the Europeans saw America as ripe for the picking. A steady swell of youth soccer players, "soccer moms," and their families had provided a strong base for the United States' successful hosting of World Cups in 1994 (men's) and 1999 (women's). Major League Soccer, hatched after the 1994 World Cup, was averaging crowds over 15,000 by 2004, better than those in Argentine and Dutch leagues. By 2011 the MLS average had increased to 17,872, a respectable size when compared with other leagues, as shown in table 1.1. North America appeared to have arrived as a market for world football.

TABLE 1.1   Average Attendance in Selected World Football Leagues

League	Country	Average	Season
Bundesliga	Germany	45,134	2011–2012
Campeonato Brasileiro Série A	Brazil	14,976	2011
Chinese Super League	China	17,651	2011
Eredivisie	Netherlands	19,538	2011–2012
J League 1	Japan	15,797	2011
La Liga	Spain	30,275	2011–2012
Major League Soccer	USA	17,872	2011
Premier League	England	35,283	2010–2011
Primera División de México	Mexico	25,837	2010–2011
Serie A	Italy	24,031	2010–2011

List of attendance figures at domestic professional sport leagues.

Data from http://en.wikipedia.org/w/index.php?title=List_of_attendance_figures_at_domestic_professional_sports_leagues&oldid=497203914, accessed 15 June 2012.

ACTIVITY 1.2 The Global Marketing Strategy

College sport marketing has traditionally been centered in the United States. In this WSG activity, you will learn how a globalized marketplace is changing college sports.

Weathering Recessions

Global competition was shifting the realities of the sport marketplace at the turn of the 20th century. So were the economic booms and busts. As early as 1998, *Street & Smith's SportsBusiness Journal* asked the headline question "Is Sports Business Recession-Proof?" The answers were mixed. Most industry insiders said yes (no surprise). But some bankers and economists were less certain. Randy Vataha, an investment banker (and an NFL alum), worried about the 1990s buildup of luxury seats that would likely be threatened by a recession. As the stock market bubble reached its peak, the ESPN Chilton poll announced that the last half of the 1990s had seen a *decrease* in the percentage of Americans who considered themselves fans of the NFL (–3.06 percent), the NBA (–11.38 percent), the NHL (–8.57 percent), college basketball (–8.45 percent), and college football (–6.37 percent), all this despite general increases in aggregate attendance.[14]

The next decade saw both dot-com and real estate bubbles burst—the first in 2000, the second in 2008—unleashing recessions to wreak havoc on economies at the national and household levels. The effects on sport were palpable, as a few examples suggest:

- Sport-related construction slipped 7.9 percent in the United States between 1999 and 2001. This decrease was in contrast to the 22.3 percent increase in overall construction spending during the same period.[15]

- Overall attendance in Major League Baseball went significantly down and up twice over the decade, in tune with the economy. The downturn in 2009 was an aggregate 5,220,345 (6.64 percent), the highest overall decline in history and the fourth largest percentage decline. Only slightly behind was the 2002 decline of 4,448,769 (6.30 percent). League attendance bounced back in both cases, but it was a tense roller coaster ride.[16]

- Franchises, especially in the minor leagues, were stressed to their limits. In early 2009 the Southern Professional Hockey League lost two franchises. Richmond (VA) Renegades GM Allan B. Harvie Jr. repeated the obvious and painful reality: "The economy has driven a spike into the heart of the leisure-time market and fans have very hard choices to make with their money." Successful teams were not spared. Although the EPL's Chelsea sold out all 24,000 season tickets in 2011, they had softness in sales of premium seats that went for $1,000 per game and with luxury boxes.[17]

- Corporate sponsors, especially in the financial sector, were forced to rethink their expensive partnerships with sport properties. Many reduced or dropped their deals. The Royal Bank of Scotland was a good example. In February 2009 the venerable institution, which faced nearly £30 billion in losses, announced that it was cutting its sport funding by half.[18]

- In 2012 the Football League, the English association of 72 professional clubs playing in tiers below the Premier League, saw a 26 percent decline in its three-year television broadcast package with the Sky network, from $420.5 million to $316.6 million.[19]

- Sport wasn't the only sector affected. The wider entertainment industry was also reeling. *Rolling Stone* reported that attendance at North American music shows dropped an "astonishing" 24.4 percent in 2010 compared with 2009. Gross sales were down 26 percent, in part because the number of concerts was down 16 percent. Promoters weren't taking chances.[20]

Teams and leagues responded in emergency fashion. In the fall of 2008, the New Jersey Nets gave season-ticket holders an extension on payment until January 2009. The Indiana Pacers didn't even charge their season-ticket holders for preseason games, a loss they estimated at $2 million. That same year, English Premier League clubs started to slash ticket prices; for example, Newcastle cut prices by 9 percent on average, and Manchester City reduced prices by 7 percent.[21]

Even the NFL, about as close to bulletproof as a sport league can be, had to respond to soft demand. Ticket sales were way off for the 2009 Super Bowl, held in Tampa. Only days before kickoff, StubHub could not unload 3,000 tickets. A spokesman quipped, "In terms of pricing, this game has become the Limbo Bowl—how low can it go?" *SportsBusiness Journal* surveyed the league's 32 teams in late summer 2009 as the national and world economy kept sagging. The basic question was this: How have you responded

to the recession? All but three franchises reported either a ticket price freeze or new initiatives in sales closer to those used in the NBA or MLB. Only four teams had raised prices across the board—almost a given in the good old days. Many teams rolled out new group-ticket packages, staged special meetings between coaches or executives and season-ticket holders, or offered miniplans. All these tactics have been outlined in earlier editions of *Sport Marketing*. The recession had prompted NFL action. As the St. Louis Rams COO put it, "The days of rolling out the football and expecting to sell out are done."[22]

Longtime pollster Rich Luker remained gloomy about the American market in late 2010 after two solid years of surveys indicated nagging consumer concerns about the ability to spend on sport. He said, "Let's face it: We are not getting past this any time soon." That same fall a reader's survey by *SSSBJ* found that 28.9 percent of respondents, the largest segment of respondents by a wide margin, ranked rising ticket prices as the biggest threat to sport. The next top threat was disconnect with fan base, a reason chosen by 19.8 percent of respondents. Luker's pessimism seemed confirmed by some striking attendance drops among college basketball powers. In early 2012 the *Chronicle of Higher Education* analyzed NCAA Division I men's basketball attendance. Although overall numbers had held steady, some significant drops had occurred at local and regional levels. Between 2009 and 2012, Arizona State dropped over 40 percent in attendance. The Pac-12 overall dropped 14 percent. Missouri dropped by 21 percent, and Indiana declined by 15 percent. The Atlantic Coast Conference slid 7 percent overall.[23]

The Competitive Marketplace

Economists and journalists have occasionally cobbled together estimates on the size of America's sport industry. Unfortunately, each study has employed different methods and different assumptions. Consequently, we have no longitudinal data tracking sport industry growth over time, using generally agreed-upon methods. In any case, one must recognize that the sport industry, by any calculation, is a small piece of the economic pie. For instance, one study pegged the

1995 gross domestic sport product at $152 billion, claiming that sport was the 11th largest industry in the American economy. That figure would equal $229 billion in 2012 dollars. The overall 1995 GDP, however, was $7.4 trillion (in 2012 dollars), meaning that despite widespread media attention, sport accounted for just 3 percent of overall GDP. A more recent, and more conservative, approach found that the aggregate demand and aggregate supply of the 2005 sport industry ranged between $44 and $73 billion. Given that year's $12.6 trillion GDP, even the higher number ($73 billion) amounted to a paltry .6 percent of overall GDP.[24]

Other data suggest that the American sport market is growing only slightly. For instance, past Census Bureau figures have shown that in 1970, recreation accounted for 4.3 percent of total personal consumption. By 1980 recreation had grown to 5.3 percent of total personal consumption. As table 1.2 illustrates, recreation's piece of the consumption pie continued to expand until it plateaued in the 9 percent range in the last two decades. The statistics were mixed, however, for spectator sports. In 1970, Census figures suggested that spectator sports admissions accounted for 3.9 percent of the total recreation consumption pie. That number shrank over the next decade to 2.8 percent in 1980. Table 1.2 shows that spectator sports continued the slump to a mere 1.52 percent in 1990 before seeing a small but steady increase. And where is the recreation dollar going? As table 1.2 suggests, the video,

audio, computer, and musical goods segment has grown more steadily in the last decade as a percentage of all recreation expenditures. One might argue that spectator sports events simply can't expand like DVRs or iPods or smartphones. Sport requires an infrastructure of fields and stadiums, which are slow to develop. And some argue that many people are using their smartphones or tablets to view sport. All this is true. At the same time, competition for the discretionary dollar is heated. This competition is especially fierce inside the sport industry.

Of course, competition is the nature of sport. For well over a century, entrepreneurs and investors have jostled for market space, particularly in professional team sports. Sport in America offers several examples. The troubles of professional baseball are internal these days, but the history of the game is punctuated by a number of wars among rival leagues, the last threat being the Continental League in the early 1960s. Football took center stage in the 1960s with the rivalry between the American and National Football Leagues. The World Football League and the U.S. Football League followed in the 1970s and 1980s. In 2000 two sport magnates—Dick Ebersol of NBC and Vince McMahon of the World Wrestling Federation—announced a new competitor, the XFL. Like many of its predecessors, however, the XFL died after its inaugural 2001 season. Another interesting market battle was in women's pro basketball, in which the Women's National Basketball Association (WNBA) and the

TABLE 1.2   Spectator Sports, Amusements, and the Consumption Pie, 1990–2009

Product or service (in billions)	1990	1995	2000	2005	2008	2009
Total recreation expenditure	314.7	449.8	639.9	807.4	916.0	897.1
• As a percentage of total personal consumption	8.2	9.0	9.4	9.2	9.1	9.0
Spectator sports admissions	4.8	7.4	11.6	16.3	20.5	20.7
• As a percentage of total recreational expenditures	1.52	1.64	1.81	2.01	2.23	2.30
Video and audio equipment, computers, and related services	81.1	119.3	184.4	239.4	273.3	265.2
• As a percentage of total recreational expenditures	25.77	26.5	28.8	29.65	29.8	29.56

Dollar amounts in billions, indexed or chained to 2005 dollars.

Adapted from U.S. Dept. of Commerce, Statistical Abstract of the United States, 2012, Table #1233 Personal Consumption Expenditures for Recreation 1990–2009, 761; dollar values (2005 index) explained on 431–42.

American Basketball League (ABL) offered consumers alternative visions of a "big league" until the ABL dissolved in early 1999. The successful Women's World Cup of 1999 spawned the first women's professional soccer league (WUSA), which opened in 2001 with eight teams. By September 2003 the league had collapsed. Another attempt (WPS) in 2009 lasted three seasons, but was shut down in 2012.[25]

In December 2011 *SportsBusiness Daily* published Harris Poll data from 1985 to 2011 that tracked the favorite sports among U.S. fans (defined as adults who follow at least one sport). The results are suggestive. Baseball had been the favorite of 23 percent in 1985, a close second to pro football (24 percent). By 2011, however, baseball had slipped steadily to be a favorite of only 13 percent of American adults—tied with college football. Meanwhile pro football had grown to be the heads-on favorite at 36 percent. Auto racing had grown slightly—from 5 percent to 8 percent, as had hockey—from 2 percent to 5 percent. Tennis had dropped from 5 percent to 2 percent. Other sports had been flat or shifted 1 or 2 percent in a very low range. Of course, a fan might avidly follow more than one sport. But the data clearly suggested that pro football had grown in the public's imagination, while baseball had slipped.[26]

Action sports had been an industry darling in the late 1990s and beyond, but something ominous was happening. Data from the National Sporting Goods Association and the Sporting Goods Manufacturers Association indicated significant downward participation trends in skateboarding and BMX biking since 2000. Snowboarding had flattened. Ratings for the X Games and the Dew Tour had declined. Worse yet, polls indicated that the cohort of avid action sports fans among 12- to 17-year-olds had been declining for nine years. Action sports had been the hot ticket for access to youth. What was happening? Consumers were shifting their sports allegiance, as they had been doing for decades.[27]

Consumers had many choices, and these options were only multiplying. But polls don't stop the entrepreneurs, especially in the global marketplace. Take cricket, which had moved into the top echelon with the arrival of the Indian Premier League (IPL) in 2007. Cricket had always been popular among countries of the British Commonwealth, and its robust markets included India, which has the world's second largest population. The IPL looked to be a cross between NBA showtime and MLS salary restraint. And yes, throw in celebrity owners like Bollywood actor Shah Rukh Khan. In 2007, 13 bidders vied for one of eight franchises that cost $90 million each. By 2008 matches were averaging 58,000 in attendance. In 2010 the television audience was an estimated 67 million per match. By 2011 one franchise had sold for $370 million, and the league had snagged a $1.69 billion, 10-year television deal.[28]

Media Challenges

For over two centuries, sporting events have benefited from innovations in media technology. A big boxing match or horse race attracted a big audience. Newspapers and magazines wanted to write those stories and circulate them widely and quickly. All this depended on technology. One of the first breakthroughs was the electrical telegraph, developed commercially in 1840s America by Samuel Morse and Alfred Vail. As telegraph lines slowly connected the nation's cities and regions, newspaper magnates like James Gordon Bennett (*New York Herald*) jumped on the value of instant reports of sporting events. The telegraph enabled, as one historian has written, "instantaneous reporting of ball games, horse races, prize fights, yachting regattas . . . box scores, betting odds, and all kinds of messages." When John L. Sullivan fought Jake Kilrain in New Orleans in 1889, Western Union employed some 50 operators to handle over 200,000 words of special reports on the bout. By this time, sports news was filling whole pages of major daily newspapers like the *Herald*, the New York *Sun*, and the New York *World*. Hence the rise of the sports section, which has provided abundant and free publicity for sport properties ever since—as long as the sport property knew how to work with the press. It is no wonder that smart athletes like Jack Dempsey hired press agents like "Doc" Kearns or that universities like Knute Rockne's Notre Dame developed offices of sports information.[29]

Each decade has seemed to bring a new media technology with new opportunities and new challenges—silent movie newsreels, radio, broadcast television, cable and satellite television, the Internet, and the World Wide Web. All have required adjustment and action by media and sport properties. Those with the skills and the drive could build market share at the expense of technological laggards. The last decade has been no different. Perhaps the biggest change has been in the newspaper business. Newspapers thrived in the ages of radio and television. A synergy that seemed to be present has disappeared with the advent of the Internet and the World Wide Web. As newspapers fiddled with an online presence, they could not stop the bleeding of subscribers and advertisers. Total circulations of American weekday and Sunday papers slid from the 60 millions in 1990 to the low 40 millions in 2011. Ad revenues were surprisingly stable because the ads moved to online versions, at least until 2007. The standard response was to cut staff. Sports reporting suffered, at all levels. A 2009 *SportsBusiness Journal* survey revealed that 50 major dailies had cut sports staffs by 20 percent in the previous 16 months. Fewer beat writers were making road trips. A fan survey reinforced editors' worse nightmares; 42 percent of respondents said they preferred a team website for information. Coverage of college and high school teams was even worse; no beat writers, or even correspondents, attended games.[30]

The Internet started on cable. Wireless technology both spawned and fed the rise of cell phones, smartphones, and tablets, all of which changed the game of reporting and consuming sports news. Blogs, podcasts, YouTube, Facebook, Twitter, Tumblr—the list of new forms and new formats for delivering, sharing, and reading information will continue to lengthen. And every sport property at every level, from the top professional team to the local recreation league, must learn how to use them. New sports media technology is always developing. The need to adapt is not new.[31]

Jacksonville Jaguars CFO Bill Prescott said in 2010, "Our biggest competitor, everyone's biggest competitor, is HDTV. There's no doubt, to view a game in your own living room, the beer is colder and cheaper, the restroom is closer, and there's no line." In May 2012 executives at YouTube and Google (which had purchased YouTube) announced plans to develop over 100 new channels of original programming, including a Team USA channel focused on the Olympics. World Wrestling Entertainment already had a Google channel that drew over a million views per week. Google executive chairman Eric E.

Schmidt predicted, "We're about to see another large explosion in the use of video." By his estimation this was part of a third wave of media change for properties and sponsors to address. The first was broadcast TV to cable, the second was cable to Internet, and the third was everything to smartphones and tablets.[32]

New media were just part of a squeeze on modern lifestyles. As Seattle Seahawks COO John Rizzardini put it in 2010, NFL clubs, like all sport properties, were pressured by a tight economy that simultaneously pinched consumers in several ways—be it the need for multiple incomes, intrusive media and communications, or overscheduled kids' activities. "People's time is that much more precious these days. . . . People are more cautious about how they spend their time and money." And in the end, a consumer has only a finite amount of time to spend. An evening spent watching a Netflix video could not be redeemed for a sport event. Steve Hank, associate athletics director for revenue at Arizona State summed up the reality: "Honestly, time is the greatest commodity someone has."[33]

ACTIVITY 1.3 The Competitive Marketplace

In this WSG activity, you will propose marketing approaches for the Brooklyn Cyclones Baseball Club, a minor league baseball team in the short-season New York Penn League. The Cyclones are located in Brooklyn, New York and are affiliated with the New York Mets, who also are located in Brooklyn. The Cyclones are in a competitive marketplace. They not only have two Major League Baseball teams to compete against but also face additional competition from sport programming on TV and other forms of entertainment.

Grassroots Stress

Times were especially tough for high school athletics, long the great talent developer in American sport. In the heartland of American basketball, 40 miles (65 km) outside Indianapolis, Anderson High School was a case study in grassroots struggle. The Wigwam—the nearly 9,000-seat field house—had once packed in crowds that included 5,000 season-ticket holders. Fifty years ago, nothing was bigger than high school basketball. The state high school boys' tournament—the stuff of *Hoosiers* legend—drew 1.5 million fans in 1965. As late as the 1980s the Anderson High School Indians outdrew the NBA's Pacers. But that was yesterday. State tournament attendance was down 50 percent in the early 1990s. By 2012 Anderson High School had closed the Wigwam and was playing in a gym with a 2,800-seat capacity. As the *New York Times'* Craig Fehrman wrote in a poignant story, many reasons contributed to the attendance collapse. General Motors had once run more than 20 factories in the area. By 1999 they had left town and with them 14,000 people, triggering school closings, consolidations, and identity crises. Top that with expanded sports coverage on television and the Internet, as well as students and adults being forced to work more part-time jobs, and the recipe for low ticket sales is in place. In 2012 the Indians sold only 450 season tickets.[34]

Cities and towns around the country faced tighter budgets, often restricted by tax caps. If pension systems were under stress, everything was up for grabs and cuts. Local athletics directors had to be nimble. They had been revving up their local sponsor deals for some time. They had also established user fees. By fall 2010, programs in at least 43 states were dependent on such fees, which normally ran from $100 to $150 per athlete per sport. School boards played chicken with athletics directors, voters, and city councils by saying, "Find more money or we will cut these sports." In Lowell, Massachusetts, the cut list included freshmen and middle school teams, as well as 37 assistant coaches. In Greenville, Mississippi, tennis, golf, soccer, and baseball were among the sports that went on the chopping block. The Los Angeles district ripped $650,000 from transportation, effectively cutting a host of away games or forcing players to find their own ways to travel.[35]

Times were tough. In January 2012 Robert B. Gardner, executive director of the National Federation of State High School Associations, wrote an open letter to the American sport industry. He believed that high school sports were being overlooked in the industry press; its leaders were never included among lists of the most influential people. He noted, "19,000 high schools provide nearly 8 million young people opportunities to play high school sports. More people attend high school sporting events than college and professional sports events combined. The growth of web streaming will widen the gap." Given this reach, he urged industry and business leaders to "recognize the key role of high school sports in developing the next generation of employees and entrepreneurs, not to mention the current generation of consumers." Gardner had a point. At the same time, local athletics directors were probably more interested in funding than in making a list of the most influential leaders.[36]

Local businesses, some national corporations, and numerous professional leagues and teams have generously put money back into high school sports. The investment has been wise. As Rich Luker noted in 2011, ESPN Sports Poll data revealed that "more Americans are avid fans of high school sports than are avid fans of NASCAR, the NBA, or the NHL. Fifty-five percent of all Americans are fans of high school sports, making it the sixth-largest fan base in sports." More important were avidity rates. Although young males aged 12 to 17 have been expressing less interest in sport, 85.8 percent of that age cohort were high school sports fans, and 48.3 percent were avid fans. Adult fans were not just parents of competing athletes. As Luker added, "Seventy percent of high school sports fans don't have kids at home between the ages of 12 and 17, nor do 57 percent of those who are avid fans." Clearly, there is both great potential and great need for more sustained and more effective marketing of grassroots sports.[37]

Sport Marketing Defined

As the needs and demographic makeup of sport consumers have become more complex and as competition for the spectator and participant dollar has increased, the demand for professional marketing has also grown. Professional teams, small colleges, high schools, sport clubs, and youth programs have all looked for a better way to attract and maintain consumers. Among other things, they know that they compete for time and money with a host of rivals, including malls, mega movie complexes, Internet providers, concerts, and museums. Today's marketers clearly need a rational, coherent system that can match sport consumers with sport products. We may call this sport marketing. The term *sports marketing* was coined by *Advertising Age* in 1979 to describe the activities of consumer and industrial product and service marketers who were increasingly using sport as a promotional vehicle. Even a casual television viewer cannot help noticing the use of sport images and personalities to sell beer, cars, and a whole range of other products.[38]

This text recognizes two components in sport marketing: marketing *of* sport and marketing *through* sport. A professional team engages in the former; a brewery or an auto dealer employs the latter. Although most of this book addresses the marketing of sport, we also consider (especially in chapter 9) the corporate sponsor, who markets through sport. We will also use the singular *sport marketing* rather than *sports marketing*. We do this because we see a need to conceptualize sport industry segments (e.g., pro, college, and club leagues; various media) as a homogeneous entity. In the chapters that follow, we hope first to provide a general theory of sport marketing across all segments.

Given these notions about the sport industry and marketing, we offer the following definition of sport marketing, adapted from standard definitions of general marketing:

> Sport marketing consists of all activities designed to meet the needs and wants of sport consumers through exchange processes. Sport marketing has developed two major thrusts: the marketing of sport products and services directly to consumers of sport and the marketing of other consumer and industrial products or services using partnerships and promotions with sport properties.

As we will see, the terms *sport consumers* and *sport consumption* entail many types of involvement with sport, including playing (both real and virtual games), officiating, watching, listening, reading, blogging, and collecting memorabilia.

Marketing Myopia in Sport

If sport marketing ideally consists of activities designed to meet the wants and needs of sport consumers, then historically the industry has been guilty of what Theodore Levitt called marketing myopia, or "a lack of foresight in marketing ventures." We like to call it the vision thing.[39]

Following are some of the standard symptoms of sport marketing myopia:

- **A focus on producing and selling goods and services rather than identifying and satisfying the needs and wants of consumers and their markets**. Spencer Garrett, part owner and general manager of the successful Pierpont Racquet Club, recognized a problem that plagues many sport teams: "There are industry people who still focus on closing the sale. Membership retention [we can add fan retention] is where the future of the industry lies, so selling has to focus on benefits to the potential member." Selling is a critical component of marketing, but it is not the end all.[40]

- **The belief that winning absolves all other sins**. Longtime Buffalo Bills owner Ralph Wilson expressed this sentiment when he questioned some expenditures. "You go about marketing by winning," he insisted. "That's how you do it. A couple years ago we spent $700,000 on television, advertising the Bills, and we didn't sell five tickets. . . . This is sort of an anomaly, this marketing. Everybody gets carried away with it." Unfortunately, winning does not guarantee a rise in attendance. Take the case of the New Jersey Devils. Under the leadership and genius of Lou Lamoriello, the franchise has enjoyed extended excellence on the NHL ice. Their record between 1988 and 2012 included 17 straight winning seasons; playoff berths almost every year; nine Atlantic Division championships; and Stanley Cups in 1995, 2000, and 2003. Few professional franchises in any sport can match that record. Nonetheless, despite the record and concerted marketing efforts, the Devils' average attendance record was a downward staircase from 1998 to 2007. It had peaked above 17,000 in 1998, but by 2007, when the Devils moved to a new arena, it was barely above 14,000. Attendance is a constant challenge.[41]

- **Confusion between promotions and marketing**. Promotion—including advertising and special events—is only one part of a marketing mix, or strategy. Many fail to see the difference between promotion and marketing. Not long ago, *NCAA News* ran a feature story titled "Professional Marketing Finds Its Way into

College Basketball." The article hardly described professional marketing—only the influx of promotional tactics such as NBA-style laser shows, cheerleaders, and halftime shows. Said Jim Harrick, UCLA coach at the time: "In the past, UCLA has had a history of its game being its main attraction. Marketing has become a great asset." Good promotions can certainly be the "sizzle that sells the steak," but promotions must be part of an integrated strategy that begins with knowing consumer wants and needs.[42]

- **Ignorance of competition inside and outside sport**. Not enough teams are smart enough to recognize competitive trends and use them to advantage. For instance, the Atlanta Hawks had data that showed that their fans were 30 percent more likely than the general population to attend movies four or more times in the last three months. What did they do? They began to use ticket promo ads on the big screen before the movies. Research found that moviegoers have an 80 percent recall the next day, compared with a 15 to 20 percent recall rate from television ads. The Hawks made good use of competition.[43]

- **A shortsighted focus on quick-return price hikes or sponsorships rather than long-term investments in research and in relationship marketing**. This predisposition is especially true at the professional level, where escalating salaries have prompted front offices to focus resources on selling corporate signage, often at the expense of building a large database around small groups, families, and individual ticket buyers. Worse yet, too many teams gouge their fans whenever they sense that demand is greater than supply. In the new millennium, some NFL teams began to charge fans to see preseason practice. In the enlightened opposite camp was Robert Kraft, owner of the New England Patriots, whose Super Bowl champs have enjoyed a long train of sellouts. Rather than alienate preseason fans, Kraft understood that they represent future generations of Patriots Nation. To this end, New England's preseason camp had free admission, free parking, free rosters, and players lingering to sign free autographs. Said well-known Boston Globe columnist Dan Shaughnessy, "It's the best sports deal in New England."[44]

- **Poor-quality research**. When Matt Levine, who we consider the father of modern sport marketing, broke into the NBA in 1974, the cutting edge of market research belonged to the L.A. Lakers, who collected patron names and addresses on raffle entries available at Forum ticket gates. Levine's boss, Golden State Warriors GM Dick Vertlieb, posed a simple question to Levine: "Isn't there more we could learn than their names and addresses?" Since our first edition in 1993, the sport industry has come a long way with research. But common problems remain. For instance, as we discuss in chapter 4, the sport venue requires special considerations of sampling. Simply handing out surveys at the front door will not always do the trick. Further, questions on sport participation require much more clarity than we see in an average survey. Does playing one round of golf per year, with someone else's clubs, make a person a golfer? Some surveys have suggested this sort of thing. Quick, sloppy surveys will not suffice. The authors of this book have experienced firsthand some of the frustrations in selling research to executives. A few years ago we developed a machine-readable fan survey for a big-league team. A few weeks after the surveys were administered, a team employee brought us the completed surveys—dumped and mangled in four Hefty trash bags! Myopia can't get much worse. Professional teams and major universities are now investing hundreds of thousands of dollars in developing, maintaining, and using databases. Managers at the youth club, high school, and small-college levels obviously lack the resources for sophisticated systems. But research can begin with simple Excel files or even paper files.[45]

- **Poor sales and service**. Although many sport firms have equated sales and promotions with marketing, until the last decade few even invested in the sales effort. Historically, sales have been driven by quota and commissions mentalities, and little emphasis has been placed on training, tactics, or sales as part of the larger marketing strategy. We should not conflate the notion of sales with boiler-room operations using untrained and exploited staff and interns. The philosophy there seems to be this: If they can't do it, we'll just fire them and bring in more from the hundreds who have sent in resumes. In all this, no thought is given to the value of training and incentives, both of which might improve the interaction between the sport organization and its consumers.

- **Arrogance and laziness**. Simon Kuper, a well-known world football writer, recently recalled his attempts to reach the chairman of an English club. The press officer kept asking for fax requests, which Kuper called "a 1980s technology revered by soccer clubs." Kuper sent them, but the press officer claimed that none were received. Only after a month of this did Kuper get permission to send an e-mail request. His frustration grew: "Because soccer clubs are the only businesses that get daily publicity without trying to, they treat journalists as humble suppliants instead of as unpaid marketers of the clubs' brands. The media often retaliate by being mean. This is not very clever of the clubs, because almost all their fans follow them through the media rather than by going to the stadiums."[46]

- **Failure to adapt to industry, market, and consumer change**. As we noted earlier, adapting to new technology has been a constant necessity for sport executives and their media counterparts. Something new is always shaking up the status quo, and calling an innovation a fad or a waste of time is easy. People said that about the telephone and the cell phone, video games, and Facebook. But each of these innovations changed the way that many people lived their everyday lives. The business world, in and out of sport, it littered with the carcasses of firms that failed to adapt.

Change in the Profession

Sport marketing has a long history, dating back to spectacle promoters in ancient Greece and Rome. Many golden ages and growth spurts have occurred. David Stern has hundreds of predecessors, including the legendary Bill Veeck, one of the most imaginative sport entrepreneurs and marketers of the past century (see the sidebar about Veeck). Boxing had Tex Rickard, who made a name in the first quarter of the 20th century promoting boxing matches with the likes of Jack Johnson and Jack Dempsey. He later ran sports at Madison Square Garden, where the press referred to his young hockey franchise as Tex's Rangers. In 1928 he was asked by a pundit, "What do you regard as the secret to your success as a promoter—what psychological impulse guides you?" Rickard answered quickly: "It's no secret. By merely reading the newspapers most anybody can tell what the public wants to see."[47]

The field was not much farther along in 1975 when *Sports Illustrated's* Frank Deford wrote a brilliant profile of Michigan's athletics director, Don Canham, a man widely recognized for leading college athletics into a new age of marketing. Deford focused on Canham's frenetic pace and his hustling personality. He was way ahead of his time in the use of direct mail and aggressive advertising (including using airplane banners over nearby Detroit's Tiger Stadium), and in recognizing the need for commercial sponsorship. More than anything, Canham saw the need to sell the overall experience of big-time college football or basketball. As he said to Deford: "We've got to promote what we have. We've got to ballyhoo the pageantry. . . . We've got to sell the spectacle." To many fellow athletics directors (ADs), Canham's approach threatened the purity of "amateur" sport. Deford recognized this, but he also recognized the key to Canham's success: "There is very little that Don Canham does not take into consideration, and that, indeed, is the first mark of a promoter: concern for the tiniest detail while retaining the broadest vision." We would make only one correction in Deford's description. Canham was more than a promoter. He was a marketer. It is all in the vision thing.[49]

The authors of this book have interviewed thousands of young people who want to work in sport marketing because they "love sports." Like millions of others among the ESPN generation, they are deluded by visions of mingling with Robbie Cano, LeBron James, Maria Sharapova, or Lionel Messi. Reality is much more of a grind—heavy competition for entry-level jobs (the XFL reportedly had over 50,000 people apply online for 112 positions), low salaries, and long hours. A 2012 survey of pro franchises showed that the median income of workers in marketing, broadcast, and communications departments was $79,510. Still, those with strong sales skills (where salaries are higher) and an equally strong work ethic have a chance to be discovered by a team or by an executive recruiter such as Buffy Filippell, whose TeamWork Online LLC (www.teamworkonline.com) is highly respected and widely known inside the industry.[50]

Despite lingering myopia, the last 15 years have seen many encouraging signs of professional approaches to sport marketing. Among them are the following.

Bill Veeck: Sport Marketing's Foremost Prophet

Bill Veeck (b. 1914) was bred to sport marketing. His father, William Veeck Sr., was a Chicago sportswriter who switched fields to become president of the Cubs. In the cozy confines of Wrigley Field, young Bill Jr. learned the trade of the baseball magnate, from the bottom up—working with the grounds and concessions crews or with the ticket office, like any good intern today. The short biography on his plaque in the National Baseball Hall of Fame sums up his rich and varied sports life:

> Bill Veeck, owner of Indians, Browns and White Sox. Created heightened fan interest at every stop with ingenious promotional schemes, fan participation, exploding scoreboard, outrageous door prizes, names on uniforms. Set M.L. attendance record with pennant-winner at Cleveland in 1948; won again with "go-go" Sox in 1959. Signed A.L.'s first black player, Larry Doby, in 1947 and oldest rookie, 42-year-old Satchel Paige in 1948. Champion of the little guy.

He was a champion of the little guy not because he once used a midget as a pinch hitter, but because he believed that everyday fans were baseball's true royalty. His two classic books, *Veeck as in Wreck* and *The Hustler's Handbook,* still hold up as invaluable guides for any would-be sport marketer or executive. He happily considered himself a hustler, but here was his definition: "An advertiser pays for his space. A promoter works out a quid pro quo. A hustler gets a free ride and makes it seem like he's doing you a favor." For high school and small college athletics directors or youth program administrators who need to cut deals on slim budgets, Veeck's hustler should be a prototype.

Bill Veeck also left a legacy of 12 commandments that capture an enduring vision for successful sport marketing:

1. Take your work very seriously. Go for broke and give it your all.
2. Never ever take yourself seriously.
3. Find yourself an alter ego and bond with him for the rest of your professional life.
4. Surround yourself with similarly dedicated soul mates, free spirits of whom you can ask why and why not. And who can ask the same thing of you.
5. In your hiring, be color blind, gender blind, age and experience blind. You never work for Bill Veeck. You work with him.
6. If you're a president, owner, or operator, attend every home game and never leave until the last out.
7. Answer all of your mail; you might learn something.
8. Listen and be available to your fans.
9. Enjoy and respect the members of the media, the stimulation, and the challenge. The "them against us" mentality should only exist between the two teams on the field.
10. Create an aura in your city. Make people understand that unless they come to the ballpark, they will miss something.
11. If you don't think a promotion is fun, don't do it. Never insult your fans.
12. Don't miss the essence of what is happening at the moment. Let it happen. Cherish the moment and commit it to your memory.

Bill Veeck's 12 commandments offer an effective antidote to marketing myopia.[48]

12 commandments reprinted, by permission, from P. Williams, 2000, Marketing your dreams: Business and life lessons, In *Baseball's marketing genius*, edited by Bill Veeck (Champaign, IL: Sports Publishing), xiv.

Robust Improvements in Sales

Few sport properties have the luxury of waiting to take ticket orders—what is now called an inbound sales approach. To succeed in a competitive environment, organizations need to use a proactive outbound sales approach. Yet until recently the industry did little to train a sales force. That circumstance has changed rapidly, of necessity, because a strong sales program depends on having people who understand and can implement activities that integrate database development, prospect identification, dynamic pricing, primary and secondary market sales, and (ultimately) customer satisfaction. Professional teams and Division I universities have led the trend, either building an in-house staff or outsourcing to companies like IMG, Learfield Ticketing, Get Real Sports Sales, or the Aspire Group.[51] For instance, faced with a steep decline in men's basketball attendance, Arizona State hired the Aspire Group, led by coauthor Bernie Mullin, to boost sales in four ticketed sports. As part of the deal ASU also hired 30 full-time sales and service representatives. The goal was to build relationships. Aspire implemented tactics that included "occasional conference calls between coaches and season-ticket holders, giving supporters a chance to dial in with questions," as well as a young alum ticket package.[52]

Institutionalization of Knowledge and Training

When we started this book in the 1980s, some two dozen universities in the United States and Canada offered programs in sport management. Now there are hundreds around the world. On the professional side, Ron Seaver's National Sports Forum has served the industry since 1996, bringing the top marketing executives together for keynotes, roundtables, and workshops (www. sports-forum.com). Along similar lines, the National Association of Collegiate Directors of Athletics (NACDA) sponsors professional groups such as the National Association of Collegiate Marketing Administrators (NACMA). Many other formal organizations and consultants like IMG and NASCAR are providing information, training, and professional identity to men and women in the field. Universities are develop-

ing more structured internship programs (see the sidebar about the 'Cat Crew). A number of journals and magazines, such as *Street & Smith's SportsBusiness Journal*, *Sports Business Daily*, *SportsPro Media*, *Sport Marketing Quarterly*, and the *International Journal of Sports Marketing & Sponsorship* provide forums for sharing the latest best practices, research reports, and convention calendars.

Coauthor Bill Sutton and Dick Irwin have filled industry needs by developing the Sport Sales Combine, a unique event held periodically around America in partnership with professional franchise staffs. Fashioned along the notions of the scouting combines that evaluate player talent, the Sport Sales Combine is designed for entry-level to advancing sport industry ticket sales representatives looking to develop and refine sales and management skills. Combine trainees are engaged in an authentic sales training environment working with seasoned professional sales team leaders as well as hiring sales managers. Over the course of two high-action days, combine attendees receive training and then get to display their talents in real auditions at real events. Eager and effective sales "athletes" may leave with four or more job offers.[53]

Broadening Diversity

Historians have recently rediscovered the genius of minority marketers like Rube Foster, who built the first stable professional baseball league for African American players in the 1920s, and Senda Berenson, who was a central steward of women's basketball in the 1890s. Although the industry still shades heavily to male and white, minorities have made progress. A good example is Sportivo, an agency "dedicated to harnessing the muscle of sports to drive brand acceleration among the nation's fastest growing population" (www. sportivo.us). The market segment is covered by the blogspot *Marketing to Latinos and Hispanics Sports News* (http://marketingtolatinossports. blogspot.com).

As the field continues to progress, sport marketing will move back to a future that was recognized clearly by old-time promoters and hustlers such as Tex Rickard, Bill Veeck, Rube Foster, and Charlotte Perkins Gilman—who all knew how to leverage sport for media attention.[54]

University of New Hampshire 'Cat Crew Sports Marketing Team

Amber Lilyestrom, Associate Athletic Director for Marketing and Communications, University of New Hampshire Athletics

'CAT CREW
2012-2013

One of the most important parts of my job as a collegiate sport marketer is to serve as an educator. The University of New Hampshire Department of Intercollegiate Athletics serves not only as a learning environment for student-athletes but also as a training ground for young sports marketing professionals.

When I began my role at UNH in 2004, I quickly realized that to meet the many demands of seven revenue-generating programs I would need a lot of help. After one year of working with any student who walked through my door, I learned that a more formalized internship program would be the answer. This is when the 'Cat Crew was born.

Fast forward to 2012. The 'Cat Crew Marketing Team consists of 15 undergraduate students in majors varying from sport studies to business administration. The group is responsible for the marketing and game presentation of UNH's ticketed sports as well as the activation of elements contained in the department's corporate sponsorship agreements. UNH is home to some of the nation's most competitive programs in the sports of ice hockey and football (FCS). UNH's athletics department, like many other collegiate athletics departments, works with lean budgets on an annual basis. Therefore, a hearty volunteer-based internship program has become the lifeblood of UNH's marketing department.

The 'Cat Crew Marketing Team internship program is unpaid, but the students are eligible to receive academic credit hours for their participation. More important, the program prepares them for a career after they graduate. Some of the keys to success are as follows:

- **Provide titles that match responsibilities**. Our marketing team members earn titles for their specific roles. This arrangement not only increases accountability but also outlines expectations and responsibilities (e.g., student marketing director for men's ice hockey). Directors must staff all events for their sport; write PA scripts; direct fellow team members on game day; and write a comprehensive year-end report that analyzes the attendance figures, marketing initiatives, and methods of their sport.

- **Support teamwork**. Most of the members who have gone on to earn great jobs upon graduation have participated in the 'Cat Crew for two years. In year 2, they have the opportunity to maximize their leadership skills by training their new teammates. They also have time to expand on projects and initiatives that they dreamt up in year 1 and now have the time and experience to implement them. Through this internship program, these students not only increase their sport marketing knowledge but also significantly develop their confidence, public-speaking ability, and creativity.

- **Create opportunity**. The 'Cat Crew is responsible for all ticketed home athletics events at UNH, but we also have the opportunity to work at NCAA championship events and large-scale events taking place at neutral sites (e.g., 2010 and 2011 Colonial Clash football game at Gillette Stadium, 2012 Frozen Fenway hockey game). Through these opportunities, the students get to meet other sport professionals in the industry, broaden their networks, and experience events at alternate venues.

To date, 95 percent of those who have participated in the 'Cat Crew Marketing Internship program have earned full-time jobs in a marketing or sales position upon graduation. We have found that employers are impressed with the level of experience and responsibility that these interns were given during undergraduate years and the skills that they have developed as a result. Placements of recent 'Cat Crew grads include regional sales manager at Monumental Sports & Entertainment, new business development account executive at Pittsburgh Pirates, group sales and marketing coordinator at the University of New Hampshire Athletics Department, inside sales representative at AEG, account manager at Genesco Sports Enterprises, event coordinator at Octagon Sports Marketing, and selection tour representative at All-American Games.

The 'Cat Crew takes a good bit of my time. But we see a very high ROI.

Uniqueness of Sport Marketing

Overcoming sport marketing myopia requires an appreciation of this particular domain of human experience. Our book, in fact, rests on a simple premise: that humans view sport as a special experience or as having a special place in their lives, and that marketers must approach sport differently than they do used cars, donuts, or tax advice. John Staffen, chief creative officer of Arnold Worldwide, planned ad campaigns for dozens of consumer products and services, including McDonalds, Progressive Insurance, and Volvo. He compared them to events like tennis's U.S. Open: "Sports are so multifaceted. The Open is sports, sure, but it's also part fashion, part people watching, part cuisine-fest and part New York City happening—balancing all those things isn't easy." Much of the marketing process is similar, and some of the sharpest industry minds came from outside sport, such as Sarah Levinson (from MTV), who served as president of NFL Properties in the late 1990s.[55]

But the sport domain has distinct features, which we discuss in the following sections, and there is no simple road to mastery. This book can provide an overview, but hard experience is also needed. Just ask Tim Leiwicke, president and CEO of AEG, governor of the NHL's L.A. Kings, and CEO of Maple Leaf Sports and Entertainment. It all started in 1979, when Leiwicke began as assistant general manager of the St. Louis Steamers, a franchise in the Major Indoor Soccer League. Although to some extent we can argue that marketing is marketing, the field is full of failures who treated tennis, golf, and basketball as though they were the latest fashion design or tooth whitener. In the following sections, we suggest components that, collectively, make sport a unique phenomenon.

Sport Product

A product can be described generally as "any bundle or combination of qualities, processes, and capabilities (goods, services, or ideas) that a buyer expects will deliver want satisfaction." A peculiar bundling distinguishes the sport product, including at least the following elements:[56]

- Playful competition, typically in some game form
- A separation from normal space and time
- Regulation by special rules
- Physical prowess and physical training
- Special facilities and special equipment

Figure 1.1 illustrates the importance that this special bundling has for the sport product. At its core, the sport product offers the consumer some basic benefit such as health, entertainment, sociability, or achievement. Of course, many other products may offer the same core benefit. The sport marketer must understand why a consumer chooses to satisfy a given want or need by purchasing a sport product rather than some other type of product. Why do some people seek achievement in sport whereas others prefer to raise prize tomatoes? Although research on such a question is sparse, we may assume that

FIGURE 1.1   The bundle of characteristics of the sport product.

the preference relates partially to the generic product components of sport—emphasis on physical activity that is regulated in special game forms. At the same time, the golfers among this sport group might scorn tennis and vice versa. The tennis players may be split into groups that prefer public courts and those that prefer private club membership. We can recognize the complex dynamics behind each level of segmentation (considered in later chapters), but the fundamental point is that the sport product is unique.

Additional elements of the basic sport product—the game or event—make it unusual. Some of these elements reflect the nature of sport as a service.[57]

• **An intangible, ephemeral, experiential, and subjective nature.** Sport is an expression of our humanity; it can't be bottled like tonic water. Even tangible elements like equipment have little meaning outside the game or event. Few products are open to such a wide array of interpretations by consumers. What each consumer sees in a sport is subjective, making it extremely difficult for the sport marketer to ensure a high probability of consumer satisfaction. As baseball executive Peter Bavasi once said: "Marketing baseball isn't the same as selling soap or bread. You're selling a memory, an illusion." Each fan and each active participant creates a different illusion. Each round of golf, each tennis match,

each softball game brings a different experience. Equally important, consumers use sport to brand themselves in multiple ways. The same person in Seattle can easily say, "I am a Jimmie Johnson fan (NASCAR); I am a Storm fan (WNBA); I am a Red Sox fan; I am a Huskies fan." Each of these identities may embrace different aspects of the sport experience—speed and risk in NASCAR, team play in the WNBA, hope and redemption with the Red Sox, and community with the UW Huskies. Thus, selling the benefits of consuming sport (compared with those of a car) is difficult because they are hard to pinpoint or describe.[58]

• **Strong personal and emotional identification.** As we discuss in chapter 3, few products or services elicit passions and commitments as sport does. Most readers will remember the first time they were bitten by a sports bug—golf, tennis, baseball, hockey, or whatever. The addiction for more is striking. Fan identification with players and teams has spawned its own nomenclature. For example, there's BIRGing, or "basking in reflected glory," which can be seen in fans' use of the words *we*, *us*, and *our* when their favorites win, or CORFing ("casting off reflected failure"), as seen when the words *them* or *they* are used to discuss a loss. This strong identification is connected to the general feeling that "I could do that if only I had the chance." In the world of sport it sometimes seems that everyone is a passionate expert. No wonder that fantasy games, talk radio, and sport blogs are successful.

• **Simultaneous production and consumption.** Sports are perishable commodities. As events, they must be presold, and there are no inventories. Sport consumers are typically also producers; they help create the game or event that they simultaneously consume. Although DVDs, on-demand videos, and newspaper accounts extend product life in a different form, the original event is fleeting. No marketer can sell a seat for yesterday's game. Day-of-game sales alone are not sufficient, because inclement weather or some other factor may diminish gate sales. Preselling, especially of season-ticket programs or yearly memberships, guarantees a minimum revenue.

• **Dependence on social facilitation.** The loneliness of the long-distance runner notwithstanding, sport usually occurs in a public setting. Enjoyment of sport, as player or fan, is almost always a function of interaction with other people. Typically, less than 4 percent of those attending collegiate and professional sport events attend by themselves. Only a few sports, such as running, can be undertaken by a single person. And who watches the Super Bowl or the World Cup alone? Consequently, sport marketers need to recognize the central role of social facilitation.

- **Inconsistency and unpredictability.** A baseball game played today will be different from next week's game even if the starting lineups are the same. Numerous factors such as weather, injuries, momentum, rivalries, and crowd response create the logic of "On any given day . . ." Who can predict a no-hitter, or a dog of a game, or the sudden squall on a mountain? Unpredictability is one of the lures of sport, but it makes the marketer's job more complex. One baseball marketing executive, who previously spent 13 years with Clairol, put it this way: "Before, I had control of the product. I could design it the way I wanted it to be. Here the product changes every day and you've got to adapt quickly to the changes."[59]

- **Core-product control beyond marketer's hands.** As suggested, most sport marketers have little control of their core product—the game itself. General managers make trades. Leagues make schedules and game rules. Although some core-product decisions are clearly made with an eye on marketing (in baseball, one such decision was the designated-hitter rule to create more offense), these decisions are still typically made by coaches and administrators whose agendas are often the game's "purity" or equalizing offense and defense. Sport team marketers must sell the sizzle as much as the steak. Boston Marathon managers sell T-shirts, collector's item lithographs, and special marathon-label wine. Only one person finishes first, but everyone can have a winning memento. That objective will be doubly important in the aftermath of the 2013 Boston Marathon bombings.[60]

Sport Market

Following are some special features of the sport market.

- **Many sport organizations simultaneously compete and cooperate.** Few sport organizations can exist in isolation. To have meaningful competition, professional, intercollegiate, and interscholastic sports require other franchises and schools. The same is true for private and amateur sport clubs.

- **Product salience and strong personal identification lead many sport consumers to consider themselves experts.** The expert mentality was clearly revealed decades ago in a famous national survey. Among the respondents, 52 percent said yes when asked, "Do you think you could play for a professional team if you practiced?"; 74 percent said yes when asked, "Do you think that you could do a better job of officiating than most officials?"; and 51 percent said yes to the question, "Do you think that you could do a better job of coaching than the average coach?" No other business is viewed so simplistically and with such personal identification by its consumers.[61]

- **Demand tends to fluctuate widely.** Each sport form tends to have an annual life cycle, and spectator sports fans are especially prone to quick changes in interest. Season openers bring high hopes and high demand; but midseason slumps, injuries, or weak competition may kill ticket sales.

- **Sport has an almost universal appeal and pervades all elements of life.** Although most of the world's most popular sports clearly have a Western tradition, a wide world of sport is also clearly in place. A recent book even took as its title *How Soccer Explains the World*. What appear to be simple games—soccer, hockey, or basketball—link easily to other facets of our humanity, for better or worse.[62]

Sport Financing

The financing of sport encompasses the following special features.

- **Pricing the individual sport product unit by traditional job costing is difficult.** For example, it is virtually impossible for the sport marketer to allocate fixed and operating costs to the individual ticket or membership. How can one account for the possible use of an usher, an instructor, an attendant, or a shower? Further, the marginal cost of providing an additional product unit is typically small. Therefore, pricing the sport product is often based on the marketer's sense of consumer demand—for certain seats, for certain times of day, for certain privileges.

- **The price of the sport product itself is invariably small in comparison with the total**

cost paid by the consumer. As we will see in chapter 8, marketers must recognize the hidden costs of sport. The cost of tickets to a ball game may be only one third of a family's total costs, which include travel, parking, hot dogs, drinks, and merchandise—all perhaps controlled by someone other than the team hosting the event.

• **Indirect revenues are frequently greater than direct operating revenues.** Because consumers are (and should be) cost sensitive, income from fans is often not enough to cover total expenses, especially debt service to the shiny, high-tech facilities that consumers demand. The direct income–expense gap has focused more attention on media and sponsor revenues. The quest for television and sponsors extends to all levels and segments of the sport industry, in part because the money is there. A good example is the NCAA. Of the NCAA's total revenues for 2010–11 ($845.9 million), 81 percent came from television and marketing rights fees. And most of this amount was from rights associated with March Madness, the men's Division I basketball tournament.[63]

Sport Promotion

Promoting sport is not as easy as it seems, despite widespread media attention. Consider the following.

• **The widespread media exposure is a double-edged sword.** Unlike a hardware store, sport teams get free promotions daily, in the newspapers, on the radio, and on television. Cases in point: In 1997, the *Chicago Sun-Times* and the *Chicago Tribune* published 6,259 articles mentioning Bill Clinton, the elected president and the "leader of the free world." Michael Jordan was mentioned in 4,173 articles. An economic impact study by Price/McNabb (North Carolina) estimated that the University of Tennessee at Chattanooga men's basketball team generated

$22 million of free media exposure through its 1997 Sweet Sixteen run. At a time of great competition in college admissions, any president or trustee would take notice. On the one hand, this exposure is a blessing, particularly for financially strapped programs at the grassroots level. At the same time, free exposure can lead to laziness, arrogance, and amnesia toward fans.[64]

• **Media and sponsors emphasize celebrities.** Sport marketers work hard to shape their organization's image. This purpose becomes problematic because the bulk of sponsor and media attention is focused on a few celebrities, whose expanded egos can lead to wholesale problems both inside and outside the locker room.

ACTIVITY 1.4 The Uniqueness of Sport Marketing

In this WSG activity, you will consider how to market the U.S. Open tennis tournament, which is the fourth and final major in the tennis Grand Slam. You will discover that the Open is more than just a sporting event.

Wrap-Up

Sport is a distinct enterprise. It cannot be marketed like soap or tax advice. A sport marketer is asked to market a product that is unpredictable, inconsistent, and open to subjective interpretation. The marketer must undertake this task in a highly competitive marketplace with a much lower promotional budget than those of similarly sized organizations in other industries. Finally, the sport marketer must do all this with only limited direct control over the product mix. On the bright side, the media are eager to give wide exposure to the general product, and many opportunities exist to generate revenue through associations with business and industry.

Activities

1. List three reasons for the great need for better sport marketing.
2. Define marketing myopia; give three examples in the sport industry.
3. On the basis of figure 1.1, discuss how two golf players might consume different products in terms of benefits, sport forms, or marketing mix.

4. Find the names of four sport organizations from a major newspaper to illustrate each segment of the industry identified in this chapter.

5. Discuss the three elements of sport that you believe most contribute to the uniqueness of sport marketing.

6. Identify a sport or a sport organization on the rise and one on the decline. What types of evidence support the notions of either rise or decline? Is the change caused by the invisible hand of the market or by the visible hand of marketing?

Your Marketing Plan

In the following chapters, you will be asked to develop your own marketing plan, step by step. This activity will allow you to apply the topics that are presented in each chapter. Take advantage of these opportunities and have fun!

Endnotes

1. Quoted in Pablo Torre, "From Couch to Clutch," *Sports Illustrated*, 20 February 2012, 46; Pablo Torre, "A Run Like No Other," *Sports Illustrated* 27 February 2012, 32; Harvey Araton, "Disappointing Defeat Fine Tunes a Frenzy," *New York Times*, 25 February 2012, D2; Howard Beck, "Lin Craze Has Left the Building," *New York Times*, 16 March 2012, B12; Howard Beck, "Knicks' Push For Playoffs Will Go On Without Lin," *New York* Times, 31 March 2012, SP1; Howard Beck, "Clock Strikes 12: Fairy Tale Ends," *New York Times*, 18 July 2012, B10.

2. Chip Heath and Dan Heath, *Made to Stick: Why Some Ideas Survive and Others Die* (New York: Random House, 2007).

3. Keith Bradsher, "In China, Lin Is a Star and a Symbol," *New York Times*, 15 February 2012, B12; Ho quote in Torre, "A Run Like No Other," 32; Adam Fraser, "Brand Design's: Basketball's FIBA World Championships Were Screened in 183 Countries," *Sports Pro Magazine*, December 2010, 60–64; Nielsen Co., "State of the Media: Year in Sports 2010," Supplement in *Street and Smith's SportsBusiness Journal* (hereafter cited as *SSSBJ*), 24–30 January 2011, 7.

4. Keith Bradsher, "In China, Lin Is a Star and a Symbol," *New York Times*, 15 February 2012, B12; Michale Wines, "China Tries to Add Cultural Clout to Economic Muscle," *New York Times*, 8 November 2011, A8.

5. Ken Belson, "Chinatown Can Cheer, but Can't Watch, Rise of an Adopted Star," *New York Times*, 16 February 2012, A1, www.nytimes. com/2012/02/16/sports/basketball/cable-tv-blackout-frustrates-lins-chinatown-fans.html?ref=cabletelevision&pagewanted=all; Howard Beck and Richard Sandomir, "Time Warner and MSG Resolve Cable Dispute, With Help of Lin and Cuomo," *New York Times*, 18 February 2012, D5; www.nytimes.com/2012/02/18/sports/ time-warner-cable-and-garden-resolve-dispute. html?ref=timewarnercableinc.

6. Pablo Torre, "A Run Like No Other," *Sports Illustrated* 27 February 2012, 33–34; Richard Sadomir, "As Lin's Legend Grows, MSG's Ratings Keep Rising, Too," *New York Times*, http://offthedribble. blogs.nytimes.com/2012/02/22/as-lins-legend-grows-msgs-numbers-continue-rising/; Richard Sandomir, "Lin Is Gone, and So Is the Buzz," *New York Times*, 19 July 2012, B12.

7. M. Swift, "From Corned Beef to Caviar," *Sports Illustrated*, 3 June 1991, 75–89, quotation on 80.

8. Ibid.

9. Jeff Coplon, "The People's Game," *New York Times Magazine*, 23 November 2003, 73–77.

10. L. Jon Wertheim, "The Whole World Is Watching," *Sports Illustrated*, 14 June 2004, 72–85; John Lombardo, "Game Plan Calls for Growth Overseas," *SSSBJ*, 27 October–2 November 2003, 25; John Lombardo, "Stellar Rookies Help Lead NBA to Heights It Hasn't Reached Since Jordan Left," *SSSBJ*, 19–25 April 2004, 36; John Lombardo, "Global Trade: NBA Imports Talent and Exports the Game," *SSSBJ*, 25–31 October 2004, 21–25; Jack McCallum, "Wake-Up Call," *Sports Illustrated*, 27 June 2005; Johnny Ludden, "Argentina in Love With Its Hoop Star," *Globe and Mail*, 7 July 2005.

11. For an excellent look at Chinese basketball in 2012, see Jim Yardley, "Away Game," *New York Times Sunday Magazine*, 5 February 2012, MM33, www. nytimes.com/2012/02/05/magazine/NBA-in-China.html?_r=1&pagewanted=all; investment growth in "China Sports Industry Report," published by Research in China, www.researchinchina.com/Htmls/Report/2010/5847.html.

12. Adam Frazer, "Net Growth," *SportsPro Magazine*, February 2011, 94–95.

13. FIFA.com, "Almost Half the World Tuned in at Home to Watch 2010 FIFA World Cup South Africa," 11 July 2011, www.fifa.com/worldcup/ archive/southafrica2010/organisation/media/ newsid=1473143/index.html. For a good overview of sports broadcasting, see Rodoula H. Tsiotsou, "Entrepreneurship in Sports Broadcasting," in *Sports Entrepreneurship: Theory and Practice*, ed. Dorene Ciletti and Simon Chadwick (Morgantown, WV: FIT, 2012), 97-120.

14. Daniel Kaplan, "Is Sports Business Recession-Proof?" *SSSBJ*, 19–25 October 1998, 37; Marcy Lamm, "Sports' Grip on Public Slips in Poll," *SSSBJ*, 31 January–6 February 2000, 47.

15. Bill King, "Passion That Can't Be Counted Puts Billions of Dollars in Play," *SSSBJ*, 11–17 March 2002, 32.

16. David P Kronheim, "Major League Baseball 2011 Attendance Analysis," http://numbertamer.com/ files/2011_MLB_Attendance_Analysis.pdf.

17. John Raby, "Minor-League Hockey Taking a Hit in Recession," *Fosters Sunday Citizen*, 1 March 2009, C5; Fred Dreier, "Key Business Issues Facing EPL Franchises," *SSSBJ*, 15 August 2011, 35.

18. BBC Sports, "RBS Cutbacks to Hit British Sport," 26 February 2009, www.sports-city.org/news_ details.php?news_id=7248&idCategory=1.

19. Tom Love, "A Different League: The Football League," *SportsPro Magazine*, April 2012, 60–64, TV rights deals at 61.

20. Steve Knopper, "Concert Biz Collapses as Fans Flee," *Rolling Stone*, 20 January 2011, 19.

21. Bloomberg News, "NBA Reacts to Tough Economic Times," 6 October 2008, www.sports-city.org/ news_details.php?news_id=5771&idCategory=1; Reuters, "English Football Clubs Cut Prices to Help Fans During Recession," 25 February 2009, www.sports-city.org/news_details.php?news_ id=7240&idCategory=74.

22. AP, " 'Big Game' Not Quite as Big This Year," *Foster's Sunday Citizen*, 1 February 2009, A3; Daniel Kaplan, "Teams Tackle Tough Ticket Market," *SSSBJ*, September 7–13, 2009, 1, 24–27, quotation at 24.

23. Rich Luker, "Industry Must Adapt to Decline in American Spending on Sports," *SSSBJ*, 27 September 2010, 13; "About the Industry," *SSSBJ*, 29 November 2010, 18; Brad Wolverton and Alex Richards, "Crowds Shrink at Men's Basketball Games," *Chronicle of Higher Education*, 25 March 2012, http://chronicle.com/article/ Basketball-Draws-Shrinking/131294/?sid=w-b&utm_source=wb&utm_medium=en.

24. Alfie Meek, "An Estimate of the Size and Supporting Economic Activity of the Sports Industry in the United States," *Sport Marketing Quarterly* (hereafter cited as *SMQ*), 6 December 1997, 15–22; Brad R. Humphreys and Jane E. Ruseki, "Estimates of the Size of the Sports Industry in the United States," IASE/NAASE Working Paper Series, No. 08-11, August 2008, http://college.holycross.edu/ RePEc/spe/HumphreysRuseski_SportsIndustry. pdf; U.S. GDP levels found at http://knoema. com/gdp-by-country?gclid=CKGFl6LC07AC-FUZN4AodDDvq2g.

25. Terry Lefton and John Ourand, "X Years After: The Brash, Bold XFL Played Only One Season, but a Decade Later Its Images and Impact Live On," *SSSBJ*, 16 May 2011, 1, 26–7; http://msn.foxsports. com/foxsoccer/usa/story/womens-profession-al-soccer-league-shut-down-051812.

26. "Poll Shows Popularity of Pro Football Continues Growing While Baseball Slides," *SportsBusiness Daily* (hereafter cited as *SBD*), 26 January 2012, www.sportsbusinessdaily.com/Daily/ Issues/2012/01/26/Research-and-Ratings/ Harris-Poll.aspx?hl=Research%20and%20Ratings&sc=0.

27. Tripp Mickle, "Balancing Act: With Some Metrics Leveling Off, Action Sports Industry Pushes Ahead With New Strategies," *SSSBJ*, 23 January 2012, 1, 15–17.

28. Tripp Mickle, "Billion Dollar Baby: In Four Short Years, the Indian Premier League Has Put Cricket on a Wicket Growth Curve," *SSSBJ*, 18 April 2011, 1, 15–18; "Global Growth Markets: India," *SSSBJ*, 18 April 2011, 20; David Hoyt and George Foster, "Sports Entrepreneurship: The Case of the Indian Premier League," in *Sports Entrepreneurship: Theory and Practice*, ed. Doreen Ciletti and Simon Chadwick (Morgantown, WV: FIT, 2012), 34–50.

29. John R. Betts, "The Technological Revolution and the Rise of Sports, 1850–1890," *Mississippi Valley Historical Review*, 40 (September 1953): 231–56, quotation at 239.

30. Pew Research Center, *State of the News Media 2012*, http://stateofthemedia.org/2012/newspapers-building-digital-revenues-proves-painfully-slow/newspapers-by-the-numbers. Bill King, "No News Is Good News," *SSSBJ*, 20–26 July 2009, 1, 28–32.

31. For more on technological innovation and sport products, see Stephen Hardy, Brian Norman, and Sarah Sceery, "Toward a History of Sport Branding," *Journal of Historical Research in Marketing*, 4 (4) (November 2012): 482–509.

32. Jaguars quotation in Albert Breer, "Teams Finding Their Product Is a Tougher Sell," *Boston Sunday Globe*, 4 July 2010, D-9; Stuart Elliott, "YouTube and Kin Woo Marketers, Seeking to Siphon Dollars From TV," *New York Times*, May 3, 2012, B2, www. nytimes.com/2012/05/03/business/media/ youtube-channels-court-advertisers-at-newfronts. html?ref=todayspaper.

33. Albert Breer, "Teams Finding Their Product Is a Tougher Sell," *Boston Sunday Globe*, 4 July 2010, D-9; Brad Wolverton and Alex Richards, "Crowds Shrink at Men's Basketball Games," *Chronicle of Higher Education*, 25 March 2012, http://chronicle.com/article/Basketball-Draws-Shrink-ing/131294/?sid=wb&utm_source=wb&utm_medium=en.

34. Craig Fehrman, "The End of an Era in Indiana," *New York Times*, 25 March 2012, SP1, www.nytimes.com/2012/03/25/sports/farewell-to-wigwam-and-heyday-of-high-school-basketball-in-indiana.html?_r=1&pagewanted=all.

35. Bill King, "High School Sports Running on Empty," *SSSBJ*, 2 August 2010, 1, 15–19.

36. Robert B. Gardner, "Influence of High School Sports Goes Overlooked," *SSSBJ*, 30 January 2012, 24.

37. Rich Luker, "Local Power, Grassroots Appeal Make High School Sports Compelling," *SSSBJ*, 28 March 2011, 21.

38. L. Kesler, "Man Created Ads in Sport's Own Image," *Advertising Age*, 27 August 1979, 5–10.

39. T. Levitt, "Marketing Myopia," *Harvard Business Review* (July–August 1960): 45–56.

40. D. Cooke, "Packaging for Prestige: The Tennis Advantage," *IRSA Club Business*, July 1987, 62.

41. *SBD*, 22 August 1997, 11; Andy Bernstein, "Despite Stanley Cup Win, Devils Play to Few Fans," *SSSBJ*, 11–17 December 2000, 1, 58; Matthew Ventolo, "2010–2011 New Jersey Devils Attendance Analysis," www.inlouwetrust.com/2011/4/22/212580 3/2010-2011-new-jersey-devils-attendance-analysis.

42. Laura Bollig, "Professional Marketing Finds Its Way Into College Basketball," *NCAA News*, 6 December 1993, 12.

43. Marcy Lamm, "Teams Take Their Pitch to the Big Screen," *SSSBJ*, 21–27 February 2000, 13.

44. Dan Shaughnessy, "Eyes of Many Are Trained on Workouts," *Boston Sunday Globe*, 8 August 2004, C-1, 4.

45. "Profile/Interview With Matt Levine," *SMQ*, 5 (2) (September 1996): 5–12.

46. Simon Kuper and Stefan Szymanski, *Soccernomics* (New York: Nation Books, 2009), 85.

47. Bozeman Bulger, "Twenty-Five Years in Sports," *Saturday Evening Post*, 26 May 1928.

48. Hustler definition in Bill Veeck with Ed Linn, *The Hustler's Handbook* (New York: Fireside Books, 1989), 12.

49. Frank Deford, "No Death for a Salesman," *Sports Illustrated*, 28 July 1975, 56–65.

50. Bill King, "What's the Payoff in Sports? Salary Survey Sheds Light on Challenges College Grads Face," *SSSBJ*, 13 August 2012, 1, 16–25.

51. Michael Smith, "Survey: More Schools Beefing Up Ticket Efforts," *SSSBJ*, 4 June 2012, 8.

52. Brad Wolverton and Alex Richards, "Crowds Shrink at Men's Basketball Games," *Chronicle of Higher Education*, 25 March 2012, http://chronicle.com/article/Basketball-Draws-Shrink-ing/131294/?sid=wb&utm_source=wb&utm_medium=en.

53. Description taken from www.sportsalescombine.com.

54. For an outstanding introduction to the broader roles of these people (and many more) in American sport history, see Gerald Gems, Linda Borish, and Gertrud Pfister, *Sports in American History* (Champaign, IL: Human Kinetics, 2008).

55. Terry Lefton, "9 Rules for Making the Most of Sports Property/Ad Agency Relationships," *SSSBJ*, September 24–30, 2007, 23–28, quotation at 25; www.arn.com/creative/client-list.

56. B. Enis and K. Roering, "Services Marketing: Different Products, Similar Strategy," in *Marketing of Services*, ed. J.H. Donnelly and W.R. George (Chicago: American Marketing Association, 1981), 1. The classic definition of sport comes from John Loy, "The Nature of Sport," *Quest*, 10 (May 1968): 1–15.

57. Scott Edgett and Stephen Parkinson, "Marketing for Service Industries," *Service Industries Journal*, 13 (3) (July 1993): 19–39.

58. B. Stavro, "It's a Classic Turnaround Situation," *Forbes*, 1 July 1985, 70.

59. R. Poe, "The MBAs of Summer," *Across the Board*, October 1985, 18–25.

60. Tom Moroney, "Hopkinton Finds Itself in the Winner's Circle," *Boston Globe*, 3 April 1996, 1, 24.

61. Research and Forecasts, *Miller Lite Report on American Attitudes Toward Sports* (Milwaukee, WI: Miller Brewing Co., 1985), 131–136.

62. Franklin Foer, *How Soccer Explains the World: An Unlikely Theory of Globalization* (New York: HarperCollins, 2004).

63. www.ncaa.org/wps/wcm/connect/public/ncaa/finances/revenue.

64. "NBA News and Notes," *SBD*, 20 February 1998, 5; "Marketplace Roundup," *SBD*, 20 March 1998, 4.

Chapter 2

Strategic Marketing Management

OBJECTIVES

- To identify the key stakeholders in sport marketing and the interaction between them that creates brand perception

- To recognize the interacting components of the marketing management process

- To appreciate the core elements of market analysis, product concept, and product position

- To understand the distinctions among the five Ps of sport marketing: product, price, place, promotion, and public relations

Many professional musicians make no secret of their dream to be a professional athlete, yet since the late Italian tenor Luciano Pavarotti and Scottish rocker Rod Stewart's flirtation with professional soccer over four decades ago, precious few in the music entertainment business have ever come close. Similarly, many professional athletes make no secret of their love of music and their desire to be professional musicians, but equally few possess the necessary talent to carry it out. Maybe it's the love of performing in front of an adoring fan base. Maybe it's the bond of people with God-given talent that places them far above average mortals. Or maybe it's something more fundamental than that. Whatever the case, sport and entertainment clearly go hand in hand, and music will always play a part in dramatizing and enhancing the sport experience.

No surprise, then, that the National Basketball Association leads the way in producing a comprehensive sport and entertainment experience that appeals to a broad base of fans. In the 1990s the NBA was the first league to recognize the need to enhance its product with a fully choreographed entertainment package. More than any other league, the NBA acknowledges that the product outside the white lines is as important as the product inside the white lines in terms of inducing fans to repeat purchase and come back to the arena again. Sometimes, to the chagrin of fans, particularly older ones, the comprehensive production that wraps around NBA games means that there is never a dull moment, or even a silent moment.

Music is frequently the main emotive force that unlocks the passion of sports fans and facilitates their expression of support. Mark Cuban, owner of the NBA's Dallas Mavericks, the 2010–11 champions, once said that anyone on his ticket or sponsorship sales staff that sold based on wins and losses would be fired immediately: "We sell a basketball entertainment experience, of which the music, video, promotions, and other entertainment off the court is a vital part of the product we sell and exactly how we are able to attract every member of the family.[1]

Consistent, marketing-minded leadership, complete with a vision and a plan, is a necessity in today's competitive environment. For the high school athletics director, the racket sports and health club manager, or the commissioner of a professional league, the absence of this type of leadership is a sure ticket to disaster. Of course, having a plan does not ensure success. The NFL's 2004 Super Bowl halftime fiasco, thanks to Janet Jackson's "wardrobe malfunction," and the failures of the WUSA and the XFL were fundamental miscalculations in marketing strategy.[2] The lack of a strategy, however, simply multiplies the odds of failure. In this chapter, we lay out the basic elements required for strategic marketing leadership. We refer to these elements as marketing management, but we emphasize that the key to successful marketing management lies in the development of a comprehensive, strategic, and creative marketing plan. This plan must involve

a process that combines both strategy (the big picture) and tactics (the details of a plan). Note that throughout this text we purposefully don't just call it a marketing plan; we emphasize the concept of a marketing planning process (MPP) to delineate a calculated process formed from direct input from all sport marketing stakeholders. Subsequent chapters in this book flesh out the various tactical steps in the marketing management process. This chapter places each step in the broader perspective of strategy.

Sport Strategy Is More Than Locker Room Talk

The NFL, like the NBA, remained an industry leader over the last two decades by having clear strategies to develop and position their products in the marketplace of consumer needs. Although these leagues face their own challenges to retain prominence and profitability, their success came from carefully developed visions and plans—game plans, to use a sport term. In fact, many successful organizations have borrowed the notion of game plans from the successful coaches, who have always evaluated their own talent, carefully scouted their opponents, and developed their tactics and playbooks accordingly. In simple terms, that process is the essence of strategy, and it has spread from the locker rooms to the front offices of the sport industry.

In its simplest sense, strategy entails setting long-term goals, developing plans to achieve those goals, and then outlining tactical programs for execution. This process requires a continual analysis of the environment and the organization. The challenges of today's marketplace have forced sport executives to think more strategically, as shown in the following examples from tennis, golf, and ice hockey.[3]

Tennis

In 1960 American tennis had some 5.6 million participants (people who played at least once per year). By 1974 tennis was booming, and the number of participants had grown to 34 million. Then came the big slump in the 1980s as participation dwindled to 13 million in 1985. By 1995 tennis was still only half as popular as it had been 20 years before. The problems in tennis were recognized in 1995 when the Tennis Industry Association, or TIA (a trade association), announced their strategic Initiative to Grow the Game from the grassroots level upward. As Brad Patterson, TIA executive director, put it, each tournament, manufacturer, club, association, and pro tour had been marketing itself: "The fact is that nobody was marketing tennis." Tennis, in effect, had lost its position to aerobics, in-line skating, basketball, and other competitors. In the last decade, the United States Tennis Association (USTA) and the TIA have developed a range of programs under such banners as Play Tennis America and Tennis Welcome Center, which included free clinics, free equipment, and organized leagues for all ages. As Patterson reminded his colleagues, "What was missing was that we were not telling people to come out and play tennis." Gauging the success of these campaigns is difficult. The tennis industry claims that participation is on the rise, but

statistics from the Sporting Goods Manufacturers Association and the National Sporting Goods Association (NSGA) suggest flat or declining participation among both casual and frequent players. In the spectator arena, the USTA recently sought to boost its sagging tournament ratings by creating a series with a point system, along the lines of NASCAR. They needed to do something fast. A 2002 ESPN poll had reported that almost 57 percent of respondents had indicated they were "not at all interested" in the U.S Open—the marquee event. In a 2004 Turnkey Sports Poll, 52.4 percent of sport industry executives believed that getting recognizable players was the biggest challenge facing pro tennis. Tennis has a long way to go, but at least it has begun to pursue an integrated strategy.[4]

As of March 2011 the most recently released USTA membership data showed 700,000 individual members, 7,000 organizational memberships, and an estimated 25 million people playing tennis. Public interest in the sport, however, continues to decline. The *New York Observer* noted that TV ratings were down for the 2010 Wimbledon match featuring Rafael Nadal against Tomas Berdych, which scored a 1.8 rating, the lowest rating since 1988 and one of the lowest in history. The interesting story of Novak Djokovic in 2011 and the rebirth of U.K. favorite Andy Murray in 2012, under the tutelage of Ivan Lendl, have added some freshness and hence increased interest in men's tennis among existing tennis fans. But these events have not been enough to raise overall ratings by drawing new fans to the sport.

Golf

In the mid-1990s golf participation was stagnant. In 1997 the World Golf Foundation (WGF)—a nonprofit entity funded by the PGA, USGA, LPGA, Calloway, Titleist, and others—announced a campaign called the First Tee, which aimed to develop hundreds of new golf facilities around the country in the next decade. Former president George Bush agreed to serve as honorary chairperson of the initiative. The effort stemmed from a simple conclusion that the game of golf was limited only by the availability of facilities. Tiger Woods might excite millions, but millions couldn't take up the game without available, affordable facilities. At the WGF's first GOLF 20/20 conference in November 2000, Chairman

Tim Finchem set three major goals for golf to achieve by 2020:

- Reach 55 million participants
- Reach 1 billion rounds played
- Achieve a level of interest in the United States comparable to that of professional football

By 2002 the number of courses in the United States had increased to 14,725 from 13,528 in 1998. NSGA statistics indicated a rise in the number of one-time players—up to 28.3 million. At the same time, however, the number of frequent players (40 or more days per year) had plateaued at 6 million. The number of rounds played had actually decreased in the near term, from 518 million in 2000 to 502 million in 2002. Rounds played continued to slip in 2003, to 495 million. The industry was still struggling to unite around a clear strategy. Many experts thought that too many courses had been built, that the issue was oversupply, not too little demand. Although Finchem and the WGF stood firmly behind a grassroots strategy that built the base of novice players, including those in inner cities, Acushnet's chairman, Wally Uihlein, was less sanguine: "GOLF 20/20 is a noble effort, but it's in default and denial of golf's middle-class requisite." Uihlein claimed that Finchem was "a little bit naive as to our ability to bring in non-middle-class components to prop up the numbers." To Rich Luker, who guided the Chilton Sports Poll in the 1990s and then headed up the Leisure Intelligence Group, the major problem was not the availability of golf greens; it was the availability of time. Spending five or more hours to play a round of golf is considered too much in an age of multitasking: "Golf doesn't meet the relevance of a generation for whom option, speed and simplicity are the most important things." Like tennis, golf had a long way to go, but at least it recognized the need for strategy.[5] Hence, the PGA initiated its Tee It Forward program featuring Jack Nicklaus to encourage players who do not hit the ball that far to use the forward tee boxes to speed up play and enjoy the game more.

According to the National Gold Foundation (NGF), the independent resources dedicated to supporting all the people, companies, facilities, and associations that earn their living in golf:

- The United States lost nearly four million golfers from 2007 through 2012.

- Golf participation in the United States in 2012 fell to levels not seen in 25 years; only 9.2 percent of the population played golf.
- The numbers of female and junior golfers dropped 23 and 35 percent, respectively, over the previous five years.
- Golf continued to be viewed by many as an expensive game, which goes hand in hand with perceptions that it is an elitist game.[6]

The number of annual rounds of golf played in the United States fell from 518 million to 475 million in the past decade, and it declined for the fifth consecutive year in 2011. The number of players peaked at 30 million in 2005 and has been sliding since, to 26.1 million golfers in 2010, the most recent year for which numbers were available. Based on these findings, the PGA launched Golf 2.0, an initiative to increase the U.S. golfer participation and increase frequency of play. Coupled with the grassroots participation programs, such as First Tee, the USGA, PGA, and LPGA have set a goal of increasing the U.S. golfer population to an unprecedented 40 million by 2020.[7]

Golf 2.0 initiatives include the Get Golf Ready and Play Golf America programs as the most important initiative ever undertaken by the 96-year-old PGA organization. Golf 2.0 is a targeted, focused, long-range strategic plan for the golf industry to achieve a substantial increase in the number of golfers, the number of rounds of golf played, and the revenue generated from golf over the next decade among current and potential consumers of the game. Golf 2.0 is a philosophy based on the belief that golf must change now. "Millions of people love this game, but the staggering statistic is that (in 2010) we lost 4.6 million people. It's terribly important that we recognize that golf doesn't fit currently into the lives of consumers," said Darrell Crall, senior director of Golf 2.0. Goals of the plan are to

- retain and strengthen the existing core golfers,
- engage the 61 million lapsed golfers who still have an interest in playing, and
- drive new players.[8]

Golf is expensive and time consuming—two major factors that have led to continual decline in participation despite the proliferation of new golf courses and hence the availability of the sport. The major organizations in golf are clearly now addressing this widespread defection, but it remains to be seen whether it is too little, too late or just in time to sustain the future of the sport.

Hockey

In the fall of 2004, 32 stakeholders met in St. Paul, Minnesota, for the Grow Hockey Summit under the aegis of the International Hockey Industry Association. The IHIA's founding members include major manufacturers such as Itech Sport Products, Nike Bauer Hockey, Sher-Wood Hockey, Hespeler Hockey, and Louisville Hockey, all of whom have an obvious stake in growth. The summit attracted representatives from the NHL, the NHLPA, USA Hockey, Hockey Canada, and the International Ice Hockey Federation. Although the group was helpless to stop a lockout of the world's top hockey league, they did agree on an issue demanding concerted effort: the slow overall participation growth of 1 to 2 percent, although much better for females. The summit also recognized the importance of three youth segments: 5- to 8-year-old entry-level players, 10- to 14-year-olds thinking of leaving the sport, and 18- to 34-year-olds entering or reentering. In all cases, the obstacles to growth revolve around cost, time, availability of ice, and perceptions of violence. Attendees circulated a press release in which they committed to developing a strategic plan that included the following:

- Increasing accessibility through an emphasis on fun
- Partnerships with kids' organizations
- Increased skill focus
- Renewed focus on ice, in-line, street, and other types of hockey
- An international Grow Hockey Day
- Ties with the retail community, such as a Welcome to Hockey kit
- Targeted communication to hockey moms

- Development of First Goal, a collaboration to include equipment discounts and a mass media campaign

With the NHL in lockout mode for the entire 2004–2005 season and again for the first half of the 2012–2013 season, hockey is clearly in dire need of a grassroots growth strategy.[9]

The two factors that have hurt hockey the most are the frequent NHL labor strife at the highest level of the game in North America and the lack of consistent coverage on major television networks in the United States. Even though NBC started its latest broadcast rights agreement in 2007, the limited game schedule and changing start dates and times have not driven the desired increase in ratings. ESPN's increased coverage of the sport in the past two years through their *SportsCenter* show has increased the visibility of hockey. NBC's addition of regular weekend broadcasts during the second half of the season and the playoffs coupled with extremely competitive series on the ice led to ratings for the 2013–14 NHL Conference Championships and Stanley Cup that were among the highest in 17 years. Nonetheless, hockey's 4.8 TV rating, the highest ever for the NHL on NBC for game 1 of the 2013 Stanley Cup Championships, and double the rating for the prior year, paled in comparison to ABC–ESPN's 14.7 rating for the Heat versus Spurs NBA Championship game 6. Hockey's fan base is loyal and passionate but still limited in the United States.

The Harris Interactive poll in December 2011 surprisingly showed hockey to be at least as popular as basketball in the United States. This survey, conducted since 1985, asked participants what their favorite sport was. Among the 2,237 adults surveyed online, men's professional and men's collegiate hockey each rated at a consistent 5 percent level of interest in the past decade, significantly ahead of the 1985 level and substantively higher than the level in 2003. Table 2.1 is adapted from this poll and reveals the significant

TABLE 2.1 Harris Interactive Poll

1985 (%)	1989 (%)	1992 (%)	1993 (%)	1994 (%)	1997 (%)	1998 (%)	2002 (%)	2003 (%)
2	3	3	3	5	4	3	3	3

2004 (%)	2005 (%)	2006 (%)	2007 (%)	2008 (%)	2009 (%)	2010 (%)	2011 (%)	Change 1985–2011 (%)
4	5	4	5	5	4	5	5	+3

Data from Harris Interactive Poll, Dec. 2011.

growth in interest among men in both professional and collegiate hockey in the United States during the past decade, although at 5 percent hockey remains very much a niche sport.

Hockey has clearly developed an avid core group of fans who support the game with fervor and whose average attendance frequency is the highest of fans of all the major professional leagues. One of the major reasons cited for the growth in interest among more casual fans is the increased scoring in the NHL. Before the lockout in 2004, many hockey games were viewed as boring defensive battles. The league noted this perception and implemented significant rule changes designed to reduce the neutral zone trap and other negative defensive strategies. These changes led to a speeding up of the flow of the game and produced more scoring chances and goals.

Tennis, golf, and hockey leaders began to realize that marketing their sports required broad, integrated efforts—campaigns that would transcend old divisions between amateurs and professionals, between grassroots and elites, and between manufacturers and governing bodies. As the golf, tennis, and hockey industry groups demonstrate, marketing strategy is not a privilege reserved for the big-time leagues and teams. It is a necessity for all organizations, all the way down to the grassroots level. In fact, given the financial squeeze at the grassroots level, marketing strategy may be even more essential there. Grassroots leaders cannot defer their marketing efforts simply because they lack a support staff. David Hoch, former athletics director at Eastern Technical High School in Baltimore County, Maryland, stated the matter clearly: "For many athletics directors, the first stumbling block to starting a marketing program is the work it adds to your already hectic schedule." But, added Hoch, marketing can no longer be viewed as an "extra or frivolous effort. Marketing is just as important as scheduling facilities, evaluating coaches, and the numerous other responsibilities" that any high school AD must address on a daily basis.[10]

Marketing Planning Process

The elements of marketing strategy can be conceptualized in models. Marketing theorist

Philip Kotler has called one model the marketing management process (MMP). We have blended Kotler's model with others (see figure 2.1) to create our version, which we consider both a step-by-step process and a way of thinking. As some of the activities at the end of the chapter suggest, the MMP can be used to develop a marketing plan. But the marketing plan must be integrated into an organization's larger strategic plan, which includes finance, asset management, resource allocation, and personnel management, among other elements. The MMP is the backbone of marketing; it emphasizes interdependencies at all stages.[11]

Although subsequent chapters examine the MMP steps in greater detail (e.g., research, product development, pricing, and promotion), a brief introduction is important here if only to emphasize that decision making is an ongoing, circular process. The business side of sport really has no off-season (see the sidebar on strategic opportunism later in this chapter). As figure 2.1 suggests, a marketing plan aligns tactical details and operations (such as pricing) with broader organizational strategies (such as setting attendance goals). To use a sport metaphor, tactics are the offensive and defensive plays or sets, used for various situations, that collectively make up a strategic game plan for victory. The game plan provides a broad direction to the coach or quarterback, who picks the specific tactics to be used during the game itself. This chapter introduces that important blend of strategy and tactics. Just as it is on the field, court, and ice, all elements of the plan must be synchronized and fully integrated.

The strategic steps of the MMP and their relation to the remaining book chapters are as follows:

- Develop vision, position, and purpose (chapters 3–5, 16)
- Develop strategic goals and objectives (chapter 5)
- Develop a marketing mix plan (chapters 6–13)
- Integrate the marketing plan into the broader organizational strategy (chapter 15)
- Control and evaluate all elements of the marketing plan (chapters 14, 15)

Tactical components   Strategic components

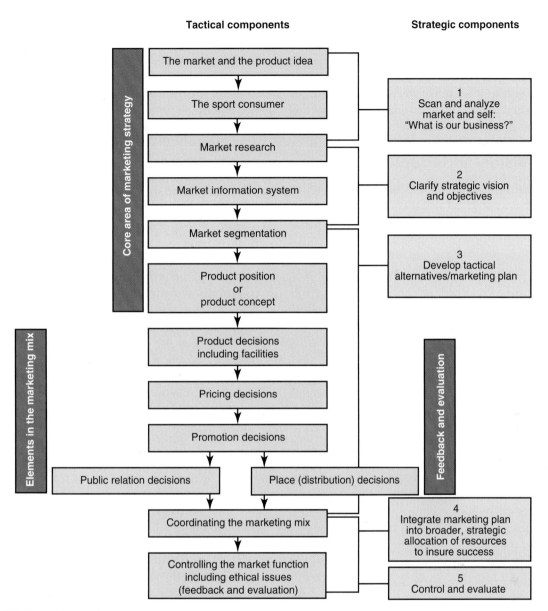

FIGURE 2.1   The marketing management process in sport.

Adapted, by permission, from B. Mullin, 2000, Characteristics of sports marketing. In *Successful sport management*, edited by H. Appenzeller and G. Lewis (Durham, NC: Carolina Academic Press), 123.

ACTIVITY 2.1 The Marketing Planning Process (MPP)

For this WSG activity, assume you were just hired as the new director of marketing for the Tulsa Shock. The Shock is a professional basketball team based in Tulsa, Oklahoma, playing in the Women's National Basketball Association (WNBA). As of 2012, they had never qualified for the WNBA playoffs in their years in Tulsa. The Shock does not share a city with an NBA counterpart.

Strategic Step 1: Develop Vision, Position, and Purpose

In the following sections, we provide examples of the way that core vision and ideology should inform decisions and position the sport product or service. We also discuss the importance of using a technique known as a SWOT analysis (strengths, weaknesses, opportunities, threats) that involves the use of data-based marketing (DBM) systems and customer relationship management (CRM) systems to provide market intelligence and identify fads and trends (and determine which is which). DBM systems house fan contact data and essential information such as purchase history. CRM systems provide a 360-degree record of all customer interactions with the organization, such as complaints about traffic, fans sitting nearby, and broken seats.

Core Vision and Ideology

When we talk about developing a vision, we mean visualizing the organization. We borrow the concept from sport psychologists, who teach athletes to visualize the process and outcomes of performance. Above all, any strategic plan must operate within the framework of the organization's core vision and ideology, as James C. Collins and Jerry I. Porras argued in *Built to Last: Successful Habits of Visionary Companies*, one of the most successful management books of the millennium. Collins and Porras examined the performance of a set of companies over the last century. What distinguished the firms that seemed "built to last"? In their words,

> The fundamental distinguishing characteristic of the most enduring and successful corporations is that they preserve a cherished core ideology while simultaneously stimulating progress and change in everything that is not part of their core ideology. Put another way, they distinguish their timeless core values and enduring core purpose (which should never change) from their operating practices and business strategies (which should be changing in response to a changing world).

With increasing frequency of on-field violence and off-field negative behavior problems by NFL players, the league has had to review its strategic plan, check its core purpose, and ask itself whether extremely negative player behaviors like the New Orleans Saints' Bountygate, or former San Diego Chargers player Junior Seau's suicide (attributed to concussion-related injuries that apparently led to permanent brain damage), or Kansas City Chiefs player Jovan Belcher's murder of his girlfriend and subsequent suicide at the team's practice facility fit with the NFL's core vision as an organization whose product appeals to all segments of society, including youth

and women. Such questions have been equally troubling for school and college athletics, whose leaders must balance commercial realities with educational core visions. The path has not been easy. Again, the fundamental task lies in the effort to develop, recognize, and sustain a core vision, even as the organization changes.[12]

In the early 2000s Ohio State University made such an effort under the leadership of then athletics director Andy Geiger. OSU athletics is a mighty big boat to steer; its 36 programs make it one of the nation's broadest and largest departments (with a budget over $80 million at that time, which has now grown closer to $200 million per annum, it's not surprising that in January 2013 the school announced a 25 percent increase in premium-seating ticket prices for its perennially sold-out football home games). Its operating waters are filled with shoals and sharks, as the Maurice Clarett, Jim O'Brien, and Jim Tressel episodes in the past decade demonstrate. In early 2005 Andy Geiger announced his retirement because, in his own words, "I find that my work is no longer fun." Some things haven't changed for Buckeyes AD Gene Smith. In 2012, following major NCAA penalties, the football team was not allowed to play in a bowl game despite an undefeated season. But Smith's ability to be proactive and get ahead by reporting those transgressions led to a strengthening of his position with the school's board of trustees under the leadership of Bobby Shottenstein. Despite major problems, Ohio State has been extraordinarily successful both on the field and in the classroom. One reason is the recognition of a core vision and consistent dedication to that ideal, developed during a series of staff meetings based on a shared reading of *Built to Last*.

OSU's core vision rests on six elements, which are spelled out on its website and in numerous publications. These elements are considered when hiring a coach or developing a marketing plan:

- Education and enrichment of the student-athlete
- Integrity in all aspects of behavior
- Innovation in approach and spirit
- Excellence throughout the organization
- Respect for the individual
- A tradition of leadership

As Andy Geiger and his staff knew full well in the early 2000s and as Gene Smith and his staff currently live every day, a core vision can't prevent mistakes or public relations nightmares, but it can steer a big boat.[13]

SWOT Analysis

All strategy begins with an understanding of the environment and the organization or the place of the product within it. As executives in tennis, golf, and hockey realized, the organization must know where they are before they can decide where they want to go or how to get there. Knowing where the organization is requires a knowledge of consumers and their behavior (see chapter 3), which in turn requires careful research and the development of a data-based marketing (DBM) system or customer relationship management (CRM) system (see chapter 4) that supplies timely, accurate, and usable data to decision makers. As we will explain, the elements of the DBM and CRM systems range from magazine clippings to vast computer databases that describe the customer's every interaction with the organization.

Step 1 often includes what is called a SWOT analysis, a careful analysis of the strengths and weaknesses of the organization as well as the opportunities and threats in the marketplace or beyond. The SWOT analysis relies on the DBM system and reinforces its importance. Unless marketers understand their industry and their business,

Studies on Member and Fan Preference Change Put the "O" in Opportunity

Perhaps no segment of sport business has undergone more metamorphological change than the health club business. When the principal author became a consultant in this field in 1977, the big growth business was racquetball clubs. Tennis was becoming too expensive for many people, and the cardiovascular benefits of the more vigorous workout obtained playing the wristy racquetball game drove a customized-facility building boom.

Although new purpose-built racquetball clubs were sprouting up in many suburbs of large cities throughout America, IRSA (International Racquet Sports Association), then the leading association in the racket, fitness, and health club industry, noted that many of the racquetball courts were being built at tennis clubs. On the space required for one tennis court, six racquetball courts could be built instead. Instead of 2 or at most 4 players occupying the one tennis court, the club could instead have 12 members using the club at the same time, driving more revenue at the bar, restaurant, and pro shop afterward. Only a few short years later the racquetball craze began to die, and those racquetball courts were quickly transformed into variable-resistance exercise machine centers as the Nautilus craze took off. Shortly afterward, the spaces became aerobic dance studios. But in true renaissance fashion, the health and fitness industry continued to morph and add exciting new features each year to retain their members. In quick order came free weights, personalized trainers, and prescriptive evaluation of strength, flexibility, and endurance. The addition of personal trainers led to diversification into performance enhancement, diet and nutrition supplements, and eventually "juicing" (the legal kind). Juice bars located within the health and fitness facility offered patrons a postworkout way to replenish energy.

The latter-day desire for more effective and efficient workouts has led to highly specialized equipment and the creation of spinning classes, CrossFit training, Pilates, kick boxing, Zumba, Insanity, and a myriad of exercise methodologies. These activities have been incorporated into today's health clubs, YMCAs, YWCAs, JCCs, and community fitness facilities to such an extent that racquet sports are rarely emphasized.

Such rapid and constant change in consumer taste is, of course, a marketing consultant's and researcher's dream because the facility owner cannot exist without having expert advice, constantly talking to customers, and interpreting consumer trends.

they are doomed. Later in this chapter, we consider some megatrends in the sport industry and offer some tips on culling trends from fads.

Ideally, the SWOT analysis involves the full range of key stakeholders and staff constituents in the organization. In the early 2000s two of the authors (Mullin and Sutton) helped the NBA develop an internal consulting group (the Team Marketing and Business Operations Group, or TMBO), which, among other things, helped individual franchises develop SWOT analyses. As the NBA's TMBO insisted, narrowly crafted, top-down planning, whether farmed out to consultants or not, rarely succeeds because it invariably misses the mark and few workers are willing to buy into the effort. Knowing your organization means paying close attention to what Peter Drucker called the theory of the business, which he defined as assumptions about the environment, the organizational mission, and the core competencies needed to accomplish the mission. Managers must be sure that the theory is realistic and widely understood.[14]

The Detroit Pistons provide an excellent example of how the location of an arena can have a massive effect on the composition of attendance. Despite the fact that Detroit has the second highest percentage of African American population among U.S. cities at 82.7 percent, according to the U.S. Census Bureau's *Quick Facts*, updated in June 2013, the team draws less than 10 percent of its fan base from the African American community. Of course, the dreadful economy in the Michigan city may have something to do with this disparity, but current management is convinced that the location of the Palace of Auburn Hills, in an affluent suburb 25 miles (40 km) north of the city, is by far the larger contributing factor.

Under the leadership of President/CEO Dennis Mannion, the Pistons used SWOT analysis and sophisticated fan and market research programs to identify that mass media advertising to the downtown Detroit African American population is futile, even with the disproportionate interest among African Americans for watching NBA basketball on television. Consequently, the team has adapted their strategy specifically for this segment to drive in-arena attendance sampling. A comprehensive school student award voucher program targeted African American families of good students (those with B plus or better grades, perfect attendance, or good behavior),

offering two complimentary tickets for the student and a sibling or friend. The voucher program had no adult purchase requirement for those schools offering free lunches (primarily those of low-income inner-city families). For the city and suburban schools not in free lunch programs, the complimentary tickets were contingent on the purchase of at least one adult ticket.

In this manner, a situational strategy was devised that varied with each target segment. Further, this strategy was communicated directly rather than via the mass media, which was essential in order to protect the integrity of the Pistons broader offerings to the more affluent market area surrounding Auburn Hills. Following are a few additional examples of strategies devised through understanding the organization's place within its environment and its target segments.

- Athletics club manager Marla Chavetz built a strong clientele by knowing her consumers. When member surveys showed that a large number of older members had orthopedic problems and that asthma was far more prevalent than expected, Chavetz responded with clearer guidelines on dealing with knee and shoulder rehabs and working with people who had asthma. Says Chavetz, "The whole point is to identify your clients' needs and to develop programming to meet those needs."

- Burton Snowboards increased market share from 30 to 40 percent in the latter half of the 1990s by carefully culling the opinions of some 300 professional riders, whose opinions on product design often overruled those of Burton's top designers.

- The Florida Panthers, the NFL, and the USTA have employed the Sports Management Research Institute to conduct in-depth fan research, using both traditional methods (focus groups, surveys) and more innovative ones such as mystery shoppers. As SMRI's CEO Kathy Davis explained: "We put on a hat and pretend we're Joe Fan to experience all the elements. We take pictures, test out toilets. Is there a baby-changing amenity? Is the ATM functioning? Are they friendly when you come into the parking lot?" Ohio State University hired the Aspire Group to conduct extensive fan research with the many committees and constituent groups within the university community before rolling out its aggressive price increases for the 2013 football season. The organization believed that the price increases were essential to sustaining a financial structure that would allow the university to offer its 36 sports at the desired level of excellence, which is to compete perennially for conference and national championships.

Sport Megatrends in the New Millennium

Marketing strategy is not an easy game, especially when the environment is rapidly changing, as it has been pretty much since the 1950s. An annual SWOT analysis is essential. This analysis can be conducted internally by any sport management team willing to take time out and think (as recommended by Rich Horwath in his *New York Times* best-selling book *Deep Dive*). But this essential, annual internal reflection process must begin with an objective evaluation of strengths and weaknesses. The S and W portion of this exercise is highly dependent on the staff being honest and not fearing reprisals from the boss. Consequently, outside facilitation is frequently critical to success. The O and T portion of this exercise refers to a constant scanning of the environment, a search for trends and clues about the future, and objective analysis of the competition and economy. Of course, recognizing trends (more of a historical analysis) is far different from forecasting the future. Some trends, such as population growth and demographic shifts, have real predictive power. Consumer tastes are a different matter. Take automobile styles, for instance. In the late 1970s spikes in the price of gasoline prompted a trend toward smaller, fuel-efficient cars. No one predicted the surge of demand two decades later for tanklike, gas-guzzling sport utility vehicles. Just ask the executives who banked on the continued demand for minivans! By 2005, however, sales of big SUVs were again pinched by price increases at the gas pump. Forecasting is an art, not a science. A rigid faith in forecasts has led many an executive, in the words of *American Demographics*, to "plan for a future that never arrives, while a different future passes them by." We have already described two key trends in chapter 1—globalization and consolidation. Here are a few more worth noting.[15]

Women's Sports Continue to Crest   In 1970, 1 in 27 girls played on high school teams—less than 4 percent. By 2002, 33.5 percent of girls in high school were playing on sport teams. According to the 2010–11 NFHS (National Federation of State High School Associations) participation study, athletics participation grew for the 22nd straight year and the participation rate for girls was growing at double the rate for boys. Now, 42 percent of all high school sport participation is by girls.[16] The reason is simple—Title IX. And the Title IX generation has come of age, causing marketing implications that we will examine throughout the book. To be sure, stumbles have occurred at the big-time level, most notably the failure of the Women's United Soccer Association (WUSA) and Women's Professional Soccer (WPS). The WUSA began play in 2001 following the success of the U.S. national team in the 1999 World Cup, but the league was out of business by late 2003. The WPS was founded in 2007 but folded a few years later. Analysts blamed the WUSA's demise on the lack of financial controls, poor media strategy (including the decision to spurn a TV deal with TNT in favor of one with the Pax network), and an over-reliance on soccer moms as the target audience. As one consultant said, "For Gen-X moms, the whole 'soccer moms' concept is dead."[17] In 2013 the National Women's Soccer League played its inaugural season, which reinstated top-division women's soccer in the United States.

The failure of the WUSA is a reminder that a strong participant market does not guarantee the success of a professional league. But this does not diminish the growing importance of girls and women to the sport marketplace. Over the last decade, attendance at NCAA women's basketball games has tracked sharply upward in all three divisions, while it has been relatively flat or declining on the men's side. Or, take the case of ice hockey:[18]

- In 1991 USA Hockey had 5,533 registered female players. By 1997 the number was almost 21,000. By 2012 USA Hockey had a total of 66,692. In Canada, female participation had been growing steadily for several decades, tripling from 2000 to 2005. According to Hockey Canada, overall youth hockey participation in Canada from 2005 through 2011 declined by 15 percent overall and would have been a greater decline had it not been for continuing increases in girls' participation.[19]

- The NHL has estimated that 45 percent of NHL game attendees are female.
- A Fox–TMG poll taken after the Nagano Olympics indicated that over 80 percent of the people who watched the U.S. women's hockey team were either somewhat likely or very likely to watch a women's hockey game in the near future.
- Equipment manufacturers have begun to make hockey gear designed for girls and women. For instance, Louisville's pants for women have wider hips, a narrower waist, and more pelvic protection than the men's version. CCM's women's Tack brand skate is narrower through the heel.

More Action at the Grassroots   Women and girls both forged and reflected important links across sport levels, from the grassroots to the elite professionals. Female athletes often seemed to be throwbacks to an earlier age of unspoiled athletes who played for the love of the game and not for the next deal. Sponsors noticed this characteristic as they sought to spend their dollars more effectively. The most appealing segment of sport were the extreme or action sports—skateboarding, snowboarding, motocross biking, surfing. In the 1980s these sports were considered alternative and minor. By 2001 they had become mainstream and major, and skateboarding had more participants than baseball did. Television had the X-Games and the Gravity Games. Tony Hawk became the new Larry Bird. Experts wondered whether the growth would slow or fizzle, but the NFL was not taking any chances. Partnering with the NFLPA, the league channeled some $130 million into the creation of USA Football, whose prime objective was to boost participation in youth and amateur football.[20]

Digital Revolution Expands   In 1999–2000, Internet ticket sales accounted for less than 25 percent of individual game tickets sold in the NBA. By 2012–13 this figure has risen to over 90 percent of individual game tickets sold in advance of the game. People of all ages, especially the young, are seeking basic information instantly provided on their personal device of choice by the Internet.

In June 2004 the Pew Research Center released its Biennial News Consumption Survey based on telephone interviews with a national probability sample. Two-thirds of Americans (66 percent) indicated that they used the Internet for e-mail and for information, a 12 percent increase from 2000. One of the major shifts in the new millennium has been the steady increase in regular online news consumption—from 23 percent of Americans in 2000 to 25 percent in 2002 to 29 percent in 2004 and to a whopping 84 percent of U.S. adults having been online in 2013. The trend crosses categories of age, gender, race, ethnicity, and education and appears to be a key driver of Internet use. Two amazing 2013 statistics reveal the ubiquity of electronic communications in America: An estimated 72 percent of adult Internet users are now using social network sites, and 20 percent of U.S. adults are using Twitter.

The move to Internet news is part of a larger interactive digital trend. Like television and radio decades before, the Internet and the cell phone did not cause people to become less active couch potatoes. The digital age has simply rechanneled their activities. Fans now expect an interactive website that gives them a peek at the sight line they will have when they buy a ticket in a certain section. Drive-time commuters seek a piece of the "juice" by calling their favorite sports talk radio show. At a sport venue, they expect interactive kiosks and more. In 2006 Sprint Nextel and NASCAR were experimenting with fourth-generation cell phones that fans could rent at racetracks. These devices would provide video views from cameras attached to race cars, stream live chatter from the drivers and their pit crews, and deliver stats from a NASCAR database. In the future, fans will play the role of television or radio producer and director. And between live events, weblogs (a.k.a. blogs) and podcasts allow the everyday fan to develop a fan following of his or her own. In short, people are not just consuming the new technology; they are active producers. And the new technology promises new and cheaper avenues to reach these consumers. School, club, and college programs should begin to rethink their heavy reliance on newspaper ads and public service announcements to drive consumer awareness. The emerging markets have been digitized. As *BusinessWeek* summed up the digital revolution as of 2005, when some billion people were online, the Internet has nurtured the "power of us."[21]

More Battles Over Ambush Marketing In 1998 a post–Nagano Olympics survey of 512 consumers revealed that 55 percent incorrectly named Pepsi as an official Olympic sponsor. One reason for the confusion was the practice of ambush marketing, in which a nonsponsor corporation's ads create the image of sponsorship without using any official logos or symbols reserved for sponsors. At those same Olympics, Wendy's ran ads with a hockey theme, even though McDonald's was the official sponsor. Events such as road races or marathons, held on open, public venues, face special difficulties. At the 2005 Boston Marathon, one ambush marketing firm hired "guerrillas" to wear sandwich-board signs promoting a nonsponsor. One of them ran onto the course itself and joined a pack of competitors—all for $50 and an arrest by Boston police. Such antics have given rise to a new class of consultants. Before the 2000 Olympics in Sydney, an Australian sponsorship expert, Kim Skildum-Reid, offered a series of workshops promising "to teach marketers how to mount and protect themselves from ambush marketing campaigns," although ambush marketing is a problem with no clear solution in sight. A 2010 Turnkey Research survey found that 88.9 percent of responding sport marketing executives agreed that "ambush marketing can confuse consumers into thinking that a nonsponsor is actually a sponsor." As more sport organizations and athletes push their brands in the marketplace, further confusion among consumers is likely to occur. The sorting of multiple sponsorships is an escalating problem, especially in professional team sport where leagues, players, teams, and venues are all looking to push their brands. Short of costly lawsuits, there seem to be few effective antidotes to clever ambush marketing. Jeff Long, the former Atlantic 10 Athletic Conference's assistant commissioner for corporate sponsorships, summed up today's reality: "Frankly, as well as it can be done now . . . I'm always surprised there's not more."[22] Whether brands are ambushing or just being active in the market place, a recent study by Alan Mitchell of *Marketing Magazine* of sponsor recall at the 2012 London Olympics revealed that while Olympic sponsors Coca-Cola and McDonalds received recall scores above 25 percent of survey respondents, non-Olympic sponsors Nike and Barclays Bank received erroneous association scores above 10 percent of respondents. Mitchell's

obvious conclusion is that the latter two iconic brands receive a halo effect from their other sport sponsorships in the market place, which in this case was the United Kingdom.

Culling the Fads From the Trends

As marketers scan the environment, some trends jump out clearly. The rise of aerobics in the 1980s is a good example. Even the casual observer could see this. Nike, however, was slow to respond to the growing popularity of aerobics and lost that huge market to Reebok (now absorbed by Adidas). But sport history is punctuated by many fads that lit up the skies for a few years and then fizzled.

Examples are the roller-skating craze of the 1860s, the bicycle boom of the 1890s, the miniature golf mania of the 1920s, the racquetball boom in the late 1970s and early 1980s, and the roller-hockey craze of the 1990s. So how can the marketer distinguish between a solid trend and a short-term fad? Consultant Martin Letscher suggested a few simple questions that can help:

- Does the new development fit with other basic lifestyle trends or changes in the consumer world?
- How varied, immediate, and important are the benefits associated with the new development?

Sport marketers must be good at recognizing fads versus trends.

- Can the product or service be personalized or modified to meet individual needs?
- Is it a trend in itself or is it merely the manifestation of a larger trend?
- Has the new development been adopted by key consumers who drive change?
- Is the new development supported by changes in unrelated or surprising areas?

Although these questions are useful, no system is foolproof. After all, Letscher predicted a long boom for in-line skating, which has declined in popularity over the last two decades. Still, Letscher's questions provide an effective framework for analysis. In an industry in which racquetball is hot one year and fly-fishing the next, in which changing tastes in color create wild swings in merchandise from bright pastels to earth tones, to teal and black, to neon colors, the marketer must be careful to distinguish fads from trends.[23]

One significant trend that appears to be here to stay is the massive decline in print media readership. The proportion of Americans who read news on a printed page, in newspapers and magazines, continues to decline, even with online readership offsetting some of these losses:[24]

- According to Pew Research's October 2012 study, only 23 percent of U.S. adults surveyed said that they read a print newspaper the day before. This figure was down from 26 percent in 2010 and massively down from 47 percent in 2000. Of the adult population who read the *New York Times*, 55 percent said that they read it online; of those who said that they read the *USA Today*, 48 percent read it online.
- At the same time, the percentage of Americans who said that they saw news or news headlines on a social networking site the day before has doubled, from 9 percent to 19 percent, since 2010.
- Among adults younger than age 30, one-third said that they saw news on a social networking site the previous day, roughly the same proportion (34 percent) of this group who said that they saw any television news. Only 13 percent said that they read a newspaper either in print or digital form.

After the SWOT Analysis

After a SWOT analysis, the organization may need to adjust their strategy and steer a slightly or drastically different course. But an organization must always be careful not to stray from its core vision. As Collins and Porras argued in *Built to Last*, management should (1) develop new alignments to "preserve the core and stimulate progress" and (2) eliminate misalignments—"those that drive the company away from the core ideology and those that impede progress toward the envisioned future." Nike, for instance, expanded its strategy in the 1990s from its original focus on designing and marketing running shoes. Part of the reason was the lesson Nike learned from missing the aerobics market. By the mid-1990s, Nike had expanded into multiple lines of sport apparel and sport equipment, including ice hockey. With its many successful ties to athletes and events, the company even dabbled in the marketing and agent business. Would Nike expand too far from its core vision as a company?[25]

In the late 1990s Stanford University athletics decided that corporate signage was moving its programs too far from its educational mission. As then president Gerhard Casper explained, "Although the financial realities of collegiate sports probably make some corporate sponsorship inevitable, I look forward to a day when this is no longer true. In the meantime, at Stanford we will always make a point of saying that ours are student-athletes, with the emphasis on students." Therefore, Stanford told its sponsors, in effect: "We value your partnerships, but we will limit our exchange to tickets and hospitality. Corporate signs will be removed from our venues." After then athletics director Ted Leland explained the policy to one alumni group, they gave him a standing ovation. As Leland put it, "You usually don't get a standing ovation for anything but going to the Rose Bowl or disciplining the band." Leland also understood that Stanford's huge endowment enabled it to stay true to a core vision: "If the choice had been either to have advertising or drop sports, we might have come to a different decision."[26]

Like all organizations, Nike and Stanford must constantly assess the realism of their theory of the business—what Peter Drucker called the assumptions about (1) the environment, (2) the organizational mission, and (3) the core competencies needed to accomplish the mission. Following are some key triggers for testing these assumptions:[27]

- When you achieve original goals
- When something prevents goal attainment
- When you think you know your consumers well
- When you don't think that you know your consumers well
- When you sustain rapid growth
- When growth is unexpectedly slow
- When you are surprised by success
- When you are surprised by failure
- When a competitor enjoys unexpected success or failure
- When the environment is changing quickly
- When you haven't seriously questioned your assumptions in two years

Strategic Step 2: Develop Strategic Goals and Objectives

The development and reassessment of goals and objectives should emanate from ongoing analysis. Although people sometimes interchange the terms *goals* and *objectives*, goals are typically broad statements, whereas objectives provide more detailed, usually quantified targets. Jim Collins and Jerry Porras found that "visionary companies" typically articulated a few "big, hairy, audacious goals" (BHAGs) that could stimulate progress while preserving a core vision. The Denver Grizzlies Professional Hockey Club, a minor league expansion franchise that was establishing itself in a major-league market and a highly successful member of the International Hockey League in the mid-1990s, included both BHAGs and ordinary goals in its Community Relations Plan:[28]

1. To create high awareness and visibility for the Grizzlies in the community, we want positive publicity for all the programs in which we are involved. (It is not enough for us to do these programs; people have to see pictures, read about us, or see our involvement on TV.)

2. To generate goodwill and positive feelings about the Grizzlies in all areas of the community.

3. To develop new programs and support existing programs, which encourage youth participation in ice hockey and street hockey.

4. To identify quality organizations and provide them with Grizzlies tickets to be distributed to 100,000 underprivileged, handicapped, at-risk, or deserving youths throughout our market areas.

Goals 1 and 2 might be characterized as BHAGs for any sport organization. Positive publicity and goodwill for the whole organization in "all areas of the community"—those are surely big, hairy, and audacious goals. But the Grizzlies' goals also clarified direction in a number of ways. First, they call for publicity that will be measured in media exposure. Specific objectives might be exposure in a certain number of newspaper column inches or features on the evening television news. Second, the goals require goodwill in all areas of the community, measured perhaps by surveys in Denver's various inner-city neighborhoods and suburbs. As the fourth goal suggests, the Grizzlies did not want to be the team of only upscale, professional families. They wanted to be a team for all of Denver. And they set a specific target of distributing 100,000 tickets to particular groups of kids, particularly school-aged children with good grades, perfect attendance, or good behavior in school. This goal was big, hairy, and audacious indeed for a minor league team in a major league market.

Clarifying goals and objectives is what sets the manager apart from the caretaker. This step is necessary at all levels. At Technical High School in Baltimore County, Maryland, athletics director David Hoch made a clear choice in his marketing objectives. As he put it, the mission was not to boost revenue, but to promote greater awareness. Raising money by having hard-core families conduct a car wash would have been far easier. But that activity would not expand awareness and loyalty. At Technical High School,

"Success is measured by how our school's athletic programs are perceived—are we garnering more support? —not in how many dollars are added to the coffers." For Hoch, awareness and knowledge would be the foundation for steadier streams of financial support.[29]

Strategic Step 3: Develop a Ticket Marketing, Sales, and Service Plan

With a mission and objectives in place, the marketer must develop a plan at both the broad (strategic) and specific (tactical) levels. We have emphasized starting with a ticket marketing, sales, and service plan (TiMSS plan, as it has been dubbed by the Aspire Group), based on the notion that ticket sales and attendance is the trunk of the sport business money tree that feeds all the other sport marketing revenue streams (marketing partnerships and sponsorships, food and beverage and hospitality, merchandise and licensing, and so on). This process requires a return to the database to identify the targeted consumer segments (the way that the Grizzlies identified inner-city neighborhoods and suburbs as a specific segment for one of their programs). One of the most important ways for sport marketers to segment consumers is by their position on the escalator of involvement, a concept that we examine later. After identifying target segments, the marketer must develop products; prices; distribution systems; promotions; and public relations, media, and sponsorship programs that will ensure the successful attainment of objectives and mission. These functions make up the core of this book—chapters 6 through 16.

ACTIVITY 2.2 Capture the Fans
In this WSG activity, and based on your work with the Tulsa Shock (see activity 2.1), assume that one of your favorite sport teams hires you away from the Shock to serve as their director of marketing. Your first two assignments are to create a fan data capture plan and to create a Ticket Marketing Sales and Service plan (TiMSS plan).

Market Segmentation and Determining Key Targets

People are different. That goes without saying. Some sport businesses (e.g., personal training services) treat every consumer as an individual, creating a program tailored to individual needs and capabilities. This solution is not practical or profitable in all situations. The Portland Sea Dogs of AA baseball, for instance, may tailor ticket plans for corporate sponsors or for special group outings, but they do not have the staff or resources to approach each person in southern Maine with an individual message. At the same time, the Sea Dogs have more than one message for more than one target market. They recognize market segments consisting of consumers grouped with others with similar characteristics. Marketing theorists have typically considered several bases for segmentation, which we discuss in detail in chapter 5:

- Demographic information—age, sex, income, education, profession
- Geo-market information—location of residence by zip code
- Psychographic information—lifestyle factors such as activities, interests, and opinions
- Product usage rate—attendance or activity frequency, or size of donation
- Product benefits—product attributes or benefits that are most important to the consumer and consumers' perceptions regarding the major benefits of the product and its competitors

Obviously, any segmentation strategy relies on the DBM system to distinguish marketable clusters. Although marketing theorists differ on definitions, some clusters may be called niches—small groups of consumers who share special, often unfulfilled needs or interests. One might view Fantasy GM Football or Rotisserie Baseball (initially at least) as a niche market of statistics-hungry fanatics who relish any chance to argue about player talent and trades and are willing to spend hours and considerable money for league registration, for player trade fees, and even for services like CSA's ScoutPro, which won a competition as the most accurate predictor of

The market strategy you employ affects what audience you target. If you're selling luxury cars, the typical college student isn't your target audience.

NFL player performance. These days, such sport consumers appear to make up more than a niche. According to the Fantasy Sport Trade Association (FTSA), 34.5 million people played fantasy sports in the United States and Canada in 2012.[30]

Marketing databases also create the potential for something closer to individual marketing strategies, sometimes called *relationship marketing*. For instance, a database of information on season-ticket holders would allow a marketer to send birthday greetings along with information on special events (such as concerts) or special group deals (for children's birthdays).[31]

Market Development Using the Escalator Concept

User segments are especially important in the sport business because they constitute the sport

consumer escalator (see figure 2.2)—perhaps the most important concept in this book. We discuss the escalator from many angles in the chapters that follow, but for now a simple explanation will do. The escalator is a graphic representation of consumer movement to higher levels of involvement in a sport, as a player or a fan. The escalator concept was developed by Bernie Mullin (who adapted baseball executive Bill Giles' simpler staircase concept) in a 1978 manuscript that was the original basis for this book. The escalator suggests that sport organizations should invest first and foremost in nurturing existing consumers (retain). The second step is focusing on casual fans (grow) to make them more avid fans. The final step is trying to create new fans (acquire). Although campaigns to attract new fans are important, they cannot match for impact a strategy that moves current consumers a few steps up the escalator of involvement and commitment.

The escalator concept has been supported by consumer research among both participants and spectators. In the 1970s, for instance, Dick Lipsey began national, syndicated research on the sporting goods business. These studies, one of which is now the annual National Sporting Goods Association survey, supported some important elements of the sport escalator, including the fact that new participants represented a minor portion of total purchases (from 5 to 12 percent of dollars and from 10 to 20 percent of units sold). The conclusion was that sport participants moved up an escalator of involvement and that most equipment buyers were already playing the sport and looking for ways to improve.[32]

For team sport marketers, the escalator is crucial, in part because fan surveys indicate clear intentions to move up the escalator. For instance, fans who currently attend three games per year typically indicate their intention to attend five or six games the next year. The key is to create a ticket marketing sales and service plan marketing plan, using an array of elements and tactics, that can satisfy the needs of various consumer clusters and thereby move user groups up the escalator.

Later in this text we go into more depth about the applied strategy and execution of the escalator concept. We identify the three essential stages mentioned earlier: retain—keep avid fans high up on the escalator; grow—move more casual fans up to a higher level of attendance or

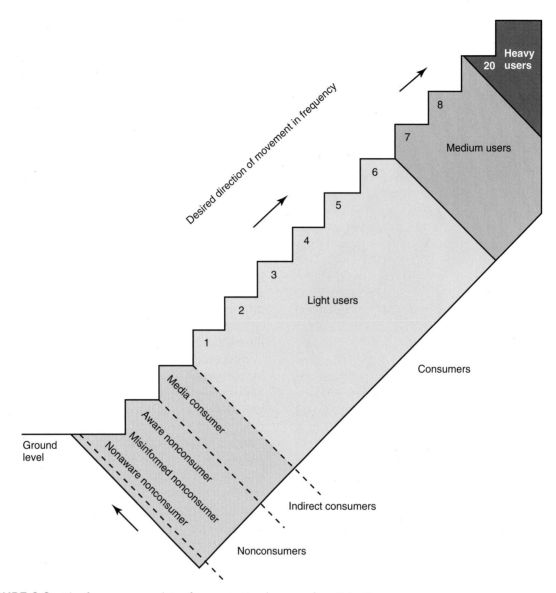

FIGURE 2.2   The frequency escalator for sport attendance and participation.

participation; and acquire—intelligently attract new fans or sport participants from those most likely to respond to the marketing efforts. At the same time, even a casual fan knows that great numbers of consumers can fall off the escalator at any time. Nike and Reebok suffered serious sales dips in the 1990s, in part because sport had lost its luster as a fashion statement in the youth market. More earthy shoes, like the ones that Timberland made, became trendy. Similarly, fan defections can become hemorrhages for many reasons beyond a long losing streak. For this reason, as we explain in chapters 5, 8, 10, 11, and 12, the smartest

organizations have multiple tactics and plans to reach user segments all along the escalator. The NHL, for instance, had problems translating the rabid devotion of local core fan groups into anything resembling a strong national consumer base. Television ratings demonstrate clearly that outside its immediate markets, hockey has not caught on with consumers at the bottom of the escalator. In 2003 the league began running ads in which entertainers like Shania Twain and Jim Belushi explained the finer points of rules, coaching tactics, and playing styles. As an NHL executive put it, "We wanted to have a diverse group of celebrities who would appeal outside of hockey." The NHL and its member teams used a concerted TiMSS campaign, emphasizing strategies and tactics all along the escalator, to rebound after the lockout of 2004–2005, and it no doubt was dusted off and used again for the restart after the 2012–13 season labor stoppage.[33]

Product Development and Positioning

One way to move consumers up the escalator is to design, redesign, and promote products to capture special space in the minds of target consumers. This strategy is sometimes called positioning. The concept was promoted in the 1980s by two advertising executives whose book title captured their argument: *Positioning: The Battle for Your Mind.* Their basic mantra was simple: "Positioning is not what you do to a product. Positioning is what you do to the mind of the prospect. That is, you position the product in the mind of the prospect." As we discuss in chapter 6, product positioning is not simply a matter of branding and advertising; it also involves research, development, and design. Some leagues use rule changes to reposition themselves. Baseball redesigned its basic product with the designated hitter, largely to reposition itself as a more exciting and offensive sport in the face of football's smashing popularity in the 1960s. Ice hockey clamped down on the worst of its street-fighting image with tough rules against the third man in and against leaving the bench during a fight.[34]

There are many positions to occupy in the sport industry. Take the notion of "major league" sport. The marketplace is fluid. In the past, many viewed NASCAR as blue-collar entertainment for Southern Bubbas and their women. If that was ever completely true, it is no longer: NASCAR became the hottest growing major league sport for the high-class corporate suits, male or female. One way that NASCAR shifted its position was with new, modern megatracks, complete with hundreds of corporate boxes and upscale dining facilities.

By 2004 NASCAR had a 10-month season that included 1,500 races held in 100 venues that ranged over 36 states. One of the most successful was in Loudon, New Hampshire, far from Bubbaville. As NASCAR's communications director told the *Boston Globe*, the term *NASCAR dads* proved NASCAR's national impact: "NASCAR dads are everywhere. They're in New England." The Northeast, in fact, accounted for a full 20 percent of NASCAR's fan base. The West had 19 percent. More than 13 million spectators watched live NASCAR events in 2003. The association claimed to have 40 million passionate, hard-core fans who crossed all demographic lines.[35] Sadly for NASCAR, the extended economic recession that started in 2007 hit their fan base harder than that of any other major league sport, given the high percentage of its fans who have lower incomes. As a result many tracks have downsized, and NASCAR stopped announcing the attendance at its events in the 2013 season.

While NASCAR aspired to corporate embrace, the Major League Soccer (MLS) commissioner at the time, Doug Logan, looked to position his league as an alternative to the corporate glitz of his higher-profile counterparts. Logan articulated his position at the start of the 1998 season: MLS fans were an amalgam of soccer purists, young soccer players (and their moms, no doubt), Hispanics, and the disenfranchised fan (especially the baseball fan) "who reads his newspaper back to front" and is "tired of the player actions." Emphasizing MLS as an alternative, Logan threw down the gauntlet at the "big" leagues and their emphasis on corporate revenues: "The biggest piece of garbage in American sports is the luxury box, with its couches faced away from the field . . . with everybody eating sushi." Logan's successor, Don Garber, moved the MLS along a track that emphasized new soccer-specific stadiums that combined big-league amenities with a grassroots feel for closeness. Although the amazing success of Toronto FC, the Seattle Sounders, and Portland Timbers is not to be overlooked, the boom in interest in soccer in North America, particularly among young males, appears to result largely from the rise in interest in the Barclays Premier League, as evidenced by strong increases in TV ratings on ESPN and Fox Soccer Channel. MLS' conscious shift in strategic emphasis by the league's Team Services staff has been away from the soccer mom accompanied by a hoard of grade school children, the so-called Chuck E. Cheese

Successful sport organizations know that they must evolve their marketing position in order to gain a larger audience.

approach, to young and middle-aged men, the way the game has been grown in Europe and Latin America for a century.[36]

Successful athletics clubs have also expanded their product concepts. As one expert argued, a tennis club member will have a hard time justifying her investment if she thinks only in terms of playing time. If cost per play is the driving mechanism for members, they're not going to be satisfied. Members are now renting space with a full range of amenities. On those terms, $20 per person per hour is a good investment.[37]

In a final example, the city of Lancaster, California, repositioned its entire city image by upgrading an athletics facility. An old (and debatable) song at the big-league level is to build a big, new stadium and get a big-league franchise that will make you a big-league city. Lancaster had a different idea: become one of America's major venues for softball tournaments. With a

clear vision, Lancaster expanded the city park to include six high-quality diamonds to go with assorted tennis courts, soccer fields, and basketball and volleyball courts. With a new logo and promotional campaign called Big 6, Lancaster increased its number of softball tournament days from 27 in 1994 to over 75 in 1996. Now expanded to the Big 8 complex, the Lancaster venue is a regular host for regional and national championships that attract revenue in hotel and restaurant fees and taxes from well outside the area. With a careful strategy, Lancaster repositioned itself on both the sport and revenue maps.[38]

Five Ps in the Sport Marketing Mix

The product is often referred to as one of marketing's four Ps:

- Product (development and positioning)
- Price
- Place (or product distribution)
- Promotion (personal selling, advertising, special events)

Because sport enjoys so much media attention, we treat public relations (usually considered part of promotion) as a separate P.

- Public relations

In a service-oriented industry like sport, all the Ps are influenced by how well employees interact with consumers; we could call this process management. We will see how critical process management is to the running of any promotion. For instance, if stadium personnel are surly to fans looking to exchange giveaway T-shirts (often for a different size), those fans, who might well be at their only game of the year, will likely fall off the escalator in the belief that the stadium is a hostile place to bring a family. In a wireless age, staying connected to consumers is possible 365/24/7. But that connection must always be positive. Nothing can replace the human touch. Great customer service will always be the major force moving fans up the escalator.

The mix of any marketing plan contains many elements and tactics. The bulk of this book is dedicated to describing the best practices that we have discovered in our four-plus decades in the field. Here are a few suggestions from one of the best practitioners of our time, John Spoelstra, whose work with the Portland Trail Blazers ensured his induction into anyone's sport marketing hall of fame.

- Bring radio and television production in house.
- Sell at least 80 percent of all tickets before the opening game.
- Develop a full menu of season-ticket packages, such as three-game, five-game, and weekend.
- Don't wait for a superstar. Find other ways to sell your team.
- Remember that, on average, 50 percent of a sport property's locally generated revenue comes from ticket sales and that all revenues are directly tied to ticket sales by the sport business money tree.

In which of the five Ps would you place each of these pointers?[39]

Integrating the marketing mix is the ongoing challenge for managers, even when they have a clear sense of strategy. Phil Guarascio, who worked at General Motors before taking over the NFL's top marketing position, put it clearly in describing the need to coordinate efforts: "This all has to be orchestrated to work. Fan development, sponsorship activation, and brand management can't be three entities; they have to be one." This idea is as true for a Pop Warner league as it is for the NFL.[40]

Strategic Step 4: Integrate the Marketing Plan Into a Broader, Strategic Resource Allocation

Before, while, and after developing the five Ps—product, place, price, promotion, and public relations—into a plan for action, the marketer must ensure that senior executives will support the plan. There's nothing worse for a marketer than to develop an imaginative, can't-miss plan that fails because it lacks support at a higher level. College athletics staffs often face this problem. Surefire plans for creating a bigger fan base in women's sports linger on the shelf because the limited funds go into promoting the traditional revenue sports (usually men's sports) that have historically helped fund everyone else. Although shifting money to a promotion of women's sports might result in a greater revenue yield, the risks seem too great. This scenario is almost a self-fulfilling prophecy. Successful marketers make sure that they have support as they move along, so step 4 must be ongoing. The key to developing and executing any successful sport marketing plan is to include research and input from all the key stakeholders (ticket buyers and users, corporate marketing partners or sponsors, the media and broadcast rights holders, and the community as a whole). Additionally, the input and the buy-in of senior and middle managers and the programs directors who will implement

Managing the Plan With Strategic Opportunism

Although planning is a crucial feature in any effective organization, managers must be prepared to act—to strike or respond—when the situation presents itself, which may not be in keeping with the timetable or outline of a particular plan. As Collins and Porras argued in *Built to Last: Successful Habits of Visionary Companies*, effective companies "distinguish their timeless core values and enduring core purpose (which should never change) from their operating practices and business strategies (which should be changing in response to a changing world)." Sergio Zyman, longtime marketing whiz at Coca-Cola, put it another way in his book, *The End of Marketing as We Know It*, "The reality is that marketing, like science, isn't about knowing all the answers when you start out. It's about experimenting, measuring the results, analyzing them, and then making adjustments based on what you find out. . . . Change my mind, you bet! New info, new tactics. Same strategy. Fixed destination [to sell more]." Zyman knew all about experiments, because he supervised one of the biggest backfires in cola history—the introduction of New Coke in 1985. Within months, the product was pulled and the company reintroduced "Classic" Coca-Cola. A blunder? For sure. But it was a blunder that reinforced the strength of the original Coke brand.

The ability to blend both core continuity and change is one of the hallmarks of effective managers. Daniel Isenberg called this strategic opportunism "the ability to remain focused on long-term objectives while staying flexible enough to solve day-to-day problems and recognize new opportunities." Isenberg's research led him to outline certain habits of thinking and acting as the keys to strategic opportunism.

Habits of Thinking

- **Collecting ideas.** "In combing the beach or watching for flies, senior managers often collect ideas whose relationship to strategic goals may appear murky at first." These managers create mental maps that Isenberg defined as a "rich, multidimensional set of associations among the myriad tasks, people, problems, issues, and goals the manager is dealing with at any one time." One mental map may conceptualize staff responsibilities, especially regarding a marketing plan. One BCS athletics director we know used his mental map during a chance encounter with an alumnus who was an experienced fund-raiser. Knowing that his current director was about to leave, the athletics director quickly assessed the potential match between the alumnus and the soon-to-be vacant opening. On the spot, he planted the seed for a more formal visit and interview.

- **Summarizing.** How can a manager make sense of the daily mountains of data? "The answer is, by climbing up on a hillside every now and then to take a look around, to assess accomplishments, to see how much work is left, even to make sure that draining the swamp is still important." One executive, for instance, would gather notes from the day's or week's meetings to see whether any patterns emerged. Summarizing data in this way can reduce cognitive burden, detect new goals, and maintain a sense of direction.

Ways of Acting

- **Being plan-less by design.** Effective managers leave gaps in plans and avoid rigid detail in plans, knowing that chance encounters might lead to new ideas and subtle shifts in direction—zigging and zagging.

- **Binding to goals.** Even while leaving gaps, effective managers find ways to keep pursuing the most important things. They do this by creating tickler files and to-do lists, and by scheduling priority meetings well ahead of time.

- **Piecing the puzzle.** Effective managers understand that ordering the phases and efforts in any plan is not as important as their ultimate integration. They know that sometimes a sequence of ready–fire–aim may be appropriate.

Thinking both strategically and opportunistically is clearly not easy. It requires a tolerance for ambiguity, intellectual intensity, mental hustle, and a vigilant eye for new ideas. It requires, in other words, a tough-minded approach to an inherently messy process, the ability to take action in the midst of uncertainty, to "sin bravely."

Based on Collins and Porras 1999; Zyman 1999.

---

the plan are essential. For those reasons, we call it the marketing planning process—an intellectual process of creating ideas and testing them with the key constituents.

Once adopted, a strategy may require some changes in personnel or in the organizational structure. The historical studies of Harvard's Alfred Chandler demonstrate that successful organizations design and redesign themselves around their strategies, not the other way around. In Chandler's words, "structure follows strategy." The alert executive has an eye on environmental changes that might require restructuring. Quick changes can be traumatic. In the late 1990s Coca-Cola walked away from its huge league-wide sponsorship with the NFL, leaving individual clubs with greater control and autonomy in making sponsor deals in the soft-drink category. Alan Friedman, editor of the influential *Team Marketing Report*, immediately saw the implications: "While NFL clubs have upgraded their front office marketing talent over the last few years, some clubs still don't have executives with full-time sponsorship development and service responsibility." In the new world of soft-drink sponsorships, restructuring became a priority.[41]

An effective marketing plan will carefully blend all the Ps into a portfolio of activities that move a range of consumer clusters up the escalator. An enlightened school, college, or professional sport program will blend several of the Ps into packages differing in cost and benefits, promoted with different messages, and targeted at different segments or even niches. A college program might offer special plans for students, area families, distant alums, and corporate sponsors. Careful coordination of efforts is required. The athletics director, coaches, players, sports information personnel, facilities managers, and the ticket office must all be on board. Marketing is not the work of just a few people.

A lack of coordination can dump fans off the escalator in a series of waterfalls. This is what happened to the Kansas City Wizards of MLS in the late 1990s, when average attendance slipped from 12,900 to 8,661 over a single season. The MLS commissioner emphasized, "There are no excuses. Kansas City has a terrific team that plays in a great stadium in a town that prides itself on its sports teams." The only excuses were what one local reporter called marketing blunders and gaffes, including unwarranted price hikes and tinkering with the team's name and logo, which muddled any attempts at a brand image and merchandise sales. The Wizards responded to the challenge; by 2004 their attendance averaged 14,816. Marketing blunders crippled the chances of the National Lacrosse League's Washington Power. The organization entered the market only 60 days before the first game and refused to buy advertising. The team's owner oozed marketing myopia when he assumed that the area's rabid lacrosse players and fans would automatically show up: "I figured if we put a great product on the field, that product would sell itself." The next year the franchise packed up and moved to Colorado. A missing or mismanaged marketing plan is a sure way to negate a hot market or a great product.[42]

Strategic Step 5: Control and Evaluate Implementation of the Plan

Step 5 is another ongoing step. Waiting for the end of the season to see whether you're in last place makes little sense.

Marketers (and their bosses) are quick to analyze failures. But analysis, evaluation, and control should be everyday events. Sergio Zyman, longtime marketing mogul at Coca-Cola, warned marketers to grab the moment and debrief success as well as failure. "Don't be blinded by your assumptions," he stressed. "Just because you run a promotion and it works doesn't mean that it worked for the reasons that you thought it would." He is correct. Especially in the sport industry—in which marketing plans can unfold on a game-by-game basis—don't wait until the end of the season to debrief. Evaluation must be done on an event-by-event basis.[43]

Evaluation (or control) requires not only discussion and debriefing sessions but also rigorous quantitative analysis. Spending marketing dollars on hunches is a high-risk game—one that the University of Oregon played in the summer of 2001 when it paid $250,000 (donated by boosters) for a large billboard near Madison Square Garden promoting Joey Harrington for the Heisman Trophy. Was it worth the investment? A Portland *Oregonian* editorial thought so: "From where we sit, that $250,000 is beginning to look like the smartest public-relations money ever spent, dollar for dollar." Harrington finished fourth in the Heisman race, but the Ducks created a buzz and enjoyed many stories in the mass media, including a cover story in *Sports Illustrated* (which also included Oregon State's Ken Simonton). Oregon could have (and may have) quantified the return on investment by calculating the cost of advertising in national outlets such as *Sports Illustrated* or the *New York Times* and comparing that with the number of free promotions they received in the stories. At the same time, they would need to ask whether national media exposure stemmed from a $250,000 billboard or from the Ducks' and Harrington's success on the field. Ultimately, the point is not whether one finds the true answer; the point is in the pursuit of the answer.[44]

Ultimately, success in marketing is determined only through the consumer's eyes. It is a simple equation:

**Consumer satisfaction =
Product benefits – Costs**

Consumers provide the answers to the equation. Do they buy the product? Do they use the product? Do they repeat the purchase, or do they try something else? Although marketers must control their own budgets and costs, their more important control function is to ensure customer satisfaction. This measure must be tempered by the long-term effect of various strategies. The Vancouver Giants of the Western Hockey League, the major junior hockey league in Western Canada and Northwestern United States, faced a dilemma common in the minor leagues in the first round of the 2010–11 playoffs. Having minimal notice of the game date and opponent for their first-round game, they feared an embarrassingly small home crowd, especially going up against the hometown Vancouver Canucks, who had the best record in the NHL's Western Conference. The Giants ran a fantastic promotion on Groupon that more than doubled their crowd by selling over 4,000 tickets in just four days. The $20 offer included a ticket and a $10 food and beverage voucher for the fan. The promotion prima facie was a huge success, but it was actually a major faux pas. As owner Ron Toigo stated, "We upset the 4,000 season-ticket holders who paid $20 for their tickets and received no food voucher, and worse yet, we gave $10 to our food concessionaire and split the other $10 equally with Groupon. So for $5 net, we completely undermined the loyalty of our most important fans."[45]

Indicators of satisfaction, benefits, and cost must be monitored and evaluated not just in the short term but also the long term, which is why we emphasize the importance of measuring lifetime asset value (LAV) in determining the effectiveness of all sport marketing strategies and evaluating true return on objectives (ROO) and return on investment (ROI). Consider a few examples of possible indicators:

- Satisfaction
  Attendance
  Ticket or member renewal rates
- Benefits
  Food quality
  Access to and speed of parking
- Total cost of the experience
  Time spent in the parking lot after the game
  Beer spilled on children by a drunken fan
  Annoyance caused by a surly usher

The marketer must consider other issues as well, including ethical principles. At the turn of the 20th century, for instance, white baseball audiences enjoyed the antics of black mascots, who cavorted between innings like clowns and kneeled near the on-deck circle so that their white bosses could rub their wooly heads for good luck. Such were the mores of Jim Crow America. No major league team would consider this acceptable entertainment today, yet some major college and professional teams have resisted change and continue to employ Native American team names and images. In 2004 the NCAA put the squeeze on schools with potentially offensive mascots, requiring a self-study that would be examined by an NCAA committee. Some 30 institutions were forced to look carefully at the influence of tradition. A year later, the NCAA Executive Committee announced that Native American mascots or images would be banned from all NCAA tournament venues. In announcing the decision, the *NCAA News* was emphatic: Event management and marketing would be driven by core principles in the NCAA strategic plan for diversity and inclusion.

Florida State was granted a waiver by the NCAA because of the unique relationship between the university and the Seminole tribe of Florida. The tribe officially sanctioned the use of Seminole as the nickname and Chief Osceola as the school mascot. FSU took extraordinary steps to be respectful in its association with the Seminole nickname, such as ensuring accuracy of portrayals of Chief Osceola, and in 2006 the university launched a history course focused on the Seminole tribe. Professors met with tribe members to develop the course outline, and the Seminole leaders urged that the class include discussion of other Southeastern tribes that pre-dated theirs.

Any marketing management process (MMP) must consider social responsibility. Beyond the legal issues (see chapter 14), any marketing plan or decision includes ethical dimensions. More-over, numerous frameworks can guide ethical decisions—in business, in marketing, in sport, or in any domain of activity. In our experience, however, we haven't found anything better than Laura Nash's simple framework of 12 questions, in her article "Ethics Without the Sermon," to consider when confronting a problem:[46]

1. Have you defined the problem accurately?

2. How would you define the problem if you stood on the other side of the fence?

3. How did this situation occur in the first place?

4. To whom and to what do you give your loyalty?

5. What is your intention?

6. How does this intention compare with probable results?

7. Whom could your decision or action injure?

8. Will you discuss this with affected parties before making the decision?

9. Will your position be valid over the long run?

10. Could you disclose your decision or action without qualm?

11. What is the symbolic potential of your action if understood? If misunderstood?

12. Under what conditions would you make exceptions?

Questions reprinted, by permission, from L. Nash, 1981, "Ethics without the sermon," *Harvard Business Review* 79–90.

In the late 1990s sport ethics seemed focused on Nike's labor practices in the developing countries in Asia. Was Nike exploiting labor with wages clearly unacceptable by American standards? Or, as Nike argued, was the company creating economic opportunities with wages in keeping with local standards? More issues were involved, to be sure, and Nike was not alone in trying to justify its management and marketing decisions.

Eight-Point Ticket Marketing, Sales, and Service Plan Model

The Aspire Sport Marketing Group LLC, a leading global outsourced ticket marketing, sales, and service consulting business, has developed an eight-point plan (figure 2.3) that speaks to the key elements in developing a comprehensive ticket marketing and sales plan. This plan logically starts with market research, which has the purpose of determining who the existing fans of the sport property are, who they attend with, what they like and don't like, why they attend, and what it will take to get them to attend more games. It also provides information on those not currently attending and what it will take to get those who have interest in the sport, the team, or the university product to attend.

The essential strategies of retain, grow, and acquire are then outlined as mentioned previously in this chapter, followed by the recommended tactics for executing these strategies:

• Capture the essential fan contact data, clean it, removed the duplicates, review past purchase patterns, and segment the various fan groups by level of interest and their desired product alternatives (the appropriate offer from the ticket product ladder).

- Communicate the offer that will most likely resonate best with that fan segment through the fans' preferred communication medium (e-mail, text, tweet, direct

mail, and so on). In this manner, digitally prequalify sales leads by targeting those who respond to the offer, next to those who open, click through, and make social media postings.

- Close by having staff in the fan relationship management center (FRMC) call those fans who purchased as the result of the offer to build a relationship, better identify their needs, and possibly upsell to a higher-level ticket plan. Staff members also call those who opened and clicked through the electronic communication because they have clearly qualified themselves as warm leads. Those who do not open the communication are then retargeted electronically with another offer that the marketer thinks will have the best chance of being accepted.

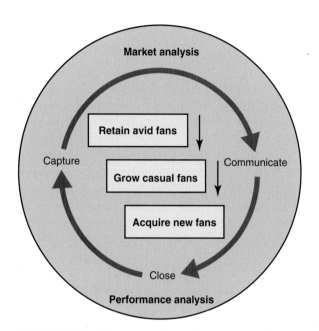

FIGURE 2.3   The Aspire Group's unique TiMSS plan structure, which drives their fan relationship management philosophy.

All ticket marketing and sales campaigns are then fully reviewed for return on objectives (ROO) and return on investment (ROI), using standard performance analysis that involves measurement and production of critical analytics on such items as open rates, click-through rates, and sales or revenue response measured against campaign costs. This review is done for every initiative using embedded promotional codes that enable sales response tracking through the ticket service vendor software (Ticketmaster, Paciolan, Veritix, Agile, and so on).

Wrap-Up

Sport organizations clearly face many unique challenges and demands, not all of which they can meet with frenzied marketing action. Many challenges require considerable thought and a well-planned response. Yet the majority of demands have comparatively simple solutions after all the data are put together. In the new millennium, sport will continue to be unique, but it will follow one principle experienced without modification in all industries: The organizations most likely to succeed will be the ones that have the best handle on the marketplace. Such a handle comes only with a disciplined approach to research and input from all stakeholders, including the staff, followed by the development, analysis, and integration of every function of marketing. In the following chapters, we consider all these steps in detail.

Activities

1. Define the five Ps of the sport marketing mix.
2. Find evidence of a sport organization that does an excellent job of recognizing market trends and adjusting its strategy accordingly. How does the organization stay true to a core vision while also repositioning its products?
3. Describe a new product concept that you think would meet unfilled consumer needs in your favorite sport.

4. List the market or consumer segments that most clearly relate to a tennis or golf club near you.

5. From the stories or ads in any newspaper sports section, try to find examples of the five Ps of the marketing mix.

6. Consider the case of the American Basketball League (ABL) versus the WNBA—one of the most interesting contests of sport marketing strategy in the late 1990s, at least until the ABL declared bankruptcy in 1999. Make a table that compares elements of the leagues' strategies. For instance, the leagues made clear choices on the placement of their products. The ABL played during the traditional basketball season, whereas the WNBA played during the summer. Their media packages also differed. How did their products, including player talent and rules, differ? How did their promotion through ad campaigns differ? Think of all the ways that the leagues differed in the Ps of marketing. Was the WNBA's marketing strategy a key component of its victory over the ABL?

7. Conduct a marketing postmortem on the XFL, which lasted barely one season, despite the backing of NBC Sports and the WWF. What were the strengths and weaknesses of the XFL's marketing strategy?

8. Look closely at the list of Laura Nash's ethics questions. Discuss a recent example of an ethical issue in sport marketing and analyze the issue using those questions.

Your Marketing Plan

The first step in this project is to choose (or create) an organization for which you will develop a marketing plan, or perhaps just a ticket marketing sales and service plan. Your ultimate goal is to prepare a 20- to 30-page plan that helps the organization attain strategic objectives. This plan should become an item in your personal portfolio. Do you aspire to work for a particular organization? Do you have an idea for a sport product that will fill some existing consumer needs or wants?

1. Identify the key stakeholders and a market research and data capture plan.

2. Identify resources for internal and external scanning.

3. Identify the three most important market trends affecting your firm or product.

4. Begin to define your business and your product.

5. Develop the draft of your mission statement.

6. Conduct a SWOT analysis (strengths, weaknesses, opportunities, threats).

7. Set specific objectives for each element of the eight-point marketing plan.

Endnotes

1. Personal conversation with Mark Cuban and Bernie Mullin in May 2000, while Mullin was SVP, Marketing and Team Business, at the NBA.

2. The most comprehensive account of the NFL–MTV debacle is Lawrence Wenner, "Recovering (From) Janet Jackson's Breast: Ethics and the Nexus of Media, Sport, and Management," *Journal of Sport Management*, 18 (2004): 315–334. See also Michael Miller, "Say It Ain't So, Joe: NFL Cans Ad Over Lyrics," *SSSBJ*, 15–21 November 1999, 6.

3. For an excellent discussion of strategy in sport organizations, see Trevor Slack, *Understanding Sport Organizations* (Champaign, IL: Human Kinetics, 1997; 2nd ed. with Milena Parent, 2006).

4. Andrew Cohen, "Can the Game Return," *Athletic Business*, March 1996, 40; Joe Burris, "Repairing the Damage," *Boston Globe*, 24 June 1997, C-1, C-7; www.TennisWelcomeCenter.com; Dan Kaplan "Tennis Courting Irrelevance," *SSSBJ*, 26 August–1 September 2002, 22; Ross Nethery, "Watching and Waiting," *SSSBJ*, 23–29 August 2004; Michael Popke, "Serving Up an Ace," *Athletic Business*, March 2000, 43–52.

5. "Golf's Biggest Supporters," *SBD*, 14 November 1998, 4; Uihlein and Luker quotations in Noah Liberman, "Luring More Players to the Links," *SSSBJ*, 14–20 June 2004, 20–21; golf data in *GOLF 20/20 Vision for the Future: Industry Report*

for 2002, available at www.golf2020.com/frip/resources/2003frip.pdf; *Summary 2003 National Golf Foundation Rounds Played in the United States Report 2004*, 2, www.golf2020.com/wgf/; SBRnet, *Golf Participation: Total vs. Frequent Participation*, www.sbrnet.com/Research/Research.cfm?sub-RID=199. On the issue of overbuilding, see E.M. Swift, "If You Build It, They Won't Necessarily Come," *Sports Illustrated*, 15 November 2004, np.

6. United States Golf Association, January 2012 Market Research Study.

7. PGA Golf Statistics Report, "Golf Participation in the US – 2013," National Golf Foundation, Jupiter, FL.

8. "Golf 2.0—Friends, Family, Fun 2013." www.met.pga.com. The PGA of America, Palm Beach Gardens, FL.

9. "Grow Hockey Summit," press release from Bill Hattem, executive director of the IHIA, 7 Melbourne Ave., Mont-Royal, QC, Canada H3P 1E9.

10. David Hoch, "Signs of the Times," *Athletic Management*, August–September 2001, 47–48.

11. Philip Kotler, *Marketing Management*, 9th ed. (Upper Saddle River, NJ: Prentice Hall, 1997); William A. Sutton, "Developing an Initial Marketing Plan for Intercollegiate Athletic Programs," *Journal of Sport Management*, 1 (1987): 146–158; Shelly Reese, "The Very Model of a Modern Marketing Plan," *Marketing Tools*, January–February 1996, 56–65. For a detailed checklist for marketing planning, see the 50-page appendix in David M. Carter, *Keeping Score: An Inside Look at Sports Marketing* (Grants Pass, OR: Oasis Press, 1996), 262–310.

12. James C. Collins and Jerry I. Porras, *Built to Last: Successful Habits of Visionary Companies* (New York: HarperCollins, 1999), 220.

13. Personal communication from Andy Geiger, 6 June 2003; Jennifer Lee, "Geiger Blends On-Field Success With Overall Mission," *SSSBJ*, 9–15 June 2003, 17.

14. Peter Drucker, "The Theory of the Business," *Harvard Business Review*, 72 (September–October 1994): 95–104; Carole Hedden, "Build a Better Image," *Marketing Tools*, May 1996, 68–72.

15. John Mahaffie, "Why Forecasts Fail," *American Demographics*, March 1995, 34–40; John Kelly and Rod Warnick, *Recreation Trends and Markets: The 21st Century* (Champaign, IL: Sagamore, 2000).

16. National Federation of State High School Associations Athletic Participation Survey 2013. NFHS.org. National Federation of State High School Associations, Indianapolis, IN.

17. Erik Brady and MaryJo Sylwester, "More and More Girls Got Game," *USA Today*, 1 July 2003, 1–2C;

Grant Wahl, "Rebound Attempt," *Sports Illustrated*, 29 March 2004, 34. For an excellent postmortem on the WUSA, see Richard Southall, Mark Nagel, and Deborah LeGrande, "Build It and They Will Come? The Women's United Soccer Association: Collision of Exchange Theory and Strategic Philanthropy," *SMQ*, 14 (3) (2005): 158–167.

18. www.stats.ncaa.org/; www.usahockey.com; "Women Love the NHL," *SBD*, 7 May 1998, 9; "Can Men's Hockey Ride on Coattails?" *SBD*, 21 April 1998, 15; Paula Hunt, "Gear," *Sports Illustrated Womensport*, Fall 1997, 166–167.

19. "Raw Numbers: Hockey Participation Up in USA Hockey 2011-2012." USA Hockey, Colorado Springs, CO. May 31, 2012.

20. Jeff Ostrowski, "Corporate America Making Pitchmen of Pariahs," *SSSBJ*, 12–18 August 2002, 19, 26; Russell Adams, "Sports No Longer Going to Extreme for Identity," *SSSBJ*, 12–18 August 2002, 21; Russell Adams, "League, Players Team to Expand Youth Football, *SSSBJ*, 2–8 September 2002, 20; www.usafootball.com.

21. "Turnkey Sports Poll" at *SBJ* online, 26 July–1 August 2004; http://www.sportsbusinessjournal.com/index.cfm?fuseaction=search.show_article&articleId=39990&keyword=turnkey,%20sports,%20poll; Pew Research Center for the People and the Press; *Biennial News Consumption Survey*, 2004, 5, 17, 21; "Special Report, the Future of Tech," *BusinessWeek*, 20 June 2005, 73–82; Hiawatha Bray, "Race Fans' View Goes Wireless," *Boston Globe*, 26 July 2006, C-1, C-7. For a cautionary note, see Eric Fisher and John Durand, "Analysts Put Mobile ESPN on the Defensive," *SSSBJ*, 31 July–6 August 2006, 4.

22. Suzanne Smalley, "New Advertising Ploy Runs Afoul of Marathon," *Boston Globe*, 20 April 2005, B-5; "Ambushing 101: Socog, Sponsors to Face Educated Guerrillas," *SBD*, 9 June 2000, 4; Peter Graham, "Ambush Marketing," *SMQ*, 6 (March 1997): 10–12; "Well, Who Does," *SBD*, 12 February 1998, 15; Terry Lefton, "Ambush Tactics Evil, Effective," *SSSBJ*, 3–9 November 2003, 9; Alycen McAuley and William Sutton, "In Search of a New Defender: The Threat of Ambush Marketing in the Global Sports Arena," *International Journal of Sports Marketing and Sponsorship*, 1 (1) (1998): 64–86.

23. Martin Letscher, "How to Tell Fads From Trends," *American Demographics*, December 1994, 38–44; Martin Letscher, "Sports Fads and Trends," *American Demographics*, June 1997, 53–56; L. Jon Wertheim, "Trout May Jump for Joy," *Sports Illustrated*, 23 March 1998, 22.

24. Pew 2012 Research. The State of the News Media 2012. stateofthemedia.org

25. Collins and Porras, *Built to Last*, 238. For a view of Nike at its height of power, see Donald Katz, *Just Do It: The Nike Spirit in the Corporate World* (Holbrook, MA: Adams, 1994).

26. "Post No Billboards," *Stanford Magazine*, 2000, online edition, www.stanfordalumni.org/news/magazine/2000/sepoct/farm_report/billboards.html.

27. Drucker, "Theory of Business"; Carole Hedden, "Build a Better Image," *Marketing Tools*, May 1996, 68–72. List of bullets adapted from Edward Pitts, "Imagination Is Better Than Knowledge," *Fitness Management*, March 1995, 33–35.

28. Collins and Porras, *Built to Last*, 111–112; Denver Grizzlies Hockey Club, *Draft Community Relations Plan, 1994–1995 Season*.

29. David Hoch, "Signs of the Times," *Athletic Management*, August–September 2001, 47–48.

30. The Demographics: Fantasy Sport Trade Association 2013. ftsa.org/industry_demographics.

31. David Shani, "A Framework for Implementing Relationship Marketing in the Sport Industry," *SMQ*, 6 (June 1997): 9–15.

32. Hardy, "Dick Lipsey," 6. For a closer look at the fan escalator, see William Sutton et al., "Escalating Your Fan Base," *Athletic Management*, February–March 1997, 4–5.

33. Terry Lefton, "Hockey Tips From the Stars," *SSSBJ*, 6–12 October 2003, 5.

34. Al Ries and Jack Trout, *Positioning: The Battle for Your Mind* (New York: Warner Books, 1982).

35. Peter May, "Zooming Into Prominence," *Boston Globe*, 17 September 2004, E-1, E-16; Michael Smith "NASCAR Tracks Roll Out Upscale Seating Options," *SSSBJ*, 17–23 July 2006, 6.

36. "MLS Faces Tests," *SBD*, 24 March 1998, 12.

37. D. Cooke, "Packaging for Prestige," *IRSA Club Business*, July 1987, 65.

38. Rachel Sherman, "Softball City," *Athletic Business*, July 1997, 28–29; www.big8softball.com, 2 February 2005.

39. Marianne Bhonslay, "Selling the 'Less Than Best,' " *SSSBJ*, 8–14 March 1999, 25.

40. Terry Lefton, "Guarascio: Research Will Help NFL Understand Its Fans," *SSSBJ*, 8–14 November 2004, 6.

41. Alfred Chandler, *Strategy and Structure: Chapters in the History of Industrial Enterprise* (Cambridge, MA: MIT Press, 1962); Alan Friedman, "Coke Agreement May Leave NFL Teams Scrambling," *SSSBJ*, 8–14 June 1998, 6.

42. "Is There a Spell Over the MLS Wizards' Marketing Efforts?" *SBD*, 25 July 1998, 12; Bruce Schoenfeld, "Pro Team Takes a Hit in Lacrosse's Stronghold," *SSSBJ*, 18–24 March 2002, 38.

43. Sergio Zyman, *The End of Marketing as We Know It* (New York: Harper Business, 1999), 51.

44. "Oregonian Editorial Calls Harrington Promo a Good PR Move," *SBD*, 13 August 2001, 24.

45. Ron Toigo, owner of the Vancouver Giants, personal conversation with B. Mullin.

46. Laura Nash, "Ethics Without the Sermon," *Harvard Business Review* (November 1981): 79–90; G.B. Laczniak and Patrick Murphy, "Sports Marketing Ethics in Today's Marketplace," *SMQ*, 8 (December 1999): 43–53; C. Spindel, *Dancing at Halftime: Sport and the Controversy Over American Indian Mascots* (New York: New York University Press, 2000); Ellen Staurowsky, "Privilege at Play: On the Legal and Social Fictions That Sustain American Indian Sport Imagery," *Journal of Sport and Social Issues*, 28 (February 2004): 11–29; Amalie Benjamin, "Sense and Sensitivity," *Boston Globe*, 21 June 2005, F-1, F-7; Sean Smith, "NCAA: Mascot Ruling," *Boston Globe*, 6 August 2005, D-1-D-2; Gary Brown, "Policy Applies Core Principles to Mascot Issue," *NCAA News*, 15 August 2005, 1, 19.

Chapter 3

Understanding the Sport Consumer

OBJECTIVES

- To recognize the differences among socialization, involvement, and commitment for sport consumers
- To understand the various individual and environmental factors that shape consumer involvement and commitment in sport
- To understand the decision process for sport consumers

In June 2006 Gilad Shalit was a 19-year-old soldier serving his required national service on the Gaza border as a member of the Israeli Defense Forces. Abducted by the militant Islamist group Hamas, Shalit was held in isolation for over five years until he was released as part of a controversial prisoner exchange. In the months after his release he was a high-value target for the Israeli media, but he managed to keep a low profile with a few exceptions that included a trip to watch a Maccabi Tel Aviv basketball game and a longer excursion to the NBA's All-Star events in Orlando. In June 2012 Shalit announced that he was going to work as a sportswriter for Israel's most popular newspaper, *Yediot Aharonot*. When he began to make public remarks about his captivity, he spoke expansively about the importance of sport. Given some access to radio and television, sportscasts had kept him mentally and emotionally whole. "I drew a lot of strength" from listening and watching, he noted, "despite the conditions I was under there." The Israeli national football and basketball leagues were on radio. European football was on Arabic television. But the language did not matter. He figured it out. Most important, he added, was the sense of humanity he felt when his guards watched some events with him, including a Champions League match between Lyon of France and Hapoel Tel Aviv. While they never discussed politics and had little to say about much else, sport was different. During the Lyon–Hapoel match he noticed that even the Hamas militants were in shock at the skills shown in one Israeli score on an overhead strike. "In those conversations, around the games," he said, "we had a common denominator, sport."[1]

That same June, news sources were filled with less sanguine stories about sports fans before and during the UEFA Cup championships, hosted by Poland and Ukraine. Both nations had long histories of xenophobia, the latest versions unleashed by the collapse of the Soviet Union. These fears were fanned by a BBC documentary displaying hard-core groups making Nazi salutes, beating fans from India, and making monkey chants at black players. Some feared that Ukraine and Poland would not protect black players and black fans. Sol Campbell, who had once served as England's captain, suggested they stay home "because you could end up coming back in a coffin." Nationalist, ethnic, and racial taunting is well known, of course, in and out of many sport venues around the world. For every warm and fuzzy story about football or basketball bridging cultural differences, another seems to be exposing sport as a vessel of humanity's worst forms of behavior—most of it bubbling among large groups of rabid fans.[2]

How and why can sport be such a strong medium of both hate and humanity, of both connection and separation? Why do fans behave as they do? As we noted in chapter 1, the marketing concept begins and ends with the consumer. The marketer of any commodity—golf, grain, or gasoline—needs to understand who might be interested in buying her product. Therefore, the intelligent marketer constantly seeks to answer a series of questions, including the following:

- Who are my consumers—past, present, and future—in terms of both demographics (age, sex, income) and psychographics (attitudes, opinions, lifestyles)?

- Where do my consumers reside? Where do they work? How do they travel to and from the places where they consume my product?

- Where, when, and how have my consumers been exposed to my product?

- How and why did they become involved with my product?

- If they have been committed to my product, why? Why have some lost that commitment?

Chapter 2 provided the big picture of how consumer research may drive effective marketing strategy. This chapter explores the literature on some of the how and why questions about sport consumers. Chapter 4 examines research methods to address all the preceding questions and develop a database on consumers—the foundation for all the subsequent chapters. As we discuss here and in chapter 4, sport marketers must look beyond basic demographic research (who, what, and where) to examine the reasons consumers are (or aren't) aware of, involved in, or committed to their organization or product. Galen Trail, a professor who studies sport consumer behavior, once lamented to *Street & Smith's SportsBusiness Journal* that "the problem with the sports organizations and their marketers is that when they do market research, they get stuck on the demographics," which Trail claimed explain only 3 to 5 percent of fan attendance. "You can do all the demographic research in the world," he concluded, "and you aren't learning diddly. It's the psychographic research that matters. That's what tells you why people are or aren't going to show up." Demographics are clearly worth more than "diddly," but Galen Trail is correct to say that they are but a small piece of a large puzzle.[3]

Although countless studies, theories, and models attempt to get into the mind of the consumer, we may characterize the factors that influence behavior as either environmental or individual. Environmental factors may include significant others such as family, peers, and coaches; social and cultural norms; social class structure; race and gender relations; technology; and market behavior of firms in the sport industry. Individual factors include stage in the life or family cycle, learning, perceptions, emotions, motivations, and attitudes. In the end, a host of variables influences a person's self-concept and social identity, an aspect of humanity that research has linked to consumer decisions about embracing or abandoning sport.[4]

As we noted in chapter 1, the core sport product—a game or event—is simultaneously produced and consumed, by players and spectators alike. In this chapter we will use the term *consumer* to refer more to those who watch, or listen to, or read about an event. But we must remember that players do the same thing, so they are also consumers. Some researchers distinguish mere spectators from fans based on social bonds, that is, the strength of their association with other spectators and the sport property (e.g., team,

player, venue). Fair enough. In this chapter, however, we will use multiple terms to describe sport consumers.[5]

Socialization, Involvement, and Commitment

Environmental and individual factors influence how and how much people become involved with and committed to sport. Think about your own sport activities, whether as a child, a youth, or an adult. Something or somebody got you interested, somehow, in an activity. Perhaps it was a trip to watch a game, an afternoon playing with a parent or friend, a television broadcast of an exciting event or championship, or a cool new app. A trigger of interest prompted your involvement and perhaps your socialization into a sport.[7]

Sociologists typically consider socialization to be the process by which people assimilate and develop the skills, knowledge, attitudes, and other "equipment" necessary to perform various social roles. This process involves two-way interaction between the individual and the environment. Socialization, in turn, demands some kind of involvement, in our case with sport. Involvement takes one of three basic forms:

- Behavioral involvement: the hands-on doing. This behavior includes playing at practice or in competition; it also includes the activities of fans at a venue, at home, or on a mobile device, watching and listening and rooting.

- Cognitive involvement: the acquisition of information and knowledge about a sport. Players sitting through a chalk talk and fans at a boosters club meeting listening to the coach explain how last week's game plan worked so well both exemplify cognitive involvement. Magazines, newspapers, game programs, radio, television, and wired and wireless devices are key media for cognitive involvement by consumers eager to know more about a sport. Almost a decade ago, sport industry executives predicted a significant swing over the next five years in where fans most often get information—from heavy reliance on television and radio to an overwhelming future focus on the Internet and wireless devices. It is no wonder that newspapers and television stations duplicated and expanded their best sports features on their web and social media sites.[8]

Crowds, Mobs, Fans, and the Fancy

In September 2007 the Chicago Cubs celebrated a real first. Paul and Teri Fields had named their newborn son Wrigley Alexander Fields, in homage to the Cubs home venue. Parents have named their children after famous athletes, but ballparks and stadiums? Obviously, the Fields were serious fans, the kind who have been analyzed for centuries. The Romans, for instance, had the crowd or the mob or the factions who filled the circuses to cheer chariots and horses that were organized into stables of reds, whites, blues, and greens. By the empire's second century, Pliny the Younger complained of the "childish passion" that he saw among the racing crowds. It was not the driver's skill or the horse's speed they cheered, Pliny lamented. That might be understandable. "But in fact," he claimed, "it is the racing colors they support." If the drivers changed colors in midrace, the crowd would change allegiance—"such is the popularity and importance of a worthless shirt." Such avid consumers are now called fans. Where did the name come from? Many assume it is simply a shortened version of the word *fanatic*, and that notion has some logic to it. But there is another possibility.

In a 1929 *American Mercury* essay, William Henry Nugent gave his readers a detailed history of sports writing from its British beginning in 1824 with Pierce Egan's weekly *Life Sporting Guide*. Irish by birth (1772), Egan found his calling on his days off from work as a compositor for *London's Weekly Dispatch*. Walking the streets and alleys later made famous by Dickens, Egan was enamored of the cockfights, prizefights, hangings, and other blood sports popular with the city's underside. He wrote about what he saw and in 1813 published *Boxiana: Or Sketches of Ancient and Modern Pugilism*. Four more volumes would follow. A century and half later, A.J. Liebling would dedicate his own volume on boxing, *The Sweet Science*, to Egan's memory, calling him "the greatest writer about the ring who ever lived."

One of Egan's projects was an 1823 revision of Francis Grose's *Dictionary of the Vulgar Tongue*, a book that took readers into the auditory world of the "sporting character" who was "attached to pigeons, dog-fighting, boxing, etc." Egan called such characters collectively "The Fancy." A century later, Nugent wrote, "*The fancy* was long a class name in England and America for followers of boxing. Baseball borrowed it and shortened it to the *fance, fans*, and *fan*." Nugent did not agree with those who claimed that *fan* was an abbreviation of *fanatic*.

Much evidence supports Nugent (and Pierce Egan). The *Oxford English Dictionary*, first compiled beginning in 1857, includes a short meaning of *fan* as "a jocular abbreviation of fanatic." Unfortunately, *OED* definitions of *fanatic* include no sporting references. On the other hand, the word *fancy* is clearly identified with boxing and the prize ring (as well as with bird and book lovers).

We are hard pressed to find early accounts of baseball that use the term *fan* or *fancy*. When New York area rivals began to face off in the late 1850s, spectator groups might be called club followers or spectators in general. If misbehaving (which happened early and often), they were called roughs, the blackleg fraternity, or factions, all terms unrelated to sport. A few decades later, baseball writers developed other names for rabid followers, including the term *cranks*. Ice hockey fans in the 1920s were sometimes called bugs, and they were prone to litter the ice with lemons or eggs.

Selecting the origin of a word like *fan* is always dicey. But the available evidence tilts toward Nugent's theory. Fans are often fanatical, but the term more likely emanates from the thriving commercial and entrepreneurial underworld of Regency London captured in the work of Pierce Egan—a world populated by The Fancy.[6]

• Affective involvement: the attitudes, feelings, and emotions that a consumer has toward an activity. Pep rallies and pregame festivities are standard fare for affective involvement. But so too are the best advertisements. Just think of any Nike ad. Like them or not, these ads stir the emotions about a sport (or about Nike). A 2012 study of NFL fans revealed a range of ways in which consumers were involved with the sport (table 3.1). These are aggregated numbers, so a given fan may range widely within each category. But the overall picture suggests that sport involvement is media driven.[9]

Commitment refers to the frequency, duration, and intensity of involvement in a sport, or the willingness to expend money, time, and energy in a pattern of sport involvement. Movement up the escalator normally indicates a deeper commitment. For some sports, like tennis and golf, the ties between involvement and commitment can be dramatic. For instance, a random sample of 468 fans at a Men's Clay Court Tennis Championship displayed the following types and levels of tennis involvement:

• 89 percent were tennis players.

• 45.7 percent rated their own skills as intermediate.

• 42.1 percent rated their own skills as advanced intermediate.

• 71.8 percent rated tennis as a favorite participant sport.

TABLE 3.1 2012 Study of NFL Fans

Type of activity	Percentage of time in activity
Watching game through media	39%
Watching other NFL info	13%
Discussing	10%
Listening though media	9%
Reading print	8%
Reading the web, mobile	7%
Video games	5%
Fantasy football	5%
Attending NFL games	4%

Adapted from NFL 2012.

• 52.9 percent rated tennis as the most frequent sport attended.

• 39.6 percent rated tennis as the most frequent sport viewed on television.

• 75.5 percent owned a racket worth $100 to $199.

• 27.8 percent owned a racket worth more than $200.

These consumers were highly committed, spending considerable time, money, and energy on the sport of tennis.[10]

The marketer must clearly understand the types of involvement and commitment that consumers represent. The WNBA season-ticket holder who subscribes to fan magazines, attends every game, follows player tweets, tracks game statistics, pays for special-content websites, downloads team information onto her cell phone, plays in a fantasy league, and roots with great emotion is obviously different from the father who takes his child to one game to satisfy a sense of parental duty. The casual spectator who attends a game with a free ticket is distinctly different from the rabid fan watching the same game at home. The act of attendance may or may not reflect or develop a deeper commitment. The committed fan thinks more, feels more, and does more.

Research on sport consumers has segmented respondents along levels of involvement and commitment, even if only into two categories, such as casual and avid. A 2010 Turnkey survey, for instance, reported some interesting differences between casual and avid NFL and NBA fans. When asked about attending an upcoming game if tickets became available for purchase, only 11 percent of casual NFL fans indicated that they would attend the game in person; 89 percent preferred to watch the game on television. Among avid fans, 45 percent would attend in person, and only 55 percent would prefer to watch on television. The top reason for staying home was cost. Another survey by Catalyst Public Relations and the *SportsBusiness Journal* found that 55 percent of NFL fans and 61 percent of MLB fans "consider themselves bigger fans of the respective leagues since they started following their favorite teams on Facebook, Twitter and similar sites." About half of both groups "said they spend more time watching and following the league now than they did prior to their social-media engagement."

Social media have been a powerful force in building commitment.[11]

Nurturing the committed consumer is a key goal. So is better research on commitment to sport. As several experts recently asked, "What effect does being a professional football fan have on consumption of football at other levels, or consumption of other spectator sports, or recreational sport involvement?" In the last decade, sport marketing researchers have begun to look much more closely at the nature of consumer involvement, but a great deal of work remains to be done on these important topics.[12]

Environmental and individual factors interact constantly to influence involvement and commitment. Although people are influenced by their environment, they are also capable of reshaping the social, physical, and cultural landscape around them. If this were not so, life would be static. Change is part of existence in politics, in art, in music, and in sport. For this reason, the sport marketer must understand the complex dynamics that shape consumers. The model in figure 3.1 depicts the interaction that determines the outcomes of importance to this chapter: socialization, involvement, and commitment in sport.

Like all models, figure 3.1 is a picture of a complex process, not a formula that guarantees understanding and correct decisions. This figure should serve to remind the marketer of key factors to sift through to understand and develop consumer interest, involvement, and commitment.

Environmental Factors

Consumers are surrounded by a host of factors that may influence their decisions about sport involvement. As we consider some of the most prominent factors, we stress again the constant interaction between and among them.

ACTIVITY 3.1 Commitment to a Sport Team

In this WSG activity, you will learn about a cricket club and a football club. The cricket club is the Melbourne Cricket Club. The football club is Manchester United Football Club. Based in part on what you learn about these two clubs, you will consider how the fans' personal and business behaviors, attendance at sport events, and culture indicate their commitment to their sport team or organization.

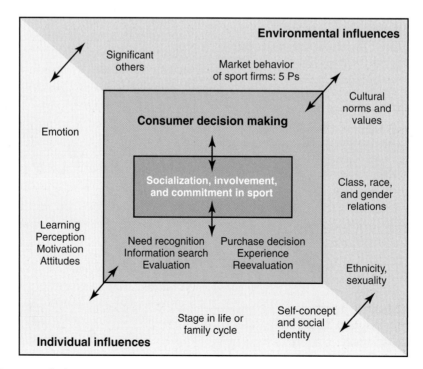

FIGURE 3.1 Consumer behavior in sport.

Significant Others

Much of a person's socialization into sport roles occurs through interaction with significant others, who may actively shape patterns of involvement or who may act as role models. Some of the most important are family members, coaches, teachers, and peers. Although these relations are personal, consumers may also have impersonal, distant reference groups that are also significant. Sport consumers recognize the importance of family and friends. A study of professional wrestling fans showed that only 27.3 percent had found the sport on their own; 22.4 percent had been introduced by parents; 11.1 percent by grandparents; 19.2 percent by other family members; and 20.2 percent by friends.[13]

These results parallel general consumer behavior. For instance, a study by the *Yankelovich Monitor* showed the following responses from American consumers:

- Forty percent said that advice from friends had a strong influence on buying behavior.
- Fifty-seven percent considered advice from a friend or relative a good reason to try a new grocery brand.
- Sixty percent said they seek advice from friends when considering products they know little about.

Sport is no exception: Pals have power. Family and friends may be the most powerful force in sport socialization; their influence colors behavior and attitudes. One study of baseball spectators determined that their perceptions of event quality (e.g., stadium, service) varied according to how they believed their family and friends viewed baseball's popularity and acceptability.[14]

At the same time, consumers have reference groups, heroes, or role models who may be distant and impersonal but nonetheless important. The hit movie *Bend It Like Beckham* showed the power of cultural heroes. For sixth graders in any middle school, the heroes could be the seemingly Olympian cool kids in the eighth grade. For many adolescents, the idols may be the cool kids on MTV, who influence both school and sport fashions. As we explain in chapters that follow, teams, leagues, and corporate sponsors have much at stake in linking the right products, prices, and promotions with the appropriate fan groups.[15]

Cultural Norms and Values

Significant others tend to convey the beliefs, attitudes, and behaviors that typify their own cultural settings. In a society's broader framework, however, alternative cultures, subcultures, and countercultures nurture different lifestyles. This point is as true in sport as it is in all areas of living; if not for the dynamics of culture, society would not change over time. A stagnant society would greatly affect sport. Consider, for example, that as late as the 1920s, many U.S. communities outlawed organized sports on Sunday. Can you imagine being arrested for golfing on a Sunday? That circumstance is unthinkable today, yet at the turn of the 20th century it happened with some regularity in U.S. cities where cultural groups fought over secularism and the Sabbath. And 40 years ago, who would have predicted that sellouts for the Minnesota high school hockey championship were for the girls? Or that the star hockey team at the 1998 Olympics was a women's team?[16]

Some aspects of culture are based on climate and topography. For instance, Minnesota and Massachusetts still dominate the production of U.S. hockey players. Northern cities with long hockey traditions—Pittsburgh, Buffalo, Detroit, and Boston—tend to have higher local ratings for hockey telecasts than do Southern cities. Similarly, the mountainous areas of North America and Europe produce far more world-class skiers than other parts of the world do. Regional weather patterns have been, concluded GOLF 20/20, "far and away the biggest factor impacting rounds of golf." The dry sun and long coast of California spawned both surfing and skateboarding. Geographer John Rooney identified 11 distinct regions of American sport involvement, from the Eastern Cradle to the Pigskin Cult of the deep South to the Pacific Cornucopia of surfing, skiing, and just about everything else. Each region had a different array of emphases. A *New York Times* Google traffic search reached the conclusion that "there are probably about 5 times as many football fans in Birmingham [Alabama] as there are in New York, even though the New York market is 10 times larger." Why is that? American historians have begun to look at the evolution of Southern approaches to sport, including hunting, auto racing, and baseball. Regional sport cultures demand much greater analysis.[17]

Sport involvement often begins, and continues, as a family affair.

Class

The influence of social class can be subtle. Researchers do not agree on exactly what constitutes social class distinctions or how to assess a person's class rank. For some, class is a function of income, education, or occupation. For others, it is a matter of inherited prestige and status, which derive from residence and lifestyle. Numerous scales attempt to describe various strata in the class system. Clearly, though, differences in class standing relate to differences in lifestyle, including sport involvement. This complexity is especially acute among many middle-class Americans, to which may be added some people from skilled working-class jobs, such as plumbers and

carpenters. Most of these people consider themselves middle class, and many have household incomes higher than those of their white-collar counterparts. But important differences are also present. White-collar middle-class people may spend money on tennis and golf, whereas their blue-collar counterparts may choose to invest in bowling and hunting. In this case, the difference between purchasing power and purchase behavior is significant.[18]

The linkage of certain sports with certain classes requires ongoing research. Some activities appeal to the upper ranks because of their esoteric and historically exclusive nature. Golf, polo, and yachting are examples of what Thorstein Veblen called conspicuous consumption—clear expressions of wealth and privilege, particularly through membership in exclusive clubs. At the other end are what some sociologists have called "prole sports"— working-class, or proletarian, activities such as roller derby, motorcycle racing, and demolition derby. Such sports, with their speed, machinery, and danger, may express the peculiar regimentation of the work worlds of this social class. Although both elites and working-class folks have focused on expressive uses of their bodies in sport, the middle class has tended to use sport as an instrument for achieving the disciplined life ingrained in the American corporate lifestyle. Hard work, sacrifice, teamwork, and precision, closely tied to football and baseball, dominate the ethos of middle-class sport.[19]

Of course, life can't be put into boxes. The complexities of history usually confound simple models. Auto racing, especially NASCAR, is a good example. A prole sport that started on dirt tracks, it is now produced on highly rationalized, modern tracks for the highest levels of the American elite, who sit in glassy boxes above the crowd. Some critics complain that the big-time sports are provoking elements of class struggle. Bigger and gaudier skyboxes, expanded areas of expensive club seats, and endless rounds of price hikes seem to indicate to the everyday fan that America's teams have been transformed into private clubs for corporate suits. Regardless of perspective, the marketer must recognize the complexity and fluidity of class structure.

Race and Ethnicity

Race and ethnic relations have a similar association with patterns of sport involvement. Racial and ethnic groups (problematic categories to begin with) are represented in all levels of social class. At the same time, many have endured continued discrimination resulting in overrepresentation in urban areas and in low-income, low-education levels. In the case of sport participation, even a casual observer can see the dominance of black athletes in basketball, football, and track, as well as their underrepresentation in hockey, golf, and tennis (despite the prominence of Tiger Woods and Venus and Serena Williams). Does this mean that participation is dictated by genes? That notion is doubtful. Contemporary medical and genetic studies have uncovered some differences among population groups (including racial and ethnic minorities) in their proclivity to certain illnesses and their responses to certain drug treatments. At this time, however, little credible research has been done on genetic disposition in sport. Rather, people of any group are likelier to excel in the sports that are available through school and recreation programs and appear as viable avenues to status and achievement. As one distinguished geneticist argued, behavioral differences among racial groups may have some genetic basis, "but it may also be environmental, the result of diet, or family structure, or schooling, or any number of biological and social factors."[20]

Several studies have quantified market discrimination against minority players:[21]

- Two studies on the market for baseball cards suggested that white players are valued more highly than minority players of equal productivity.

- A study of revenues and racial composition at 42 NCAA Division I basketball programs concluded that "on average, a team replacing a black player with a white player of equal skill gains in excess of $100,000 in annual gate receipts, providing a strong incentive for college basketball programs to discriminate against black recruits."

- A study of 259 local NBA broadcasts concluded that a team's local ratings went up almost one-half of a rating point for every additional 10 minutes of playing time given to a white player.

The links between race, ethnicity, and sport consumption are not simple. For instance, one study of WNBA fans in Atlanta and Columbus, Ohio, found that white spectators were more likely to "make their sport experience an extension of a social outing at a bar or restaurant," and were more likely to buy their tickets in advance. At the same time, Southern black spectators were more attracted to promotional giveaways and were more likely to get team information by radio. The authors of a study on the Latino community, however, concluded, "Sports marketers should not create marketing campaigns solely based on the assumption that Latinos or any ethnic group are necessarily fans of any particular sport (e.g., soccer)." Instead, they argued, marketers "should focus on an individual's motives for attending sporting events and attachment to a team or to a sport, instead of an individual's identification with an ethnic group." More research needs to be focused on consumer behavior among racial and ethnic minorities, in the United States and elsewhere.[22]

Gender and Sexuality

Over the last three decades historians have steadily recovered evidence suggesting that women have been far more involved in the sport market than we have typically remembered or celebrated. In the 1920s, for example, girls' and women's teams filled the sports pages, often described by female beat reporters. The current robust levels of female participation and fan experience have been hard fought, but they should be recognized more as a renaissance and less as a novelty. In any event, girls and women are a major force among spectators, across a host of big-time sports. Fan surveys have shown that females make up over 40 percent of the American fan base in football, indoor soccer, and auto racing. Australian data suggest a similar ratio.[23]

Do women derive different satisfaction than men do from sport involvement? Early studies of sport television viewing—dominated by traditional male sports—showed interesting differences between male and female viewers:

- Men were more emotionally involved in viewing.
- Men engaged in pregame rituals to pump up for the game.
- Women were more likely to watch sport because others were watching.
- Women were more likely to work while they watched.

Additional research suggests that compared with women, male viewers exhibit higher levels of eustress (pleasant stress), escapism, and focus on aesthetics, whereas women had higher family motivations. At events, women view parking, seating, and accessibility as more important than do men.[24]

Sexuality has long been a taboo subject, especially in the sport world. In the 19th century, sports were defined as "manly." Straight women had a hard enough time breaking into this masculine territory, let alone gay, lesbian, bisexual, or transgendered (GLBT) athletes. Yet the tennis world did not crumble when Richard Raskind became Renee Richards. The Olympics were not threatened by Greg Louganis' homosexuality, or by the Gay Games. In the last decade, scholars have begun to examine sexuality and sport, and GLBT activists have pressed more vigorously for opportunities to pursue sport opportunities free of harassment, as athletes and as fans.[25]

Culture in the Global Marketplace

Over the last few decades, as global capitalism returned to levels not seen since before World War I, marketers naturally became more concerned with how their products played out when they crossed borders and cultures. As one researcher warned, "People who grow up in one culture have learned to see things in certain contexts that people in other countries have learned to see in different contexts. . . . Knowledge of the differences is of utmost importance to international marketers and advertisers." In an age when sports events such as the Super Bowl, the World Cup, and the Olympics are viewed by billions, this issue is obvious. But it is also true for a high school athletics director whose teams and fan groups are filled by increasingly diverse groups of people. A 2009 account estimated that more than 80 languages were spoken at Central High School in Manchester, New Hampshire. If basketball or any other sport was to have an influence on students and families, that issue would have to be addressed.[26]

The English Football League's chief commercial officer, Richard Heaselgrave, has seen fans close up—in England, Europe, and America—where he has served as VP of business development for the NBA. He recognized some clear cultural differences. "I think there's a zeal in America for the nonpitch, off-court entertainment, something like the All-Star games fan fests, which can take three or four days," he said. That kind of event might not fly in England, where the game itself is the sole event. There are, he admitted, "definitely some things you can pick up [in America], but others better 'to leave in New York.'" The trick, of course, is knowing which is which.[27]

In 2010 VisitBritain, the national tourism agency, circulated guidelines for sport and hospitality properties who would be negotiating dozens of cultural gaps during the London

Olympics of 2012. With hundreds of thousands arriving and billions at stake, the idea of better cultural awareness made sense. Among the agency's cautions were the following:

- Poles are sensitive to suggestions that they drink too much.
- Belgians don't like finger snapping.
- Japanese take offense to prolonged eye contact.
- Americans are informal to the point of being very direct or even rude.

Perhaps these were just stereotypes. And clearly, research is needed on behaviors of various cultures of sports fans. There is no denying, however, the importance of recognizing and negotiating differences.[28]

Market Behavior of Sport Firms

Psychologists suggest that much of fan behavior relates to the wins and losses of their favored teams or players. Although marketers cannot control game or match results, they can control how the product (including past or future performance) is packaged and presented to consumers. The behavior of teams, leagues, suppliers, and distributers clearly influences consumers. We cover much of this in subsequent chapters, but some examples bear emphasis here.[29]

Take the adaptation to technological innovation. One hundred and twenty years ago, railroad and streetcar systems expanded and created networks of teams and fans without which a national pastime would not have developed in the United States or elsewhere. Around the same time, entrepreneurs in leather goods and paper products recognized the possibilities in focused production of sporting goods. Firms like Spalding and Brothers shrewdly drove increased demand with slick packaging, pricing, and promotions— in ways that have been copied ever since. The telegraph, the motion picture, radio, television, and the Internet each influenced the development of sport consumers. America's big leagues

Sport has both universal appeal and culturally different manifestations.

in football and baseball had danced with radio, and they feared and then embraced live television broadcasts by the 1960s. Always, they worried about effects on the home gate—the lifeblood of every team. The English Football League waited until the 1980s to permit live televised broadcasts. Each generation has faced a new technology. Twenty years ago, marketers viewed television as the most important medium for mass marketing. How could we ever go beyond satellite broadcasts? And then along came the Internet, WiFi, and 4G. How will new technologies affect sports fans? Will improvements in virtual gaming increase or reduce viewing of live or on-demand game broadcasts? In an age when just about any high school, college, or club program can find the resources and people to produce live streaming of home events over the Internet, the questions should be everywhere.[30]

Corporate social responsibility (CSR) has grown in importance over the last few decades. Research indicates that increased awareness of a firm's CSR improves consumer attitudes and inclinations to purchase products. The notion of cause-related marketing need not trigger cynicism. Good works are good works. Hence, sport properties have elevated CSR in their hierarchies of objectives. Examples include the following:

- NFL's Make the Pledge campaign
- Orlando Magic Youth Foundation
- Major League Baseball's Reviving Baseball in Inner Cities (RBI) program
- Boston Red Sox's long relationship with the Jimmy Fund

If such programs are to be effective in both community building and marketing, they must

- focus program objectives more on community building than on ticket sales and
- develop and report rigorous metrics that measure program success in building physical capital (e.g., acres of fields built), human capital (e.g., improvements in kids' reading scores), and social capital (e.g., increase in a volunteer network).

We discuss these ideas in more detail in chapter 12.[31]

Sport property marketing campaigns increasingly appeal to all five senses—the sights, smells, tastes, sounds, and touches that make for memorable events. Packaging all the senses is important in building brand affiliation. The special signature song in the stands, the voice of the announcer, the aroma of the sausage and onions, the sight of the field, the feel of the seats—all these link to consumer identity, learning, and motivation, which we discuss in the next section.[32]

Individual Factors

Environmental factors swirl constantly around the consumer, but individual or internal factors influence the way that the consumer interacts and makes sense of that larger world. Among the most important factors are self-concept, the learning process, perception, motivation, and emotions. We look now at how these may affect involvement in and commitment to sport.

Self-Concept and Social Identity

Consumers or spectators or fans develop as humans amid a continual interaction between their internal and external selves and consciousness. Some researchers call this personal and social identity. Some call this combination the self-concept. Whatever the technical definitions, the notions are powerful. Our being is a fusion of individual and environmental, personal and social, internal and external. Among other things, the results may link us to associations with sport. As several researchers recently put it, "Few associations inform an individual's self-concept to the extent found in sports." One of the reasons is that "sport presents challenges that help individuals determining their own limits while providing accessible comparisons to others." This idea is true for the participant on an Olympic team and for the fan wearing a school team sweater at a stadium or sports bar. The links between a person's overall self-concept, social identity, and what we might call sport identity are still being discovered. As two leading scholars of the subject recently put it, some academic research on sports fans has suggested that levels of team identification may stay "fairly constant across different levels of fan avidity during a single season." But more research is needed on how these levels may vary in the off-season, when marketers are planning and implementing campaigns for the next season. Longitudinal research is needed here—tracking cohorts of fans across longer stretches of time.[33]

Stage in Life or the Family Cycle

The self-concept is a dynamic entity, often changing as a person interacts with the environment. One path of self-development is the life course or the family cycle. Although our notions of marriage and family are changing (as they have for centuries), each of us passes through a series of stages that often correspond to transitions in our values, identities, feelings of competence, and attitudes. Such stages may include some of the following:

- Adolescence
- Teen years
- College years
- Single but independent, without children
- Living with a partner or married, but without children
- Living with a partner or married, but with children
- Single with children
- Empty nester, still employed
- Retired

Transitions from one stage to the other may have a profound effect on our sport involvement and commitment, even as sport may be an important ingredient in our quest for identity at any stage.

These stages, of course, vary from person to person, and much more research is needed on their effects. For instance, some data suggest that the youth period is especially important in fan development. Research by NFL Properties indicated that 43 percent of fans claimed to have become fans of a particular sport by the age of 8. And 60 percent said they had become fans by age 11. This number is staggering.[34]

Learning

A formal definition of learning is "the acquisition of new responses to behavioral cues in the environment, occurring as the result of reinforcement." This definition includes several components common to learning theories. The first encompasses drives or arousal mechanisms that cause a person to act; the desire for esteem is an example. The second includes cues or environmental stimuli that may trigger an individual

drive. Advertisements for luxury cars during televised golf tournaments are good examples of cues that attempt to trigger esteem drives. The third component includes reinforcements or outcomes (usually positive rewards) that serve to reduce the drive. The golf fan who purchases a Cadillac may (or may not) learn the connections between lifestyle and esteem.[35]

Several areas of learning theory have special relevance to the sport marketer. For example, cognitive, affective, and behavioral types of involvement correspond to the hierarchy of effects sometimes used to describe consumer purchase behavior. The basic hierarchy suggests that consumers first process information about a product (cognitive involvement), often through advertising. If additional messages succeed, consumers next develop a new feeling about the product (affective involvement), which may in turn lead them to buy the product (behavioral involvement). This hierarchy is displayed as

$$\text{Learn} \rightarrow \text{Feel} \rightarrow \text{Do}$$

One way or another, product knowledge is an important variable in consumer behavior. Knowledge links to involvement and commitment in an endless loop. Anyone who has ever been bitten by the golf bug understands this. The more you play, the more you want to learn about the game and its nuances. The more you learn, the more you want to play. The same is true for sports fans. One study of minor league hockey fans showed that hockey knowledge—measured by a set of simple questions (e.g., What does icing mean?)—accounted for over 12 percent of the variance in games attended. All things being equal, the more fans knew about hockey, the more they attended. On the one hand, this point is just common sense. But then consider how little effort many organizations put into teaching their consumers about their sport.[36]

ESPN used aggressive teaching tools such as television ads and an Internet site when it launched the X Games. In 1998, three years into the games, ESPN was still helping consumers learn the basics; for instance, it put a 20 page magazine insert into *Rolling Stone* magazine, a perfect medium for reaching the target audience. The insert included basic information on all the events, which ran from bicycle stunts to sport climbing, wakeboarding, and street luge. Exquisite visuals were surrounded by text on "the point," or the rules; "the tools," or the equipment; "the names," or the prominent contestants. The "Guide to the X Games" was an excellent primer. Even a casual reader would feel empowered with the information.[37]

Some researchers suggest that the standard hierarchy Learn → Feel → Do may not apply to services, which are intangible and therefore less conducive to initial cognitive messages about product, price, and the like. This notion is certainly true for many sport products, which often involve intricate physical activities. In sport, consumers may be more responsive to information that triggers their emotions about an overall experience, even if the initial image is limited in its detail. Consumers may be willing to act on such information, try the sport product, and then learn more about it after the trial. In sport, then, the hierarchy may be more like

Feel → Do → Learn

This approach is the one used by most Nike ads, which look to stir emotions before anything else.

Social media have increased the opportunities for sport properties to engage fan emotions and attachments while also learning about players, events, and venues. Such approaches using multimedia, however, would do well to absorb some of the research findings on multimedia learning (see the sidebar on multimedia learning).

Some activities demand this hierarchy:

Do → Feel and Learn

As the U.S. Army ratcheted up its recruiting efforts in 2009, it opened an Army Experience Center in Philadelphia, where young men and women could experience simulated gunfights and helicopter rides. This hierarchy was Do → Feel and Learn. Likewise, special sales or promotional efforts, targeted at youth and family groups, are often packaged in a way to attract casual fans. The hope is that in coming with friends, eating together in a special area, getting group recognition on a big screen or PA announcement, smelling the aromas, hearing the unique sounds, and cheering together will, in combination, create consumers who want to return. Fan fests that offer kids the chance to swing at a big-league pitch or test their slap-shot ability also follow a Do → Feel and Learn approach.[38]

Some fantasy game makers have recognized the need to create simpler versions of their products to attract and retain consumers with a casual interest. In 2007 the NFL expanded its NFLRush.com site with a fantasy game targeted at kids. Bloomberg Sports' fantasy baseball product began in 2010 to include utilities that made it easier for novices to manage rosters and enjoy the action—in short, to Do → Feel and Learn. Likewise, in an age of interactivity, the most progressive organizations use exhibits, fan zones, and websites to promote all three elements of the learning hierarchy. The smartest sport marketers understand the centrality of learning to sport consumption. To that end, they even modify their notions of sales, especially with corporate clients. Marketers become teachers, and selling becomes what Bill Sutton has called "edu-selling."[39]

ACTIVITY 3.2 Individual and External Factors in Sport Marketing

Major League Baseball and almost all the other sport leagues offer fans a chance to play their fantasy sport leagues. In this WSG activity, you will explore how these fantasy leagues affect the fans and the organizations.

Perception

Learning requires the consumer to use perception, which may be defined as the process of scanning, gathering, assessing, and interpreting information in the environment. Much work needs to be done on how consumers use the five senses in perception and decision making. One study, for instance, found that the sense of touch "influenced impressions and decisions formed about unrelated people and situations." Among the effects, "heavy objects made job candidates appear more important, rough objects made social interactions appear more difficult, and hard objects increased rigidity in negotiations." Martin Lindstrom has argued, "The more sensory touch points leveraged when building brands, the higher the number of sensory memories activated. The higher the number of sensory memories activated, the stronger the bonding between brand and consumer." What are the implications for stadium design and game presentation?[41]

Multimedia Learning

Sarah Sceery, Development Project Assistant, Brown University Sports Foundation, and Brian Norman, Sales Manager, Philadelphia 76ers

What is it that you remember from the last newspaper coupon, television advertisement, or in-store promo you saw? Could it have been an image, a catchy slogan, a musical jingle? The combination of how consumers learn or what consumers remember from any type of advertising, promotion, or other form of marketing communication today could be classified as multimedia learning. The concept, developed by Richard E. Mayer, is defined as "learning from words and pictures. The words can be printed text or spoken text. The pictures can be in static form . . . or in dynamic form." This research has great implications for sport marketers at all levels.

According to Mayer, learning is defined as a "change in a learner's knowledge that is attributable to experience," and in this case, the experience is a consumer's exposure to a marketing communication such as an ad, a promo coupon, or a video on an arena screen. Mayer has developed 10 principles of multimedia learning. We highlight five, with examples from what we consider effective communications in the sport industry.

- Signaling principle. The signaling principle concludes that "people learn better when cues that highlight the organization of the essential material are added." At the collegiate level, the Brown University Sports Foundation has used Mayer's signaling principle to send a targeted message with a year-end postcard (see the following image). As the fund-raising branch of Brown athletics, the card is used in an effort to increase support for Brown's 37 varsity and club athletics teams. The layout is designed to highlight key words and attract the reader's attention toward the successes of athletics programs throughout the year. In doing so, the essential connection is made between the Bears' ability to win championships and the financial support of the programs.

> continued

- Spatial contiguity. Mayer defines the spatial contiguity principle as "students learn better when corresponding words and pictures are presented near rather than far from each other on the page or screen." The photos and word *championships* on the Brown postcard depict this principle, providing a direct message to encourage support for the Bears.

- Pretraining principle. As Mayer describes in his pretraining principle, "people learn more deeply from a multimedia message when they know the names and characteristics of the main concepts." In Washington, DC, Monumental Sports and Entertainment (www. monumentalsports.com) has used Mayer's pretraining principle to educate fans on the rich history of their core business units. Founded in 2010, MSE owns and operates the Washington Capitals (NHL), Wizards (NBA), Mystics (WNBA), and Verizon Center. To educate fans about the newly formed, integrated sport and entertainment company, MSE runs a preevent video on their video monitor that displays the past, present, and future of their business units. Images of the nation's capital kick off this 60-second time capsule as music and play-by-play clips make their way across the screen. Famous shots of Alex Ovechkin, Dale Hunter, and the 1978 NBA champion Washington Bullets fill the arena and ignite applause among fans. As the video concludes, MSE's "M" logo appears. This video ties in to the pretraining principle by displaying images, sounds, and text that fans know and understand, making it easy to link the past, present, and future of Washington's NHL, NBA, and WNBA team to the Monumental Sports and Entertainment brand.

- Modality and temporal contiguity. Mayer's modality and temporal contiguity principles are used in the advertisement and promotion of golf's largest event each year—the Masters at Augusta National. To use the modality principle effectively, Mayer explains, "People learn more deeply from pictures and spoken words than from pictures and printed words." The homepage of the tournament (www.masters.com) captures the learner through the rotating videos on the site, which pair images and footage of iconic history, the current tournament, and the prestigious course with corresponding descriptions. Similarly, each year Jim Nantz and CBS Sports promote the event through commercials and introduction videos. Nantz speaks of the triumph and despair that have taken place on those hallowed grounds as images of Tiger Woods, Arnold Palmer, Jack Nicklaus, and Magnolia Lane flash across the screen. The temporal contiguity principle is used alongside the modality principle on the Masters website and in CBS promotional videos as well. Mayer identifies the temporal contiguity principle in use when "corresponding word and pictures are presented simultaneously rather than successively." This principle is used often when ads or videos describe the legendary Green Jacket while corresponding pictures of past winners in their prized jackets flash simultaneously across the screen.

This concept of multimedia learning is similar to the idea of multisensory learning. In an article from the *Boston Globe*, Courtney Humphries stated, "In broader commercial applications, meanwhile, the science is already providing a new basis for what marketers have long surmised: They are selling customers more than just the core sensory experience. Restaurant owners, for instance, know that choosing decor, lighting, music, and table settings that complement their food can boost their bottom line, and companies have long market-tested food products for texture and packaging as well as taste." Multimedia learning is more than the core experience for learners in the sport industry. It is not only seeing the Ivy championship trophy, Stanley Cup, or Green Jacket presentation but also viewing and feeling those moments through a combination of visuals, sound, and text. Through these means all levels of the sport industry are able to influence consumers.[40]

Although perception employs the five senses, it involves far more. Perception depends on the characteristics of the person, situation, or thing perceived (stimulus factors) and on the characteristics of the perceiver (individual factors). A roaring crowd may be an exhilarating and uplifting experience for a knowledgeable fan but a threatening mob to someone else. Our perceptions, then, are something of a filter, influenced by our values, attitudes, needs, and expectations. This filter contributes to selective exposure, selective distortion, and selective retention of the innumerable stimuli that confront us daily.[42]

Consumers and prospective consumers are constantly filtering and interpreting cues about sport products in relation to their self-concepts. Failure to provide congruent and consonant images to consumers will typically reduce involvement. For example, perfume companies keep their high-priced products out of discount stores because the place of purchase enhances the perception of quality.

Like many product and service providers, sport teams have often attempted to develop perceptions among fans that tickets are going fast, thus elevating a sense of risk over missing something big. Recently, marketing researchers demonstrated that the scarcity factor does work.

Sport marketers must be particularly sensitive to a number of perceptual issues, including the following:[43]

• Facility cleanliness. Long ago, Bill Veeck realized that clean restrooms were critical to attracting women and families to the ballpark. But men don't love a mess either. Some research suggests that cleanliness is especially important to people in certain counties, including Japan.

• Exposure to violence. This perception can work both ways, as shown in ice hockey. Some fans love a good brawl; others abhor the goons. The NHL continues to walk a fine line, with Commissioner Gary Bettman trying to distinguish between goonism and a spontaneous altercation. Can the casual fan tell the difference? Worse than player violence is the fear of rowdy, drunken fans. No parent wants to expose children to that form of entertainment. Some clubs have responded with no-alcohol family zones.

• Waste of time, money, effort. As we will see in chapter 8, consumer costs include far more than the event ticket, the lift ticket, or the greens fee. In an age focused on quality time, every choice is a risk.

Motivation

Amid a constant swirl of stimuli, can we identify any individual triggers of sport involvement? According to motivation theory, environmental stimuli may activate the drive to satisfy an underlying need. Theorists like Abraham Maslow, Henry Murray, and David McClelland have outlined elaborate models explaining how physiological, psychological, and social needs influence human behavior. In the last decade, a number of researchers have focused their efforts on explaining what makes sport consumers tick. At the same time, historians have outlined a number of long-residual factors that have motivated involvement in sport across vast extents of time and space. The research is extensive and growing, but some motivational factors have emerged rather clearly:

• Achievement and self-esteem. The notion of winning does matter, for players and fans. In one USTA survey, serious players listed winning as a major reason for playing. Likewise, numerous studies show that fans tend to bask in reflected glory when their team wins.

• Craft. Winning isn't all that counts. For many, developing or enjoying physical skill prompts sport interest. Learning a new skill typically ranks high among reasons people list for playing. And the chance to watch a star display great skill brings a crowd to any game.

• Health and fitness. This is an obvious motive for club membership and equipment purchase. Even golfers can argue that a "good walk spoiled" beats watching television or an afternoon at the office.

• Fun and festival. Humans have a long history of framing their games with circles of spectators and fun lovers, who exchange money for sight lines, food, and merchandise. Descriptions of ancient festivals sound much like those of modern events. There was and is more than the contest. What is big-time football without the tailgating? For similar reasons, most new venues contain a concourse, which is the locus of fun and festival—the midway, if you like. Perhaps the most visible symbol of festival is the team mascot, now almost a necessity.

• Eros. Evidence is clear that many players and fans have erotic motives. Sweaty bodies in motion, not all of which are clad in tights or a leotard, have a certain sexual attraction. In 1975 the Golden State Warriors ran a promotional campaign to attract female fans. The tag line was this: "We've got five men in shorts who can go all night." Pay-per-view promos for boxer Oscar De La Hoya included female voice-overs saying, "You know, Oscar, I could sit around and watch you sweat all night. And that's exactly what I'm gonna do." A study of Florida Gators fans showed that they were more aroused at football action shots than at patently erotic photographs. The erotic motive is still somewhat taboo as an academic subject; it demands more attention.

• Affiliation or community. Being with friends or family is a common reason that people give for any sport involvement, as indicated in studies of tennis participation, athletics club membership, and fan motivations. Fan communities have existed for thousands of years, represented in the Roman factions of blues, greens, reds, and whites, who passionately rooted for their color in the chariot races. Their modern counterparts may wear official merchandise, but the motives are the same. Research has clearly shown that few fans (1 to 3 percent) attend games alone. Fantasy football is on the rise, particularly among teenage boys. According to one researcher, participation is a way of belonging. "Dropping a league," he said, "is like ending a dozen friendships." Being a fan or a participant can become of paramount importance to a person's social identity, which links to the notion of self-concept that we discussed earlier. For some, fan identity was welded in place by adolescence. Dan Mahony, sport marketing scholar, spent only the first half of his life in New York, but that was enough: "I can live in Louisville for the rest of my life and I'm still going to be seen as a Yankee. It's part of my personality." Green Bay Packers transplants to New York City may cultivate their cheesehead personality in a Greenwich Village watering hole called the Kettle of Fish. For others, adopting a new loyalty is part of any move. NBA studies clearly show that transplants readily attach themselves to their new city. Although historical research shows clearly that Americans have always been a people on the move, some wonder about fan identity in an era when players and franchises seem to swirl around like rootless sagebrush.

• Eustress, risk, and gambling. The emotional ride of rooting is much like that of gambling—an addictive combination of euphoria and stress. It is no wonder that sport and gambling have gone hand in glove as far back as our literary and archeological records will take us.

• Entertainment and escape. Many fans believe (and report on surveys) that a day at the ballpark or an evening in front of their TV, rooting and cheering, takes their minds off their everyday troubles. Social activists have sometimes attacked this "bread and circuses" aspect of sport, and an escape motive and a eustress motive may be in contradiction. After all, rooting for the Cubs may be simply trading work troubles for leisure troubles. But who's to tell a fan what is best?

Researchers are beginning to tease out the differences between the motives of fans of men's sports and women's sports, or revenue sports and nonrevenue sports. Although motivations are elusive and difficult to quantify, they will remain essential constructs for understanding consumer behavior in sport. A better understanding of fan motives promises to help marketers develop better communications with their consumer base through promotions, ads, or newsletters.[44]

Emotion

In 2012 the managing director of the 155-year-old Brooklyn Philharmonic Orchestra posted an online plea for a change in the norms of classical music audiences. He wanted less of the silent treatment and restrained applause that he thought was stagnating the field. He wanted more cheering, whooping, and hollering—the kind that we associate with a stirring performance in sport. Reaction from his peers was tepid at best. Bach seemed a long way from Beckham. Sports fans, on the other hand, are usually vocal and emotional. As one experienced executive explained to *SSSBJ*'s Terry Lefton in 2007, "The passion and engagement that goes along with sports is very different from the emotion a consumer feels when buying a box of Tide." Unfortunately, he went on, too many advertising agencies overlooked that distinction.[45] Researchers like Dae Hee Kwak have sharpened our understanding of the role of emotion in the development of sport consumers (see the sidebar).

Emotion and Sport Consumer Behavior

Dae Hee Kwak, University of Michigan

On July 11, 2010, millions of Spaniards rushed into the streets of the capital city and danced, cheered, and set off fireworks all night to celebrate the country's first FIFA World Cup triumph. After the final match against the Netherlands, the center of Madrid became a sea of red and gold, the national colors, as huge crowds poured onto the streets. Similar strong emotional outbursts in crowds are also seen in collegiate sports. Nothing rivals a college basketball buzzer beater followed by a court storming by students and fans. People are motivated to seek out behaviors that are congruent with their current emotions (e.g., intense joy or pride) to maintain or even increase those feelings at that moment. This enthusiasm can contribute to a consumerist approach toward the situation to extend the experience of elation and positive feelings, as seen when fans line up to buy team-licensed merchandise or reserve tickets for the next game or season.

On the other hand, fans may experience strong negative feelings when their team loses to a vicious rival or loses a playoff game. When people experience strong negative emotions, they are motivated to avoid situations or events that exacerbate those emotions. Avoidance tendencies are triggered in such situations. For instance, a basketball fan might leave the arena if the team she is rooting for is trailing by many points at the bottom of the fourth quarter. Although regulating negative emotions is more complex than dealing with positive ones, some fans may want to distance themselves temporarily from the losing team to alleviate their temporary negative feelings (e.g., shame, frustration).

As such, sport consumption experiences are experiential and emotional in nature. Emotions are pervasive and readily accessible when consuming sport. Researchers in various disciplines have contended that sport provides unique opportunities to understand how emotions operate in people. Sports fans report greater levels of arousal and suspense when viewing sport on television than they do when viewing other types of entertainment genres. Therefore, exploring emotional and experiential aspects of decision-making processes is critical for developing better understanding of sport consumers. But in comparison with traditional information-processing paradigms, relatively little is known about the role of emotions in the behavior of sport consumers. In particular, the motivational effect and influence of emotions on fans' subsequent cognition, beliefs, and behaviors is much less understood.

Sport marketing research has shown that fans' emotional states can be manipulated by sports articles. Researchers have found that such article-induced emotions have significant influence on respondents' cognitive and behavioral responses to team-related marketing stimuli.[46] For instance, research participants experiencing positive feelings were more likely to choose to receive a team's promotional items than were respondents experiencing negative feelings. Additionally, positive emotions had significant direct effects on value perception toward the team-licensed product. Positive emotions derived from a team's success are transferred to favorable evaluations of team-related marketing stimuli. Overall, the findings suggest that emotions had significant biasing effects on how fans respond to team-related marketing stimuli. Understanding fan emotions is critical in predicting consumption behavior and planning marketing communication campaigns.

Figure 3.2 demonstrates a model of consumer behavior that incorporates both the emotional system and the cognitive system. Previous consumer research has established that both the emotional and the cognitive systems contribute to decision making but provide different types of inputs from the same stimulus (e.g., event, game outcome, advertising). In general, the cognitive system has been characterized as being more analytical, logical, and active, whereas the emotional system is relatively more holistic, affective, and passive. Figure 3.2 indicates that the two systems interact with each other in responding to a stimulus. The

> continued

> continued

model also suggests that various individual characteristics (e.g., personality, identification, attitudes, and needs), environmental factors (e.g., culture, subculture, family, and friends), and genetics influence how people respond to stimuli. The strength of a fan–team relationship may affect how individuals respond to the outcome of a game. For instance, research has found that die-hard fans express greater levels of emotions before, during, and after the event than fair-weather fans do, regardless of the outcome of the game. Strong affective dispositions (rooting for a team) emerge as a precondition for greater emotional outcomes. As such, emotions are extremely important to sport consumer behavior and sport marketing research because consumers react most immediately to their feelings.

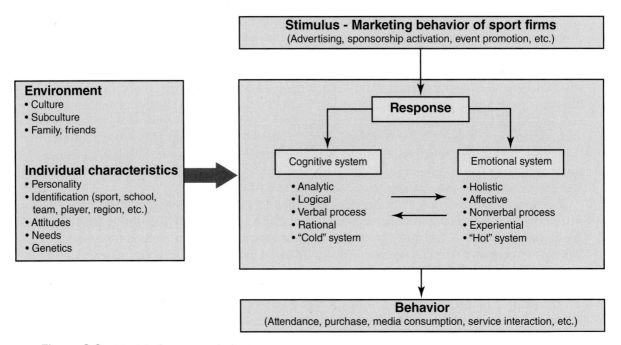

Figure 3.2 Model of consumer behavior.

Consumers' emotions can be measured in several ways. Self-report measures using established items like the Positive Affect and Negative Affect Schedule (PANAS) and the Pleasure–Arousal–Dominance (PAD) scale have been widely used by researchers. Self-report emotion measures usually require consumers to recall their emotional state from a recent experience or to report the emotions that they are feeling at the moment. Although these paper-and-pencil measures are less obtrusive than physiological measures (e.g., skin conductance, heart rate, electroencephalography), the results are valid enough to be useful to consumer and marketing researchers. More recently, researchers have been employing more innovative techniques to understand consumers' decisions and behavior. For instance, consumer neuroscience can allow researchers to identify brain activity in response to marketing stimuli. Functional magnetic resonance imaging (fMRI) measures brain activity by detecting associated changes in blood flow and can provide hidden information about the consumer experience in the marketing context. Although brain image research may be far less cost effective than traditional measures, it may be useful in answering many interesting questions about the complexity of emotions pervasive to sport consumers.

Decision Making

The array of factors discussed in this chapter contributes to the difficulty of establishing a standard process by which consumers make decisions about becoming or staying involved with sport products. Nonetheless, such models, even if they are imperfect, can be helpful tools for marketers. We offer one such model, based on a series of steps generally seen as part of consumer decision making (figure 3.3). As displayed, the consumer's decision to become involved in sport includes several stages:

1. Need recognition. Any number of cues, particularly images in the mass media, may trigger the arousal of a need or motive, which may be related to achievement, esteem, affiliation, health, or other sport motives. In short, any of the individual or environmental factors may trigger an arousal of need. Over the last decade, researchers have acknowledged team identification as one of the most important factors in determining attendance. In that respect, team identification might be seen as the starting and ending place for each cycle of fan decision making.[47]

2. Awareness or information search. The consumer may have prior awareness of, or may seek information about, products that can satisfy aroused needs. Marketers must never underestimate this critical stage. Countless studies of sport involvement point to the importance of information about distance to venue, time to travel, and cleanliness of venue. Given the consumer's perceptual filter, the marketer cannot make any assumptions about the accuracy of the consumer's perceptions. Worse yet is the possibility that consumers are unaware of the product. In these respects, social media have become game changers as more consumers base decisions on their social media world. In a 2011 study of 8,000 American and Canadian Ticketmaster users, researchers found that 14 percent were influenced to attend a particular event because of Facebook posts and that 20 percent invited friends to attend through Facebook posts or Twitter tweets.[48]

3. Evaluation of choices. Consumers make product choices at a number of levels. Philip Kotler distinguished these levels as follows:

- Product family. Within the realm of leisure, people make choices between broad families such as competitive sports, outdoor recreation, and hobbies (like making jigsaw puzzles).
- Product class. There are many classes of sports, such as motorsports, water sports, field sports, and team sports.
- Product line. Within the team sport class are lines of products such as bat and ball sports, ball-only sports, and stick and ball sports.
- Product type. Within the ball-only line are product types such as rugby, world football, and American football.
- Product brand. Within the product type of American football are various brands including the NFL brand and the NCAA brand, and even more specifically the Packers brand and the SEC brand.

Consumers are surrounded by levels of choice as they engage the world around them.

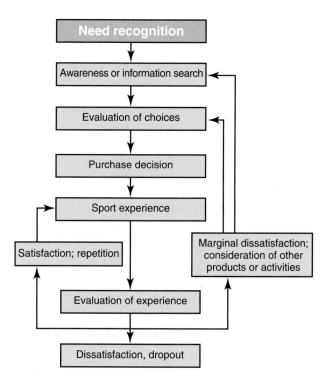

FIGURE 3.3 The decision process for sport involvement.

They may be steered toward decisions at any of the preceding levels, which may influence their attitudes at other levels. As we noted earlier, young people may be socialized by family or peers to adopt specific sport brands, which may then limit their interest in other product types or classes.[49]

4. Purchase decision. Numerous questions demand research concerning the sport consumer's purchase decisions. For instance, to what extent are decisions to purchase a sport experience (with time, money, effort) planned and calculated or unplanned and impulsive? As one review of research reminded marketers, "Studies of sport fans indicate that a majority—especially in baseball, basketball, and hockey—make purchase decisions only a few days before the event." Walk-up fans and season-ticket holders obviously require different messages, as we discuss in chapters to follow.[50]

5. Sport experience. As Chubb and Chubb have suggested, this stage may include a period of anticipation after a person has made the decision (thinking about the big game a month before it is to occur), a period of preparation (readying the tailgating food, drink, and grill the night before), travel to the site of the experience, the main experience, and travel from the main experience.[51]

6. Evaluation of experience. An effective illustration of evaluation is the consumer satisfaction equation:

Satisfaction = Benefits – Cost

Satisfaction can relate to social experience, self-concept, skill, reliability, or other elements. Benefits relate to characteristics like quantity and duration. Costs can include money, time, ego, effort, and opportunities to do other things. In the end, benefits must outweigh costs. Marketers attempt to maximize satisfaction through the various elements in the marketing mix. But consumers continue to filter the stimuli around them. They can develop positive or negative attitudes for a host of reasons. One of the most important is the consumer's assessment of competence, as a player or a fan. Has the experience enhanced the person's sense of competence and self-worth? Has it strengthened his or her identity? The answer has a major influence on subsequent behavior.

7. Postevaluation behavior. After evaluating, the consumer has three basic choices:

- If satisfied, to repeat the experience, and perhaps build a stronger identity or affinity with the activity. Fans of NASCAR reflect high levels of satisfaction, which spills over into brand loyalty to NASCAR sponsors. Satisfied fans typically indicate that they plan to attend more of a team's events in the future—that is, they intend to move up the escalator.

- If dissatisfied, to reduce or abandon the activity. Some participants and spectators move down or even off the escalator.

- If marginally satisfied or dissatisfied, to reevaluate information and decisions about product choices at various levels (family, class, line, type, and brand).

Researchers need to study those who drop off the escalator. Although information is increasingly available on youth sport dropouts, we know relatively little about adult fan dropouts. One of the few studies of adult dropouts involved extensive interviews with NHL Hartford Whaler fans (the Whalers left Hartford in 1997 for Carolina). The researcher, Craig Hyatt, discovered that most of these abandoned (betrayed?) fans did not follow either the Carolina Hurricanes or the NHL, but they still considered themselves Whalers fans. We can only guess how many sports fans drop off the escalator of present-day involvement and live in the world of memories. What prompts voluntary dropouts? We know little about how financial contingencies or other life-altering events such as marriage, divorce, or employment change affect sport consumption patterns. We have much to learn, most of which will require the kind of in-depth interviews that Craig Hyatt conducted.[52]

All the decision loops require much more attention from sport marketers. Consumers are constantly constructing preferences bases on changing contexts. At the same time, they may be driven by habit. Over the last decade, research in brain science has exploded. Some of it has focused on decision making. As Dae Hee Kwak's

Consumers make all kinds of purchase decisions before, during, and after events, including what to eat!

sidebar on emotion suggests, we employ both a conscious, analytical, and rational process and an unconscious, fast, intuitive process. One would think that the purchase of season tickets would be deliberate and rational, whereas walk-up sales would be more of a snap judgment, perhaps made by thinly slicing the odds of a great experience based on weather and opponent. Along these lines, a Corporate Executive Board (CEB) study of 7,000 consumers and hundreds of marketing executives concluded that people value simplicity. The CEB boiled things down to a decision simplicity index, a "gauge of how easy it is for consumers to gather and understand (or *navigate*) information about a brand, how much they can *trust* the information they find, and how readily they can *weigh* their options." Those brands that scored in the top quarter of the index were 86 percent more likely to be purchased than brands in the bottom quarter of simplicity. But it may not be so simple with decisions about events.[53]

Wrap-Up

In this chapter we examined some of the theories that may indicate why people consume sport. Specifically, we considered the literature on sport consumers within the larger context of general

All sorts of sport consumer studies are available in print or on the Internet. Scholarly research has exploded in the last decade, finding outlets like *Sport Marketing Quarterly*. Governing bodies like FIFA, the NCAA, and the NBA post information about fans. So do industry trade associations like the National Sporting Goods Association. In reading any such reports, however, we must remember the limitations of any study. All market research is limited by time and resources. Researchers make choices about many elements, including the following:

• Definitions. For instance, what constitutes a fan or a participant? Casual or careless use of definitions will severely limit the utility of any statistics. Take, for example, one poll commissioned by MLB in the late 1990s to examine fan support for league realignment—a controversial issue. The poll, of 801 fans aged 16 or older, supposedly represented the vast population of the baseball nation. When the Associated Press looked more carefully at the sample, however, they discovered that 70 percent of the people in the sample were not aware that MLB was considering realignment. Worse yet, 44 percent had never heard of the expansion Diamondbacks or Devil Rays, and 13 percent had never heard of the Colorado Rockies. Almost half of the sample planned to attend only one game or no games during the season. As the Associated Press concluded, these were casual fans at best—hardly the type of fans who should have input into realignment decisions.[54]

• Methodologies. Researchers must make choices about methods. How should they interact with their subject consumers? Interviews? By phone? By mail? At an event? Personal observations? Each approach has strengths and weaknesses, including relative time and cost.

• Sampling. Researchers must also make choices about samples. Should they attempt a random sample of the whole population? Several random samples grouped, or "stratified," by some criterion (e.g., ticket type)? A convenience sample? A snowball sample? One of the problems with academic literature on just about anything, including sport consumers, is the overreliance on samples of undergraduate students. Although they are an important segment of the potential market, they are hardly the entire market. As a 2010 article in *Science* put it, they are WEIRDos: "people from Western, educated, industrialized, rich, and democratic cultures" . . . who "aren't representative of humans as a whole," despite the tendency of psychologists to "routinely use them to make broad, and quite likely false, claims about what drives human behavior." Thus, readers must look carefully at the samples behind models or theories of sport consumer behavior.[55]

Anyone trying to make sense out of published studies must consider all these questions. We will discuss them further in the next chapter.

---

consumer behavior. We discussed various factors that help to explain the process whereby people are socialized into involvement in or commitment to sport. We have seen that factors influencing behavior may be either environmental or individual. Environmental factors include significant others; cultural norms and values; class, race, and gender relations; and the market behavior of sport firms. Individual factors include self-concept, a person's stage in the life or family cycle, perception, and motivation.

We have been able to provide only a brief introduction to some of the components in the complex area of consumer behavior. Further research is sorely needed before sport marketers can build effective theories on decision making. In the next chapter, we provide some information on how the marketer should conduct such research.

Activities

1. Define socialization, involvement, and commitment in sport consumer behavior.

2. Describe the most logical indicators of commitment for the following sport consumers: (*a*) Montreal Canadiens fans, (*b*) members of a local gymnastics club.

3. Discuss which environmental factors most influenced your involvement in your favorite sport.

4. Why is it likely that the normal hierarchy of effects (learn → feel → do) is less applicable to sport consumers than to consumers of detergent?

5. Find a magazine ad for a sport product or team. Analyze how, in your opinion, the ad is trying to influence consumer perceptions of the product.

6. List the steps in the decision making process for sport consumers. Reconstruct your most recent decision to attend a major sport event. How did your experience compare with the decision making model?

Your Marketing Plan

This chapter outlined many of the factors that influence how people become involved in and committed to sport. As you organize and conduct research on the current and possible consumers for your product, event, or organization, pay close attention to the most prominent environmental and individual factors that influence their behavior. This analysis, in turn, should influence your decisions about product development, pricing, promotion, distribution (place), and public relations.

Endnotes

1. Isabel Kershner, "Israel: Ex-Captive to Be a Sportswriter," *New York Times*, 16 June 2012, A9; Yitzhak Benhorin, "Shalit Will Watch NBA All-Star Game in Orlando as Part of Second Overseas Trip Since His Return From Captivity," ynetnews.com, 26 February 2012, www.ynetnews.com/articles/0,7340,L-4194739,00.html.

2. Jeré Longman, "Racism and Soccer Are in Play at a Big Event in East Europe," *New York Times*, 30 May 2012, A1.

3. Bill King, "What Makes Fans Tick?" *SSSBJ*, 1–7 March 2004, 26.

4. Our general list of topics follows that found in most texts on marketing and consumer behavior. See, for instance, Michael Solomon, *Consumer Behavior*, 6th ed. (Upper Saddle River, NJ: Prentice Hall, 2004); Leon G. Schiffman and Leslie Lazar Kanuk, *Consumer Behavior*, 8th ed. (Upper Saddle River, NJ: Prentice Hall, 2004); Curtis P. Haugtvedt, Paul M. Herr, and Frank R. Kardes, eds., *Handbook of Consumer Psychology* (New York: Erlbaum, 2008).

5. D. Zillman and P. Paulus, "Spectators: Reactions to Sports Events and Effects on Athletic Competition." in *Handbook of Research on Sports Psychology*, ed. R. Singer, M. Murphey, and L. Tennant (New York: MacMillan, 1993), 600–619.

6. AP, "Indiana Couple Name Baby Boy Wrigley Fields," www.foxnews.com/story/2007/09/24/indiana-couple-name-baby-boy-wrigley-fields/. Pliny quoted in Allen Guttmann, *Sports Spectators* (New York: Columbia University Press, 1986), 30. See also Alan Cameron, *Circus Factions: Blues and Greens at Rome and Byzantium* (Oxford: Clarendon Press, 1976); William Henry Nugent, "The Sports Section," *American Mercury*, March 1929, 329–338; A.J. Liebling, *The Sweet Science* (New York: Viking, 1956, repr. New York: Penguin, 1982); *Fan* and *Fancy* definitions in *Compact Edition of the Oxford English Dictionary* (Oxford, 1971), Vol. 1, 960–61. Early baseball crowds in George Kirsch, *The Creation of American Team Sports: Baseball and Cricket, 1838–72*, Ithaca: Cornell University Press, 1989), 178–200, and Mel Adelman, *A Sporting Time: New York City and the Rise of Modern Athletics, 1820–1870* (Urbana: University of Illinois Press, 1986). Early hockey fans in Stephen Hardy, "Long Before Orr: Placing Hockey in Boston, 1897–1929," *The Rock, the Curse, and the Hub: Random Histories of Boston Sports*, ed. Randy Roberts (Cambridge: Harvard University Press, 2005), 245–89.

7. On sport socialization, involvement, and commitment, see J. Loy, B. McPherson, and G. Kenyon, *Sport and Social Systems* (Reading, MA: Addison-Wesley, 1978), 16–23, 215–248; R. Brustad, "Integrating Socialization Influences Into the Study of Children's Motivation in Sport," *Journal of Sport and Exercise Psychology*, 14 (1992): 59–77.

For an interesting study of sport consumers, with implications about socialization, see A. Shohlan and L. Kahle, "Spectators, Viewers, Readers: Communication and Consumption Communities in Sport Marketing," *Sport Marketing Quarterly*, 5 (March 1996): 11–20.

8. Bill King, "The 24/7 Fan," *SSSBJ*, 7–13 March 2005, 25.

9. "NFL: For Stoking Insatiable, Year-Round Demand for Professional Football," *Fast Company*, March 2012, 98. For some of the literature on affect, see Joel B. Cohen, et al., "The Nature and Role of Affect in Consumer Behavior," in *Handbook of Consumer Psychology*, ed. Curtis P. Haugtvedt, Paul M. Herr, and Frank R. Kardes (New York: Erlbaum, 2008), 297–329.

10. P. Graham, "A Study of the Demographic and Economic Characteristics of Spectators Attending the U.S. Men's Clay Court Championships," *SMQ* 1 (1) (March 1992): 25–30.

11. Bill King, "What Makes Fans Crazy About Sports?" *SSSBJ*, 19 April 2010, 22; David Broughton, "Survey: Social-Media Use Builds Fan Avidity," *SSSBJ*, 26 July 2010, 9.

12. Daniel Funk, Daniel Mahony, and Mark Havitz, "Sport Consumer Behavior: Assessment and Direction," *SMQ*, 12 (4) (2003): 200–205; D. Wann et al., *Sports Fans: The Psychology and Social Impact of Spectators* (New York: Routledge, 2001), 2–3; Bob Stewart, Aaron Smith, and Matthew Nicholson, "Sport Consumer Typologies: A Critical Review," *SMQ*, 12 (4) (2003): 206–216; Hyungil Harry Kwon and Ketra Armstrong, "An Exploration of the Construct of Psychological Attachments to a Sports Team Among College Students: A Multidimensional Approach," *SMQ*, 13 (2) (2004): 94–103; H. Kwon and G. Trail, "The Feasibility of Single-Item Measures in Sport Loyalty Research," *Sport Management Review*, 8 (2005): 69–89.

13. Frank B. Ashley et al., "Professional Wrestling Fans: Your Next-Door Neighbors?" *SMQ*, 9 (3) (2000): 140–148.

14. "The Power of Pals," *Marketing Tools*, March 1997, 39; C. Walker, "Word of Mouth," *American Demographics*, July 1995, 38–44.

15. K.L. Wakefield, "The Pervasive Effects of Social Influence on Sporting Event Attendance," *Journal of Sport and Social Issues*, 19 (1995): 335–351.

16. For excellent history on dominant sports cultures, see S.W. Pope, *Patriotic Games: Sporting Traditions in the American Imagination, 1876–1926* (New York: Oxford University Press, 1997); M. Dyreson, *Inventing the Sporting Republic: American Sport, Political Culture, and the Olympic Experience, 1877–1919* (Urbana: University of Illinois Press, 1997).

17. "GOLF 20/20 Vision for the Future: Industry Report for 2002," www.golf2020.com/research/participation-reports/2002/2002-industry-report.aspx, 2003; John Ourand, "NHL Viewership Rends Tied to Hockey Tradition, Northern Exposure," *SSSBJ*, 7 February 2011. Contemporary sports regions are described in Rooney and Pillsbury, *Atlas of American Sport* (New York: MacMillan 1992); B. Hunnicutt, "Sports," in *Encyclopedia of Southern Culture*, eds. C.R. Wilson and W. Ferris (Chapel Hill: University of North Carolina Press, 1989), 1239; Nate Silver, "The Geography of College Football Fans," *New York Times*, 19 September 2011, http://thequad.blogs.nytimes.com/2011/09/19/the-geography-of-college-football-fans-and-realignment-chaos/. On the South and baseball, see K. Greenburg, *Honor and Slavery* (Princeton, NJ: Princeton University Press, 1996). For a more expansive analysis of southern styles, see T. Ownby, *Subduing Satan: Religion, Recreation, and Manhood in the Rural South, 1865–1920* (Chapel Hill: University of North Carolina Press, 1990).

18. R.P. Coleman, "The Continuing Significance of Social Class to Marketing," *Journal of Consumer Research*, 10 (December 1983): 265–280.

19. D. Booth and J. Loy, "Sport, Status, and Style," *Sport History Review*, 30 (1999): 1–26; T. Veblen, *Theory of the Leisure Class* (New York: New American Library, 1899); concerning prole sports, see D.S. Eitzen and G. Sage, *Sociology of North American Sport*, 3rd ed. (Dubuque, IA: Brown, 1986), 244–245; G. Lipsitz, *Class and Culture in Cold War America* (South Hadley, MA: Bergin, 1982), 173–194; R. Gruneau, *Class, Sports, and Social Development* (Amherst: University of Massachusetts Press, 1984).

20. James F. Crow, "Unequal by Nature: A Geneticist's Perspective on Human Differences," *Daedalus*, Winter 2002, 84. For a fine review of the historical literature, see J.T. Sammons, " 'Race' and Sport: A Critical, Historical Explanation," *Journal of Sport History*, 21 (Fall 1994): 203–278; D. Wiggins, " 'Great Speed but Little Stamina': The Historical Debate Over Black Athletic Superiority," *Journal of Sport History*, 16 (Summer 1989): 158–185.

21. R. Brown and R.T. Jewell, "Is There Customer Discrimination in College Basketball?" *Social Science Quarterly*, 75 (2) (June 1994): 401-413; "Do NBA Ratings Increase With White Athletes' Playing Time?" SBD, 20 April 1998, 4.

22. Ketra L. Armstrong and Terese Peretto Stratta, "Market Analyses of Race and Sport Consumption," *SMQ*, 13 (1) (2004): 7–16; Michelle G. Harrolle and Galen Trail, "Ethnic Identification, Acculturation and Sports Identification of Latinos in the United States," *International Journal of Sports Marketing & Sponsorship*, 8 (3) (April 2007): 234–253, quotation at 234.

23. John Hall and Barry O'Mahony, "An Empirical Analysis of Gender Differences in Sports Attendance Motives," *International Journal of Sports Marketing and Sponsorship*, 7, 4, (July 2006): 334–348.

24. W. Gantz and L. Wenner, "Men, Women, and Sports: Audience Experience and Effects," *Journal of Broadcasting and Electronic Media*, 35 (2) (Spring 1991): 233–243; Robert Madrigal and Vassilis Dalakis, "Consumer Psychology of Sport," in *Handbook of Consumer Psychology*, ed. Curtis P. Haugtvedt, Paul M. Herr, and Frank R. Kardes (New York: Erlbaum, 2008), 857–76; Hall and O'Mahony, "An Empirical Analysis of Gender Differences."

25. See Judy Davidson, "Lesbian Erotics at Women's Hockey: Fans, Flashing, and the Booby Orrs," *Journal of Lesbian Studies*, 13 (2) (July–Sept. 2009): 337–348; Vikki Crane and Heather Barber, "Lesbian Experiences in Sport: A Social Identity Perspective," *Quest*, 55 (2003): 328–346. See also Dan Woog, *Jocks: True Stories of America's Gay Male Athletes* (New York: Alyson Books, 1998); Steven M. Kates, "The Protean Quality of Subcultural Consumption: An Ethnographic Account of Gay Consumers," *Journal of Consumer Research*, 29 (3) (December 2002): 383–399.

26. Marieke de Mooij, *Consumer Behavior and Culture*, (Thousand Oak, CA: Sage, 2004), 225; Tom Long and Stacy Milbouer, "Inside Multicultural Manchester," *NHMagazine.com*, 1 December 2009, http://www.nashuatelegraph.com/towncity/481525-115/story.html.

27. Tom Love, "A Different League: The Football League," *SportsPro Magazine*, April 2012, 60–64, quotation at 61.

28. David Stringer, "UK Issues Olympics Etiquette Primer," *Boston Globe*, 12 August 2010, A-20; www.visitbritain.org/insightsandstatistics/markets/index.aspx.

29. Robert Madrigal and Vassilis Dalakis, "Consumer Psychology of Sport," in *Handbook of Consumer Psychology*, ed. Curtis P. Haugtvedt, Paul M. Herr, and Frank R. Kardes (New York: Erlbaum, 2008), 857–76.

30. John Betts, "The Technological Revolution and the Rise of Sport," *Mississippi Valley Historical Review*, 40 (September 1953): 231–256; Terry Lefton, "Survey Results Push NFL.com to Increase Fantasy Content," *SSSBJ*, 9–12 September, 2002, 4; Bill King, "Reaching Today's Sports Fans," *SSSBJ*, 14–20 March 2005, 17–21; Tracy Mayor, "What Are Video Games Turning Us Into?" *Boston Globe Magazine*, 20 February 2005, 18–37; Simon Kuper and Stefan Szymanski, *Soccernomics* (New York: Nation Books, 2009), 80.

31. Stephen Hardy, Robert Barcelona, Randi Hickox, and Caitlin Lazaro, "Image Isn't Everything: Community Relations and Community Building for Sport Organizations," *Athletic Business*, May 2006, 50–56; Pamela A. Kennett-Hensel, Russell Lacey, and Matt Biggers, "The Impact of Corporate Social Responsibility on NBA Fan Relationships: A Conceptual Framework," in *Consumer Behavior Knowledge for Effective Sports and Event Marketing*, ed. Lynn R. Kahle and Angline G. Close (New York: Routledge, 2011),135–57.

32. Martin Lindstrom, Brand Sense: *Build Powerful Brands Through Touch, Taste, Smell, Sight, and Sound* (New York: Free Press, 2005).

33. Jesse King, Lynn R. Kahle, and Angeline G Close, "Introduction: The Study of Sports and Events Consumer Behavior," in *Consumer Behavior Knowledge for Effective Sports and Event Marketing*, ed. Lynn R. Kahle and Angline G. Close (New York: Routledge, 2011), 1–28, quotations at 2, 3. On team identification, Madrigal and Dalakis, "Consumer Psychology of Sport," 866. For an excellent article on the links between fan segments, social identity, team marketing behavior, and brand equity, see B.A. Boyle and P. Magnusson, "Social Identity and Brand Equity Formation: A Comparative Study of Collegiate Sports Fans," *Journal of Sport Management*, 21 (4) (2007): 497–520. See also G.A. Akerlof and R.E. Kranton, "Economics and Identity," *Quarterly Journal of Economics*, 115 (August 2000): 715–53.

34. R. Burton, "Profile/Interview With Sara Levinson," *SMQ*, 6 (4) (December 1997): 5–8.

35. Berkman and Gilson, *Consumer Behavior*, 273.

36. J.J. Zhang et al., "Spectator Knowledge of Hockey as a Significant Predictor of Game Attendance," *SMQ* 5 (September 1996): 41–48.

37. ESPN and ESPN2, "Guide to the X Games," insert in *Rolling Stone*, 25 June 1998.

38. John Leland, "Urban Tool in Recruiting by the Army: An Arcade," *New York Times*, 5 January 2009, A11.

39. Beth Teitell, "Fantasy Football Scores With More Kids," *Boston Globe*, 23 October 2012, A1, A9; Eric Fisher, "A More Casual Approach: Fantasy Industry Rolls Out Simpler Products Aimed at Attracting Casual Gamers," *SSSBJ*, 1 March 2010, 15–19. On the links between expertise and learning, see J. W. Hutchinson and Eric M. Eisentstein, "Consumer Learning and Expertise," in *Handbook of Consumer Psychology*, ed. Curtis P. Haugtvedt, Paul M. Herr, and Frank R. Kardes (New York: Erlbaum, 2008), 103–115. For edu-selling, see Bill Sutton, "Educate Your Buyer to Be a Satisfied Client," *SSSBJ*, 23 February 2004, 29.

40. Richard E Mayer. *Multimedia Learning*, 2d ed. New York: Cambridge University Press, 2009), quotations on 108, 135, 153, 189, 200, 761; Courtney Humphries, "The New Science of our Cross-Wired

Senses," *Boston Globe*, 11 December 2011, http://shamslab.psych.ucla.edu/lay-articles/Boston-Globe_Dec2011.pdf; for The Masters, visit www.masters.com.

41. Joshua M. Ackerman, et al., "Incidental Haptic Sensations Influence Social Judgments and Decisions," *Science*, 328 (2010): 1712; Martin Lindstrom, *Brand Sense: Build Powerful Brands Through Touch, Taste, Smell, Sight, and Sound* (New York: Free Press, 2005), 68.

42. B. Berelson and G. Steiner, *Human Behavior: An Inventory of Scientific Findings* (New York: Harcourt Brace, 1964), 88; P. Kotler, *Marketing Management*, 5th ed. (Upper Saddle River, NJ: Prentice Hall, 1984), 140.

43. Marieke de Mooij, *Consumer Behavior and Culture* (Thousand Oak, CA: Sage, 2004), 142; D. Wann, C. Bayens, and A. Driver, "Likelihood of Attending a Sporting Event as a Function of Ticket Scarcity and Team Identification," *SMQ*, 13 (4) (2004): 209–215; B. Veeck, *Veeck as in Wreck* (New York: Signet, 1986); D. Kerstatter and G. Kovich, "An Involvement Profile of Division I Women's Basketball Spectators," *Journal of Sport Management*, 11 (1997): 234–249. For an excellent ethnography of Chinese consumer perceptions during the 2008 Beijing Olympics, see Ha Gunagtian and Kevin Caffrey, "Olympian Ghosts: Apprehensions and Apparitions of the Beijing Spectacle," *International Journal of the History of Sport*, 26 July 2009, 1065–83.

44. Fantasy football in Beth Teitell, "Fantasy Football Scores With More Kids," *Boston Globe*, 23 October 2012, A1, A9; Cheeseheads in Ryan Goldberg, "Bratwurst, NYC," *New York Times*, 13 January 2012, B9. For overviews of fan motivations see D.L. Wann and N.R. Branscombe, "Influence of Level of Identification on a Group and Physiological Arousal on Perceived Intergroup Complexity," *British Journal of Social Psychology*, 34 (1995): 223–35; Edward R. Hirt and Joshua J Clarkson, "The Psychology of Fandom: Understanding the Etiology, Motives, and Implications of Fanship," in *Consumer Behavior Knowledge for Effective Sports and Event Marketing*, ed. Lynn R. Kahle and Angline G. Close (New York: Routledge, 2011), 59–85; Bill King, "What Makes Fans Tick?" *SSSBJ*, 1–7 March 2004, 26, 32; Robert Cialdini et al., "Basking in Reflected Glory: Three (Football) Field Studies," *Journal of Personality and Social Psychology*, 34 (1976): 366–375; Lynn Kahle and Chris Riley, eds., *Sport Marketing and the Psychology of Marketing Communication* (Mahwah, NJ: Erlbaum, 2004), 67–79; G. Trail et al., "Motives and Points of Attachment: Fans Versus Spectators in Intercollegiate Athletics," *SMQ*, 12 (4) (2003): 217–227; S. Hardy, J. Loy, and D. Booth, "The Material Culture of Sport," *Journal of Sport History*, 36 (1) (Spring 2009): 129–52; Wann et al.,

Sports Fans; L. Kahle, K. Kambara, and G. Rose, "A Functional Model of Fan Attendance Motivations for College Football," *SMQ*, 5 (December 1996): 51–60; H. Hansen and R. Gauthier, "The Professional Golf Product: Spectators' Views," *SMQ*, 3 (4) (December 1994): 9–16; M. Grunwald, "Taking Funny Business Seriously," *Boston Globe*, 5 January 1998, A-1, A-12; A. Guttmann, *The Erotic in Sports* (New York: Columbia University Press, 1996); "Gator Bait" [Scorecard], *Sports Illustrated*, 19 May 1997, 29–30; "Oh Oscar," *SBD*, 9 September 1997, 5; J. James and S. Ross, "Comparing Sport Consumer Motivations Across Multiple Sports," *SMQ*, 13 (1) (2004): 17–25.

45. Daniel J. Wakin, "A Loud Call for Cheering at Classical Concert Halls," *New York Times*, 9 June 2012, C1; Terry Lefton, "9 Rules for Making the Most of Sports Property/Ad Agency Relationships," *SSSBJ*, September 24–30, 2007, 23–28, quotation at 25.

46. Kwak, D.H., Kim, Y.K., & Hirt, E.R., 2011, "Exploring the Role of Emotions on Sport Consumers' Behavioral and Cognitive Responses to Marketing Stimuli," *European Sport Management Quarterly*, 11 (3): 225–250.

47. D. Wann et al., *Sports Fans*; Funk et al., "Sport Consumer Behavior"; R.J. Fisher and K. Wakefield, "Factors Leading to Group Identification: A Field Study of Winners and Losers," *Psychology and Marketing*, 15 (1998): 23–40; Sutton et al., "Creating and Fostering Fan Identification."

48. Eric Fisher, "Research Shows Social Media Moves Tickets," *SSSBJ*, 7 May 2012, 4.

49. Kotler, *Marketing Management*, 464; J. Faircloth et al., "An Analysis of Choice Intentions of Public Golf Courses," *SMQ*, 4 (March 1995): 13–21. For a good introduction to factors influencing spectator choice, see J. Zhang et al., "Factors Affecting the Decision Making of Spectators to Attend Minor League Hockey Games," *International Sports Journal*, 1 (Summer 1997): 39–53.

50. Daniel Funk, Daniel Mahony, and Mark Havitz, "Sport Consumer Behavior: Assessment and Direction," SMQ, 12 (4) (2003): 200–205.

51. M. Chubb and H. Chubb, *One Third of Our Time? An Introduction to Recreation Behavior and Resources* (New York: Wiley, 1981), 230–250.

52. Craig G. Hyatt, "Who Do I Root for Now? The Impact of Franchise Relocation on the Loyal Fans Left Behind: A Case Study of Hartford Whalers Fans," *Journal of Sport Behavior*, 30 (1), (2007), 36–56. See also Craig G. Hyatt, W.M. Foster, and G.H. Duquette, "Where Have All The Good Fans Gone? A Study of NHL Fans and Why They Stopped Cheering for Their Teams," paper presented at Putting It on Ice III: Constructing the Hockey

Family conference, Halifax, Nova Scotia, July 2012, which includes an excellent review of literature on the few studies that consider consumer dropouts.

53. Patrick Spenner and Karen Freeman, "To Keep Your Customers, Keep it Simple," *Harvard Business Review*, May 2012, 108–14. See also Malcolm Gladwell, *Blink: the Power of Thinking Without Thinking* (Boston: Little, Brown, 2005); Daniel Kahneman, *Thinking, Fast and Slow* (New York: Farrar, Straus, and Giroux, 2011); James R. Bettman, Mary F. Luce, and John W. Payne, "Consumer Decision Making: A Choice Goals Approach," in *Handbook of Consumer Psychology*, ed. Curtis P. Haugtvedt, Paul M. Herr, and Frank R. Kardes (New York: Erlbaum, 2008), 589–607; Charles Duhigg, *The Power of Habit: Why We Do What We Do in Life and Business* (New York: Random House, 2012); Adam L. Penenberg, "Have They Hacked Your Brain," *Fast Company*, September 2011, 85–89, 123–25.

54. "The Fans," *SBD*, 19 August 1997.

55. "A WEIRD View of Human Nature Skews Psychologists Studies," *Science*, 328 (25 June 2010): 1627.

Chapter 4

Market Research in the Sport Industry

Steve Seiferheld
Haynes Hendrickson
Nikolay Panchev
Jaclyn Cranston
Leigh Buwen
Evelyn Dwyer

OBJECTIVES

- To become aware of the various sources of data and information available within the sport industry and how businesses go about obtaining or collecting data

- To understand which business functions benefit the most from data-driven decision making

- To understand how the sport industry uses market research methodologies in daily business activities through case study examples

What Price Glory?

Think of all the points of purchase that exist within the sport industry. Sports fans and consumers at any given time may spend money on an array of goods and services. Speaking only of the live game-day experience, attendees may need to pay for tickets, parking, concessions, and merchandise. Beyond game day, fans can lay out cash on TV packages (e.g., NFL Sunday Ticket), apps, merchandise, and more. One lingering question spans all these potential purchases: How much are people willing to pay?

Readily available data have empowered stronger decision making in some of these areas. For example, sport teams maintain robust databases of ticket buyers and their spending behavior. By combining this information with data from the secondary market and dynamic pricing algorithms, the sport industry today is more armed than ever to price tickets for maximum profit. But the picture is not complete; if a team wants to offer a new ticket package never before sold, it must connect a bunch of dots to form an educated guess on price.

Of course, we can figure out what people might pay for things in another way. We could simply ask them.

Simply asking people what they are willing to pay for something, however, has its risks as well. As humans, we have an inclination to seek out the best deal. If asked as part of a survey how much they would be willing to pay for, say, a team jersey, respondents may answer with a number that is in fact lower than what they would pay, hoping to skew the price downward in their favor (should the jersey actually be for sale).

Some research methodologies use indirect questioning techniques to get around consumer pricing bias. One of the stronger methodologies, called Van Westendorp analysis, presents each respondent with a product concept (e.g., a retro away jersey) and asks a battery of four questions:

- At what price would you begin to think that the jersey is too expensive to consider?
- At what price would you begin to think that the jersey is so inexpensive that you would question the quality and not consider it?
- At what price would you begin to think that the jersey is getting expensive, but you still might consider it?
- At what price would you think that the jersey is a bargain—a great buy for the money?

Proper analysis of the resulting data yields (a) an optimal price point and (b) a range of suitable prices. Although an optimal price point provides a clear target number, having a range of suitable prices provides decision makers some flexibility should conditions change, such as having more or less jersey inventory than planned.

- How much money are Team K's season-ticket holders spending on merchandise throughout the season?
- How much of Team Z's brand equity is tied to the head coach and star player?
- In which market should Bank Q invest its sponsorship dollars?
- What out-of-home media platform will create the most impressions for advertising a new ticketing website?

Questions such as these used to be difficult if not impossible to assess accurately. But technological advancements have facilitated opportunities for the sport industry to make sounder, more educated business decisions. Not unlike other major business verticals, sport properties and related businesses can tap into numerous sources of consumer data, ranging from terabytes of information stored by credit bureaus to 140-character opinions from Twitter.

The term *market research* means different things to different people. Perhaps the simplest and most direct way to define market research is "research on the market." A market researcher's job involves providing insight and wisdom about consumers in the brand's target market. Generally, a market researcher working in health care addresses topics relevant to health care providers and patients. A market researcher working on Kraft Macaroni & Cheese looks at a target market of mothers. Within the sport industry, market research is then defined as the provision of insight and information about sports fans. As referenced earlier, the 21st century has brought us a plethora of data sources from which to derive this insight. We consider those sources of data now.

Sources of Information

As acclaimed statistician Stu Hunter once spoke, "Data is not information; structure within data is information."[1] Of course, to characterize that structure requires a data source or sources. Some people in the industry hear the words *market research* and instantly think *survey*. Surveys certainly provide valuable feedback for sport marketers, and these tools will be addressed throughout this chapter. But researchers have many sources of data beyond surveys. Data sources are commonly broken out into two general categories—syndicated data and custom research. We will define each category and provide examples of data types as follows.

Syndicated Data

Syndicated data refers to data that have been collected, organized, and repackaged for consumption. Syndicated data suppliers typically monetize their businesses by selling subscriptions to their data sources; the ongoing subscriber fees more than offset the investment required to accumulate and process the data collected. Because multiple clients purchase the data, the supplier can charge a lower price than would be required had the data been compiled for only one client. On the other hand, buyers of syndicated data do not necessarily receive information that has been customized for their exact needs. Many brands make this tradeoff, and in some cases syndicated data provide the only real source of

usable information. Consumer packaged goods manufacturers rely on companies such as NPD, Nielsen, and IRI to sell them retail sales data; without these suppliers, manufacturers would have to spend inordinate amounts of money on consumer studies that would lack sufficient sample size or granularity.

Major syndicated data suppliers are highlighted in this section. Ironically, perhaps the biggest supplier, the U.S. government, provides its information at no cost.

U.S. Census

The U.S. Census offers an often-overlooked syndicated data source that provides a plethora of helpful information about the demographic makeup of the U.S. population. Mandated by the U.S. Constitution, the U.S. Census enumerates the U.S. population every 10 years. It identifies trends in the evolving makeup of the U.S. population both for the country as a whole and by state, county, city, and even zip code. The most recent U.S. Census took place in 2010. For the period until 2020 the U.S. Census Bureau will use historical data at their disposal to provide estimates for any related information queries.

A significant advantage of U.S. Census data is that it is available online free of charge. Moreover, in recent years the U.S. Census Bureau has revamped the data presentation, providing a user-friendly tool for researchers or any other interested party with basic computer skills. The ancillary website of the U.S. Census Bureau, American FactFinder, is designed as a data bank[2]. It allows the use of various demographic and economic indicators as variables to filter and sort through the data. Table 4.1 provides an example.

Demographic Profiling

Despite its robust data supply, the U.S. Census does not fulfill all needs related to syndicated data, nor is the Census positioned only to facilitate businesses in understanding their target markets. Syndicated research companies such as Scarborough and Simmons provide a more detailed overview of the U.S. population than the U.S. Census does, and they tailor their offerings to specific clients by looking at the population as sets of consumers. Scarborough surveys more than 200,000 consumers annually in the nation's 77 most populous Designated Market Areas

TABLE 4.1   2011 Household Income Estimate for the Philadelphia–Camden–Wilmington, PA–NJ–DE–MD Metro Area

Subject	Philadelphia–Camden–Wilmington, PA–NJ–DE–MD Metro Area			
Income and benefits (in 2011 inflation-adjusted U.S. dollars)	Estimate	Margin of error	Percent	Percent margin of error
Total households	2,220,655	+/−7,438	-	-
Less than $10,000	167,485	+/−6,787	7.50%	+/−0.3
$10,000 to $14,999	112,151	+/−5,502	5.10%	+/−0.2
$15,000 to $24,999	206,906	+/−6,618	9.30%	+/−0.3
$25,000 to $34,999	203,693	+/−7,004	9.20%	+/−0.3
$35,000 to $49,999	275,201	+/−7,879	12.40%	+/−0.4
$50,000 to $74,999	378,274	+/−9,538	17.00%	+/−0.4
$75,000 to $99,999	276,089	+/−7,987	12.40%	+/−0.4
$100,000 to $149,999	329,232	+/−6,745	14.80%	+/−0.3
$150,000 to $199,999	138,715	+/−5,689	6.20%	+/−0.3
$200,000 or more	132,909	+/−5,516	6.00%	+/−0.2
Median household income (dollars)	58,322	+/−773	-	-
Mean household income (dollars)	79,850	+/−805	-	-

Data from http://factfinder2.census.gov/faces/tableservices/jsf/pages/productview.xhtml?pid=ACS_11_1YR_B19001&prodType=table

(DMAs).[3] Scarborough's measurement tactics include phone interviews, survey booklets, television diaries, and internet surveys that detail their consumer habits across leading product categories such as automotive, banking, beverage, drug and grocery, health care, lifestyle, restaurant, sport, and many others. Scarborough's database is conveniently web-based, and the company typically releases two annual data files with information collected in the previous six months. Simmons, on the other hand, offers access to a web-based data bank that provides an array of data fields and segmentation capabilities.

Although both services are well positioned in sport and live entertainment, anecdotal evidence suggests that Scarborough has higher penetration among the properties (or rights holders) in this space. Brand managers and sponsorship sales professionals working for properties mine Scarborough's data to uncover shopping habits and brand preferences within their fan bases. Rights holders often use data like Scarborough's to demonstrate the fit between its property's fan profile and a sponsor's target customers.

Table 4.2 reviews consumer information from the Miami, Florida, DMA from Scarborough data. It compares the auto products and services shopping habits of adults aged 18 to 49 (target population) to those of the general population in the market. The data show that 16 percent of adults aged 18 to 49 shopped at AutoZone in the previous 12 months. With an index of 128, this group of consumers is 28 percent more likely than the general population to shop at AutoZone.

The self-proclaimed worldwide leader in sports, ESPN offers a subscription to the ESPN Sports Poll, another syndicated research service that profiles sports fans in the United States on their interests, behaviors, and preferences.

Audience Measurement

In the last few decades, media rights fees have escalated to be the biggest and an ever-growing piece of sport properties' revenue pie. Because this escalation shows no signs of slowing down, all stakeholders will continue to have interest in measuring consumption of sports media. Anyone aspiring to work in the business of sport and live entertainment stands to benefit from having a basic understanding of audience ratings.

A property's TV and radio ratings not only dictate the nationwide and local broadcast rights fees but also play a substantial role in sponsorship rights negotiations. Nielsen remains the most

TABLE 4.2 Auto Parts and Services Buying Habits

Stores household shopped for auto products or service past 12 months	Total pop.	Total %	Target pop.	Target %	Index	Horizontal %
Total	*3,544,205*	*100*	*2,041,960*	*100*	*100*	*58*
Auto dealership	343,865	10	189,740	9	96	55
AutoZone	444,835	13	328,645	16	128	74
Bennett Auto Supply	112,340	3	75,370	4	116	67
BJ's Wholesale Club	99,815	3	60,810	3	106	61
Bridgestone–Firestone–Mastercare	75,520	2	51,505	3	118	68
Costco	130,380	4	76,505	4	102	59
Discount Auto Parts	1,111,335	31	788,300	39	123	71
Firestone–Mastercare	159,440	5	104,765	5	114	66
Goodyear Tire and Auto	145,200	4	84,370	4	101	58
Jiffy Lube	239,260	7	154,440	8	112	65
Kmart	165,860	5	111,760	6	117	67
Maaco	8,295	0	6,705	0	140	81
Meineke Discount Mufflers	24,715	1	11,390	1	80	46
Midas	44,285	1	29,800	2	117	67
NAPA Auto Parts	175,020	5	109,230	5	108	62
Pep Boys	431,320	12	296,045	15	119	69
Sam's Club	55,045	2	34,480	2	109	63
Sears	313,185	9	169,480	8	94	54
Target	75,400	2	52,650	3	121	70
Tire Kingdom	280,950	8	174,320	9	108	62
Tires Plus	118,940	3	71,835	4	105	60
Wal-Mart	347,570	10	255,605	13	128	74
Other Firestone–Mastercare	10,625	0	8,625	0	141	81
Other store	385,660	11	240,975	12	108	63
Did not shop	1,169,495	33	543,475	27	81	47
Any automotive store	2,374,710	67	1,498,485	73	110	63

Geoscape is a syndicated research company that specializes in understanding the fastest growing segment of the U.S. population—Hispanics. Similar to Simmons, they provide web-based access to consumer and demographic profiling data of Hispanics across the nation's leading DMAs. Total, target, and horizontal percentages have been rounded.

Adapted, by permission, from Scarborough Research, Scarborough USA+ 2004 (12 months). For more information contact info@scarborough.com.

used source of television metrics, such as total viewers and the eponymous Nielsen ratings. (And although website hits, app downloads, and social media followers certainly have a role in measurement, TV ratings continue to reign supreme in the space.) In each country in which Nielsen operates, the company recruits a large sample of households, representative of all households in that country who own a televi-sion. Although some families keep diaries and later report the programming that they watched, most of Nielsen's panel use devices called People Meters. The device is attached to the TV sets, and panelists indicate which members of the household watched the respective programming. Results are reported automatically to Nielsen every night. Nielsen monetizes the business through paid subscriptions for its services; these subscriptions provide detailed ratings reports (e.g., ratings breakdown by age group, gender, and geographic location) to clients across all industries concerned with TV viewership. In the sport market in particular, properties want to know how to price advertising slots for sponsors and brands that buy ad space during related programming (e.g., game broadcasts). Table 4.3 provides an example of Nielsen output for prime-time network TV programs.

In table 4.3 the "Persons 2+ rating" column indicates the percentage of households with a TV set who had tuned to the programming. The "Viewers" column is an estimated total number of viewers. Another popular ratings indicator is *TV share*, the estimated percentage of all households and viewers watching TV at that time and tuned in to the respective programming.

Critics of Nielsen ratings cite challenges in accurately accounting for out-of-home (OOH) viewers (for example, fans watching an NFL game in bars or restaurants), as well as online and mobile viewers.

Similar to the television marketplace, the radio marketplace needs to understand listenership metrics. Arbitron provides similar data in this space, using an approach to data collection analogous to Nielsen's. Arbitron has augmented Nielsen's TV rating methodology by allowing for some OOH measurement.[4]

The rise in importance of digital media has created a marketplace for measurement of online behavior. ComScore is an example of a syndicated data provider in this space. Although the company offers several products and services related to online behavior, one area of increasing importance is its Mobile Metrix solution.[5] The module provides usage data across mobile devices and mobile apps for smartphones.

One note here is that although it is considered a competitor to ComScore, Google Analytics does not generally fall under the category of syndicated data. Google Analytics deliverables are generally specific to one client's website, as opposed to being a mineable source of data for multiple clients.

The high-speed evolution of the media landscape has served as a catalyst for introducing service models for summarizing publicly available information, which by itself is also syndicated data. As an example, Critical Mention tracks brand references across news outlets, live event broadcasts, and other various media platforms. It qualifies the direction and tone of the brand-related sentiments mentioned by TV anchors or analysts as well as on blogs and in social media. The company's services allow businesses to keep a pulse on public discourse related to their brand on TV, online, and in social media.[6]

TABLE 4.3   Prime Broadcast Network TV, United States, Week of October 15, 2012

Rank	Program	Network	Persons 2+ rating	Viewers (000)
1	*NBC Sunday Night Football*	NBC	10.7	17,469
2	*60 Minutes*	CBS	10.0	15,857
3	*Big Bang Theory, The*	CBS	9.7	15,733
4	*Dancing With the Stars*	ABC	9.2	13,640
5	*Dancing With the Stars, Results*	ABC	8.8	12,917
6	*Person of Interest*	CBS	8.7	13,928
7	*Two and a Half Men*	CBS	8.5	13,604
8	*Voice*	NBC	7.6	13,008
9	*Criminal Minds*	CBS	7.5	11,809
10	*Modern Family*	ABC	7.3	12,276

Viewing estimates on this page include live viewing and DVR playback on the same day, defined as 3 a.m. through 3 a.m. Ratings are the percentage of TV homes in the United States tuned into television.

How can Sky measure the value of Chris Froome winning the 2013 Tour de France and millions of people seeing its brand name?

Broadcast Exposure Research

Traditionally, signage and brand exposure have been one of the pillars of sponsorship rights agreements. Sponsor signage within TV camera sightlines—be it on-court signage, static in-venue or rotational signage, or brand marks on athlete uniforms—is typically considered premium inventory. But how can we assign a dollar value for the benefit of seeing Dwyane Wade drink from a Gatorade cup during a halftime interview? One widely used methodology counts the minutes (or seconds) of exposure that a brand gets during a game or event broadcast and applies a conversion factor to estimate the advertising equivalent value. In other words, a comparison is made between the cost of buying standard advertising time and the exposure gained through the sponsorship.

Joyce Julius and Repucom have established themselves as authorities in providing broadcast exposure evaluations. Each firm has a proprietary image recognition technology to analyze the time and quality of exposure that a brand receives during a live event broadcast or TV programming in general.[7,8] Sport and entertainment properties use broadcast exposure data to demonstrate the value that their marketing partners receive when their brand marks are picked up by TV cameras. Although sport sponsorship provided the impetus for broadcast exposure research, the increased use of planned product placement in traditional TV programming has expanded its use.

Custom Research

Although syndicated data offers cost-effective, readily available information, the available sources of syndicated data only sometimes adequately address the needs of a business. In many situations only customized market research will satisfactorily resolve open business questions.

Customized market research, or, more simply, custom research, refers to any situation in which researchers customize and implement a methodology for obtaining data. Unlike syndicated data suppliers, custom research produces primary data—data not already collected and available for usage.

More often than not, custom market research explores opinions, attitudes, and behaviors among the consumer marketplace. Objectives can vary of course, dictating different target populations and methodologies.

Data collected from consumers (and really any market research effort) generally fall into one of two categories: quantitative and qualitative. Quantitative data refers to any data type that can be represented numerically. Quantitative data can be nominal (in which order has no significance, such as area code) or ordinal (in which order does matter, such as weight). Quantitative data can also be categorized as discrete (meaning countable, such as number of tickets sold to a game) or continuous (meaning noncountable, such as game-time temperature). Quantitative data provide the built-in advantage of bringing into play the many available data analysis techniques, software packages, and graphical representations that allow researchers to identify higher levels of insight.

Qualitative data, on the other hand, are composed of nonnumeric metrics—text, images, objects, sounds, and so forth. Analysis of qualitative data requires more complex and less clear-cut techniques because researchers must explore the meaning and context of the data to identify common themes and patterns. Technology has facilitated advanced techniques of qualitative data analysis. Many companies offer software to aid with the analysis of open text; content analysis is one of the more common techniques. Of course, the challenge is to get computers to understand responses and people.

Qualitative consumer research offers a particular benefit to the sport industry because the evaluation of the effect of emotion and passion between fan and team or sport is better handled through dialogue than through survey. On the downside, projects involving qualitative data collection and analysis generally cost more than similar projects focusing on quantitative techniques. Driven primarily by the cost factor, most market research conducted in the sport industry tends to be quantitative. Without question, finding ways for sport marketers to access less expensive qualitative consumer research will remain an opportunity for the foreseeable future.

We now turn our attention to methods of data collection within custom consumer research. (Similar methods will apply to business-to-business research, addressed in an upcoming section.) Surveying is the overwhelmingly most common method to obtain custom quantitative research data, although how and where a survey is administered certainly matters. Qualitative research can come from a myriad of other sources. We will generally focus on the more common methodologies in play today.

Quantitative Research

As mentioned earlier, surveying provides the source of most quantitative custom market research data. Surveys allow people to provide opinions, report behaviors, and identify things that matter to them within a framework that is usually anonymous and confidential. The advent of newer technologies has allowed researchers to personalize the survey experience for respondents, at the disadvantage of removing anonymity. The experiential versus anonymous part of research can be evaluated only on a case-by-case basis.

To get completed surveys, respondents have to know that a survey exists and they must be invited to complete the survey. Common methods of inviting survey responses are described as follows.

Online With Internet connectivity in U.S. households now reaching 78 percent of adults (18 years of age or older), online surveying has become one of the most popular and easiest forms of surveying.[9] Online surveying can consist of many different forms, including

- sending a survey invitation by e-mail to a database or online panel;
- hosting a survey link on a web page or social media site;
- presenting a survey invitation through a pop-up window on a web page; or
- distributing copies of a survey URL by text, hard copy, or SMS.

Where The Home Depot Meets Market Research

Years ago, when something at your house wasn't functioning correctly, you hired someone to fix it—a plumber, electrician, or other contractor type. If you were one of the few homeowners brave enough to try to fix it on your own, you ventured to your local hardware store in search of replacement parts and perhaps expertise on how to go about the repair.

Fast forward to 1979, when the Home Depot opened its first two stores, in metro Atlanta. At that moment, the do-it-yourself (DIY) era commenced. (In all fairness, Lowe's first store dates back to the 1920s, but we defer to the Home Depot's stronger market share and larger number of retail locations.) With the Internet providing nearly infinite resources on how to fix anything from a leaky faucet to a broken lawnmower engine, virtually everyone has some level of handyman skills.

The DIY phenomenon doesn't stop at home repair. In the business world, few if any industries have been as affected as much as market research when it comes to the influence of DIY. Just as anyone with a hammer feels empowered to fix something, thousands of marketing, sales, communications, and public relations professionals have been armed with straight-forward, inexpensive DIY market research technology. Want to run a survey? Tools such as SurveyMonkey, Google Surveys, QuestionPro, and SurveyGizmo provide users the ability to do simple to moderately complicated research at commoditized prices. For those who desire more advanced software platforms, options such as Turnkey's Surveyor (powered by Verint) or ConfirmIt allow organizations to conduct survey research and analyze results across numerous projects for about $10,000 per year, less than the cost of a typical one-off project.

The sport industry has boarded the DIY train, motivated by the low cost and availability of bright, young data analysts who welcome the chance to work in sport. Just as a homeowner taking the DIY approach risks breaking a pipe and having to pay a plumber thousands of dollars, DIY research has its hazards. A poorly written questionnaire renders the resulting response data worthless, even detrimental. Failure to analyze data correctly can easily lead to incorrect business decisions, which we all know can be costly. (See JCPenney's 2012 attempt at forgoing sale prices.) And tapping the same database for survey respondents repeatedly can alienate an organization's most loyal customers.

In truth, data-driven decision making benefits all in the long run. And DIY research technologies have certainly enabled more organizations to use data for decision making. All involved are advised to proceed carefully and with all necessary precautions in place. As any do-it-yourselfer would agree, one wrong cut of the electrical wire can cause all the good work to go up in flames.

In addition to the large Internet presence within households, the birth of numerous survey software companies has made online surveys easier than in the past. Companies such as Verint, Survey Monkey, QuestionPro, ConfirmIt, SurveyGizmo, and others provide solutions ranging from simple do-it-yourself options to full panel-management and data analytic capabilities. Survey software companies help make online surveying one of the fastest ways to receive data.

Most software tools offer real-time results, allowing the researcher to see data coming in as soon as a respondent completes a question.

The prevalence and ease of online research has caused ordinary people to become inundated with invitations to complete surveys. To help make the process of survey completion less burdensome on the respondent, software providers have optimized mobile devices' formatting and adapted features to help respondents avoid

Including yourself, how many people were in your party?

[⌄]

Did you attend the event with any children under the age of 13?

○ Yes
○ No

[Submit Survey]

Online surveying offers a simple way to obtain information about, and feedback from, consumers.

survey fatigue (e.g., drag-and-drop question types, pictures and videos). Skip logic within surveys keeps the respondent from having to answer questions that are not applicable to him or her. For example, the Los Angeles Dodgers send a game-day satisfaction survey after every home game to all individual-game ticket buyers who purchased their tickets online. The respondents are asked whether they bought concessions at the ballpark. If the respondent bought concessions, he or she receives a series of concessions-specific questions; respondents who did not purchase concessions skip past that battery. Because respondents are settled in at their computers or on their mobile devices, online surveys can usually incorporate longer questionnaires (as opposed to surveying at a game or event where respondents are busy rushing to seats, trying to watch the game, and so on).

Although online surveying provides an effective all-around methodology for collecting quantitative research data (and even qualitative, depending on need), it is not always the best choice. Say, for instance, that a venue wants to survey event attendees to measure experiential satisfaction. Any database held by the venue will likely contain e-mail addresses of ticket buyers, people who receive an online newsletter, or other database opt-ins, but that venue will likely not have contact information for walk-up cash buyers or guests of the ticket buyers.

More pitfalls exist within the online surveying world. Survey invitations e-mailed out to respon-

dents commonly are caught in spam filters. And spam regulations are tougher than ever; researchers and research agencies must ensure permission exists to contact potential respondents or face the wrath of e-mail domains everywhere.

Response rates for e-mailed surveys (the number of respondents who complete the survey divided by the number of respondents who received the survey) vary based on the type of respondent. Turnkey has found that respondents with more investment (financial or emotional) in the brand are more likely to complete a survey. For instance, fans who are signed up to receive a team's e-mail newsletter yield survey response rates of 2 to 5 percent, whereas single-game buyers tend to be at 5 to 15 percent and season-ticket holders are around 20 to 35 percent. If a survey is posted to a web page, the web page needs to be heavily trafficked. If it is not, the response rate will be significantly low.

Here are some examples of online surveys:

- To determine what influences fans to watch games at home instead of attending in person, the Chicago White Sox use an online survey to reach their TV and online audience. During live game-day broadcasts, the URL is shown on the screen and the broadcasters announce where to complete the survey and the incentive for their participation. TV and online viewers type in the URL on an Internet browser and complete the survey.

- To gauge the satisfaction of their online fan club, the St. Louis Cardinals send a survey to club members. The Cardinals are able to obtain the e-mail address of the members during the sign-up process.

Intercepts As the old adage states, "If the mountain won't come to Mohammed, Mohammed will go to the mountain." Sometimes the easiest way to locate survey respondents is to go physically to where they are. Intercept surveying consists of interviewing respondents in person, usually with the aid of some type of instrument for data capture. Although modern interviewers surely appreciate the development of iOS and Android devices, pen-and-paper surveys and even voice recorders provide alternative and effective means of recording pertinent information.

Numerous applications of intercept surveying exist. An earlier example in this chapter cited databases being void of contact information for event attendees; surveying onsite ensures access to those people at the event. A team may conduct interviews at a nearby sports bar to assess why fans preferred that environment to the stadium itself.

Intercept surveying can backfire if done inappropriately. Here are some guidelines to conduct intercept surveying most effectively:

- Employ objective, unbiased staff in unbranded attire. Like any other market research, the respondent must be allowed to give his or her true opinion. Staff dressed in team (or sponsor) garb or staff that talks up the company behind the research can sway responses, introducing unwanted bias into the analysis process.

- Keep the questionnaire short. Unless you have an amazingly cool incentive to give out, nobody will want to spend a long time completing the survey. As a rule of thumb, don't go over 4 minutes per survey (about the length of a typical rock song).

- Employ an adequate number of interviewers. Here's a rule of thumb. Assuming that the staff person is administering the survey (as opposed to a self-administered version) with one device (or clipboard) and no incentives are offered to respondents, expect no more than 40 minutes of surveying during a 1-hour period. If you are using a 4-minute survey, expect at most 10 surveys per hour per person.

- Have your staff employ a sampling scheme. If your interviewers want to talk only to good-looking respondents, the chance is good that your data will not accurately reflect the opinions of the whole crowd. Staff should be encouraged to select targets to approach randomly or have a scheme that forces them to consider a wide array of people. Turnkey commonly recommends inviting every nth person to take the survey, with n depending on crowd size. (Big crowd? Maybe every fifth person. Smaller? Every third.)

Some sport teams or brands are fortunate to have enough volunteers or interns to administer surveys, but often paid staff must be brought in, which of course must be accounted for in the budget. Although the objectives of any research project will determine when surveying should take place, typically interviewing will not be done while the main event is happening (e.g., before the start of a game, between matches at a tournament). As part of ongoing research about attendance motivation, the Cincinnati Reds survey fans from gate opening to first pitch.

Here's a tip. If a survey must be conducted during a game or event, asking fans who are waiting in line (e.g., for concessions) provides a good way to reach respondents looking to kill time anyway.

Telephone Once one of the more popular methodologies for market research, telephone surveying—the act of calling a respondent by telephone to administer a survey—has fallen off dramatically in recent years. Many factors have contributed to the falloff in phone surveying, such as the simplicity of Internet research, the obstacles posed by the do not call list (www.donotcall.gov), and the number of U.S. households who have only mobile phones, that is, no landline (34 percent).[10]

Phone surveying certainly is not as popular as online or intercept surveying in the sport and entertainment industries, primarily because of the comparatively expensive nature of telephone interviews. With all the aforementioned caveats, telephone interviewing still provides a viable and handy method of collecting survey data. Telephone surveying can be helpful if a sport team is trying to reach respondents who may not be in the database or easily reached by e-mail. For example, if a team is trying to conduct a survey among DMA residents who have never attended a game, that team will not have a readily available list of people to contact. And purchasing a list of DMA residents from a company such as Acxiom or Full House Entertainment Database Marketing will not necessarily provide a full array of e-mail addresses. In this situation, obtaining a list of all phone numbers in the region becomes more straightforward than assembling an e-mail contact list.

Given the abundance of unlisted phone numbers today (mainly cell phones), phone surveying projects often include random digit dialing (RDD). RDD is the process of generating phone numbers within a geographical area based on typical phone numbers given out in that area, not taken from a list. Generating phone numbers using RDD circumvents the obstacles of unlisted numbers and cell phones.[11]

When conducting telephone surveys, computer-assisted telephone interviewing (CATI) is typically used. CATI refers to computer software that helps the interviewer dial the phone number, schedule phone calls for a later time if the call is not answered, place the survey questions on the monitor for the interviewer to read, code data as the interviewer records the response from the respondent on the computer, and apply appropriate skip logic based on the answers provided.[12]

Direct Mail Similar to telephone surveying, direct (U.S.) mail has become less popular within the research industry and among sport and entertainment companies. To survey by direct mail, the company must print and mail surveys (invoking printing and postage costs), include a return envelope with postage, open the returned surveys, and manually enter them into a system to analyze the data. After all that effort, direct mail surveying tends to have lower response rates than online surveys or intercept surveys because more effort is required of the respondent to fill out the survey and mail the envelope back to the company, even though respondents are given the envelope and free postage.

One advantage offered by direct mail research is the assurance of anonymity and confidentiality. Although online and phone surveys offer those benefits, respondents have reason to be skeptical. After all, computer technology makes e-mails

and IP addresses easily traceable, and phone surveying suggests that the interviewer has the person's phone number. But with direct mail, the respondent controls the location from which she or he mails the survey and what information she or he includes.

Qualitative Research

Several chapters would be needed to describe all types of qualitative research data, namely because virtually anything can be a source of qualitative research. A person could walk around the stands at a college football game, read the emotions of the fans, and later report that "most people were having fun." Although the example may be silly, that information is in fact qualitative research.

More structured forms of qualitative research exist within the market research industry. We will touch on a few here, focusing on those most relevant for the sport and entertainment industry. For a broader view of qualitative research, you may wish to review Belk's book.[13]

In-Depth Interviews In-depth interviews, or IDIs, are comprehensive question-and-answer discussions between a respondent and an interviewer (or moderator). IDIs provide a preferred protocol when the research objective focuses on an individual's decision process or reaction to stimuli without interactions from other respondents. As an example, a sport team might want to understand the benefits most appreciated by premium suite holders. Having multiple suite holders in the same conversation could bias one (or more) respondents because of the demands of another (e.g., "Wow, I never thought to ask for a concierge.").

IDIs offer some additional obvious advantages, such as easier scheduling and absence of bias. Two additional subtle but important advantages include the following:

- **Cost efficiency**. You end up using a respondent for 100 percent of the time for which you are compensating him or her. (And at about 30 to 60 minutes per interview, cost can be significant.)[14]

- **Deeper insights**. Qualitative research moderators like to probe respondents, often using a technique referred to as laddering. Laddering is a question sequence composed of four (or more) questions related to a feature. The questions consist of asking about a feature, its functional benefit, higher benefit, and finally the emotional benefit.[15] When interviewing one person, the moderator can delve deeply into a topic and potential sensitivities without worrying about how the respondent will feel about discussing the topic in front of others.

For IDIs and focus groups (discussed in the next section), Turnkey advocates the following best practices.

- Using a discussion guide document, meant to ensure that the interactions remain in the scope of the research objectives.

- Conducting the research at a location unrelated to the client. Many clients prefer to conduct qualitative research at their office location (e.g., within a stadium or arena) to save money. In fact, the potential bias introduced by the branded surroundings has the power to render the research useless. All major cities offer professional research facilities equipped to optimize the power of qualitative research, offering amenities such as recording capabilities, transcription of conversations, and refreshments for participants.

- Having a third-party moderator lead all discussions. Despite best efforts to be objective, a company employee will naturally allow some subjectivity to slip through during the research process. Bias on the part of the moderator can lead a respondent to either overstate or suppress true feelings on a topic, which renders the research results useless.

Focus Groups A focus group typically includes between 5 and 12 respondents who are recruited based on their relevance to a particular business issue or research topic. A moderator bears responsibility for ensuring that the discussion provides feedback on the outstanding research

Focus group facilities offer clients the opportunity to watch and hear the proceedings live, while the moderator leads the discussion in an adjacent room.

issues. As with IDIs, moderators typically rely on a discussion guide to enforce the structure of the discussion.

Conducting focus groups not only allows gathering of insights unlikely to surface in survey research but also allows clients to target a group of respondents who may not be willing or able to participate in survey research. For example, an NFL team's youth program conducted a focus group in which the respondents were kids aged 7 through 14. Conducting this focus group allowed the NFL team to gain insights into their youth program from a kid's perspective, which would be impossible to do by online surveys because of federal laws.

Individual focus groups should be as homogeneous as possible in terms of participants' age, gender, and product usage. Homogeneity promotes group dynamics, which can lead to greater insights. When the demographics of one respondent are not consistent with the other participants, misleading information is often provided. If a client desires to obtain information from a variety of ages, genders, and so on, conducting multiple focus groups is recommended.

Online focus groups have become more popular, correlated with the availability of chat software, Skype, WebEx, and similar products. Online focus groups do provide some obvious benefits, such as ability to recruit respondents without geographic restriction. Online focus groups are limiting by nature; live product demonstrations, visuals, and written exercises pertaining to the topic are included more easily in person. Additionally, valuable nonverbal behavior including body posture, hand gestures, and facial expressions provide additional insight but get lost in a chat room. For example, mentioning words such as "parking egress" and "public seat license" to NFL season-ticket holders will produce negative facial expressions from some participants.

Ethnography Yogi Berra famously quipped, "You can observe a lot just by watching." Ironically, the form of market research that most follows this line is hardly ever used in the sport industry. Ethnographic research is the act of observing respondents, be it one person or a group of people, in their real-life environment. This type of research can provide deep insight into consumers' need states, daily habits, and decision-making process. Have you ever noticed that ketchup and shampoo bottles now stand on their lids? That change came through ethnographic research; consumer goods brands noticed that consumers would typically stand the items upside-down to ensure that they used the entire contents.

Often, ethnography requires the permission of the subject being studied. But simple ethnographic studies can be accomplished in the sport industry without such formal steps. Simply sitting in the stands during a game or walking around a pregame tailgate can reveal a lot about satisfaction with in-seat service and beer consumption respectively. More often than not, ethnographic research takes place at the beginning of a project and generates hypotheses for future study.[16]

Ethnography has its share of potential pitfalls. For one, people don't always act the same when they are being actively observed. The studies can also require a long time to conduct. The subject must feel as natural and unaffected during the research process as she or he does when no research is taking place. More so than other forms of qualitative research, ethnographic research requires an experienced practitioner to ensure the study's validity and success.[17]

Other Qualitative Data Sources Although much qualitative research continues to follow protocols cited in previous sections, newer technologies and social media are providing new ways for properties and brands to collect feedback from consumers.

• **Market research online community (MROC).** Businesses of all types, including the major U.S. professional sport leagues, commonly employ consumer panels for survey research. Only in 2008 did MROCs begin to flourish, and as of 2013 they really haven't taken off in sport and entertainment. An MROC is a dedicated online community created for the purpose of qualitative market research. An MROC can provide respondents for IDIs and focus groups, provide unmoderated conversation between participants, or even be a source for journal and diary entry.[18]

• **Social media sites.** Data posted on social media (e.g., Facebook or Twitter) is fundamentally observational; you get what you get. But information from these sites often comes from the most invested customers (fans), which alone makes the feedback valuable. If Nike observes a feed of basketball fans maligning the durability of a line of shoes, that information can clearly motivate action in Oregon.

Business-to-Business Research

Market research in the business-to-business (B2B) space happens more outside the sport industry than within. The reason for the gap is easy to comprehend—obtaining feedback from business people costs more than getting it from ordinary consumers. Whereas consumers willingly take online surveys just for the opportunity to win a sweepstakes or for a tiny monetary incentive, getting someone to take time out of a busy business day often requires much higher compensation.

But this is not always the case. Some businesses definitely have a stake in providing feedback to sport marketers. Here are a few examples:

- **Corporate partners**. Corporate partners provide a valuable source of revenue for sport teams. The team needs to ensure that partners are satisfied with the fulfillment of its contractual terms. Objective third-party research can provide a better understanding of where partners are satisfied and where they are not.
- **Vendors**. Teams can just as easily play the role of client. For instance, concessionaires benefit from ensuring satisfaction of their key stakeholders.
- **Premium seat holders**. Many premium seating areas, such as suites or high-level clubs, serve the hospitality needs of business development personnel. If the business developers do not see positive momentum because of using the venue for client or employee entertainment, renewal becomes an iffy proposition. Teams and venues can use research techniques to identify the needs of their clients within the premium areas.

Users of Market Research in Sport and Entertainment

We now turn our focus specifically to the sport industry. Except for conducting the occasional project, research has not held a regular role in the typical sport organization. Historically, market research in the sport world has been designed, performed, analyzed, and interpreted by a tenured market researcher sourced from a third-party vendor or partner. These people were likely to have been trained academically on how to collect and interpret data. A person with this skill set was often employed by a professional sport franchise, allowing third-party suppliers to make a living providing these services to sport teams. Examining the historical landscape of larger businesses, such as sponsors, league offices, and agencies, the likelihood grew that a market researcher would be employed in house.

In recent years tremendous growth has occurred in the use of market research to drive day-to-day business decisions in sport. With database marketing and the Internet allowing for ease in data collection and data storage, properties now have valuable data at their fingertips. Interpreting that data and putting the findings into practice is the next big hurdle, and this challenge has spurred many organizations within the sport industry to bring on staff internally to facilitate the wide array of market research needs. No longer is there a typical market researcher or analyst; that title can mean something different to each organization that employs a researcher. In one instance you could have someone who is skilled at managing an influx of syndicated research data from various sources. Another instance may present a person who is well versed in designing a survey questionnaire and performing stable data collection. Yet another organization may have a person who truly analyzes data, hunting for trends and pulling out findings. To complicate matters further, an analyst at one place may have 15 years of experience, whereas an analyst in another organization may be an intern who will be returning to school in 3 to 6 months.

Each of the aforementioned skill sets can serve a specific need. Needs for research arise from different places across the sport industry. The following examples show how different organizations use market research services.

Professional Sport Leagues

A market researcher within a professional sport league serves several purposes. Media ratings and broadcast research have high relevance because leagues typically control a portion, if not all, of their television rights. All major sport leagues employ media researchers who mine ratings data to support the rights fees and advertising fees charged. Nielsen and Arbitron provide the two primary ratings measurement systems used at league offices. Media research also helps to validate contractual obligations that leagues owe to sponsors and advertisers.

A market researcher at a professional sport league often satisfies the internal consumer research needs across multiple departments. Primary consumers of research include the sponsorship, ticketing, and marketing departments. A league office needs to understand consumer behaviors and perceptions as they affect the branding of the league, league partners, and league marks. A consumer may well have different perceptions and intentions toward the Tampa Bay Lightning brand, Tampa Bay Lightning sponsors, and the Tampa Bay Lightning experience than he or she does toward the NHL and its respective brand, sponsors, and experience. In this particular example, an NHL market researcher might seek out the league's fans for feedback regarding national broadcasts, methods for consuming the NHL, experience at league-facilitated events (the Winter Classic, All-Star Game, and so on), and behaviors relating to NHL sponsors. League offices will analyze this data market by market, region by region, and nationwide. Normal practice is to analyze the

How Much Is Enough?

The question that market researchers get all the time, and hate getting whenever they get it, is this: "How many respondents do I need in my sample?"

No one-size-fits-all answer can provide an adequate response to this question. The best answer is, "It depends," which of course raises the follow-up question, "Depends on what?" When conducting survey research, identification of an appropriate sample size requires consideration of the following issues.

- **What is the size of the population to which your inferences will relate**? Quite often the size of the population is so large that it may as well be considered boundless (e.g., the U.S. population). But sometimes the population size can be rather small (e.g., season-ticket holders for a class A minor league baseball team in the Southeastern United States).

- **How precise do you need your estimates (and hence inferences) to be**? Think carefully when evaluating this question. Although many Turnkey clients express concern about not collecting a sufficient sample, oversampling occurs quite frequently. And although an out-of-pocket cost may not be associated with sampling from a fan or ticket-buyer database, asking your customers to answer too many surveys has a hidden cost. Certain fields require incredible precision, such as spinal surgery and air-traffic control. On the other hand, when estimating the proportion of game attendees who approve of the music selection, plus or minus a few percentage points can certainly be deemed tolerable.

- **What is the budget**? More often than not, larger sample sizes result in higher cost. Even if the sample source does not require out-of-pocket spending, a higher number of respondents results in larger data files, more intricate analyses, and more resources required to compile findings. If onsite research is the methodology of choice, larger sample sizes require more time in field, which usually means higher cost for staffers to administer interviews. And, of course, online research using third-party panels produces a one-to-one correlation between cost and sample size. If your budget does not allow you to collect enough respondents to have solid, trustworthy data, you are probably better off skipping the project or identifying an alternative methodology.

Only after population size, precision, and budget are identified can a researcher adequately address sample size appropriateness. Turnkey finds that a typical survey project with only one population of interest requires anywhere from 250 to 500 respondents to generate a robust data set. Why is the range 250 to 500?

Well, it depends.

data across the various fan segments as well (avid versus casual, attendees versus viewers, young fans versus old fans, and so on).

Finally, a market researcher at a professional sport league often serves in the role of advisor or consultant to its member clubs. Not all teams have access to the same resources in terms of staff and budgets, but a league office doesn't want to look across its member clubs and see a landscape of haves and have-nots. A league office wants to provide as many resources as possible to empower member clubs and support their business operations. No league does this better historically than the NBA through its Team Marketing and Business Operations (TMBO) division. Market researchers within TMBO assist NBA clubs with ticketing research, sponsorship research, premium seating research, impression measurement research, and so on. They share best practices of clubs using market research across NBA, WNBA, and NBADL clubs.

Leagues have the ability to perform market research across multiple clubs at much lower pricing than clubs would have to pay if they performed research by themselves. Investing in these efforts ensures that teams are maximizing the margins in good times and minimizing the effect on revenues in bad times.

Professional Sport Properties

Overall, the use of market research on a day-to-day basis at the professional sport property level has grown substantially over the past five years. Some teams invest heavily across custom and syndicated research, whereas other properties employ no market research in their business operation. At the most basic level, the vast majority of professional sport properties collect fan feedback. Topics frequently covered include event satisfaction (concessions, parking, ushers, and so on), season-ticket holder satisfaction, ticket purchase intent, and fan segment profiling. These studies help an organization keep their finger on the who, what, when, where, why, and how of the fan base. Marketing and ticketing departments use this type of research to create promotions, ticket packages, and at-event features.

Because sport teams have similar business operations and desire similar fan input, Turnkey has noticed some repetitiveness to survey topics over the years. Here is a list of common survey topics:

- Ad awareness
- Brand study
- Broadcast satisfaction
- Broadcasting partner
- Community relations
- Concept testing
- Concession preferences
- Customer service satisfaction
- Demographic profiling
- Economic impact study
- Employee satisfaction
- E-newsletter content
- Fan behavior
- Fan club satisfaction
- Fan entertainment preference
- Food and beverage
- Game-day satisfaction
- Green and recycling behavior
- Group leader
- Hospitality preference
- In-game entertainment
- Internet usage and consumption
- Kids club
- Lapsed season-ticket holder
- Mascot satisfaction
- Media habits
- Media partner
- Merchandising
- New ballpark
- New customer
- Off-site engagement
- Online ticketing satisfaction
- Parking and logistics
- Partner and sponsor satisfaction
- Preferred start time
- Premium concessions
- Premium seating
- Promotional item preference
- Season-ticket holder satisfaction
- Secondary market
- Social media habits
- Special event satisfaction
- Sponsor category opportunity
- Sponsor or partner summit postevent
- Sponsorship measurement
- Suite rental satisfaction
- Theme night
- Ticketing habits
- TV viewer study
- Uniform preferences
- Unused ticket study
- Website satisfaction

Professional sport properties seem to be engaging in increasingly sophisticated research projects. Specifically, sponsorship measurement and ticket-pricing studies have proved to be highly effective in maximizing revenues within those respective departments. Sponsorship departments are under significant pressure to justify rights fees and measure the effectiveness of a corporate partnership. Brands are being held accountable internally, and they often rely on the property to provide data. Sponsorship departments can collect data respective to specific brands, categories, or perceptions of sponsors in general. These data are analyzed and translated to help convey to the brand how the partnership is moving the needle with the property's fan base.

In the ticketing world, all professional sport properties are trying to find the optimal price point to charge for a ticket. What price point will result in unsold tickets? What price point will damage the perceived value of a ticket? What variables should drive the price up or down? Ticketing departments analyze many sources of data to modify prices. Sales data from the primary and secondary market account for two of the more important sources. Knowing the available inventory, prices already paid for tickets, and advanced purchase information help identify the optimal price point going forward. Some professional sport teams use this data to make pricing recommendations every day of the year, but others perform this analysis less frequently. Despite advancements in this area, some organizations opt not perform this analysis at all.

Sponsors

The primary objective of a sport sponsorship is to use the assets (marks, hospitality, fan reach, event access, and so on) of the property to drive the business objectives of the sponsor more effectively than it could without the sponsorship. Generalizing about how sponsors use their

What metrics did these sponsors of the Arnold Sports Festival measure to assess the effect of their sponsorships on brand performance?

sponsorships is difficult. Comparing the use of sponsorship by a global company like Coca-Cola to that of NovaCare, a Philadelphia-based rehabilitation company, makes little sense. More broadly, one brand may want to build awareness of a new product to a male audience. A second brand may want to incentivize partners and employees with exclusive hospitality. And a third partner may be sponsoring purely as a defensive measure to keep a competitor from doing so and effectively building their market share. Objectives should be clearly identified during any sponsor relationship.

Because every sponsor and sponsorship has different objectives, market research related to sponsorship can vary. Before beginning any activation, a sponsor should put effort into identifying baseline metrics of any key performance indicators (KPIs). All measurements from that point on will be compared with the baseline metrics to show the effectiveness of the activation. Without a baseline measurement, no metric is available against which to base conclusions on the effectiveness of the sponsorship.

Generalizing about the use of market research in regard to sponsorship is challenging. Generally, the sophistication of market research within a sponsor organization exceeds that of a typical professional sport property. Many sponsor brands have a market research department at their disposal to facilitate studies related to all marketing, including the sport sphere.

As in many situations, budget constraints limit sponsorship measurement. Brands have been known to comingle their research, trying to reduce cost by including sponsorship-related questions in broader brand-tracking studies. Doing so masks the differences between typical consumers and sports fans. Brands sometimes divest the measurement process to their agency of record, which is arguably the equivalent of the student grading herself.

Application of Market Research in the Sport Industry

The following section provides case-study examples of how market research can be used throughout the sport industry to facilitate data-driven decision making. Research applications span far beyond the case studies in this chapter, although areas such as marketing, ticketing, and sponsorship tend to benefit especially from fan feedback. All data cited in the case studies are real, although team names may be blinded because of confidentiality agreements.

Sponsorship: Milwaukee Bucks

The 2010–11 NBA season marked the first time that the league's Team Marketing and Business Operations office spearheaded a large-scale research study to bolster the performance of sponsorship sales departments. The Milwaukee Bucks, like other participating teams, identified several top-tier sponsors whose renewal could be favorably influenced by demonstrating the effect of sponsorship on fans. One of the two sponsors included in the study by the Milwaukee Bucks was their official casino—Potawatomi Bingo Casino.

Methodology and Sample

The Milwaukee Bucks distributed invitations for an online survey to their database of ticket-plan holders (full and partial season), individual game buyers, and e-newsletter subscribers. All respondents were screened to ensure that they resided in the Milwaukee market. A control group of Milwaukee residents with no interest in the team was sourced through an online consumer panel provider. The study consisted of three waves: preseason (to set benchmarks), midseason (to allow the team to act in underperforming areas), and at the end of the season (to recap all findings).

Key Findings

- Familiarity and affinity for Potawatomi Bingo Casino among Bucks fans were higher than among nonfans.
- Potawatomi Bingo Casino was by far the number one casino destination for fans who visit regional casinos.
- Specific brand perceptions of Potawatomi Bingo Casino (e.g., "offers the best restaurants/dining options," "features the best entertainment acts") scored notably better among fans than among nonfans.

Outcome

The Bucks included the data from this study in their sponsorship recap, demonstrating return on objective (ROO) to Potawatomi. During the 2012–13 NBA season, the Milwaukee Bucks and Potawatomi Bingo Casino announced the extension of their partnership for an additional six years.

Ticketing: Seattle Sounders FC

Seattle Sounders FC is one of the most popular teams in Major League Soccer (MLS). Because of high demand for tickets, the organization has had to increase the capacity in CenturyLink Field multiple times since the inaugural season in 2009. (CenturyLink Field is shared with the Seattle Seahawks from the NFL. Stadium capacity for soccer matches had been artificially reduced from the total capacity of 67,000.) In 2011 the Sounders had the highest average attendance in MLS, best-ing the L.A. Galaxy, which had the next highest attendance, by over 60 percent.[19] Because of the strong attendance, the Sounders organization wanted to figure out how to sell as many tickets as possible throughout the stadium while offering the best ticket packages for their fans at the right price points. To do this, they needed to determine what fans deemed most important when buying tickets and what prices they would be willing to pay for various ticket packages.

Methodology and Sample

Sounders FC distributed online surveys in June 2011 and obtained data from full and partial season-ticket holders, single-match ticket buyers, and a small number of other Sounders fans.

Key Findings

- Sounders FC fans focused primarily on price, even more than they did on seat location.

Seattle Sounders FC continues to draw substantially more fans than any other MLS team, and their ticketing options help them do so.

○ Seat location in the upper versus lower bowl had little effect on the fans who were willing to pay for their seats.

○ Corner seats could be priced the same as or slightly lower than midfield options.

- All-you-can-eat packages had no incremental value to the fans, who preferred the cheapest tickets regardless of whether concessions were included.

Follow-Up

During the 2012 season (the season after the research), average attendance at Sounders FC matches increased another 9 percent, buoyed in part by a franchise-record attendance of 66,452 against the Portland Timbers.[20] The match had the second highest attendance of any regular-season match in the 17-year history of MLS.[21]

Event Operations: Las Vegas Motor Speedway

Each spring Las Vegas Motor Speedway (LVMS) hosts over 300,000 visitors during a three-day NASCAR weekend that includes Sprint Cup and Nationwide Series races. Historically, LVMS had used online research to create a profile of event ticket buyers. In 2012 track executives began shifting the focus of consumer research efforts toward better understanding the background and behavior of race-day attendees. Of particular interest to LVMS were fans in the 18- to 34-year-old age range.

Methodology and Sample

LVMS used two separate onsite surveys, administered by pen and paper to a random sample of attendees throughout (*a*) the venue itself and (*b*) in the Neon Garage, a VIP-type fan area. Research staff members were strategically positioned throughout the venue to ensure that they would interview a representative sample of attendees. To allow fans to sample what LVMS had to offer on race day, any customer experience questions were included in a survey that was administered after the race started.

Key Findings

Regarding 18- to 34-year-old fans in attendance at LVMS,

- they were less avid NASCAR fans than attendees aged 35 and older,

- 40 percent were attending their first NASCAR race ever (or first in the past five years),

- they were looking for less expensive food and beverage options,

- they enjoyed the Neon Garage experience, and

- they probably learned of the Neon Garage through the LVMS website or word-of-mouth rather than mass media.

Key Action Items

- Exploration of options regarding bundling ticket price with food and beverage credit

- Bounce-back offers for first-time LVMS attendees

- Buy one, get one (BOGO) ticket opportunities, given likelihood that attendees would bring friends and family

Social Media: St. Louis Cardinals

MLB's St. Louis Cardinals, having devoted substantial energy to sustaining a Facebook page and Twitter feed, wanted to gain better understanding of their fans' social media habits and preferences. A research study took place that sought to assess attitude and usage, in regard to both general social media and the Cardinals' specific accounts.

Methodology and Sample

The Cardinals used online survey research, sourcing respondents from their fan database and Facebook and Twitter accounts.

Key Findings

- Although the Cardinals have a strong following on both sites, Facebook followers strongly outnumber Twitter followers, consistent with the general dynamics of Facebook versus Twitter.

- Facebook and Twitter serve different purposes for the Cardinals' social media efforts:

Facebook	Twitter
Maintaining relationships	Receiving news
Keeping connected	Keeping up with events
Sharing personal information	

- Overall satisfaction with the Cardinals' social media platforms is strong. Fans express interest in having more chances to interact with the Cardinals and more ticket offers and giveaways.

- Cardinals fans who use social media are less active at the Cardinals' sites compared with their behavior at other Facebook and Twitter pages. At Cardinals' accounts, they are less likely to

  ○ like or comment on posts, pictures, or videos; or

  ○ retweet or reply.

- Poor internet connectivity at Busch Stadium hinders fans from accessing Facebook and Twitter while attending games. This problem is common at sport venues, as seen in other Turnkey Intelligence research.

Key Action Items

- The Cardinals will be exploring separate strategies for their Facebook and Twitter pages, playing to the strengths of each platform and the expectations of the sites' users.

- For Facebook they will offer content that promotes connections with the players, team, and organization.

- For Twitter they will keep the user informed about all things Cardinals.

- Content should be curated for the sites' visitors and match what they are looking for. Ideally, the information will create a VIP experience for fans.

- The team will offer a Wi-Fi hot spot within the stadium for social media users to check in.

Performing the Right Research

In the sport industry, a sizeable amount of revenue is converted into salaries for players, coaches, and managers. Still other money goes to stadium leases, team travel, and other on-field expenditures. Off the playing surface, a sport franchise functions on a lean budget that must pay for marketing, payroll, community outreach, data

infrastructure, and all the way down to pens and a cleaning staff after hours. Nowhere is the budget leaner than in market research. In some cases, sport marketers just don't value research enough to devote significant money to it. And even in cases in which research brings tremendous value to the organization, funds simply might not be available. The reality is that in all businesses, market research is a cost center whose ROI frequently comes under question.

Thankfully, the readers of this book understand that customer feedback has a place in the operation of any sport-related business. The key issue becomes performing research for the right reasons, at the right times, and within appropriate budgetary constraints. The main question becomes how best to use limited research resources and get the optimal bang for the buck out of market research projects.

In other words, what is the right research project?

Of course, that question has no answer. But by abiding by the following set of tips, chances are that the research project at hand will provide the level of insight required to make powerful, informed decisions.

- **Identify the business objective at hand as it pertains to your business.** Amazing as it may seem, through the years Turnkey has encountered more than our fair share of projects in which the key stakeholder or project manager could not identify the purpose of the project. Sometimes the project was simply routine; for example, "We always collect data after every home game." Other times, the project was done "because other teams are doing it." Neither of these examples constitutes a business objective. A business objective pertaining to market research should involve an open question whereby consumer feedback will provide a way to answer that question and move the business forward. Here are some examples frequently encountered at Turnkey:

  ○ How can we improve the in-game experience for the attendee?

  ○ Does our advertising improve brand perception?

  ○ Is our sponsorship of Team X helping to improve brand recall in market?

- **Let your objective define your methodology, and never vice versa (i.e., the Turnkey** research motto). We often have a client contact us and say, "We need a vendor to do onsite research." After probing why the client wants to do onsite research, we find that the client wants to understand future attendance habits. Because this protocol resembles asking a college student at a frat party whether he wants to come to another frat party, we end up steering the client toward online research two weeks after the event at hand.

This scenario provides one example of trying to determine methodology beforehand, but plenty more are in the coffers. Clients commonly get into the habit of trying to shoehorn research goals into a model simply not made for them. A common example relates to any organization, sport or otherwise, that licenses online survey software. Because this software comes relatively cheap these days, businesses try to use online surveys for an array of projects.

As alluded to earlier in the chapter, sport and emotion go hand in hand; qualitative research provides a much more effective method of understanding the emotional component to avidity and behaviors. Expecting a survey to provide the right type of data to account for the emotional piece is expecting something unfair.

• **Plan as much as possible**. One study or another will always need to be fielded ASAP because of an unforeseen PR nightmare or similar issue. Putting that aside, realize that conducting quality custom research and data analysis takes time. As a simple rule of thumb, assume that writing a comprehensive questionnaire from scratch takes 8 to 10 business hours and that creating an insightful research report can easily take from 40 to 80 business hours. Computers facilitate the process to a point, but human thought is required to formulate the story, that is, the findings that address the business objective, and provide actionable recommendations.

• **Have a sense of budget before moving forward**. Some people go to look at a new car, check its price, and then figure out a way to come up with the money to buy it. Other people decide how much money they can afford to spend on a new car and then look at cars that fit their budget. Which method is better? Let's leave that for the psychology books. Within the sport industry, Turnkey believes it best to lean toward the latter approach. Identify a cost that the team would willing spend to solve the business issue

at hand. Then explore methodological options that meet that objective. If the project costs significantly exceed budget, chances are that the information from the project will not merit the amount required to do it. That said, an organization should not just abandon a research project without exploring options for reducing the cost. To ensure that research is done efficiently, follow the advice in the next bullet.

• **Search out a research partner, not just a supplier**. Chances are that your sport organization has an ad agency of record, an accounting firm on retainer, a concessions partner, and even a preferred shipping company. Why then would you try to shuffle market research companies in and out as if they were interns? Research agencies will provide more insightful information at streamlined cost by having the opportunity to work consistently with individual clients. The firms get to know the business, nuances of the brand, habits of the fans, and methodologies that work. As any market researcher will tell you, knowledge of the client's business is vital to delivering impactful work.

ACTIVITY 4.1 Market Research

In this WSG activity, you're a market researcher for your school's sport organization. Assume the sport organization wants you to conduct market research, and based on that research, make recommendations for implementing new marketing strategies.

Wrap-Up

Successful businesses have come to rely on a multitude of data sources to create a solid understanding of their markets. The sport business works no differently, because all types of organizations in the industry employ data-driven decision making to varying degrees. Data may be obtained from syndicated sources such as Nielsen, Arbitron, and Scarborough or similar companies. When suitable information is not available through syndicated offerings, researchers turn to customized data-collection methodologies, resulting in qualitative or quantitative data. Typical data-collection methodologies include surveying, individual interviews, and focus groups, just to name a few. Of course, the objectives of an individual project will dictate the correct methodology.

Within the sport industry, the most frequent usage occasions for market research apply to sponsorship, ticketing, and marketing, not surprisingly, given the contributions of these areas to revenue streams. Sponsorship measurement has taken off because of the need for brands to monitor budgets carefully and understand what they get in return. Ticketing research helps ensure the value proposition of ticket packages, and sport marketers have begun seeing the parallels between branding in sport and in more traditional marketing arenas.

Despite the sport industry's increasing investment in research and data analytics, budgets in these areas remain tight. Performing optimal research at the lowest cost involves having full understanding of objectives and careful planning to ensure that all aspects of a project run smoothly.

Activities

1. Beyond the sources cited in this chapter, identify three syndicated data sources that could have value in helping sport organizations determine optimal sales and marketing strategies.

2. For each of the following scenarios, identify what custom research approach would be of most value. First, specify a quantitative or qualitative approach and then add any specifics (e.g., quantitative onsite surveying, qualitative focus groups).

   · A minor league hockey team wants to find out how game attendees feel about the at-game experience.

   · A brand of baseball gloves and gear, looking to develop a new advertising campaign aimed at parents of Little League players, wants to understand what emotional ties kids and their parents have to equipment handed down.

   · A motorsports venue is considering offering various ticket packages that include multiday passes, varying food and beverage options, and merchandise offers. The venue needs consumer feedback to identify appropriate pricing and interest in the offers.

   · A professional sport league wants to gain an understanding of how avid and casual fans' opinions of the league change when athletes run afoul of the law.

   · A major sports drink brand wants to know how its sponsorship of college football is driving purchase behavior among people ages 18 to 25 who are athletically active.

3. What are the potential obstacles to conducting successful business-to-business research as it relates to a sport teams' current partners? How can a team solicit feedback from partners to avoid these pitfalls?

4. What market research topics might cause a respondent not to answer honestly? What methodologies allow the research to obtain data that is honest and objective?

Your Marketing Plan

1. Data-driven decision making is becoming the way of life for the sport business, even on the field! How can you use familiarity with market research to improve your marketing plan?

2. What are the open business questions related to your organization where market research can fill the holes?

Endnotes

1. Stu Hunter, presentation given at Nabisco, Inc., East Hanover, NJ (1999).

2. U.S. Census, *American Fact Finder*, http://factfinder2.census.gov.

3. Scarborough. *Scarborough Methodology*. http://en-us.nielsen.com/sitelets/cls/documents/scarborough/Scarborough-Methodology-2012.pdf

4. D. Goetzl, "Arbitron Data Gives NBC a Crown of Sorts," *MediaPost*, 21 June 2012, www.mediapost.com/publications/article/177355/#axzz2botNZDfW.

5. comScore, *Mobile Metrix*, www.comscore.com/Products/Audience_Analytics/Mobile_Metrix.

6. Critical Mention, www.criticalmention.com.

7. Joyce Julius, www.joycejulius.com.

8. Repucom, www.repucom.com.

9. K. Zickuhr and A. Smith, *Digital Differences*, Pew Internet (13 April 2012), http://pewinternet.org/Reports/2012/Digital-differences/Main-Report/Internet-adoption-over-time.aspx.

10. S. Blumberg and J. Luke, *Wireless Substitution*, Centers for Disease Control (June 2012), www.cdc.gov/nchs/data/nhis/earlyrelease/wireless201206.pdf.

11. Pew Research Center for the People and the Press, *Random Digit Dialing—Our Standard Method* (2012), People-Press, www.people-press.org/methodology/sampling/random-digit-dialing-our-standard-method/.

12. United Nations Economic and Social Commission for the Asia and the Pacific, *Computer Assisted Telephone Interviewing (CATI)*, United Nations Economic and Social Commission (October 1999), www.unescap.org/stat/pop-it/pop-guide/capture_ch04.pdf.

13. R. Belk, *Handbook of Qualitative Research Methods in Marketing* (Northampton, MA: Elgar, 2006).

14. C. Azzara, "Qualitatively Speaking: The Focus Group vs. In-Depth Interview Debate," *Quirk's*, June 2010, p. 16.

15. FocusGroupsTips.com, *How to Use Laddering in Qualitative Market Research*, www.focusgrouptips.com/laddering.html.

16. T. Fidgeon, *Ethnography—When and How to Use*, Spotless Interactive, http://www.spotlessinteractive.com/articles/usability-research/ethnography-when-and-how-to-use.php; T. Brogdon, "Qualitative Techniques That Go Beyond the Focus Group Room," *Quirk's*, February 2011, p. 50.

17. Ibid.

18. J. Henning, *MROC = Market-Research Online Community*, Vovici (24 October 2008), http://blog.vovici.com/blog/bid/17991/MROC-Market-Research-Online-Community.

19. MLS Attendance, *September 30th Attendance Update* (September 2012), http://mlsattendance.blogspot.com/2012/09/september-30th-attendance-update.html; J. Boyle. "Sounders Beat Timbers 3-0 Before Record Crowd," *Washington Herald*, 7 October 2012, www.heraldnet.com/article/20121007/SPORTS/121009835.

20. Ibid.

21. Ibid.

Chapter 5

Market Segmentation

OBJECTIVES

- To appreciate the essential role of segmentation in the marketing process in order to match the right product offer to the correct target
- To recognize the standard bases of market segmentation in sport

Mass Customization

The heading is a deliberate use of an oxymoron to make the point that the original foundation of market segmentation was the concept of recognizing different clusters or groups within a market that shared similar characteristics, such as demographics or usage patterns, and then targeting their needs with a similar product (such as an all-inclusive business entertainment ticket and hospitality package or a family ticket package that includes food and drink and a souvenir). The key to accessing the segment relied on having a media vehicle that would permit access to that target segment. With the advent of the Internet, just about every person within the cluster can now be accessed individually by a text or e-mail campaign. Using Acxiom Corporation's PersonicX household-level segmentation system, spending data, and a review of social network site postings such as Facebook, a personalized product offering can be made.

The ability to segment a market is made possible by the kind of market research we discussed in chapter 4. In this chapter, we explain segmentation, its centrality to the marketing process, and its feasibility. Next, we look at the common bases for segmenting the sport market: state of being (demographics), state of mind (psychographics), product benefits, and product usage.

What Is Market Segmentation?

Market segmentation is a key concept in this text because it creates the bridge between managerial analysis and managerial action. It provides a conceptual framework on which a sport marketer builds direct marketing and promotional strategies.

In simple terms, market segmentation is the process of dividing a large, heterogeneous market into more homogeneous groups of people, who have similar wants, needs, or demographic profiles, to whom a product may be targeted. The Jane Blalock Company, for instance, does not target its clinics to all golfers, or even all female golfers.[1] Instead, the focus is the female executive golfer. Such segmentation is basic to most successful marketing efforts throughout the world. Even within the massive global marketing strategies of corporate giants such as McDonald's and Coca-Cola, marketers recognize that consumers in Germany are different from consumers in Japan. If technology has made the world smaller, it has not homogenized the world's cultures. Neither has television created a mass mentality within a nation of television viewers such as the United States. To the contrary, the scores of channels now available on cable television systems and the even more diverse media available through the Internet reflect the fragmentation of the general and niche media marketplace.[2]

The sport marketplace is equally segmented. As chapters 3 and 4 indicate, no single profile describes the sport consumer. The consumer profile varies by sport, by place of residence, by life situation, and by a host of other factors. But one thing is clear: Segmentation rules. Sport television provides clear evidence. Twenty years ago, the broadcast networks dominated sport television. Sport junkies (an important segment of men) had little choice in their viewing. Then came HBO, TBS, ESPN, CNN, Fox networks, and now NBC Sports Network, which have significantly widened the choices. ESPN wagered its program schedule (and its corporate life) on the sport junkies to whom the old networks had appealed a few times per week. In recent years, "narrowcasting" has spawned even more clearly defined segment strategies, such as the Golf Channel.

Given the competitiveness of the sport market and the intangible nature of most sport products, market segmentation is both logical and necessary. A product is nothing more than a bundle of benefits. The deeply committed fan may want special privileges that come with a season ticket (newsletter, special functions with the team), whereas the infrequent fan may need a telephone or Internet ticket-ordering system that reduces anxieties and hassles over ticket purchase. The young executive who uses a fitness health club on a frequent basis may require a club that provides laundry service. Another member may prefer fewer amenities for lower fees. Segmentation, then, is designed to maximize consumer satisfaction, but it is also a marketing tactic to maximize market response. Thus, segmentation should not be carried to the point beyond which it no longer provides meaningful returns. The WNBA's Seattle Storm might wish to maximize attendance by individualizing ticket packages to suit the desires of every individual fan, but that method would not be feasible. The Storm's marketing staff identify and target segments that they can reach by offering a flex plan (11 ticket coupons for the price of 10) that the fan can redeem as she or he sees fit. They also offer a "modern family plan" that starts with a purchase of two tickets, two meals, and two drinks, not the typical four, four, and four plan offered by most teams. To meet the needs of all varieties of families, additional packages of one ticket, one meal, and one drink can be purchased individually as needed to suit the smallest family to the largest.

Identifiability, Accessibility, Responsiveness

Several issues are important in choosing whether to segment a market—the identifiability, accessibility, and responsiveness of potential segments.[3]

Just a decade ago, the sport marketer would have to ask, Can the segment be identified or measured in terms of its size and purchasing power? The marketer would have to make this determination using the kind of research discussed in chapter 4. Today, the ubiquitous nature of electronic media, the widespread involvement in social networks, and the proliferation of purchases through the Internet make possible the gathering of segmentation data on an individual fan or consumer basis. Major League Baseball clubs did not spend time in the last decade trying to determine the size or strength of the market for a souvenir pin or bobblehead giveaway promotion. The raging success in other markets was enough for them to go with a gut instinct that the items were hot everywhere, at least for the moment. A golf course developer, however, would want to research a local or regional market

in depth before making a $30 million investment to develop a new course, particularly during the recession that has gripped the world economy since 2007.

The second question that the marketer once had to ask was, Can the marketer access the segment? With today's electronic marketing, this question is less relevant, but an essential question remains: Is it possible to gain access to those groups of consumers individually without upsetting marketing efforts aimed at other segments? Our souvenir pin and bobblehead promoters had no problem with this. A few weeks of promotional ads brought out more than enough collectors. Things are not so easy, however, for a state high school association trying to promote its championship games, especially in minor sports. The time between playoff rounds is often short, upsets happen with regularity, and fan bases are segmented by community identity. Most state associations cannot feasibly prepare special contingency plans for each team that might advance. Hence, campaigns tend to be broad-based promotions of high school sports and focus heavily on group sales. Exactly the same problem exists for minor league teams, the early rounds of the Men's NIT and Women's NCAA Division I basketball tournaments, and even early round CHL or Major Junior Hockey playoffs in Canada.

The final segmentation question that the marketer must ask remains unchanged: Will the segment be responsive? Two questions need to be answered here. The first is whether the product will match the wants of the chosen segment. With customer and prospect propensity scoring, that point is particularly prevalent in ticket marketing. Using Ticketmaster's Ticket Analytics, SSB's Ticketing Intelligence, Turnkey Intelligence, or Axiom prospect scoring, this portion of segmentation strategy has become increasingly targeted, more effective, and less costly. The second question concerns the significance of the segment. Is it worthwhile (given segment size and response) to break down product characteristics and promotional efforts sufficiently to reach a segment? The significance question is less relevant in the era of e-mailing because the cost of e-mail and text campaigns is so low that the ROI is still individually beneficial.

The marketer must address all these factors in deciding whether (and to what extent) to pursue segmentation. In professional team and collegiate sport marketing, the consensus has evolved over time that at a minimum certain segments need to be identified and targeted with a different product menu and unique direct marketing and sales promotional strategy (table 5.1).

Segment or Niche?

You may occasionally hear the term *niche strategy;* the concept is not quite the same as segmentation. Marketing theorists distinguish segments from niches largely based on size and competition. Segments are large but also prone to competition. Consider, for instance, adult male football fans. Colleges and pro leagues compete for this audience at live gates, on television, and with merchandise. A niche may be smaller (perhaps even women executive golfers), but in the past, larger firms typically ignored a niche. But in today's society of mass customization and individual communication strategies through the Internet and smartphones, large companies are much more willing to target smaller niche segments. In sport marketing, niches have also been distinguished from segments based on sport specificity. Niches arise from the sport market; segments are imposed on the sport market. For example, the Sled Dogs Company developed its product in the early 1990s—a miniski and boot combination—with an eye on a part of the existing in-line skater population. Specifically, it targeted skaters (most of whom are young) who had no winter activity. Sled Dogs were simply a way to skate on snow. The niche started in a group within sport—in-line skaters who had no winter counterpart. Unfortunately for the Sled Dogs Company, much of this niche market has since adopted snowboarding, in part because ski resorts recognized the same market potential and began embracing snowboard shredders and building terrain and boarding and extreme skiing parks and half pipes.[4]

In the early 1980s most skiers would have considered snowboarding a small (and annoying) niche. Jake Burton thought otherwise. He saw a niche that could grow. The Burton Company has memorialized its history in the company's poetic vision statement, which captures the early mentality of an alienated niche market. This idea has been further reinforced in the past 20 years as successive younger generations (the so-called millennials) have valued authenticity and heavily rewarded Burton for their originality and first-to-market position.

- We stand sideways.
- We sleep on floors in cramped resort hotel rooms.
- We get up early and go to sleep late.
- We've been mocked.
- We've been turned away from resorts that won't have us.
- We are relentless.
- We dream it, we make it, we break it, we fix it.
- We create.

TABLE 5.1   Typical Sport and Entertainment Segments for Ticket Marketing

Segment	Product offer
Corporate business	Premium seating location, high-end hospitality, close-in parking
Male fans	Meal and a Match—game ticket, pie, and a pint for an EPL team
Female fans	Ladies night—offer a female fan clinic
Children	Youth plan—discounted or free ticket with a kid's meal or souvenir
Student (high school and college)	Thursday night ticket and food and drink
Full season-ticket holders	Offer to experience premium seating and hospitality
Partial- and miniplan holders	Early bird price offering for buying a plan with more games
Group leaders	Group leader appreciation night with complementary ticket when the leader brings a guest who buys, plus fan experience packages (FEPs) for group attendees
Families	Modern family plan

- We destroy.
- We wreck ourselves day in and day out and yet we stomp that one trick or find that one line that keeps us coming back.
- We progress.
- Burton Snowboards is a rider driven company solely dedicated to creating the best snowboarding equipment on the planet.

Of course, the history of many popular sports is a progression from niche to mainstream markets. And who is to say what the next wave will be? The 2004 feature film *Dodgeball* spurred a spike of adult interest in the game. Bill DePue, vice president of the National Amateur Dodgeball Association, told *Athletic Business* magazine, "Our website got 2,000 hits a month before [media coverage of the movie]. . . . Since then, we've had days in which we get 4,000 hits." As we discuss later, niche marketers have used the Internet aggressively.[5]

Niches or segments? Much of the distinction is semantic, especially within the sport industry, where many firms exist in a single-sport domain. In both cases, however, the key questions of identification, accessibility, and responsiveness remain.

Four Bases of Segmentation

With the advent of the Internet and because the overwhelming majority of people in the Western world have their own personal communication devices (smartphones, whether Droid or iPhone; iPads; or other mobile wireless communication devices), the temptation is to assume that we no longer need to segment. But sport marketing best practice reveals that opportunity to every individual consumer. Although such strategies are clearly available to mass retailers such as Amazon and major sites such as Google, in particular the ability to search massive amounts of data, most sport organizations with limited marketing resources must still rely heavily on broader segmentation strategies.

Market segments are formed based on differentials in consumer wants and desires; that is, segments derive from consumer satisfaction. Four bases are commonly used for segmentation, each of which rests on an assumption that homogeneity in one variable may relate to homogeneity in wants and desires. Following are the four common bases:

- Consumers' state of being (demographics)
- Consumers' state of mind (psychographics)
- Product benefits
- Product usage

Typically, marketers employ cross-sections of segments such as middle-income, Hispanic families living within a baseball team's metropolitan market or affluent and active older people who live within 20 minutes of a particular golf and country club. We discuss integrated, or nested, approaches to segmentation at the end of this chapter. The following sections, then, must be understood to represent fluid categories.

State-of-Being Segmentation

State-of-being segmentation includes the following dimensions, which are generally easier to measure than state-of-mind or product benefits:

Geography

Age

Income

Education

Gender

Sexual orientation

Race and ethnicity

These dimensions are discussed in the following sections.

ACTIVITY 5.1 Consumers' State of Being (Demographics)

In this WSG activity, you have just been hired as the new director of marketing for Bellator MMA. Mixed martial arts (MMA) is a full-contact combat sport that allows the use of striking and grappling techniques, both standing and on the ground. Your boss asks you to research Bellator's demographics, review how NASCAR is broadening its fan base (for insight), and report back to him.

Geography

Several clear principles apply to geographic segmentation in sport:

- **First, proximity rules**. A simple survey of participants will typically support the long-recognized relationship between proximity and activity or involvement. The closer a person lives to a sport facility, the more likely she is to become involved with activities there.

- **Know your clusters**. Good internal marketing data from ticket applications, membership inquiries, and similar sources often reveal especially important geo-demographic clusters of these consumers. Abundant software is available to help with "heat mapping" (the nine-digit zip codes or postal carrier routes that typically have a disproportional distribution of ticket buyers, members, or participants in high-income locations). All the marketer needs are consumer codes to couple with other data, such as types of purchases (season tickets, full membership, and so on), frequency of participation, and income. Mapping allows the marketer to see whether certain suburbs or neighborhoods are especially prone to a certain product. Those areas can be targeted for special campaigns, especially direct marketing campaigns (e-mail, text, direct mail, or outbound calling campaigns). Claritas is one of the best-known companies for this kind of analysis, especially its Prizm system. Full House is one of the best lead list suppliers for targeted lists for the sport industry. For example, the Aspire Group uses Full House to target Georgia businesses that would most likely be interested in buying a Club One ticket (exclusive seating with all-you-can-eat food and drink with Atlanta Motor Speedway's Labor Day NASCAR Sprint Cup Series race). The 4,000 mostly automotive-related, heavy manufacturing, or blue-collar-worker companies were targeted for an e-mail and phone call follow-up campaign that cost $4,000 and produced over $20,000 in sales.[6]

- **Value your outer rims (or secondary market radius)**. Some consumer clusters may come from considerable distances. These represent outer-rim markets that can repay extraordinary attention in terms of advertising, promotions, radio, or television networking. The recognition of outer rims in sport date at least as far back as baseball's early radio broadcasts.

Midwest major league teams such as the St. Louis Cardinals developed fan bases at great distances, nurtured largely by radio. Outer-rim markets (typically defined as more than 50 miles [80 km] from the venue but within a 100-mile [160 km] radius in most markets or within a 150-mile [240 km] radius in larger geographic markets) are now primarily reached through cable TV, and they represent logical targets for group sales and special events. But in football, which has relatively few home games (the NFL plays mostly on Sunday afternoons and college football plays mostly on Saturday afternoons), outer rims can mean season tickets. When the Rams and the Raiders deserted Los Angeles, the city was left without an NFL team, so the San Diego Chargers spent several hundred thousand dollars on an ad campaign in the Los Angeles area. In effect, Los Angeles became an outer-rim market for the Chargers. First, the Chargers had to seek an exemption from the NFL rule that prohibits marketing outside a franchise's 75-mile (120 km) radius. That was no problem. Second, and more difficult, the Chargers had to cultivate a potential market of fans as far as 160 miles (260 kilometers) away (for those in northern Los Angeles County and eastern San Bernadino County).

The Chargers are not alone in their campaign for outer rims. The Seattle Seahawks have long maintained an outer rim of Alaskan fans, over 1,000 miles (1,600 kilometers) from CenturyLink Field. The Miami Dolphins have looked to develop a wider rim of markets, to both the north and the west, possibly through partnerships with media outlets and corporate sponsors in places such as Naples, Vero Beach, and Port St. Lucie. State universities have cultivated outer rims by scheduling some "home" games at venues in other parts of their home states.[7]

Some outer rims are what might be called borderlands, in that they rub against the territory of a competing organization. A good example is the central swath of Connecticut, which is the borderland between the Yankee Empire and Red Sox Nation. A 2003 survey showed a clear line of demarcation running through Hartford and Middlesex counties. The turf is important because it contains the several counties that have the highest per capita income in the country and represents a gold mine in cable TV revenues when winning the ratings war. The Red Sox have been aggressive in courting this borderland. At one

Hartford rally, owner Tom Werner announced, "We want to welcome all those Connecticut Yankees who don't want to be in King George's court," a reference to the now-deceased Yankees owner George Steinbrenner. Some of the jousting has been in good fun, but it has been a marketing competition as hot as that on the field.[8]

Age

The old notion of the generation gap contains obvious truth—the young have different tastes and lifestyles from their parents, who in turn diverged from their own parents. Marketers talk about cohorts rather than generations (e.g., the Depression cohort, the millennials cohort). Musical tastes, sexual mores, approaches to debt and savings, and fashion sense are but a few of the cohort touchstones. In some cases, we may include sporting tastes. For instance, an ESPN Sports Poll survey of fan interest in the USTA's U.S. Open tennis championship suggested significant differences between those under and over 25 years of age. In particular, tennis had serious work to do with the teenage market (table 5.2). Tennis was not alone.

Sport organizations have learned that kids in the above-average family income bracket can be most effectively found through the Internet, where they download music and movies, shop, and participate in text and social networking sites such as Facebook and Twitter. Facebook alone had 1.11 billion active users as of March 2013. Not surprisingly, a recent survey found that 46.7 percent of males aged 14–19 used the Internet to find information about sport.[9]

Youth have been a target of sport promotions for over a century, often with the idea of building character through baseball, basketball, or just about any sport. In the early 20th century, the sport curriculum swept gymnastics and calisthenics to the background of the burgeoning physical education programs in U.S. public schools. After World War II, organized youth leagues exploded in the suburbs, first in baseball and then across a broad range of sports. Starting ages drifted downward, so that today, under-8 travel teams are the norm. But registration does not ensure commitment. In fact, American youth appear less committed to mainstream modes of fitness, exercise, and sport, at least as measured in national surveys. Young people are no longer interested in their parents' sports. The industry has responded in two ways:

- **Get 'em to the action to do → feel → learn**. Baseball in particular has recognized the need for special efforts to get kids on the escalator in terms of both their participation in the game and spectatorship. The logic of nurturing fans at a young age was accentuated in MLB because of the long strike in 1994–1995, which dropped many longtime fans off the escalator. In luring kids back, teams got kids more engaged with on-field mass autograph sessions and started letting kids run the bases between innings of some games. They let kids sing the national anthem or throw out the first pitch. They dropped ticket prices for kids 14 and under. The National Hockey League needed similar aggressive strategies as it sought to repair damage from the lockout that cancelled the entire 2004–2005 season and again after the 2012–2013 lockout.[10]

- **Repackage the product for youth**. A number of bowling alleys have created late-night, weekend slots devoted to the youth of either Generation Y or X or today's under-15-year-olds, who have been dubbed Generation Always Connected because they are rarely seen without an electronic device in their hands or next to their ears. Using tag lines like "Extreme Bowling" or "Rock 'n' Bowl," proprietors transformed their premises with night-glow balls, strobe lights, and heavy-metal music. Bowling was not alone. *Sports Illustrated* launched *SI for Kids* in 1989, and now in 2013 its readership has reached 8.1 million. Most of those fans view the magazine online. In 2003 the New York Jets launched the Generation Jets—a culturally diverse and hip set of young cartoon characters who all happen to be Jets fans. The Generation Jets have their own television

TABLE 5.2 USTA Participation Rates by Age: 2009

Age range	Participation rate (%)
6–11	16.25
12–17	20.51
18–24	18.44
25–39	10.99
40–49	8.79

Percentages are based on total tennis participants.

Reprinted from Tennis Industry.

Ethics of NASCAR for Kids

In the late 1990s NASCAR (like most sport organizations) aggressively targeted the family and youth markets. Said NASCAR's director of communications worldwide, John Griffin, "We're going after youth as a whole. We want to continue in our direction of becoming more of a white-collar sport, where it's mom, dad, and the kids sitting around the TV and rooting for their favorite driver on Sunday. We're going after urban youth as much as any other youth." The youth campaign has included NASCAR toys, games, theme parks, cafes, a cartoon show, and even a NASCAR Barbie doll. These pieces were all logical, but NASCAR had to make one major alteration in these youth and family products. It had to cut out the alcohol and tobacco references that were prominent in the wider NASCAR image. The NASCAR Barbie might have a Pennzoil patch, but not a Winston decoration. But one had to wonder: What would kids compete for with their toys and their imagination, if not the Winston Cup? And when Mommy and Daddy took the kids to the live event, how could they prevent the clear link between NASCAR and the Budweiser and Winston brands? Winston has since dropped its NASCAR sponsorship, but until 2007 NASCAR still had the Busch Cup. One might argue that NASCAR was no more responsible for protecting kids from alcohol images than the NFL or any number of universities was. That argument is correct. But if sport claims to stand for healthy lifestyles, it must be especially vigilant in the way that it pursues kids. Sport marketers must continually ask several of Laura Nash's 12 ethics questions:

- What is your intention?
- How does your intention compare with probable results?
- What is the symbolic potential of your action if understood? If misunderstood?[12]

---

show and form the core link for other Jets initiatives such as youth football camps and school–community outreach programs. The campaign was a brilliant twist on traditional kids clubs that exist at collegiate, minor, and major league levels. Rather than offer membership in an amorphous club, the Jets created characters—with names like Blitz, ASKA, and XL—who would become the kids' friends.[11]

Sport marketers will always have an eye on youth campaigns. As the case study on NASCAR suggests, however, these often raise special ethical issues.

The senior, or maturity, market is another target for special marketing plans. As the baby boomers and Gen Xers grow older, they bring their vast cohort into another life or family stage. In the next quarter century, the over-50 market will grow far faster than the under-50 market. Increasingly, baby boomers will move from their family stages to empty-nest and single stages. More research is needed on the sporting attitudes, lifestyles, and subsegments of this maturing market, but the implications are obvious for sport marketers from the major leagues to the local athletics club. In the past, most seniors did not want to attend as

many games in person, particularly night games and games in inclement weather. But the behavior of today's 60-year-olds, in particular their sport participation and spectatorship needs and interests, has been likened to that of their parents in their 40s. So how does this notion affect today's silver-haired generation? Marketers should ask some simple questions about marketing and sales plans proposed for any older segment:

- Does the program speak to the possibilities of aging, as opposed to its limitations?
- Does the program have motivated leadership?
- Is the program user friendly?[13]

Education and Income

Education, not surprisingly, is related to income. Like their counterparts in the golf industry, members of the tennis industry target affluent, highly educated consumers (although not exclusively). The data suggest that this segment is more inclined toward involvement and commitment to tennis. For instance, a recent survey by Scarborough Research indicated that 70 percent of loyal professional tennis fans had at least some

Gen X, Gen Y, Millennials, and Generation Always Connected

Although it is not easy or always logical to create clear generational cohorts that represent distinct lifestyles and outlooks, some demographers and marketers revel in developing and using catchy terms to describe just such phenomena. Baby boomers (people born between 1946 and 1964) have been analyzed for decades. Gen X and Gen Y are two of the most recent groups of interest. Gen Xers were born roughly between 1965 and 1981 (years vary in the literature), whereas Gen Yers were born after 1981. Gen Xers were described as independent, cynical, and slackers. They were the original snowboard and skateboard shredders, the children of grunge music, the target of the X Games. Of course, they are now at a different place in their life cycle, so parenting, PTA meetings, and coaching soccer are more central to their lives. Among the subgroups of Gen X are the yoga and Pilates mamas, who are affluent and spend lavishly on their kids and on their own fitness as mothers. Yoga mamas have boosted sales of $200 designer diaper bags and $800 strollers that they can push while jogging.

The youngest yoga and Pilates mamas may also belong to Gen Y—a cohort also called the millennials and the baby boom echo generation. They are about 78 million strong in America, three times larger in number than their predecessor, and they represent some 16 percent of the population. But they have great buying power. In contrast to Gen Xers, they are described as traditional in their values, optimistic, tolerant, and committed to diversity. Like their predecessors, only more so, they are media-savvy multitaskers who demand interactivity. As one expert advised marketers, "Today's youth expect interactivity within their various interests. Passive entertainment is rapidly being replaced by active participation across virtually all types of media." Marketers have scrambled to reach Gen X, Gen Y, yoga and Pilates mamas, millennials, and now Generation Always Connected (GAC) and many other special consumer segments.[14]

Members of Generation Always Connected (GACs) are indeed a unique breed. Besides having a seemingly insatiable need for electronic communication with their friends even when seated in the same room, they much prefer to play electronic games than play sport. When they watch sport, they invariably pay equal attention to their smartphones. Sport applications offering content to spectators are therefore becoming increasingly in demand. GACs value authenticity. Communication with and from their peers trumps anything that comes from an adult or parental source. They do not want to do what their parents did at the same age, and they expect to be in positions of authority within a few years of college graduation. This generation is clearly the most demanding segment to market to. Principal author Dr. Bernie Mullin once called them the easiest generation to communicate with but the hardest to reach because of the ease of electronic communication but the difficulty of getting through the "last two inches" and driving a purchased sport experience decision.

---

college education. Thirty-two percent enjoyed at least $75,000 in household income. Similar Scarborough research indicated that almost 44 percent of Boston Red Sox fans enjoyed over $75,000 in household income. With Fenway's average ticket prices the highest in baseball and in all North American major leagues, they need it.[15]

Geo-demographic clustering matches income with residence and, presumably, lifestyle. Although a certain income is no guarantee of a particular lifestyle, it is frequently a central index. The National Football League can demand high television-rights fees because it delivers males with relatively high disposable incomes. Golf does not draw as many fans, but its income profile is even higher, which explains why luxury car companies advertise during golf telecasts. Some sports are even more closely tied to high incomes. Take polo. The U.S. Polo Association (USPA) claims to have some 250 clubs and 4,500 members, and it would like to grow even faster than its recent rate of 1 to 3 percent per year. But when novice-level group lessons cost $100 per person, advanced instruction runs at double that cost, and polo ponies run from $50,000 to $70,000, we expect that polo will stay linked to the wealthiest demographics. In fact, polo is so valuable that in the late 1990s, the Polo Ralph Lauren Company sued the USPA's magazine, insisting that it drop the name "Polo." The Lauren Company, which had obtained a trademark for the term *polo*, complained that *Polo* magazine was now overstepping its bounds, focusing "not on equestrian sports but on sophisticated fashions and elegant lifestyles." We might ask, was there ever a difference in the world of polo?[16]

Gender

As sport marketers have recognized the importance of a female market, they have discovered two distinct facets to segmentation strategies. First, women and girls are a special group of consumers who have special needs and wants. Second, women's and girls' sports are a special type of product and have benefits distinct from those of men's and boys' sports. The first is appropriately considered demographic segmentation. The second is really benefits segmentation, considered later in the chapter.

Sport firms have recognized women as a special segment for over a century. For the most part, however, marketing strategies focused on rather glib visions of the "fair sex"—white, relatively affluent, and limited in capabilities. Bicycle companies made V-shaped women's frames to avoid criticism that cycling forced women into unladylike positions. Golf and tennis firms made smaller clubs and rackets for women. Baseball teams promoted ladies' days to elevate the image of their crowds. This was segmentation, but it was very different from Jane Blalock's intent. The women's sport market is no longer an afterthought to the market for men. Title IX and Billie Jean King ushered in a new era that has been fully of age for more than two decades. The female fan base for the dominant men's sports is nearing equity—by one account, some 43 percent for the NFL, 46 percent for MLB, and 46 percent for the NBA.[17] No wonder leagues now have a full line of specifically designed merchandise for women including differently sculptured women's authentic game jerseys and golf-style polos with a different cut and look. This merchandise is now prominently featured during NFL game broadcasts and has driven massive increases in the percentage of licensed apparel sold to women and girls.

The words of one NFL executive capture the widespread desire to win with women: "Women are of critical importance to us. They control the TV dial on Sunday afternoons and decide what sport their kids will get involved in. We have to make these gatekeepers comfortable." One national survey found that male respondents who were avid or somewhat avid sports fans and whose wives were also avid fans attended 57 percent more games than did avid male fans whose wives were not. The NFL has been ahead of the game in cultivating these female gatekeepers, launching a series of seminars in 1997 in 10 cities. The tag line was "Football 101." For a nominal fee, women could hear presentations on equipment, rules, and tactics. In Pittsburgh the class also toured the locker room and practiced plays on the field. Susan Gray, a shipping clerk from Irving, Texas, said she came to the Cowboys' clinic because she no longer wanted to be left out of football talk at the office: "It might be nice to know the difference between a running back and a wide receiver." Other women were not amused, including Jeanne Clark, a former national board member of the National Organization for Women. In Clark's view, "Football 101 sounded like long-ago stories in teen girl magazines, warning the football novices that a little inside knowledge of quarterbacks and linebackers was necessary if you wanted to catch that handsome football hero." Concluded Clark, "They're making a lot of gender assumptions that are unwarranted." Especially critical for the future of the NFL and participation in football are the moms who share President Obama's concern about whether he would allow his son (if he had one) to play a physically damaging sport such as football.[18] In 2013, the NFL and a group of more than 4,800 players reached a $765 million settlement over a class action concussion lawsuit. However, in January 2014 Judge Anita Brody postponed the settlement over concerns that it would not adequately cover the existing plaintiffs' needs, let alone potential future needs.[19] It remains to be seen exactly how large a financial settlement the NFL will be required to pay out. Whatever the cost, the financial setback will likely pale in comparison to the long-term cost that will occur if parents discourage their sons from playing and potentially watching the sport. The female sport consumer market will only grow stronger, with more specialized equipment, more magazines, and television networks that recognize special interests, wants, and needs. More firms, such as the Women's Sports Foundation, SPANX, and Moving Comfort (running wear) are run by and for women. Regardless of a marketer's gender, a patronizing message or a one-shot, low-budget program provides little return. As Donna Lopiano, executive director of the Women's Sports Foundation, concluded, "Selling to women is different from selling to men." One recent survey at four Midwest university basketball games found that women were far more concerned about venue cleanliness, restroom experience, quality of the sound system, and overall staff service. Men were far more concerned about parking. One might say that Bill Veeck knew this long ago from casual fan interaction and that social science has just supported his insights.[20]

At the same time, sport marketers must avoid lumping women into an amorphous category. Some critics argue that such gender myopia doomed the WUSA, the women's professional soccer circuit that started in the euphoria of the 1999 Women's World Cup and was out of business by 2003. James Chung, a marketing consultant who studied WUSA consumers, claimed that the league lumped too many women into the soccer mom category. As Chung put it, "For Gen X moms, the whole 'soccer mom' concept is essentially dead. They don't view themselves the same way as Baby Boomer moms. But that's what the WUSA tried to sell, and the strategy fell on deaf ears."[21]

Gay and Lesbian Market

Historically a taboo market to target within the sport world, gays and lesbians continue to struggle for recognition, opportunity, and understanding. The last few years, however, have seen clear progress. A 2005 national survey commissioned by NBC and the USA Network reported that although 61 percent of respondents agreed that homosexuality should not be accepted as a way of life, 86 percent agreed that "it is OK for male athletes to participate in sports even if they are openly gay."

In 2001 the Minnesota Twins ran a promotion called Out in the Stands, sponsored by *Lavender* magazine, the area's major GLBT (gay, lesbian, bisexual, transgendered) publication. A Twins VP stated emphatically that they were open and accessible to any fan. Perhaps the Twins were responding to an incident the year before, when two lesbians were ejected from Dodger Stadium for allegedly kissing in the stands. The Dodgers had to apologize profusely and promise to train their stadium attendants better. The Los Angeles WNBA franchise, the Sparks, was much more aggressive in courting GLBT fans, kicking off L.A.'s Gay Pride week in 2001 by partnering with Girl Bar, a 12,000-member lesbian club. Such targeted marketing campaigns (as opposed to mass media campaigns) are probably more effective ways to reach GLBT groups. Such strategies are also more sound than having a gay pride day at a WNBA game or LPGA event that could alienate the heterosexual community. Marketers must ensure that they embrace every market, every day. At the same time, they must be prepared to stand their ground if a public backlash develops among conservative groups. Corporate sponsors have watched the success of the Gay Games, where they have enjoyed high (33 percent) recall rates among attendees. Those high levels of commitment, coupled with high income and education profiles, led *American Demographics* to label the gay and lesbian market "an untapped goldmine."[22]

Race and Ethnicity

American history has been heavily influenced by enduring struggles between natives and immigrants and among races and ethnic groups. The nation's motto—*e pluribus unum* ("out of many, one")—captures part of this ethos. Opinions still diverge on whether the motto represents an achievement or a goal. Battles over bilingual education reflect opposition on the emphasis: Is it the *unum* or the *pluribus*. And minority groups increasingly challenge the right of white European immigrants to control the definitions of the American *unum*. Despite popular beliefs, America is less a melting pot and more a mosaic. America's presidential and congressional elections throughout the past decade have sadly defined the increasing diverseness and animosity among the races, particularly in light of the economic downturn. Consequently, ethnic marketing, much like marketing to the alternative lifestyle community, requires sensitivity and communication strategies that use direct methods through predominantly niche channels.

Cultural diversity is both the American strength and the American conundrum. In some ways, the sport world has provided the most vivid theater for this struggle. Jack Johnson, Joe DiMaggio, Eddie Gottlieb, Althea Gibson, Jackie Robinson, and Roberto Clemente are just a few names that represent millions of athletes, promoters, and fans for whom sport has been a touchstone of racial and ethnic pride and tension. Although the dominant leagues, teams, and clubs have gradually opened their doors to qualified athletes of any color, they have been slower to pursue minority fans. That situation is changing, however, in response to the obvious. Americans of African, Asian, Hispanic, and Middle Eastern descent now represent more than a third of the population, and their numbers are growing rapidly. In some markets, minorities are a majority, including the student body at the University of Texas at Austin. By some estimates minorities will be a national majority by 2020. Clearly, minorities represent important consumer bases that demand diligent respect, not benign neglect.

Blacks have been historically underrepresented as targeted consumers in professional and collegiate sport spectatorship. Some numbers bear this out. For instance, ESPN Sports Poll data in 2002 indicated that only 18.3 percent of NBA fans were African American, despite the overwhelming dominance of black players. At the same time, another poll reported that nearly 50 percent of African American respondents were somewhat or very interested in the U.S. Open tennis championship—more than double the level of white respondents. We may guess that the Williams sisters had something to do with this. But was the tennis industry also more engaged with African American consumers? As we discussed in chapter 4, we must be careful in using secondary data, especially in teasing out the definition of the term *fans*. At the same time, the numbers cry out for more analysis.[23]

A growing Latino population provides sport marketers with an expanding market.

The Hispanic market has been pursued more aggressively than other ethnic markets, perhaps because it is the fastest growing minority segment, projected to represent one-quarter of all Americans by 2050. Latino nights are common in baseball venues, as are grassroots events such as the MLS's four-on-four Futbolito tournaments and Spanish radio and television broadcasts. As one expert put it: "If you really want to get at this growing market, you need to do this all the time: Do marketing in Spanish, have ticket sellers who speak Spanish, sell foods that Latinos like."[24]

Sport marketers are beginning to recognize several important principles for success in reaching minority segments:[25]

• **Use minority firms, individuals, and icons**. In 1998 the St. Louis Cardinals engaged FPM/Fuse, a minority-owned ad agency (now Fuse Advertising, www.fuseadvertising.com), to create a campaign aimed at attracting more black fans to Busch Stadium. They did so with good reason. Although the St. Louis metropolitan area was 17.4 percent black and although the Cardinals had enjoyed Hall of Fame careers from a host of African Americans including Bob Gibson and Ozzie Smith, black attendance had lagged behind—making up between 1 and 3 percent of all fans for over a decade. The FPM/Fuse $100,000 campaign used bus, billboard, and radio ads featuring black players such as outfielder Brian Jordan, who said, "God gave me the ability. My parents gave me the opportunity. Everything else I earned." Clifford Franklin, FPM/Fuse partner, expressed the gist of the campaign message as "hard work, dedication, and focus." Major League Baseball has expanded such efforts with its Baseball's Diverse Business Partners Program.[26]

• **Recognize diversity and change within minority groups**. Major League Soccer franchises have been active in addressing their Hispanic fan base, and for good reason: Hispanics accounted for 23 percent of all Major League Soccer fans in the late 1990s. But the rapidly evolving Hispanic population will require changes in strategy. Said consultant Dean Bonham, "The Hispanic market is lower to middle income right now, but can be described as a soccer-educated demographic with disposable income that's growing at a very rapid rate." The NBA's Miami office is the center of the league's efforts to reach Hispanic fans. The staff is made up of people from diverse backgrounds, including Cuba, Panama, Brazil, Uruguay, Costa Rica, Argentina, Puerto Rico, and Peru. The lesson is simple: There is no single Hispanic market.[27]

• **Recognize minority consumer loyalty**. In the summer of 1998 Street & Smith Publishers announced a new annual football preview magazine: *Street & Smith's Black College Football*. The prospectus ad for this joint effort with the Historically Black Collegiate Coalition noted some of the superstars who had played at HBCUs (historically black colleges and universities), including Jerry Rice and Walter Payton. But it also emphasized that "black college sporting events are attended by more African Americans than any other type of sporting event in the country."[28]

State-of-Mind Segmentation

State-of-mind segmentation assumes that consumers may be divided by personality traits; by lifestyle characteristics such as attitudes, interests, and opinions; and by preferences and perceptions. The most noteworthy approach to state-of-mind segmentation was developed by the Stanford Research Institute (SRI). Called the values and lifestyle (VALS) typology, it assumes that attitudes, opinions, desires, needs, and other psychological dimensions collectively govern daily behavior. VALS identifies eight segments of the adult population, based on resources and primary motivations (ideals, achievement, and self-expression):

Innovators

Thinkers

Achievers

Experiencers

Believers

Strivers

Makers

Survivors

VALS is used extensively in proprietary research. For instance, telecommunications companies have used VALS to identify components that will be attractive to early adopters. We are not aware, however, of recent studies of sport consumers using VALS as a base. The possibilities of state-of-mind segmentation, however, are intriguing. For instance, Discovery Communications, which runs The Learning Channel and the Discovery Channel, uncovered eight segments among its viewers. "Machos," who comprised 12 percent of viewers, were 76 percent male, largely blue collar, average in income, and oriented toward action programming, including sport and war. In contrast, the 15 percent of viewers who were "Scholars" were 54 percent female, urbane, upscale, and favored programming in archaeology, history, and anthropology. Discovery Communications can use the knowledge to create and promote programming for the various segments. We might project similar segments among ice hockey fans—"Rumblers" who revel in aggressive hitting and fighting and "Aesthetes" who focus on skill, craft, and grace.[29]

Recent research in sport consumer behavior has opened up other prospects for state-of-mind segmentation, particularly in terms of fan loyalty and identification. Galen Trail and his research team, for instance, have developed a point of attachment index that measures fan identification with product elements such as team, coach, players, and university. Along similar lines, Dan Mahony, Bob Madrigal, and Dennis Howard developed the psychological commitment to team (PCT) scale that measures fan loyalty to a particular team. Sport organizations, at any level, with a substantial fan database could administer such instruments to discern possible state-of-mind segments based on levels of identification or loyalty. In other words, marketing research can now provide empirical substance to old notions such as hard-core and marginal fans. Marketers could then develop different marketing plans for each segment, which may now be identifiable, accessible, and responsive.[30]

Much is at stake. Major League Soccer, for instance, has grappled with the problems of appealing to both hard-core soccer fans and casual fans (think youth soccer families), who always seem to represent the future. This lack of focus has led MLS to make wild swings in rules. For instance, in the 1990s MLS rules required the official time to be shown on a clock and dispensed with draws by conducting shootouts to determine a winner after drawn matches. These rules were intended to please casual fans whose frame of sport reference was the NFL. But these rules flew in the face of FIFA (Federation of International Football Association) and world soccer tradition, in which the referee kept the official time and a tie was honorable and even exciting. In 1999 MLS commissioner Don Garber announced a change of direction—no shootout and no official clock. The MLS, it appeared, was ready to stick with a hard-core base that it hoped was growing as Americans learned more about world football. The results have been positive for MLS as stadiums in Toronto and Portland have sold out and lower-level sellouts have been the norm in Seattle.[31]

ACTIVITY 5.2 US VALS™ Survey

The US VALS™ Survey provides psychographic market segmentation information that companies use to tailor their products and services in order to appeal to the people most likely to purchase them. The information helps companies determine how to place a product for a certain consumer niche. In this WSG activity, you will complete the survey and consider its implications.

Product Benefits Segmentation

Benefits segmentation is closely related to state-of-mind segmentation. After all, the sport product is a bundle of benefits. If those benefits don't exist in the consumer's mind, then they don't exist at all. Sport marketers have adopted benefits segmentation in many ways. The most easily illustrated applications are in the sporting goods industry. Take athletics shoes. The competitive runner who logs over 60 miles (100 km) per week seeks the product benefits of support, shock reduction, and long wear; the intermediate tennis player seeks sound grip and comfort; and the casual sneaker purchaser is just looking for a light and fashionable shoe to use as regular footwear. Each purchaser is looking for different benefits and will be best served by different shoes.

The motivational factors discussed in chapter 3 provide insights into the benefits sought by sport consumers. Affiliation, achievement, status, health, and fitness, in various forms and configurations, are certainly related to benefits that consumers perceive from sport consumption. Team marketers, for instance, know that season-ticket holders expect exclusive benefits such as access to inside information (often through newsletters); special events (autograph sessions); or participation in on-field, on-court, or on-ice fan experience packages (FEPs). Large groups, on the other hand, look for scoreboard recognition, on-site liaisons, discounts, and team promotional materials to drum up interest. The most successful sport organizations understand the importance of identifying the core benefits that define their products in their consumers' minds. For example, in the late 1990s the NFL defined its six core equities (with sample symbols) as follows:

- Action and power: hitting, circus catches, the NFL shield
- History and tradition: autumn leaves, NFL legends, tailgating
- Thrill and release: fans and players laughing and screaming
- Teamwork and competition: the "steel curtain" defense of the Pittsburgh Steelers Super Bowl champions
- Authenticity: the pigskin, muddy field, blood
- Unifying force: groups of fans, teams

These core equities may be viewed as core benefits to be cultivated and promoted in live events, broadcasts, videos, programs, and merchandise.[32]

The steady rise of high-performance, commercialized women's team sports (e.g., college and pro basketball, international soccer, and ice hockey) appears to be a case in alternative benefits more than demographics. To be sure, fan research suggests that women's team sports attract a wider age range than their male counterparts. And the generally lower prices are more attractive to families. But the strong male base—30 percent in the arena and 50 percent on television for the WNBA—belies notions that women's sports are a "chick thing." As an NCAA survey revealed, fans of women's basketball, regardless of gender, enjoy a game that in their minds is distinctly different (e.g., "below the rim"), played by athletes who are more articulate, more accessible, and, yes, more appropriate as role models than the men. Women's sports are evolving rapidly; time will test the margins of these product differences. The WNBA, for instance, suffered a 4.5 percent decline in average attendance during the 2005 season—enough to spur league president Donna Orender to promise to work harder at branding and positioning: "Everyone has a sense

of what the WNBA is, but we have to refine it." The league would do well to focus on benefits segmentation.[33]

Unfortunately, sport managers are often out of touch with the benefits segments in their fan base. In this state of ignorance, they can hardly hope to fashion a strategy that does not alienate one group or another. One recent investigation of an NHL franchise and its fans found that the team envisioned a strategy that would appeal to both tradition (classic merchandise for the hard-core fan) and dynamism (rock music for the casual, especially young, fan). Unfortunately, the team strategy belied an ignorance or avoidance of other key segments revealed in fan research. In particular, the franchise was neglecting social fans who needed special group rates and better fan rituals (like signature songs or cheers) to encourage their attendance. Marketing researchers have found ways to identify segments of benefits in sport consumers' minds. Managers must start to use that research. We look closer at such strategies in chapter 6, when we consider product positioning.[34]

Product Usage Segmentation

We know that product usage segmentation is also significant and that it interacts with consumers' state of mind. Here, marketers have predominantly concentrated on the heavy half, the heavy users of the product. In many markets, the so-called 80-20 rule applies, according to which 80 percent of market consumption comes from only 20 percent of the consumers. Sensitivity to factors of the marketing mix has been shown to vary significantly with product use. In sport, we have long been cognizant of the various usage patterns (e.g., the season-ticket holder versus the individual-game ticket purchaser). This point is true across most sports, for players and fans alike. Research on the women's 1990s golf market, for example, showed that occasional golfers (1 to 7 rounds per year) made up over 50 percent of all the golfers but accounted for only 12 percent of the total rounds played. Meanwhile, avid golfers (25 or more rounds per year) accounted for 64 percent of the total rounds played. Along similar lines (table 5.3), the "light" fan segment of one MLB club made up an estimated 43 percent of 1990 total attendees (unique people attending), but only 19 percent of total tickets sold. "Heavy"

TABLE 5.3   User Segments and Estimated Attendance Effect on a Major League Baseball Club—1976, 1990

Segment	Number of games	Year	Percentage of people	Estimated percentage of attendance
Heavy	11 or more	1976	4.2	20.4
		1990	14.4	29.6
Medium	3–10	1976	29.4	45.5
		1990	42.7	51.1
Light	1–2	1976	66.4	34.1
		1990	42.9	19.3

fans accounted for only 14.4 percent of the attendees but almost 30 percent of typical tickets sold. In the NBA, suite, club, and season-ticket holders account for just over 60 percent of all tickets sold but over 80 percent of team ticket revenue. Whether the sport is basketball, golf, tennis, or weightlifting, the heavy-half rule seems to apply.[35]

Table 5.3 also illustrates how a baseball club shifted from a reliance on light users in 1976 to a distribution more weighted toward heavy and medium users. In effect, this club had moved fans up the escalator of involvement. Although heavy users may return greater immediate dividends, the sport marketer must aim to satisfy the needs of each group as much as possible to ensure a steady stream of light, medium, and heavy users, because the light user of today may be the medium user of tomorrow and the heavy user of next year. Chapters 8 and 10 address the need for special promotions for different user groups. For instance, special groups may fit into the category of light users, but they have special needs and interests. Many have particular interests in some charitable cause (fund-raising), seating in a special area, or special recognition on the scoreboard. The smartest marketers offer a full menu of group benefits and fan experience packages (FEPs).

Several summary points about usage segmentation demand emphasis:

- Not all consumers consume at the same rate.
- Levels of consumption (e.g., heavy, medium, and light) vary from sport to sport, so the relative importance of usage rates (in terms of total attendance or participation) differs from sport to sport.

- Levels of consumption are likely to vary from age group to age group. Thus, sport spectatorship and consumption show a life cycle pattern. For any given set of consumers, levels of consumption are likely to vary by other variables (state of being, state of mind, benefits).
- The sport marketer needs to maintain opportunities for consumers to consume at many usage levels. That is, the marketer should not depend too heavily on season-ticket sales and thus exclude the occasional user. This latter problem is well known to the Boston Bruins, who were sold out for many years in the 1970s, primarily through season-ticket sales. After Bobby Orr left the club in 1976 and fan interest declined, no light users and few medium users were on hand to replace the defecting season-ticket holders.
- An increase in sales volume is much more likely to be generated by increased frequency or a higher consumption rate of existing users than it is from an increase in sales to first-time users.

Sport organizations should also conceptualize (and segment) use in terms of breadth of activities. In this case, the notion of a heavy user should include the number of different activities as well as the frequency of participation. Marketers could develop a grid to visualize segmentation along the dimensions of breadth and frequency. Internal marketing data can be placed within the grid. Figure 5.1 provides a sample grid for a hypothetical Boston Bruins fan base. Only three cells are filled in here, but the concept of such a grid is the important point. Specific group names are not crucial, but as seen in tables 5.4 and 5.5, they are sometimes used as shorthand. For instance, "Captains" are clearly committed in breadth and frequency; they are the hard-core fans. On the opposite end, "Cubs" represent the bottom of the involved fan base. They are highly prone to falling off the escalator and may well turn their attention to another sport before they even attend a game. Such a frequency and breadth grid with all the cells filled in would provide the basis for

Breadth \ Frequency	High frequency (>10 times/month)	Medium frequency (5-9 times/month)	Low frequency (1-4 times/month)
High breadth (>3 activities)	"Captains": read game stories daily; attend five games/month; buy programs; watch all away games on TV		
Medium breadth (2-3 activities)		"Growlers": Share miniplan; wear Bruins hat; watch weekly telecast	
Low breadth (1 activity)			"Cubs": Watch big game on TV

FIGURE 5.1   Sample frequency and breadth grid for Bruins fans.

TABLE 5.4   User Segments Identified by the PGAA

Name	Percentage of golfers	Average household income ($)	Rounds per year	Amount spent per year ($)	Sex
Dilettantes	27	64,200	16	1,100	M
Tank tops	17	36,700	13	570	M
Pull carts	15	32,200	32	1,400	M
Public pundits	13	50,600	52	2,000	M
Junior league	13	57,800	24	1,600	W
Country clubber	9	77,300	69	4,400	M
Swingin' seniors	6	31,300	42	1,600	W

Data from *American Demographics* 1995.

TABLE 5.5   National Thoroughbred Racing Association User Groups

Name	Frequency and breadth	Number
Core	Handicappers who know the sport and bet five or more times per year	3 million
Light	Love social aspects more than the sport and bet fewer than five times per year	28 million
Socialites	Mostly female who love the track atmosphere but do not bet	9 million
TV fans	Mostly female, do not attend track, do not bet	33 million

Data from L. Mullen, 1999 "Demographics survey surprises NTRA," *Street & Smith's SportsBusiness Journal* pg. 7.

promotional campaigns. Indeed, a strategy that aims for breadth of activities may provide the club with a buffer to prevent members from becoming bored and burned out and thus from defecting.

Tables 5.4 and 5.5 present similar user groupings developed by the National Thoroughbred Racing Association and the Professional Golfers' Association of America. The point is that users can be conceptualized along the lines of frequency and breadth to create targets for separate marketing plans.

Integrated Segmentation Strategies and Tactics

As noted earlier, our divisions of segmentation—state of being, state of mind, benefits, and usage—are simply organizational conveniences. Sport marketers must recognize that successful marketing plans will typically require the integration of these divisions. For instance, the PGAA user groupings outlined in table 5.4 link rounds played (usage) with household income (state of being). And, as most organizations with an extensive database know, certain geographic areas may have a higher proportion of avid fans than other areas, related to proximity, income, or some other demographic or lifestyle variable.

Today's myriad cable networks often represent particular clusters of demographic and psychographic consumer segments. This development has encouraged new integrated advertising strategies. For instance, when the TNT network looked to promote Steven Spielberg's spring 2005 miniseries *Into the West*, it developed an integrated strategy that recognized a division of the target audience into six separate segments—history lovers, family saga watchers, action seekers, truth seekers, western lovers, and Generation Y—each of which represented a slightly different combination of age, gender, and television viewing habits. TNT's research also demonstrated that each of the segments was prone to particular media habits, so rather than run the same advertisement across a number of different media outlets, TNT developed separate ads for each target audience. Ads that focused on the Battle of Wounded Knee or the gold rush were placed on the History Channel and on a wrapper cover of *National Geographic*. Ads that accentuated the multigenerational drama of several families

were placed on the finale of *Desperate Housewives* and in *People* magazine.[36]

The Miami Heat are even more sophisticated. With financial support from the NBA, the Heat developed a database of some 700,000 entries containing data on age, income, zip code, lifestyle and consumption patterns, and website activity, among other variables. The Heat used e-mail campaigns to reach targeted clusters in the database. For instance, when 150 season-ticket blocks were shifted from group to individual sales, the Heat quickly identified a cluster of names that fit a particular profile of income, residence, and past purchase behavior. Targeted e-mail campaigns have thus replaced cold calls, print, and broadcast advertisements as the primary method of introducing an offer with a dramatic increase in return. During the 2004–2005 season the Heat received almost $11 in revenue for every dollar spent on database research and staff.[37]

In similar fashion, the Aspire Group has developed its own version of this highly segmented "intelligent marketing" approach that it calls "24:48:48—capture, communicate, close." The *24:48:48* stands for capturing essential fan contact data (first and last names, zip code, and mobile phone number) within 24 hours of a fan's contact with the sport property (buying or using a ticket, buying merchandise, visiting the website, completing an enter-to-win ballot, and so on). The data is then entered into the DBM–CRM system, run through data hygiene filters (cleaned and de-duplicated), and checked against purchase history. If the property has purchased data append capabilities (Axicon, PersonicX, and so on) or has data-mining capabilities such as Ticketmaster's live analytics suite, then these data can be scored for propensity to buy in the future. The more sophisticated web analytic tools permit people to be assigned a core to identify their probability to buy various ticket or hospitality packages. Most models of predictability use the RFM method (R = regency of last purchase; F = frequency of the customer's purchases; and M = monetary value of how much the customer spends). The RFM method indicates the lifetime asset value (LAV) of the fan and the likely responsiveness to an offer.

After the data have been stored, the customer or prospect is automatically or manually assigned to a specific segment or cohort. Examples of segments are those most likely to buy season tickets or those most likely to buy an individual game ticket offer, such as a modern family plan (starting with the purchase of just two tickets, two meals, and two drinks rather than the typical four, four, and four offering).

After the prospect has been assigned to a segment and matched with the most appropriate offer, the next stage is communicating, which is to be done within 48 hours of data capture. Again, if the sport property has sophisticated analytic tools, the consumer's or prospect's preferred method of communication can be used (e-mail, text, direct mail) or the offer can be posted on a social network site (Facebook, Twitter, and so on). If these tools are not in place, the property should e-mail the offer if they have an e-mail address, text the offer if they have a mobile phone number, or do both in some cases.

The final stage of Aspire's intelligent marketing approach that relies heavily on effective segmentation is to use a personal touch—an outbound call from one of their staff in their Fan Relationship Management Centers (FRMC). The close stage ideally needs to occur within 48 hours of the consumer's or prospect's receipt of the offer. Those who responded to the e-mail or text offer by purchasing receive a thank-you call. The sales consultant uses the opportunity to learn more about the customer and then, by identifying the customer's needs, tries to up-sell the fan, when appropriate, into buying more tickets, more benefits, or a more expensive seating location. Those prospects who opened the e-mail or text are treated as qualified prospects and also receive a phone call from an FRMC staff member, who again attempts to build a deeper understanding and a better relationship, gathers data about what the fan really wants, and attempts to make a sale. Those prospects who did not open the e-mail or text receive a retargeting e-mail or text with a different offer, or the same offer in a different format or style or a different message, to see whether they are interested enough to open the communication.

Although the efforts of TNT, the Heat, and the Aspire Group can be more expensive than many sport organizations can afford, the principle of developing a consumer database (see chapter 4) that contains demographic, psychographic, lifestyle, and product usage data may be applied at any budget level. Data analysis may identify consumer clusters or segments that are accessible

and responsive to marketing plans. Sport marketing researchers have already developed survey instruments that measure lifestyle characteristics related to game attendance in professional ice hockey and basketball. These could be adapted for use in other sports. Identified clusters of fans could then be sent special electronic advertisements or promotional offers by e-mail, text, or direct mail, or the offer could be posted on appropriate social networks and Internet sites.[38]

ACTIVITY 5.3 Product-Usage Segmentation

In this WSG activity, you will explore how the Professional Golfers' Association uses product-usage segmentation to establish and elevate the standards of the profession and to grow interest and participation in the game of golf.

Wrap-Up

Segmentation is truly central to the notion of knowing the sport property's consumers, because segmentation recognizes that consumers vary along a number of dimensions that the marketer may use to form the basis of specialized strategies. Therefore, the sport property's database system should be keyed in to the notion of segmentation, and research should examine the possible bases for meaningful segmentation of the marketplace. Whether segmentation makes the most sense in terms of psychographics, demographics, usage, benefits, or some combination depends on the marketer's knowledge of and feel for the market. Indeed, it makes sense to pursue a relational approach to segmentation. That is, consumer segments distinguished by benefits sought should be evaluated for any internal homogeneity in demographics, psychographics, or usage. Discoveries of such relationships will provide fruitful insight for improved communication with such target segments. An example of such combined segmentation might be the targeting of a fan in a sport property's database who has purchased multiple individual game tickets in the past, has a six-figure income, and lives in a prime zip code for season-ticket purchases. This fan could be sent an offer to purchase a premium club seat or high-end package hospitality offer. In any case, the decision maker must recognize that people can and must be distinguished from one another. Whether the business is pro basketball, high school lacrosse, or public parks and recreation programs, it is hard to consider any plan a marketing plan if it doesn't incorporate some aspect of segmentation.

Activities

1. Define segmentation. Describe the differences among segment identification, segment access, and segment responsiveness. Think of examples in the sport world of segments that might be identifiable but not accessible or responsive.

2. What are the basic components of state-of-being segmentation? Give examples of the state-of-being segments most important to your local college women's basketball team.

3. Define state-of-mind segmentation. Try to find an ad for a sport product or team that appeals to a state-of-mind segment.

4. Explain why the heavy-user segment is important to sport marketers. Use table 5.3 to explain.

5. How would you relate the notion of benefits segmentation to the discussion of motivation in chapter 3? List and compare the benefits of attending an MLB game and playing golf at the nearest public golf course.

6. How would you set up a segmentation plan for your favorite sport property and match each segment to a unique or customized product or ticket package offering?

Your Marketing Plan

Can you define the core benefits of your products? Will any of these benefits link to consumer segments defined by demographics, psychographics, or product usage? You should begin to clarify, at the least, the product usage segments in your consumer base. Try to fill in a frequency and breadth grid for your consumer base. Use figure 5.1 as a guide. Then use your answer to question 6 to detail your specific market segmentation plan and match each segment with the most relevant product offering.

Endnotes

1. For more on the LPGA clinics, see www.lpgagolf-clinicsforwomen.com/; K. McCabe, "Lowering a Gender Handicap," *Boston Sunday Globe*, 27 July 1997, C-1, C-4; "Women Golfers: By the Numbers," *Golf Market Today*, September–October 1998, 4; Jolee Edmondson, "Queen of Clubs," *Sky*, March 1999, 59. The authors thank Melanie Bedrosian of the Jane Blalock Company for research assistance on this vignette.

2. On the notion of global marketing, see T. Levitt, *The Marketing Imagination* (New York: Free Press, 1984).

3. For a general discussion, see P. Kotler and K. Keller, *Marketing Management*, 12th ed. (Upper Saddle River, NJ: Prentice Hall, 2005), chapter 8, "Identifying Market Segments and Targets."

4. P. Kotler, *Marketing Management*, 9th ed. (Upper Saddle River, NJ: Prentice Hall, 1997), 251; S. Ruibal, "Horwath Seeks Niche for Snow Skating," *USA Today*, 31 January 1997, 2C; G. Milne, W. Sutton, and M. McDonald, "Niche Analysis: A Strategic Measurement Tool for Sport Managers," *SMQ*, 5 (3) (29 September 1996): 15–22; Martin Kaufmann, "Small Sports Dream Big Despite Woes," *SSSBJ*, 18–24 March 2002, 19, 24.

5. www.burton.com/company; Marvin Bynum, "Target Audience," *Athletic Business*, September 2004, 40.

6. See www.claritas.com.

7. Langdon Brockinton, "Miami May Look to Lure Far-Off Fans," *SSSBJ*, 22–28 October 2001, 9; L. Mullen, "Chargers' New Campaign Will Test Drawing Power in LA," *SSSBJ*, 6–12 July 1998, 13; M. Levine, *Making Marketing Research Hustle: The Essential Sweat of Attendance Building and Fund Raising* (paper presented at the annual Athletic

Business Conference, Las Vegas, NV, December 1987).

8. Ross Kerber, "Sox, Yanks Fight for Conn. Viewers," *Boston Globe*, 6 August 2003, A-1, B-8.

9. Andrew Grossman, "Where Have All the Young Viewers Gone?" *SSSBJ*, 22–28 November 2004, 8; Bill King, "Where The Teens Are," *SSSBJ*, 20–26 February 2006, 17–24; Bill King, "Reaching the 18–34 Demo," *SSSBJ*, 17–24 April 2006, 1, 19–26.

10. Sean Brenner, "Reaching Tomorrow's Fans," *SSSBJ*, 13–19 September 2004, 19–23.

11. C. Cox, "Rock 'n' Bowl," *Boston Herald*, 20 August 1997, 37; www.newyorkjets.com/community.

12. "NASCAR Targets Kids, but Must Dance Around RJR's Sponsorship," *SBD*, 22 May 1998, 7.

13. J. Rude, "Making the Mature Decision," *Athletic Business*, January 1998, 31–37.

14. Tim Mask, "Gen Y a Gold Mine for Marketers Who Dig It," *SSSBJ*, 12–18 August 2002, 29; Gregg Bennet, Robin Henson, and James Zhang, "Generation Y's Perceptions of the Action Sports Industry Segment," *Journal of Sport Management*, 17 (2003): 95–115; D. Turco, "The X Factor: Marketing to Generation X," *SMQ*, 5 (1) (March 1996): 21–26; Christopher Palmeri and David Kiley, "In Hot Pursuit of Yoga Mama," *BusinessWeek*, 7 November 2005, 128–130.

15. Ross Nethery, "Watching and Waiting," *SSSBJ*, 23–29 August 2004, 22; "Who the Fans Are," *SSSBJ*, 9–15 December 2002, 26.

16. Harry Hurt, III, "Sure, It's Not Bowling, but Polo Is Catching On," *New York Times Sunday*, 22 August 2004, BU-9; M. Babineck, "Ralph Lauren's Firm Sues Magazine to Drop Polo Name," *Boston Globe*, 27 May 1998, C-3.

17. "Fan Breakdowns," *SSSBJ*, 16–22 June 2003, 24.

18. Andy Bernstein, "Do Sports Market to the Right Sex?" *SSSBJ*, 2–8 November 1998, 44; T. Cassidy, "Football 101," *Boston Sunday Globe*, 26 October 1997, C-1, C-11; N. Kapsambelis, "Football 101," *Foster's Sunday Citizen*, 16 November 1997, 9B; "On and Off the Road with Barack Obama", David Remnick. www.newyorker.com, January 22, 2014.

19. "Judge rejects initial $765M NFL concussion lawsuit settlement." Will Brinson, January 14, 2014.   www.cbssports.com/nfl/eye-on-football/24409040/judge-rejects-initial-765m-nfl-concussion-lawsuit-settlement

20. S. Hardy, "Profile/Interview With Donna Lopiano," *SMQ*, 5 (4) (December 1996): 5–8; Galen Trail, Dean Anderson, and Janet Fink, "Examination of Gender Differences in Importance of and Satisfaction With Venue Factors at Intercollegiate Basketball Games," *International Sports Journal*, 6 (Winter 2002): 51–64.

21. Grant Wahl, "Rebound Attempt," *Sports Illustrated*, 29 March 2004, 34.

22. "Gay in Sports: A Poll," *Sports Illustrated*, 18 April 2005, 64; "Dodgers Apologize," *SBD*, 24 August 2000, 10; "Debate Over Marketing to Alternative Lifestyles Continues," *SBD*, 15 May 2001, 18; "Sparks' Alterative Marketing Effort," *SBD*, 15 June 2001, 18; "WNBA Teams' Marketing Toward Lesbians Continues to Draw Reax," *SBD*, 2 August 2001, 17; Tom Weir, "WNBA Sells Diversity Marketing, Recognizes Lesbian Fans," *USA Today*, 24 July 2001, 1-C; H. Kahan and D. Mulryan, "Out of the Closet," *American Demographics*, May 1995, 40–47.

23. Daniel Kaplan, "Tennis Courting Irrelevance," *SSSBJ*, 26 August–1 September 2002, 22; "NBA Fan Demographics," *SSSBJ*, 29 December 2004, 41. Ketra Armstrong is the leading researcher on African American sport consumers. See, for example, "An Examination of the Social Psychology of Blacks' Consumption of Sport," *Journal of Sport Management*, 16 (2000): 267–288.

24. Cindy Rodriguez, "At Fenway, It's Fiesta Time," *Boston Globe*, 6 June 2001, A-1, A-11; Scott Warfield, "MLS' Grassroots Tournament Grows by 58%," *SSSBJ*, 27 September–2 October 2004, 6.

25. K. Armstrong, "Ten Strategies to Employ When Marketing Sport to Black Consumers," *SMQ*, 7 (3) (September 1998): 11–19; L. McCarthy, "Marketing Sport to Hispanic Consumers," *SMQ*, 7 (4) (December 1998): 19–24.

26. R. Desloge, "Cards Make Pitch for Blacks," *SSSBJ*, 18–24 May 1998, 9; Tom Cordova, "Building a Diverse Network of Suppliers Can Pay Big Dividends," *SSSBJ*, 12–18 September 2005, 29.

27. "USA Today Looks at MLS' Target Marketing of Ethnic Groups," *SBD*, 3 March 1998, 9; Sean Brenner, "A World of Opportunity," *SSSBJ*, 31 May–6 June 2004, 16.

28. Announcement in *SSSBJ*, 6–12 July 1998, 15.

29. Information on VALS may be found at www.strategicbusinessinsights.com/. For information on discovery segmentation, see R. Piirto, "Cable TV," *American Demographics*, June 1995, 40–47.

30. Galen Trail et al., "Motives and Points of Attachment: Fans Versus Spectators in Intercollegiate Athletics," *SMQ*, 12 (4) (2003): 217–230; Daniel Mahony, Robert Madrigal, and Dennis Howard, "Using the Psychological Commitment to Team (PCT) Scale to Segment Sport Consumers Based on Loyalty," *SMQ*, 9 (1) (2000): 15–25.

31. A. Bernstein, "MLS Narrows Its Aim to Game's Core Fans," *SSSBJ*, 15–21 November 1999, 4.

32. J. Seabrook, "Tackling the Competition," *New Yorker*, 18 (August 1997): 42–51.

33. WNBA fan data at http://aol.wnba.com/about_us/historyof_wnba.html; John Lombardo, "WNBA Looks for Answers to Attendance Dip," *SSSBJ*, 5–11 September 2005, 7; NCAA data from "NCAA Study Shows Extent of Basketball's Popularity," *NCAA News*, 30 March 1998, 1, 17. For information on women's team fans, see D. Antonelli, "Marketing Intercollegiate Women's Basketball," *SMQ*, 3 (2) (June 1994): 29–33; S. Hardy, "Profile/Interview With Donna Lopiano."

34. André Richelieu and Frank Pons, "Reconciling Managers' Strategic Vision With Fans' Expectations," *International Journal of Sports Marketing and Sponsorship*, 6 (3) (April, 2005): 150–163.

35. M. Nowell, "The Women's Golf Market," *SMQ*, 4 (2) (June 1995): 40. See also the excellent usage segmentation analysis in D. Howard, "Participation Rates in Selected Sport and Fitness Activities," *Journal of Sport Management*, 6 (September 1992): 191–205.

36. Joanna Weiss, "TV Marketers Seek Audience With You," *Boston Globe*, 10 June 2005, D-1, D-4. For a valuable review of research on consumer categories, see Bob Stewart, Aaron Smith, and Matthew Nicholson, "Sport Consumer Typologies: A Critical Review," *SMQ*, 12 (4) (2003): 206–216.

37. John Lombardo, "A Whole New Ball Game in South Florida," *SSSBJ*, 28 March–3 April 2005, 1, 38–39.

38. James Zhang et al., "Understanding Women's Professional Basketball Game Spectators: Socio-demographics, Game Consumption, and Entertainment Options," *SMQ*, 12 (4) (2003): 228–38. For a valuable orientation to "nested" segments, see Mick Jackowski and Dianna Gray, "SportNEST: A Nested Approach to Segmenting the Sport Consumer Market," in *Sport Marketing and the Psychology of Marketing Communication*, eds. Lynn Kahle and Chris Riley (Mahwah, NJ: Erlbaum, 2004), 271–292.

Chapter 6
The Sport Product

OBJECTIVES

- To recognize the elements of the sport product that contribute to its uniqueness in the wider marketplace of goods and services

- To learn the process involved in product development as well as its relation to the concept of the product life cycle

- To understand product positioning, product image, and product branding, and their roles in successful sport marketing

In March 2011 the Maryland Jockey Club introduced the public to a new mascot that they hoped would drive interest in the Preakness, the second leg of American horse racing's Triple Crown. The industry overall had been in the doldrums for over a decade. The national Jockey Club had stopped reporting nationwide attendance in 1993. Everyone seemed to agree on the need to lure a younger demographic to the track. Their efforts had included forming the National Thoroughbred Racing Association, whose first promotional campaign had used the theme "Go Baby Go." The Maryland Jockey Club was taking things a step further with a huge festival on the large infield inside the actual racetrack. Infield Fest looked to bring the buzz back to infield partying, which had collapsed when the Preakness banned BYOB a few years earlier.

Chief buzz-maker was a new mascot named Kegasus, a CGI character described in the *Baltimore Sun* as a "party manimal . . . a centaur with a nipple ring, body hair and ample beer gut," who would appear in various media spots promoting Infield Fest. Kegasus' mission, said the *Sun*, was "reassuring young people that this year's infield festivities will indeed be rowdy, raunchy and booze-soaked." The play on Pegasus, the mythical centaur, was telling. Kegasus was a figure right out of contemporary feature films like *BeerFest* and *Old School*. He was a clear signal that the Jockey Club wanted and needed a younger generation. If thoroughbred horses didn't attract them, a massive good time would. As Jockey Club president Tom Chuckas responded, "We have never hidden the fact that we want people to come to the infield and party."[1]

The infield has always been part of horse racing, a place for both watching and partying, a place that combined tailgating with standing-room tickets. As with much of the sport and entertainment mix over the last decade, however, the sizzle had been elevated a few decibels. The United States Naval Academy Glee Club represented the old infield atmosphere at the Preakness (although they had been performing only since the late 1990s). They would not be

> *continued*

As noted before, any sport product is best understood as a bundle of benefits. Like countless organizations, the Baltimore Jockey Club was tinkering with their bundle in hopes that it would attract a wider audience. In this chapter we review the elements that make the sport product unique. These items include the core event, the ticket, the organization, the facility, and equipment and apparel, to name a few. We discuss the intricacies of developing products, including the concepts of line, item, and mix; issues in launching new products; and the product life cycle. We also introduce positioning and branding, the most critical parts of contemporary product development. Chapter 7 will dig much deeper into branding.

What Is the Sport Product?

The sport product is a complex package of the tangible and the intangible. When you hear the word *golf*, you think of little dimpled balls and oversized metal "woods" that are, in different ways, standardized. They are tangible elements of the golf product. But the golf experience is hardly standardized: It can be total frustration for the occasional duffer and total infatuation for the addict. It is no different in any other sport, because all sports depend on human performance—by the players, the fans, and the marketers. As we discussed in chapter 1, this makes the marketer's job challenging in several respects.[4]

• **The sport product is inconsistent from consumption to consumption.** As Fox Sports president David Hill concluded, "If there's one great thing about sports, it's that it's unscripted. And the guy in the white hat doesn't always get to kiss the horse. Sports is the last frontier of reality in television." Part of the inconsistency stems from the sensual and emotional nature of involvement. Every game, every event is a unique mix of touch, smell, taste, sight, and sound. For the fan or the player, it is the uncertainty and the spontaneity of the sport product that make it the headliners at Infield Fest. That honor would be saved for rapper Wiz Khalifa, Grammy winners Maroon 5, and other hipper bands who would rock on the Beer Garden Jagermeister Stage. Loud music would be complemented by a bikini contest, professional beach volleyball, and a cornhole competition tent—all washed down with copious quantities of beer. Infield Fest was to be spring break and Octoberfest rolled inside a great horse race. As one media analyst put it, "They're not talking to the ladies with the big flowered hats in the grandstand."[2]

The Baltimore Jockey Club was trying to reposition the Preakness to make it more attractive to a younger audience. Product repositioning can be difficult, and this situation was no different, especially the use of Kegasus. Baltimore's health commissioner complained that "the star of the show isn't the beautiful horses, or the determined jockeys who ride them to glory. Instead, we're given Kegasus, a centaur who loves to party. Really? Why not Barney from the Simpsons, or other media symbols of alcohol overindulgence that appeal largely to adolescent boys?" The Jockey Club held fast. Kegasus and Infield Fest were credited with increasing infield attendance by 8,000 at the 2011 Preakness. Tom Chuckas announced the centaur's return for 2012: "We experienced one of the most successful Infield Fests in history last year and are certain that Kegasus brought the spirit of fun and energy tailored toward a younger demographic." The festival, he added, was "just one of the many components" that make the Preakness "as magical as it is." Kegasus did not return in 2013. But Tom Chuckas could take heart in the fact that overall attendance at Pimlico Race Course was up for the fourth straight year, and ticket sales for the Preakness were 10 percent above 2012. Still, Infield Fest and its success raised a question posed a few years earlier by Peter Land, a marketing executive who had worked with the Breeders Cup: "Do you market to your core audience, people who are already going to the track, or to a younger demographic who are choosing between several entertainment options? Or go somewhere in the middle?" As the Kegasus story suggests, knowing how to adjust and reposition the product and its components is an ongoing challenge.[3]

attractive. As Rick Jones of the GEM Group put it, the consumer, not the marketer, is in control of the final experience.[5]

- **The core game or performance is just one element of a larger ensemble.** Players and fans rarely consume the game, event, or contest in isolation. The sport experience includes the atmosphere of the venue, the equipment, the apparel, the music, the concessions, the pre- and postgame festival, and the in-game entertainment (see the later section on game presentation). All these elements extend the sport product beyond the contest itself, for players and fans alike. In some cases, the contest is almost secondary. Satellite television and the Internet, with their instantaneous, worldwide reach, have prompted an increase in sport events that exist less for their intrinsic value and more for their ability to deliver product extensions. One industry executive expressed the widespread belief that more events would "be created purely to sell specific brands and products such as shoes and apparel. Events

will be the integrated marketing sales engine of the future." A casual look at the Olympics, the Super Bowl, or the X Games suggests that this future has been slowly arriving for some time.[6]

- **The marketer typically has little control over the core product and consequently must focus efforts on product extensions.** In the new millennium, Real Madrid of Spain's La Liga fashioned a strategy that leveraged the core product (soccer games) to generate product extensions. The team broke world transfer (purchase-price) records in buying the contracts of star players like Luis Figo, Zinedine Zidane, and David Beckham. Although Real Madrid expected to win games with its all-star cast, the team was even more confident that it would expand its global sales of merchandise and sponsorships. And although the stars and the team stumbled, failing to win a major trophy in 2004, a study by the Harvard Business School certified the success of the strategy. By 2004 ancillary revenue was expected to double from its 2001 mark. Marketers cannot control the contest, especially the winning and losing. But it is worth repeating Don Canham's decades-old wisdom: "We do not market that Michigan football is number 1, because next year we may not be! Instead we market a fall weekend in Ann Arbor." In sport marketing, winning can never be the only thing![7]

Questions always arise in developing a product. Many professional teams have partnered with state lotteries to create sports "games." But how does that action align with continual league positions against gambling? Although playing a scratch card is not quite the same as betting on a point spread, it is still gambling. Likewise, should a college marketer, looking to juice the entertainment package, pursue a deal with an auto body shop that wants to sponsor the toughest collision at each home hockey game? This idea sounds innocent enough, but what if it prompts fans to cheer loudest at each hit, no matter how vicious or illegal? And what if the sponsor runs newspaper and television promos that juxtapose pictures of tough hockey hits and auto wrecks? What is the message to fans? What is the message to families who have lost children in vehicular collisions? We

go back to three of Laura Nash's questions in her article "Ethics Without the Sermon":

- What is your intention?
- How does this intention compare with probable results?
- What is the symbolic potential of your action if understood? If misunderstood?

Ethics require both principles and common sense, as do marketing and maintaining sport products with enduring value.[8]

The Sport Product: Its Core and Extensions

As figure 6.1 suggests, the sport product is both an integrated ensemble and a bunch of components with lives of their own. At the core is the event experience, or the game presentation, composed of six components:

- Game form (rules and techniques)
- Players (star power)

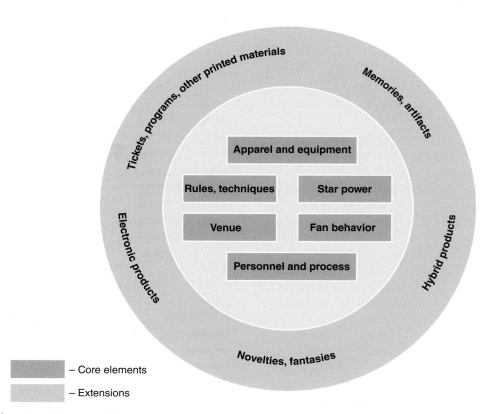

FIGURE 6.1   Core elements of the sport product and a sample of extensions.

- Fan behavior
- Equipment and apparel
- Venue
- Personnel and process

Game Presentation: Core Product

Whether we consider a friendly game of three on three on a hot asphalt court or a Memphis Grizzlies game in the lush surroundings of the FedExForum, we will find the common features of game, players, equipment, fan behavior, personnel, and venue. Everything else builds on those components. Take the game of golf. Although the duffer has a different experience from the scratch golfer, the particular nature of rules and techniques, equipment, and venue joins the two players and distinguishes golf from tennis. Moreover, it is the playing out of rules and techniques, equipment, and venue that makes sport products distinct from all other products.

As figure 6.1 also suggests, the event experience may include an abundance of extensions. Several elements move us from the playground to the FedExForum: tickets, luxury boxes, programs, video, music, memorabilia, and mascots. An extension is simply a product component that enhances the value (and often the price) of an event experience. At the same time, any product component—from the player to the mascot—can also become a product extension, with a life (and sales) beyond an event or even a season of events.

Teams, schools, colleges, clubs, and leagues are the entities that commonly prepare and sell the experience. But at least one company, Fandeavor, saw a market in helping universities package and sell product elements as commodities. The trick is packaging components to fit customer desires. A ticket is a given, but then what? A handshake with the head coach? Sideline access? A tour? Postgame meet and greet with some players? Fandeavor CEO Tom Ellingson said, "You have to understand what the fan wants, and how the experience at [one school] might be different than the experience at [another]." This is a marketer's philosophy that the smart athletics director or club executive should embrace.[9]

Combining all elements on game night is an art and science called game presentation. At the top levels of sport the supplements sometimes outweigh the game itself, at least in terms of time. For instance, in 2009 the *Boston Globe* examined the overall presentation of a February Celtics–Lakers game. The games don't get much bigger in the NBA. The event itself ran from 7:45 to 11:11 p.m.—a total of 207 minutes. Of that total, 83 minutes were actual game time when players were on the court. The other 124 minutes were pregame show, halftime show, and timeouts with other entertainment, which included cheerleader dances, special on-court promotions, over 300 crowd shots, fan contests, and game-action replays on the Jumbotron, as well as 125 pieces of music. All this took place at high decibel levels and was prepared according to a 75-page event script, executed by a staff both on the floor and in the ninth-floor control room, where 41 monitors demanded attention. Said Celtics director of game presentation Sean Sullivan, "Trying to keep track of everything going on is like air traffic control." But the payoff was huge. Surveys showed that 92 percent of all attendees were "satisfied or extremely satisfied with game presentation," and 70 percent said that they would "likely" return "*because of* game presentation" (our emphasis).[10]

Some high school and college administrators worry that fans, especially those familiar with all the promotions and giveaways at professional events, will expect the same at the grassroots level. Deidre Jones, sports information director at Jackson State, put it this way, "When people come to the game, they expect to get something for free. If we don't do something, I hear about it. . . . It is eclipsing the game somewhat for a smaller school. . . . I think people are going to get so caught up in the entertainment that they're going to overlook the actual talent of the athletes." Ohio State's Dave Brown, past president of the National Association of Collegiate Marketing Administrators, played on an old hockey joke to capture the conundrum: "I went to a concert and a baseball game happened." Ultimately, the answer at any level involves a return to core mission and strategy (as discussed in chapter 2).[11]

The game presentation, the core product, is made up of the following elements.

Game Form: Rules and Techniques

Each sport has unique special features that may make it especially attractive to certain consumers. For instance, basketball has speed, agility, physical contact, power, and grace. If James Naismith, who invented the game in 1891, could see the San Antonio Spurs play today, he would be surprised at the radical changes in his product. Senda Berenson, who quickly adapted Naismith's game for women, would be even more surprised at a WNBA game. Of course, game forms change all the time. Players invent new moves, and rules committees tinker with this or that as they work to balance offense and defense. Three classic basketball examples are the 24-second shot clock, the three-point line, and the goaltending rule.

We might argue that changes in rules and techniques are comparable with design changes in any consumer product, sort of like making a tastier, low-fat potato chip or a faster computer chip. Changes are made to satisfy consumer wants and needs. American college football's rules committee first allowed forward passing in 1906, clearly concerned with public opinion about the deadly nature of the "mass" game. Likewise, American League owners approved baseball's designated hitter rule in 1973 in an effort to jack interest and attendance; National League owners, with higher average attendance and more new ballparks, felt no such urgency.

Star Power: Players, Coaches, and Owners

The most memorable event experiences build drama from the playing surface outward. Players and coaches are the keys, as all successful promoters have learned. The architects of the golden age of American sport in the 1920s (e.g., Tex Rickard) recognized the need to accentuate the struggles of hero against villain or mind against muscle. Their strategy was simple—star power. Babe Ruth, Jack Dempsey, Helen Wills—these are names we remember and associate with that fabulous era.

In some respects, things have not changed much; the drama of sport still requires star power. On the other hand, today's players and coaches are extended beyond the event far more than their predecessors were. Players still provide most of the script in sport. They can make or break teams and leagues. The great Pelé is a good example. Before he signed with the New York Cosmos of the North American Soccer League, the team averaged 5,000 fans per game at Randall Island. With Pelé, the team moved to Giants Stadium and

Helen Wills was a star athlete during the golden age of American sport. She competed in the 1924 Olympics in Paris where she and doubles partner, Hazel Wightman, won the gold medal.

drew over 50,000 on a regular basis. In recent history, American youth soccer phenom Freddy Adu signed a $2 million, four-year contract with Major League Soccer in 2004, purportedly the league's biggest contract ever. No matter that Adu was only 14 years old. Nike had already signed him to a two-year, S1 million deal. And even if Adu was never an impact player on the field, he was credited with boosting league-wide attendance over 4 percent. In some cases, his presence doubled attendance at rival venues. Pundits called it the Freddy Factor or the Freddy Effect.[12]

Something called the Q-score attempts to measure the American public's embrace of celebrity figures. As Terry Lefton explained, "Hundreds of millions of advertising decisions are predicated" on the annual Q-score reports, one of which is specific to sport. Marketing Evaluations Inc. annually surveys several thousand 12- to 64-year-olds in a national probability sample. Respondents rate over 500 sport figures along scales such as "never seen or heard of" or "one of my favorites." The big news for 2012 was the rise of Tim Tebow from a recognition rate of 62 percent to 80 percent, a score that put him in company with LeBron James and David Beckham.[13]

Coaches and owners can also be stars and fundamental parts of a product. For instance, John Madden ranked above Tebow in the 2012 Q rating. When many people think of the NFL, they still think of John Madden. Bill Parcells had similar stature. When he left New England for the New York Jets, Parcells' presence alone helped boost ad sales 20 percent for televised Jets games. He generated similar enthusiasm when he went to Dallas. Then there are the owners; just think of George Steinbrenner and the New York Yankees. For three decades the names and the images have gone hand in hand. A popular and effective owner like the NFL's Robert Kraft or the NBA's Mark Cuban can be a positive brand attribute.[14]

Over the last five decades, athletes have felt more empowered to take antiestablishment positions (see the sidebar on Chinese athletes). And the media have felt more comfortable exposing bad behavior, especially if it was criminal. Although neither agents nor teams can control all elements of players' or coaches' performances or behavior, the last decade has seen greater efforts to enhance their interpersonal skills and their product value. One example was the Corel WTA Tour and the United States Tennis Association, which promoted a media skills training program for players in the late 1990s. The NCAA Champs/Life Skills program for Division I athletes is an even more comprehensive example. This mandatory educational program covers not only communication skills but also such

Rebels in Chinese Sport

Multimillionaire professionals are not the only ones who can suddenly cause a problem or a stir with their actions—whether a contract holdout, a DUI, or an assault charge. And problems are not limited to the capitalist Western teams and leagues. In August 2011 members of China's national junior basketball team sent a letter to the Chinese Basketball Association (CBA) protesting the physical and verbal abuses and demanding the ouster of coach Fan Bin. As the *New York Times* put it, "Chinese athletes, once dutiful ambassadors who obediently spent their lives in pursuit of patriotic glory, are no longer willing to just grin and bear it." The letter was leaked on the Internet and social media, creating a buzz and a problem for Chinese officials who oversee a national sport system of schools and coaches who train over 250,000 athletes with one goal—to win world and Olympic championships. But Chinese players were no longer quiet and obedient, noted Jiang Yi, *Sports Illustrated China*'s managing editor: "What's happening now is the younger generation of athletes has so many options to communicate, through microblogs and social networking, that they want to stand up and speak out." The CBA's head of game operations responded that corporal punishment had a long history in Chinese coaching. Coaches acted just like parents, he maintained, "and it's completely normal for parents to hit their kids." The problem, he went on, was with the players who were products of a more prosperous and softer age. For anyone who played or followed college sports in 1960s America, this was déjà vu of the "Athletic Revolution."[16]

issues as substance abuse, eating disorders, and stress management. Some firms have begun to offer services to college prospects, helping them create promotional packages to sell their skills to recruiters more effectively. The National Scouting Report, for example, offered packages ranging in cost from $895 to $2,495, for which high school prospects received a range of benefits including DVDs, websites, promotional e-mails, and fancy resumes. Whether the products were worth the price remains to be seen.[15]

Fan Behavior

Nothing is quite so energizing as sitting among tens of thousands of sports fans who begin to sing in unison some signature song or perform some special movement, such as Wisconsin partisans who leap to the 1992 song "Jump Around" by House of Pain. Live spectators are fundamental to the sport product, just as they are to opera or theater. Their responses are central to the unscripted "script" of action. Fan groups and their behaviors—so much a part of the live experience—can even become commodities of their own. For instance, the Green Bay Packers' Cheeseheads spawned a hot piece of novelty headwear.[17]

Players are subject to rules that proscribe abusive taunting or profanity. What about fans? They are an essential part of any event. Fans move the core product into the realm of spectacle; they expand the drama. But they can also poison the atmosphere and promote violence. There is nothing new in this. Fan riots occurred in the ancient world. In the 19th century, gangs of hooligans stormed fields of play with some regularity. Still, whether accurate or not, the news is filled with stories suggesting that fan behavior is getting worse.

In December 1997 a mob of Alabama high school football fans attacked two officials. Just before the melee, the game's announcer had berated the officials over the public address system, taunting them and complaining that they "needed to go back to school." In February 1998 spectators cheered as a New York high school hockey player was hauled off in handcuffs for assaulting a referee. A 2004 fan brawl at an Illinois boys' high school regional tournament game ended with five people in the hospital including one coach who was hit by a bottle. By July 2012 the website Bleacherreport.com posted a story with video and slides on the "25 most awesome

fan fights in the stands." The writer began the story with this: "If you think things get intense on the field during a sporting event, that's nothing compared to what's going on in the stands sometimes." Mercifully, at least one commenter posted that there was "nothing awesome" in such behavior; it was "just stupid."[18]

But what can be done about it? Because the worst behavior has been linked to alcohol consumption, people regularly call to prohibit or restrict sales and consumption at or near events. At the professional level, such a policy would eliminate major sources of revenue, so franchises have used technology and staff training to control aggressive fans. Modern venues have infrastructure that allows text-message reporting of unruly behavior. By 2009 every NFL team had a text system set up, and the NBA, NHL, and MLB expanded their text operations. As a Miami arena executive put it, "Everyone has a different tolerance level for behavior. This system allows each person to reach us discreetly so we can address it when they find someone else's actions offensive." In an odd way, such a system expanded the events staff, with a twist on the notion of crowdsourcing.[19]

In 2008 the NFL established a fan code of conduct that banned the following, which could result in "ejection without refund and loss of ticket privileges for future games:"

- Behavior that is unruly, disruptive, or illegal in nature
- Intoxication or other signs of alcohol impairment that result in irresponsible behavior
- Foul or abusive language or obscene gestures
- Interference with the progress of the game (including throwing objects onto the field)
- Failing to follow instructions of stadium personnel
- Verbal or physical harassment of opposing team fans

A year later the NFL followed many college football programs in suggesting a reduction in the time that fans would be allowed to tailgate in the stadium parking lots. Eight league teams then began a special class for ejected fans, designed by a psychotherapist to educate them in proper

Rowdy fans are an ongoing problem for effective game presentation and necessitate ever harsher policies and procedures.

behavior, including responsible drinking. In the words of one spokesperson, it was all "part of the NFL's ongoing effort to further improve the game-day experience for all fans." In August 2012, 11 of Southern California's top sport venues, including the Rose Bowl, Dodger Stadium, and Pauley Pavilion, embraced a uniform code of conduct for fans.[20]

School and college programs have also developed fan codes. When profanity and taunting reached intolerable levels, the University of Maryland established a special student committee to prepare a code of conduct for fans at Comcast Center. Some critics argued that restraints on student behavior would violate First Amendment rights, but State Attorney General John Anderson supported the university's efforts to maintain a civil environment at its sports events. Even with legal cover, however, controlling a student section of fans is not easy, especially if several hundred

chant a profanity in unison. Ejecting an isolated drunk is one thing, but attempting a mass ejection of an entire section is quite another. In one Maine gym recently, a game official grew frustrated by the reluctance of one fan group to give up a noisemaker—an item banned by the state association. At his insistence, the home team administration emptied the entire section of fans.[21]

The most successful initiatives have seen partnerships between administrators and students. As Lehigh University's athletics director Joe Sterrett put it, the best way to get student support of a fan behavior policy "is to involve them in creating the plan." Lehigh administrators identified a core group of student fans who established imaginative but positive chants and songs as alternatives to profanity-laced taunts. Among other guidelines in creating a set of "house rules," the Lehigh group considered a fundamental question: Would you be embarrassed to have your parents or little brother or sister sitting next to you? Lehigh students now promote the house rules at fall orientations, on arena video displays, and by in-game announcements.[22]

Equipment and Apparel

As noted earlier, equipment is part of the core product for any sport consumer. No sport is played today without equipment and uniforms. But equipment, apparel, and merchandise take on a life beyond the core-event experience. Uniform designs and colors have been part of sport events for centuries. Fans in the ancient Roman stadiums cheered for chariot drivers of particular stable colors—red, white, green, blue. Many of today's teams are known by their colors. If you say, "the Crimson" around Boston, most fans will think of Harvard. If you say, "Crimson Tide," any American football fan will think of Bear Bryant and Alabama. In the last several decades, uniform design became part of broader strategies that extended the event into everyday apparel. Every major league team expanded its properties division to oversee the careful development and sale of merchandise, including official team jerseys. Among other things, this meant that two basic uniforms—home and away—were no longer enough. Teams developed secondary home and away uniforms. Some were retro, some were avant-garde, and some (like the wild UnderArmour football jerseys unveiled in 2011) were off the charts. But they shared a rationale. If big-league players showcased new uniforms at the live event, plenty of people would buy replicas at their local department stores.[23]

Sport-related T-shirts, jackets, and ball caps became badges of personal identity over the last three decades. Even casual research into crowd shots over the years will show a sharp contrast from workaday (and often rather formal) clothing before 1980 to team-branded apparel today. And sport brands are truly global. Manchester United apparel sells briskly worldwide. We discuss the growth of branded and licensed apparel in the next chapter, but we cannot overstress the high stakes involved in careful development, distribution, and control of a team's or school's or league's sport marks and logos. When the Boston Celtics began the 2008 NBA Finals against the L.A. Lakers, the planning among merchandisers was as intense as it was among the coaches. A small team from the NBA, Adidas, Reebok, and local apparel printers met to perform a code-blue operation. Two graphic designers visited selected sports bars in hopes of hearing a possible slogan or catch phrase. Inside the "design lounge" bunker, lots of brainstorming occurred about slogans and images. Some were obvious—"Go Green" or "Beat LA." Some were more inventive—"17 Cigars" with an image of Red Auerbach lighting up. Many ideas were generated, and few were chosen. But the challenge was to move from idea to finished product in the 48 hours between game 1 and game 2. "It's organized chaos," said one silk screener. Tens of thousands of shirts and hats needed to be made and shipped in time to cash in on fan frenzy.[24]

Venue

All sports have a venue, a field, or a facility as part of the product package. We look more closely at the sport place in chapter 13, but we note here that teams and franchises are closely aligned with their venues, which are cauldrons of powerful memory and community. Historian Bruce Kuklick captured this well in his monograph on Philadelphia's historic Shibe Park, longtime home of the city's major league teams: "Meaning and the items that bear it are fragile. The meanings accrue over time in their visible embodiments, artifacts like Shibe Park. Memories do not exist in the mind's isolation but are connected to objects and stored in them." A fan's identity, particularly in a large city, often resides in the stories or the recollections that link people and events with a place. A place like Shibe Park offered special rituals that made Irish or Italians into Philadelphians. Old Trafford has a similar, but global, effect on Manchester United fans. The same may be true for any venue. Small towns everywhere have sport venues ripe with tradition and collective memory.[25]

Many of today's venues have such broad appeal that they provide significant revenue streams outside normal game days. With the success of the NHL's Winter Classic, we can expect to see more ice hockey played in baseball or football venues such as Wrigley Field or Michigan's "Big House." Such is the power of their brands. A place like Fenway Park attracts consumers for much more than baseball. When the new owners of the Boston Red Sox looked to reverse the "Curse of the Bambino," they had to find revenue to compete with the Yankees. But ticket prices were already the highest in baseball. And the options for expansion were limited—a few hundred seats atop the Green Monster and a new section in right field were all that could be added. But the Fenway Park calendar had plenty of open dates—some 284 of them. So the Red Sox began to advertise for parties, weddings, and business meetings inside Fenway's friendly confines. Rentals were not cheap. The price was anywhere from $1,000 to $100,000, depending on numbers, location, and quality of food. But in baseball-mad New England (a.k.a. Red Sox Nation), everybody wanted to get to Fenway. The Red Sox were not alone in this approach to product extension. Seattleites could enjoy dinner for two at home plate in Safeco Field. Michigan fans can rent Michigan Stadium for a one-hour wedding ceremony. Price: $6,000. Memories: incalculable.[26]

Personnel and Process

If the core sport product is a performance or an event, then successful marketing depends on the people who process the product. A.J. Magrath argued persuasively that personnel and process are additional Ps in the marketing mix. Any fan who has gone to numerous giveaways at sport events knows the frustration of receiving the wrong size or of being told, "Sorry, we're all out . . . . We didn't expect so many fans today." The actions of a surly attendant or the hopelessness of a botched promotion can never be repaired. The consumer cannot return or exchange the experience. In the consumer's eyes, personnel and process are inextricably linked to the product.[27]

Brian Crow, a faculty member at Slippery Rock University, has done extensive research on event management, fan perceptions, and staff training at multiple levels of the sport industry. In a recent study of football games within the Pennsylvania State Athletic Conference (NCAA Division II), he and his students found problems that are far too common:

- "Limited security presence at entrances," which could well trigger perceptions of risk.
- Lack of "clear and visible signs for venues and parking areas"—a good way to get fans frustrated before they even find their seats.
- Sportsmanship signs (an NCAA requirement) "not clearly visible in most venues," although half the sites did use PA announcements to convey expectations and codes.

- Although concession and restroom lines were reasonable, the locations were "not as clean as expected."
- Event staff were "often students who seemingly were not trained to answer basic questions."

All the preceding reduce the quality of the game experience for fans.[28]

Charles L. Martin's research on customer relations in bowling centers led him to coin a telling phrase: All sports are "contact" sports. Although formal training is desirable, there are simple things to remember:

- Emphasize common courtesy, especially sincere thank-yous, even when making change.
- Employ "aggressive hospitality." Make extra-transactional encounters with customers, going beyond what they normally expect. This approach shows extra concern for their satisfaction.
- Be proactive. Offer assistance before being asked. Work to solve problems immediately. Treat consumers as though they were guests in your home.
- Increase complaints. Encourage consumers to speak their minds. In the language of Disney, "Ask the guests what they want . . . then give it to them." Only then will the organization know how to satisfy the consumer.
- Use some kind of consistent, professional dress code, uniform, and grooming for events staff.
- Develop a theme and a consistent ethos of service that cascade through the venue—in signage, color, cleanliness, personnel appearance, and a tenacious belief that all consumers have special needs.
- Incorporate personnel procedures and training into organization policy.

Little things matter. The various processes involving event personnel—ticket taking, front desk management, locker room attending, concessions operations, skills instruction, and field maintenance—are essential features of the product. They cannot be overlooked or taken for granted.[29]

The Wide World of the Glocal Sport Experience

Few sports have anything approaching universal appeal on this little planet of ours. World football is at the top of the list, embraced as it is with great passion across oceans and continents. Yet even within world football there are distinct notions about national systems of play—the flair of the Brazilians, the tiki-taka short passing of the Spaniards, the brute force and long ball of the English. Do these emanate from culture, or are they figments of media imagination? Those are ongoing questions for scholars of the game. But what about the overall event experience? How does that differ by culture? At least some elements seem to be both global and local, or "glocal," to use another phrase.

- **Fan shouting and singing**. Most North American sport marketers invest enormous time and money developing and delivering triggers to raucous but controlled fan involvement. Cheerleaders and pep bands are old assets; big-screen television cues are new. In much of the world, however, the fans themselves control the orchestrated songs, the chants, and the prompts. Some songs are appropriated, such as Irish national team fans and "the Fields of Athenry" or Liverpool fans and "You'll Never Walk Alone" (ironically, an old American show tune). In Japan's top baseball league, fan groups are equally robust and boisterous, led by cheer captains. In a country like Myanmar, where government protestors can suffer 100-year prison sentences, the football pitch is an oasis of freedom. The government encouraged the 2008 creation of the Myanmar National League, and tickets are cheap at 70 cents. Challenging a state official is illegal, but challenging a football official or a rival player is fair game. As one high school student told the *New York Times*, "I don't come here to support any particular team. I come for the freedom to yell anything I want."[30]

- **Music and dance**. North American fans may jump and sway in unison, or do the wave, but they don't seem to dance the way that Brazilian fans do. That circumstance will probably change as world football in the United States grows through Major League Soccer and its specialized venues and its dedicated fan groups who are hip to global cultures. Will there soon come a day when a vast NBA crowd is swaying to the salsa and blowing vuvuzelas?

- **Food**. American crowds love their hot dogs, popcorn, and peanuts; they are solid traditions. In Japan their counterparts are grilled eel, soba noodles, and rice balls with eggs. In England it might be minidoughnuts or a mince beef pie. When French spectators watch American football, in a French league, they eat their hot dogs with mayonnaise on baguettes.[31]

When the NFL first pushed itself into Europe in the 1980s, the league had a cocky sense that its product was so good that marketing could be a simple inoculation of the American game, using television to sell the public and corporate sponsors. Articulation of how an American product might be adapted to European culture was lacking. Has that changed in three decades? NFL Hall of Fame player (and now broadcaster) Troy Aikman seems doubtful. In his words, "I think there is a little bit of arrogance on our part in thinking that these other countries are just excited about watching American football."[32]

We may live in a global economy, but markets and consumers are still local. Granted, Russia's Kontinental Hockey League has NFL-like cheerleaders, and the cultures of world football are changing the experience in North America. But we must recognize the existence of several versions of any sport product or experience. The league—NBA, NFL, EPL—has a version that it would like to distribute. Local media and local marketers would like to present another version to their local audiences. And then the local consumers themselves affect and experience another version. As scholars have teased out, there is no simple inoculation. It is constant negotiation.[33]

Product Extensions

The core product, the game experience, is supplemented by numerous product extensions that often have a life of their own. Some of those extensions include the following.

Memories

One thing is clear in sport: History captivates and motivates consumers. Arguments about the best player of all time, interest in retro sweaters or hats, and the proliferation of halls of fame at every level in every sport all testify to the power of the past. In 2007 readers of *SportsBusiness Journal* voted on the best NHL team logo as well as the one most in need of change. The top five logos were among the six oldest—Red Wings, Blackhawks, Canadiens, Rangers, and Leafs. Tradition ruled. The five most in need of change included three of the leagues' newest—Atlanta Thrashers, Columbus Blue Jackets, and Anaheim Ducks.[34]

Some historical artifacts have reached staggering values. In December 2004 Sotheby's auction house sold a baseball bat for $1.28 million. Of course, it was not your everyday bat; it was the gargantuan 3-foot-long (91 cm), 46-ounce (1,300 g) stick that Babe Ruth swung to hit the first home run in Yankee Stadium, the "House that Ruth Built." Sport memorabilia has a long history, and collectors have sought investments for well over a century. Counterfeiters have followed closely behind, so the major leagues have hired authenticators such as Deloitte and Touche, who attend events such as the World Series, to slap artifacts with special holograms and numbers that are used to register the authenticity of a ball, bat, hat, glove, base, or even an empty champagne bottle. But the frauds continue. Some are exhibited on a cool website entitled haulsofshame.com. Despite charlatans, the memories that swirl around historical data and artifacts are a key component to fan commitment, a phenomenon recognized by the smartest sport organizations, who carefully manage halls of fame, historical exhibits, retro apparel, and other elements of memory.[35]

Novelties and Fantasies

Sport toys and novelties go back over a century, but they were never as clearly tied to integrated marketing strategies as they have been in the last two decades. The NBA–WNBA had a Barbie Doll line. The NFL had a Pro Action Athlete collectible line. NASCAR had driver figurines. NASCAR teams saw another market in recycling old tires, which fans happily bought for $5 to $10 each. Said one consumer about his purchase: "I'm going to keep it on my floor at home, next to my bed. You know, so that I can see it first thing in the morning when I wake up." Teams have continually searched for hot collectibles to drive promotions and fan loyalty. Beanie Babies were hot in the 1990s. Bobblehead figures were strong in the last decade. In 2001 the Chicago Cubs partnered with Topps to create a set of 10 trading cards of current and former Cubs to be given away at various points in the season. More recently, many clubs linked with local newspapers to sell collectible pins and coins. In 2011 old-fashioned T-shirts were the number one giveaway item in Major League Baseball. But organizations are constantly searching for a new twist. The NHL tried to up the ante in 2011 with the Guardian Project, a set of superheroes developed by Stan Lee, the genius behind Spiderman and other legends. Each NHL team was to have its own superhero—the Bruin, the Predator, and so forth—who could be called in to save the local community from some force of evil. Video clips on the big screen would sell ministicks, T-shirts, wood signs, posters, pennants, and graphic novels. As of fall 2013 the project had not generated much positive buzz.[36]

Then there are the fan fests, fantasy camps, and cruises, which have developed for two simple reasons. The first is the meteoric rise in price of tickets, concessions, and parking at big-league events. The standard event in any sport has become less accessible to the majority of potential consumers. If fewer people can afford to get on the consumer escalator, how can they sample the sport product up close and personal? At the same time, even the most committed consumers want to learn, feel, and do more. Fan fests, fantasy camps, and cruises were the answer. Free or low-cost fests are offered at the entry level, and high-cost cruises and camps are available to consumers willing to pay for closer contact with past or present-day players. For example, the LPGA event included the following features:

- Fan–player photo opportunities
- Rules and technique seminars
- Health and fitness forums
- Club-fitting and hitting areas
- Pictorial time line of LPGA highlights
- Video and computer displays

Colleges and universities have also developed their own fan fests. Notre Dame was among them. In 2004, 52 campers paid $4,290 each to practice in real Notre Dame equipment under the tutelage of present and past Fighting Irish coaches and then play in a final flag football game in Notre Dame Stadium. The Chicago Bulls took it one step further, offering fans the chance to be a floor sweeper during a game. The price tag? $1,200. For $1,500, a fan could play reporter and file a story on the club's website.[37]

Ticket, Programs, and Other Print Materials

Few people realize the full value of a ticket to an event. The obvious uses are to provide a receipt, to guide people to their seats, and to communicate the terms and conditions of purchase. Statements of limited liability are standard these days. But these mundane applications are just the tip of the iceberg in terms of marketing potential.

The look and feel of a ticket may vary in ways that represent the different experiences that the ticket symbolizes. Thus, tickets represent a ladder of products that parallel the escalator:

- Premium seating
- Full-season plans, partial plans, and miniplans
- Group ticket sales
- Single-game ticket plans and promotions
- Complementary tickets and sampling programs

As the phrase *sampling programs* suggests, the ticket can clearly be used both as a promotional tool and as a source of revenue. Many collegiate and minor league baseball teams use the ticket as an advertising medium for sponsors. Other organizations have been quick to use it for a promotional tie-in, such as drawings of ticket numbers for prizes or printing redeemable coupons

Even in a high tech age, the simple game day program still attracts consumers.

(often for fast food) on the back of the ticket. We discuss these ideas in more detail in chapters that follow. Beyond the game experience, tickets often carry prestige (not to mention scalping value) that turns them into souvenirs. World Cup and Super Bowl tickets include an embedded hologram that makes counterfeiting much more difficult. High-tech printing companies can create personalized, plastic tickets for high-end customers at golf, tennis, or other events.[38]

Other print materials can extend the product. Programs are one example. Besides including player, coach, or game profiles and statistics, rules, and records, programs can include lucky numbers used for special prize drawings. And like tickets, programs can be tailored for big events, with added features that make them collectibles. Teams, clubs, and leagues can also publish magazines and newsletters. Few sport organizations in North America match the reach of Manchester United, whose magazine can be purchased at newsstands all over Britain, although NASCAR, with its magazine *Inside NASCAR*, may be one of them. Many groups have high-quality serials that circulate to members and season-ticket holders.

Hybrid Products and Electronic Products

Internet and wireless technologies have opened new opportunities to extend a fan's involvement with a player, a team, or an event. New hybrid products merge print and electronic media. One development has been QR (quick response) codes, which allow linkage between print and wireless mediums. In 2010, for instance, the Detroit Red Wings switched their game program from the older, magazine style that might cost $4 or more to a smaller, free, book-size item supported by advertisers. The coolest part of the new format, however, was the embedded QR codes that allowed a reader to scan the code against a cell phone or other reading device and link to videos on YouTube or (the Red Wings planned) to other Internet content. Said a Wings executive, "We're looking to enhance our published program, as well as drive usage of our online material." In 2011 the Philadelphia Eagles announced plans to include QR codes in smartphone apps that allowed fans to access information about game-day events. Wherever there is new technology, there is a new sport product.[39]

FanVision is a smartphone-like mobile device formally known as Kangaroo. It works with NASCAR, Formula 1, the NFL, and some college football properties to allow owners or renters to view, from their stadium seats, replays, alternate video angles, real-time statistics, radio broadcasts, fantasy football content, and other information with a high degree of user control. The next step for FanVision will be smartphone apps. MLB already had an app with similar functions called AtBat (free for limited version or $15 for a full-season pass), and the Pittsburgh Penguins have an app called YinzCam.[40]

Electronic sports games have been around since at least the 1940s when Norman Sas developed a vibrating metal board that served as the base for horse races and car races. His Tudor Electric Football game took the technology to new levels and markets in 1949. Sport has been a focus of video games since the days of Pong. New technologies have improved quality and marketability. When ESPN and the NFL combined with Sega to create ESPN NFL 2K5, they sold two million copies (at $20 each) between July and September 2004. That success put some heat on the industry frontrunner, Electronic Arts Inc.'s Madden NFL, which had achieved worldwide domination for a decade. Consumer loyalty allowed Madden NFL to charge $50 and still move four million units. Crowds can now play new types of video games at live events with products like CrowdWave, which "uses cameras and software to interpret body movements of fans in specific seating sections and then uses those combined fan movements to power games or surveys on a video board." This innovation reduces downtime during time-outs. Now fans can go to an NHL game and also play tug-of-war or have a Zamboni race on the big screen.[41]

Although music and sport have been linked for over a century (football fight songs, "Take Me Out to the Ball Game"), recent years have seen more aggressive connections. NASCAR formalized its marriage to Nashville with CD compilations such as *NASCAR: Runnin' Wide Open*, which featured songs by Billy Ray Cyrus, Rick Trevino, and even Kyle Petty. Alphabet City Music Productions began creating in-venue music videos tailored to rally fans of client franchises. Alphabet's special-edition Chicago Bulls CD sold over 300,000 copies. Sport properties also moved their stories to DVD. Within a month of winning the 2004 World Series, the Boston Red Sox and MLB Productions had a DVD on the market that had advanced sales of 300,000.[42]

Fantasy leagues are growing. Fans want to pretend that they are general managers; they want extra passion when they watch games. What better adrenaline boost than to follow a set of players whom you have drafted to your team—even if in reality they all play on different teams. As one fan noted to *Time* magazine in August 2012, the upcoming football draft would be a formal affair: "At our draft, the commissioner wears a sport jacket, and there is a speaker system, just like the real thing." *Time* estimated the 2007 fantasy sports economic impact at $1.5 billion. By 2012 it had grown to a projected $3 billion. In 2012 fantasy football had an estimated 23.8 million players. Baseball had 12.2 million players, and basketball had some 7 million players.[43]

In August 2011 one of the Internet's pioneers—Marc Andreessen, who cofounded the first great web browser (Netscape)—wrote an article titled "Why Software Is Eating the World." His basic point was that electronic and digital products had changed the way that we worked, banked, drove a car, read books, took classes, and did just about anything. For some reason he omitted an obvious segment of life—producing and consuming sport.[44]

The Organization

Ultimately, all product elements can add value to the individual team, club, league, or association, which is the ultimate objective of a careful marketing strategy. Players, equipment, venues, merchandise, books, movies, and websites can all combine in the consumer's mind as representations of a particular organization. For that reason, all major leagues have business divisions that include in their names terms like *enterprises* or *properties*. Integrated product strategies yield values through synergy, meaning that the whole is more than just the sum of the parts. Therefore, professional franchise values continue to escalate despite salary pressures and fan antagonism. Sometimes we gasp at franchise selling prices—$530 million for the NFL expansion Cleveland Browns or $1.5 billion for Manchester United. But if we begin to add up all the value associated with the core and extended product elements, those selling prices make more sense.

Grassroots Ideas

A million-dollar marketing budget isn't required to benefit from the concepts discussed in the preceding sections. After all, fight songs and signature songs developed at high schools, clubs, and small colleges just as fast as they did at the big-time institutions. The same programs have long sold tickets and food, and employed event staff. Many have halls of fame, summer camps, and stores that sell apparel. The program director might benefit, however, from making a checklist (apparel, food, event staff, venue, tickets, store, hall of fame, camps, phone apps) and asking a few questions about each item:

- Do we employ this component in a way that advances our brand integrity?
- If not, how shall we respond?
- Do we have the people and resources to respond?

Directors typically review coaching performance and equipment needs. Likewise, they should review the complex product that they offer to the public and assess whether it is driving the desired level of involvement and commitment.

Key Issues in Sport Product Strategy

As we discussed in chapter 2, strategy is essential. Here we discuss the major issues of sport product strategy: differentiation, product development, product position, brands, and product and brand cycles.

Differentiation

If consumers don't recognize the club, the team, the player, the event, or the equipment as meeting their needs, then marketing becomes a one-way drive to oblivion. Like successful coaches who must tinker with their lineups and strategies, marketers must continuously revise, delete, and add elements to their comprehensive product. Unlike coaches, however, marketers must consider their consumers and their competitors simultaneously. Whether the product is new, established, or old, the ever-present challenge is to make the product distinctive and attractive in the consumers' minds.

As an example, take Nike's image battles. The Nike swoosh is as recognizable today as Mickey Mouse or McDonald's golden arches. Despite ups and downs in sales and profits, Nike looms as a dominant force in the wide world of sport. As Nike's Phil Knight is the first to recognize, however, staying at the top requires constant reinvention and reconfiguration. In the early 1980s, for instance, Nike was temporarily toppled from preeminence by Reebok, which captured the swelling aerobics market. As Knight recalled later, "We made an aerobics shoe that was functionally superior to Reebok's, but we missed the styling. Reebok's shoe was sleek and attractive, while ours was sturdy and clunky." Nike survived and then thrived by repackaging and reconfiguring its products to include style as well as performance. Moreover, Nike began to use aggressive television ads to focus consumer attention on this shift. In Knight's words, "Our advertising tried to link consumers to the Nike brand through the emotions of sports and fitness. We show competition, determination, achievement, fun, and even the spiritual rewards of participating in these activities." Nike ads have succeeded because of these emotions. But in the 1990s Nike's foreign manufacturing and labor practices stirred equally strong emotions, forcing Knight to admit that Nike had "become synonymous with slave wages, forced overtime and arbitrary abuse." Nike could do without this reputation, so the company had to continue repositioning itself in the public's imagination.[45]

The epic competition between the ABL and WNBA offered another example of differentiation. In 1997 women's professional basketball provided sports fans with two new products—the ABL and the WNBA. The war between the leagues revisited product battles that had dotted the sport landscape back as far as the 1880s, when the American Association challenged the National League's chokehold on big-time baseball. Issues included the following:

• **Markets and venues**. The ABL played in midsized markets and venues, such as Columbus (Ohio) and Richmond (Virginia). The WNBA played in the big-market venues of the parent franchises—New York, Los Angeles, Cleveland, Phoenix.

• **Star appeal**. Both leagues pushed for star talent. The WNBA had the best-known players (Lisa Leslie, Rebecca Lobo, and Sheryl Swoopes), but the ABL grabbed eight members of the 1996 Olympic team.

• **Television**. What counted most here was NBA leverage; the WNBA enjoyed secure television packages with NBC and ESPN, whereas the ABL got limited exposure on BET and regional sports channels.

• **Season of play**. The ABL played in the traditional period (October to February), whereas the WNBA played a summer schedule.

The WNBA and the ABL pressed their product distinctions to the public in 1997. Gary Cavelli, the ABL's founder, hammered away at the WNBA for relegating women to secondary status with a summer season that was little more than filler for NBA arenas. But the public didn't seem to care. If the ABL were to survive, it would not be because of its playing season. The choices were clear, for players and fans. The contest was almost David against Goliath, except that David was offering higher average salaries than Goliath was. And that was the rub. Without the clout of big markets and big media, the ABL strained to stay afloat with a higher payroll than its rival had. In early 1999 the ABL declared bankruptcy, but the brief league war will be remembered for providing one of the starkest product contrasts in sport history.[46]

As the ABL case suggests, marketers must constantly evaluate and reevaluate their products, especially as they exist in consumers' minds. Philip Kotler defined differentiation as "the act of designing a set of meaningful differences to distinguish the company's offering from competitors' offerings." Sport products can be differentiated based on any or all of the elements that we have discussed. Many people, for instance, see women's basketball as more of a team game, requiring more precision passing, and men's basketball as more of a one-on-one, above-the-rim, slam-dunk game. Marketers must use their knowledge and imagination to recognize the ways that their products may be distinct in the consumer's mind. As a simple exercise, take a standard LPGA event and compare it with a standard NFL event. How are they different? Table 6.1 offers some possibilities. The nature of the game, the way that fans are framed around players, their proximity to players, and their chances of interaction with players all help to distinguish pro football from tour golf. All of these could be

TABLE 6.1   Sport Product Differentiation: The LPGA and the NFL

Element	LPGA	NFL
Game form	High skill, slow pace	High skill, high pace
Framing of fans around players	Clustered around course; fans can move with players	Uniframe, determined by venue seating; little or no movement by fans
Proximity to action	Very close	Distant
Chances of exchange with players	High	Low

helpful in developing surveys and promotions that might clarify important distinctions for other sport products. Marketers are limited only by their imagination.[47]

Product Development

Marketers must continuously develop the product. They may need to delete, revise, or add any one or more of the elements that make up the comprehensive bundle of benefits. Product development includes two standard steps:

- Generation of ideas
- Screening and implementation of ideas, which includes refinement of the product concept, market and business analysis, development of the actual product, market testing, and commercialization

An excellent example of a brilliant development strategy was the introduction by hockey's San Jose Sharks of their colors and marks in the early 1990s, largely under the leadership of Matt Levine, long regarded as the father of modern sport marketing. A small task force developed a list of key criteria to be used in name selection. These criteria included clarity, regional links, brevity, and graphic potential. With the name *Sharks* in the forefront of their minds, the team held a name sweepstakes to generate even more ideas, as well as interest. More than 2,300 different names came in, with the name *Sharks* running second to *Blades*, which was never seriously considered because of its gang implications.

With a name and an image under design, the next step was selecting colors. Here the Sharks used a number of steps, including bypass interviews with 800 season-ticket depositors who rated various color schemes and consultations with expert designers such as L.L. Bean. The final product was a raging success—teal and black colors that accentuated a cartoonlike "Sharkie," who was crunching a hockey stick. In 1992, after one year of public distribution, sales of San Jose Sharks merchandise had reached $125 million. By the end of 1994 the Sharks were the number one seller of NHL merchandise. In the ever-changing market of popular taste, however, Sharks merchandise sales drifted downward, so that by 1997, they ranked 21st in the NHL. Other teams had jumped on the Sharks' innovations and had redesigned their uniforms. By the late 1990s the Sharks were back at the drawing board.[48]

Product innovations and repositioning efforts often walk a fine line between success and failure. In the end, of course, consumers determine the results. Theories of innovation suggest that consumers grapple with five perceptual issues as they decide whether to adopt a product innovation:

- Relative advantage of the new product over old preferences
- Complexity or difficulty in adoption and use
- Compatibility with consumer values
- Divisibility into smaller trial portions
- Communicability of benefits

Researchers studying a small sample of Cleveland Cavaliers fans (who had attended at least one game) in the Akron–Canton area found that all five issues came into play when the Cavs moved in 1994 from Richfield Coliseum near Akron to the new Gund Arena in downtown Cleveland:

- **Relative advantage**. The greater travel distance often outweighed the benefits of the beautiful new arena.

- **Complexity**. Issues of distance, time, parking, and safety might be too daunting.
- **Compatibility**. Of the women sampled, 91 percent said they rarely or never visited downtown Cleveland.
- **Divisibility**. Some fans could not link higher ticket prices to the benefits of a new facility.
- **Communicability**. Aggressive ad campaigns did not register with some fans; one respondent was not even aware of the new arena.

The Cavs did address these issues in the promotional campaign associated with their move, and the success of Gund Arena (now Quicken Loans Arena) supports the Cavs' move to downtown Cleveland. The research results listed, however, reinforce the virtues of careful planning for all product innovations.[49]

Product Position

The elements in any sport product should contribute to a coherent image; product development should not be pursued haphazardly. Further, the sport organization must get this image across to the consumer. When all elements of the product provide the same message, the image is clear and distinct. A major factor influencing the reception of this image is consumer perception. As the Cleveland Cavs study suggests, consumer perceptions may be selective and inconsistent. Just think of the prospects if the sport organization is also inconsistent in the images that it sends out!

When Mannie Jackson purchased the Harlem Globetrotters from the International Broadcasting Company in 1993, the legendary franchise was a ghost of its glorious past. Attendance and profits had decreased drastically in only six years. Jackson brought the Trotters back to prominence and profitability by repositioning them away from the clown image that they had acquired. While retaining their humor, the Trotters took on more legitimate competition, ran clinics for kids, and made speaking appearances wherever they played. This approach, in turn, made them much more attractive to corporate sponsorships, which further increased their standing in the public eye.[50]

The bottom line is the product's position in the minds of the target consumers. Marketing campaigns often focus on positioning or repositioning the product in consumers' minds. Positioning strategy, however, is especially tough in the sport industry, where media images are public and where they are often beyond the control of team and league marketers. In 2007 the Chicago Blackhawks began a successful turnaround after years of failure on and off the ice. Rocky Wirtz, who inherited the team, made several important decisions that signaled a new product. Said Wirtz, "I knew we had to do something. It had to be dramatic and it had to be now." These changes included replacing an "old-hockey guy" general manager with a popular executive from the Chicago Cubs, televising home games (something his father refused to do), and mending fences with old Blackhawks heroes like Bobby Hull, who had signed with the rival league World Hockey Association in 1972 after a bitter contract dispute with the father. In a flash, Rocky Wirtz looked like an owner who cared for the fans. Ticket and sponsorship sales went up.[51]

The battle for positioning occurs at all levels, in all sports. Horse racing and bowling have mounted multi-million-dollar campaigns to reposition their products as hip and hot, especially in the minds of younger consumers. If high school sports are to remain solvent, their administrators must emulate Novi, Michigan, athletics director John Fundukian, whose annual *Athletics Highlights* bulletin focuses attention on the distinct contributions of high school athletics to the local community. Among other things, Fundukian has emphasized statistics showing the relation between participation and academic performance.[52]

Sergio Zyman, longtime marketing whiz of Coca-Cola, described positioning as a matter of managing the five images of any organization or product:

- **Trademark imagery**. The mark or logo on a hat or shirt must represent something of interest or value. Think of the Nike swoosh or the New York Yankees "NY."
- **Product imagery**. Nike shoes and the Yankees' on-field performance have been consistently exceptional in the minds of their many fans.
- **Associative imagery**. Nike has battled against negative associations (e.g., cheap overseas labor), but it is also associated with top performers like Michael Jordan and the Oregon Ducks.

- **User imagery**. Yankees fans conjure different images among Bostonians than they do among New Yorkers.

- **Usage imagery**. The swoosh on a new, high-tech shoe makes many people think of a more efficient or effective workout.

All images are at play in product positioning. It is not just a matter of placing a new mark on apparel. No simple formula can make the images congruent. Ed O'Hara, a senior partner at one of the sport industry's top brand image builders (SME), noted in 2007, "Every team we've ever worked with wants to say they are fast, fierce and aggressive. Even if that's true, it's not unique." Teams and leagues, he added, "need to determine the real point of difference and build out from there." This idea is true at all levels of sport.[53]

Positioning strategies can benefit from the use of perceptual space maps, which are formed by asking consumers to rank certain product attributes. The critical attributes vary from product to product and from sport to sport, but the following example illustrates the principle (figure 6.2). Suppose the University of Durham wanted to conceptualize the position of its successful women's ice hockey team in the minds of local (25-mile, or 40 km, radius) consumers, including students at the university. The U of D women's team draws only 900 to 1,200 fans per game, at low prices, whereas the less successful men's hockey team sells out every game, at four times

the price. Many factors drive the attendance levels, but the athletics marketers want to get a better sense of where women's hockey fits in the minds of current and potential fans.

To do this, they would develop a survey (such as those described in chapter 4) to administer at local malls and at athletics events on campus. On the survey, they might ask consumers to indicate their levels of attendance at or involvement in a number of activities, including U of D events. They also might ask consumers to indicate their perception of the cost (time and money) and the excitement or action levels in the same activities. The levels are rated on a 10-point scale. Using the results, the marketers could construct a product-space map that suggests the relative positions of these activities along the dimensions of cost and excitement or action.

The results might look like those in figure 6.2. Note that U of D women's ice hockey had a position in the minds of overall area consumers that reflected low cost but also low action. Respondents saw the games as more exciting than watching television but much less exciting than high school basketball. But suppose the marketers also noticed that U of D women's hockey had a more favorable position among consumers who indicated high interest in or involvement with women's hockey (women's hockey fans). For those people, U of D women's hockey was low cost and high action. This positioning would be even more significant if consumers with high

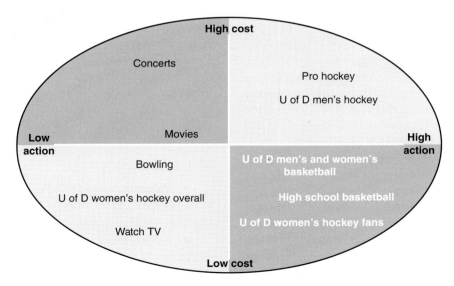

FIGURE 6.2   Product-space map of U of D women's ice hockey.

interest or involvement in other activities (say, bowling) didn't have the same sense of increased action in their sport. It would indicate that U of D women's hockey had real upside potential for a shift in image and position. Women's hockey might simply need more aggressive promotion of its excitement and action.

Product-space maps can also be useful in conceptualizing market segments. The U of D research might include demographic information that reveals different market segments for women's hockey. For instance, U of D students will likely perceive women's hockey as a low-cost product because their ID cards get them into all games free. Older people outside a 5-mile (8 km) radius, however, may mistakenly believe that U of D women's hockey costs as much as U of D men's hockey. This segment is worth addressing, because research shows that women's athletics generally attract a wider age range of fans than men's athletics do.[54]

ACTIVITY 6.1 The Sport Product—Differentiation and Position

Robert Morris University (RMU) Athletic Department is home to 23 intercollegiate athletic teams, including men's and women's Division I hockey squads and a Division I men's lacrosse team. In this WSG activity, you will learn more about RMU sports and the strategies they use to maximize one sport product: the men's basketball team. Then you will compare RMU's approach with the approaches of one professional team and one interscholastic or club team.

Brands and Branding

Over the years, coaches, writers, and fans have discussed certain "brands" of play—the Oregon Duck's brand of football, the Soviet brand of hockey, the Brazilian brand of soccer. In recent years, the concept of branding has swept the sport industry. Branding is both a means and an end to product differentiation. Brands can be created or retained in the names, marks, designs, or images of any one or more of the product elements described in this chapter. Nike successfully built its overall brand (the swoosh) as well as special product brands (Air Jordan). Phil Knight explained how the ad firm of Wieden and

Kennedy helped to build the special image of the Nike brand that was so hot in the late 1980s and early 1990s: "They spend countless hours trying to figure out what the product is, what the message is, what the theme is, what the athletes are all about, what emotion is involved. They try to extract something that's meaningful, an honest message that is true to who we are." Brand building never really ends.[55]

Over the last decade, the king of sport branding has been ESPN, whose parent corporation, Disney, pushed the ESPN brand as a major weapon in its marketplace showdown with Fox and Time Warner. ESPN brand products have included the following:

- ESPN flagship network with its *SportsCenter* core
- ESPN2, ESPN News, and ESPNU
- ESPN Radio
- ESPN Sports Zone website
- ESPN Espy Awards show
- *ESPN the Magazine*
- ESPN CDs and video games
- ESPN Zone restaurants
- ESPN Wide World of Sports Complex

Other properties that moved into the restaurant-retail business were Fox, CBS, Sporting News, the PGA Tour, the NBA, the NHL, and various franchises such as the Dallas Cowboys.[56]

ESPN, like Nike, was conscious about building brand equity, a crucial concept for sport marketers. On its face, brand equity is a relatively simple concept: the added value, or equity, that a certain product has by virtue of its brand name. Coca-Cola, Disney, and ESPN are good examples. Put their name or image on a product, and it is worth more than a generic product of similar quality.

Several components of brand equity have special interest to sport marketers, especially in events in which the product is an intangible perception or memory:

- Name recognition or awareness
- Strong mental or emotional associations
- Perceived brand quality
- Strong customer loyalty

Marketers can build brand equity through any of the various product elements. Even the strongest organizations have analyzed their brand equity. In 2005, for instance, the National Football League hired a specialty firm to study its brand presence and strength. One of the outcomes was a "brand book" that contained rules to govern the use of NFL images in any sponsors' ads. Such strategies are discussed in detail in chapter 7.[57]

Product and Brand Cycles

Product and brand development has a long history in sport, which is only beginning to be organized. Figure 6.3 offers an overview of some of this process. Each stage of development, from family to line to type to property and brand, required the work of entrepreneurs who took advantage of new technologies to design rules, equipment, apparel, stories, and images that might win the embrace and loyalty of consumers. We sometimes take for granted the existence of a popular sport like Major League Baseball. But its success was not a given in 1850 when North Americans and Europeans played a variety of

bat and ball games that might have evolved to become the national pastime of the United States. The same is true with football, a sport with at least five distinct national brands.[58]

ACTIVITY 6.2 Product Life Cycle

Sport products vary in the shape of their developmental and life cycles, as you will learn in this WSG activity. Assume you are the director of marketing for Bellator MMA, and the CEO asks you report on the differences in product life cycles for Bellator MMA and professional boxing. To complete the CEO's request, you will analyze where Bellator MMA is in its product life cycle compared to professional boxing. Then you will consider how you will use what you learned to Bellator MMA's advantage.

Many products seem to have stages, which some theorists have referred to as the product life cycle:

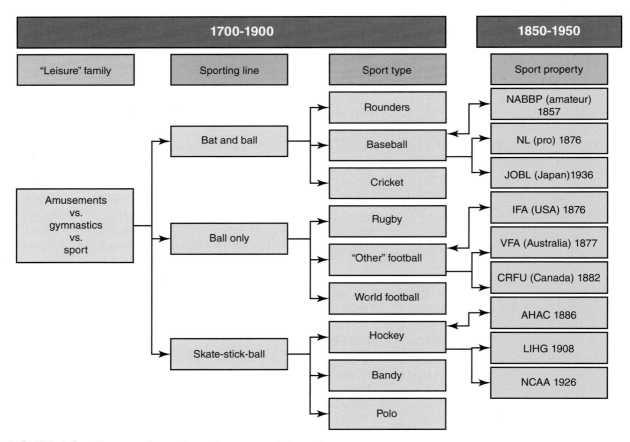

FIGURE 6.3   The tree of sport branding, general chronology.

Copyright Stephen Hardy and used with permission.

- Introduction
- Growth
- Maturity
- Decline

Other theorists have attacked the notion of a standard life cycle as an unsupported concept that, in the worst scenarios, could become a self-fulfilling prophecy whereby managers would reduce support for a product because it had reached its decline stage. Sport products vary in the actual shape of their developmental and life cycles. The following are speculations about sport product life cycles:

- Game forms that enjoy any kind of maturity seem to be resistant to decline. Baseball's popularity hit a low in the 1960s and early 1970s, rebounded in the 1980s, and then had to rebound from the strike of 1994. But MLB is in solid shape. Many people wondered whether the NHL would stagger from lockouts in 2004-2005 and in 2012. But it bounced back. NASCAR had a long, flat maturity. The last decade saw a huge spike of rejuvenation. Will NASCAR's good times last? Both MLS and the WNBA have moved beyond the introduction stage. What will their growth curves look like?

- Teams and franchises have much more volatile and unpredictable cycles than those of their overall sports. Team and franchise cycles are more subject to owner or management whims, economic downturns, and labor issues.

- Equipment cycles appear to be more technology driven than apparel cycles are.

- Apparel cycles blend the more stable trends in game forms with the wide fluctuations of fashion.

The concepts of product or brand life and competitive cycles deserve much greater attention from researchers. Discernible trends may be important to practicing marketers.[59]

ACTIVITY 6.3 Key Issues in Sport Product Strategy—Marketing Danica Patrick

In this WSG activity you will learn that differentiating yourself and having a positive image are ways to market your brand. Picture yourself as the upcoming NASCAR driver that brings sex appeal to the sport. How will you select your endorsements, and how do you want to be positioned in the eyes of the consumers?

Wrap-Up

In this chapter we have begun our investigation of the marketing mix, or the five Ps of sport marketing—product, price, promotion, place, and public relations. We reviewed the features that make the sport product unique and outlined its various components. These include the game or event and its stars, equipment and apparel, novelties and fantasies, the venue, personnel and process, the ticket, electronic and digital products, and finally the organization itself. We also discussed the intricacies of product development, including developing new products, positioning, branding, and the product life cycle. As much as possible, products must be shaped to meet the needs and wants of the consumers targeted in prior research.

Activities

1. Investigate the website of your favorite sport organization. List the various product components (as discussed in this chapter) that you find on the website.

2. Fans are a key part of the core sport product. Develop a set of policies and plans for ensuring that your organization's fans or consumers will be a source of positive energy and not vulgar profanity or complaints. Explain how you will train and use stadium or arena staff, coaches, and players in this effort.

3. Try your hand at a new product image, mark, or logo for the merchandise of your favorite sport organization. What are the key elements of this image that you think will make it attractive to consumers? How will you protect the value of your product?

Use ideas from readings (note page numbers). Be sure to consider how the new marks truly capture the core of your product.

4. Prepare an outline that shows at least three dimensions on which brand image differs between Nike, the World Wrestling Federation, and the WNBA.

Your Marketing Plan

1. Briefly outline a new digital, virtual, or interactive product for your organization (perhaps to be placed on your website or on an app).

2. Create a product-space map like the one in figure 6.2 that indicates where your product can be positioned in a competitive marketplace.

Endnotes

1. Jill Rosen, "Putting a New, Strange Face on Preakness," *Baltimore Sun*, 29 March 2011, h t t p : / / articles.baltimoresun.com/2011-03-29/entertainment/bs-ae-preakness-campaign-20110329_1_infield-festivities-club-president-tom-chuck-as-preakness; Liz Mullen, "Place Your Bets: Horse Racing Industry Faces Long Odds," *SSSBJ*, April 28–May 4, 2008, 13, 14, 20, 22.

2. www.preakness.com/infield/infieldfest; analyst quotation in Rosen, "Putting a New, Strange Face."

3. Oxiris Barbot (female) MD, Baltimore Health Commissioner, http://takecarebmore.blogspot.com/2011/03/kegasus-really.html; "Kegasus Back for 2012 Preakness," http://espn.go.com/horse-racing/triplecrown2012/story/_/id/7747051/kegasus-back-preakness-infieldfest. Peter Land quote in Liz Mullen, "Place Your Bets: Horse Racing Industry Faces Long Odds," *SSSBJ*, April 28–May 4, 2008, 22; Kevin Cowherd, "Preakness 2013 Shaping Up to Be Another Great Showcase for Baltimore, *Baltimore Sun*, 12 May 2013, http://www.baltimoresun.com/sports/horse-racing/preakness/bs-sp-cowherd-preakness-0513-20130512,0,5546044.column.

4. Theodore Levitt, "Marketing Intangible Products and Product Intangibles," *Harvard Business Review* (May–June 1981): 94–102.

5. "Adios Sportschannel, Hola Fox Sports Net," *SBD*, 29 January 1998, 6; Rick Jones, "Sponsorship as Experiences," *Team Marketing Report*, March 2001, 8.

6. "Names in the News," *SBD*, 9 June 1998, 16.

7. "The Real Deal," *Economist*, 3 July 2004, 53.

8. Laura Nash, "Ethics Without the Sermon," *Harvard Business Review* (November 1981): 79–90; David Broughton, "Massachusetts Sets Pace in Team Lottery Games," *SSSBJ*, 7 February 2011, 10–11.

9. Michael Smith, "Firm Extends Corporate Perks To Schools' Fans," *SSSBJ*, 3 September 2012, 12.

10. Shira Springer, "A Garden Party," *Boston Sunday Globe*, 8 March 2009, A1, A12.

11. Michelle Brutlag Hosick, "More Than a Game," *NCAA News*, 27 September 2004, A1–4.

12. James Trecker, "The Freddy Factor," *SSSBJ*, 10–16 May 2004, 10; Scott Warfield, "Adu Mania Spurs MLS Attendance," *SSSBJ*, 8–14 November 2004, 1, 38–39.

13. Terry Lefton, "Retired Players Still Scoring in the Latest Sports Q-Scores," *SSSBJ*, 23–29 May 2005; www.qscores.com; http://qscores.blogspot.com/2012/05/tim-tebow-recognition-now-at-83.html.

14. "Tuna Helps Boost Ad Sales," *SBD*, 1 August 1997.

15. National Scouting Report products may be found at www.nsr-inc.com. For an attempt to analyze the NBA's management of race, see Glyn Hughes, "Managing Black Guys: Representation, Corporate Culture, and the NBA," *Sociology of Sport Journal*, 21 (2004): 163–184.

16. Quotations taken from Dan Levin, "Saying No to the System," *New York Times*, 19 August 2011, B-10; www.nytimes.com/2011/08/19/sports/chinese-athletes-begin-to-challenge-governments-tight-grip.html?_r=1&pagewanted=all.

17. Zachary Woolfe, "The Screen Can't Hear When You Yell 'Bravo,' " *New York Times*, 6 May 2012, AR1; Pete Thamel, "A Tradition Reverberates at Wisconsin," *New York Times*, 1 October 2011, D2.

18. Jack McCallum, "The Ugliest Game," *Sports Illustrated*, 29 November 2004, 44–51; Laura Smith, "Cheer Pressure," *Athletic Management*, June/July 2004, 43–49; "Football Hooligans," *Economist*, 12 June 2004, 54; http://bleacherreport.com/articles/1272302-25-most-awesome-fan-fights-in-the-stands.

19. Don Muret, "Reporting Troublemaker Just a Text Away," *SSSBJ*, 16 November 2009, 18, www.usatoday.com/sports/football/nfl/2008-08-05-

fan-code-of-conduct_N.htm; "Pressure Mounts to End Alcohol Sponsorship," www.sports-city.org/news_details.php?news_id=8972&idCategory=1.

20. Michael McCarthy, "NFL Unveils New Code of Conduct for Its Fans," *USA Today*, 6 August 2008, www.usatoday.com/sports/football/nfl/2008-08-05-fan-code-of-conduct_N.htm; Michael McCarthy, "NFL vs. Unruly Fans: League Out to Protect Game Day Experience." *USA Today*, 19 November 2009, www.usatoday.com/sports/football/nfl/2009-11-18-1a-cover-nfl-fans_N.htm; Michael McCarthy, "Misbehaving NFL Fans May Get Detention at Online School," *USA Today*, 16 April 2012, http://content.usatoday.com/communities/thehuddle/post/2012/04/ejected-nfl-fans-may-have-to-pay-for-online-course/1; Don Muret, "Major Southern California Sports Facilities Team Up to Create New Fan Code of Behavior," *SSSBJ*, 27 August 2012, 4, www.sportsbusinessdaily.com/Journal/Issues/2012/08/27/Facilities/Fan-code.aspx.

21. Mark Hyman, "Maryland Concocting a Code to Kick the !@#$% Out of Its Arena," *SSSBJ*, 10–16 May, 2004, 13; John Doyle, "ADs Try to Balance Spirit, Sportsmanship," *Foster's Daily Democrat*, 21 March 2010, C1, C4.

22. Kay Hawes, "Sportsmanship: Why Should Anybody Care?" *NCAA News*, 1 June 1998, 1, 18; "Strides in Sportsmanship Require First Step From All," *NCAA News*, 15 June 1998, 1, 6, 7; Laurie Smith, "Cheer Pressure," *Athletic Management*, June–July 2004, 43–49.

23. Mike Tanier, "There's an Exciting Clash on the Field. Oh, That's the Uniform," *New York Times*, 15 September 2011, A1.

24. Shira Springer, "Shot Clock Ticks for Sloganeers," *Boston Globe*, 8 June 2008, A1, A10.

25. Bruce Kuklick, *To Everything a Season: Shibe Park and Urban Philadelphia, 1909–1976* (Princeton, NJ: Princeton University Press, 1991), 191, 193.

26. Naomi Aoki, "Red Sox Owners Fielding More Nongame Revenue," *Boston Globe*, 16 October 2004, D-1, D-3; Jeff Klein, "The Game Is Big, but the Crowd Should Be Enormous," *New York Times*, 10 December 2010, www.nytimes.com/2010/12/11/sports/hockey/11hockey.html?_r=1&emc=eta1&pagewanted=print; AP, "College Football: Go Bride! Michigan Stadium Available for Weddings," naplesnews.com, 22 July 2011.

27. A.J. Magrath, "When Marketing Services, 4 Ps Are Not Enough," *Business Horizons*, May–June 1986, 44–50.

28. Gary Brown, "PSAC Events Undergo Peer Review," *Champion*, Spring 2009, 68.

29. Charles L. Martin, "The Customer Relations Dimension of the Employee-Customer Interface: An Empirical Investigation of Employee Behaviors and Customer Perceptions," *Journal of Sport Management*, 4 (January 1990): 1–20; Randal Ross, "Creating the Service Experience," *Fitness Management*, September 1993, 32–33.

30. Ingrid K. Williams, "Root, Root, Root and Buy Me Some Eel, *New York Sunday Times*, 5 July 2009, TR5; "Myanmar Soccer Fans Given Freedom of Raucous Speech," *New York Times*, 1 September 2011, A4, www.nytimes.com/2011/09/01/world/asia/01iht-myanmar01.html?_r=1.

31. Williams, "Root, Root, Root and Buy Me Some Eel," Scott Sayare; "Football, American Style, Is Alive in France," *New York Times*, July 12, 2009, SP11.

32. "Aikman: NFL in Europe 'Arrogant,'" http://chicago.cbslocal.com/2011/10/24/aikman-nfl-in-europe-arrogant/.

33. Mark Falcous and Joe Maguire, "Imagining 'America': The NBA and Local-Global Mediascapes, *International Review for the Sociology of Sport*, 41 (2006): 59–78; Joe Maguire, "More Than a Sporting Touchdown: The Making of American Football in England, 1982–1990," *Sociology of Sport Journal*, 7 (1990): 213–237, quotations at 224–225.

34. "2007 *SBJ/SBD* Reader Survey—Hockey," *SSSBJ*, 26 November 2007, 35.

35. "Babe Ruth Bat Hits Auction Record," *Boston Globe*, 3 December 2004, A-2; www.haulsofshame.com.

36. Bill King, "Cubs Try Topps Twist on Traditional Promotion," *SSSBJ*, 11–17 June 2001, 3; Terry Lefton, "Extra, Extra! Sports Pins and Coin Programs Hot With Newspapers," *SSSBJ*, 20–26 September 2004, 14; Bill King, "Finding the Pop for Kids, Teens," *SSSBJ*, 16–22 July 2005, 1, 28–29; Andy Bernstein, "Sports Leagues Get Serious About Toys, *SSSBJ*, 10–16 August 1998, 9; "One Man Gathers What Another Man Spills," *SBD*, 4 December 1997, 4; David Broughton, "How Best to Use the Bait? MLB Teams Continue to Tweak Their Promotion Schedules, Searching for the Offers That Boost Attendance, Improve the Fan Experience and Increase Sponsor Exposure," *SSSBJ*, October 17, 2011, 17–20; Bill Keveney, "Stan Lee Teams Up With the NHL For Superpower Promo," *USA Today*, 8 October 2010, 2D; Greg Wyshynski, "Stan Lee's NHL Guardian Project Failure Cost Tech Firm Millions," *Yahoo Sports*, 4 December 2011, http://sports.yahoo.com/nhl/blog/puck_daddy/post/stan-lees-nhl-guardian-project-failure-cost-tech-firm-millions?urn=n-hl,wp18962

37. "Fielding Football Fantasies," *Athletic Management*, August–September 2004, 10; LPGA news release,

8 January 1997; Peter Mandel, "A Week Playing With the Big Boys," *Boston Globe*, 2 April 2004, M-10, M-11.

38. Jon Snow, "LPGA Moves Toward Customized Tickets," *SSSBJ*, 5–11 November 2007, 10.

39. Eric Fisher, "Codes Link Program to Red Wings' Online Video," *SSSBJ*, 15 February 2010, 9; Dan Kaplan, "Eagles Add Apps for Fans With Smartphones, *SSSBJ*, 22 August 2011, 7.

40. Eric Fisher, "Smartphones Next Target for FanVision," *SSSBJ*, 30 August 2010, 3; www.fanvision.com; Bob Tedeschi, "Tracking Major League Baseball, a Perfect Sport for an App," *New York Times*, 29 March 2012, B9; Eric Fischer, "Attention Getter," *SSSBJ*, 12 July 2010, 15–16; "YinzCam application offers stats, replays," *SSSBJ*, 7 February 2011, 16.

41. Hiawatha Bray, "Sega Blitzes EA's Madden With NFL Hit," *Boston Globe*, 1 November 2004, B-1, B-8; http://en.wikipedia.org/wiki/Norman_Sas; "CrowdWave Getting Fans out of Their Seats," *SSSBJ*, 7 February 2011, 16.

42. "NASCAR: Moving to the Music" insert, *Sport Illustrated*, 3 August 1998; "Marquee Group's New Team Service," *SBD*, 24 June 1998, 3; "Alphabet City," *SBD*, 5 September 1997, 4; Russell Adams, "Red Sox DVD Already a Record Breaker," *SSSBJ*, 15–21 November 2004, 4.

43. Eliana Dockterman, "Good $ports: Inside the Rise of Fantasy Everything," *Time*, 27 August 2012, 18.

44. Marc Andreessen, "Why Software Is Eating The World," *Wall Street Journal*, 20 August 2011, C-2.

45. Geraldine Willigan, "High-Performance Marketing: An Interview With Nike's Phil Knight," *Harvard Business Review*, July–August 1992, 92, 99; "Nike's Knight Announces Reforms," *SBD*, 13 May 1998, 3.

46. Michael Hiestand, "NBA Puts Clout to Test," *USA Today*, 5 February 1997, 3C.

47. Philip Kotler, *Marketing Management*, 9th ed. (Upper Saddle River, NJ: Prentice Hall, 1997), 282.

48. Stephen Hardy, "Profile/Interview with Matt Levine," *SMQ*, 5 (September 1996): 5–12; Douglas Robson, "Sharks Sink in Sales Rankings," *SSSBJ*, 2–8 November 1998, 40.

49. Susan Higgins and James Martin, "Managing Sport Innovations: A Diffusion Theory Perspective," *SMQ*, 5 (March 1996): 43–48; E.M. Rogers, *Diffusion of Innovation*, 3rd ed. (New York: Free Press, 1983).

50. Lawrence Fielding, Lori Miller, and James Brown, "Harlem Globetrotters, Inc." *Journal of Sport Management*, 13 (1999): 45–77.

51. Tripp Mickle, "Turnaround Teams: How Rocky Wirtz and Team President John McDonough Brought the Blackhawks Back," *SSSBJ*, 6 October 2008, 1, 15, 16, 20.

52. Brett Mendel, "Up Against the Pros: Converting the Community," *Athletic Management*, September 1993, 13.

53. Sergio Zyman, *The End of Marketing as We Know It* (New York: Harper Business, 1999), 80–82; O'Hara quoted in Terry Lefton, "9 Rules for Making the Most of Sports Property/Ad Agency Relationships," *SSSBJ*, September 24–30, 2007, 23–28, quotation at 28.

54. For suggestions on the use of perceptual maps, see James Martin, "Using a Perceptual Map of the Consumer's Sport Schema to Help Make Sponsorship Decisions," *SMQ*, 3 (3) (September 1994): 27–33.

55. Geraldine E. Milligan, "High Performance Marketing: An Interview With Nike's Phil Knight," *Harvard Business Review* (July–August 1992): 91–101. For world football brands, see Sue Bridgewater, *Football Brands* (Basingstoke; New York: Palgrave Macmillan, 2010).

56. Terry Lefton, "*SI* Enters Retail Market With Detroit Location," *SSSBJ*, 15 September 2008, 4.

57. "ESPN's Full-Court Press," *Men's Journal*, March 1998, 30; Kotler, *Marketing Management*, 442–460; Jay Gladden, G. Milne, and W.A. Sutton, "A Conceptual Framework for Assessing Brand Equity in Division I College Athletics," *Journal of Sport Management*, 12 (1) (1998): 1–9; L.E. Boone, C.M. Kochunny, and D. Wilkins, "Applying the Brand Equity Concept to Major League Baseball," *SMQ*, 4 (September 1995): 33–42; D.A. Aaker, *Building Strong Brands* (New York: Free Press, 1996); Terry Lifton, "Study Helps NFL Unify Branding Efforts," *SSSBJ*, 5 September 2005, 34.

58. For a detailed discussion see Stephen Hardy, Brian Norman, and Sarah Sceery, "Toward a History of Sport Branding," *Journal of Historical Research in Marketing*, special issue "Marketing Sport Through the Ages," 4 (4) (November 2012): 482–509.

59. Nariman Dhalla and Sonia Yuspeh, "Forget the Product Life Cycle Concept!" *Harvard Business Review* (January–February 1976): 102–112.

Chapter 7

Managing Sport Brands

Jay Gladden

OBJECTIVES

- To understand the scope and importance of brand management and branding in the sport setting

- To demonstrate an understanding of how brand equity is developed in a variety of sport settings

- To identify and discuss the sources of brand associations for teams, athletes, agencies, and other sport entities

And the World's Strongest Team Brand Is . . .

It's not the Miami Heat, the Dallas Cowboys, or even the New York Yankees. Think globally! Think soccer, or football, as it is called throughout the rest of the world. Manchester United of the English Premier League is the world's strongest sport team brand. In 2012 *Forbes* magazine estimated that the Manchester United brand was worth US$2.24 billion.[1] This figure is nearly US$400 million more than the valuations associated with the Yankees and the Cowboys.[2] At the core of this valuation is the fact that Manchester United has 330 million fans around the world.[3] As a point of reference, that total is larger than the entire population of the United States. This large fan base allows the Red Devils to secure large-scale global media and sponsorship contracts. For example, in 2013 Manchester United signed an eight-year sponsorship deal with the Aon corporation. In return for commercial rights associated with the training complex and the training uniform (or kit, as it is called in soccer), Manchester United will receive approximately US$23 million annually.[4]

The Red Devils have been the highest valued team since *Forbes* first released valuations of English soccer clubs in 2004.[5] Because significant value is associated with Manchester United's brand, the organization carefully manages where the logo appears and how it is used. In fact, if you visit the Red Devils website (www.manutd.com), you will be able to navigate to a specific page that discusses the brand protection of Manchester United's marks. The page stipulates what logos Manchester United owns and how to gain permission to use those logos.[6] All this is done to protect and nurture the brand. If Manchester United allowed any company to use their marks, the value associated with the brand and the revenue that they could generate from commercial agreements with sponsors would decrease. This is an example of brand management.

Since the mid-1990s *branding* has become a popular term in the spectator sport industry. Almost every day, it seems, you can read about a sport organization embarking on some new branding initiative. The story of Jeremy Lin, highlighted in chapter 1 of this book, is a good illustration of a rapidly emerging brand management opportunity for an athlete. In many ways, that case is similar to that of Manchester United, just shorter in duration. Lin's likeness quickly received much publicity and corporate interest. There was a need to protect certain marks (Linsanity) and opportunities to generate significant revenue.

The fact that branding is a prevalent part of today's discourse is a good sign for the sport industry. Chapter 1 of this book described the sport marketing myopia that has often pervaded the sport industry. This myopia was characterized by a short-term focus on revenue generation rather than a long-term focus on developing loyal customers. Sport organizations that look at themselves as brands to be managed are taking an important step away from such myopic tendencies. As you will soon see, branding is vitally important to the long-term health and success of a sport organization.

This chapter begins by answering the question, What is branding? In doing so, it provides an understanding of branding and brand management with a particular focus on the spectator sport setting. Following the introduction and definitions of concepts, an in-depth discussion on the development of brand equity is provided. Central to this discussion is a focus on how brand associations are formed by organizations involved with sport, including teams, sponsors, athletes, and sport management and marketing agencies. Throughout this chapter, examples from the sport setting are provided so that you can see how those concepts are at work in the sport setting.

What Is Branding?

Branding starts with a brand, which includes the name, logo, and symbols associated with the sport organization.[7] For example, the Nike name and the Nike swoosh are both important components of the Nike brand. Similarly, both the nickname *Liberty* and the logo that includes a version of the Statue of Liberty are important components of the WNBA's New York Liberty brand. Ultimately, the brand name and marks associated with a sport organization provide a point of differentiation from the other sport, leisure, and entertainment-oriented products in the marketplace. These names and marks are important facets of branding as evidenced by the fact that more than half of the teams in the NBA, NFL, NHL, and MLB have modified their uniforms (and sometimes their logos) since 1995.[8]

But thinking of branding as simply the management and manipulation of an organization's marks would be myopic. The brand name, logos, marks, and colors of a sport organization serve as a starting point in the brand management process, serving to trigger other feelings and attitudes toward the organization. When a Boston Red Sox fan hears the team's name mentioned, a variety of thoughts may come to mind, including the Red Sox's 2004 World Series victory (its first in 86 years!), the 2007 and 2013 World Series victories, the fabled "Green Monster" outfield wall at their home field Fenway Park, or great players who have worn a Red Sox uniform such as Ted Williams, Carlton Fisk, and Curt Schilling. The brand is, as author Daryl Travis suggested, "like a badge that lends you a certain identity."[9] Thus, a key point about branding is that it goes much deeper than the names, symbols, and marks of an organization. Branding is really about what a customer thinks and feels when she sees the marks of a particular brand.

As it relates to the sport setting, what consumers think and feel toward a sport-related brand is developed based on experiences that they have when consuming sport (for example, attending a game, watching a game on television or through a portable electronic device such as an iPhone or iPad, or watching highlights of a game on ESPN's *SportsCenter*). The benefits provided by consuming sport are much more experiential than tangible. You cannot touch or taste a baseball game, whereas you can taste the toothpaste that you put into your mouth. Additionally, what makes the experience of consuming sport unique is the emotion tied to sport. Sport has the ability to trigger emotions that are arguably unlike those activated by other leisure or entertainment products available. Can you think of an experience that triggers your emotions (good or bad) more than watching your favorite team play its rival in a game that has playoff implications? Despite the fact that we live in a time when we regularly record or TiVo shows, we are hesitant to do that with sporting events because reviewing the event later is just not the same as seeing it, or experiencing it, live.

Being experiential and emotional lends sport organizations some advantage here. As author Marc Gobé stated,

> In this hypercompetitive marketplace where goods and services alone are no longer enough to attract a new market or even to maintain existing markets or clients, I believe that it is the *emotional* aspect of products and their distribution systems that will be the key difference between consumers' ultimate choice and the price that they will pay. By emotional I mean how a brand engages consumers on the level of the senses and emotions; how a brand comes to life for people and forges a deeper, lasting connection.[10]

Think about your favorite team for a minute. Beyond its name and marks, how long does it take you to come up with a memory that has some emotion attached to it? Spectator sport is unique in the variety of emotions that are generated and in the level of emotional involvement that consumers have with their favorite sport team or athlete brands. This emotional involvement can be favorably transferred to sponsors of sport. How else can you explain the fact that many NASCAR fans buy only the products of the corporations that sponsor their favorite drivers? Logic goes out the window when brands are able to create such emotional connections.

Therefore, one of the key goals of branding is to create such a strong impression in the consumers' minds that when they see or hear something that includes a brand's name or see its logo, marks, or colors, they experience intense positive feelings. As Declan Bolger, vice president of club services for Major League Soccer has said, "People make decisions based on emotion, and reinforce them with logic."[11] If a sport brand triggers positive emotions, the sport marketer can more easily engage fans and consumers in the products of that sport brand.

Importance of Brand Equity

When a sport organization is able to achieve a strong image in the consumer's mind, it realizes brand equity. According to David Aaker, a leading expert on branding, brand equity is "a set of assets and liabilities linked to a brand, its name and symbol, that add to or subtract from the value provided by a product or service to a firm and/or that firm's customers."[12] Strong positive emotional connections formed between the fan and a team are an example of the assets to which Aaker refers. The New York Yankees' 27 World Series wins have helped create a number of strong emotional connections with the Yankees brand that can be seen as assets. But the sport marketer must also be wary of creating negative feelings toward the sport organization. For example, during the late 1990s and early 2000s, the NBA's Portland Trail Blazers experienced several incidents in which players were arrested for running afoul of the law. Similarly, in 2004 the Indiana Pacers were one of the best teams in the NBA. In November of that year, however, two Pacers went into the crowd to fight with several Detroit Pistons fans during a game. This fight and the resulting penalties not only thwarted the Pacers' championship aspirations but also created negative brand associations with the fans. In this case, a series of events created negative impressions in consumers' minds that could be viewed as liabilities linked to the brand.

Benefits of Brand Equity

When a team such as Manchester United of the Barclay's Premier League is able to generate a wealth of assets linked to its brand, the team is thought to have high brand equity. This position is the ultimate goal for the sport franchise manager because a number of benefits result from having high brand equity. Perhaps most important, loyalty to the team brand increases when brand equity is high. Which team has higher brand equity—Major League Baseball's Chicago Cubs or Kansas City Royals? Although the Cubs have not won a World Series in more than 100 years, they regularly sell out games at their home field, Wrigley Field. In contrast, the Kansas City Royals struggle to fill half of their stadium, Kauffman Stadium, for most games. Although neither team has had much success recently, the Cubs have a stronger brand because of unique brand assets such as Wrigley Field, which is located in a nice Chicago neighborhood about 1 mile (1.6 km) from Lake Michigan and just a few miles from the downtown business district. Achieving a high level of brand loyalty allows the sport marketer to realize increases in revenue through ticket and merchandise sales. Brand loyalty also typically results in a larger viewing audience for events, which in turn allows the sport organization to realize higher broadcast fees for the rights to televise a property's games or events and attract more sponsors looking for widespread television exposure.

The case of the Cubs also underscores the fact that winning is *not* the only important factor in the creation of brand loyalty. Research has documented that factors other than winning are more predictive of brand loyalty for North American professional sport teams.[13] Again referring back to chapter 1, do you remember how a winning-is-everything mentality was an example of sport marketing myopia? Researchers have documented that winning is *not* everything and that other factors contribute to the realization of ticket sales, corporate sponsorship sales, and other positive revenue outcomes.[14] In fact, sport marketers can create equity for their brands in a variety of ways, many of which are discussed later in this chapter. The important point here is that brand equity creates brand loyalty. As chapters 8 and

11 point out, relationship marketing is central to the development of loyal customers. Similarly, building relationships with the customers of a sport organization can enhance the brand.

Less Drastic Revenue Declines When the Team Loses

Because strong brands have high levels of loyalty, they are better able to withstand downturns in fortunes on the field. Although winning is not the only creator of brand equity, teams clearly reap short-term benefits when they win. Few teams, however, are able to compete for championships year in and year out. The myopic sport marketer sees the organization's fortunes tied to the performance of the team on the field. The sport marketer who adopts a longer-term view, however, focuses on other things that can be done to enhance brand equity so that when the team loses, fortunes do not drastically decline.

Again, take the Chicago Cubs as an example. Here is a team that has not won a World Series in more than 100 years, yet it still draws large crowds for its home games. The Cubs posted a record of 61 wins and 101 losses in 2012 but still drew nearly 2.9 million fans to Wrigley Field! This figure is only about 425,000 fewer fans than they drew in 2007 when the Cubs *won* nearly 100 games.[15] So yes, performance may affect attendance, but when a team has high brand equity and high brand loyalty, the drop-offs are much less extreme. Figure 7.1 depicts the revenues

over time of two teams that experience cycles of winning and losing, one with high brand equity and the other with low brand equity. When brand equity is high (team A), revenue declines are less drastic over time as the team's fortunes change. Meanwhile, when brand equity is lower (team B), more drastic revenue changes are seen as the team wins and loses.

Ability to Charge Price Premiums

Another potential benefit of high brand equity is the ability to charge price premiums.[16] In the sport setting, where having revenues exceed expenses is often challenging, this benefit can be particularly important. Team Marketing Report annually publishes a report called the *Fan Cost Index,* which highlights both the average ticket price for a professional sporting event and the average cost of attending for a family of four. Table 7.1 documents the five teams with the highest ticket prices in Major League Baseball, the National Hockey League, the National Football League, and the National Basketball Association. Although some teams regularly made the playoffs before 2012, such as the New England Patriots, Los Angeles Lakers, and New York Yankees, quite a few teams, such as the Chicago Cubs, Edmonton Oilers, and Minnesota Twins, had not been in the playoffs in several years before the season listed in table 7.1.

Another interesting point of comparison can be found when looking at the NFL data. The average ticket price for the New York Jets was higher than that for the New York Giants in 2011. This disparity is particularly illustrative of brand equity for several reasons. First, the two teams share a stadium, thus eliminating the possibility that one team's attendance was higher because of stadium design, amenities, or history. Second, the Giants, not the Jets, had most recently won a Super Bowl (in 2008, and they would go on to win the Super Bowl again in 2012), while the Jets had not even played in a Super Bowl since 1969! How else can we then explain the ability of the Jets to charge a higher average ticket price? The strength of the Jets brand, going back to the historic 1969 upset of the Baltimore Colts by the Namath-led Jets allowed for revenue generation despite a lack of Super Bowl championships.

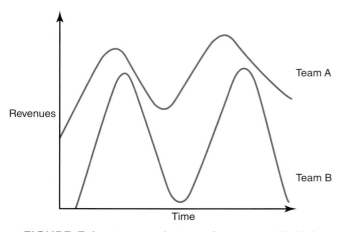

FIGURE 7.1   Revenue fortunes for teams with high and low brand equity.

TABLE 7.1   Teams With the Highest Ticket Prices in the Major Professional Sport Leagues for Teams Playing in 2011-13

NFL (2011)	Average price	NBA (2012)	Average price	NHL (2013)	Average price	MLB (2012)	Average price
New York Jets	$120.85	New York Knicks	$123.22	Toronto Maple Leafs	$124.69	Boston Red Sox	$53.38
Dallas Cowboys	$110.20	Los Angeles Lakers	$100.25	Winnipeg Jets	$97.84	New York Yankees	$51.55
New England Patriots	$117.84	Boston Celtics	$72.96	Edmonton Oilers	$79.27	Chicago Cubs	$46.30
New York Giants	$111.69	Miami Heat	$72.50	Vancouver Canucks	$87.38	Philadelphia Phillies	$37.42
Chicago Bears	$101.55	Chicago Bulls	$71.90	Montreal Canadiens	$78.56	Minnesota Twins	$33.04

Data from *Fan cost experience*. Available: http://fancostexperience.com/pages/fcx/fci.php.

More Corporate Interest

As noted in chapter 9, corporate sponsorship is an ever-increasing presence in sport today. Although corporations clearly see the benefits in this marketing method, another reason for the increased presence may be sport organizations' efforts to seek new revenue streams. But more events than ever are looking for sponsorships, and sponsors are becoming more discerning about which events they sponsor. One factor that sponsors may consider is the strength of the sport organization's brand. For example, NASCAR sponsors realize that both the governing body (NASCAR) and a number of the individual drivers (Jeff Gordon, Jimmie Johnson, Danica Patrick) have high brand equity. One contributing factor to this high brand equity is the emotional connection and commitment that fans have toward the race teams. As a result, sponsors are attracted to NASCAR teams because they know that these brands hold powerful places in the minds of consumers.

Sport organizations with high brand equity increase the price of the sponsorship package to take advantage of the fact that many corporations might be interested in becoming sponsors. Think for a minute: What sport event or organization can charge some of the highest rates for a sponsorship? If you said the Olympic Games and soccer's World Cup, you are correct. Taking the Olympic Games as an example, the International Olympic Committee (which oversees the Olympic Movement and has the responsibility for selling Olympics sponsorships) is able to charge approximately $60 million for Olympics sponsorships for a four-year period.[17] Similarly, according to the International Events Group (IEG), FIFA, which oversees the World Cup, has increased its revenues from $584 million between 1998 and 2002, to $1.6 billion between 2007 and 2010 by charging between $24 and $44 million to the sponsors at the highest level.[18] Without question, the equity associated with the Olympic Games and World Cup events create the opportunity to charge high sponsorship fees for affiliation.

Licensing and Merchandising Opportunities

Sport organizations with strong brands are also better able to develop brand extensions, or to use "a brand name established in one product class to enter another product class."[19] Sport organizations can use the organization's name to launch new products to enhance revenue streams. Some sport organizations have taken advantage of their brand strength to sell team-logoed merchandise in a team-owned merchandise store, open restaurants bearing the organization's name, and create television programming and even channels bearing the organization's name. For example, the Pittsburgh Pirates have Pirates Clubhouse Stores from which they sell Pirates-logoed merchandise. At the league level, the National Basketball Association has a merchandise store (the NBA Store) and a TV network (NBA TV). Adopting a slightly different perspective, the NBA has also used its brand to extend into professional women's basketball (with the WNBA) and into minor league basketball (with the National Basketball Development League, or D-League). Such licensing opportunities are also available for teams and players. In 2013 the New York Giants partnered with the Hackensack University Medical Center to create the HackensackUMC Fitness and Wellness Center Powered by the Giants.[20] In this venture, the Giants are lending their brand name to a state-of-the art, 112,000 square foot (10,400 sq. m) health club.[21] Coming off two Super Bowl victories between 2008 and 2013, the Giants brand lends credibility and uniqueness to this new venture.

How Brand Equity Is Developed

Now that we have established the important benefits of brand equity (and their relationship to long-term revenue generation), you are probably thinking, OK, how is brand equity developed? That is a good question. According to brand researcher Kevin Keller, two components are essential to developing brand equity: (1) the creation of awareness about the brand and (2) the creation of a brand image.[22] Think about your favorite professional athlete for a minute. First, and most obviously, you are aware that the athlete exists. That is brand awareness. The second step is a little more challenging. What adjectives come to mind when you think of that athlete? Why is that athlete your favorite? Your answer probably has something to do with the way that the person plays the sport or his or her personality both in and out of competition. The combination of these elements is what we call the brand image.

Brand Awareness

As brand researcher David Aaker put it, "An unknown brand usually has little chance."[23] If a potential consumer is not aware that a minor league hockey franchise exists 20 miles (32 km) from her home, then the minor league hockey franchise has no brand awareness. For that reason, brand awareness is often seen as the starting point in developing brand equity. The easiest way to define brand awareness is to refer to it as *the ability of a consumer to name the brand's existence when its product category is mentioned.* For example, if we were to ask a resident of Charlotte, North Carolina, to name all the professional sport franchises in the area and he did not name minor league baseball's Charlotte Knights, then the Knights would not have brand awareness.

The two most important components to building brand equity are brand awareness and brand image, but brand image cannot be developed without brand awareness. Developing brand awareness is typically not an issue for major league sport franchises such as NBA, NFL, NHL, MLB, and MLS teams, but it does become more challenging for events, facilities, and minor league sport franchises. Additionally, a primary challenge for a sport agent representing a new athlete is to create brand awareness for her client. Similarly, you may be familiar with "Heisman hype," the publicity campaigns that colleges and universities undertake to promote their star athletes for college football's most outstanding player award. Past efforts to promote athletes for the Heisman Trophy include Rutgers University's sending out binoculars so that people could "see" running back Ray Rice and the University of Southern California's sending out highlight videos of receiver Marqise Lee set to music by the legendary Beatles rock band.[24] These are great examples of efforts to develop brand awareness.

The development of brand awareness is also important for corporations that sponsor events. Sponsors pay to be associated with athletes, teams, events, and leagues (often called sport properties). Part of their expectation is that fans of those sport properties will feel better about the corporate sponsor because they are supporting the property. Such a transfer of goodwill cannot happen if the consumer is not aware of a corporation's sponsorship efforts. If you have even the most remote interest in professional race car driving, you are probably aware that Sprint is the sponsor of the overall points championship. But are you aware of the other NASCAR sponsors or the individual team sponsors? How many of Dale Earnhardt Jr.'s sponsors can you name? For this reason, sponsorship evaluation usually involves measuring the level of awareness of the sponsorship.

Brand Image

Although the concept of brand awareness is easy to grasp, understanding brand image is more difficult because brand image is the cumulative influence of all the associations with a particular brand.[25] Take out a piece of paper and think about your favorite team. Now, time yourself. Spend one minute writing down all the words and phrases that come to mind when you think of that team.

The words and phrases that you have written down are called brand associations, because they represent the thoughts that the mention of a brand name triggers. If you were thinking of the New York Yankees, you may have been thinking such things as "world champions," because of the many World Series that the Yankees have won. Or you may have been thinking about Monument Park, the area in the outfield of Yankee Stadium where statues of Yankees greats stand. In both cases, these thoughts are unique, strong, and favorable. That is the goal in developing a brand image—to develop unique, strong, and favorable brand associations. Marketers of sport may have an advantage when it comes to creating unique associations. Where else is the product so packed with drama because of an unknown outcome? Where else is the emotional involvement between the consumer (the fan) and the product (the game or event) so high?

The key is making sure that these brand associations are both strong and favorable. This task is not necessarily easy given that the outcome of the event is unknown. And, as noted earlier in the text, the marketer cannot control when a team performs well or when an athlete gets hurt. In an ideal world, we would be able to know when the team we were marketing was going to succeed. That way, we would know that fans would have strong and favorable associations with winning. The team's ability to win in the current or upcoming year, however, is undetermined. Thus, although winning can certainly create a strong, unique, and favorable brand association, sport marketers should focus their energies on

nurturing this association in advance of a team's actual performance.

One aspect of winning can serve as a valuable brand association—past success. After Michael Jordan retired from the Chicago Bulls in 1998, the Bulls immediately entered a rebuilding era. For six consecutive years, the Bulls did not make the playoffs, and in three of those years the Bulls did not even win 20 games.[26] At the same time, the Bulls led the NBA in average attendance between 1999 and 2009.[27] This success may have resulted from their marketing efforts, which reminded fans of the six NBA championships that the Bulls won in the 1990s and suggested that the period following Jordan's retirement was the time to get tickets because the Bulls would again become a championship-caliber team. Thus, a *tradition* of past success can be an important brand association. Given the traditions of competing for national championships at schools such as Duke University (men's basketball), the University of Michigan (football), and the University of Connecticut (women's and men's basketball), fans of those schools have strong associations with the past accomplishments of their teams.

Beyond success and tradition, a variety of other sources of brand association exist in sport. A sampling of these are discussed in the following sections.

Sources of Brand Association With Teams

The success of the team is one source of brand association, but other aspects of the team and its marketing, promotion, and publicity efforts can develop strong brand associations. These include, but are not limited to, the following:

- Logo, marks, nickname, and mascot
- Owners
- Players
- Head coaches
- Rivalries
- Entertainment package surrounding the game or event
- Stadium or arena in which a team plays

Although branding is more than just managing the organization's logo, the logo, marks, nickname, and mascot can all create strong, unique,

The NFL's Oakland Raiders create many brand extensions from their nickname and colors. The "Black Hole" is a good example of one such extension.

and favorable brand associations. Take team colors as an example. Los Angeles Lakers fans would probably mention the purple and yellow uniform colors, Oakland Raider fans often refer to their team as the silver and black, and University of Michigan fans have strong associations with the maize and blue. When creating or changing a logo, teams should take great care to consider the ways in which brand associations can be developed. For example, should the nickname represent a unique feature about the location of the team, as is the case with the Phoenix Suns (referring to the perpetual sunny, warm weather in Phoenix) and the Pittsburgh Steelers (hearkening back to Pittsburgh's history as a steel town)? Or, should the logo contain colors that are fashionable and attractive (such as the San Jose Sharks' use of teal in the early 1990s when that color was popular)? Or, should the nickname be easily translatable into a mascot that can create strong brand associations in the minds of kids (as is the case of Benny the Bull, the mascot of the Chicago Bulls)? All these things need to be considered when changing the logo or nickname.

The owner or owners of the sport franchise are often the most visible team personnel aside from the head coach and the players. Through their actions, owners can generate positive brand associations. For example, when John Henry and Tom Werner purchased the Boston Red Sox of MLB, they publicly stated initiatives geared toward pleasing their fans and making their fans more proud of the team. In a similar vein, Mark Cuban has responded directly to e-mails from fans of the Dallas Mavericks of the NBA on a daily basis. By doing this, he creates the impression that he cares about the fans' opinions, thus creating a favorable brand association. Now consider the Steinbrenner family, owners of MLB's New York Yankees. Although baseball fans who do not like the Yankees tend to have negative associations with the Steinbrenners, Yankees fans tend to have favorable associations with the family because they are committed to winning championships and do everything in their power to do so.

A more obvious source of brand associations for teams is the players themselves. A variety of associations can be developed in association with the players. For example, associations could be formed based on how a player actually performs. Michael Jordan was perceived to walk on air, particularly in his early years with the NBA's Chicago Bulls. Zdeno Chara of the NHL's Boston Bruins is a 6-foot-9-inch (206 cm) defenseman. Besides his perennially excellent play, his unique size (for a hockey player) creates brand associations. Associations can also be formed around a player off the court. An interesting case related to developing associations based on behavior is Metta World Peace (formerly named Ron Artest) of the NBA's Los Angeles Lakers. When he was with the Indiana Pacers in 2004, Peace was one of the players who left the game floor and entered the stands to fight with fans at Detroit's Palace at Auburn Hills. From that incident and his subsequent suspension (73 regular season games), Peace created negative brand associations in the minds of fans who found the behavior inexcusable. Following his suspension, Peace became involved in causes related to mental-health counseling. In recognition of this effort, the Pro Basketball Writers presented Peace the J. Walter Kennedy Citizenship Award.[28] Through this off-court work, Peace may have offset the previous negative associations with his brand by creating positive associations.

Similarly, the head coach of a team can serve as a significant source of brand associations. If you are a football fan, think about the brand associations that Coach Jim Harbaugh of the NFL's San Francisco 49ers generates: successful coach, great motivator, entertaining person, and a man players respect. Similar to players, coaches have the potential for associations that go beyond their performance on the field or court. Given the fact that high-profile college athletes play for their teams for a maximum of four years, head coaches can be a more important source of brand associations on college campuses. For example, Mike Krzyzewski, or Coach K as he is most often called, has generated a number of brand associations during his long tenure as the head coach of the men's basketball team at Duke University. Besides directing the significant success that Duke has experienced on the court, Coach K has developed a variety of associations such as an academic focus and integrity. Beyond the fact that Coach K has graduated student-athletes at a high percentage and has never experienced a rules violation scandal, he has been a significant benefactor to Duke and its surrounding community. Coach K's name is on an academic leadership center, and his Duke basketball legacy fund has helped create a large community center in downtown Durham, North Carolina.[29]

A word of caution must be offered with respect to players and coaches as sources of brand associations. Player mobility at the professional team sport level is as great as ever; few players remain a member of the same team for their entire careers. Further, many high-profile collegiate athletes now stay at their universities for only one or two years before turning professional. For that reason, a team should not focus its brand-building efforts on one player, particularly when that player's contract is nearing an end. Professional and collegiate coaches are also mobile these days. Thus, although coaches can be tremendous sources of associations, their departure can cause a significant loss of brand associations that ultimately hurts the team's brand. One way to counteract such departures is to understand whether and how the player or coach played a role in building the team brand and then sign players and coaches who either have the potential to build similar associations or have the potential to build their own unique and favorable associations. Does this mean that owners and athletics directors should consider the marketing implication of their coaching decisions? Based on the preceding discussion of how they create brand associations, the answer is yes.

Opponents can create strong brand associations for a team. For example, the Boston Red Sox–New York Yankees rivalry serves as a strong brand association for both MLB teams. Such rivalries and the crucial games that are played between teams (such as the historic 2004 American League Championship Series that the Red Sox won after being down three games to none) create long-lasting memories that motivate sports fans to follow teams. At the college level, rivalries at all levels create strong associations not only among sports fans but also among alumni. Although they play at the Division III level (the lowest level of college competition in U.S. intercollegiate athletics), the Amherst (Massachusetts) versus Williams (Massachusetts) and DePauw (Indiana) versus Wabash (Indiana) football games are so popular that they are typically televised by regional sports providers. Thus, strong brand associations can be reinforced not only by attending one of these games but also by watching them on television all over the country.

As noted in chapter 10, the effective use of promotional elements can greatly enhance the experience that people have at games. This enhancement of the entertainment package through promotional tactics such as giveaways and on-court, on-ice, or on-field promotions during time-outs and intermissions can serve to create strong brand associations. Earlier it was mentioned that the NBA's Chicago Bulls were able to maintain large crowds in the post-Jordan era despite poor performance on the court. Although their nurturing of brand associations tied to past success might be part of the reason for the high attendance, another reason could be the fact that Bulls games are highly entertaining. Time-outs, halftime, and the breaks between quarters are used to provide additional entertainment for those in attendance. In college athletics, several unique factors can create strong brand associations tied to teams. For example, at the University of Mississippi, "the Grove" serves as a popular tailgating area both before and after games. At Ohio State University, fans are often in Ohio Stadium 30 to 45 minutes in advance of the game so that they can see the nationally renowned marching band enter the stadium and execute its pregame routine. Finally, where college athletics events attract large and loud student sections (such as at Duke University men's basketball games), the exuberant, youthful crowd can also serve as a source of brand associations. In fact, when asked what would enhance their enjoyment of college athletics events, season-ticket holders (who are not students) often mention larger and louder student sections.

Another way that the entertainment experience can be enhanced is through a focus on the service elements that a consumer experiences when attending a game. Think about all the experiences that you have when attending a game; any of these could theoretically form a brand association. Some facilities offer unique cuisine items at their concession stands, whereas others have unique features built into the stadium, such as the swimming pool in the outfield at Chase Field in Phoenix.

Now more than ever, the stadium or arena can serve as a source of brand associations. Strong brand associations are typically formed around two types of arenas these days: (1) those with long histories and traditions and (2) new facilities that are built with many features to enhance the customer experience. Facilities such as Wimbledon (tennis), the Daytona International Speedway (auto racing), Yankee Stadium (MLB), Fenway Park (MLB), Lambeau Field (NFL), Old Trafford (English Premier League), and Notre Dame Stadium (college football) all have long histories of hosting significant sporting events. Because of the tradition associated with these venues, consumers may form strong brand associations. The stadium construction boom that started in the early 1990s focused on building facilities that not only generate more revenue but also have unique features that form strong brand associations. This trend is particularly noticeable when considering baseball stadiums. Since 1992, stadiums such as Camden Yards (Baltimore), Progressive Field (Cleveland), Coors Field (Denver), and Safeco Field (Seattle) have incorporated features that are reminiscent of baseball a long time ago. Because baseball stadiums have no standardized size, the unique features can be tied to the dimension of the park, such as the hill in center field at Minute Maid Park in Houston. Or, the actual location of the park can create a unique association. At both AT&T Park in San Francisco and PNC Park in Pittsburgh, home runs can land in bodies of water.

Brand Associations Based on the Benefits of Consumption

Beyond the features and aspects of the sport product, brand associations can also be developed based on the consumer needs that are satisfied or the benefits that consumption provides. For example, nostalgic (remembering and perhaps glorifying an experience) memories can serve as a source of brand associations. Whether it is a recollection of following a team with a family member or friend or remembering the elation felt when a team won a championship, nostalgic memories can serve as a strong source of association. For these reasons, a hidden benefit for teams that own or partially control their own cable networks (often called regional sports networks, or RSNs) is the ability to generate programming that will foster these nostalgic memories of team accomplishments. For example, New England Sports Network (NESN) is owned by the Boston Red Sox and distributed through cable networks free to most of New England. That arrangement affords the Red Sox a unique opportunity to create programming (particularly in the winter months) that reminds people of the march to the 2004, 2007, and 2013 World Series titles.

Social benefits can also serve as a source for brand associations. A parent could form a strong association to a minor league baseball team because it provides a platform for the parent to do something fun with his or her children. Think about the athletics programs at your college or university. You may have some associations tied to attending games with a large group of friends.

A person's feeling of identification with a team can serve as a source of brand associations as well. Identification with a team entails several things, mostly tied to what it means to be a fan of a particular team. In the case of the Boston Red Sox, being a Red Sox fan means that a person is a member of Red Sox Nation. In essence, *Red Sox Nation* is a term that creates a sense of belonging to a group, or even a special club. Up until the 2004 World Series, membership in this club meant being a part of a group that often suffered when the team failed to win a big game. But with the 2004 World Series championship and the additional titles in 2007 and 2013, the Red Sox Nation celebrated as a group. For example, 3.2 million people turned out for a parade in Boston to celebrate the 2004 World Series title. Just as identification can form with a team, so too can it form with a particular geographic location. In this sense, identification with a city can be exhibited by someone following a sport team. For example, someone from Chicago living in another part of the country could demonstrate to people that he is from Chicago by wearing a Chicago Cubs hat. Further, when the Cubs finally win the World Series, people will see it as a positive reflection on *their* city.

ACTIVITY 7.2 Brand Association

The Chicago Blackhawks, New York Yankees, and Boston Celtics are just a few of the teams that have created a positive brand image of their team with their logo. As you will learn in this WSG activity, other sport organizations have perhaps not fared as well.

Brand Associations in Other Realms of Sport

Beyond team sport, brand management is important throughout the sport realm. For example, the development of brand associations is also important to the following segments of the industry:

- Sponsors
- Athletes
- Agencies
- Health clubs

ACTIVITY 7.3 Developing a Brand Image

Congratulations! Bubba Watson, who won the Masters Golf Tournament in 2012, has hired you to be his marketing manager. In this WSG activity, you will provide some marketing and brand image advice.

How Sponsors Create Brand Associations One motivation for companies to sponsor sporting events or programs is to enhance or reinforce the brand associations with their company. This motivation is based on the belief that image attributes of the entity being sponsored can be transferred to the sponsor. A sponsor such as Gatorade or Powerade might seek to align itself with the best college basketball or football teams to reinforce the perception that their sports drink is of high quality and is used by the best athletes. Similarly, Nike, Reebok, Adidas, and others often fight for the footwear and apparel rights associated with professional sport leagues, college athletics programs, and athletes. This competition is probably at least partially because of the desire to be associated with the best.

Positive brand associations tied to Jimmie Johnson, such as success and quality, can be transferred to his sponsors, Lowe's and Kobalt Tools.

Besides perceptions of quality, other brand associations might be transferred to the sponsor. Several classic examples include the Air Jordan basketball shoe and the Mountain Dew sponsorship of action sports. Coinciding with the launch of the Air Jordan basketball shoe (containing Nike's then-revolutionary air-pocket technology), Nike ran an advertisement featuring a young Jordan running and jumping to the background noise of a jet engine.[30] This ad provided the nexus for Nike to create the perception that the Air Jordan helped people jump higher. Whereas Nike used an athlete endorsement to create a brand association, Mountain Dew used a new sporting genre to redefine its image. Dating back to 1960, Mountain Dew was perceived to be a drink of people in rural areas (mostly in the southern United States). In 1992 Mountain Dew launched a new campaign under the tag line "Do the Dew" that featured people taking part in risk-taking activities such as skydiving. Mountain Dew followed this up by becoming one of the first sponsors to become involved with the emerging action sports captured by events such as the X Games and the Dew Action Sports Tour (note the title sponsor). By undertaking these actions, Mountain Dew completely redefined itself as cool, edgy, and exciting.[31]

The Air Jordan and Mountain Dew cases demonstrate how the image of a sport entity can help create strong, unique, and favorable associations for the sport brand. They also raise a practical point for all sponsorship decision makers: The image of the sport entity that a company is thinking about sponsoring should have the potential to either reinforce or positively alter the brand associations as a sponsor.[32] Consider the potential for negative associations that occur when an athlete runs afoul of the law or a college athletics program is found to have violated NCAA rules. Might such occurrences create a negative association with a sponsor by virtue of its involvement with that particular sport entity? Perhaps! Following news accounts of Tiger

Woods extramarital affairs in late 2009 and 2010, a number of the companies that endorsed Woods discontinued or terminated their contracts. International brands Tag Heuer, Accenture, Gillette, and AT&T discontinued their relationship with Woods.[33] Did you know that corporations often embed morals clauses into their endorsement contracts that allow termination of the relationship if the athlete does something that is illegal or immoral and draws significant negative attention? Another interesting aspect to the Woods situation was that Nike did not discontinue their relationship. Do you think that maintaining the relationship negatively affected the Nike brand?

As discussed in chapter 9, successful sponsorships require a strong relationship between the buyer and the seller of the sponsorship program. For this to happen, both must receive benefits. In some cases, the sponsorship seller may receive image benefits beyond the cash and in-kind contributions they might receive from the sponsor. For example, take the case of the WNBA. Upon formation of the league, the ability of the WNBA to secure visible name brands such as Spalding probably helped lend credibility to the league. On a smaller scale, think about an event in your local area, such as a road race or grassroots soccer tournament. These events probably tried to secure brand-name sponsors as a means of generating credibility for their event, particularly in their first years of existence.

Because some of these associations with corporations may be formed based on the experience that users have when consuming the brand, a new form of branding through sponsorship has emerged—branded entertainment. Have you ever attended a fan festival affiliated with a pro or college team that has interactive games for people to participate in? For example, Boston College turns one of its campus recreation centers into a Fan Zone on football game days. If you walk into the Fan Zone on a football Saturday, you will see kids in line waiting to participate in various football-related activities, such as throwing a football with accuracy. This effort is an example of a team's branded entertainment. Another example is the Richard Petty Driving Experience, in which people pay to drive a NASCAR car on a racetrack. This experience is sponsored by a variety of companies, including Goodyear and DuPont.[34] As existing NASCAR sponsors, DuPont and Goodyear are likely just

trying to add a branded entertainment element to their involvement with auto racing. A related form of branding is the use of branded content to further the influence of a brand. The sidebar at the end of this chapter explores the concept of branded content and explains its importance to branding efforts.

How Athletes Create Brand Associations   As noted in the previous section, one of the associations with Michael Jordan was that he could walk on air. Other associations might have been clutch player, prolific scorer, and champion, based on his style of play and his achievements. Because professional athletes can make money from corporate endorsements, having strong, unique, and favorable associations is important for an athlete. In fact, player agents should view the players they represent as brands and attempt to develop strong brand associations with their clients.

The Jordan example illustrates the two ways that athletes can generate brand associations for themselves. First, they can generate associations based on their performance in athletics competition. These associations are derived from their accomplishments, from their style of play, and from any signature moves that they create. A great example of this is tennis player Andrea Petkovic. Following any match that she wins, she does what is now called the Petko dance on the court. The celebration dance started after her coach encouraged her to do something unique if she was successful in a first-round U.S. Open match.[35] A second way that athletes can generate associations is through their actions off the court. For example, former soccer star Mia Hamm raises money to help female athletes and patients who are seeking bone marrow transplants.[36] In each case (Petkovic and Hamm), the associations serve to create an image that may or may not be appealing to sponsors.

How Agencies Create Brand Associations   Sport marketing and management agencies are typically not visible entities to the average consumer, although they are visible behind the scenes of events—to the athletes they represent, the sponsors they are helping to activate sponsorships, or the event management crew responsible for the logistics of the event. So how do these agencies (at which some of you will invariably be employed) generate brand associations? The easiest answer is through the clients that they represent. David Falk made a name for himself as a player agent at least partially through his representation of Michael Jordan. Another answer is through the people who work for the agencies. For example, before his passing, Mark McCormack, founder of IMG and a sport marketing industry leader, was a strong association linked to IMG. Sport marketing agencies also generate brand associations through the way that they deliver their services. For example, Just Marketing International (JMI) has differentiated itself in the agency world by focusing heavily on corporate consulting and activation within the motorsports industry.

How Health Clubs Create Brand Associations

Do you work out? Do you use health club services such as cardiovascular and weight equipment? If so, you are a member of the market targeted by health clubs. Some of you may have facilities on your campus that are free of charge. If so, what brand associations exist in your mind with respect to those facilities? Are they too crowded at peak times? Do they offer enough hours? Embedded

in these two questions are potential associations for health clubs. Those of you who are not satisfied with the facilities on campus may have looked at health clubs in your town. If so, do you hold brand associations with each of them? One might be big and spacious but perhaps a little more expensive. Another might be smaller but less expensive. These perceptions represent potential associations. What do you think about the staff at the various health clubs? Are they friendly? Are they helpful? As is the case with professional sport teams, brand associations can be formed based on the service provided by the front-line personnel.

ACTIVITY 7.4 Branding the Road Warriors

In this WSG activity, you have just been hired by the Greenville Road Warriors to improve the team's branding. The Greenville Road Warriors is a professional ice hockey team located in Greenville, SC.

Branding Through Content Development

It all started, a while ago now, with the creation of ESPN. The megabrand that has resulted from all-sports content provision (through the ESPN family of stations and websites) is both the envy and model for many others. Through the CBS Sports Network, the NBC Sports Network, and Fox Sports 1, the other three traditional U.S. broadcast networks (CBS, NBC, and Fox) now all have a cable station exclusively dedicated to sport programming to compete with ABC's sister company, ESPN.

Major League Baseball (through MLB Network), the National Football League (NFL Network), the National Basketball Association (NBA TV), and the National Hockey League (NHL Network) followed suit by establishing cable television outlets geared toward the distribution of content. Similarly, starting with the YES network (to broadcast Yankees games and deliver content related to the Yankees), professional teams have increasingly either created their own regional sports networks or partnered with cable providers to develop such cable networks. We now live in a time when the delivery of media is extremely segmented and fragmented. Although the landscape is more competitive, opportunities continue to emerge for sport organizations to extend their brands and generate significant revenue. In 2013 the Los Angeles Dodgers agreed to terms with Time Warner Cable on the creation of a regional sports network featuring the Dodgers that will provide the Dodgers $8 billion of revenue over the next 25 years![37]

Everywhere you look, a sport organization or group of sport organizations is leveraging their brands to generate more content for consumption. Think for a minute about college sports in the United States. First on the scene was the Big Ten Network, which was followed

> continued

by the Pac 12 Network. Now even individual colleges are creating networks where brand strength and interest is sufficient. The University of Texas received $300 million from ESPN to create the Longhorn Network.[38] Meanwhile, Texas' rival to the north, the University of Oklahoma, reached agreement with Fox Sports Net to create a variety of branded content on Fox regional stations in Oklahoma, Texas, Louisiana, and Arkansas. The agreement will pay the University of Oklahoma approximately $7 million per year.[39]

All the aforementioned efforts strive to create content and programming that will generate revenue linked to a strong, or potentially strong, brand. Content can also be a brand accelerator, irrespective of the revenues that it generates. For example, the existence of the Big Ten Network throughout the country allows the mostly Midwest-based conference to further its emotional connections with fans while also reaching fans who might not live near one of the member institutions. Similarly, the Dodgers sports network will not only allow fans great access to Dodgers games but also provide a variety of programming that will further a fan's engagement with the team, thus enhancing the brand.

In some cases, the creation of ancillary content has fueled brand popularity. Consider the Ultimate Fighting Championships (UFC). Were the fights the foundation of early popularity for UFC? The answer is no. UFC saw its popularity skyrocket after the creation of the cable television show *The Ultimate Fighter*, which tracked the lives and progress of aspiring UFC fighters.[40] The show inspired followers of UFC and helped drive viewership in the televised events. As UFC has expanded its brand globally, it has continued to use the reality television show strategy, launching versions of *The Ultimate Fighter* in Brazil, India, and Australia.[41]

The use of shows in the promotion of brands is now a common strategy. The Big Ten Network has *The Journey*, which features Big Ten coaches, athletes, and families in pieces that fuse on-field or on-court performance with stories about individuals and their lives. Action sports organizer Alli is behind *The Octane Academy*, a show that features established Alli motorsports stars competing against up-and-coming competitors.[42]

Networks and shows are only the beginning. Sport organizations are increasingly pushing the boundaries of content delivery using all available elements of the digital space. The NHL's Montreal Canadiens launched 24CH through television, smartphones, and the team website to provide inside information about the team. The goal is to bring "the Canadiens closer to current fans and, perhaps, win some new ones along the way."[43] To deepen its relationship with children, the NBA created Hoop Troop, an interactive website focused exclusively on kids.[44] Even Olympic sport organizations are employing these strategies. USA Swimming created Deck Pass, a digital platform focused on helping swimmers manage their performance and progress.[45]

The results of these strategies are staggering in many cases. For example, the NFL's New England Patriots were one of the early innovators in the provision of digital content when they launched their own website in 1995.[46] Since that launch, the Patriots have continued to innovate and populate their website with programs such as Locker Room Uncut, which literally takes fans into the Patriots locker room.[47] The efforts have paid off; Patriots.com receives approximately 10 million page views every month.[48]

The success experienced by sport properties with content has not been lost on sponsors of sport. Informed by the interest and activity related to this variety of digital efforts, most large-scale sponsorships now include some form of digital element. When the University of Alabama football team won the 2013 national championship, Coke Zero ran a commercial featuring the wife of Alabama coach Nick Saban discussing the history of her husband's career.[49] Although the piece originally aired as a 30-second commercial, it was also distributed through other outlets, such as YouTube and CokeZero.com.[50] Similarly, linked to the 2013 NBA All-Star Game, automaker Kia used a Facebook page to encourage fans to submit videos arguing for the right to be the "Kia All-Star" reporter at the All-Star Game.[51]

Wrap-Up

Regardless of the sport setting, you likely now recognize that branding entails much more than managing logos and marks. Sport organizations that successfully manage their brands create both awareness and a strong image for their products. Organizations that are successful in this endeavor receive a variety of benefits, including increased fan or consumer loyalty and increased revenue.

Activities

1. Manchester United, Real Madrid, and Chelsea are three of the strongest professional soccer (football outside the United States) brands. Visit their websites—www.manutd.com; www.realmadrid.com; and www.chelseafc.com—and identify how the websites are used to create, reinforce, and nurture strong, favorable, and unique brand associations.

2. Identify the brand associations with your school's athletics program. A useful way to do this is to ask some friends what comes to mind when they think of your school's athletics teams. You may want to focus on one team in particular. After you have prepared your list, identify which of these associations are strong, unique, and favorable. Are there negative associations that need to be overcome?

3. Based on your assessment of the strong positive and negative associations with your school's athletics program, develop three strategies either to nurture these brand associations or to overcome the negative brand associations.

4. Let's say that Major League Baseball has decided to put an expansion franchise in Portland, Oregon. What would be a good nickname for that team? Why would that be a good nickname? (Hint: The answer needs to have something to do with brand associations.)

5. After news of golfer Tiger Woods' extramarital affairs became public, a number of his endorsers chose to discontinue their association with him. But Nike did not. Considering what you have learned about branding, why might Nike have made that decision?

Your Marketing Plan

1. Analyze the name and logo of your product. Does it trigger positive memories in consumers? If not, should it be changed?

2. Identify the various associations that are created by your product. Are they positive or negative? Are they unique? Develop strategies to reinforce and nurture the positive associations and brainstorm what must be done to manage the negative associations.

Endnotes

1. Mike Ozanian, "Manchester United Again the World's Most Valuable Team," *Forbes*, 18 April 2012, www.forbes.com/sites/mikeozanian/2012/04/18/manchester-united-again-the-worlds-most-valuable-soccer-team.

2. Ibid.

3. Ibid.

4. Oliver Joy, "Manchester United Pen New Multi-Million Dollar Naming Deal," CNN.com, http://edition.cnn.com/2013/04/08/business/manchester-united-aon-deal.

5. Ozanian, 2012.

6. "Brand Protection," www.manutd.com/en/Club/Brand-Protection.aspx.

7. D.A. Aaker, *Managing Brand Equity* (New York: Free Press, 1991), 7.

8. P. Williams, "Franchise Rebranding: Out With the Old . . . In With the New," *SSSBJ*, 23 February 2004, 17.

9. D. Travis, *Emotional Branding: How Successful Brands Gain the Irrational Edge* (Roseville, CA: Prima Venture, 2000), 15.

10. M. Gobé, *Emotional Branding: The New Paradigm for Connecting Brands to People* (New York: Allworth Press, 2001), xiv.

11. D. Bolger, speech delivered to the University of Massachusetts Sport Management Program, Amherst, MA, 10 September 2004. At the time, Bolger was chief marketing officer for the NBA's Portland Trail Blazers.

12. Aaker, *Managing Brand Equity,* 15.

13. James M. Gladden and Daniel C. Funk, "Understanding Brand Loyalty in Professional Sport: Examining the Link Between Brand Associations and Brand Loyalty," *International Journal of Sports Marketing and Sponsorship,* 3 (1) (2001): 45–69.

14. For examples of studies that have shown that winning is not the only important factor to realizing brand loyalty and positive marketplace outcomes, see James M. Gladden and George R. Milne, "Examining the Importance of Brand Equity in Professional Sport," *SMQ,* 8 (1) (1999): 21–29; and Gladden and Funk, "Understanding Brand Loyalty."

15. www.baseball-almanac.com/teams/cubsatte.shtml, http://chicago.cubs.mlb.com/chc/history/year_by_year_results.jsp.

16. Aaker, *Managing Brand Equity,* 22.

17. Justin Bachman, "UPS Pulls Out as Olympic Sponsor," ABC News, http://abcnews.go.com/Sports/story?id=100047&page=1#.UWVybGbD-70.

18. International Events Group, "FIFA Secures $1.6 billion in World Cup Sponsorship Revenue," 3 June 2010, www.sponsorship.com/About-IEG/Press-Room/FIFA-Secures-$1-6-Billion-in-World-Cup-Sponsorship.aspx.

19. Aaker, *Managing Brand Equity,* 208.

20. Terry Lefton, "N.Y. Giants Make Rare Move, Extend Brand to Health Center," *SSSBJ,* 1 April 2013, 4.

21. Ibid.

22. K.L. Keller, *Strategic Brand Management: Building, Measuring and Managing Brand Equity* (Upper Saddle River, NJ: Prentice Hall, 1998), 50–51.

23. Aaker, *Managing Brand Equity,* 19.

24. Greg Bishop, "Texas A&M Hushes the Heisman Hype Over Manziel," *New York Times,* 14 November 2012, www.nytimes.com/2012/11/15/sports/ncaafootball/texas-am-hushes-the-heisman-hype-over-johnny-manziel.html?pagewanted=1&_r=0.

25. Keller, *Strategic Brand Management,* 93.

26. *NBA Teams: Chicago Bulls Records Year by Year,* NBAUniverse.com, www.nbauniverse.com/teams/records_chicago_bulls.htm.

27. "Bulls Top NBA Attendance Over the Past Decade," Bulls.com, www.nba.com/bulls/news/bullstopnbaattendance_091028.html.

28. Kevin Ding, "Ron Artest Wins NBA's 2010–11 Citizenship Award," *Orange County Register,* 26 April 2011, www.ocregister.com/articles/artest-437789-award-lakers.html.

29. Michael Sokolove, "Follow Me," *New York Times,* 5 February 2006, www.nytimes.com/2006/02/05/magazine/05coachk_96_101__116_117_.html?pagewanted=all.

30. D. Katz, *Just Do It: The Nike Spirit in the Corporate World* (Holbrook, MA: Adams, 1994), 7.

31. G.W. Prince, "Give Them Their Dew: Credit Pepsi for Marketing a Mountain of a Brand," *Beverage World,* 54 (January 1998): 54–60.

32. For more on this topic, see James M. Gladden and Richard Wolfe, "Sponsorship and Image Matching: The Case of Intercollegiate Athletics," *International Journal of Sports Marketing and Sponsorship,* 3 (1) (2001): 71–98.

33. "Gatorade Cuts Ties With Woods," ESPN.com, 26 February 2010, http://espn.go.com/espn/print?id=4950137&type=story.

34. www.drivepetty.com

35. Georgina Robinson, "How a Bet Triggered the Petko Dance," *Sydney Morning Herald,* 24 January 2011, www.smh.com.au/sport/tennis/how-a-bet-triggered-the-petko-dance-20110124-1a1rb.html.

36. G. Bruce Knight, "Big Players in Charity," *Wall Street Journal,* 28 April 200, http://online.wsj.com/article/SB117771735737385480.html.

37. Eric Fisher and John Ourand, "MLB Clubs Look to Follow Dodgers," *SSSBJ,* 1 April 2013, p. 1.

38. Michael Smith and John Ourand, "Oklahoma Will See $7 Million a Year From TV Deal," *SSSBJ,* 17 September 2012, 10.

39. Ibid.

40. Jesse Baker and Matthew Thomson, *The Ultimate Fighting Championships (UFC): The Evolution of a Sport,* Richard Ivey School of Business, University of Western Ontario, 16 June 2010, 4.

41. Bill King, "UFC's Global Ambitions," *SSSBJ,* 11 June 2012, 15.

42. Tripp Mickle, "Ford-Alli Deal Steers 'Octane Academy' to NBC," *SSSBJ,* 3 December 2012, 15.

43. Christopher Botta, "Canadiens Join All-Access Crowd With '24CH,' " *SSSBJ,* 4 February 2013, 5.

44. John Lombardo, "NBA Youth Push Includes Branded Website," *SSSBJ,* 31 January 2011, 11.

45. Tripp Mickle, "USA Swimming Cheers on Fans With New Program," *SSSBJ,* 24 October 2011, 10.

46. Daniel Kaplan, "New England Patriots: Going Long Online," *SSSBJ,* 1 April 2013, 28.

47. Ibid.

48. Ibid.

49. Michael Smith, "Coke Zero Drinks Up Bama Win," *SSSBJ,* 14 January 2013, 6.

50. Ibid.

51. Tripp Mickle, "Digital Theme Dominates All-Star Activation," *SSSBJ,* 11 February 2013, 4.

Chapter 8

Sales and Service

OBJECTIVES

- To define what sales *is* and what sales *is not*
- To provide an overview of the various sales methodologies used in sport business
- To analyze pricing techniques and strategies as they relate to the sport industry
- To examine the influence and role of the secondary market in sport sales
- To explore the concepts of yield management and lifetime value
- To show the importance and influence of retention and service activities as they relate to the sales process

The First Sales Coach: Knute Rockne

The influence of Rockne as a salesperson cannot be overstated. Rockne was the coach who brought Notre Dame into prominence and packaged and sold the Irish as a football product to the more established schools that he needed to play to build a reputation as a national power. Rockne was so successful that he was able to persuade the Notre Dame administration to build a 57,000-seat stadium, which opened in 1930. Here, we share some of Rockne's thoughts and practices for today's sales managers to aid them in the selection, training, motivation, and development of their respective sales teams. We hope that they find Rockne's thoughts and words about sales useful in structuring their own "workouts, scrimmages, and contests" because, according to Rockne, "It seems to me that the same psychology that makes for success in a football organization, will make for success in any organization, particularly in a selling organization." What follows is the Rockne philosophy of relating how he coached football to how he worked with the sales managers at Studebaker.

- "You must have the ability to cooperate with the men [and women] around you." A sales manager, like a coach, is always searching for talent and then must work diligently to get those talented people to work together and follow a game plan.

- "Successful men [and women] have the ability to persevere—the ability to stick in there and keep giving the best of one's self." Salespeople succeed less than 5 percent of the time (and we are being generous). Given that they will fail 95 percent of the time or more, perseverance is essential to long-term success and a career in sales.

- "Competition is a challenge you should thrill to." The thrill of competing against others and chasing a goal is an essential part of the sales culture. To that end, sales managers need to have short-term and long-term forms of competition designed to motivate and provide numerous opportunities to compete and succeed.

- "A sales manager is the trustee of the potential worth of every salesman in his employ. It's his job to put enough time and effort into training every individual so that the maximum worth of each will be brought out." Although bringing in sales trainers from time to time is a good idea and provides salespeople with another perspective, a great sales manager will have a personal development plan for each member of the staff and will work with those people almost daily to help them realize their full potential.

- "It is the job of the sales manager to know where his men [and women] are every day and what they are doing." The sales manager must be present in the workplace, not

> *continued*

Sales are the lifeblood of any sport organization. Whether the item is tickets, media rights, corporate partnerships, digital assets, advertising, premium seating offerings, merchandise, or any other component or product of the sales inventory, sales accounts for most, if not all, of the revenue.

According to Ron Seaver, former San Diego Padres executive and founder of the National Sports Forum, "Nothing happens until somebody sells something."[2] Unfortunately, the word *sales* or the term *salesperson* usually conjures up images of hucksters—people using guile and persuasion to talk customers into buying products that they might not want or need at prices they sometimes cannot afford. This type of salesperson and sales organizations has been depicted in such Hollywood films as *Wall Street*, *Boiler Room*, and *Glengarry Glen Ross*.

In this chapter, we attempt to alter this perception by exploring the various sales methodologies employed in the sport industry, distinguish between product-oriented and customer-oriented sales, and examine the concept of aftermarketing, or what should happen after the sale to ensure that the purchase is a win–win situation for both the seller (the sport organization) and the purchaser (the sport consumer). This emphasis on relationship selling and marketing (creating and building long-term relationships that grow and removed from the sales floor in an office. He or she needs to understand goal and sales numbers not only for the department but also for every member of the sales team.

- "Selling is dependent upon strong fundamentals. The sales manager must understand the blocking and tackling aspects necessary to be successful." After the sales manager has identified the fundamental skills that need to be practiced and perfected to achieve success, he or she must incorporate a repetition and review of those skills on an individualized basis for each member of the sales team.

- "I have a control plan, or as I refer to it in football terms, a chart of play. This chart tells us everything we want to know about what happened in previous games and shows us just where we can improve on the individual performance of every team member." Sales managers employ sales charts, call records, and lead scoring, as well as call volume, call length, and sales-to-call ratios to determine how to improve the performance of every sales team member. As in Rockne's world, the preparations, practices, and strength of the fundamentals are the best measures of predictive success.

- "A handler of men [and women] must be willing to break his group down into units and study, work and understand each one. He must understand the minds of each and know something of the mental hazards confronting him." To understand someone, the sales manager must understand him or her not only professionally but also personally. Is the person going through a divorce? Expecting a child? Is something interfering with the person's ability to perform? The best chance to achieve success is to remove the obstacles blocking that success.

- "The thing we insist upon and stress with men on a competitive team like a football team can be put into one word: *pep*." In Rockne's world, pep stood for purpose, enthusiasm, and perseverance. Although we have already examined perseverance, purpose and enthusiasm merit some explanation.

Rockne was a highly organized, focused, inspirational leader who created a system that maximized efficiency and produced results at the highest levels on the football field and at the dealerships. Every sales manager needs such a consistent coaching approach to be effective. And if they're Irish, well, a little bit of luck never hurts.[1]

increase in value) and lifetime value (the true measure of a consumer's value to the organization over time—the length, depth, and breadth of the relationship) will illustrate the value of the sales process to a sport organization and the professionalism of the sales approaches used in this industry.

As we have discussed earlier in this book, sport marketing differs from other forms of marketing in a variety of ways. One difference is the presence of emotion. This attribute also applies to the sales dimension of sport marketing. In sport the sales process may involve an emotional element that may be, but is usually not, an element of the majority of sales taking place throughout the world every day. This emotional element can be either an aid or a hindrance, usually depending on the public perception of the sport product at that time. Updating our comparison from 2007, we find that little has changed in terms of success and attendance between MLB's Chicago Cubs and Chicago White Sox. On September 9, 2012, the Chicago Cubs ranked 7th overall in attendance in terms of percentage of capacity filled at 88 percent, averaging 36,343 per game for a total attendance to that date of 2,471,238. The Cubs were fifth in the National League Central with a record of 53-86 (wins and losses). Their crosstown rivals, the first place Chicago White Sox, had a record of 75-63 yet were ranked 20th in attendance in terms of percentage of capacity filled at 59.9 percent, averaging 24,326 per game for a total attendance to that date of 1,678,558, or 792,680 fewer fans despite offering a better product in terms of performance. Why is this still the case? The Cubs, historically described as "lovable losers," play in Wrigley Field, and much of the experience starts before the game in Wrigleyville, the neighborhood entertainment district outside the venue. The White Sox have no such area. The emotional ties manifested in pride in place combined with the tourist attraction of Wrigley Field and the tradition for area residents makes a poor on-field product a more attractive purchase in terms of the emotional experience for the consumer.

This chapter addresses the types of sales strategies and tactics most commonly employed in the sport industry. We illustrate these strategies and tactics through examples and insight from expert practitioners from a number of sport organizations, primarily within the context of tickets or sponsorship sales.

Relationship Between Media, Sponsors, and Fans and the Sales Process

Figure 8.1 depicts a critical relationship among the media (now defined to include all forms of social media, the Internet, and traditional print and electronic media), sponsors, and fans. This relationship is essentially symbiotic, because the three elements feed off each other to create the conditions that attract additional fans.

The media, in all its forms, provide coverage and express opinions according to the interest that fans have in sport. The media then are influenced by attendance, website utilization and followers, Twitter content and activity, Facebook likes and activity, and so forth. The media are also influenced by the credibility the sport or organization has with its sponsors—how many there are, how much they invest, and, of course, who they are. Sponsors make their investment largely in the target markets that are following the sport, whether that following is in venue (attendance), on television or mobile devices (viewership), or online. The more fans there are, the more opportunities there are for interactions to occur between the sponsor, the product, the respective media outlets, and the fans (target demos and markets). Fans and their support of the organization are used to attract sponsors, and fans' level of support, interest, and spending influences media interest, coverage, and ultimately, contracts for rights fees.

Baseball Hall of Famer Yogi Berra once said, "Nobody goes there anymore; it's too crowded." In his inimitable style, Yogi captured the goal of any event marketer—to create a crowd, because a crowd attracts a crowd. The game or the venue must be the place to be. The crowd is important

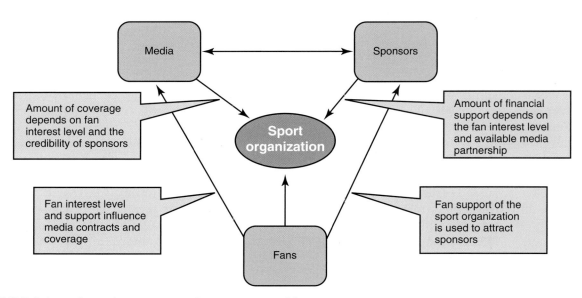

FIGURE 8.1   Relationship among media, sponsors, and fans.

"Meat in the seats" may seem to be less important to the National Football League (NFL) than to the other big five sports in the United States and certainly in comparison with other sports throughout the globe. According to Mike Florio of nbcsports.com, despite unprecedented growth of television audiences, attendance at NFL games that reached an all-time high in 2007 has dropped ever since, falling to its lowest number in 2011 when attendance was 16,562,706, a drop of 4.5 percent since the all-time high of 17,345,205 in 2007.[3] Despite this slight decline in attendance the NFL is alive and well in your living room, on your mobile device, or wherever you care to consume the broadcasts. According to the Nielsen Company, in 2011, NFL regular-season games reached more than 200 million unique viewers, averaged 17.5 million viewers, and accounted for 23 of the 25 most watched TV shows seen on cable that fall. *NBC Sunday Night Football* ranked as the most watched primetime program for the second consecutive year, averaging 21.5 million viewers.[4]

because it provides credibility to media decision makers and content creators, who then deem the event worthy of coverage and attention. Media coverage and interest function to create value for sponsors, who rationalize their costs on a per exposure basis. The larger the crowd is, the more exposure and value sponsors receive. In the words of many sport marketers, the goal is to put "meat in the seats." That goal is accomplished through ticket sales.

What Is Sales?

Sales is the revenue-producing element of the marketing process. In the strictest sense of the word, selling is the process of moving goods and services from the hands of those who produce them into the hands of those who will benefit most from their use.[5] Sales usually involves a questioning process to assess needs and find a product match. The salesperson needs listening skills to gain an understanding of the needs and wants of the prospect and the concerns or objections that the prospect may have. The process usually involves the application of conversational skills that might include persuasive skills and may be supported by print, audio, video, websites, technological aids, and appropriate sampling—all designed and used to promote the brand or product as essential, appropriate, desirable, and worthy of consideration.

In this chapter, we define and explain sales by referring to the thoughts and ideologies of a famed sport marketer, the late Mark McCormack, author and founder and chairman of IMG (International Management Group), arguably

the world's leading sport marketing and athlete management organization at the time of his death. As McCormack explained, selling consists of

- identifying customers,
- getting through to them,
- increasing their awareness and interest in your product or service, and
- persuading them to act on that interest.[6]

We can also explain sales as customer performance: When a customer purchases a product, he performs the act of buying.[7] In sport, four main factors cause customers to perform or fail to perform:

- **Quality**. How well is the product or service performing? Consider the star power of the 2011–12 NBA World Champion Miami Heat; the road followers of the Pittsburgh Steelers, Dallas Cowboys, and Green Bay Packers of the NFL; and the 27 World Series championships of the New York Yankees.

- **Quantity**. In what quantity is the product sold? Miniplans, flex plans, and other smaller ticket packages offer the consumer a variety of purchasing options to consider.

- **Time**. Does the consumer have time to consume the product? For example, family obligations, work schedule, hobbies, and other interests and everyday life might dictate that she does not. To make the purchase of a golf membership worthwhile, for example, the potential purchaser probably must be able to play on a weekly basis.

- **Cost**. Cost relates not only to the overall cost but also to such aspects as payment plans and value received for the purchase price. Many health and fitness clubs position the cost of membership as cost per day: Isn't your health worth 74 cents per day?

In many cases, a fifth consideration is social perception: Is it cool? What do my friends and peers think about it? Does it make them think differently about me? The difficulty here is figuring out how to make things cool, which is the "burning issue of our time."[8] Unfortunately, cool cannot be created and controlled.

Getting the customer to purchase and retaining that customer will dictate how successful a salesperson or a sales organization is and how viable the future of the person or the organization will be.

What Makes a Good Salesperson?

Are salespersons born or made? The debate has raged for centuries. In the opinion of experts, the naturally born salesperson is a myth; salespeople are made, not born, although for some it is a much easier development.[9] People usually learn the skills needed to be successful by developing good listening skills, being comfortable speaking to strangers, and having an aggressive attitude in the context of wanting to succeed. These traits are generally learned and developed through experience and modeling; over time they form another critical element in a successful salesperson—confidence. Mark McCormack looked for these qualities in salespeople in his sport-marketing agency:

- Belief in the product
- Belief in yourself
- Seeing a lot of people (sales call volume)
- Timing
- Listening to the customer (but realizing what the customer wants is not necessarily what she is telling you)
- A sense of humor
- Knocking on old doors
- Asking everyone to buy
- Following up after the sale with the same aggressiveness that you demonstrated before the sale
- Common sense[10]

One notable omission from the list is preparation. Author and consultant Jeffrey Gitomer defines this preparation as "visiting the prospect's website and printing out several strategic pages, reading them and making notes so you can ask good questions about the prospect's business."[11]

One of the best developers of sale talent we have observed is Jeff Ianello, VP sales and service for the Phoenix Suns. The Suns have long had a talent for developing potential sales managers, so we asked Ionello to share with us his thoughts about developing talent.

What Is a Good Sales-Oriented Organizational Structure?

The organizational structure and style of the organization form a key element in determining the overall success and effect of the sales department's efforts. Organizational structure for sales includes the following:

- The reporting structure (whom you report to, your immediate supervisor) in an organization.

- The relationships between departments that are integral in the sales process. For example, in structuring any organization involved in the sale of tickets, the relationship between the box office manager and the ticket-sales department is critical because of possible offers and incentives and the subsequent redemption of those offers. Similarly, the relationships between ticket sales and marketing, ticket sales and corporate partnerships, and ticket sales and game-day operations are all critical because of messaging, advertising, up-selling opportunities, and implementation issues. Figure 8.2 illustrates a model NBA team organizational chart for ticket-sales and service departments.

- The organizational style or philosophy with regard to producing support materials (e.g., brochures, direct mail pieces, e-offers, advertising, in-game announcements, website page development and design) used in the sales process.

- The sales development process within the department. Most sales departments begin their salespeople in entry-level sales positions. In sport, this often involves starting

Develop Core Strength

Jeff Ianello, VP Telemarketing and Business Operations, NBA

I have always enjoyed hitting the gym. Since my high school days the majority of my workouts have consisted of lifting, lifting, and more lifting. I would often skip stretching and anything to do with core or cardio. That is, until about five years ago, when I was swinging a golf club and threw my back out. For about two weeks, I was on the proverbial shelf. After a tip from a friend I set an appointment with a physical therapist. The prognosis was simple: My lack of core strength and flexibility caused the injury and now nothing else worked. I got by for a while, but eventually the inevitable caught up with me.

As I have been reviewing the past year in leading Sales and Service, I couldn't help but pull from the lesson of this experience. With more responsibility comes the pull of identifying new projects as well as trying to improve current ones.

What types of ticket plans should we have? How do we gain more group experiences to sell? What events should we host, and what should the creative programming entail? What vendors should we use to help support our new variable and dynamic pricing models? What should the pricing be?

These are all important questions that need to be answered, but the current most important processes need to remain as the most important process to maintain strong core business execution. We must remember that if what I mentioned were the silver bullet to sell 90 percent of the tickets in the building, then we wouldn't need a sales and service staff! Having a staff that can maximize the variety of offerings and efforts of marketing is not possible without having the right people in place and the support of an elite training and development program. This will be the core that greatness will grow from, and all else will be maximized. A basic four-pronged actionable philosophy is as follows.

1. Hire Great

Everything starts here. If you do not make strong hires, then the training and development program will be ineffective and underapplied. Look for these attributes when hiring or promoting sport sales and service reps:

- Attitude
- Work ethic
- Coachability
- Leadership
- Commitment to the industry (both sport and sales)

Where do you find these folks?

- Develop relationships with both local and key national colleges and universities.
- Consistently interview candidates for your entry-level sales program (one to two phone interviews a week).
- Don't miss a resume! Look at them all! Or at least have some administrative support to pull ones that fit basic criteria that you identify. I always remember this when I think of my first phone interview with Nic Barlage for an entry-level sales position in Phoenix. Nic was surprised that I had reached out because he had applied online for half a dozen other entry-level jobs with teams and never even got an interview. Nic was one of our top producers and is now the vice president of sales and service for the Cleveland Cavs—a rising star in our business.
- Use your industry connections to inquire about talent throughout the industry. You never know who may be looking for the next step in their career. You may find a superstar.

> continued

2. Invest in Sales Training Through External Consultants

This item is probably the last thing that should be cut from any sales and service budget, but inexplicably it is usually the first. Many of us have an inexperienced sales force in which three- to five-year reps make up the most tenured portion. They need more coaching and learning.

Another voice, messaging something that you have attempted to message, can cause a breakthrough. What is it worth to you to increase the productivity in gaining referrals or setting appointments? Do you have data that can track historical conversion rates in these areas? If so, you can measure the success of the training by comparing the month following the training session with that historical record. The increment will be your ROI to validate future investment.

It only takes one! One sale, that is, to pay for that training, let alone the rep that absorbs and activates the training to the tune of hundreds of thousands of dollars. This is typically the big miss among sales managers. They expect that every one of their reps should leave the training better and in a few months all will have explosive growth. In reality I have experienced that a great trainer is more likely to have a large influence on only a handful of reps. These reps are yearning for a breakthrough, and that is just what they get. This breakthrough leads to more sales as well as a desire to learn more about great sales technique and strategy. This process is how a great sales culture will start and spread!

3. Create and Activate a Strong Internal Coaching and Development Program

One of the most important turning points in my professional life was hiring Keith Rosen to deliver his program on sales coaching to the sales managers and me. Rosen, the author of *Coaching Sales People Into Sales Champions*, teaches about how to communicate more effectively with your team by putting them in the driver's seat of their career by creating new possibilities of learning and growth. These teachings have led to great professional success, a healthier sales culture, and more personal happiness.

- Consistently practice. (Most refer to this as role-play, as I once did. Based on a tip from one of our trainers, we have shifted this vernacular. The term *practice* has a more positive connotation that most can pull a great result from past practice experience.) This should happen at least three to five times a week. I prefer to have some of these interactions occur voluntarily so that you can judge which reps really want to hone their craft.

- Message strong techniques through testimonials from call observations and rep feedback. Make referrals a priority to teach and champion. We have found that referral leads produce four times the dollars per lead as the next most successful lead campaign.

- Create opportunities for the reps to champion learning. If the reps feel ownership of a project or piece of a business, it should help discipline develop as well as help the reps gain important skill sets for their professional development. Our new business manager, Dave Baldwin, has formalized our management development program. We select two or three current sales and service reps from a pool of applicants. These reps are assigned a team of reps from our entry-level program. They meet with their team a few times a week to review learning from the week on the phones and on appointments. They also lead book-club style training with the team. The team leaders rotate managing the reps during sessions when the manager may not be present. This process helps identify future department leaders.

4. Inject Yourself in the Sales Process Through Observation

It is impossible to know whether the training you have invested in (time and money) is being activated without observation. I'm always surprised by the large number of sales and service people who do nothing on their own time to get better—no reading, or practice, or seeking help from the sales manager. This observation time, combined with coaching, could lead to new possibilities of learning and practice that the rep self-generates. We have found that listening to reps on the phone as well as observing them at their desks while they make calls is helpful, as is shadowing them during appointments in and out of game. Recording calls and having a worksheet that the reps fill out after observation and before manager dialogue has been helpful for both parties to reflect on before discussion. Two other benefits of this observation time could be the following:

- You are the expert, not the rep. You will increase your closing rate the more you assist in the process.
- Identify top prospects and coach on strategy.

Much like the human body, if the core of your sales department is weak, nothing else can be maximized.

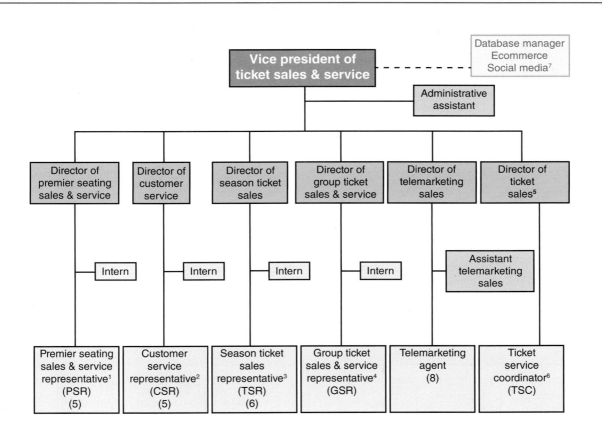

Notes:
1. One premier seating sales & service representative (PSR) per every 500 premier seats.
2. One customer service representative (CSR) per every 750 season-ticket accounts.
3. One season ticket sales representative (TSR) per every $500,000 of new season-ticket sales revenue to be generated.
4. One group ticket sales & service representative (GSR) per every $500,000 of group business (new and renewed).
5. Director of ticket sales may also be the director of box office operations in many teams' structures.
6. Ticket service coordinators (TSC) are responsible for building season-ticket and group accounts, processing payments, printing tickets, and delivering tickets. The number of TSCs depends on the degree of support provided by arena box office personnel.
7. Dependent on structure of database. May or may not have a direct reporting function. These positions might report directly to VP of marketing or, more recently, to the VP of business strategy.

FIGURE 8.2   NBA organizational chart.

them in telemarketing or, as it is often referred to, inside sales (discussed later in this chapter) and letting them progress according to performance. The typical sales-development progression begins with telemarketing and leads to opportunities in group sales or season-ticket sales that may lead to premium sales or possibly to corporate sales, which often involves corporate partnerships and other high-priced inventory such as luxury suites. According to sport sales consultant Jack Mielke, organizations should establish separate and distinct departments for ticket and sponsorship sales and divide ticket sales into season, group, corporate, and telemarketing.[12] Although the major U.S. sport leagues commonly employ this model, the structure obviously depends on the size and scope of the organization. We recommend this structure as a best practice because it produces specialists who can develop into experts in their particular area.

- Determining the composition of the sales force and compensation mix for the sales staff. In this process, the organization determines the number of full-time sales staff, the number of part-time sales staff (if any), the use of outside sales services (usually operating a telemarketing sales center, such as the Aspire Group or IMG College), and the way that sales personnel will be compensated. Compensation is usually a combination of salary and commission (a percentage of the sales revenue generated), and in some cases bonuses. Commission percentages vary according to what the salary-to-commission ratio is, what product is being sold, and whether the sale is a new sale or a renewal.

What Is a Recommended Sales-Oriented Structure?

Figure 8.3 depicts a possible organizational structure for a marketing department in a professional sport franchise, specifically how the ticket-sales

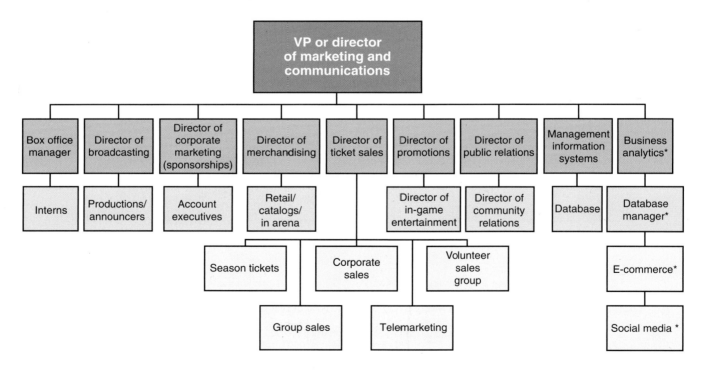

*May also report to the CFO, CRO, or VP of business strategy

FIGURE 8.3   How the ticket-sales department fits into sport marketing.

department could be structured and how it fits within the context of a marketing department.

As we have previously mentioned, the relationship between ticket sales and the box office is essential, but so are other relationships such as that between data-based marketing and ticket sales. This relationship is critical because of the practice of data-based marketing or customer relationship management (CRM), which would be asked to provide targeted segments of the database to the sales department for use as leads (names of potential consumers who through some action or activity have indicated an interest in or ability to purchase the product) or for the purpose of conducting a campaign, either an e-mail campaign or possibly direct mail (although this is becoming less common in sport). Similar relationships are necessary for providing tickets to sponsors as part of their packages, to community-relations personnel for use in their efforts, and to the promotions department and social media coordinators to assist in their promotional activities.

What Do I Have to Sell?

Sales inventory refers to all the available products and services available to the sales staff to market, promote, package, and sell through the sales methodologies described in this chapter. Table 8.1 categorizes the types of inventory available to sellers within the sport marketing industry.

TABLE 8.1 Inventories—What Do I Have to Sell?

Naming rights	Electronic inventory	Signage inventory	Print inventory	Assets related to ticket sales
Arena or stadium	Television	Dasher, score, matrix, and message boards	Game program	Court, ice, or field time
Practice facility	Radio	Marquees	Media guide	Clinics
Team	Web page	Floor, field, ice	Newsletters	Fan tunnels and high-five lines
	E-newsletters	Medallions	Ticket backs	Ball boy and ball girl opportunities
		Concourse	Ticket envelopes	
		Blimps	Scorecards, roster sheets	
		Turnstiles	Faxes	
		LED signage		

Tickets and hospitality inventory	Promotions inventory	Community programs	Miscellaneous inventory	
VIP parking	Premium items	School assemblies	Fantasy camps	
Stadium or arena clubs	On-floor promotions	Camps, clinics	Off-season cruises, trips with players	
Season tickets	Diamond Vision (or similar brand)	Awards, banquets	Road trips	
Club seats, suites, PSLs	Contests	Kick-off luncheons, dinners		
Group tickets	Pre- and postgame entertainment	Golf tournaments		
Parties, special events				

ACTIVITY 8.1 What Do I Have to Sell?

The Brooklyn Nets is a professional basketball team based in the New York City borough of Brooklyn. After 35 seasons in New Jersey, the team returned to the state of New York in 2012 to play in the new Barclays Center in Brooklyn as the Brooklyn Nets. In this WSG activity, you will learn more about the inventory the Brooklyn Nets have to sell. Based on what you learn, you will determine how to sell unsold inventory items for a particular sport at your school.

Direct Data-Based Sport Marketing and Sales

According to the Direct Marketing Association, the industry trade group for direct marketing, the definition of direct marketing is "an interactive process of addressable communication that uses one or more advertising media to effect, at any location, a measurable sale, lead, retail purchase or charitable donation, with this activity analyzed on a database for the development of ongoing mutually beneficial relationships between marketers and customers, prospects or donors."[13] The Direct Marketing Association estimated that $149.3 billion was spent on direct marketing in 2009.[14] In 2012 commercial and nonprofit marketers spent $168.5 billion on direct marketing, which accounted for 52.7 percent of all ad expenditures in the United States.[15]

Simply stated, database marketing involves the collection of information about past consumers, current consumers, and potential consumers. This information can be generated from membership records, lists of past purchasers, credit card receipts, contests, and so forth. The organization then cleans the data to improve accuracy and avoid duplicate records and compiles the information into a database or, ideally, a multifaceted CRM system. They can then create campaigns based on past purchasing behavior, demographic segment, or other factors according to organizational intent and the suitability of the target market as it relates to that intent. With the acceptance and growth of sport business analytics and research, the database manager works closely with (and in most cases reports to) the director or VP of analytics. The data is analyzed, targeted, and packaged to assist the sales team in focusing their correspondence and efforts with regard to prospecting and setting up sales calls. Regardless of the sales approach or process that the sport organization uses, some type of database is necessary to generate leads.[16] Table 8.2 illustrates how a ticket-sales database can be generated and how the data could be used.

It has long been considered the best practice for every organization to attempt to secure contact information of everyone who purchases its products or services. Technology that allows paperless tickets and other forms of electronic entry are making this goal much easier to achieve. A product called Flash Seats employs a paperless ticketing system designed to identify and provide the contact information for every person in the venue.

Management of the database is also a key element in the process. Each group or segment in the database should be tested and its responsiveness to certain appeals measured—ticket plans, telephone solicitation, online offers, e-marketing campaigns, and special offers through social media outlets. Responses should be measured to test ROI (return on investment) or ROO (return on objective) and should be documented to increase the targeting and the effectiveness of future efforts.

Lead scoring, identifying the likelihood of potential purchase and spend amount, is becoming a highly effective management tool. Lead scoring is designed to identify the prospects most likely to buy, and it can also be used to identify the best salesperson to make the solicitation based on the success of that salesperson and the qualifications of the prospect. Turnkey Sports has created a lead scoring system called Prospector. The sidebar illustrates how such a program is used and what benefits can result from employing such an approach.

Typical Sales Approaches Used in Sport

One of the keys to successful sales is having a product that everyone wants. Another key is to have products that people can afford, and yet another key is to have a product that considers the amount of time required to consume the

TABLE 8.2 Sample Construction and Use of a Ticket Database

Type of ticket purchaser	Source	Use
Season-ticket holders	Ticket applications	Renewals, upgrades, additional tickets, playoff tickets, PSLs, merchandise, special events, fantasy camps, youth clinics
Co-account holders (share season tickets)	Not usually listed on the application—provided by season-ticket holders in exchange for an incentive (extra tickets, gift item)	New season tickets, partial plans, additional individual game tickets, playoff tickets, PSLs, merchandise special events, fantasy camps, youth clinics
Corporate	Chamber of commerce, vendor lists, Dun and Bradstreet, ticket applications	Season tickets, club seats, luxury suites, PSLs, sponsorships, groups, additional tickets, playoff tickets
Partial-plan holders (ticket plans less than a full season)	Ticket applications	Upgrades, renewals, additional tickets, playoff tickets, merchandise, special events, fantasy camps, youth clinics
Groups (usually defined as parties of 20 or more)	Group leader lists, surveys of group attendees, contest participants	Partial plans, group brochures, group leader packet, individual game tickets, merchandise, promotional schedule, special events, fantasy camps, youth clinics
Advance-ticket purchasers (tickets purchased from the team or in-house box office)	Credit card slips, ticket form	Partial plans, promotional schedule, single-game ticket brochure, playoff tickets, merchandise, special events, fantasy camps, youth clinics
Phone sales	Ticketmaster or other software phone sales list	Partial plans, promotional schedule, single-game ticket brochure, playoff tickets, merchandise, special events, fantasy camps, youth clinics
Outlet (walk-in other than the stadium or arena, such as department stores, grocery chains)	Point-of-sale record (voucher documenting the sale provided to the team), contest entries	Partial plans, promotional schedule, single-game ticket brochure, playoff tickets, merchandise, special events, fantasy camps, youth clinics
Day-of-game walk-up sales	No set format—could use intern-run booths, kiosk computer terminals, and related formats	Partial plans, promotional schedule, single-game ticket brochure, playoff tickets, merchandise, special events, fantasy camps, youth clinics
Sweepstakes or contest entries	Entry forms	Merge and purge with other sources—promotional schedule, single-game ticket brochure, merchandise, special events
Opt-ins	Web visitors	Introductory offers, welcome packages, survey information

The Charlotte Bobcats began using Turnkey Prospector, a lead scoring system built by Turnkey Intelligence, to identify strong sales leads during the 2010–2011 NBA season. Over the course of the season, "hot leads" (i.e., individuals given 4- and 5-star ratings by Prospector) closed at rates over 200 percent higher than lower-rated leads (1 to 3 stars). Most significantly, the best leads identified by Turnkey (i.e., leads that were given 5-star ratings) closed at more than three times the rate of 1- and 2-star-rated leads.

To increase the efficiency of their sales staff, the Bobcats elected to evaluate and prioritize all incoming leads using Turnkey Intelligence's Prospector lead scoring system. At the Bobcats' request, Turnkey created a single custom-scoring model to help identify strong leads for either a full-season or half-season ticket plan. Ultimately, nearly 20,000 prospects (i.e., individuals who did not hold either ticket plan at the time they were scored) were called by the Bobcats as part of their outbound sales efforts. All leads were processed by Prospector and then, based on the scores they received, sorted into priority groups by the Bobcats. These leads came from the team's nightly ticketing feed or were imported lists of leads obtained from other sources (concert ticket buyers, names collected on the concourse, and so on).

As the 2010–2011 regular season ended, the Bobcats examined the sales associated with their Prospector-scored leads to determine the success of the integrated lead scoring system. As shown in figure 8.4, the club found that close rates were over 200 percent higher for hot leads (customers given ratings of 4 and 5 stars) than for all other leads (1-, 2-, and 3-star leads) and over three times higher for the best leads (5-star leads).

Effectively profiling incoming leads

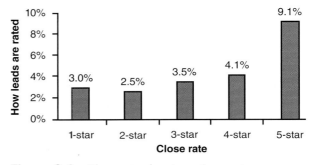

Figure 8.4 Close rates by star rating.

and their likelihood to purchase played a crucial role in enabling the Bobcats to distribute leads and effectively prioritize outbound phone calls. Although the hot leads represented only about 25 percent of all called prospects, they clearly drove sales by closing at more than double the rate of all other leads.

The same can be said for the best leads, the 5 stars. Although they represented just 9 percent of all called prospects, their significantly higher close rates emphasized their value and enforced the Bobcats' philosophy that the best leads should receive call priority over lower-rated leads.

When asked to discuss his club's direct marketing efforts, Flavil Hampsten, VP of ticket sales and database marketing at the Bobcats, noted the challenge of deciding which leads deserve the bulk of his sales team's resources. "In any given e-mail campaign, we might send an e-mail to 100,000 people, but we know our reps cannot possibly call 100,000 people to follow up," said Hampsten. "At best, we might be able to call 15,000 leads in a given campaign. As a lead distributor for the Bobcats, the difficult question becomes, "Which 15,000 of the 100,000 do I assign to the reps?" Because there's a finite number of leads that your reps can actually call for a given campaign, you'll need to create some sort of hierarchy to determine which leads receive those calls." Hampsten then stressed how crucial the Prospector platform has become in helping his team prioritize the leads that must be called every day. "Turnkey's Prospector scoring model has helped us identify which leads give our reps the best chance of success at selling," said Hampsten. "Using that information, we've made it a priority to assign the best 5-star leads first in any given campaign."[17]

Reprinted by permission from Turnkey. Available: http://www.turnkeyse.com/2011/04/charlotte-bobcats-lead-scoring

product (number of games). Full-menu marketing is having something for everyone. A fan of the Miami Heat can wear a $500 leather jacket or a $10 T-shirt. A New York Yankees fan can sit in the bleachers, in a luxury suite, or even in a steakhouse behind home plate to watch the game. The key is that the clubs or retailers recognize that demand for the product is present at a variety of price points. Our experience as practitioners and consultants has taught us that full-menu marketing is necessary not only because of price but also because of time and the depth and breadth of the fan's level of interest and commitment.

As the ability to pay, interest in the product or service, and availability of the product vary, so too must the approaches used to sell those products or services. A successful sport organization will employ a variety of sales approaches. And as the levels and types of products or services offered for sale within a sport organization vary, so should the sales approaches that aim to inform and convince consumers of a product's value to them. Certain approaches are more appropriate and consequently more effective in selling types or volume of the sport product. In this section, we examine the most common sales approaches used in sport.

Unlike food, clothing, and shelter, sport is not a necessity of life; it is a want rather than a need. As such, value is more important than price. Remember, unlike most purchases that consumers make, sport purchases ask them to invest not only their money but also their time and emotions. What value are they receiving in exchange for their investment? Selling, then, is not just about being the low-cost provider. It's about providing the best fit for the consumer in terms of ROI, ROO, and ROE (return on emotion), no matter how expensive or luxurious the product may be.

Telemarketing

Telemarketing (or, as it is commonly called, inside sales) can be defined as a marketing approach that "utilizes telecommunications technology as part of a well-planned, organized and managed marketing program that prominently features the use of personnel selling, using non-face-to-face contacts."[18] Telemarketing by telephone links can be used to complement, support, or substitute for a direct sales force. Telemarketing can be one-dimensional—handling inbound calls from consumers inquiring as a response to a promotional campaign, catalog, e-mail message, or other source.

Sport organizations are beginning to examine the benefits of expanding incoming phone-line capabilities to provide not only information but also revenue opportunities. To satisfy the desire of fans to stay abreast of team and player information and to increase sponsorship revenues (either in terms of the price the sponsor paid or by revenue sharing in a B-to-C [business-to-consumer] opportunity), several teams are offering 24-hour-a-day interactive phone lines.

Websites have also become an integral part of the telemarketing process in a number of ways:

- Links on the team web page to pose a question that someone in the organization will answer

- Links on the web page that will immediately connect the visitor with someone in the ticket office

- Applications on the website such as Virtual View and other integrated applications that help the caller visualize seating locations and other opportunities that can be discussed online or over the telephone with a sales representative

Telemarketing can also be two-dimensional, as an outward-oriented vehicle to prospect for customers, follow up leads, research prospects, solicit existing customers for repeat or expanded business volume, or set up appointments to bring the prospect to the place of business to learn more about the product or possibly for an opportunity to sample the product. A 2010 study conducted by Global Industry Analysts, Inc. projects telemarketing revenue in the United Sates alone at $15.5 billion by 2015. This growth is driven by the advent of advanced telecommunications technology coupled with the growing popularity of direct response advertising.[19] Additionally, 27.1 percent of respondents in a study conducted by the Direct Marketing Association chose telemarketing as the single most important direct marketing activity for business-to-business sales.[20]

Telemarketing offers considerable possibilities for enhancing the productivity of the sales force by permitting more specialization by account type and better focus on high-yield accounts. Telemarketing is also valuable in terms of sales

Telemarketing: The In-House Alternative

Adam Haukap, Associate Athletic Director Sales and Marketing, Oklahoma State University

I came to Oklahoma State in the fall of 2007. The decision to hire an in-house sales team was made before my arrival. This decision was one of the better ones that administrators could have made at the time, because OSU was about to enter a period of unprecedented growth in fan base and revenue. The ability to capitalize on this growth was one of the greatest advantages of having an in-house sales team, but not the only one. Having a sales team in house offers many advantages, including the connection with your alumni, control of the message, the flexibility that an in-house department provides, and, best of all, no revenue sharing.

We started with humble beginnings—eight part-time students in a small-box office setting. We have since grown to handle all ticket sales, ticket marketing, season-ticket retention, customer service, and all inbound phone traffic. Our department consists of seven full-time members (associate AD, analytics manager, sales coordinator, and four full-time customer service and retention representatives) along with 10 to 15 students who are focused on selling 20 to 30 hours per week.

I like the in-house model that we have developed because we can connect with alumni and fans. Most of our season-ticket holders are alums and have spent time on this campus as students, so we can reconnect them to that time in their lives. Our sales reps are students who may have lived in the same dorm or had the same professor as the people they are calling. Developing that relationship between prospects and students at their alma mater has paid dividends for us in ways I could not have imagined. An instant connection is present that many sales calls do not initially have and that many sales reps struggle to develop. We also have great working relationships with departments across campus. Whether we collaborate with our admissions department to help recruit students to campus by offering a discounted group seat or meet with our alumni association to plan events around a road game or bowl, the great relationships that we have on campus are mutually beneficial. We all are working to improve OSU. We also have complete control of the message that we want to get out. We focus on football revenue, but we also have the flexibility to sell all other ticketed sports. We can turn our attention in an instant if we hire a new baseball coach, or our women's basketball team makes a run to the WNIT Championship, or we are hosting a national wrestling dual. We are fully integrated with the entire athletic department. Our setup allows us to process annual fund donations in addition to season-ticket sales. Our customer service is improved because we act as a concierge, not a gateway to transfer to other departments conducting business. This arrangement helps us promote a consistent message to our fan base. We have one focus—to provide the best experience and customer service to our fans. Of course, we have an eye on revenue generation, but we can afford to take a long-term, relationship-building approach. The nature of the third-party agreement has an end date, and their goal may not be in accord with the long-term goals of the entire department. I have no concern of delivering a mixed message. Best of all, we do not share revenue. Hiring a company with an area of expertise and agreeing to split revenue with them may make sense in some aspects of the collegiate athletics department. Ticket selling is so important to the overall health of the company that, in the case of Oklahoma State athletics, an in-house sales department is the best model.

I'm often asked what the return on investment is for our department. I am a strict bottom-line numbers kind of person, but my take on the ROI aspect of this department is a little different. The long-term return is what I am focused on. It's hard to measure in future dollars what providing outstanding customer service and developing a relationship today will mean. We anticipate turnover in personnel, but the consistency of our message will be true through that turnover. Having an in-house sales department with flexibility and the connection to fans has positioned OSU to maintain its new position near the top of the Big 12.

support—scheduling sales calls and deliveries, conducting surveys, checking the status of a customer, and providing customer service. Long a staple approach by sport organizations, particularly professional sport franchises, telemarketing offers advantages that have finally persuaded one of the latecomers in outbound ticket sales, namely, college athletics departments, to embrace these practices either internally or through an outside vendor.

Although most professional sport franchises have in-house sales activities, college athletics departments vary in their setups. As we have learned in this chapter, Aspire and other outsourcing groups can be highly effective in providing outsourced sales services. Nevertheless, some athletics departments opt to conduct these activities themselves, preferring to control all messaging and interaction with their customers. Adam Haukap, who had previously worked in a professional sport setting and currently serves as associate athletics director at Oklahoma State University, offers his thoughts about why he prefers the in-house model.

ACTIVITY 8.2 Telemarketing

In this WSG activity, you will learn more about the telemarketing sales process as explained by Eric Kussin, vice president of sales, New Jersey Devils, and as demonstrated in a roleplay. You will also develop guidelines for telemarketing a product that you select.

Telemarketing Sales Process

Telemarketing involves training sales personnel to follow a script, become effective listeners, identify the objections to the sale (if any), and complete the sales process by countering the objection and selling the original offer or modifying the offer (by up-selling or down-selling) to fit the needs of the consumer better. This process could look like the following:

1. Precall Planning
   - Review client information including lead scoring (if available)
   - Plan the objective for the call
   - Psych-up—get in the proper mental frame for the call

2. Approach and positioning
   - Identify who you are and who you represent
   - Specify the purpose of your call
   - Make an interest-creating statement
   - Build rapport
   - Navigate through the gatekeeper (secretary or receptionist) to the decision maker

3. Data gathering
   - Build on the knowledge obtained from the preplanning investigations and research
   - Move from general to specific questions about practices and interests
   - Identify a personal or business need

4. Solution generation
   - Tailor communication to the specific client need
   - Ask in-depth questions to test the feasibility of the possible solutions
   - Gather data for a cost–benefit analysis
   - Prepare the client for the recommendation or the possibilities that have been identified

5. Solution presentation
   - Get client acknowledgment and agreement on the areas of need
   - Present the recommendations clearly and concisely
   - Describe benefits—ROI, ROE, and ROO—to the parties who will benefit from the purchase

6. Close
   - Decide on timing—when to close or, if the call was made to set up an appointment or visit to make the close, set the date and time of that appointment
   - Listen for acceptance or buying signals
   - Handle objections
   - Use closing techniques

7. Wrap-up
   - Discuss next steps, notably implementation issues
   - Thank the client for his or her business
   - Confirm client commitment

- Position the follow-up
- Ask for referrals

Applying the Telemarketing Process

To see how the process works, let's imagine the following scenario. Jane Micelli is a telemarketer employed by the Gotham Batmen, a professional baseball team that qualified for postseason play after the 2013 regular season but did not win the championship. Jane has been provided a list of leads, derived from people who used their credit cards to purchase tickets to one or more games during the past season. Jane's goal is to sell partial plans of 40, 20, or 10 games for the 2014 season. For the first time she has the opportunity to sell a game-of-the-month plan, a six-pack. Here are the steps that Jane follows:

1. **Precall planning**. Jane reviews the file on Mary Stuart, an attorney who bought individual tickets to four games during the past season. Jane notices that Ms. Stuart purchased two tickets for each of the four games and attended once per month in June, July, August, and September. Jane reviews her script and places the call.

2. **Approach and positioning**. "Hello. My name is Jane Micelli, and I am calling from the Midwest Division champion Gotham Batmen. May I please speak to Mary Stuart? Good evening, Ms. Stuart. As I stated, I'm calling from the Gotham Batmen, and we want to thank you for your interest and support of the team during the past season. I hope you enjoyed your experiences, and I would like to take this opportunity to talk to you about the upcoming season. We are excited to have made the postseason last year, but that is just a step on the way to our ultimate goal—winning a championship for the people of Gotham. We anticipate tickets being more difficult to obtain for next season because of our performance last year, our prospects for next year, and the new players we have added to our roster. We would like to make sure that our fans who have supported us in the past have access to better seating location and options before the tickets go on sale to the general public. Do you have just a few minutes?"

3. **Data gathering**. "According to our records, you purchased tickets to see the Penguins, Riddlers, Jokers, and Cats last season. Is that correct? Did you attend any other games? Were you able to go the postseason games? Were you attending for your personal enjoyment, or was there a business aspect involved? Did you always attend with the same person?"

4. **Solution generation**. "We have designed several ticket plans that are less than our traditional full-season plan with people such as you in mind. We have plans ranging from 40 games to as few as 6 games, and even with our 6-game plan you have priority over the general public to have the opportunity to purchase playoff tickets, and I know that is important to you. We also realize that these games are important to a businessperson such as you to host clients and conduct business meetings in a fun and entertaining setting. Would you be interested in considering a 6-game plan for next season?" (The number of games offered is selected based on the previous step.)

5. **Solution presentation**. "The Gotham Batmen have designed a new ticket plan especially for the business person. Our game-of-the-month plan offers one game per month located in our premium seating areas, including food and beverage, meeting space, and the opportunity for a dinner seating at three different times. It also guarantees you the option to purchase postseason tickets for at least one game in each of the postseason series in which we are competing. How would that fits your needs?"

6. **Close**. "I am sure that this game-of-the-month plan will meet your needs and be much more convenient and consistent than your current ticket purchasing options. Can I reserve two Big Game plans for you and schedule a time when we can select your seat location? If it is inconvenient for you to select the seats, we can do that right now using our seat finder, which we can access online. I can assist you with that right now. How does that sound?"

7. **Wrap-up**. "Thanks for taking the time to select your location online. I am sure that you will be happy with your seats. If there is anything that we can do during the season, please contact either me or Thomas Fagan, who will be your account representative. Thomas will contact you in the next 48 hours to provide further explanation of the benefits that we discussed that are part of your account. One last question: Is there anyone else at your firm or anyone in your business circles who you think could benefit from a similar ticket package?"

Outsourcing Telemarketing

Nearly all major college programs outsource something, whether it is multimedia and marketing rights sales, licensed logo and image rights, naming rights, merchandise sales, or concessions. Outsourcing ticket sales was a logical evolution that was based on the success of the previously listed outsourced areas, the financial and competitive pressures that colleges and universities helped to create, the challenging post-2008 economy, and the inability or unwillingness of colleges to add employees and implement a compensation system of bonuses and commissions that is common in sales and marketing enterprises but is a radical departure from compensation models employed at colleges and universities.

Since 2009 more than one-third of the 124 schools (in 2013–14) in the NCAA's elite-level Football Bowl Subdivision have instituted outbound telemarketing sales initiatives, either on their own or by outsourcing to an outside vendor. Although a number of outside vendors provide such services, the two major players in this space are the Atlanta-based Aspire Group, led by former NBA and MLB executive and college athletics director, Dr. Bernie Mullin, and IMG College, which already enjoyed a strong presence and history of being the outsourcing vehicle for marketing and media rights with many of the same colleges and universities. "The colleges, for many years, were almost in an arms race for who could have the most seats, and they were able to fill those seats, for the most part," says Mark Dyer, a senior vice president for IMG College, whose menu has recently expanded to include ticket sales. "That has changed. . . . Most schools across the country have an issue with their football or basketball seating demand versus seating capacity."[21]

Aspire's Bill Fagan manages the Fan Relations Management Centers for the Aspire Group, including the initial center at Georgia Tech, which serves as the epicenter for Aspire's sales activities. Fagan explained the setup: 12 to 14 staffers working on commission, each making 80 to 100 phone calls per day from a database of Georgia Tech–connected names, and trained and supervised by a sales manager. The sales team solicits these contacts for sales as well as sales referrals and new leads. Aspire generated $2.7 million in gross sales for Georgia Tech through 2011, and

the agreement has been extended through 2013. Fagan goes on to say, "If you (athletic departments) can do it in house, we encourage you to do it. But not everybody can. (Schools) don't have the core competency or the expertise to build it, and many schools can't pay commissions to their sales consultants because of university rules or state regulations. They don't have the flexibility and the nimbleness to hire and fire quite like we can in the private sector."[22]

Look for this trend of outsourcing ticket sales to continue, not only by these two major players but also by smaller organizations and by professional franchises at both the major and minor league levels who want to capitalize on their off-season or slower periods by using their sales departments to sell for colleges or other sport and entertainment venues.

Direct Mail

We know your first reaction when you saw this: "In this day and age? With social media as prevalent as it is?" The answer is yes. According to Dale Berkebile of Brandwise, direct mail is as effective as ever if you follow one simple rule: know your target audience.[23] Salesforce.com and other CRM (customer relationship management) systems should provide you with an excellent up-to-date portrait of your customers or donors, their purchasing or giving history, and their anticipated interests and patterns of behavior.

Like telemarketing and other forms of direct marketing, direct mail has distinct characteristics and advantages:

- **Direct mail is targeted**. The appeal is to certain groups of consumers who are measurable, reachable, and sizable enough to ensure meaningful sales (or fund-raising) volume.

- **It is personal**. The message can be personalized not only according to the name and other demographic characteristics but also with regard to lifestyle interests and past behaviors (football fan, Cowboys alumnus, merchandise purchaser, fantasy camp attendee, and so on).

- **It is measurable**. Because each message calls for some type of action or response, the organization mailing the message is able to measure the effectiveness of the marketing effort.

- **It can be tested**. Because the effectiveness is measurable, marketers can devise accurate head-to-head comparisons of offers, formats, prices, terms, and so forth.

• **It is flexible.** There are few constraints (other than cost) with regard to the size, color, timing, shape, and format of the mailing. Also, the marketer determines the mailing date and anticipated arrival of the campaign piece.

As with any approach, direct mail has limitations. Because it does not involve any personal contact (face to face as in personal selling or mouth to ear as in telemarketing), no opportunity is available to explain the program and the offer, to counter objections, or even to answer questions. Thus, the sender must clearly communicate the material, including the offer itself, so that the targeted recipient can clearly understand it.

In formulating the direct-mail offer, the sport marketer should consider the following:

• **Differentiating the product to be offered from other products offered.** In other words, in the case of a ticket brochure being mailed to a target audience, is each ticket package option clearly distinguishable from the others? Can the recipient easily assess the benefits of each, make a decision, and act accordingly?

• **Offering options or variations of the product to fit the price considerations, time constraints, and abilities of the marketplace.** This approach, sometimes referred to as the good, better, best approach, was an essential part of Sears' catalog marketing for decades. The Sears approach was to list three items in the catalog with different features and at slightly increasing prices relative to the number of features. Each was then described (in ascending price order and feature order) as a good model, a better model, or the best model. The Golfsmith Store, a direct mail merchandiser that specializes in golf equipment and apparel, offers a range of options from factory closeout specials for the budget conscious to the newest state-of-the-art equipment (to find prices for the latter, the prospective buyer is directed to call the company for the most recent pricing). In one recent catalog (and on the website) the price for a new driver ranged from a low of $49.99 to a high of $399.[24]

• **Providing an attractive range of benefits or exclusivity.** Since the 1990s sport marketers have appealed to consumers to "join them" in various direct-mail membership initiatives. These memberships, such as those offered by the National Baseball Hall of Fame and Museum, the Special Olympics, and others, sometimes entailed various levels that had different fees and a set of benefits, publications, admission privileges, premium items, special access, and special events to join at a particular level.

• **Using discounts, sales, refunds, coupons, premium items, and other incentives to enhance the perceived value of the offer.** Direct mail seeks to cause an action, and the perception of getting a deal in making the purchase is often the catalyst in producing the action. These deals can take many forms. The most popular forms of catalog discounting allows a consumer to receive free shipping or receive a certain portion off if the order exceeds a certain amount, perhaps an offer of $10 or $15 off on an order that exceeds $100. This offer is prevalent in apparel marketing, but teams often use it with their own merchandise catalogs or stores. Likewise, sport mass merchandisers may offer certain deals to move merchandise or to attract new buyers.

• **Offering flexible payment or deferred payment terms.** Some consumers may be intrigued by the opportunity to purchase merchandise now and pay for it at a more convenient time.[25] This retailing practice is common in the United States, and payment plans have become a fixture in the sport industry, particularly for higher priced items such as season tickets. Some professional sport teams allow their season-ticket purchasers to agree to pay for their season tickets over an extended period. The NFL Tampa Bay Buccaneers offer a payment plan for season tickets that can be extended to a full 12 months. According to the Buccaneers website, "After gathering the opinions of existing Season Pass and Stadium Club Members, the Buccaneers have created a new 12-month payment option for the 2013 season that creates the flexibility fans desire. On Friday, the team mailed a description of the plan to all current members, inviting them to take advantage of the option immediately. Members may do so by filling out and returning a detachable portion at the bottom of the mailer."[26]

• **Offering a money-back guarantee.** This type of offer permits the consumer to purchase (by payment in full) the product and consume at least some portion of it. Consumers who are not satisfied with the product for a specified, or

Dr. Sutton's Favorite Direct-Mail Promotion

Going back to the critical marketing concept that we introduced regarding direct-mail—namely, know your target audience—Tommy Bahama, an island lifestyles clothier, has created a direct-mail campaign that has motivated me to purchase on numerous occasions. The direct-mail piece came in the form of a holiday greeting card and contained a gift card for $50. The most interesting aspect of the $50 gift card is that it required no minimum purchase. In fact, it required no purchase whatsoever. The no-strings gift card invited me to visit a Tommy Bahama retail store or restaurant and use the card as cash. If I picked up a T-shirt for $48, I just gave them the gift card and walked away. (A minimum purchase of $100 was required to use the card online, so the customer had to spend $50 to use the free $50, still an incentive.) How effective was it? In my particular case, I have redeemed such a card three times, and in all three instances I never spent less than an additional $200. I would judge that an effective direct-mail campaign. I feel appreciated, and because the company knows my shopping habits, the incentive on their part is worth it to encourage me to continue shopping with them—a place where I feel appreciated and valued.

in some cases an unspecified, reason may return it for a full refund of the purchase price. Jason Rowley, president of the NBA Phoenix Suns, says that the ticket rebate will go to fans who leave the arena unsatisfied after experiencing what he termed the excitement of Suns basketball, regardless of whether the team wins or loses.[27] This approach was pioneered by long-term sports executive John Spoelstra during his days at the then New Jersey Nets. His direct-mail piece even specified, "You can ask for a refund if you don't like my tie or the way I comb my hair."[28] Both guarantees have proved effective because they not only sold tickets and motivated consumers to try the product but also generated significant local, regional, and even national publicity.

According to Ron Contorno, founder of Full House Entertainment Database Marketing, the key to successful direct marketing is its ability to target potential customers accurately. Full House has analyzed customer databases from numerous teams and venues. Having access to customer data takes the guesswork out of prospecting. Contorno's company offers a product called Current Fan Profile Reports that provides a full analysis of an organization's business and consumer accounts. A separate report is generated for each type of buyer: full seasons, partial plans, groups, and premium seating. The research allows the organization to target its customers more effectively by penetrating further into the business segments and consumer demographics to identify proven buyers.[29]

ACTIVITY 8.3 Direct Mail

You are the director of marketing for Hawk Pointe Golf Club located in Washington, NJ. The club membership is declining due to newly opened public golf courses within a 15 miles radius and a struggling economy. In this WSG activity, you will consider the value of direct mail and how you can use it to increase memberships for Hawk Pointe Golf Club.

E-Mail Marketing

In many ways e-mail marketing has experienced a healthy metamorphosing into part of a long-promised broader digital marketing arsenal focused on what matters most for most businesses—making money. New and growing businesses are strategic and continually evolving in how they embrace e-mail. Marketing automation, cloud-based marketing platforms, digital messaging, and CRM are all ways to deliver e-mail. The companies that are successful in this space and delivering significant ROI include ExactTarget, Pardot, Eloqua, HubSpot, and Infusionsoft. These companies all showcase proven technology platforms designed to persuade customers to buy more often and to turn prospects into customers.[30]

We should also acknowledge that e-mail marketing is also mobile marketing. The number of e-mails opened on a mobile device (Smartphone or tablet) during the first half of 2012 overall rose to 36 percent.[31] New content, technology, and savvy testing can accomplish a lot on the mobile front. In addition to understanding the audience and building a game plan with that in mind, the execution of campaigns to a mobile readership is crucial. The right message on the right device can be the difference between a read, a click, and a purchase.[32]

Developing the E-Mail Offer

Eloqua, which includes among its clients the Miami Heat, Boston Bruins, Golden State Warriors, and a number of other professional sport franchises and venues, has a variety of tools and e-mail campaigns designed to assist in reaching and converting fans into buyers with highly targeted offers, not unlike direct-mail campaigns. Eloqua offers a platform named the All Star that provides a variety of tools that provide the following, which we view as essentials to an e-mail campaign. Many (but not all) of these concepts and services are highly desirable in direct-mail campaigns as well.

- Fan profiling and web tracking
- Fan acquisition, append, and cleanse
- Fan segmentation
- Fan (lead) scoring
- One-to-one personalization
- Campaign and conversion metrics
- Segment analysis
- Real-time, multichannel marketing[33]

One of the more intriguing e-mail marketing and sales campaigns surrounded the sale of the New Orleans Hornets (now the Pelicans as of the 2013–14 season) when the team (which at the time was owned by the NBA) was sold to New Orleans Saints owner Tom Benson. Fans received an e-mail that directed them to a website (www.nba.com/hornets/NOLAIMIN.html?source=release) where they were asked to declare their support of the team by clicking an "I'm In" logo and viewing several ticket-purchasing options to declare their support for the Hornets.

The marketing campaign featured icons of the Crescent City alongside everyday fans, each bearing the message that living in New Orleans—and being a Hornets fan—is not an effort that can be done halfway. Well-known residents voicing their "I'm In" pledges included Governor Bobby Jindal, Mayor Mitch Landrieu, political commentator James Carville, Archbishop Gregory Aymond, jazz musician Jeremy Davenport, and Arnold Young, the beloved usher from section 124 of the New Orleans Arena.

Fans showed their support and said, "I'm In" by joining the Krewe of Hornets as season-ticket holders for the 2011–12 season with two great offers. The Balcony Buster season-ticket pack allowed fans to buy two season tickets in the balcony and get two free while supplies lasted. Or, fans could put down an initial payment for any other seat location and receive all April regular-season home games free. Purchasing season tickets for the 2011–2012 season also locked in playoff priority for the 2011–12 playoffs.[34]

E-mail (and Direct Mail) Can Be More Than an Offer

Organizations that use e-mail or direct mail to do nothing more than initiate the sales process through an offer do not understand relationship marketing. As we discuss later in this chapter, the long-term goal of sales efforts is to develop lasting and deep relationships with the consumer. If the only time the consumer hears from the organization is at renewal time or when the aim is to sell more of the product, the relationship will never be strengthened or expanded. Regular communication through these two channels can be used to enhance sales opportunities through several means:

- By providing a regular method of communication to keep the customer informed (through letters, newsletters, video blasts, and other ways of sharing content that might be of interest to the recipient and be interesting enough for the recipient to share through social media with a wider audience)
- By soliciting input, opinions, and feedback with questionnaires, surveys, chat rooms, and other ways to create two-way dialogue
- By showing accountability and expanding the knowledge of the consumer with an annual report
- Through thank-you correspondence that acknowledges the support of the consumer over the past year and asks for continued support

- By delivering invitations to special events and opportunities that may be of interest to the consumer or a member of her or his family or organization

Making an organization's annual report available to customers is just one of the ways that a team can keep communication between the fans and the team open. The concept of sharing an annual report with stakeholders has been around for the past 20 years in one form or another. Technology has been a huge innovator in this area because the annual report can now be shared electronically, which is not only green and financially efficient but also brings the report to life because video and audio elements can be added to the content. The annual report thus becomes a multidimensional experience that is both informative and entertaining and includes content that may be shared through both e-mail and social media channels.

The annual report, which can be described as having the purpose of updating the shareholders and various interested publics on the state of the franchise, organization, institution, or campaign, usually contains the following elements:

- A letter from the ownership (could also be a video)
- An overview of the season and a preview of the next season (direction of the team or product discussion)
- A synopsis of charitable activities, ideally including player involvement, which is the type of content that is viewed and shared most frequently
- An explanation (and listing) of the benefits of being a season-ticket holder, donor, or similar role
- Thank-you notes and messages from the players to the fans
- A video or photograph montage of the previous season's highlights and activities
- Video or photographs of stakeholders at various special events held in the past year
- A thank-you offer from sponsors or the team

The intent of such mailings or e-mails is to make the stakeholder feel special and informed. The annual report can take the form of a printed

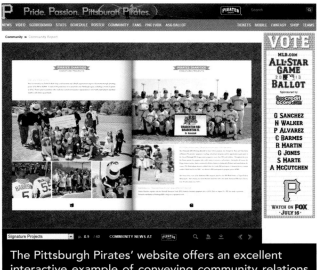

The Pittsburgh Pirates' website offers an excellent interactive example of conveying community relations programming.

document or be produced on a DVD or flash drive, but the best way may be to e-mail a link to a website so that the message can take advantage of all the technology available and have a more multidimensional feel that brings the content to life. For an excellent example of such an annual report go to http://pittsburgh.pirates.mlb.com/pit/community/report_flip.jsp to view the 2012 Community Report of the Pittsburgh Pirates.

Personal Selling

"Face-to-face selling is the art of convincing, the use of learnable techniques to close a transaction and the application of basic rules to show a prospect or customer that you have something he or she needs."[35] Although more costly than telemarketing, direct mail, and e-mail, personal selling can be more effective because it enables the seller and the prospect to engage in dialogue. In most sport situations, personal selling is done at the seller's place of business because of the opportunity to offer sampling, comparisons, and other two-way interaction and capitalize on the assets at hand. Developing and maintaining a strong sales force can be one of the most expensive elements of the promotional mix, and the management and motivation of this sales force require an experienced, gifted sales manager with exceptional observational, communication, and motivational skills. But the return on investment

(ROI) in the sales force may be well worth the cost if a few simple rules are followed as outlined in table 8.3.

Personal selling involves the integration of data-based marketing, relationship marketing, and benefit selling to communicate effectively to consumers. Because data-based marketing has been discussed previously in this text, we will examine the other two elements to assess the contribution and importance of each to the personal-selling process.

Relationship Marketing

Palmatier defines relationship marketing (RM) as the process of identifying, developing, maintaining, and terminating relational exchanges to enhance performance.[40] We believe this performance to be on the part of both the supplier and the customer and believe that besides enhancing performance, the goal is to extend the relationship. Relationship marketing implies finding a way to integrate the customer into the company to create and sustain a relationship between the company and the customer.[41] Gronroos, an expert on relationship marketing, identified three main

conditions under which relationship marketing is a successful and productive marketing approach:

- The customer has an ongoing desire for service.
- The customer of the service controls the selection of the service supplier.
- Alternative service suppliers are available.[42]

These conditions are present in the sport marketplace, and they provide an excellent application forum for relationship marketing. In general, people who consume sport are highly involved consumers who have a desire for long-term association with a sport team, event, or branded product. The extremely competitive sport marketplace includes many providers for each sport product or service (not necessarily in the same sport type, but as a sport entertainment option), enabling the consumer to select among many providers.[43] For example, a customer looking for athletics footwear conducted a brand search and identified 78 possible choices by manufacturer alone, not even counting the specific models

TABLE 8.3   Rules for Effective Personal Selling

Rule	Rationale
Use data-based marketing	Generate leads with a high likelihood of interest and ability to purchase. Score leads whenever possible.
Follow the LIBK rule—let it be known that you are in sales and what you are selling.[36]	Be proud and enthusiastic about what you do and what you are selling.
Overcome objections and perceived barriers to the sale.	Be familiar with the most common objectives or barriers to the sale and modify the product or provide examples showing that people with the same objection have enjoyed the product.
Manage the conversation by being an effective listener as well as by stating your case.[37]	Consumers want to be heard; they want affirmation to their concerns.
Employ consultative selling.	You are consulting by proposing possible solutions to the various needs and wants of the consumer.
Build your world and your customer's world around the strengths of your product, your service, and yourself.[38]	Customers want to buy from strength; explaining a weakness detracts from their belief in the salesperson.
Match the consumer with the appropriate product.	A good sale fits the needs, budget, and lifestyle of the purchaser.
Always follow up.[39]	Show the same level of interest during and after the sell; the sale doesn't end with the first sale.

available.[44] Therefore, building a relationship with a customer is essential to retaining that person as a repeat customer.

Benefit Selling

Benefit selling involves the creation of new benefits to offset existing perceptions or assumed negatives related to the sport product or service.[45] For example, for consumers who state that they cannot commit to a ticket plan because they don't know where they will be or what their schedule will look like several months in advance, benefit selling may be the answer. The concept of benefit selling has been responsible for the creation of new products in the sport industry such as the flex books, such as the one developed by the State College (Pennsylvania) Spikes minor league baseball team in response to the frequent objections of potential consumers that they could not commit to a certain number of games on specific dates. The Flex Book contains coupons for 12 games sold for the price of 10 game tickets. The coupons have no date or specific seat location, just a price category, and they can be redeemed (exchanged for a ticket) in advance of a game that the customer wishes to attend or even that same day based on ticket availability. Purchasers can use the tickets in any way that they choose—all at once, in multiples of two or one game at a time, or any combination adding up to the number of coupons purchased. Consumers benefit because they are not restricted to particular dates, and in some cases they receive an extra coupon for a game to choose as an incentive to purchase the Flex Book. The incentive for the organization is that the tickets are presold, so filling the seats does not depend on team performance, weather, or any other factors. The only limitation is that the coupon does not guarantee admission; redemption is based on availability and on whether the game is a premium game, such as opening day and concert dates. In addition, the number of coupons that can be used for a particular game against an opponent that draws well is limited.

The State College (Pennsylvania) Spikes, minor league affiliate of the St. Louis Cardinals, offer the Flex Book plan:[46]

- Each book contains 12 undated vouchers for the price of 10. Vouchers can be redeemed for tickets to any State College Spikes regular-season home game, based on availability.
- The plan is affordable and makes a great gift.
- It offers great flexibility. You can use all 12 vouchers at one game or come to 12 different games.
- Vouchers can be redeemed in person at the Medlar Field at Lubrano Park Box Office in advance or on the day of the game.
- Each voucher includes a money-saving coupon to be used at any State College or Milesburg McDonald's location (12 coupons per book).
- Each flex book also includes one (1) coupon for either ten (10) free ball launch balls or five (5) free "Closest to the Pin" golf balls to be used after any 2013 Spikes home game.

When these three approaches—data-based marketing, relationship marketing, and benefit selling—are integrated into the formulation of a personal-selling campaign and fine-tuned into a sales style involving the personality and experience of the salesperson, the results can be highly effective.

When combined with concepts such as sampling, trial usage, and open houses, personal selling can be even more effective, especially in certain segments of the sport industry such as fitness clubs, sporting good sales, and the sale of high-end professional sport seating options such as club seats, loge boxes, and luxury and party suites. Sampling, trial usage, and open houses are designed to let the consumer experience the product. One of the most innovative trial programs of all time was the "test drive" designed by Apple to introduce the Macintosh (now referred to as the Mac or iMac) computer in 1984.[47] Consumers could pick up a Macintosh at a selected retailer, leave a credit card deposit, and take the computer home for the test drive.

Personal selling complements the experience by educating consumers about what they are experiencing and what benefits they are receiving. The fitness industry, for example, is a proponent of trial visits with professional instruction and attention. A sales presentation in the form of an interview between the salesperson and the prospective member usually follows the trial workout. The topics of the interview usually include patterns of physical activity, health and fitness goals, and the importance of wellness and regular physical activity, all in relationship to the facility, equipment, and staff that the prospect has just experienced.

Professional sport teams such as the Cleveland Indians, New York Mets, Pittsburgh Pirates, and Orlando Magic often use the open house concept, sometimes branding it as a select-a-seat event. The open house type of event usually occurs in the preseason (making weather a distinct factor for baseball teams in northern climates) and can include stadium tours, anthem singer auditions, and entertainment activities, such as mascots, clinics, and autographs. Most important, as potential consumers, attendees have the opportu-

Basketball mini plans, such as this one from Kansas State University, are another way to entice fans to purchase tickets. In this example, the mini plan includes a ticket to the in-state rival game with the University of Kansas.

nity to sit in the seats available for sale. Balloons or flyers often designate available seats so that potential customers can identify the existing inventory and check out the view. After they are seated (indicating at least some level of interest), sales staff introduces themselves and, usually armed with a special offer that expires that day, initiate the personal-selling process.

One common misperception about personal selling is that it is nothing more than verbal interaction between the parties. Remember the axiom "Actions speak louder than words." The consumer often interprets the actions taken by an organization, or for that matter the actions not taken, as evidence of what they may expect in the future. Thus, hospitality management, staff interaction, and the way that informational inquiries are handled are key elements of the personal-selling process.

Personal selling is ideal for some types of ticket sales such as group sales, but it is most important when used in the sale of premium seating options such as suites, loge boxes, and courtside seats with club amenities—all products with significant hospitality and entertainment benefits to consider and sample in addition to the seating location. In regard to these particular products, personal selling becomes experiential selling because a visit and trial methodology is an important aspect of the sale and because the sales process usually begins with an invitation to sample by attending a game. The visit to the game usually includes some type of orientation, tour, and education for the buyer along with sampling the other benefits such as food and club access. In a similar vein, corporate partnership sales and their related visits are best suited for personal selling.

Innovative Promotional Approaches for Selling Sport Products and Services

The unique nature of sport allows us to become highly imaginative in the sale of the sport product. Here are some additional reminders:

- **Education can sell the fan base**. Albert G. Spalding discovered more than 150 years ago that if people understood what his products were (at that point, baseball equipment) and how to use them and benefit from them, they would be more likely to play the game and have a need for his products.[48] Professional team sports, in particular football and hockey, have taken a similar approach and created courses such as Football 101 and Hockey 101 to educate fans on the rules, strategies, nuances, and complexities of the game by simplifying and explaining the terminology. The NFL Tennessee Titans have an extensive Football 101 section on their website (www.titansonline.com/fans/kidzone/football-101.html), and About.com provides a basic guide to Football 101.[49] Teams have also been known to offer clinics and demonstrations to help accomplish this educational process. Using educational activities to help create an understanding and a need for the product that is addressed through the sales process has been defined as edu-selling.[50]

• **Remember your packaging.** Promotional activities (discussed in chapter 10) can be effective in driving sales for a specific game, event, or period. One such promotion, implemented by the then New Jersey (now Brooklyn) Nets, is relevant because of its ability to attract new trial purchasers and because of its dramatic effect on sales. The Nets' speaker package was a three-game ticket plan targeted to New Jersey corporations and businesses as a way to enhance their companies. Lou Holtz, Tom Peters, and Harvey Mackay, packaged as authors and motivational speakers, spoke for an hour before one of the three Nets games. Each speaker appeared on a particular date. The dates chosen were weeknight games against some of the lesser-performing teams in the NBA, but all sold out through this package.[51]

• **Remember that fun is good.** The film *Field of Dreams* made famous the quotation "If you build it, they will come." This quotation now epitomizes the emphasis and dependence on building new stadiums and arenas not only to generate new revenue streams but also to provide an experience and level of entertainment that is essential to the live experience of attending a game. Beginning in the 1940s with Bill Veeck's giveaways and promotions and continuing today with his son Mike and his minor league baseball franchises, the rally cry has been "If it's fun, they will come." The Veecks believed, and rightly so, that to attract fans teams can't just sell their win-loss record. Teams have to sell the experience of a good time and the possibility of winning. Through promotional flair, understanding of hospitality management (cleanliness and com-

fort), and their commitment to fun, the Veecks established attendance records at all levels. Veeck staples such as giveaway days with items like bats, fireworks nights, and special theme nights and concerts have become commonplace not only in baseball but in professional sports at all levels.[52]

• **Couponing is not just for groceries and fast food.** One of the most common complaints about attending a sporting event is cost, particularly for families. Creative packaging can answer the need for affordable family entertainment options. Many sport organizations in both professional (major and minor league) and amateur sports (including those at colleges and universities) have developed and implemented one-price tickets for families. The package is usually based on four admissions, parking, and refreshments. Given that in today's world the traditional family of four is less prevalent than in was when this packaging began 20 to 30 years ago, it might make more sense to offer the pricing on an individual basis by pricing packages as low as $11 per person or whatever makes up 25 percent of the price of the traditional family four-pack. In this manner larger families will feel more welcome and single-parent households will recognize that this promotion is targeted to them as well. Inclusivity should result in increased sales. Some organizations elect to provide a souvenir (e.g., a cap, T-shirt, or other team novelty item), whereas others may elect to provide a voucher for a sponsor's product. Some organizations use a restaurant or pizza chain to provide the food items instead of providing them at the ballpark. This arrangement is a good traffic driver to the sponsor's place of business.

• **Remember the profitability and effect of group sales.** As discussed earlier in this book, sport consumers usually do not attend sporting events alone. Research has shown that fewer than 2 percent of fans attend games by themselves. We also noted that for some fans the social interaction defines their enjoyment of the event and that for others the social component may be their sole reason for attending. For these reasons, sport organizations should make every attempt to attract and sell tickets to large groups (25 or more). Discounts ranging from $1 to $5 per ticket depending on the size of the group and the retail price of the ticket, and special seating sections, menus, and dining options (from catered sit-

Tampa Bay Buccaneers star Vincent Jackson and his foundation, Jackson in Action 83.org, teamed up with the Tampa Bay Lightning to offer specially priced group tickets for the Lightning's Seats for Soldiers Night. Jackson purchased and donated 2,000 tickets for military personnel at nearby MacDill Air Force Base to attend the game.

down dinners to picnics) are all effective means to attract a group to a sporting event. Groups can be Little League teams, scouts, church choirs, employees, military units, and college students—any collective that meets or exceeds the organizational minimum.

Use Your Assets to Sell, Part I

One of the most successful sales campaigns in the history of the then New Jersey Nets was the Influencer Program implemented before the 2005–06 season. The signature marketing tool of Nets CEO Brett Yormark generated over $1 million in new season-ticket sales in its first year and was a best practice emulated by many professional teams in various leagues.[53] The program was, and is, built on connectivity, hospitality, star power, face-to-face selling, and, of course, the perceived and actual influencing ability of the host. The program begins by having a current season-ticket holder host 30 or so friends and business connections who are not season-ticket holders at his or her home or at another setting such a business or country club. At this point the Nets (or any team employing this strategy) take over, providing

hospitality and catering services as well as entertainment (mascot, dancers) and a representative from the coaching staff or a current or retired player. The business side is usually represented by the team president. In some cases, the owner, accompanied by members of the marketing and sales staff, attends and provides a state-of-the-team overview before asking for the sale.

This form of influencer marketing, novel at the time, initially was related to celebrity and athlete endorsement and is now a large part of social media because trust, experience, nonaffiliation, and firsthand knowledge by previous consumers or users can dictate the financial fortunes of restaurants, music, film, apparel, equipment, and almost anything you can imagine. Influencer marketing is an updated approach to marketing and public relations in which marketers target the people who prospects turn to for information. These influencers help generate awareness and sway the purchase decisions of those who seek out and value their expertise, read their blogs, converse with them in discussion forums, attend their presentations at industry events, and so on.[54] In sport, other season-ticket holders, corporate partners, suite owners, and the like are considered influencers. Their opinions, whether positive or negative, can sway prospects who are involved in the decision-making process.

ACTIVITY 8.4 Using Your Best Assets

You've been hired as the director of marketing for your school. As discussed in this chapter, one of the best ways to spread the word is to give customers some personal connection to the event that anchors their experience. This WSG activity asks you to use your "assets" to increase sales. Can you handle the challenge?

Use Your Assets to Sell, Part II

The goal of every sport marketer in the repeat attendance business is to provide consumers with an enjoyable experience and a lasting, positive memory that will encourage them not only to attend again but also to become customer evangelists by spreading the word to their friends and associates. One of the best ways to do that is to give them some personal connection to the event that anchors their experience. Group sales (previously discussed in this chapter) provide an ideal target for the selling of assets to create a memory and a story that can be shared and retold. Assets come in many forms—honorary captains, ball kids, anthem singers, halftime performers, and a variety of others. Many professional sport teams offer dance clinics conducted by the team's dance team as part of a group ticket package. The ticket price usually includes a clinic with the dancers during the day when the participants are taught a routine that they will perform with the dance team during halftime of that night's game, which is the asset. Another option used by baseball, hockey, and basketball teams to sell group tickets is offering the opportunity for two high school teams (can also be grade school, junior high, and so on) to play a game on the field, ice, or court of the professional team. This event is usually called Field of Dreams, Court of Dreams, or Arena of Dreams, depending on the sport. Selling these types of assets can turn into another asset for the buyer. Many teams provide fund-raising opportunities for organizations in their communities to raise funds. A charitable tie-in might not only let the girls' basketball team sell enough tickets to play on the court but also receive a portion of the proceeds.

Online Sales

Websites can be used as standalone sales tools or as part of an interactive sales approach that brings the website to life through other technological aids or pairs it with a telemarketer to assist in the sales process. The trend in developing websites as a sales tool is to make the process as simple as possible by using technology and interactive video components to enable the visitor to see all available seating options, compare them, price them, and purchase them online. A number of teams have added a live chat button in case the visitor has questions or issues and wants to speak to someone on the sales staff. Even teams and organizations that employ a variety of pricing techniques have been able to create web pages that explain the process clearly and enable visitors to purchase tickets.

The Golden State Warriors, despite using a dynamic pricing scheme whereby ticket prices vary according to demand, which is influenced by the opponent or day of the week, have a site that is simple to navigate and make purchases from. When the visitor clicks on the game that she wishes to see, a price map of the arena pops up. The visitor can then place an order online or elect to call and speak with a group sales representative.

One of the best examples of an interactive web sales approach was introduced by a number of professional sport teams over the past three seasons. The Hornets were one team that used this approach, produced by Chanel1Media. The e-mail link that the customer receives connects him to a website; once on the website, the customer is asked to enter his favorite jersey number and telephone number. After entering the information, the customer watches a video of the Hornets coach and GM talking about how important the customer is to the franchise. At the conclusion of the video, the customer's phone rings. The caller is a representative of the Hornets sales team who offers the opportunity to purchase a ticket plan. This approach integrates e-mail, a website, and telemarketing to capture the customer's attention and induce him to act and possibly forward it to friends and associates because of the coolness factor alone. This viral referral process then identifies additional

An e-mail from Boston College Athletics that includes a link to their website to purchase during their Black Friday and Cyber Monday sales.

prospects for the Hornets or whoever originated the message and content.

Total Inventory Plan: The Club Sandwich

During our time working in the Team Marketing and Business Operations Division of the NBA, teams always inquired about what type of full menu that they should offer to have a balanced ticket-sales inventory. To illustrate our recommendations, we created the "club sandwich" (figure 8.5). The intent of the club sandwich model is to ensure balance and thus minimize dependence on any one ticket-purchasing segment. The model ensures that consumers will always be on all levels of the frequency escalator (see chapter 10). The NBA World Champion Miami Heat (2011–12 season) were in a position to sell all their inventory as season tickets for the 2012–13 season, but having learned from the previous championship season (2006), President Eric Woolworth structured the available inventory to include miniplans, groups, and limited advance tickets available for purchases for single games. According to Woolworth, "Access is essential in building a long-term fan base and even though

our demand is at record levels, it is important to grow a fan base through a variety of purchasing channels and not just season tickets."[55]

In our club sandwich model, the "meat" (our apologies to vegetarians and vegans), or main course, is the full-season-ticket holders. Because this group is the one that attends the highest percentage of games, it is the most important ingredient in the club sandwich, but as in any good sandwich, it can be complemented by a variety of other ingredients. Partial plans (entailing some level of precommitment and purchase of a large number of games) and groups (involving a large volume of tickets) are the next most important ingredients in our sandwich. Our final stage of sandwich construction consists of the "condiments" ingredients, selected according to individual preference. A sport organization may prefer to use more than one condiment or to rely heavily on one condiment because the proverbial refrigerator is bare. Condiments include advance ticket sales (sold by in-house telemarketing, web sales, and social media sales, including Groupon, Facebook, and Twitter offers), walk-up and day-of-game sales, and complimentary tickets disbursed through community relations program and activities. Because the flavor of the club sandwich will change with the type and amount of ingredients added or the combination of those ingredients, so too will organizational profit margins (e.g., if there are too few season-ticket holders and too many groups or walk-ups). We recommend ingredients in the following proportions for a good-tasting and profitable club sandwich:

- Season-ticket equivalencies (full and all partial plans): 50 to 65 percent*
- Advance sales (telemarketing, web, and social media): 15 to 25 percent
- Group sales: 10 to 25 percent
- Day-of-game and walk-up sales: 5 percent

*Because NFL and college football teams have significantly fewer games in their plans, the meat should be 80 percent or more of the sandwich.

Because team performance can have a significant influence on the construction of your club sandwich, we have identified certain activities in terms of sales and retention to undertake depending on team performance. Table 8.4 illustrates situational selling factors as they relate to team performance.

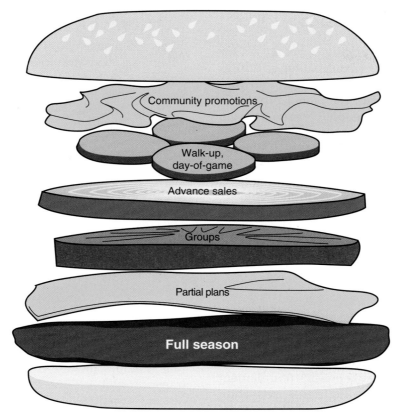

FIGURE 8.5 The "club sandwich" components of an effective ticket sales plan.

TABLE 8.4 Situational Selling Factors Related to Team Performance

Declining or losing team	Improving team	Successful team
Add staff to sell inventory	Add staff to capitalize on perception and move inventory	Lay off staff because of lack of inventory
Add discounts to attract buyers	Use discounts to create up-sell opportunities	Eliminate discounts
Add ticket plan options—a plan for every fan	Offer a variety of ticket plan options but push higher cost plans	Offer few plans, possibly only full- and half-season options
Emphasize group sales to create a few sellouts, offer a variety of discounts	Use groups to sell out, leverage attractions by forcing purchase of a lesser game, offer limited discounts	Limit group inventory, no discounting
Heavily emphasize sales training and sales contests	Heavily emphasize on sales training and sales contests	Focus sales training or sales contests on increasing account value
Offer payment plans	Offer payment plans	Offer incentives for payment in full
Add promotional nights and giveaways	Use promotional nights as peak on peak to sell out targeted games	Use premium giveaways for sponsor activation purposes, not to attract attendance

Pricing Basics

Knowing the basics of pricing, whether it's for tickets, merchandise, or luxury suites, is critical for a sport organization. For example, knowing how to price each part of the club sandwich is important because the people consuming each part of the sandwich have different wants and needs.

Marketers must recognize the vast range of product elements that require pricing. In the sport world, these elements include the following:

- Hard or soft goods (equipment or apparel)
- Tickets
- Memberships
- Daily usage fees (court times, tee times, lift tickets, and so on)
- Concessions (food, novelties)
- Content (magazines, cable, satellite TV, sports apps, videos, and so on)
- Access for corporate entities (entitlement space, signage, naming rights, activation platforms, banner ads, web links)
- Image (logo, photo, LED signage)
- Hospitality
- Premium seating
- Exclusive association
- Commercial time and exposure

These elements are priced according to a range of variables, including location, time, uniqueness, demand, quality, quantity, and desirability.

Price is a critical element in the marketing mix for a number of reasons. First, prices can be readily changed. Second, in certain market conditions (specifically, where demand is elastic), price is one of the most effective tools. Third, price is highly visible; therefore, changes are easily communicated, resulting in possible changes in consumer perceptions. Finally, price is never far from the consumer's mind and is often a key determinant in the decision of whether to buy.

Availability of data has had a significant effect on determining pricing strategy. In the following sidebar, Leigh Castergine explains the factors that she uses when making a recommendation to ownership on setting ticket prices.

ACTIVITY 8.5 Pricing Strategies

This WSG activity will examine how your team's pricing strategies and prices are affected by how your team plays. You will review how different teams use different pricing strategies, and you will consider some of the challenges for determining seat prices for your team.

Price, Cost, and Developing a Cost Index

The core issues in any pricing situation are cost, value, and objectives. Customer satisfaction can be expressed as

Satisfaction = Benefit − Cost

Cost is the most visible and often the most compelling part of the equation. For the consumer attending a sporting event, the price of a ticket does not represent the real cost of attendance, which would include travel, parking or public transportation, concessions, and possibly souvenirs of the experience. The ticket might also contain service charge or handling fees depending on how it was purchased. The difference between a marketer's sense of price and a consumer's sense of cost applies to most forms of sport involvement, such as golf, bowling, hunting, fishing, skiing, tennis, and so forth. For instance, the real cost of golfing in addition to the daily greens fee being charged includes any or all of the following:

- Clubs (purchase or rental)
- Shoes
- Golf bag
- Golf balls
- Golf glove
- Lessons
- Cart rental (sometimes included with the greens fee to enhance value)
- Transportation to and from the course
- Accommodations (if a resort)
- Food and beverage
- Tips

The golfer (skier, tennis player, or other participant) might also pay a range of prices for

Pricing Considerations and Strategy

Leigh Castergine, Senior VP of Ticket Sales and Service, New York Mets

> Do you remember when gas was only . . .? Back in my day you could buy milk for . . . ! Look at the price on my ticket stub from 1980!

Although significant price changes have occurred over the years in many product categories, our industry is unique in that prices have been affected not only by inflation but also by significant shifts in our overall pricing strategies, especially in recent years. When I first started selling tickets, it was simple. We had one price for every ticket in the lower level and three prices in the upper level based on location. We also had a special group ticket price if a customer bought 25 or more tickets. Only 10 years later, some teams have over 40 price categories. Prices vary for different plans such as for full-season ticket packages, half-season packages, 10-game packages, groups of 25 to 100, groups of 100 to 1,000, groups of 1,000 or more, and special discount prices for promotions through groups like Groupon. Now, with the introduction of dynamic pricing, the number of prices for a given event can be limitless. Already overwhelmed?

The trend for professional sport teams in their pricing strategy has been compared with how player acquisition strategy has changed. With better technology came more data. But what do we do with all this new data and information? In *Moneyball*, Michael Lewis explained how baseball clubs, specifically the Oakland A's, shifted their strategy by using metrics such as on-base percentage rather than traditional scouting to determine a player's likelihood of success. On the business side, we now have access to ticketing data such as the following:

- When a ticket was purchased
- How much that ticket cost
- Whether that ticket was resold on the secondary market and what price was paid for the resold ticket
- Where fans purchased the ticket (online, kiosk, phones, team store, secondary market)
- Who the ticket buyer was in terms of demographic information

These data can help us as we explore these topics:

- Changes in volume of daily ticket sales based on weather projections
- The effect that a bobblehead or other promotional giveaway item has on game attendance
- Fan seating preferences and price sensitivity

Just as the baseball operations staff strive to put a better product on the field using their data and analysis, the ticket operations team use their data to maximize revenues and grow the fan base.

When I graduated with a degree in economics and began selling tickets for the Philadelphia 76ers, I could not have imagined that all that time spent learning about supply-side policies, secondary markets, regression analysis, and sticky pricing would come in handy. Back then, most ticket prices were set by veteran sales and box office managers who were given an overall ticket-sales revenue goal by senior leadership or ownership. Many times they would estimate the number of seats that would be sold for the season and divide that by the given budget number. After they had that average ticket price, they could decide whether they needed to increase overall ticket prices or at least increase the price in certain categories based on their gut feeling.

Under this strategy there were only two ways to grow ticket revenues:

- sell more tickets or
- increase prices before the season started.

> continued

The tricky part is that if the organization is setting all the prices before the season even begins, they could be leaving a lot of money on the table or overprojecting.

The old pricing model had a few flaws. First, without using the data that we now have access to, accurately projecting the number of tickets sold was difficult. Second, with few price categories, gauging a fan's preferences was difficult. We all know that center ice above the glass and directly behind home plate are premium locations. The old model suggested that tenure determined seating priority. But we did not know what motivated our ticket purchasers more—their seat location or the price they paid. Few choices needed to be made.

But the biggest flaw in the old pricing model was its inflexibility. One of my favorite parts about working in sport, although it can also be one of the worst parts, is how unpredictable a team's success can be. We don't control our product. Sometime we have the hottest team in town, and other times we can't give away tickets. Although we can stimulate demand using special promotions like fireworks and postgame concerts, creating demand is extremely difficult. Therefore, we need to maximize the demand that we do have and, in particular, maximize our revenues and sold seats at those times.

Thanks to companies like Qcue, all the data that we now have access to can be easily digested. Barry Kahn's company helps teams understand their data and, more important, gives them a platform to maximize sales and revenues by offering a more flexible solution. Flexibility is not just important—it is vital! The secondary market and sites like StubHub offer fans a marketplace to buy and sell tickets for prices that are set by the seller. A Mets versus Atlanta game on a cold Tuesday in April would surely not be sold for the same price that the buyer purchased it for months earlier. Therefore, to adjust to the demand and to the prices available through the secondary market, more teams are turning to Qcue to help them price their tickets better initially and, more important, to price tickets dynamically throughout the season.

As the trend shifts to more analytically based pricing decisions, the ticket-sales staffs have evolved as well. Our senior director of ticket operations and analytics never worked a day in sport. He has an undergraduate degree in mathematics, a master's degree in engineering, and an MBA. Previously these roles were filled with people who had spent their entire careers working in ticket operations. Today, most major league teams have separate reporting and analytics departments that are setting prices and helping the sales managers and sales representatives sell more tickets. All those economics terms I learned in college are now part of conference calls and my daily pricing discussions.

A quick overview of the new pricing strategy typically begins with an analysis of the current season. We look at factors such as renewal rates, tenure of accounts, and new sales, to name a few. Using data from previous seasons, regression analysis helps project future sales. Then, initial season-ticket pricing is established in the last trimester of the season based on feedback that we receive from Qcue.

But the real shift in strategy is the move to dynamic pricing of individual games. Qcue's platform takes all the data that we provide and runs algorithms that make pricing recommendations on a daily basis for each price category for each event that we are selling. This means that I can see the increase in demand for a game that is going to feature a pitcher who threw a no-hitter the last game he pitched and adjust my price upward to match the demand. On the flip side, for a game that is not selling well we can adjust ticket prices in the opposite direction to encourage buyers who are looking for a better value.

Simply put, ticket pricing is no longer simple.

Just as general managers are always looking for the next metric that will help them identify the next all-star, ticket executives must continue to analyze the data and adapt to new technologies so that they can sell more tickets and maximize revenues while still offering an affordable option for young families and fans.

those elements according to certain demand factors such as location; seasonality; and course difficulty, reputation, and aesthetic appeal. The obvious point is that marketers must appreciate total cost from the consumer's perspective, which often includes elements priced by three or four distinct providers.[56]

In the team sport industry, this approach to total cost was first recognized and championed by *Team Marketing Report*, a leading industry newsletter. For the past 19 years, *Team Marketing Report* has tracked the fan cost index (FCI) for every team in MLB, the NBA, the NFL, and the NHL. The FCI includes the following price elements (and related costs) for a family of four:

- Two adult average-price tickets
- Two child average-price tickets (if available)
- Four small soft drinks
- Two small beers
- Four hot dogs
- Two programs
- Parking
- Two adult-size caps[57]

(In 2013 we, the authors, believe that the notion of a family of four does not produce the best measurement device; the index might better be broken down to adult cost and child cost. We also do not think that a family would purchase two programs; more likely they would buy and share one. Although we would like to see *Team Marketing Report* revisit its formula, it is an accepted standard of measurement in the sport industry.)

In 2012, for example, the NFL average FCI was $443.93, up 3.9 percent from the prior year. The Dallas Cowboys had the highest FCI at $634.78 but had only the fifth highest priced tickets. Their high cost related to a parking cost of $75, almost twice as high as that of the next highest priced team. The Jacksonville Jaguars had the lowest FCI at $342.70, but not the lowest priced ticket, which was offered by the Cleveland Browns at $54.20.[58]

Overall, MLB (baseball) is a much less expensive proposition as measured by FCI. In 2013 the average FCI was $207.88. The Boston Red Sox had the highest FCI at $336.99 and the highest priced tickets at $53.38. The Arizona Diamondbacks had the lowest FCI at $122.53, but the San Diego Padres offered the lowest ticket prices at $15.99.[59]

The fan cost index, now widely distributed by publications such as the *Wall Street Journal* and *USA Today*, has been an invaluable service to fans and marketers alike, even if the release prompts a round of criticisms and justifications from the higher-priced teams and a bevy of press releases from the lower-priced teams showing their rankings and implying that fans in that market are getting a good deal.

ACTIVITY 8.6 Developing a Cost Index

To start this WSG activity, imagine you have two children who would like to take ice skating lessons at Howell Ice World; imagine you live thirty minutes from the rink. This activity will help you develop a cost index for ice skating lessons and apply it to professional sports.

Yield Management and Pricing Strategies

An effective sales organization employs a variety of pricing strategies from time to time to ensure that the product, particularly tickets, can be purchased by the broadest range of potential buyers. This overall concept, often referred to as yield management, includes not only pricing but also packaging of tickets to ensure the highest yield on the sale of the product. In the following sidebar we focus on yield management as it relates to pure pricing initiatives. Later, yield management is explored in terms of packaging and promotional activities.

Secondary Ticket Market

One of the biggest challenges to sport organizations is the availability of tickets in the secondary market and the ease of purchasing them in that way, often at prices below the current asking price of the team producing the event. Forrester Research VP and principal analyst Sucharita Mulpuru estimated that the secondary ticket market is worth $3 billion a year. The number of tickets bought on sites such as StubHub has risen steadily.[60] We can almost argue that in the current

Yield Management for Sport Organizations

Lou DePaoli, EVP/CRO, New York Mets

Over the past 20-plus years the concepts of yield management and revenue management have become prevalent in most industries as a way to grow revenues strategically. In its simplest form, yield management is the process of understanding the supply and demand curve specific to your inventory and knowing how to find the right price for your product so that you can sell it to the right customer at the right time to maximize revenues, preferably without sacrificing units sold. The best known example of this concept in action would be the airlines. As an example, two people sitting next to each other on a flight from New York to Chicago might pay very different prices for their flights. Why? The airlines have implemented complex algorithms based on many variables, predominantly supply and demand, to determine how to price their product at that moment to maximize revenues and have full flights to cover the costs associated with operating each flight.

Similar to the airlines, sport organizations are implementing yield management in an effort to increase revenues and fill ballparks, arenas, and stadiums while also managing to remain an affordable live entertainment option. Unlike the airlines customers, sports fans have multiple options to engage with their favorite sport teams without attending a game, such as watching from the couch on a giant high-definition TV, watching through a personal smart device, or listening on radio. Thus, teams and leagues have become even more cognizant of maintaining the proper balance between available inventory and pricing of that inventory to manage brand perception. If they charge too much, they may have empty seats that damage the perception of demand and curb future sales. If they charge too little, they may not generate enough revenue to cover their costs, which then leads to reductions in payroll and eventually a reduction in sales. Thus, finding the proper balance of pricing and inventory is critical for sport organizations. The following are my recommended steps to ensure successful yield management for sport organizations.

- **Organizational buy-in**. The entire organization needs to understand that their supply, demand, and perception of demand are all in a constant state of change and that the organization needs to be nimble to adapt to changing market conditions. What worked last season or 10 years ago might not be the right strategy going forward to the next season or three seasons from now. For decades pricing decisions in sport were made by a small group within an organization, and data were rarely an input in the decision. Typically, someone would suggest a price increase of $X per ticket or an increase of X percent because they were trying to back into a revenue target based on an assumed attendance goal. Within the last decade organizations have started to understand that poor yield management as it relates to ticketing inventory can have disastrous consequences for years to come.

- **Understand your marketplace**. What may work in one market or sport might not work in yours. Although a team in your league or in your market may be successfully handling yield management a certain way, the same strategy may not be correct for you. You can learn a lot from peers and by what is happening in your market, but you need to be cognizant of how these decisions can affect your brand. Successful yield management is definitely not a one-size-fits-all approach. That said, you need to look at your peers within your league, other teams in your market, general costs for other forms of entertainment, and so on to provide context.

- **Data, data, and more data**. One of my favorite sayings is "You can never have too much data," especially in the area of yield management. Gather as much data as possible down to the individual seat level and look at the sell-through, yield, retention rate, the timing of when the seat was sold, by which channel the seat was sold, the demographics of who purchased the seat, and so on. These data will provide a snapshot of the supply, demand, and pricing on a per-seat level that can be turned into a heat map of your primary market sales.

- **Understand the secondary market**. The secondary, or resale, market has been around forever, but it was something of an underground business that many teams and fans didn't necessarily want to admit existed or partake in. The advent of the Internet has allowed fans and resellers to connect more easily and transact business on the secondary market, which became a $15 billion business in 2012. Accessing the same sell-through information from the secondary market as you do for the primary market is another valuable data point that you should add to your seat-by-seat sell-through analysis. The secondary market data can be helpful in improving ticket pricing, but careful analysis is crucial. Proper analysis of secondary market data in conjunction with primary market analysis will generate better pricing strategies for sport organizations.

- **Understand the implications**. One item related to effective yield management for sport organizations to understand is that supply and demand often affects pricing in ways that are outside theoretical expectations. At times demand becomes so high that pricing skyrockets as fans become willing to pay whatever it takes to attend a specific game or event (e.g., World Series, Super Bowl, the Masters). When that happens for a team or league, second-guessing often occurs: "Did we leave money on the table by pricing too low?" Some would describe that situation as a good problem to have. The flip side, however, is not.

  When demand drops significantly, yield management models will show that the price of the tickets should go down dramatically as well. At that point an organization needs to look at the effect of having prices drop and the way in which they want to address the major issues related to reducing pricing. For example, if a team's pricing drops 20 percent below the expected level, then they need to generate 25 percent more sales volume to be even in terms of revenue. Generally, that doesn't occur because after demand falls significantly, the demand for tickets is nil until the price is almost zero.

- **Remember the fans**. Yield management and other strategies are all theoretical. You need to get your fans to engage with and embrace the strategies, which is not always an easy task. Remember that the goal of effective yield management is to find the proper balance between pricing and sales volume to increase volume and revenues. If that balance gets upset in either direction, in all likelihood the effect of yield management will diminish significantly and will potentially have a negative effect on your brand as a whole. Proper messaging containing clear and concise wording along with key data points is recommended when rolling out price changes.

As sport organizations have begun to look closer at yield management, three distinct pricing strategies have emerged—premium pricing, variable pricing, and dynamic pricing. None of these concepts is new, but they are now becoming more widely used by organizations and accepted by fans. The following is a brief synopsis of how each strategy affects yield management:

- **Premium pricing**. This approach is used for games that come with inherently high demand (opening day for most MLB clubs, a rivalry game in college football, and so on). Because these events will sell out immediately, prices are increased based on that demand. The pricing is higher than the other games on the schedule based on the theory that these specific games have much higher demand. Although something may change during the season to affect demand negatively or positively, the prices for these games are locked in.

- **Variable pricing**. In this strategy, different price scales are applied based on factors such as opponent, event, time of season, day of week, and so on. As an example, a team might have three tiers of pricing for games in an MLB season. "Gold" games would feature the highest prices and could include opening day, matchups with rivals, the final weekend,

> continued

> continued

and marquee interleague matchups. "Silver" games would have the next highest prices for games of above-average demand, such as certain weekend games in June, July, and August. "Bronze" games would the lowest demand games of the season, typically weekday games early in the season, and would make up the lowest price tier. As with premium pricing, prices for these games are locked in, so no adjustment can be made if something changes during the season that has a negative or positive effect on demand.

- **Dynamic pricing.** The newest of the pricing strategies, which has seen increased adoption every year, is dynamic pricing. This approach allows ticket prices to change on a specified basis (daily, hourly, and so on) based on the demand for that game. This methodology is exactly how the secondary market operates. More organizations are implementing dynamic pricing because it allows them to raise and lower prices as the season goes along, depending on the change in demand. If a team is on a hot streak and demand increases, prices will climb as well, which generates more revenue on a real-time basis. The risk is that the opposite can occur; if demand drops sharply, pricing would then adjust downward, potentially generating less revenue than expected. Sport organizations need to be careful when implementing and executing dynamic pricing because it has the potential to drive incremental revenue when demand is stable or increasing but could severely hurt revenue if demand is decreasing. Thus, many dynamic pricing models are currently in play across the sport industry.

Organizations that understand and maximize yield management will perform better than their peers, all things being equal.

---

marketplace, the secondary market, which includes not only StubHub but also other vendors such as TicketLiquidator.com, TicketNetwork.com, TicketsNow.com, Vividseats.com, SeatGeek.com, TicketCity.com, TicketZoom.com, EventTicketsCenter.com, GoTickets.com, and ScoreBig.com, has become the primary ticket market for consumers.[61] Why is this the case? To state the matter simply, for a price-based decision the secondary ticket market offers a variety of prices, all usually less than the team offers because the team has a higher cost of doing business. The team or organization must pay the talent, produce the game, and maintain the stadium and the costs related to the fan experience. The secondary market has none of those costs because resellers purchase inventory from consumers (and in some cases knowingly or unknowingly directly from the team itself) who have previously purchased from the team and are not planning to attend the games.

The secondary market has always existed. In the past it was referenced under the collective term *scalper*. The original role of scalpers was to buy low and sell high for high-demand games and special events. Now their role is to buy and sell at a profit, regardless of whether the game is sold out or is a high-demand game. What has changed is that the primary market, and the sport leagues in general, have legitimized the idea of buying tickets from a source other than the team itself by signing sponsorship agreements with these secondary market sources, particularly StubHub (whose parent company is eBay, Inc.). In effect, sport organizations have granted them the only thing they lacked—recognition as a credible, trustworthy source for purchasing tickets. We might argue that the sponsorship deals offered the leagues and their teams a way to benefit financially from at least one aftermarket source because the fans were already routinely buying and selling their tickets offline and online anyway.

According to Mike Janes, FanSnap CEO (and former StubHub CMO), "Fans benefit from the ticket market, empowered with choices—the power to buy the tickets they want, in the quantity they want, most importantly when they want. This is key as teams are competing against all other entertainment choices for the fans' attention and dollars."[62] The StubHub website identifies the teams and organizations that are their featured partners (MLB.com, EPSN, Philadelphia Flyers, Washington Redskins, Outside Lands, San Francisco Giants, University of Texas [Longhorns], University of Alabama [Crimson Tide], and University of Southern California [Trojans]) and provides a list of all of their partners—sport teams and organizations with whom they have a signed working agreement.[63]

But the issue is much more complicated than just the fact that the secondary market sells tickets. Many season-ticket holders purchase their tickets from the team knowing that they will not be attending all the games in their plan. Thus, the opportunity to resell their tickets to offset the costs and in some cases to resell them at a higher price than they paid for them can be a critical factor in the decision to purchase the season tickets in the first place. All Ticketmaster teams and organizations offer their season-ticket holders a special web page where they can sell their tickets online. The money is first credited to their season-ticket account. The team encourages the sellers to apply the funds to the next year's season tickets, but they can also request a payment from those funds at the end of the season. Thus, ticket-reselling options are a real benefit to the season-ticket holder.

In a 2010 column he penned for CNBC, sport business analyst Darren Rovell predicted the death of season tickets. (You can read the article at www.cnbc.com/id/39152141.) Although we agree that there will always be some type of season ticket interest we don't feel that the season ticket of the future is going to require the purchase of every game or event. Given the growth and willingness to customize, as well as capabilities of the secondary ticket market, we are inclined to agree that Rovell's position has merit for a variety of reasons:

1. Internet access and competition in the marketplace has made customization king, while also providing reach to secondary market resellers regardless of their location and their proximity to sport franchise and sport and entertainment venues.

2. The issue of buying more than is wanted or needed at a lower price has given way to buying what's wanted at a higher price, and thereby, not having to deal with trying to resell or give away unwanted tickets.

3. Secondary market sellers have the ability to offer packages containing games or events from every team or entertainment venue in the same market, allowing the consumer to enjoy a variety of sport and entertainment experiences without owning multiple ticket plans. This is also becoming more common with regard to suites and other premium seating options.

4. Package flexibility has also emerged. Although some innovative sport organizations are allowing a flex spending approach to ticket buying where the buyer agrees to spend a certain amount of revenue but elects to purchase different types of seating options at prices and locations based upon their needs throughout the season, secondary sellers have offered this option for years and it has been very successful.

Consider this comparison; everyone knows that if you go to a pizza shop it is always less expensive to purchase the whole pie rather than a number of slices customized to the buyer's preference. Yet in our current marketplace, customization, and as Burger King would say "having it my way", appears to be king.

The NBA and Ticketmaster have created a centralized online portal for fans that has been designed to serve as one-stop shopping for all NBA tickets because it consolidates the teams' primary and secondary ticket selling options in one place. Users will be directed to a page containing all available ticket options for each team, including secondary ticket listings. According to Ticketmaster COO Jared Smith, "Our goal is to create something where the fan is presented with a complete, overall view of all safe, trusted ticket options."[64]

What does the future hold for secondary ticket suites and their relationships with sport organizations? Perhaps a battle. As we have pointed out, StubHub is the official secondary ticket partner of Major League Baseball (MLB). But two large-market teams—the New York Yankees and Los Angeles Angels—elected to opt out of the five-year contract extension between Major League Baseball Advanced Media (MLBAM) and StubHub. Both the Yankees and the Angels worked with Ticketmaster for the 2013 and 2014 seasons. The Chicago Cubs stayed with StubHub for the 2013 season, but it's uncertain what they will do for the 2014 season. Developing resale marketplaces with rival giant Ticketmaster allows minimum resale listing prices that have long been the anathema to StubHub and its parent company eBay Inc.[65] This battle between Ticketmaster and StubHub will bear monitoring through the future.

Aftermarketing, Lifetime Value, and the Importance of Retaining Customers

Aftermarketing is a term used to describe the relationship between the marketer and the customer after all the marketing and sales efforts have been completed, a purchase has been made, and the prospect has become a customer. The relationship changes to one of support and sustainability. The best way to understand the importance of this new relationship is through the concept of customer lifetime value (CLTV). The customer's lifetime value is defined as the present value of expected benefits (e.g., gross margin) minus the obligations (e.g., direct cost of servicing and communicating) associated with the customer.[66] Customer lifetime value is a formula that helps

a marketing manager arrive at the dollar value associated with the long-term relationship with any given customer, revealing both the cost and the net worth of that relationship over time.[67] Thus, for example, in terms of value we should look at a season-ticket holder not as a $4,000 annual spend but as someone who, depending on current age, could spend at least that amount every year and in addition pay for price increases, parking, and per capita spending on concessions, parking, merchandise, and other possible spending options each year, possibly exceeding $100,000 over a 20-year period.

Obviously, customers have different values to an organization depending on the type of customer (sponsor, corporate buyer, personal buyer), the amount of revenue they contribute in relationship to the cost of servicing them, and the estimated time that they are projected to be with the organization. The more valuable the customer is, the more effort the staff must expend to retain that customer.[68] Figure 8.6 illustrates how the value of a customer can be moderated.

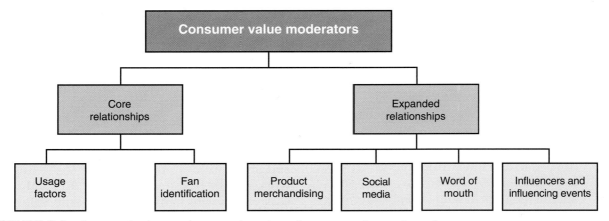

FIGURE 8.6 An organization can increase the value of a customer in a variety of ways.

Given the potential lifetime value of a customer, it is clear that certain activities and efforts must follow completion of the sale to ensure that the customer renews and continues an ongoing relationship, or becomes a repeat buyer. The value of the fan as a customer is epitomized by former San Francisco Giants senior vice president of business affairs, Pat Gallagher, who developed an upside-down organizational chart (figure 8.7) to illustrate to the Giants' staff just how important fans really are.

Sport organizations should develop customer service and retention programs that encompass at least the following:

- Offering customized or personalized customer contact and treatment
- Conducting regular customer satisfaction surveys or audits
- Creating and sponsoring special events and activities for preferred customers
- Maintaining a database of current customers and defectors
- Creating a website with special content and features for members
- Producing a newsletter and distributing that content on a regular basis
- Offering frequency incentive programs
- Conducting stakeholder meetings or luncheons to gather feedback
- Creating special members-only events to demonstrate and show appreciation
- Providing special access to players and other organizational assets that are not available to the public[69]

The activities and efforts undertaken to demonstrate value in being a member should be unique to that type of customer. A common practice in professional sport organizations is to employ a retention team whose responsibilities are to

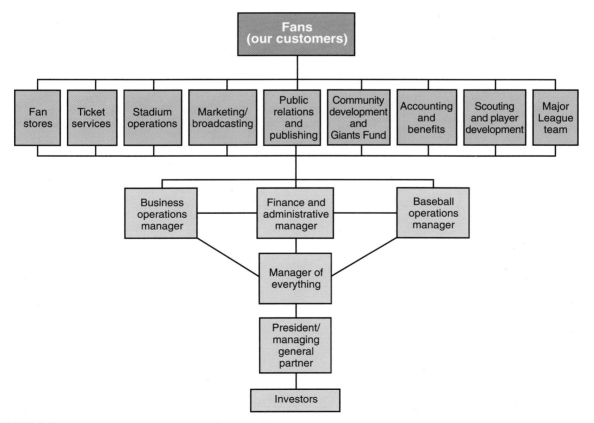

FIGURE 8.7 Upside-down organizational chart of fan importance.

Courtesy of Pat Gallagher, San Francisco Giants.

communicate and build relationships and retain or renew those relationships whenever possible. The New York Mets have created a program for their season-ticket holders referred to as Amazin' Mets Perks. Season-ticket holders who renew are eligible to participate in these perks, which can be as simple as taking batting practice on the field or as exclusive as attending a wine-tasting clinic with Mets Hall of Fame player Tom Seaver and receiving an autographed bottle of wine from his vineyard. Or the customer might be able to trick or treat on Halloween with the Mets' beloved mascot, Mr. Met. The goal is to demonstrate the value through events and activities that are not only enjoyable but also exclusive to those participating as Mets' season-ticket holders.

No matter how successful an organization is at servicing its clientele, some will discontinue their purchasing and thus end their relationship for one reason or another. Research has shown that customer loyalty is based on the consumers' feel-ings about the brand in the areas of confidence, integrity, pride, and passion, as well as their satisfaction, utilization, and enjoyment of what they have purchased.[70] Customers who leave an organization are often referred to as defectors because in effect they defect to another product or brand. Defectors are costly to an organization, not only because the organization loses their potential lifetime value but also because replacing them is expensive in terms of time and resources. According to some estimates, replacing a customer costs up to five times more than servicing an existing customer.[71] To prevent defection and at the same time attract new customers, professional sport teams and other organizations are viewing their customers as members and developing benefits accordingly. The San Diego Padres have developed such an approach, which is described in the following sidebar.

Maybe everyone can't be a member, but in the words of Blanchard and Bowles, everyone

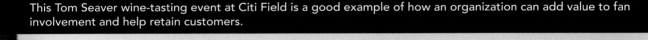

This Tom Seaver wine-tasting event at Citi Field is a good example of how an organization can add value to fan involvement and help retain customers.

How One Franchise Is Making Membership More Meaningful

Bill Sutton, founding director of the sport and entertainment business management MBA at the University of South Florida and principal of Bill Sutton and Associates

"Membership has its privileges" is the guiding, core principle of the American Express card. The consumer pays an annual fee and in exchange he or she is entitled to earn points by way of their spending in the Membership Miles Program. The miles can be converted by the member to purchase a variety of products and experiences ranging from vacations to golf clubs to electronics to unique golfing and driving experiences to meals and travel. It is up to the members to decide the benefits most important to them and to act accordingly (by spending) to acquire those benefits. It's more than a loyalty program because the member pays a membership fee, and unlike most loyalty programs, the benefits are more varied and appealing, dependent upon one's interests.

Loyalty programs in professional sport have seen varied degrees of success over the past 20 years. They have failed usually because of the lack of quality incentives, or because of the level of spending or attendance necessary to accumulate enough points to earn a meaningful reward. For the most part, these programs have been free and thus the enrollment numbers have been large, but the actual participation and involvement has been much smaller.

European sport franchises, particularly those in football, have referred to their supporters as subscribers or members for some time. The level of benefits usually correlates to the amount of the ticket purchase and, in some cases, the length of the relationship between the subscriber or member and the club. There has been growing interest in this approach in the United States, particularly among MLS teams. A particular concept and implementation by the San Diego Padres has caught my attention.

The Padres have launched a new membership program, the first phase of which focuses on season-ticket holders whose purchase of a ticket plan qualifies them as a member. The second phase will focus on general ticket sales before the 2013 season. For these prospective new members, signing up to become a member is free, and then they can move into blue-, gold-, and platinum-level memberships that include 21-game, 41-game, and full-season plans, respectively. (Consider the ticket purchase as the membership fee or dues.)

Blue, gold, and platinum members select which type of membership best fits them (fanatic, social, business, or family). As the members' status increases, so do their benefits. It isn't a loyalty program based on points, but a membership program designed to give fans a greater sense of belonging with the team, and benefits and opportunities reflecting their interests and type of relationship with the team and the organization.

For example, a business member can select to participate in the Padres golf tournament and bring a client; a family member may elect to have a birthday party or an overnight campout in the outfield at Petco Park; and a fanatic member could choose to attend a Padres away game or an exclusive autograph session. In all of these cases, the choice belongs to the member.

"The membership program is something we've been working on for a long time, and we're excited to finally roll [it] out for 2013," said Padres president Tom Garfinkel. "It started with a few core themes. First was the idea that we needed to tap into fan psychology more and create a sense of belonging. Being a fan is emotional, not rational, yet somehow we keep going to market trying to rationalize with people. Second, we needed to create benefits that can't be transferred on a secondary market and create more reasons to be a season-ticket holder than ever before. Finally, we needed to have more of a direct relationship year-round with our fans and have more information about what is important to them so that we can deliver on it."

Jeremy Walls, senior director of ticket sales and membership services, believes the program has been a huge success thus far and points to the statistics:

> continued

- 75 percent increase in "membership revenue" year over year (with that "membership revenue" being the club's designated season-ticket revenue)
- Membership renewals running 44 percent ahead of last year at the same time
- 110 percent more full (platinum) plans and 100 percent more half (gold) plans than the previous year, and 36 percent fewer 21-game (blue) plans—which suggests that membership benefits are driving customers to upgrade their memberships

At a time when fans are spending heavily in the secondary ticket market, the season ticket, or any ticket plan, needs to be much more meaningful than just a place to sit and watch a baseball game. This membership concept being touted by the Padres, and under development by some NBA and MLS clubs, offers a meaningful attempt at creating a relationship through a membership that seeks to form a 12-month bond with the member much like a country club, or perhaps a civic club, or even a church. The most intriguing part is that this is only the beginning.

"This is just Membership 1.0," Walls said. "It's a foundation that we can build on, and layer new ideas and benefits using technology. In the future, it could include benefits from corporate partners, community initiatives, in-park gaming, instant seat upgrades, concessions, merchandise, fan-to-fan communication, nonbaseball events like concerts. . . . The possibilities are endless."

Membership has its privileges and also its rewards, but maybe because it is in a sport context, the best thing might be belonging to a community of fans.

Reprinted, by permission, from B. Sutton, 2012, "How one franchise is making membership more meaningful," *Street & Smith's Sports-Business Journal* pg. 11.

---

can be a "raving fan"—those consumers who are so excited and pleased with the product that they not only remain loyal but also help attract new customers through word of mouth and now through social media by blogging, tweeting, and sharing content and experiences.[72]

Some of these experiences need not be limited to members; they can be sold to casual fans for business purposes, for special occasions, or for that special gift for a sports fan who is hard to buy for or already has everything. The NFL's Dallas Cowboys are selling the following experiences through a new agreement with the social commerce website LivingSocial:

- Access to the Cowboys' war room for the NFL draft
- A chance to try out for the Dallas Cowboys cheerleaders
- Attending a photo shoot of the cheerleaders
- Shadowing a team reporter
- Appearing in a Dallas Cowboys' official team photo[73]

How can sport consumers become raving fans? Given the emotional nature of sport, sport consumers are already more emotional about their product than other consumers are about theirs. Sport consumers have stronger feelings that elicit higher highs and lower lows. Because sport marketers don't control product composition or performance, they must aggressively strive to ensure customer satisfaction as it relates to product extensions and the experience itself, which usually involve high levels of interaction and service. All sport organizations should develop a customer service and retention program in the hopes of retaining current customers, growing relationships with those customers, and attracting new customers through their overall service quality and their demonstrated interest in the well-being of their customers. The integral aspects of retention are satisfaction, utilization, and enjoyment of what the customer has purchased. Although that might seem simple (and in many ways it is), the subjectivity of customers with regard to the sometimes emotional purchase of a sport-related product may complicate the decision to renew or buy again. Thus, the overall approach to this problem is to improve the fan experience. This goal was clearly the focus of the Padres, who achieved it through a segmentation process of how tickets are purchased and used. But can this approach be used for one-time visitors for a special event that happens only once per year? Can the organization create experiences to increase customer visits to the venue at other times during the year? The Kentucky Derby, Indianapolis 500, and induction weekend at any of the halls of fame face this challenge. All these venues have a season when they are open, but they need to find ways to attract visitors to other events or activities that are often significantly less hyped and promoted.

Horse racing is a sport that has suffered in popularity for a variety of reasons including competition from other sport properties, a consumer shift to other forms of gambling, and limited media coverage and television presence. The media hype and attention seems to start when a horse has the possibility of becoming a Triple Crown winner and ends when that possibility ceases to exist. But most horse-racing tracks don't have a premier race in the Triple Crown series, and even those that do have only one race in an entire racing season. What is the horse-racing industry doing to enhance the customer experience? Rodnell Workman, a former Madison Square Garden and NFL executive, was appointed as the first chief marketing officer for the New York Racing Association in 2012. Workman wants to change the image of the racetrack from a place for hardcore gamblers, mostly older men, to an entertainment option for younger people and families: "We want horse racing to be in the discussion when you are debating going to the movies or a park or whatever—thus we need to change the way we present our business."[74]

Horse-racing tracks are also learning to edu-sell. The sport has been positioned in the past as the only sport that people can watch and play (bet) at the same time, but that was before the emergence of fantasy sports, which obviously present a similar opportunity. In addition, the odds and various betting combinations (daily double, trifecta, and so forth) unique to horse racing can be so confusing to first-time attendees that they may choose not to participate in betting and thus may not return to the track. Therefore, clinics, tutorials, and online apps that can be accessed to help the attendee to feel more

comfortable making a bet could all enhance the fan experience.

Promotions and special pricing can also be used to enhance the fan experience. Besides simplifying betting information, Keeneland Race Track in Lexington, Kentucky, hosts a college day that offers free T-shirts, the opportunity to win $10,000 scholarships, and tailgating activities. The event draws nearly 5,000 students.[75] By attracting new customers and allowing them to sample the sport, the program attempts to make horse racing part of their entertainment mix. (Although the focus is entertainment and food and beverage sales, expenses are associated with gambling and waging activities, which we are not endorsing.)

Technology can also be an effective and valuable way to enhance the in-venue experience for fans. Some sports, in particular the NFL, are facing challenges from the at-home viewing experience. Home theaters, HD televisions, the possibility of more 3D programming, and subscription services through vendors such as DirecTV that offer all the games of all the teams for a fee significantly lower than season tickets for one team are creating attendance-based challenges. Table 8.5 examines some of the technological innovations that can enhance the stadium, arena, or ballpark experience for attendees.

Wrap-Up

A sale is the revenue-producing element of the marketing process. Marketing is communication, and as such the sales process involves a high level of two-way communication; a salesperson must be able to listen and assess as well as talk. Most organizations have developed to the point where members of the sales staff function as experts who sell a specific type of product. But in smaller organizations, salespeople must function as sales generalists and be able to sell all types of inventory. Regardless of the size of the sales team, sales training and the development of the sales personnel may be the most critical aspects of sales success.

Pricing is a vital component of the sales process. Because of the wide array of sport and entertainment products for sale in any market at any given time, consumers who think that the price is too high or the package is too large will seek out their own purchasing solutions.

TABLE 8.5   In-Venue Technological Fan Enhancements[76]

Enhancement	What is it?	Who has it?
FanVision	In-venue handheld device that provides access to TV programming such as NFL RedZone, fantasy statistics, and more	12 NFL teams, University of Miami, and University of Michigan; owned by Dolphins owner Stephen Ross
Yinzcam	Smartphone application that gives fans access for replays, live stats, VOD content, and NFL RedZone	Various NFL and NHL teams
Augmented Reality Mobile Applications (Thermopylae)	An "around me" mobile app that connects the fan with venue	U.S. Open, Wimbledon, Las Vegas Motor Speedway
MLB At Bat concessions app	Allows fans to order food and pay by credit card from their seats and to receive exclusive video highlights	MLB venues
Command Center touchscreen device	Enables team personnel to track a variety of aspects of their game-day operations that affect fans	New York Jets
Massive stadium LED video boards	Enhanced viewing and information	Dallas Cowboys, Tampa Bay Lightning, Indiana Pacers, Houston Rockets, Charlotte Motor Speedway, University of Texas
Internet protocol TV (IPTV)	Integrated messages and signage that appears on every television monitor and LED signage simultaneously	Orlando Magic

Reprinted, by permission, from GMR Marketing, 2010, *GMR white paper emerging technology is constantly enhancing the in-stadium experience* (Milwaukee, Wisconsin). ©GMR Marketing LLC, All Rights Reserved.

They may buy from the secondary market, find the product online at a discount, or purchase what they want in a size that they find suitable from another source, perhaps by joining others to share ownership of a product and consume it as a group.

Because of the effort and time involved in the sales process, the sport organization must create programs and benefits to retain current customers over time. This lifetime customer value, or LTV, is a critical consideration for every customer. It involves expanding and extending the relationship between the seller and buyer by offering specialized benefits and more fan-related dimensions. In previous editions of this text we have always addressed the importance of placing buyers on the escalator and moving them up in terms of frequency. The expansion of sport and entertainment options, competition for the entertainment dollar, and a deteriorating global economy have made us recognize that retaining customers on the escalator at a point where they are comfortable and less likely to decrease frequency or terminate the relationship is as important as moving them up, especially as it relates to LTV.

Activities

1. Identify someone you recognize as a leader in the area of sport marketing. Obtain the person's bio or profile (usually available on the corporate or organizational website). How does the person's current position or past activities reflect sales experience?

2. Interview someone with sport marketing responsibilities in an athletics department, fitness facility, or pro sport organization and ask about the person's duties. Ask what percentage of the person's time is devoted to sales activities. What methodologies does he or she employ? How does he or she train the sales staff? How did the person begin in the business?

3. Assess your career plans. Does the job you envision have a sales component? What will you need to do to attain this position? Begin compiling a roster of people in similar positions. You can use this roster to gather information and advice as you initiate your job search.

4. Visit with a small business, athletics department, or minor league team in your area. Offer to help calculate the lifetime value of a season-ticket holder based on average per capita spending and the prices associated with the various ticket plans offered by the organization.

5. Research how nonsport companies use aftermarketing. How could these practices be applied to sport organizations?

Your Marketing Plan

In the successful implementation of a marketing plan, objectives must be identified and achieved. Sales, in terms of a revenue-production target goal, are usually accounted for in formulating the objectives leading to a goal. Sales are also viewed as strategies or tactics that are integral in achieving objectives and, ultimately, in reaching goals. In reviewing your marketing plan, how do you see sales fitting in? Do you have an objective that might be stated in sales terms relating to increasing organizational revenue? For example, an objective such as "Increase attendance (membership, if you are interested in the fitness industry or other membership-based industry segments such as golf or tennis clubs) over last year's levels by 12 percent" implies that some sales strategies and tactics are necessary to achieve the objective. Review your objectives and select sales methodologies and approaches that will help you reach your objectives.

Endnotes

1. W.A Sutton, "Sutton Impact: Rockne's X's and O's of Sales Carry Lessons for Today's Leaders," *SSSBJ*, 13 (16) (16–22 August 2010): 13. Also see Huston McCready, *Salesman From the Sidelines* (New York: Ray Long and Richard Smith, 1932).

2. R. Burton and R.Y. Cornilles, "Emerging Theory in Team Sport Sales: Selling Tickets in a More Competitive Arena," *SMQ*, 7 (1) (1998): 33.

3. Mike Florio, 8 July 2012, http://profootballtalk.nbcsports.com/2012/07/08/after-peaking-in-2007-nfl-attendance-steadily-has-declined/.

4. Michael Bean, 5 January 2012, www.behindthesteelcurtain.com/2012/1/5/2684753/nfl-tv-ratings-2011.

5. T. Hopkins, *Selling for Dummies* (Foster City, CA: IDG Books Worldwide, 1995), 9.

6. M. McCormack, *On Selling* (West Hollywood, CA: Dove Books, 1996), 7.

7. P. Honebein, *Strategies for Effective Customer Education* (Lincolnwood, IL: NTC Business Books, 1997), 25.

8. N. Kerner and G. Pressman, *Chasing Cool* (New York: Atria, 2007), xi.

9. N.J. Stephens, *Streetwise Customer-Focused Selling* (Holbrook, MA: Adams Media, 1998), 4.

10. McCormack, *On Selling*, 9–10.

11. J. Gittomer, *The Little Red Book of Selling* (Austin, TX: Bard Press), 47.

12. J. Mielke, "Specialization Through Departmentalization," *That's the Ticket*, 1 (1) (May 1997): 5.

13. http://smallbusiness.chron.com/definition-consumer-direct-marketing-3477.html.

14. Ibid.

15. http://thedma.org/2013/04/30/dma-releases-2013-statistical-fact-book

16. For an excellent discussion of the importance of building a database that has withstood the test of time and clear-cut examples of how this has been accomplished in professional sports, see J. Spoelstra, *How to Sell the Last Seat in the House* (Portland, OR: SRO Partners, 1991), 72–94.

17. http://intel.turnkeyse.com/2011/04/22/charlotte-bobcats-lead-scoring/.

18. B. Stone and J. Wyman, *Successful Telemarketing: Opportunities and Techniques for Increasing Sales and Profits* (Lincolnwood, IL: NTC Business Books, 1986), 6.

19. *US Telemarketing Revenues to Reach $15.5 Billion by 2015*, www.prweb.com/releases/telemarketing/business_to_business/prweb4247074.htm.

20. Compiled from a study by the Direct Marketing Association, April 2005.

21. Steve Berkowitz, "Marketers Reshape How College Teams Sell Tickets," *USA Today*, 5 August 2011, http://usatoday30.usatoday.com/sports/college/2011-08-05-college-outsourcing-sports-ticket-sales_n.htm.

22. Ibid.

23. www.getbrandwise.com/branding-blog/bid/54291/Does-Direct-Mail-still-work-in-a-digital-age.

24. Golfsmith International, Golfsmith Store catalog, Austin, TX, December 2012, and www.golfsmith.com/ps/search/drivers?Nao=20&N=1462&Ntk=All.

25. Susan K. Jones, *Creative Strategy in Direct and Interactive Marketing* (Raycom, 2011), 101.

26. www.buccaneers.com/news/article-1/A-New-Way-to-Pay-Season-Pass-Members-Get-12-Month-Option/5328ed51-ce49-409e-b922-cf-1c4688f097.

27. www.usatoday.com/story/sports/2012/11/30/nba-phoenix-suns-dallas-mavericks-money-back-guarantee/1738463/.

28. Jon Spoelstra, *Ice to the Eskimos* (New York: HarperCollins, 1997), 173.

29. www.fillthehouse.com/about.php.

30. Simms Jenkins, www.clickz.com/clickz/column/2235299/why-your-brand-needs-email-smarts-more-than-ever-in-2013.

31. Simms Jenkins, www.clickz.com/clickz/column/2238571/the-2-most-important-things-for-email-marketers-in-2013.

32. Ibid.

33. http://media.eloqua.com/documents/All-Star-Datasheet.pdf.

34. www.nba.com/hornets/news/hornets_launch_campaign_asking_2011_03_14.html.

35. B. Breighner, *Face-to-Face Selling* (Indianapolis, IN: Park Avenue, 1995), x.

36. Spoelstra, *Ice to the Eskimos*, 146–151

37. K. Daley, *Socratic Selling* (New York: McGraw-Hill, 1996), 5–6.

38. G.A Michaelson and S.W. Michaelson, *Sun Tzu: Strategies for Selling* (New York: McGraw-Hill, 2004), 75.

39. J. Lehman, *The Sales Manager's Mentor* (Seattle, WA: Mentor Press, 2006), 227.

40. R.W. Palmatier, *Relationship Marketing* (Cambridge, MA: Marketing Science Institute 2008), 3.

41. R. McKenna, *Relationship Marketing: Successful Strategies for the Age of the Consumer* (Reading, MA: Addison-Wesley, 1991), 4.

42. C. Gronroos, *Service Management and Marketing: Managing Moments of Truth in Service* (New York: Lexington Books, 1990).

43. D. Shani, "A Framework for Implementing Relationship Marketing in the Sport Industry," *SMQ*, 6 (2) (1997): 9–15.

44. http://dir.yahoo.com/business_and_economy/shopping_and_services/apparel/footwear/athletic_shoes/brand_names/?b=60.

45. Burton and Cornilles, "Emerging Theory," 29–37.

46. http://www.milb.com/content/page.jsp?ymd=20090409&content_id=40998078&fext=.jsp&vkey=news_t1174&sid=t1174.

47. www.youtube.com/watch?v=wgxurmQSLsc.

48. For an excellent study of how to create a market, see P. Levine, *A.G. Spalding and the Rise of Baseball* (New York: Oxford Press, 1985)

49. http://football.about.com/cs/football101/a/bl_football101.htm.

50. W.A. Sutton, A. Lachowetz, and J.S. Clark, "Eduselling: The Role of Customer Education in Selling to Corporate Clients in the Sport Industry," *International Journal of Sports Marketing and Sponsorship*, 2 (2) (June/July 2000): 145–158.

51. Spoelstra, *Ice to the Eskimos*, 91–93.

52. For an enjoyable read and examples of how to sell, see B. Veeck and E. Linn, *Veeck As in Wreck* (New York: Putnam's, 1962). Mike Veeck's successful

exploits with the St. Paul Saints is chronicled in S. Perlstein, *Rebel Baseball: The Summer the Game was Returned to the Fans* (New York: Holt, 1994). Mike Veeck has also written a book about his philosophy, *Fun is Good*, Mike Veeck and Pete Williams (Emmaus, PA: Rodale Books), 2005.

53. G. Boeck, "Winning Friends and Influencing Ticket Buyers," *USA Today*, 13 September 2005, 3C.

54. http://labs.openviewpartners.com/influencer-marketing-defined/.

55. Telephone conversation with Eric Woolworth, President, Miami Heat, Miami, FL, 8 January 2013.

56. "Getting to the First Tee," *SSSBJ*, 4 (10) (May 1998), 20.

57. www.teammarketing.com/btSubscriptions/fancostindex/index.

58. www.fancostexperience.com/pages/fcx/blog_pdfs/entry0000018_pdf000.pdf.

59. www.fancostexperience.com/

60. www.sportsbusinessdaily.com/Daily/Issues/2011/01/Jan-17/Facilities/Secondary-tix.aspx.

61. W. Sutton, "Sutton Impact: A New Approach to Ticketing: Ticket Market Could Find Fortune in FAME," *SSSBJ*, 14 (26) (October 24–30): 22.

62. www.forbes.com/sites/mikeozanian/2011/08/05/stubhub-dominates-the-secondary-ticket-market.

63. www.stubhub.com/about-us.

64. J. Lombardo and E. Fisher, "Deal Will Create NBA Portal on Ticketmaster," *SSSBJ*, 15 (18) (20–26 August 2012): 1, 31.

65. E. Fisher, "StubHub Won't Surrender MLB Opt-Outs," *SSSBJ*, 15 (35) (17–23 December, 2012): 1, 3.

66. F.R. Dwyer, "Customer Lifetime Valuation to Support Marketing Decision Making," *Journal of Direct Marketing*, 3 (Autumn, 1989): 8–15.

67. http://hbsp.harvard.edu/multimedia/flash-tools/cltv/index.html. This source provides a conceptual overview, a sample problem, and a tool.

68. M.A. McDonald and G.R. Milne, "A Conceptual Framework for Evaluating Marketing Relationships in Professional Sport Franchises," *SMQ*, 6 (2) (1997): 27–32.

69. Created based on materials from T. Vavra, *Aftermarketing* (New York: Irwin, 1987), 25.

70. http://businessjournal.gallup.com/content/745/constant-customer.aspx#1.

71. Forum Consulting, Boston, MA, Customer Service Institute, Silver Springs, MD.

72. K. Blanchard and S. Bowles, *Raving Fans* (New York: Morrow, 1993).

73. D. Kaplan, "Cowboys Sell 'Experiences' on Living-Social," *SSSBJ*, 15 (19) (27 August–2 September): 3.

74. L. Mullen, "Tracks Focus on Improving the Fan Experience," *SSSBJ*, 15 (28) (29 October–4 November 2012): 18.

75. Ibid.

76. B. Gainor, *Emerging Technology Is Constantly Enhancing the In-Stadium Experience*, GMR White Paper (Milwaukee, WI: GMR Marketing, 2010).

Chapter 9

Sponsorship, Corporate Partnerships, and the Role of Activation

OBJECTIVES

- To illustrate the relationship between the sport property and the corporate partner

- To demonstrate the importance of fit and the use of exclusivity between the sponsor and the property

- To develop a comprehension of the motivations and rationale for the use of sponsorship by corporations and sport entities

- To convey the importance of activation to engage the target market while simultaneously bringing the brand to life

The Future of Sponsorship: Total Integration?

Not content with the success of its stadium signage integrations in the past three years in such popular video games as NBA Ballers, NBA 2K, and NBA Live, Gatorade upped the ante: It made the product part of the on-court action.

Working with its media agency, Omnicom Group's OMD, and 2K Sports, Gatorade created an in-game feature for NBA 2K9 called the Gatorade Thirst Meter. It alerts users that a player is becoming dehydrated, needs a substitute, and needs a Gatorade refill.

Dario Raciti, director of Ignition Factory Gaming at OMD, said the product integration worked because it tied Gatorade's hydration attributes seamlessly into the "true experience of athletes," adding another realistic dimension to the gamer's experience. "Gamers are always looking for the most realistic experience out of sports games, and [we] felt that this feature positively contributed to making game play memorable and authentic," he said by e-mail. "The integration was designed so that all of the elements worked together to augment realism in game play and place Gatorade where thirst is tied to performance and key to winning."

After a player hits the bench and rehydrates, he can be inserted back into the game. Those who need a Gatorade break but are not given one start to show signs of fatigue and sluggishness. According to Mr. Raciti, that authenticity, introduced in a "subtle, yet impactful way," has struck a chord with the target audience of 18- to 34-year-old males.

The Gatorade Thirst Meter is accompanied by the usual branding elements of the energy drink, including signage and coolers and cups behind the bench.

Gatorade spent less than $1 million on the effort but got a sizable return on investment, according to brand research. A majority (82 percent) of gamers who recalled Gatorade in the game were able to attribute it to a specific location in which the brand appeared, and nearly three-quarters (70 percent) of those who recalled its appearance in the game said they liked it as part of the experience. More important for Gatorade, the research showed that the integration positively affected gamers' willingness to recommend the product to someone they know.[1]

In this chapter we examine the integrated nature of sponsorship. Sponsorship activities are more integrated than other promotional activities and contain a variety of marketing mix elements. Although a number of marketing mix elements can function as standalones (e.g., an open house, discounts on tickets, community relations programs), a sponsorship usually involves two or more of the elements of the marketing mix to provide sponsors with associations, recognition, value, exposure, and activation opportunities to help them achieve their marketing objectives. The term *sponsorship* includes not only funding agreements between sport organizations and corporate entities but also financial grants and assistance from governmental units and departments as well as foundations and trusts. This chapter focuses primarily on the sponsorship form of corporate partnerships because this is the predominant format globally, and in light of the current global economy it will continue to occupy that position.

What Is Sponsorship?

Consider the following activities and entities: the Capital One Bowl, Sprite NBA All-Star balloting, Orlando Magic's Amway Arena, Mattel's production of Barbie dolls in the cheerleading apparel of Oklahoma State University and other collegiate athletics programs, and General Motors' $559 million jersey sponsorship for Chevrolet with Manchester United.[2] What do all these have in common? They represent the types of promotional licensing agreements that have become commonplace in sport and lifestyle marketing. *Promotional licensing* is an umbrella term that encompasses sponsorship, but *sponsorship*, and in many cases *corporate partnership*, has become the accepted term throughout the world. Therefore, throughout this chapter and the text we will use the word *sponsorship* to refer to the acquisition of rights to affiliate or directly associate with a product, person, organization, team, league, or event (throughout the chapter any or all of these types of entities will be referred to as the sport or entertainment property) for the purpose of deriving benefits related to that affiliation or association. The sponsor then uses this relationship to achieve its promotional objectives or to facilitate and support its broader marketing objectives. The rights derived from this relationship may include retail opportunities, purchase of media time, entitlement (inclusion of the sponsor name in the event or facility name, such as FedEx Cup, Staples Center, and Tostitos Fiesta Bowl), contests or sweepstakes, endorsements, logo placement on uniforms or apparel, hospitality, website access, or other associations or benefits. Although sponsorship agreements are customized and specific to the participating parties, the following provisions and benefits are the most common elements of such agreements:

- The right to use a logo, name, trademark, and graphic representation signifying the purchaser's (or supporter's) connection with the sport property, which can be used in advertising, promotion, publicity, or other communication activities employed by the purchaser or supporter

- The right to an exclusive association within a product or service category
- The right of entitlement to an event, venue, or facility
- The right to use various designations or phrases in connection with the sport or entertainment property such as *official sponsor*, *official supplier*, *official product*, or *presented by*
- The right of service (use of the product or exclusive use of the product) or the right to use the sponsor's product or service in conjunction with the performance, event, or facility
- The right to use certain promotional activities, such as contests, advertising campaigns, sales-driven activities, and so forth in conjunction with the sponsorship agreement
- The rights to the media assets of the sport property—including broadcast and cyber rights and the opportunity to associate social media platforms with those of the sport property

Sponsorship, then, includes a wide array of activities associated with a communications process that is designed to use sport, entertainment, and other forms of lifestyle marketing to send messages to a targeted audience. The amount of money spent on sport and special-event sponsorships, as well as the number of sponsorships, has grown dramatically (table 9.1).

TABLE 9.1   North American Sponsorship Spending by Property Type

Property type	2011 Spending	2012 Spending	Increase from 2011	2013 spending (projected)	Increase from 2012 (projected)
Sport	$12.38 billion	$13.01 billion	5.1%	$13.79 billion	6.0%
Entertainment	$1.85 billion	$1.93 billion	4.3%	$2.03 billion	5.1%
Causes	$1.68 billion	$1.70 billion	1.2%	$1.78 billion	4.8%
Arts	$869 million	$891 million	2.5%	$920 million	3.3%
Festivals, fairs, and annual events	$804 million	$825 million	2.6%	$849 million	2.9%
Associations and membership organizations	$532 million	$550 million	3.4%	$572 million	4.0%

Reprinted, by permission, from IEG, "2013 sponsorship outlook: Spending increase is double-edged sword," *IEG Sponsorship Report*, Jan. 7.

Sponsorship in the Marketing Mix

As previously discussed, the marketing mix comprises variables that fall into five broad categories: product, price, promotions, place (including distribution), and public relations. The marketer's function is to manipulate these variables to meet the target market's needs in a continually changing environment (figure 9.1).

As a key component of the marketing mix, promotions are often referred to by contemporary theorists as the communications mix (figure 9.2).[3] In comparison with many other promotional activities, which are often standalones, sponsorship activities are much more integrated and are composed of a variety of marketing and promotional components.

As discussed in chapter 10, the role of promotions is to inform and persuade the consumer and thus influence his or her purchasing decision. The elements of the promotions or communications mix are traditionally considered to be advertising, personal selling, publicity, positioning, and sales promotion. Combinations of some or all these elements are inherent in sponsorship agreements (figure 9.3).

One sponsorship activity that combines personal selling, positioning, and promotion is hospitality. Hospitality opportunities are a sponsorship asset or benefit commonly associated with premier events such as the Olympics, World Cup, Super Bowl, NBA All-Star Weekend, Daytona 500, and the concert tours of major performing artists. Hospitality can be defined as the provision made for the sponsor by the sport or entertainment property of tickets in exclusive seating areas, lodging, transportation, on-site special activities, and special events and excursions related to the activity or event. The sponsor can in turn use these assets or benefits to entertain its own clients, reward its best customers for their longtime support or volume of purchases, or court new prospective clients. In this guise hospitality not only positions the sponsor as a person or entity with influence and access but also acts as a form of personal selling because the sponsor can conduct activities through face-to-face contact with key customers and prospects. This sponsorship also functions as promotion because it is promoting the company to current and potential clients.

Sponsorship benefits and relations could also be used in a combined advertising and sales

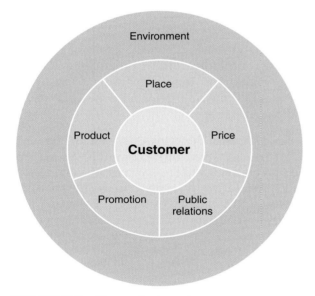

FIGURE 9.1   The marketing mix components.

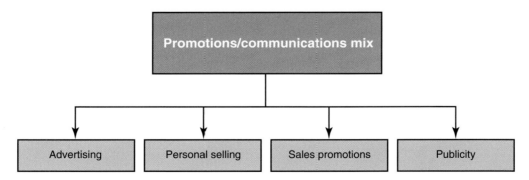

FIGURE 9.2   The traditional promotions or communications mix.

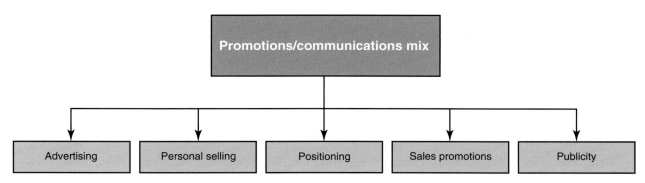

FIGURE 9.3   A broader promotions or communications mix.

campaign. For example, Quaker State Motor Oil might use a relationship with NASCAR to conduct a national sales promotion that could include any or all of the following promotional elements and rights or benefits derived from the sponsorship relationship:

- Sweepstakes to win an all-expenses paid trip for two to the Daytona 500
- Promotional presence on the NASCAR website with an enter-to-win offer
- Hospitality including a chance to meet Richard Petty
- On-track advertising
- Television advertising
- Retail point-of-purchase displays tagged with the NASCAR logo and Richard Petty image

Thus, the sponsor has the opportunity to integrate a number of the elements of the promotional or communications mix in any sponsorship relationship with a sport or entertainment property.

The costs that the sponsor incurs to promote or activate its affiliation or association comes in addition to the costs usually referred to as a licensing or partnership fee that grants the sponsor the relationship and the rights to use that relationship. Activation is commonly referred to as bringing the brand to life by creating a variety of ways for the brand to interact with its target market. Activation is defined by IEG as "the marketing activities a company conducts to promote its sponsorship. Money spent on activation is over and above the rights fee paid to the sponsored property." Sometimes activation is also known as leverage.[4]

For example, Sprite is a sponsor, actually a corporate partner, of the National Basketball Association (NBA). Sprite (through its parent company Coca-Cola) pays an annual fee to the NBA in exchange for the affiliation or association with the NBA and receives certain benefits that include but are not limited to the following:

- Category exclusivity in the soft-drink category (no direct competitors because Sprite is a corporate partner; therefore, soft-drink products not affiliated with the Coca-Cola family of products cannot be granted any sponsorship or promotional rights).
- Use of NBA registered trademarks, official product designation ("Sprite is the official soft-drink of the NBA All-Star Game").
- Preferred ticket packages and hospitality opportunities during NBA All-Star Weekend.
- The right to conduct in-store and web-based promotions and to create point-of-purchase displays featuring NBA marks and agreed-upon NBA players.
- The right to conduct national promotional activities and contests associated with NBA All-Star Weekend, such as NBA All-Star balloting.

Thus, when NBA corporate partner Sprite engages its annual All-Star balloting promotion, during which fans vote for their favorite NBA players in NBA arenas, online, and through various retail outlets, Sprite assumes all costs associated with activating this promotion in addition to paying the licensing fee to the NBA to become a corporate partner.

Marketing Through Spectacle: Peisistratus Inc. and the Ancient Art of Sponsorship

When we read about a major corporation's investment of millions in an affiliation with a venue, event, team, or league, we should recognize that there is nothing modern about marketing through sport. The strategy goes back to the ancient Greeks and Romans. Granted, there were no corporations or businesses as we think of them today. But many entities recognized the value of spectacular competition as a way to boost an image or win consumer loyalty. Among them was a whole set of political figures known as tyrants—a term that the Greeks used for those who grabbed control of a city-state by illegitimate or unconstitutional means. As historian Don Kyle has written, tyrants needed to "justify and reinforce their regimes by currying broad popular favor." One of their favorite means was athletics festivals.

Peisistratus of Athens was one such tyrant who pulled off three separate coups in Athens between 561 and 527 BCE. He needed ways to maintain broad support against any counters by the aristocratic clans that had long held power. His main strategy was to build up the new Great Panathenaic Festival, which included horse racing, running, boxing, and other competitions. Investments in facilities, administration, holy sacrifices, and prizes boosted the status of Athena and the whole community over the older tribal cults. And, of course, it all boosted the fame of the man in charge. Perhaps this explains in part why Aristotle later wrote, "Men were often heard to say that the tyranny of Peisistratus was the Golden Age of Cronos."

Similar scenes played out around the ancient world, where tyrants sponsored festivals and used victories at the Olympics and other games to enhance their reputations, especially if they could hire a poet like Pindar to write an *epinikean*, or victory ode. Peisistratus took things even further in 532 BCE when he made a trade with an exiled Athenian named Cimon, who had just won a second Olympic four-horse chariot race. Peisistratus allowed Cimon to return home, and Cimon allowed Peisistratus to be declared the official victor. Nothing like an Olympic victory to burnish the resume of Peisistratus Inc. Roman strong men like Pompey, Crassus, and almost all of the emperors used similar strategies to win and maintain favor with the growing Roman mob. The Roman satirist Juvenal summarized it all in one phrase—*panem et circenses*, or bread and circuses.

Some ideas and venues have stood the test of time. In August 2010 Italy's Culture Ministry announced that it was seeking proposals for a special kind of sponsorship, a special kind of entitlement zone—the Colosseum. Yes, that Colosseum. Finished in 80 BCE, it was still drawing over 5 million visitors per year, but the $47 million in ticket revenue was not enough to protect the structure from deterioration. By 2010 only 35 percent of the structure was open to visitors. With its triennial budget cut by $233 million, the Culture Ministry was looking for a $33 million sponsor to fund restoration. Among the returns listed by Bloomberg News would be "advertising rights," the rights to "conduct private guided tours," rights to placing the corporate name and logo on tickets, as well as "exclusive film rights to the restoration process." Signage would be mercifully limited to "posters no taller than 8.2 feet around the base of the structure." After a few months of negotiations, Rome had a deal with Diego Della Valle, the founder of Tod's Luxury Shoes. Putting some fears to rest, Mr. Della Valle announced, "I won't put Tod's Shoes on the Colosseum." Some limits were placed on activation.

So when you see a story about the Xcel Energy Center in Minnesota, watch a NASCAR race with cars wrapped in signs for Lowe's or Best Buy, or listen to the CEO of Tostitos hand out a bowl trophy, think of Peisistratus and the ways that he successfully marketed through sport.[5]

Growth of Sponsorship

As the sidebar on ancient tyrants suggests, sports events have attracted sponsors for a long time. Several factors, however, have contributed to an explosive growth of sport sponsorship over the past half century. The marketing literature shows some agreement that the emergence and growth of sponsorships coincided with the ban on tobacco and alcoholic drink advertising.[6] During the 1970s tobacco and alcoholic drink manufacturers were forced to look for ways of promoting their products other than through direct advertising channels. The banning of cigarette ads in 1971 was a triumph for antitobacco forces, but as a result those companies had to redirect their massive advertising clout (and budgets) to sport sponsorships.[7] The *IEG Sponsorship Report* noted than in 1997 tobacco firms spent $195 million on sport sponsorships, 95 percent of it in the area of motorsports, making up about 20 percent of the total sponsorship revenue for that sport segment.[8] But the landscape of the tobacco industry has undergone incredible change over the last 30 years. R.J. Reynolds departed NASCAR as the last big tobacco company to be involved with the auto-racing venture. The FDA passed new regulations that went into effect in June 2010, preventing cigarette and smokeless tobacco sponsorships in any sporting event. Thus, the tobacco industry has gone from a patron and supporter of sport to being a cancer (literally) and being banned from involvement in sport sponsorships.[9]

Companies with substantial advertising budgets gradually discovered that too much "noise" was present in the print and electronic media. The average person is exposed to more than 3,500 selling messages per day, or about 250 ads and material every 90 minutes. The number recalled is around 1, translating to a 1 in 250 chance of the marketing message, no matter how carefully crafted, having any effect on the memory, let alone the purchasing decision-making process.[10]

Moreover, advertising costs, especially on television for premier shows and events, continue to rise. Interest in sport-related ad spending in various mediums has been altered dramatically by technology, affordability, and access. Nielsen Global Ad View listed these numbers as media ad spending growth from 2011 to 2012.[11]

Internet 7.2 percent

Radio 6.6 percent

Cinema 5.9 percent

Outdoor 4.7 percent

Television 3.1 percent

Newspapers 1.6 percent

Magazines –1.3 percent

Advertising costs for the NFL's 2004 Super Bowl amounted to $2.3 million for a 30-second ad spot; a 30-second ad spot for Super Bowl XLVII in 2013 cost $3.5 million. Since 2001, Super Bowl ad prices have increased more than 60 percent. Why is so much spent on Super Bowl advertising? A look inside the numbers for Super Bowl XLV in 2011 makes the case:

- Forty-six percent of U.S. households tuned in to the Super Bowl.
- The game attracted 111 million viewers.
- YouTube registered 48 million hits (and counting) for Volkswagen's Darth Vader commercial, in addition to the television viewership.
- The Darth Vader ad generated $100 million of publicity value for Volkswagen.
- Fifty-eight percent of consumers think that Super Bowl advertising is more memorable than the average television commercial.[12]

Thus, by developing alternative channels of communication through sport sponsorships, companies found that they could achieve new levels of exposure, in many cases (the Super Bowl excluded) at lower costs than through advertising campaigns.

Table 9.2 shows the advertising spending by category, and table 9.3 shows the top 20 sport advertisers by brand.

The 1984 Los Angeles Olympics was the first privately organized Olympics in history and a landmark in the evolution of corporate sponsorship and promotional licensing through sport. The 1984 Olympic sponsors received significant media exposure and to some extent positive image building, and the Games generated a profit for the Los Angeles Olympic Organizing Committee (LAOOC). Peter Ueberroth, president of the LAOOC, inaugurated his dream of a corporately

TABLE 9.2 Ad Spending by Categories

Segment	2010	2009	2008	2007
Auto	23.80%	20.00%	21.90%	23.00%
Telecom	11.90%	10.40%	10.80%	11.60%
QSR, Pizza	9.60%	10.70%	9.90%	8.60%
Beer	7.50%	9.00%	7.50%	8.40%
Insurance	6.00%	5.70%	5.30%	5.40%
Movie	5.00%	4.50%	4.40%	3.20%
Credit cards	3.10%	2.90%	6.50%	3.80%
Financial	3.00%	1.50%	1.00%	1.00%
Soda	2.20%	1.80%	2.40%	2.20%
Pharmaceuticals	2.00%	3.70%	2.60%	2.70%

Reprinted, by permission, from D. Broughton, 2011, "Sports ad spending roars back," *Street & Smith's SportsBusiness Journal*, 14(3): 1.

TABLE 9.3 Top 20 Sport Advertisers

2010 rank (2009 rank)	Company or brand	2010 sports ad spending	2010 total ad spending	Percentage of ad spending dedicated to sport	Change in sport spending vs. 2009	Change in sport spending vs. 2008
1 (7)	AT&T Mobility	$366,313,812	$1,129,589,500	32.40%	102.80%	37.20%
2 (1)	Anheuser-Busch	$356,205,906	$440,676,094	80.80%	14.40%	8.70%
3 (3)	Verizon	$340,529,688	$1,134,530,125	30.00%	38.10%	45.90%
4 (2)	Ford	$304,976,281	$1,026,098,032	29.70%	22.70%	69.90%
5 (5)	Toyota	$240,029,368	$983,938,875	34.40%	18.00%	8.0%
6 (10)	Chevrolet	$238,965,192	$758,333,376	31.50%	43.40%	3.70%
7 (8)	Geico	$216,789,219	$544,623,000	39.80%	27.20%	58.90%
8 (4)	MillerCoors	$214,447,797	$284,931,469	75.30%	−5.40%	94.80%
9 (11)	McDonald's	$202,887,766	$721,521,000	28.10%	30.20%	18.40%
10 (6)	Sprint	$179,083,297	$512,211,688	35.00%	−10.60%	−3.50%
11 (9)	DirecTV	$175,414,641	$381,546,125	46.00%	4.20%	14.30%
12 (25)	Nissan	$160,993,935	$400,248,382	40.20%	105.90%	−0.10%
13 (24)	Coca-Cola	$144,664,359	$227,839,172	63.50%	77.80%	19.90%
14 (16)	Warner Bros.	$138,607, 172	$537,765,438	25.80%	25.30%	99.60%
15 (13)	Southwest Airlines	$131,300,672	$180,044,609	72.90%	2.00%	−0.60%
16 (14)	State Farm	$129,327,820	$392,475,125	33.00%	11.10%	14.90%
17 (35)	NFL	$125,642,688	$138,397,391	90.80%	−3.40%	−2.50%
18 (18)	Subway	$125,315,508	$432,709,188	29.00%	26.70%	21.80%
19 (17)	Lexus	$124,981,059	$273,876,320	45.60%	21.70%	67.80%
20 (15)	Taco Bell	$119,644,273	$387,067,312	30.90%	5.40%	17.00%

Adapted, by permission, from D. Broughton, 2011, "Sports ad spending roars back," *Smith & Street SportsBusiness Journal*, 14(3): 1.

subsidized Olympics by limiting the number of Olympic sponsors to 30 to avoid clutter and duplication as well as to ensure category exclusivity.[13] Thus, Ueberroth was able to increase the value of a sponsorship in relation to the increased cost of those same sponsorships. By demonstrating that as cost increased the value of the subsequent benefit increased, Ueberroth showed that sponsorships actually became partnerships because they were mutually beneficial for both the sport property (the Olympics) and the sponsor (the 30 corporations). Experiences such as the 1984 Olympics and other mutually beneficial relationships helped give rise to the term *corporate partners*, suggesting that sponsorships could be partnerships whereby corporations who hope to achieve benefits work in harmony with a sport property to create a desirable result. Founding partners in new venues and the Orlando Magic's Champions of the Community program are effec-

tive ways of limiting the number of partnerships and providing greater exposure and involvement for partners at that level.

Following the 1984 Olympics, promotional licensing and sponsorship agreements skyrocketed as the public and sport governing bodies increasingly accepted the commercialization of sport. Figure 9.4 shows the use of sponsorship, advertising, and sales promotions from 2009 through 2012. Table 9.4 depicts the amount of money spent on sponsorships throughout the world in the period between 2011 and 2013.

Because sponsorship has proved to be effective, sponsorship costs have risen. Additionally, increasing concern about the cost effectiveness of marketing expenditures has made it crucial for managers to be able to justify their marketing investments, including sponsorships.[14] To reign in those costs and exercise greater control, some deep-pocketed companies have created and own

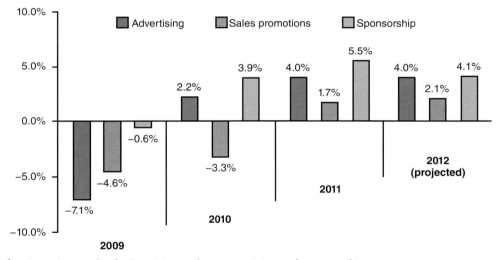

FIGURE 9.4 Annual growth of advertising, sales promotion, and sponsorship.

Based on IEG, "2013 sponsorship outlook: Spending increase is double-edged sword," *IEG Sponsorship Report*, Jan. 7.

TABLE 9.4 Global Sponsorship Spending by Region

	2011 spending	2012 spending	Increase from 2011	2013 spending (projected)	Increase from 2012 (projected)
Europe	$13.5 billion	$14.1 billion	4.7%	$14.5 billion	2.8%
Asia and Pacific	$11.2 billion	$12 billion	6.7%	$12.6 billion	5%
Central and South America	$3.7 billion	$3.9 billion	5.6%	$4 billion	2.6%
All other countries	$2.1 billion	$2.2 billion	5.1%	$2.3 billion	4.5%

Reprinted, by permission, from IEG, "2013 sponsorship outlook: Spending increase is double-edged sword," *IEG Sponsorship Report*, Jan. 7.

their own events. This practice was pioneered during the 1960s and 1970s by Donald Dell and the late Mark McCormack, founders of ProServ and IMG respectively, who sought to create opportunities for their clients. In 1997 Nike announced the launch of Nike Sports Entertainment, a division of Nike designed to initiate and control its own events. According to Ian B. Campbell, the then manager of Nike's Sports Entertainment Division, "Asset acquisition is costing more.

Online Sponsorships

Sponsorship activation is changing, according to a new report published by International Marketing Reports. The findings, published in *Driving Business Through Sport, Part 3, Activation and Case Studies*, show that a shift has occurred toward digital and experiential activation. "In the past sponsorship has been activated through traditional marketing disciplines such as advertising, PR, promotions, hospitality and merchandise," says report author Simon Rines. "The new report analyzes case studies from many of the leading sponsors across Europe and it shows that there is a move towards online activation and live events."

"Some of the findings are predictable given that the world has moved online in recent years, but what is interesting is the attitude that sponsors are taking towards the use of new media. They can see that traditional media is in decline, so activation has to shift towards new media. Instead of merely seeking to gain exposure on third-party sites, however, they are starting to take control of this media. Many major sponsors have now created their own sites to maximize their investments."

Rines points out that this doesn't merely mean that the sponsorship has its own site. The activation process has become more sophisticated than that: "What we are seeing is themed sites emerging. For example, UK sponsor Carling created a social networking site for Sunday league football. Amateur players can set up their own team site and post news, scores, video, pictures and comments. It wasn't directly linked to the brand's sponsorship of professional football, but that sponsorship gave it the credibility to own the medium."

"What is particularly impressive about this case study is that the brand then activated it further through experiential and viral marketing. They introduced a touch of glamour to a Sunday league football match by bringing a public address system, fireworks, perimeter boards, an MC and an opera singer to sing the national anthem. This alone created a huge amount of news coverage. But the significant part was the posting of videos on file-sharing sites such as YouTube and Metacafe as well as sites owned by relevant media such as men's lifestyle magazine *Loaded*. This resulted in tens of thousands of views and helped to boost site traffic and use. Without any official rights whatsoever, Carling now has a degree of ownership of Sunday league football in the UK, which is almost an institution in itself."

Case studies featured in the report show that other sponsors have used the web to great effect, and they include Coca-Cola, which leveraged its Football League sponsorship through promotions that drove fans to its site. The report also shows that live engagement is becoming increasingly important.

"There is definitely a rise in the number of sponsorship programs that seek to activate through live communication," says Rines. "In the report, the case studies in which this happens vary enormously, but include a government campaign to reduce motorcycle accidents, Samsung setting up a fan singing zone at Chelsea, CSR programs that include kids' coaching and, arguably most creative of all, Allianz leveraging its Munich naming rights deal at airports and city centers around the world."[17]

Reprinted, by permission, from W. D'Orio, 1997, "Just doing It," *Promo*, 10(4): 38.

Players and teams are more expensive than they were six months ago. I think if you are going to invest in an athlete or a team asset anywhere in the world, you've really got to justify what you're doing from an overall brand perspective and make sure it really is a total package. Why pay a third party to do that for you or to interpret that for you or screw it up for you when really you ought to do it for yourself."[15]

This philosophy of ownership and locus of control was a prime motivator for NBC and Clear Channel to create and launch, with corporate partner Mountain Dew, the Dew Action Sports Tour in 2005 and for ESPN and Capital One to launch ESPN–Capital One Bowl Week each December.[16]

Other factors in the growth of sport sponsorship relate primarily to additional sponsorship opportunities created by new sport offerings, such as the following:

- More television channels devoted to sport programming, especially at the collegiate level as conferences have added their own networks, and the success of regional sports networks and networks created by professional sport leagues such as NBA TV and the NFL Network

- Technological developments that have led to the portability of sport through cell phones, tablets, and other devices no longer tethered to viewing sport in the traditional way on television or at a specific time

- Emergence of new sport offerings such as mixed martial arts as well as the importation of programming from other countries, such as English Premier League television packages and cricket matches through satellite or cable television providers or online sources

- Sport-themed video gaming and fantasy sports attracting a broader audience to sport programming and content

- Globalization of sport, that is, importing and exporting sport programming and content from one country to another, including exhibition matches and regular-season competitions outside the home country with the intent to create a following on television and online

What Does Sport Sponsorship Have to Offer?

During the 1970s marketing through sport often served either the personal interests of top executives or as a vehicle for charitable contributions and support. But beginning in the 1980s marketing through sport became a practice involving serious research, large investments, and strategic initiatives related to corporate objectives and targets. Since 2008 it has become readily apparent that we live in a true global economy and that what happens in one country can have a serious effect of the finances and economic outlook of others. Sponsorship, in terms of structure and spending, has been significantly affected by global economics and the issues that result from those conditions. More than ever, expenditures are scrutinized not just by the companies themselves but also by the media and in certain cases governmental departments.[18] ROI (return on investment), ROO (return on objective), and ROE (return on experience) have been buzz terms in terms of the accountability and measurement expected from sponsorship investments. What rationale and benefits can sport or entertainment offer its prospective sponsors in this decade of economic uncertainty?

By marketing through sport or entertainment, a company attempts to reach its target consumers through their lifestyles. According to Hanan, "life-styled" marketing is a strategy for seizing the concept of a market according to its most meaningful recurrent patterns of attitudes and activities and then tailoring products and their promotional strategies to fit these patterns.[19] Corporate marketing executives, regardless of the size of their companies, have found that linking their messages to leisure pursuits conveys those messages immediately and credibly. The rationale is that leisure is a persuasive environment through which to relate a sales message to targeted consumers. The association of the company or product with the event or activity is also important because sporting events have good public acceptance, have a strong fan following, and are newsworthy events for all forms of media coverage. By establishing a link with an event or activity, a company shares the credibility and intentions of the event itself while delivering a message to a consumer who is apt to be more relaxed and potentially more receptive.

In addition, certain events enable the marketer to reach specific segments such as heavy users, shareholders, and investors, or specific groups that have been demographically, psychographically, or geographically segmented and identified as important. Healthy Choice became the official nutritional consultant to the U.S. Ski team, the first sport sponsorship the company had undertaken. The rationale for the sponsorship was to "create a deeper understanding of our message. Advising the team enables us to demonstrate our big strength to the consumer. Team members are young, vital people who are not willing to compromise on nutrition or taste so it's an exciting message for our consumers."[20]

Another example is Audi, which signed sponsorship agreements with equestrian events, ski races, and sailing after research indicated that participants in and followers of those events and activities were typical Audi buyers.[21]

Corporate Objectives

Not every company has the resources and global reach of Nike, Adidas, or Apple. Therefore, every approach to sponsorship or other promotional licensing activities should consider the fact that classifying corporate objectives in a uniform or clear-cut way is difficult. As they develop sponsorship objectives, corporations frequently have a number of objectives that overlap and interact. According to Meenaghan, objectives in sponsorship range from assumption of social responsibility to the commercial objectives normally associated with advertising.[22] Our review of academic writing and empirical research as well as practical findings on the subjects of promotional licensing and sponsorship indicates that no single corporate objective in the decision-making process identifies whether a company should consider sponsorship or, if they do, what they should sponsor. A study by Irwin, Asimakopoulos, and Sutton showed that company image and fit with the target market were the most important criteria in funding a sponsorship proposal.[23] Figure 9.5 is a tool that sponsors have used to screen potential sponsorship opportunities based on corporate objectives.

According to the research, the following objectives most often influenced the decision to enter into sport sponsorship agreements:

- Increase public awareness of the company, product, and or service
- Alter or reinforce public perception of the company
- Identify the company with particular market segments
- Involve the company in the community or key geographic markets
- Build goodwill among decision makers
- Generate media benefits
- Achieve sales objectives
- Showcase unique product features, technologies, or advantages
- Create an advantage over competitors through association or exclusivity
- Gain unique opportunities in hospitality and entertainment
- Secure entitlement or naming-rights visibility

Table 9.5 shows the results of an IEG/Performance research study conducted in 2011 in which corporate decision makers ranked the importance of objectives considered when making a decision regarding a potential sponsorship opportunity.

Each of those objectives can be achieved in multiple ways. They should provide the sponsor with a ROI (return on investment) that would be in monetary form or a ROO (return on objective) or ROE (return on experience) that would be measured against the goal or objective; that is, did the sponsorship accomplish what it was intended to do? In the following section we illustrate the importance of various objectives, explain what it is and why it is important, and provide examples of how objectives can be used and achieved in the context of sport sponsorship. The sponsorship paradigm depicted in figure 9.6 illustrates a simple model of what the sponsor and the sport property hope to receive because of their partnership. Each party has obligations for themselves and expectations to be delivered and fulfilled by the other.

Increasing Awareness

Sponsorship is often used with the sole aim of increasing awareness or educating the public about the capabilities of a company or the benefits of its products or services. Lenovo, a

Criteria	WT	−4	−3	−2	−1	0	1	2	3	4	Total
Budget considerations											
Affordability											
Cost effectiveness											
Management issues											
Event profile											
Organizational committee status											
Media guarantees											
Legal status											
Regulatory policy											
Athletes' cooperation											
Governing body status											
Marketing agency profile											
Positioning image											
Product and sport image fit											
Product utility fit											
Image and target market fit											
Targeting of market											
Immediate audience											
• Demographic fit											
• Size											
• Fan association strength											
Extended media coverage											
• National coverage											
• Local coverage											
Extended audience profile											
Demographic fit											
Size											
Public relations											
Hospitality accommodations											
Community leader presence											
Customer presence											
Staff sport knowledge											
Event sales and retail tie-in											
New account opportunities											
Promotional opportunities											
Promotional licensing											
Complementary advertising											
Signage opportunities											
Competition considerations											
Competition's interest											
Ambush marketing avoidance											
Sponsorship status											
Title sponsor											
Major sponsor											
Exclusivity											
Established											
Long-term involvement											
Alternative sponsorship											
Cosponsor											
In-kind supplier											
Sponsorship type											
Team											
League or championship											
Event											
Facility											
Grand Total											

FIGURE 9.5 Revised sport sponsorship proposal evaluation model. WT = weight.

TABLE 9.5   Corporate Objectives Ranked by Decision Makers in Terms of Importance

Objective	Rank	Percentage rating of importance
Create awareness or visibility	1	68%
Increase brand loyalty	2	65%
Change or reinforce image	3	53%
Drive retail or dealer traffic	4	53%
Stimulate sales or trial usage	5	43%
Showcase community or social responsibility	6	40%
Sampling, displays, and showcasing	7	34%
Entertain clients or prospects	8	33%
Gain on-site sales rights	9	17%

Data from *11th Annual IEG/performance research decision makers survey*, 2011, (Newport, Rhode Island: Performance Research), 31-32.

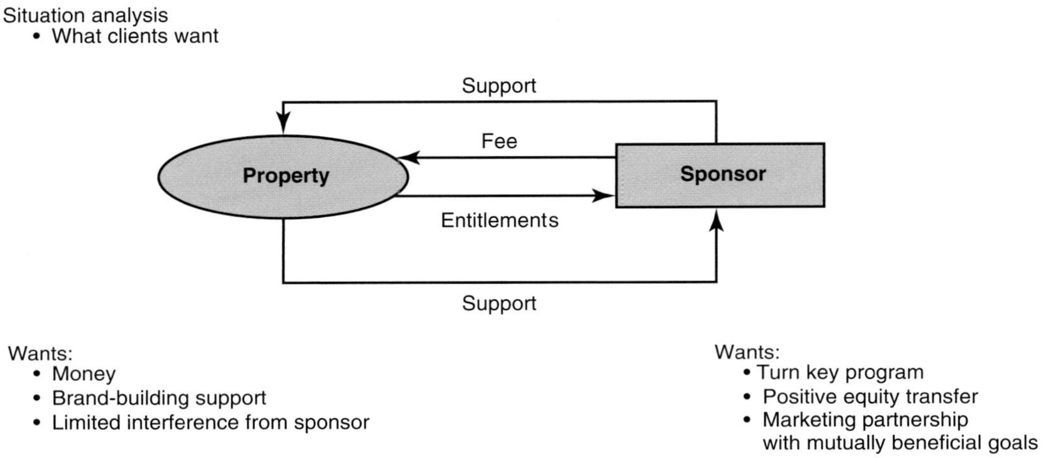

Situation analysis
- What clients want

Support

Fee

Property   **Sponsor**

Entitlements

Support

Wants:
- Money
- Brand-building support
- Limited interference from sponsor

Wants:
- Turn key program
- Positive equity transfer
- Marketing partnership with mutually beneficial goals

FIGURE 9.6   The sponsorship paradigm.

Chinese-based multinational computer hardware and electronics company, recently signed on as the official PC supplier for the National Football League. David Rabin, Lenovo's executive director of North American marketing, explains the reason for such a sponsorship agreement: "We're (Lenovo) one of the biggest brands in the tech world that a lot of people still haven't heard of, so we're picking a brand as powerful as the NFL to partner with."[24]

Influencing Public Perception

The opportunity to capitalize on image association or image transfer makes sponsorship attractive to businesses as a marketing communications tool. The choice of a sport or event with particular attributes can help a company achieve a desired image that will reinforce or change consumers' perceptions of the company or its products. Choosing the sport or event becomes less formidable when the company has an actual or logical link to the sport or event. The potential for an effective sponsorship agreement is greatest when an association exists between the target group of the company and the target group of the sport or event, between the desired image of the company and the image of the sport or event, or between the product characteristics promoted and the credibility of the sport entity helping to promote the product. In a move to create the perception that going to their restaurants can be a stadium-like experience, Buffalo Wild Wings restaurants have assumed sponsorship of what was previously known as the Insight.com Bowl, played in Tempe, Arizona. The new bowl sponsorship comes as the chain is trying to link itself to sport more closely than ever and is employing the tag line "Wings, Beer and Sports."[25]

Establishing Associations With Particular Market Segments

Selecting a sponsorship agreement that matches the target has proved beneficial for many sponsors. For example, the previously referenced Lenovo sponsorship agreement with the National Football League was done in large part because of the particular age and gender that the NFL is able to deliver. According to David Schmook, senior vice president, Lenovo Group, and president, North America Lenovo, "We want Lenovo to get in the consideration set of 18- to 35-year-olds as we continue to expand our presence in the U.S., and the power and reach of the NFL should help us do that."[26]

Another example of associating with specific target markets can be found in Coca-Cola's sponsorship of the London Olympics in 2012. Coca-Cola's global marketing team decided to develop an Olympic campaign that targeted teens, prompting the company's North American unit to create a complementary marketing strategy aimed at moms. The emphasis on moms is based on the fact that the Olympics draw more female viewers than most sports events; 49 percent of the viewers of the Beijing Olympic Games in 2008 were women aged 18 and older, many of them moms. Sharon Byers, senior vice president, North America, of sport and entertainment marketing partnerships, stated, "Moms in the U.S. are decision makers and we want to continue to push the way our company promotes healthy, active living and we want to continue to do that through Mom." One of the key activations was a sweepstakes in which moms could use Coke rewards points for the chance to have Olympic hurdler David Oliver visit their child's school.[27]

Becoming Involved in the Community

Sponsorship has demonstrated more potential than any other promotional tool in having direct impact on the community. In this context, sponsorship often takes the form of public or community relations, and its objective is usually to position the company as a concerned and interested citizen trying to put something back into the community. Companies may target community relations through sport sponsorship to specific communities, regions, or other geographic areas of influence as dictated by corporate objectives. Through licensing or sponsorship activities, the company demonstrates its awareness of local issues to influence potential customers and local social and governmental agencies. In some cases, the corporate partner provides financial or other support to an event that otherwise would not occur or could not continue. For example, a company could offer to help threatened local clubs or support interscholastic sport programs that cover a large geographic area. Evidence supports the idea of using promotional programs designed to increase corporations' involvement with the community. Meenaghan cited a survey in which 72 percent of the respondents thought that business firms should sponsor more such events and activities; 37 percent believed that companies should sponsor sport-related activities; 17 percent, children's activities; 11 percent, senior citizen programs; and 7 percent, charitable causes.[28]

Building Goodwill

Sport provides an excellent environment in which to conduct or influence business on a relaxed, personal basis. In recent years, the competition for market share among existing customers and the competition for new customers and growth (particularly in international markets) have been intense. Corporations that can deliver unique opportunities such as entertainment, tickets, and hospitality for key clients are perceived to be potentially good business partners that will always deliver good service. For example, Travelers Insurance Company is a sponsor of the prestigious Masters golf tournament. The firm's director of corporate advertising and promotion noted, "The tournament is an upscale prestigious event that provides a fit both demographically and psychographically." On each day of the Masters, a group of executives from around the United States is flown to the event site. As the director observed, "There are many golf enthusiasts in the trade and a lot of our agents conduct

This promotional poster helped to spread the word about a benefit concert for victims of Hurricane Sandy, presented by Chase.

business on the golf course. When you combine those two factors, the Masters makes good sense from a business standpoint."[29]

An excellent example of building goodwill was the 12-12-12 Concert at Madison Square Garden held to benefit the victims of superstorm Sandy that devastated a number of communities in New York and New Jersey in October 2012. Chase donated approximately $10 million in cash and services such as providing office space and helping to stage the concert, which featured the Rolling Stones, The Who, Bruce Springsteen, and Sir Paul McCartney, among others. Besides being involved in the concert-related activities, Chase offered an employee assistance program, waived all mortgage-related fees for 90 days, and offered 90 days of forbearance of mortgage fees for affected customers. Chase employees and their volunteer efforts were featured as PSAs during the international broadcast of the concert.

Generating Media Benefits

Media benefits include advertising and publicity related to the promotional efforts surrounding the product or event. Media benefits are usually equated with ROI and measured in the number of impressions generated and the source of those impressions. Impressions are the number of viewers (television), listeners (radio), readers (all print forms), unique and repeat visitors (websites), page views (websites), and members and activity (social media sites) exposed to the advertising or promotional message. The advertising or promotional message may be an actual advertisement, but it is often a logo or sign that appears during the television coverage or is evident in a news-

paper photograph or image on a website. In auto racing, for example, the driver often wears a cap with the name of a sponsor and may switch caps during a press conference, interview, or photo session to provide exposure and impressions for sponsors. The source of these impressions is also important to the sponsor. A photograph in the *New York Times* has high value because the *Times* not only has a large subscription base and circulation but also is a global newspaper and has a significant online following. Later we examine some of the methods that companies use to select events for sponsorship opportunities designed to generate media benefits.

Geico upgraded their almost 10-year partnership with the Orlando Magic to the Champions of the Community level in 2010. As part of the Champions of the Community relationship, Geico receives entitlement to the Geico Garage, a parking garage adjacent to the Amway Center and located beside Interstate 4. The entitlement to the City of Orlando parking facility brings a revenue stream to the city. As another element of the partnership, Geico receives designation as the official auto insurance of the Orlando Magic. Beginning with the 2012–2013 season, Geico received a digital signage package inside the Amway Center; presence on the Magic's official website, OrlandoMagic.com; print advertisements in the game-day program; and in-game radio spots. Geico is incorporated into a number of promotions throughout the season such as giveaways and halftime sponsorship.[30]

Showcasing Unique Product Features, Technologies, or Advantages

In recent years, an increasing number of companies have become sponsors of particular sport properties because of an opportunity to promote unique product features or technological innovations or applications. Sponsorships of this sort have always been common in technologically rich sports such as NASCAR, but the concept has also gained a foothold in traditional sports such as hockey, basketball, and golf.

Melbourne, Florida–based Harris Technology became a Champions of the Community Partner of the Orlando Magic to be able to showcase its technology in real time and under game conditions for the Orlando Magic and the 2012 NBA

All-Star Game. Harris positioned this technology on their website:

> Broadcast-quality HD is delivered to sophisticated video boards via a state-of-the-art control room outfitted with more than 800 broadcast devices. Assured interoperability among devices reduces system complexity and downtime. Increased control room capability means improved staff efficiency and shorter training periods. More robust graphics and quicker turnaround times meet a variety of event and sponsor needs and make high-impact fan experiences easy to attain.

> The world's most sophisticated high-definition broadcast center, powered by Harris technology, will enable hundreds of journalists and media to connect and report live on the NBA All-Star Game from Orlando—including video, still images, voice and data—broadcast worldwide in real time and with exceptional HD quality, including to our brave soldiers overseas. We believe no other broadcast center can currently match this HD and replay capability.[31]

Harris uses the opportunity to showcase its capabilities to other teams with their own venues as they visit the Orlando Magic.

Achieving Sales Objectives

The ultimate objective of marketing is to increase market share, notably by increasing sales volume and ultimately profitability. Sponsorship, along with other elements of the communications mix, is usually viewed as an element that can be used to influence the purchasing intention of a prospective buyer. In this sense, sponsorship constitutes an important stimulus within purchasing as a multistage, multi-influence process, but it can also influence sales in a more direct manner. BMW invests heavily in the sponsorship activities that it identifies as appropriate for its upscale audience. From placing its cars in James Bond 007 films to sailing and to fitness-related events, BMW uses sponsorships to achieve their marketing and sales goals. For example, to address the rapidly growing market segment of women who buy or lease upscale cars, BMW entered into a sponsorship agreement as the presenting sponsor of the Danskin Triathlon Series. In exchange for its financial commitment, BMW received significant media benefits that were used to promote local dealerships, because their primary marketing objective was to boost showroom traffic by suitable affluent and aware women. The program proved to be highly successful. In one local market 25 percent of the participants in the triathlon series visited the BMW dealers in that market.[32]

Sales objectives can also relate to product use as a benefit of a sponsorship or licensing agreement. A sponsorship or licensing agreement with an entity such as a cruise ship line or a venue such as an amusement park or arena may require the use of a particular product or line of products at all events or functions in the facility. Denver's Pepsi Center, home to the Avalanche (NHL) and Nuggets (NBA), is an obvious example. Supermarket sales of soft drinks have long been a battlefield for Coca-Cola and Pepsi, although Coca-Cola has been winning the market share battle by a few percentage points. But when it comes to park and recreation facilities, theaters, cruise ships, and sporting events and venues, Coca-Cola is the clear winner. The strategy of Coca-Cola is to sign sponsorship and licensing agreements that ensure product exclusivity and use whenever possible. According to Scott McCune, Coca-Cola's vice president of global partnerships and experiential marketing, "Our benchmark is that our annual report for 2010 said that the FIFA World Cup drove our business in the second and third quarter, and I would love for our 2012 annual report to say the (London) Olympic Games drove our business."[33]

Another excellent example of a sales-driven sponsorship agreement also involved the London Olympic Games, namely BMW's promotion "Drive for Team USA," which helped the company sell more than 6,000 new cars. The promotion involved a special test drive opportunity, a $10 donation to the U.S. Olympic Committee for every test drive taken, and a $1,000 allowance toward the purchase of a new vehicle. The sales promotion generated 26,535 test drives, which BMW converted into 6,633 new car sales, representing a conversion rate into purchases of approximately 25 percent. With an average new car price of $63,251 BMW's "Drive for Team USA" program generated more than $150 million.[34]

Creating Exclusivity

In some cases, particularly when the sponsorship fee is high or the commitment is long term, exclusivity of product or category is integral to licensing or sponsorship agreements. Since the economic downturn in 2007, exclusivity has not been as prevalent as it once was, obviously because of cost. The beer industry is one of the notable sport sponsorship groups that have moved away from exclusivity. Beer companies have moved more toward making their beer the prominent beer in the venue by securing highly visible areas for signage or purchasing the naming rights for a highly visible bar area within the venue.

For sponsors who insist on exclusivity, notably those that sell soft drinks, credit cards, banks, and in some case automobiles, exclusivity clauses provide that the sponsor of that particular category will be the only brand present in that category throughout the sport venue or, depending on the terms of the agreement, through any media broadcasts or on the website. Naming-rights deals, such as the Orlando Magic's sponsorship with Amway for Amway Center and the jersey naming-rights deals in the English Premier League, are guaranteed exclusivity because of the scope and magnitude of the sponsorship deal. As stated previously, the crucial benefit of exclusivity is that this type of sponsorship provides a great opportunity to drive incremental sales while at the same time denying competitors the same opportunity to interact with an audience of potential purchasers. This limitation of competition can improve the ability of the marketing message to increase sales and may affect the profitability of both the sponsor and the competition. The exclusivity, in light of the strong emotional attachment and following that sport inspires, allows the marketer to position brands or products as supporting an event or a particular team (e.g., PNC: Official Bank of the Pittsburgh Pirates) while implying that the competitors' products do

Arsenal's sponsorship with Emirates, in addition to the naming-rights deal for their stadium, leaves little doubt about Arsenal's preferred airline.

not, thereby encouraging consumer response and support where it matters most, at the cash register.

In its corporate partner agreement with the NCAA, Nabisco is guaranteed category exclusivity. As delineated by Nabisco, the category is defined as official cookies, crackers, and biscuits of the NCAA. Thus, Nabisco can promote any or all of these items as it chooses while preventing any of its competitors for any of the aforementioned types of products from doing so in a relationship with the NCAA. For example, during the NCAA basketball championships held annually in March and April, Nabisco, as part of its NCAA partnership, offers the March Madness Snack Bracket and highlights Chips Ahoy and Oreo, as well as Triscuit, Ritz, belVita, and Wheat Thins, all cracker varieties. The NCAA and its basketball tournament provide an opportunity for Nabisco to conduct exclusive association and promotions within the cookies and crackers category.

Gaining Opportunities in Hospitality and Entertainment

Although hospitality and entertainment relate to a number of the other concepts previously described, this function is worthy of examination on its own. Hospitality and entertainment play a critical role in the packaging of sponsorship and promotional licensing programs. These concepts enable the sponsor to construct certain benefits and opportunities that are often unique and unavailable in the general marketplace. Such opportunities may include trips to the Olympics, World Cup, Wimbledon, the Super Bowl, NBA All-Star Weekend, and on-site hospitality and special events that are not available to the public. This hospitality, entertainment, and access can be valuable for a sponsor to extend to clients and identified VIPs. According to William Pate, VP of advertising for AT&T (which sponsors the Atlanta Braves, the Atlantic Coast Conference, and a NASCAR Nextel Cup team), "Business people are more open to messages when they are at leisure than when they are working."[35]

Hospitality opportunities have become an integral part of sponsorship agreements for college athletics programs, which package hard-to-obtain tickets in prime locations along with tents, catering, and other amenities. Similar hospitality programs are offered on the professional golf and tennis tours, and within NASCAR and professional team sports in the United States and abroad. Such programs often form the basis for the sales of luxury suites and boxes in sporting venues throughout the globe. The key to successful use of hospitality is to ensure that the hospitality is unique, exclusive, and available only as part of a comprehensive sponsorship agreement.

Corporate partners use hospitality benefits to reward their own personnel, to serve as contest or sweepstakes prizes, to court potential new clients, or, most frequently, to induce their clients to increase product use or consumption, renew agreements, or sign new ones. An excellent example of corporate hospitality that can be extended not only to preferred clients but also to prospective clients is the NFL House presented by Verizon. The NFL House offers special benefits and opportunities for a fee to NFL House subscribers. Corporate partners can host special clients while at the same time gaining exposure for their products or services to an upscale clientele. Special seating at restaurants, player appearances, and a game room were all part of the NFL House in New Orleans for Super Bowl XLVII. As the presenting sponsor, Verizon had a branded charging station along with product demonstrations.[36]

Securing Entitlement or Naming Rights

Corporations interested in purchasing naming rights to venues or events such as concert tours, auto racing events, and bowl games have an agenda in mind when they consider such sponsorship possibilities. This agenda usually consists of the following elements and their value to the company in terms of cost and organizational priority:

- Number of impressions or exposures
- Opportunity for local, regional, national, and international media coverage
- Tax considerations
- Brand exclusivity and brand building
- Public relations and community involvement and support
- Hospitality and related amenities
- Activation platforms—sponsorship and promotional activities

Red Bull, an Austria-based sports and energy drink maker that was looking for a unique sport marketing position in the United States, purchased the then NY–NJ Metro Stars of the rising MLS and renamed them the Red Bulls so that the product name would be present at all times when reference was made to the team. According to Alan Friedman, founder and former editor of *Team Marketing Report*, "Naming rights are the most expensive sport marketing investment in the current marketplace, the best dollar-for-impression sponsorship bargain, and one of the most underutilized promotional assets in a company's marketing arsenal."[37] Corporations electing to become involved in securing naming rights or entitlements must have a strategic plan in place to leverage the opportunity and the financial resources to support that acquisition and activate the brand. One industry that has capitalized on sponsorship deals with naming rights is banking. Banks have led the way in naming-rights deals over the past decade because naming a sport venue not only communicates the impression of success and well-managed investments but also conveys the concept of permanence in that the bank is part of the community for the long term.[38]

Entitlement and naming rights have a high profile in NASCAR. In stock car racing, the corporations traditionally have a prominent role. If a company sponsors a racing event, the company's name is incorporated into the event name. For example, Mountain Dew, one of PepsiCo's soft-drink products, sponsors Darlington's Southern 500. Hence, the race itself is known as the Mountain Dew Southern 500 at Darlington. If a company becomes a sponsor of a racing team, the corporate name or brand is used in conjunction with the team name. For example, Toyota has a racing team and is a prominent participant in NASCAR's Sprint Cup Series. Although Sprint is the title sponsor of the series, Toyota and a number of other automotive manufacturers and other prominent businesses seeking exposure sponsor their own racing teams. The corporate or brand name is prominently displayed on the race car. In a study conducted by Repucom exclusively for the *SportsBusiness Journal* and *SportsBusiness Daily*, the media value generated for Toyota during the 2012 NASCAR Sprint Cup Series was $35,078,828.[39] Table 9.6 illustrates the top-performing brands and their media value.

Sponsor Activation

Activation, often referred to as engagement or experiential marketing, is one of the keys to a successful sponsorship agreement because it brings the brand to life by creating an interactive platform between the target market and the product that the brand is wishing to promote. Corporations search for unique and creative ways to leverage their association with an event or organization, an endeavor commonly referred to as activation. According to Lesa Ukman, chief insights officer of IEG (International Events

TABLE 9.6   Top 10 Brands Featured During the 2012 NASCAR Sprint Cup Series

Rank	Brand	Media value
1	NASCAR	$115,934,858
2	NASCAR Sprint Cup Series	$58,149,159
3	Chevrolet	$51,974,922
4	Sprint	$45,785,775
5	Toyota	$35,078,828
6	Lowe's	$28,354,112
7	5-Hour Energy	$23,251,148
8	3M	$22,657,734
9	FedEx	$22,517,359
10	Daytona 500	$21,552,997
Total	All brands	$1.21 billion

Group), "Sponsorship can build brand equity, sales and shareholder value, but it is mostly the activation of sponsorship that does those things."[40] According to Matt Wilkstrom, VP of partnerships for Wasserman Media Group, "Many brands today spend up to two to three times as much on sponsorship activation as they do on rights fees. As with all advertising, sponsorship dollars are intensely scrutinized for ROI. You have to be really creative not only in how you build these partnerships but how you activate them."[41]

The sponsorship activation wheel (figure 9.7) illustrates the variety of platforms that can be used to promote and communicate sponsorship activities. Social media is increasing in importance and spend and will continue to be a highly utilized platform because of reach, ease of use, and cost.

Perhaps one of the more interesting sponsorship activations is the worldwide sponsorship of the Olympic Games by Dow Chemical Company. For years, sponsors of the Olympic Games were more likely to be consumer packaged goods (CPG) companies like Coca-Cola. Dow Chemical, however, is more of a business-to-business (B2B)

company. They have approached sponsorship from a practical point of view by featuring their capabilities and products.

In July 2010 Dow became an official Worldwide Olympic Partner (TOP Programme) and the official chemistry company of the Olympic Movement through 2020. Dow Chemical has more than 5,000 products, which are produced in 36 countries around the world. Observers may not see the fit between a chemical company and the Olympics, but we only need to look at the main Olympic Stadium to see the wisdom of the partnership.

The London 2012 Olympic Games Stadium features a wrap on the outside of the structure. The wrap is made up of 306 individual panels, each 25 meters high and 2.5 meters wide. The wrap panels are made up of more than 50 colors that bear the official colors of the Games. The panels were produced by Dow and completed the stadium as the architects had intended. It became the visual centerpiece of the London Olympic Games.

Additionally, Dow products can be found all over the Olympic Park. Adhesives from Dow bind together rubber particles in the now-famous track at London's Olympic Stadium. The solution provides runners with the perfect balance of hardness and elasticity, ensuring a safe surface for both sprinters and long-distance runners. Dow also provided roofing and flooring solutions that can be found in Olympic venues all around the Olympic Park as well as materials that were used in wire and cable installations throughout London to ensure efficient and high-quality communications during the Games and beyond. On another front Dow provided 3,600 litter and recycling bins that were used in the more than 30 Olympic Venues.[42]

The biggest risk for an activation strategy is obviously at the implementation stage. Poorly planned implementation or inadequate resources can transform a well-designed consumer interaction promotion into a travesty of disappointed attendees drawing negative media coverage and using social media to voice their displeasure. The activation plan did not turn out as intended for Pepsi with their relationship with the New York Yankees. Yankees fans who showed up for a Pepsi-sponsored promotion were none too pleased after standing in line for hours to find

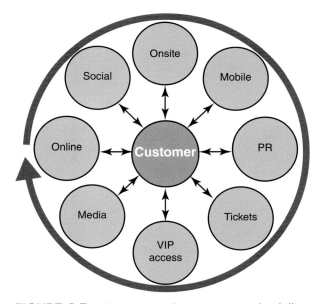

FIGURE 9.7   The sponsorship activation wheel illustrates the variety of platforms where activation can take place.

Reprinted, by permission, from T. Hughes, 2013, "How to increase fan engagement in sponsorship activation through social media," *The Migala Report*.

that fewer tickets were being given out than promised. Chanting, "Pepsi sucks! Pepsi sucks!" the overcaffeinated crowd opened cans of the soft drink and poured the liquid onto the pile of items to be handed out, sending cops racing to the scene. Video shows an angered fan who shouts, "Drink Coca-Cola!" Pepsi told the New York Post, "All we wanted to do was make fans part of the celebration, giving away free Yankee tickets and Pepsi-Cola products, but we blew it."[43] To minimize the damage, Pepsi renewed the ticket offer and extended it another day, but as they say, it's hard to take back video and social media content because it can live forever.

Social Media as Activation

Because of the emphasis on sponsor engagement with the target market, corporations have long viewed sport as an effective way to reach the most avid followers. Signage, however, has become one dimensional, and ads on television have become less effective because of the capabilities of the DVR and because television might not be the primary "screen" for the targeted audience. Marketers, particularly those who use sport as the medium, want to take full advantage of the emotional attachments between fans and the athletes, teams, and leagues that they follow.

Nowhere is this clearer than with social media, which has become the focus of the way in which brands and teams are looking to create fully integrated fan activation. Jeff Weiner, CEO of ESBL Social Media, a firm specializing in helping clients expand their social media metrics and convert them into revenue, identifies social media, along with the Internet, television, radio, and printing of the first U.S. newspaper in 1721, as one of the five most important aspects of multimedia that have evolved since the 18th century.[44] Facebook pages, Twitter feeds, location apps, and mobile platforms seem almost custom made for the obsessions and chatter of sports fans. These tools give them greater access to the leagues, teams,

Tips on Helping Sponsors Leverage Through Social Media

Here, industry insiders offer several tips and best practices about helping sponsors activate through Facebook and other social media platforms.

- Keep commercialization to a minimum. Although the point may seem obvious, rights holders should stay away from hard sales messages when incorporating sponsors into social media promotions. Instead, sponsors should be integrated into content that enhances the fan experience. "It's important to us not to have a hard sales message. We want a natural integration so that fans receive good content, not just a sales pitch," said Jeramie McPeek, vice president of digital with the NBA Phoenix Suns.

- Cap the frequency of sponsor messaging. In addition to downplaying sponsor sales pitches, rights holders also need to put a cap on the number of sponsor-themed messages. For example, the NBA Boston Celtics plan to run no more than five sponsor promotions a month. "It's a balancing act. You want to help companies engage your audience, but you don't want them to bombard your audience," said Ted Dalton, the Celtics' vice president of corporate partnerships and business development. On a more micro level, the NBA Phoenix Suns try to cap the number of sponsor-themed messages on its Facebook site to one or two a day. It also tries to cap the number of team-themed posts to three or four a day.

- Offer consumer engagement. Promotions that include questionnaires, polls, and other opportunities for consumer engagement are more likely to be effective than those without, said McPeek: "Driving consumer engagement is critical. We try to incorporate a question in every post so that fans are incented to leave a comment."[49]

MLB Fan Cave.

and athletes whom they follow, while creating virtual camaraderie between far-flung people who share their passion. This passion is what brands want to leverage.[45]

How is this passion being leveraged?

- During the London 2012 Olympic Games, McDonald's used swimming medalist Dara Torres to promote exercise and balanced eating through a branded website called Champions of Play.
- The 3 million Facebook fans of the New England Patriots can participate in a virtual tailgate on the Facebook page sponsored by JetBlue.
- Shirt maker Van Heusen sponsored fans' choice online voting for the Football Hall of Fame.[46]
- Foxwoods Casino moved a registration contest to the Facebook page of the Boston Celtics and enjoyed a seven-fold increase in the number of registrants.[47]

- Looking to build visibility for an existing in-game promotion with the St. Louis Rams, Purina rolled out the Purina Pet of the Week contest on its Facebook site. The promotion dangles tickets and a pet food prize package to consumers who post photos of themselves in team gear posing with a pet. The promo is sponsored by the Nestlé Purina PetCare Co.[48]

One of the best usages of social media activation is Major League Baseball's Fan Cave. The Fan Cave has become a virtual destination as well as an actual destination for creating content that is shared through Twitter by the inhabitants of the Fan Cave, who are chosen through social media as well. Stars (media and current and former baseball players) visit the MLB Fan Cave and help create content that is shared through Twitter, Facebook, Pinterest, and on the MLB Network. Often, news is selected to be disseminated through the MLB Fan Cave before it is available to other traditional media outlets.

Sponsorship Activation From the Property Perspective: The Case for Sponsorship Activation

Catherine Carlson, Vice President, Corporate Partnership Activation, Orlando Magic

The sponsorship landscape has transformed significantly over the past decade. Savvy sponsors are no longer just placing signage in an arena or stadium and entertaining their clients in a corporate box; they have specific objectives for a partnership and expect a greater return on their sponsorship investment. The next generation of corporate partnership account managers needs to focus on sponsorship activation rather than advertising and brand impressions alone.

The key to significant sponsorship revenue growth at the Orlando Magic has been creating a roster of sponsors that are activators versus straight advertisers. If your sponsors are activators, they are truly integrated into your brand and it is harder for them to walk away at contract renewal time. If they are just advertisers, they can always shift their advertising dollars to other mediums.

Following are two examples of how the Orlando Magic has worked with an international car brand and a locally based Tex-Mex inspired restaurant to create a fully integrated sponsor activation platform that provided results. As evidenced by these two examples, Kia and Tijuana Flats both understand the power of creating a strong activation platform, which drives their business. A sponsor that is able to connect their brand to the fans ultimately drives greater return on investment and is more likely to become a long-term partner.

Kia Motors: The Great Activator

Kia is a leader in sponsor activation. They are a National Basketball Association (NBA) league sponsor and support their platform with 15 local NBA team deals, including the Orlando Magic. At the Amway Center in Orlando, Kia has created a one-of-a-kind sponsor deck, featuring a contemporary car display visible to the entire inner bowl, called the Kia Motors Terrace. Kia leverages the deck through various in-market promotions. In one of their most successful promotions, called Kia Drive for Five, customers who purchased or leased a Kia vehicle received five pairs of tickets to a Magic game, including one game in the Kia Motors Terrace. Kia used all their sponsor assets including radio, digital advertising, website banner ads, and program ads to support the promotion. Kia uses this promotion as a closing sales tool for local dealerships. More than 300 new cars were sold during the promotional period. Although branding impressions are important to Kia, an integrated marketing promotion such as the Kia Drive for Five works for several reasons:

- Drives revenue to both Kia and the Orlando Magic through vehicle and ticket sales
- Drives consumers to local Kia dealerships and exposes them to a brand they might not have considered previously
- Provides new Kia owners an opportunity to watch the game from the Kia Motors Terrace, the most recognized sponsor space within the Amway Center among Magic fans, thereby extending the Kia car-buying experience
- Creates a brand connection between Kia Motors and the Orlando Magic
- Provides opportunities to create new Magic fans because Kia customers are exposed to the Orlando Magic game experience

Kia has transformed traditional sponsor assets such as signage, car display, and media to support a marketing platform, which drives their business. Kia understands the power of sponsor activation.

Tijuana Flats Hot Shot Promotion: Use of Social Media, Metrics, and Research

The Orlando Magic and Tijuana Flats, a locally owned fresh Tex-Mex restaurant, created a marketing platform using an in-arena promotion whereby each time the Magic scored 10 or more three-pointers in a home game, Magic fans could take their ticket stub into Tijuana Flats the next day and receive a free taco. This simple promotion was supported by in-arena digital signage, PA announcements, social media, viral videos using the team mascot, and in-store point-of-purchase signage. The key objectives of the promotion were to drive restaurant traffic to their 32 central Florida locations and to create fan engagement with Tijuana Flats—in arena, in store, and through social media. The results were clearly measurable:

- On average, 4 to 6 percent of game attendees participated in the Tijuana Flats 3-Point Hot Shot Promotion
- The introduction of a viral video in arena and through social media featuring the team mascot spiked redemptions by 50 percent
- About 12,100 ticket stubs were redeemed over 16 games
- The average incremental spend per redemption at Tijuana Flats was approximately $6.50
- The promotion generated over $78,000 incremental revenue to Tijuana Flats in 16 days

The Magic collaborated with Tijuana Flats to gain further insight into the fans who participated in the promotion. Tijuana Flats retained all ticket stubs that were redeemed for a free taco. The tickets were scanned into the Magic Customer Relationship Management (CRM) system. The e-mail addresses associated with the tickets were pulled and sent an electronic survey that aimed to increase understanding of the consumer behavior of Magic fans as it relates to the Tijuana Flats promotion. The survey results provided further data to support the value of the sponsor activation:

- Driving new customer business: 26 percent of ticket redeemers indicated that it was their first ever visit to a Tijuana Flats.
- Increasing store traffic: 66 percent of redeemers indicated that they wouldn't have visited Tijuana Flats in the same week without the Hot Shot promotion.
- Increasing brand loyalty: 85 percent of people whose first visit to a Tijuana Flats was to redeem a taco indicated that they were likely to visit again in the future because of the Hot Shot promotion (versus 72 percent of total survey respondents).

Tijuana Flats takes sponsor activation to the next level by analyzing the results from the survey to gain a better understanding of their consumer behavior, which provides valuable information to improve the promotion year after year.

Evaluating and Ensuring Sponsorship Effectiveness

The past 20 years have seen an increase in corporate accountability and responsibility, which has been mirrored by growth in sponsorship measurement, growth in business analysis, and more decision making than ever in the sport industry being driven by data. We have moved from the art of marketing (techniques and gut feeling) to the art (experience) and science (data-driven business decisions) of marketing. A declining global economy and corporate misconduct resulting in a lack of public trust has led to a demand for corporate accountability and fiscal responsibility in all business decisions. Before the turn of the century, most sponsor-related research focused on measuring impressions. Although impressions are still a key component of any measurement program, it is now only part of the assessment. The focus now is on the demographics of the audience and their ability to

Bank of America Loves Baseball and ROI

The year 2009 was a dark time for sponsorship investment not only in sport-related properties but across all sponsorship opportunities. Bank of America, however, thought otherwise. Despite engendering acres of bad press for spending on sport while collecting $45 million in taxpayer TARP funds, Bank of America maintained sponsorship deals with 10 MLB teams, including the high-profile Yankees, Dodgers, and Red Sox. It also officially sponsors 23 minor league teams and Little League, in addition to having a multitude of deals with the NFL, NASCAR, golf, and the Olympics. Why did Bank of America keep the sport deals flowing? Management believes that they make money.

"Sponsorship is about connecting the passion a fan has to our products and services," says Ray Bednar, a Bank of America senior vice president in charge of global sponsorship marketing. Bank of America claims that every dollar it spends on sport yields $10 in revenue and $3 in net income. More than 10 percent of B of A's checking accounts in the United States are sport branded through teams and leagues. The bank has raised $18 billion in debt and private equity for stadium construction and renovation since 2002. Despite the tough times for the finance industry, banks and financial services companies still represent the broadest presence in MLB; 13 firms are spending on 22 official sponsorships. No other industry has more than 6.

"It makes sense for us to be where the customers are," says Bednar. That also means knowing when to say when. Figuring that they pretty much have their potential customer base covered through the five major sports that they are involved with, the bank typically turns down offers from properties like pro lacrosse. Narrow and deep works better than broad and shallow. The biggest risk to forging ahead, of course, is a prolonged economic slump that keeps attendance subdued. When general interest drops, so does the value of a sponsorship. "If you're not getting the eyeballs, the promotion means nothing," says Chuck Costigan, a Denver-based sport sponsorship consultant.[50]

---

spend; can a particular market segment generate ROI, or at least ROO? Measurement also focuses on what the impression conveys. Is a message being communicated, and is that message being communicated effectively and being understood?

The approach described by the Orlando Magic's Catherine Carlson earlier in this chapter is becoming more common in the sport industry—a strategic and proactive partnership between the sport entity and the sponsor to ensure that objectives are being met, that the agreed-on platforms are being activated and delivered, and that the opportunity to make adjustments every month or every quarter is available. Effective activation is a key element of effectiveness. For that reason, more sport organizations are creating positions in their corporate partnerships programs that have no new business development (new sales) responsibilities. These activators focus solely on existing clients and their marketing platforms rather than selling signage. Thus, more attention is paid to each of these corporate partners by

focusing on creating marketing and promotional activation opportunities that work. The result is greater retention of corporate sponsors, increased spending among existing partners, and more new business growth because sellers are focused solely on creating new business opportunities and activators are focused on delivering on promises and building those relationships. Look for this model to continue to grow throughout the rest of this decade and beyond.

But the motivation to become a sponsor can involve many aspects besides the number of eyeballs, and documenting the reasons to sponsor and realizing those objectives is critical. When measuring this value or ROI, sponsors commonly assess the following practices:

Facts on Measurement From IEG Sponsorship Report[51]

- Eighty-six percent of the companies surveyed stated that their need for validated results from sponsorships has increased.

When speaking at the World Congress of Sports and asked about impressions, Julie Roehm (at the time director of marketing communications for Chrysler, Dodge, and Jeep) responded by saying, "Tell me what the impression of Dodge is, not how many impressions we are generating."[52]

Ms. Roehm raised an interesting point. Perhaps we have been focused on counting eyeballs for too long rather than trying to understand what those eyeballs are conveying to the consumer. The following list offers some thoughts when planning how to make a lasting, impactful impression rather than just creating something to see.

- Is the sponsorship a fit between the sponsor and their product or service and the sport property? (Think Mountain Dew, Red Bull, and Skull Candy and action sports.)
- Does the campaign create an impression with multiple anchors and touch points—heart, mind, generations—such as the highly successful MasterCard "priceless campaign" with Major League Baseball and Geico's varied campaigns?
- Is it fresh, unique, and able to stand out?
- Is the association between the image of the sponsor's product or service and the image of the property mutually enhancing and beneficial, such as that with Kia and the NBA?
- Is the property on the upswing, such as MMA, UFC, and MLS?
- What other corporate partner brands are joining in this venture?
- Does the sport property employ activation specialists dedicated to the account?

- Forty-four percent of the companies surveyed spent 1 percent or less on concurrent or postevent research to measure success, and 32 percent spent nothing at all.
- The most common factors considered when measuring sponsorship ROI are the following:
  - Brand awareness, 83 percent
  - Product or service awareness, 82 percent
  - Brand attitude, 86 percent
  - Response to promotions and ads related to the sponsorship, 74 percent
  - Product or service sales, 81 percent
  - Media exposure generated, 77 percent
  - Leads generated, 56 percent

Selling Sponsorships

Before beginning the sponsorship process to identify and locate a sponsor for a team, organization, or event, the sport entity should develop a strategic planning process about how to conduct the sales campaign. Strategic planning steps should include the following:

- Make a comprehensive list of all assets in the inventory.
- Establish a list price for each item based on the cost per impression (if media are involved) and the cost of implementing activation platforms related to the objectives of the potential sponsor.
- Conduct research with regard to sponsorships sold in the market and in similar markets; identify prospects that would be likely to have an interest based on past behavior.
- Establish packaging prices and, if appropriate, discounting for the more inclusive packages.
- Remember to determine the real cost of the sponsorship, which may include any or all of the following elements: tickets (full face value), promotions (premium items, shipping, fulfillment and labor costs), print and point-of-sale pieces, web page development, social media campaigns, signage and supporting advertising (including production, design, and layout), and other activation costs that will be borne by the organization.

- Establish the sales strategy. Which if any categories will be offered as exclusive? Are there levels such as founding partners that need to be sold first? What are the goals for each category?

- Initiate the eight-step sales process (see following section) with the top three product and service categories, followed by the next three, and so on. Sell the best inventory first.

- The order in which categories and potential sponsors are presented is critical—large categories first, major national sponsors first, easy closures first. Gain momentum; use the recognition of name sponsors to attract lesser sponsors and leverage those commitments to secure other relationships.

- Talk to competitors (Coke and Pepsi; Budweiser and Miller/Coors; Visa, MasterCard, and American Express) simultaneously to ensure a decision within a comparative period.

- Remember that all sponsorship decision makers know each other and often communicate; don't exaggerate and don't make special concessions and side deals.

Eight-Step Sponsorship Process

After an organization has agreed on and implemented the strategic planning process, it can initiate the sales process. The success of the sales process depends on adherence to the principles of the strategic planning process.

1. Research the category and then conduct research on the top prospects within that category. Know the state of their business, number of employees, outlook for the company, last year's financials, and so forth. Research should also include news or web coverage of the company, pro or con.

2. Schedule a meeting with the sponsorship decision maker at the brand within the category that you are targeting. Meet only if the decision maker is present. Don't accept no from someone not empowered to say yes.

3. At the first meeting, listen 80 percent of the time and sell only when you have to. You are there to observe and learn. Where does the prospect currently spend her marketing dollars? What is working? What isn't working? What other sport organizations or events does the company sponsor or support? What does the company like or not like about those relationships? What does the prospect do for client entertainment? For employee benefits and morale building?

4. Close with a statement that you are going back to determine whether you see a fit and to develop a possible solution that you can present next time. Ask for the next meeting before leaving and try to schedule it no more than two weeks following the initial meeting.

5. Create a marketing partnership proposal. Give the prospect something unique (creative names, program elements, or ownership). Practice consultative selling. For example, you could say, "Here are some possibilities that may work for you. Let's review them." Then get input from the activation team about time, costs, and other variables.

6. Present the proposal as a draft that you will gladly modify to meet the organization's needs. Custom-tailored proposals are much more likely to succeed than generic proposals. This is not about what you have to sell—inventory; this is about what the customer is interested in buying—a business solution.

7. Negotiate the final deal and get a signed agreement. Close the deal when you have the opportunity; ensure that the final signed deal has agreed-upon deliverables, payment terms, and a mutually agreed-upon timetable.

8. Introduce the client to the activation team.

ACTIVITY 9.1 Eight-Step Sponsorship Process

In this WSG activity assume that Fred Mangione, chief marketing officer and chief revenue officer for the Brooklyn Nets, has asked you to develop a sponsorship proposal, including a compelling story, for the Brooklyn Knight (the Nets' mascot).

Co-Op Sponsorship Opportunities

A co-op sponsorship agreement is the joining of two or more corporate partners or organizations to capitalize jointly on a sponsorship or licensing agreement. Given the economic climate and the interest in business-to-business and business-to-consumer marketing, co-op sponsorships are viable in today's marketplace for a variety of reasons. Such agreements do the following:

- Allow companies (or divisions of the same company) to share the total cost of a sponsorship
- Allow the promotion of several product lines or brands (with distinct organizational budgetary lines) within the same corporate structure (PepsiCo and Frito-Lay or Yum Brands)
- Enable corporations to use existing business relationships that make sense (McDonald's and Coca-Cola)
- Enable a newer or smaller corporation with something to offer to leverage the strength and position of a larger or more established corporation to gain the sponsorship and a position of advantage over its competitors
- Allow testing of a relationship when future opportunities are under consideration
- Create a pass-through opportunity, typically involving grocery chains that agree to a sponsorship and pass some or all of the costs (and benefits) to product vendors in their stores

Prospecting: The Key Step in Initiating the Sponsorship Sales Process

Jared Schoenfeld, Madison Square Garden Sports Division

Prospecting is using every available resource to uncover leads and ultimately to create new business partnerships. I learned the value of good prospecting in my first year as a sales consultant with the Phoenix Suns Legacy Partners, LLC. While crossing the street in Phoenix (with the right of way, of course), I was forced to jump to avoid a recklessly driven construction vehicle. Stunned, I jotted down the phone number of the company with the intention of reporting this unsafe driver. After my emotions had cooled and I hadn't called, I realized that what I held in my hand was a lead. Two months later, I had sold the CEO of the construction company a $45,000 premium ticket package. Every time that I saw him and his son at the arena, I was reminded about the importance of having my eyes and ears open at all times and treating everything as a lead.

Before you go out scouting local construction companies, let's review a few principles of prospecting that you should be doing every day to increase business. First, it is important to read newspapers, magazines, and all publications on business and the marketplace. This will keep you informed about people, business, and trends within various industries. Even more crucial, it will allow you to identify who is spending money. A great way to see who is spending money is to subscribe to a publication that showcases who is signing new commercial leases, which means they are expanding their office space and growing (www.therealdeal.com is a good example). Set automatic e-mail notifications and Google alerts about companies you have targeted to stay current on their activity. This will allow you to send touch points when you see their name in the news. Use research to learn more about your current clients as well. The objective is to identify and target other like-minded businesses with hopes of creating a partnership. Note that not all research should take place during the standard business hours of 9 a.m. to 5 p.m., because that is your best opportunity to reach out to potential clients.

> continued

Another huge element of prospecting is networking. Conferences, symposiums, and, of course, your own team's games are unbelievable opportunities to expand your network and create leads. Shaking hands is great, but make sure that you get a business card before giving your own and always follow up the next day! Networking sites like LinkedIn have made it incredibly easy not only to follow up but also to learn about people you have met and their companies. LinkedIn allows you to find background information on people, which you can use as talking points to enhance the relationship. Additionally, you're able to find friends and relationships that you have in common with the person you met or are trying to engage in conversation with, which enhance your credibility. When meeting someone, understand that your first impression is everything. The way that you dress, smile, and converse all matters, so prepare!

Referrals are my favorite form of prospecting because they usually reflect a good relationship that you have created with the referring client. All referrals begin with this basic rule: You must ask! As with many things in life, if you don't put yourself out there, you will never have the opportunity to reap the rewards. Begin by asking your current clients for referrals; if you have helped them grow their business, they should be happy to introduce you to their contacts because they see the value first hand. Sometimes you will build a great relationship with a company without their becoming a partner. In this situation, you should ask whether they know any companies that may be able to capitalize on the opportunities that you have discussed. Then ask whether they can introduce you to them. Always emphasize that you are not trying to sell them anything immediately. Just build a relationship and see whether there happens to be a fit to help grow their business.

Nothing in my sport business or entry-level sales education taught me about jumping out of the way of a construction vehicle and parlaying that into a sale. In devoting time to the aforementioned tactics, you will become more knowledgeable and build your network. But you haven't truly mastered prospecting until you're keeping your eyes and ears open at all times. Treat everything like a lead until you find out that it isn't. Don't be afraid to use unorthodox methods of identifying local businesses that are spending money. And remember, always have confidence that you can create a customized partnership for any company. It's just a matter of finding the leads!

Let Me Tell You a Story

As a society we are bombarded with thousands of messages and pieces of information every day. The Internet and social media have exploded, and no one knows what will come next. The cancellation of the 2012 New York City Marathon after superstorm Sandy hit the region occurred largely because of the many channels that people used to express their displeasure that the event was still going to take place. Some of that ill will was directed at marathon sponsors.

Most of the time what happens is dictated by the relevancy of the message to the recipient, at other times it is the timing, and sometimes it is the way that the information is presented, which may be done in a fun and engaging way.

In any case, the most effective way for a sponsor to send a message that a potential customer will receive and act on is to have an activation platform or a story that makes an impression. Sponsors must be more conscious about making a memorable impression on their audience than on counting the number of impressions that viewers, readers, attendees, and visitors generate. The point is no longer about just the quantity of impressions; it is about the quality and impact of that impression, and the circulation and life of that impression. Did it move people enough to tweet about it? If they received a tweet, did they re-tweet to their followers? Sponsors must find platforms that create a memorable impression and tell a story that brings the brand to life and will be told and retold in meaningful ways.

Having a story is the foundation for companies such as Nike. According to Adam Helfant, former Nike VP of global sports marketing, "(At Nike) we focus on . . . creating meaning . . . and we create meaning through the stories we tell."[53]

Why do we need stories, and why are they effective? Stories do the following:

- Entertain us
- Inspire us
- Inform us
- Persuade us
- Motivate us
- Engage us

Sport, because of its universal appeal, emotional connections, associations, and unscripted nature, is a uniquely effective marketing platform for sponsors to use to position their products and services to create impressions, experiences, and memories that become stories. The classic "priceless campaign" by MasterCard created vignettes that resonated with consumers because the scenes used emotional connections to sport and sport experiences that hit home with viewers who were connected to sport in some way and could relate to the feelings, emotions, memories, and experiences that the stories (actually commercials) conveyed.

Do you have a story for your products or services? Do you have customer testimonials? Do you use an athlete as an endorser or spokesperson who can draw attention to your product and create an emotional bridge from their experiences and stories to create meaning for your brand? The story and emotional connections of Lance Armstrong as a cancer survivor and his Livestrong Foundation were so strong that they insulated Armstrong and his corporate partner Nike from allegations of doping and cheating for years until he was ultimately exposed in 2012.

The 2011 NBA All-Star Game and Slam Dunk Contest was a great opportunity for NBA partner Kia to create an impression. The promotion took on a life of its own through social media and You Tube.

When Blake Griffin jumped over a car to win the Slam Dunk Contest, he wasn't just entertaining us. He was helping sell cars. The dunk was weeks in the making—there were advertisers to convince, contracts to negotiate—and Griffin's Kia jump helped the car company reach more viewers than any commercial ever could.

In case you didn't notice by looking or you didn't hear the TNT crew shamelessly touting it, the car Griffin soared above was an Optima—official car of the NBA. Griffin's people had to get the automaker on board with the plan, and then they had to convince Sprite, sponsor of the dunk contest, to allow it.

Kia liked the idea, and it paid off for both parties. Griffin won the contest (and some extra ad dollars), and the automaker got its car viewed millions of times over as the jam went viral.

According to a survey by Edmunds.com, an online resource for automotive information, the product placement worked brilliantly. Consumers said they were 20 percent more likely to consider buying a Kia on Sunday (the day after the dunk) compared with an average Sunday, and they were twice as likely to consider an Optima.

"It was the smartest type of product placement," said Karl Brauer, senior analyst for Edmunds.com. "If it is blatant and intrusive and is painfully obviously, it doesn't work with the under-40 crowd. If it's contextual and subtle, like this, it works."

> continued

Still, the product placement wasn't exactly discrete. It took several minutes to roll a sizable automobile onto a basketball court. The camera showed large Sprite stickers placed on the front doors (one of the reasons that the beverage company was willing to let Kia have such a prominent display).

And whether it was part of the product placement or simply because of Kia's NBA sponsorship, the TNT broadcasting crew was shilling heavily for the car company: Charles Barkley continually repeated, "That's a great looking car," and Ernie Johnson added, "You know what's kind of fun about this; he also jumped over the official vehicle of the NBA, the Kia Optima."

Regardless, the spectacle was clearly a marketing success (in addition to being exciting for everybody watching at home).

Those who think that props undermine the integrity of the dunk contest better get used to them. After seeing the financial implications of Griffin's dunk, props are not going to become any less prominent.

Creating Your Own Story

Essentially, five steps are needed to create a story that can become a compelling message that sponsors can use to create an emotional bond.

1. Determine your objectives. What are the essential tasks that you must accomplish this year? What is it that you want to convey to your customers and prospects?

2. Identify your appropriate assets. What potential sport or entertainment property assets can you use to achieve your objectives? The game? A player? A concert tour? A broadcast or television program? A grassroots initiative?

3. Consider a variety of platforms to achieve the desired objectives. What communication forums can you use to convey your message to your target market?

4. Design an engaging activation platform. How will you bring your message to life? How will the target market be able to interact with your product or services?

5. Create a delivery system that capitalizes on the opportunity for storytelling. After reviewing all the possible activation platforms and communication mediums, choose the one that has the best likelihood of creating a story that can be told and retold by everyone who comes in contact with it.

The late Bill Veeck, one of the pioneers of sport marketing in the United States, was a master of creating promotional activities that were fun, innovative, and engaging. One of the key considerations for Veeck was to have unique activation platforms that would cause people to tell and retell the story of their experience to their friends and relatives. It's no surprise that Veeck established attendance records in every market in which he owned a team.

Ethical Issues in Sponsorship

As sponsorship has grown in scope and impact, sport organizations have become highly reliant on sponsorship income to make a profit, secure new facilities, or balance their bottom line. In certain instances this dependence on revenue has invited scrutiny by outside parties or even regret or second-guessing by one or both of the parties participating in the sponsorship agreement. In the past decade, we have seen significant repercussions and media coverage surrounding star athletes including Tiger Woods, Michael Phelps, and Lance Armstrong in relation to their roles as corporate representatives and spokespersons. Tiger Woods' driving mishap and infidelity caused a number of his corporate partners to part ways with the golf superstar. Tag Heuer, Gillette, Gatorade, Accenture, AT&T, and Golf Digest all parted ways with Woods in 2011, giving rise to the debate about whether athletes have a moral obligation to adhere to a certain code of conduct on and off the field to be compliant with the best interests of their sponsors.

Commercial gambling providers (CGPs) have recently intensified the promotion of their products and services through sport sponsorship. Consequently, gambling products and services now gain substantial exposure to large audiences through media broadcasts of sport. Because of the mainstream appeal of some sports, television audiences and fan bases can include youth and at-risk and problem gamblers. These people may be prompted to gamble or increase their gambling because of the alignment of gambling with a healthy activity and the increased normalization of gambling, as well as direct marketing. Therefore, sport sponsorship by CGPs promotes a potentially risky behavior and may exacerbate the public health issue of problem gambling. Regulatory measures have been implemented by governments and private organizations in relation to sport sponsorship by tobacco companies in recognition of the potential harmful influence of this form of marketing. Subsequently, the involvement of unhealthy products including alcohol, junk food, and gambling in sport sponsorship has been publicly questioned. Further regulatory changes that would directly affect the management of sport organizations may be implemented. Few studies have examined these issues, and we have little knowledge of the effects that sport sponsorship arrangements have on society. Research is needed to inform prudent decision making about the appropriate regulation of sport sponsorship.[54]

Ethics, Morals, or Just Public Opinion?

Cash-Strapped Greek Soccer Team Rescued by Brothel

Voukefalas players are wearing bright pink jerseys emblazoned with the logos of the Villa Erotica and Soula's House of History, a pair of pastel-colored bordellos recruited to sponsor the Greek soccer team after drastic government spending cuts left the country's sport clubs facing ruin.

The world's oldest profession is giving a whole new meaning to love of the game.

Other teams have also turned to unconventional financing. One has a deal with a local funeral home, and others have wooed kebab shops, a jam factory, and producers of Greece's trademark feta cheese. But the amateur Voukefalas club—whose players include pizza delivery guys, students, waiters, and a bartender—has raised eyebrows with its flamboyant sponsorship choice.

"Unfortunately, amateur football has been abandoned by almost everyone," said Yiannis Batziolas, the club's youthful chairman, who runs a travel agency and is the team's backup goalkeeper.

It's a question of survival. Prostitution is legal in Greece, where brothels operate under strict guidelines. Though garish neon signs advertising their services are tolerated, the soccer sponsorship has ruffled some feathers in the sports-mad city of Larissa.

League organizers have banned the pink jerseys during games, saying the deal violates the sporting ideal and is inappropriate for underage fans. Brothel owner Soula Alevridou, the team's new benefactor, has already paid more than 1,000 Euros (~$1,350) for players to wear her jerseys.

The team is appealing the game ban, but that doesn't worry the 67-year-old Alevridou, who says she's only in it because she loves soccer. "It's not the kind of business that needs promotion," she said, dressed all in white and flanked by two young women in dark leggings at a recent game.

"It's a word-of-mouth kind of thing," she said. Alevridou watched in disappointment as her team lost its fourth straight game, 1-0, despite her promise to players of "a special time" at her businesses if they won.[55]

ACTIVITY 9.2 The Future of Sports Advertising

In this WSG activity you will determine if it's possible to have too much advertising; for consumer, for marketer, or for both.

ACTIVITY 9.3 The Future of Sponsorships

It's time to look in your crystal ball. Sponsorships have grown over time from signs on outfield walls to the naming rights of stadiums. In this WSG activity, you will think about where you see the future of sponsorships in sport.

ACTIVITY 9.4 Fans and Sponsor Activations

In this WSG activity, you will learn how teams use contests and fantasy sports in unique ways to activate their sponsors' products with the fans.

Wrap-Up

Although ample rationale may support entering into a sponsorship agreement, the key to a successful sponsorship is generating ROI, which is generally attributed to how the sponsorship agreement has been activated. Simply stated, what did you do with what you bought? What types of marketing platforms did you create to engage the target market and achieve your marketing objectives? A great sponsorship opportunity can be ineffective if it is not properly activated to engage the target market.

Sponsorships and licensing agreements should always be positioned as partnerships. Partnerships imply a mutually beneficial relationship, often referred to as a win–win relationship, in terms of consideration, negotiation, obligations, benefits, growth, and trust.[56] For example, Nike, often accused of ambush marketing in its practices, is protective of its own agreements and relationships. Nike never uses the word *sponsor* but always *partner*, believing that the term *sponsor* doesn't take into account the importance of partners' working together to meet the needs and goals of each partner.

To justify the ever-increasing cost of sponsorships, sponsors need to generate a multifaceted ROI, ROO, or ROE. Regardless of the type of return being sought, the return should contain multiple benefits that include one or more of the following: media and exposures, sales opportunities, image enhancement, effective communication with the target market, hospitality opportunities, and brand positioning.

The rationale for entering a sponsorship agreement varies according to the size, mission, vision, geographic scope, target market, and resources of an organization. Regardless of the particulars of the organization, all sponsorship decisions should be based on the suitability and fit of the opportunity with the organization and its priorities, as well as on how the sponsorship opportunity helps achieve organizational objectives.

Activities

1. Contact a local sport organization's corporate sales department and gather information about one of their corporate accounts. How does the team use various platforms to activate their sponsorship?

2. Over the course of 24 hours, track how many selling messages you are exposed to. At the end of the day, which ones do you remember? Why?

3. Give an example of a company involved in sport marketing that has tied goodwill into their campaign. Are they successful? Why or why not?

4. Think of a time when you were the recipient of hospitality benefits at a sport or entertainment event. What did they do well? What could they have added or done differently?

5. What are two things that companies should keep in mind when activating through social media?

6. List the various ways to prospect a potential sponsor.

7. What is the importance of telling a story in a sponsor's activation platform?

8. Choose a company and create a sponsorship activation platform. Use the idea of telling a story throughout your campaign.

Your Marketing Plan

In developing your marketing plan, you have generated a list of objectives, strategies, and tactics. Sponsorship can be instrumental in helping you achieve these elements of a marketing plan by providing the resources (not necessarily just financial) needed to be successful. Integrate one or more of the concepts of sponsorship discussed in this chapter into your marketing plan.

Endnotes

1. http://adage.com/article/media/gaming-platforms-festival-media-gatorade/136640/.

2. www.reuters.com/article/2012/08/04/us-soccer-manchesterunited-jerseys-idUS-BRE8730KV20120804.

3. J.Meehaghan, *Commercial Sponsorship* (West Yorkshire, England: MCB University Press, 1984).

4. www.cfmarketinginc.com/what-is-sponsorship-activation/.

5. For an excellent introduction to ancient athletics and sport, see Donald G. Kyle, *Sport and Spectacle in the Ancient World* (Malden, MA: Blackwell, 2007), 83, 157, 171, quotation on 83.   Herodotus tells the story of Cimon and Peisistratus in his *Histories*, VI, 103. Aristotle's quotation is in *Athenian Constitution*, XVI, 7–8. For the Colosseum, see Flavia Rotondi, "Cash-Poor Italy to Sell Ad Space at Colosseum," *Boston Globe*, 7 August 2010, A-5; "Rome Colosseum Repair to Be Funded by Tods Shoe Firm," *BBC News Europe*, 21 January 2011, www.bbc.co.uk/news/world-europe-12256813.

6. J. Meenaghan, *Commercial Sponsorship* (West Yorkshire, England: MCB University Press, 1984).

7. S.A. Wichmann and D.R. Martin, "Sport and Tobacco—the Smoke Has Yet to Clear," *Physician and Sports Medicine*, 19 (11) (1991): 125–131.

8. N. Meyers and L. Clarke, "No Trouble Foreseen in Finding Sponsors." *USA Today*, 23 June 1997, 3B

9. http://sportsbusinessdigest.com/2010/06/ending-an-era-tobacco-sponsorship-in-nascar/.

10. http://weare2020.com/2020/the-humbling-truth-about-how-people-respond-to-marketing-and-why-it-means-making-magic-is-not-a-luxury-its-a-commercial-imperative/.

11. www.nielsen.com/us/en/newswire/2012/worldwide-internet-ad-spend-grows-more-than-other-media-in-first-half-of-2012.html.

12. http://theweek.com/article/index/222982/the-rising-cost-of-super-bowl-commercials-by-the-numbers.

13. P. Ueberroth, *Made in America* (New York: Morrow, 1985), 61.

14. P.C. Verhoef and P.S.H. Leeflang, "Understanding the Marketing Department's Influence Within the Firm," *Journal of Marketing*, 73(2) (2009): 14–37.

15. W. D'Orio, "Just Doing It," *Promo*, 10 (4) (March 1997): 38.

16. L. Ukman, notes from Sponsorship Trends Workshop, Chicago, 2000.

17. Reprinted in its entirety from www.imrpublications.com/newsdetails.aspx?nid=22.

18. Sutton, W.A., "Sutton Impact: Proposed Legislation Has Sports Business in Crosshairs," *SSSBJ*, 15 (16) (2–6 August 2012): 11.

19. M. Hanan, *Life-Styled Marketing* (New York: AMACOM Books, 1980), 2–3.

20. "Healthy Choice Creates Integrated Promotions Around Ski Team Deal," *IEG Sponsorship Report*, 16 (16) (18 August 1997): 1–3.

21. D. Wilber, "Linking Sports and Sponsors," *Journal of Business Strategy* (July–August 1998): 8–10.

22. J. Meenaghan, *Commercial Sponsorship*.

23. R.L. Irwin, M. Asimakopoulos, and W.A. Sutton, "A Model for Screening Sponsorship Opportunities," *Journal of Promotional Management*, 2 (3–4) (1994): 53–69.

24. T. Lefton, "Lenovo Signing on as NFL's Official PC Supplier," *SSSBJ*, 15 (14) (23–29 July 2012): 1, 37.

25. T. Lefton, "Bowl Takes a Walk on the Wild Wing Side," *SSSBJ*, 15 (14) (23–29 July 2012): 8.

26. T. Lefton, "Lenovo Signing on as NFL's Official PC Supplier," *SSSBJ*, 15 (14) (23–29 July 2012): 1, 37.

27. T. Mickle, "Coke Joins Olympic Sponsors Targeting Moms," *SSSBJ*, 15 (13) (16–22 July 2012): 37.

28. J. Meenaghan, *Commercial Sponsorship*.

29. J. Carlucci, "Linking Sport Sponsorships to the Trade," *Marketing Communications*, November–December 1995, 1–2.

30. E. Rivera, www.magicbasketball.net/2010/08/30/geico-joins-orlando-magic-and-amway-center-as-'champions-of-the-community'-partner/.

31. http://harris.com/sites/amwaycenter/tour.aspx.

32. A.L. Schreiber, *Lifestyle and Event Marketing* (New York: McGraw-Hill, 1994), 140.

33. T. Mickle, "Coke's London Legacy: Higher Sales," *SSSBJ*, 15 (35) (17–23 December 2012): 1, 40.

34. T. Mickle, "BMW: USOC Deal Drives Strong Sales," *SSSBJ*, 15 (31) (19–25 November 2012): 1, 38.

35. S. Lainson, "Client Entertainment," *Sports News You Can Use* (1997), 12, 1–3, slainson@sportstrust.com.

36. T. Lefton, "NFL House Bound for New Orleans," *SSSBJ*, 15 (36) (7–13 January 2013): 4.

37. A. Friedman, "Naming Rights May Be Bargain for Companies Going National," *SSSBJ*, 1 (3) (1998): 8.

38. N. Lieberman, "Banking on Sports: Industry Aims to Score Big With the Consumers," *SSSBJ*, 7 (29) (22–28 November 2004): 19–21.

39. D. Broughton, "Higher Ad Rates Lift NASCAR Exposure Value," *SSSBJ*, 15 (36) (7–13 January 2013): 9.

40. www.sponsorship.com/About-IEG/Sponsorship-Blogs/Lesa-Ikman/july-2011/Sponsorship-Success-Depends-on-Activation.aspx.

41. S. Feil, "The Social Side of Sponsorship: Sports Marketers Take Aim at Activating Fan Engagement," www.adweek.com/sa-article/social-side-sponsorship-137844.

42. John Bevilaqua, www.examiner.com/article/activating-sponsorship, 6 August 2012.

43. http://nypost.com/2009/04/16/yankee-ticket-giveaway-goes-awry/

44. J. Weiner, "Organizations Dismiss Social Media as Fad at Their Own Risk," *SSSBJ*, 15 (13) (16–22 July 2012): 33.

45. S. Feil, "The Social Side of Sponsorship: Sports Marketers Take Aim at Activating Fan Engagement," www.adweek.com/sa-article/social-side-sponsorship-137844.

46. Compiled from S. Feil, "The Social Side of Sponsorship."

47. www.sponsorship.com/IEG/files/9e/9ef94c06-70ad-4fb0-b555-a26a17eb4827.pdf.

48. Ibid.

49. Sponsors Rely Less on Ads, Signage, 2012 Sponsorship Decision Makers Survey, IEG, Chicago (1 May 2012).

50. www.forbes.com/2009/07/07/banking-marketing-advertising-business-sports-boa.html.

51. www.sponsorship.com/iegsr.aspx

52. N. Lieberman, "Cultivating an Organic Approach," *SSSBJ*, 7 (44) (14–20 March 2005): 8.

53. Phone interview with Adam Helfant, 15 September 2005.

54. http://content.usatoday.com/communities/gameon/post/2011/08/tiger-woods-losing-another-corporate-sponsor-tag-heuer-spilt-partways-amicable/1#.UQSy8qXUNMM;

http://epubs.scu.edu.au/cgi/viewcontent.cgi?article=1573&context=tourism_pubs&seiredir=1&referer=http%3A%2F%2Fwww.google.com%2Furl%3Fsa%3Dt%26rct%3Dj%26q%3Dethical%2520issues%2520in%2520sport%2520sponsorship%26source%3Dweb%26cd%3D7%26ved%3D0CGYQFjAG%26url%3Dhttp%253A%252F%252Fepubs.scu.edu.au%252Fcgi%252Fviewcontent.cgi%253Farticle%253D1573%2526context%253Dtourism_pubs%26ei%3Dv60EUeW4FYSy9gTWrYCYBA%26usg%3DAFQjCNEWRIKTK4tKY_97pzTLCeZghD5_Bw%26sig2%3DCpBb3zx2ZkS00tX8AMsn A%26bvm%3Dbv.41524429%2Cd.eWU#search=%22ethical%20issues%20sport%20sponsorship%22.

55. http://neoskosmos.com/news/en/cash-strapped-greek-soccer-team-rescued-by-brothel.

56. W.A. Sutton and M.A. McDonald, "Building a Partnership," *Athletic Management*, 10 (4) (1998): 16–19.

Chapter 10
Promotion and Paid Media

OBJECTIVES

- To recognize the complexity of promotion with respect to the various forms it can assume as part of the marketing mix

- To understand promotion and its importance in sport through a historical context and to consider how that context has evolved because of the importance of media and sponsorship relationships

- To identify and differentiate between the integral elements of promotion and the advantages and limitations of each

- To appreciate the importance of both price and nonprice promotional strategies and the way in which they are used in the sales process to influence buyer behavior

- To recognize the key characteristics of effective promotional campaigns aimed at expanding existing consumer bases and at increasing frequency of consumption

In the second edition of this text we extolled the virtues and interest in the collectability of Beanie Babies, and in the third edition we crowned bobbleheads as the most popular promotion. Despite a big increase in T-shirt giveaways, bobbleheads were again the most popular giveaway item for Major League Baseball. Twenty-six of the MLB teams gave their fans an estimated 2.27 million bobbleheads, which were distributed over 94 promotional dates throughout the season. This figure represented a whopping 25 percent increase over the number of bobbleheads distributed in 2011, and the total was the highest number of bobbleheads distributed since the first peak in 2008.

Why are bobbleheads so popular? According to Milwaukee Brewers COO Rick Schlesinger, "Bobbleheads are an attendance driver and a key brand identifier. They have a high perceived value, high collectability, and they appeal to every demographic." Bobbleheads can be created to honor past heroes (Babe Ruth), pop culture icons (Elvis and Mickey Mouse), team mascots, team fans, radio and broadcast personalities, and accomplishments (no-hitters).

Will the trend continue? All indications are that it will for a variety of reasons. The estimated cost per item is between $3 and $3.50, depending on the number ordered. Sponsors are willing to pay for the opportunity to place their name or logo on a perceived collectible that is on display for years on someone's desk or dresser or in his "man cave." The number of subjects for bobbleheads would seem to be infinite, comprising both real people and fictional characters. One of my favorite bobbleheads (my collection includes an Elvis bobblehead from the Memphis Grizzlies) is Rick Vaughn, or more accurately Wild Thing, from the movie *Major League*, which was a giveaway several years ago in Cleveland.[1]

T-shirts and fireworks nights also rank high in popularity—T-shirts because of practicality, wearability, and cost, and fireworks because of their high cost, unique nature, and inability to be easily duplicated or provided by another source.

Based on Major League Baseball 2013; D. Broughton, 2012, "Everybody loves bobbleheads," *Street & Smith's SportsBusiness Journal* 15(3): 9.

This chapter focuses primarily on advertising and the premise of promotion. Publicity in sport and its inherent elements of public relations, media relations, and community relations is addressed in depth in chapter 11. The sales process, including personal selling, is examined in detail in chapter 8. In this chapter, after discussing how these basic activities apply to promotion, we consider their potential for attracting consumers, placing them on the escalator, and moving them up that escalator of increasing involvement.

The Catchall P: Promotion

Promotion, another of the Ps in sport marketing, is a catchall category for any of the numerous activities designed to stimulate consumer interest in, awareness of, and purchase of the product. Promotion involves the vehicles through which the marketer conveys information about product, place, and price. More important, promotion is a critical element for positioning a product and its image in the mind of the consumer. Promotion concentrates on selling the product; without sales, a company will not be in operation long. Although selling does not equal marketing, it is a vital component.

The marketing term *promotion* includes the following forms of marketing activity:

- **Advertising**: any paid, nonpersonal (not directed to individuals), clearly sponsored message conveyed through the media
- **Personal selling**: any face-to-face presentation in which the seller has an opportunity to have a dialogue and persuade the consumer
- **Publicity**: any form of exposure in the media not paid for by the beneficiary or within the control or influence of the beneficiary

- **Sales promotion**: a wide variety of activities including displays, trade shows, sampling, couponing, premium items, exhibitions, performances, and other attractions or events appropriate for the sales activity

To be successful, promotional efforts should follow the AIDA approach. That is, such efforts should include the following steps:

A: increase **a**wareness

I: attract **i**nterest

D: arouse **d**esire

A: initiate **a**ction

When we think of the term *promotion*, we are drawn to the Veeck family—the late Hall of Fame owner and legendary promoter Bill, and his son, minor league owner and impresario Mike. We refer to the Veecks throughout this text, but one of our favorite images of the term *promotion* was coined by Mike at a National Basketball Association Game Presentation Workshop. When asked what the word *promotions* meant to him, Mike responded by suggesting that to be effective in promotions, people may have to change the culture of their organizations. Mike began writing the letters used in spelling promotions on a white board. This is what he produced:[2]

P = people, publicity, price, planning, and passion

R = relevant, reward, risk, research, and reaction

O = opportunity, originality, and organization

M = motivation, momentum, money, and media

O = outrageous

T = try

I = innovate, initiate, incite, idea, and imagination

O = overdeliver

N = never say no

S = smile, shake it up, service

To get a true grasp on what the *p* in *promotion* means, think about the concepts in this list and consider them throughout this chapter.

ACTIVITY 10.1 Promotions

In this WSG activity, Ayron Sequeira will walk you through how a promotion can affect different parts of the Promotion Wheel and how AIDA is important to market the team.

ACTIVITY 10.2 Two Teams and Their Promotions

In this WSG activity, you are the director of marketing and promotions for your favorite team. You want to compare and contrast your team's promotions with the promotions of your team's archrival.

Advertising

As with all forms of promotion, the core of advertising is effective communication. That is, advertising is a communication process and is subject to the same problems as any other communication process. A major problem in advertising is perceptual distortion, which occurs when the receiver of a message interprets it differently from the way the sender intended. This phenomenon can cause misunderstanding of advertising messages, which may prevent marketers from reaching their advertising goals. Thus, in terms of advertising and other promotional activities, the sport marketer must operate under the axiom that perception is reality. In other words, the sport marketer must attempt to ensure that the message is targeted, clear, and specific so that the receiver comprehends it. If this doesn't happen, the sport marketer will have to work to address the misperception and correct it because for the consumer the misperception has become the marketing reality and she or he will act or not act accordingly.

Multipurpose athletics and fitness clubs have recognized the need to communicate to a target market that might want the same things—better appearance, social interaction, conditioning, health, and enjoyment—but with various levels of intensity, commitment, regimen, and time. Thus, the advertising message must not be limited to beautiful bodies sweating to "feel the burn." Such messages suggest too much agony and single-minded purpose for whole segments of the market that fall into the categories of deconditioned and dropped out. The fitness industry has worked diligently to create advertising campaigns that present images combining fitness, social interaction, achievability, fun, and togetherness as well as appearance and health. Perceptual distortion cannot be eliminated, but through attention to message construction, the marketer can reduce the amount of distortion.

ACTIVITY 10.3 Media in Sports

In this WSG activity, assume you're the executive vice president of marketing for a Fortune 500 company. The company's board of directors wants some information about the media and sport, and it wants your recommendations about advertising during the Super Bowl and the Olympics.

What Should Advertising Accomplish?

According to Batra, Myers, and Aaker, an advertising message can have a variety of effects on the receiver or intended audience.[3] An advertising message can create awareness, communicate information about attributes and benefits, develop or change an image or personality, associate a brand with feelings and emotions, create norm groups, and precipitate behavior. Sport shares many of these advertising goals. News releases and press conferences, common in sport, are used to create awareness about new developments such as personnel moves, product innovations, upcoming promotional events, special events and activities, and even offers that can be positioned as new or newsworthy.

The sidebar is a press release from the Phoenix Mercury, WNBA, and LifeLock. The release had multiple purposes including the following:

- Introduce and explain a new relationship between the Phoenix Mercury, the WNBA, and LifeLock
- Discuss the rationale for the relationship
- Identify what will happen as a result of this partnership
- Define the roles of each party
- Detail the potential significance of the partnership
- Provide contact information for follow up by interested parties

Although a press release is considered publicity rather than advertising, the promotional content and the way it is being presented can often blur the lines between advertising and other forms of promotion, paid or unpaid.

Advertising Communication Process

Figure 10.1 shows the Batra, Myers, and Aaker model of advertising communication system. Advertising communication always involves a perception process and four of the elements shown in the model—the source, a message, a

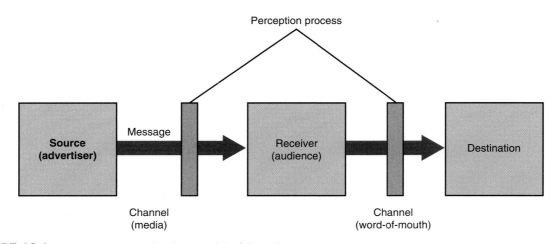

FIGURE 10.1   Batra, Myers, and Aaker model of the advertising communication system.

Reprinted from R. Batra, J. Myers, and D.A. Aaker, 1996, *Advertising management*, 5th ed. (Upper Saddle River, NJ: Prentice-Hall), 47. By permission of Rajeen Batra.

Phoenix Mercury, LifeLock Break New Ground With Partnership and the First-Ever Branded WNBA Team Jersey

Innovative Multiyear Partnership Includes Player Jersey Rights and LifeLock Memberships for All WNBA Season-Ticket Holders

NEW YORK—The Phoenix Mercury and LifeLock have entered a multiyear marketing partnership to launch the first-ever branded jersey in WNBA or NBA history, it was announced today by Phoenix Mercury President and COO Jay Parry and LifeLock CEO Todd Davis at a press conference at the NBA Store in New York City. LifeLock is an industry leader in identity theft protection.

Highlighting the innovative alliance, which runs through 2011, is the appearance of the LifeLock name on the front of Phoenix Mercury's player jerseys and on warm-up suits. The Mercury and LifeLock are the first to finalize such an agreement following the WNBA's decision this off-season to make this unique opportunity available for its teams and sponsors.

As part of the marquee partnership and a big benefit for the league's most devoted fans, LifeLock will be offering a one-year complimentary membership valued at $110 each to season-ticket holders of all WNBA teams. In addition, all fans can take advantage of a special offer to receive a free membership for one child 16 and under in their immediate family with the discounted purchase of an adult membership.

"I'm extremely proud to have LifeLock associated with the Phoenix Mercury and the WNBA," said Davis. "While this partnership allows us to be the first organization to support a team and league in a unique, pioneering way, it's also a natural fit for LifeLock to align with WNBA to reach its loyal and passionate fan base."

"This groundbreaking partnership with LifeLock represents an important next step in the growth of the WNBA," said NBA commissioner David Stern. "We are confident that its alliance with the Mercury and the WNBA will accelerate LifeLock's growth, and this deal serves as a blueprint for other associations of its kind with all our WNBA teams."

"LifeLock and the Mercury are leading organizations in our respective fields, which is why we are thrilled to be able to align our missions for the advancement of our community, our fans and the WNBA as a whole," said Parry. "This partnership will go beyond the court and will broaden the opportunities for LifeLock, the Mercury and the WNBA to continue to flourish."

In addition to player jersey rights, the partnership includes on-court apparel, in-arena signage, branding on the court, exposure on PhoenixMercury.com, including all social media outlets and e-marketing efforts. The collaboration also includes the launch of the LifeLock SafeZone basketball and life mentoring programs for underserved girls.

"Since its inception, the WNBA continues to redefine the sports landscape and this LifeLock partnership is consistent with the league's innovative mindset," said WNBA President Donna Orender. "The WNBA's iconic status continues to inspire young people around the world and we are pleased to team up with LifeLock."

Diana Taurasi, Mercury guard and three-time WNBA All-Star, emphasized the loyalty that WNBA players and fans have for those who support the league. "I join all WNBA players in thanking LifeLock for believing in our dream," said Taurasi. "I'll be proud to wear the jersey, and this great new partnership recognizes the value of our game and the power of our incredible fans."

The WNBA tips off its 13th season on Saturday, June 6. The Phoenix Mercury hosts the San Antonio Silver Stars and tickets start at just $10. For tickets and information, call (602) 252-WNBA or visit phoenixmercury.com.

> continued

> continued

About the Phoenix Mercury

The Phoenix Mercury, one of the eight original WNBA teams, tips off its 13th season on Saturday, June 6, vs. the San Antonio Silver Stars. Last season the Mercury became the first team in WNBA history to lead the league in scoring for three consecutive seasons. The franchise, which won the state's first professional basketball title in 2007, is led by All-Stars Diana Taurasi and Cappie Pondexter, who in 2008 became the first teammates in WNBA history to finish as the league's first and second leading scorers. The Phoenix Mercury organization was recently named as one of the top 20 places for females to work, by the *Arizona Republic*.

About LifeLock

LifeLock is a proactive identity theft protection service providing consumers with confidence and control as an answer for their good faith suspicion of becoming the next victim. LifeLock (www.lifelock.com) leads the charge against the crime by educating consumers, working with law enforcement, developing leading services/products, and doing what it should for members.

About the WNBA

The WNBA is a unique global sports property combining competition, sportsmanship, and entertainment value with its status as an icon for social change, achievement, and diversity. Composed of 13 teams, the WNBA is the most successful women's professional team sports league in the world. The league concluded its historic 12th regular season with increases in attendance, ratings, web traffic and merchandise sales. The 2009 WNBA season will tip off June 6 on ABC.

Through WNBA Cares, the WNBA is deeply committed to creating programs that improve the quality of life for all people, with a special emphasis on programs that promote a healthy lifestyle and positive body image, increase breast and women's health awareness, support youth and family development, and focus on education. For more information on the WNBA, log on to www.wnba.com.

---

communication channel, and a receiver (note that the receiver can also become a source by talking to friends or associates, commonly referred to as word-of-mouth communication).[4]

- **Source**—can be defined as the originator of the message. Several types of sources are used in the context of advertising, especially in sport. For example, the NBA is a source of advertising in disseminating its message "Where Amazing Happens." The Golden State Warriors, an NBA team that participated in the 2013 NBA playoffs, can also be a source for their own advertising message; they are using the message "#WeAre-Warriors."

- **Message**—can be defined as both the content and execution of the message. In practice, the message is the actuality of what the receiver of the message has perceived.

- **Channel**—refers to one or more kinds of media (such as the Internet, social media, radio, television, newspapers, magazines, billboards [fixed and mobile]), point-of-purchase displays, signage, logo placement (on scoreboards, dasher boards, ice, race cars, uniforms and apparel, caps, premiums and giveaway items, game programs), virtual signage, and special events. DVD T-shirts (DVtees) and the New Era New York Yankees cap image are excellent examples of the new types of channels being used by today's sport and entertainment marketers.

- **Receiver**—commonly refers to the target market for the message, the intended audience. The receivers (or audience), as in the case of any target market, usually share certain demographic, psychographic, or behavioral traits. In the context of sport marketing, these traits may include

DVtees are an interesting and effective way to reach millennials.

type of tickets owned, zip code, past purchasing history, children in the household, alumni status, demographic segment, and social media history.

• **Destination**—In many cases the message doesn't end with the receiver because the receiver may continue to disseminate the message through word of mouth or personal contact, thus becoming a source. This process is especially prevalent in sport, which because of its emphasis and place within society elicits significantly more interest and coverage (media) than most other topics. According to McKinsey & Co., word of mouth is the primary factor behind 20 to 50 percent of all purchasing decisions and given its influence will probably grow; the digital revolution has amplified and accelerated its reach to the point where word of mouth is no longer an act of intimate, one-on-one communication.[5] Today, it also operates on a one-to-many basis as product reviews are posted online and as opinions are disseminated through social networks.

Some customers even create websites or blogs to praise or punish brands.[6]

Advertising Media for Sport

We have examined the advertising message model and what advertising hopes to accomplish. A sport organization must decide which form or forms of media to use in an advertising campaign. In the following section we examine the various advertising mediums commonly used in sport or unique to sport. Each has its own set of advantages and disadvantages.

Signage

Signage includes electronic or printed messages or logos that identify a sponsor on any of the following types of materials: banners, street-pole attachments, billboards (fixed or movable), scoreboards, dasher boards or rink boards, electronic

LED Signage: Bringing Your Message to Life

Chris Heck, Chief Revenue Office, Philadelphia 76ers

In layman's terms, LED signage presents moving, changing, dynamic graphic images that the sport arena or stadium uses as a continuous display for general and specific advertising or visual entertainment for the audience. LED signage is a powerful vehicle for market visibility and sponsor recall. Creating a wow factor is what facility managers, corporate spokespersons, and game presentation directors should aspire to when communicating with their customers. LED signage provides displays that depict sharp images, brilliant color, and larger-than-life pictures that can capture the attention of sports fans and concertgoers who are exposed to thousands of messages every day. LED signage can be combined with sound to provide a multidimensional forum that brings the message to life for its audience.

LED signage has numerous advantages over static and rotational signage, namely the following:

- Higher resolution and clarity
- Movement
- Animation
- Sound
- Portability—can be updated by simply programming, requiring no hard production costs or delays
- Flexibility—variety of sizes and shapes
- Real-time alterations
- Life cycle—can be updated electronically as frequently as needed
- Increased inventory—no space needed to store

Perhaps the greatest advantage of LED signage is that it permits the venue, organization, or team to sell advertising based on time, not space. Thus, every purchaser's message has a prime location and can be given as much exposure as the purchaser desires.

---

message boards including LED displays, and posters. Signage also includes impressions such as in-ice and on-field messages, rotational courtside messages, on-court or on-field logos, and virtual signage (superimposed on blank stadium walls and playing surfaces but visible on television).

Virtual advertising is made possible by a live video insertion system, or L-VIS, a "proprietary technology that interrupts the broadcast feed and inserts electronic images in real time into any video stream."[7] That tool may ultimately end up creating two signage revenue streams—one for those viewing in the arena and one for those watching on television. For example, a Canadian live audience could be viewing signage for Molson while the TV audience in the United States for the same game could be watching virtual signage that converts the image to one for Coors.

The definition of signage has also been expanded to include logo placement opportunities, which are most commonly found on race cars (all types); racing boats; driver uniforms; professional golfers' caps and shirts; and professional tennis players' caps, headbands, and rackets. In some cases, the name of the sponsor is also the name of the team, as in Italian basketball (e.g., Armani Jeans of Milan).

Although signage conveys a message, it is not a spoken, scripted, or consistent message. The message that the signage conveys is more accurately described as an impression. The message is received and acted on based on the awareness and feelings of the receiver with regard to the sender. Because of the large amount of clutter (number of advertising messages and impressions) in American (and for that matter most of global) society, many messages or impressions are not received because the intended audience

Allstate's highly visible field goal nets and other stadium signage have been featured at NCAA football games, including the Allstate Sugar Bowl.

has built up an immunity, that is, has become so accustomed to advertising messages that they do not stand out. As sport marketers have become more reliant on advertising revenue from sponsors wishing to communicate to their audiences, they have had to search for new ideas and creative concepts and placements for these messages. Several studies have shown that creative placement results in higher recognition and reception of the message. Stotlar and Johnson concluded that advertising messages that have become part of the game, such as those placed on or in front of the scorer's table, were more effective than those placed elsewhere.[8] Pope and Voges found that automobile manufacturers looking to increase product awareness were effective in achieving that objective using on-site displays and vehicle and equipment signage.[9]

Exposure to corporate names and logos at sport venues can increase product awareness and may subsequently lead to loyal product consumption by spectators.[10] This potential for consumption of sponsor products and services plays a key role in the level of creativity and ingenuity we find in sport advertising. In February 2006 at the NBA All-Star Game in Houston, Toyota was able to leverage its unique position of becoming the first NBA partner to hold naming rights to the all-star venue, Houston's Toyota Center, home of the NBA Houston Rockets. Toyota was able to use February's all-star week in Houston as a launching pad for a variety of activities, including the rollout of a national sweepstakes, the introduction of new car lines, and a sponsorship of the all-star practice sessions. In addition, Toyota had the Tundra Zone, featuring a permanent vehicle display in the Toyota Center.[11] This kind of exposure was replicated to an extent by Kia, who succeeded Toyota as the official vehicle of the NBA and had a similar permanent product placement in Orlando's Amway Center, home of the 2012 NBA All-Star Game.

Signage is often one element of an integrated sponsorship purchase. It may be the most important element of the sponsorship for some companies but just a value-added component for others (i.e., not the core benefit but a benefit of secondary value or importance). For example, Allstate Insurance signed a significant deal to become a sponsor of the 2005 Bowl Championship Series. One of the platforms was the field goal net, but that was only a portion of the sponsorship agreement. The momentous marketing coup was part of Allstate's comprehensive 2005 Bowl Championship Series (BCS) college football sponsorship. In addition to the innovative goalpost net signage, Allstate has maintained a significant presence in the college football space since the inception of this agreement with a fan-friendly mobile tailgate Field Goal Fan-tastic Tour, a national consumer promotion that will award one lucky fan a trip to the BCS Championship Game, a new college football–themed television advertising campaign, and other ambient efforts to engage football fans at stadiums across the country.[12]

Endorsements

Brooks and Harris incorporated the work of McCracken and of Friedman and Friedman in defining a celebrity athlete endorser as an athlete who uses his or her fame to help a company sell or enhance the image of the company, products, or brands (table 10.1).[13] According to McCracken, a celebrity athlete can assume one product endorsement style or a combination of several styles: (1) the explicit mode (I endorse this product), (2) the implicit mode (I use this product), (3) the imperative mode (you should use this product), and (4) the copresent mode (in which the athlete merely appears in some setting with the product).[14]

According to Burt Sugar, the first recorded instance of a modern athlete's leasing his name (to endorse a sport product) occurred on September 1, 1905, when Honus Wagner (later enshrined as one of the four original inductees into the Baseball Hall of Fame) of the Pittsburgh Pirates gave the J.F. Hillerich & Son Company permission to use his name on its Louisville Slugger bats for a consideration of $75. Other athletes such as Ty Cobb and Babe Ruth soon began to endorse products for payment.[15]

The growing popularity of pro football, basketball, baseball, golf, tennis, and motorsports has led to the proliferation of the sport celebrity. Brand identity has become one of the primary reasons that advertisers closely link their products with sport; in some cases, fans seem to identify as closely with the sponsor as with the sport itself. Michael Jordan popularized Nike's Air Jordan shoe and eventually was able to create his own brand (in conjunction with Nike) called Jordan Brand. Jordan Brand, the company, is raking revenue of over $1 billion annually and dominates its market. Three out of every four pairs of basketball shoes sold in the United States are Jordan Brand, and 86.5 percent of all basketball shoes that are sold at a price over $100 are Jordan

TABLE 10.1   2012 Top Athlete Endorsement Earnings

Athlete	Sport	Endorsements ($ in millions)
Phil Mickelson	Golf	$57.0
Tiger Woods	Golf	$54.5
LeBron James	Basketball	$33.0
Kobe Bryant	Basketball	$28.0
Dale Earnhardt Jr.	Auto racing	$24.0
Derrick Rose	Basketball	$18.2
Jeff Gordon	Auto racing	$18.0
Tony Stewart	Auto racing	$15.4
Jimmie Johnson	Auto racing	$14.7
Peyton Manning	Football	$13.0

Data from M. McKnight, 2013, "Fortunate 50: The highest-earning American athletes," *SI.com*. Available: http://sportsillustrated.cnn.com/specials/fortunate50-2012/index.html?iid=EL

Brand. Jordan Brand has a 10.8 percent share of the overall U.S. shoe market, which makes it the second biggest brand in the country (behind only its parent company, Nike) and more than twice the size of Adidas' share, JB's closest competitor.[16]

The selection of endorsers should always be predicated on the product or service and its target market. One way to select an endorser who may be popular with a particular target market is to use Q Scores. Q Scores, according to their website, is the recognized industry standard for measuring consumer appeal of personalities, characters, licensed properties, programs, and brands.[17] Going back to our Michael Jordan example, Jordan has had the top Q Score among sports fans every year since 1987. The one exception was in 1990, when Joe Montana usurped him for a single year. (Tiger Woods is the only athlete to top Jordan's Q Score among the general population, which he did once in 2008.) "Jordan is unique in that he has been able to maintain that emotional connection with his consumer base for more than 25 years," says Henry Schafer, executive vice president at the Q Score Company.[18]

On the other end of the spectrum we find Lance Armstrong, at one time one of the most admired athletes and endorsers not only in the United States but globally as well. After admitting to cheating throughout his cycling career and being engaged in a variety of cover-up activities to protect his accomplishments and his reputation, he is now a pariah to those who employed him as an endorser, as well as to his Livestrong Foundation and the millions of people who bought the famous yellow Livestrong bracelets. In late April 2013 Armstrong and his reputation sustained another epic assault when the U.S. Postal Service filed litigation against Armstrong in an attempt to recover the almost $40 million they paid to sponsor the team from 1998 through 2004. Armstrong's Q Score reflects that more than one in four respondents viewed him negatively. Still, however, he was thought of more positively than was Tiger Woods, who was viewed negatively by 43 percent of those responding to the Q Score survey.[19] Armstrong lost his endorsement opportunities in a short time, led by Nike, who dropped Armstrong despite a mutually beneficial and profitable relationship that had lasted more than a decade. After Nike dropped Lance, Trek Bicycles, Giro (bike helmets), FRS (energy products), Honey Stinger, 24 Hour Fitness, Anheuser-Busch (Michelob Ultra), RadioShack, and Oakley all

soon followed suit. Nike, acting quickly and obviously concerned about how their previous endorser might damage their brand (and revenue streams) but also hoping not to alienate cancer survivors and believers in the Livestrong philosophy, released the following statement:

> Due to the seemingly insurmountable evidence that Lance Armstrong participated in doping and misled Nike for more than a decade, it is with great sadness that we have terminated our contract with him. Nike does not condone the use of illegal performance enhancing drugs in any manner. Nike plans to continue support of the Livestrong initiatives created to unite, inspire, and empower people affected by cancer.[20]

Another interesting endorsement phenomenon, which employs all four of the modes previously described by McCracken, is the relationship between high-profile rappers and various brands of liquor. Reference to the high life of liquor or drugs is nothing new to rap. A study released from the University of Pittsburgh and Dartmouth University found that for every hour that American teens listen to music, they hear more than three references to brand-name alcohol in rap, R&B, and hip-hop lyrics. Brand associations have long been a symbol of status for performers. But Pitbull and contemporaries Sean "Diddy" Combs, Ludacris, Snoop Dogg, and many others have now taken it to the next level. Instead of just referring to the products they enjoy, they're rapping about products they're selling. Pitbull has transformed his latest videos into not-so-subliminal ads for Voli, in which he owns a stake. He is the latest in a string of business savvy rappers taking the phrase "popping bottles" to the bank by aligning themselves as spokespersons for liquors, often creating their own branded vanity lines. "[Voli] gave me a great opportunity to be an owner of a brand that I really believed in," said Pitbull, born Armando Christian Perez. He became part owner of the line of low-calorie fruit and fusion-flavored vodkas in March. "That's why I got involved with Voli. It's in a market where it's needed and everybody wants it."[21]

This relationship might be referred to as a retroactive endorsement, because Primack, Nuzzo, Rice, and Sargent determined that most instances of brand-name references in song lyrics seem to be unsolicited and unpaid for by advertising companies. The authors note, however, that the line between paid advertising and brand references is difficult to distinguish because advertising companies have begun to reward artists retroactively with product, sponsorship, or endorsement deals after a song containing their product's name becomes popular.[22]

So how can corporations minimize the risk of using celebrities as endorsers? One way would obviously be to tie their compensation into product sales through bonuses and stock options. According to Lowell Traub, head of endorsements for CAA Sports, "The one trend that I've seen is athletes' willingness to take on a bit more risk and potentially forego some of the cash in a deal, depending on if there is stock available or a startup that has private shares. I would call it the 50 Cent phenomenon."[23] What Traub is referring to was the equity stake that rapper 50 Cent received form Glaceau's Vitaminwater as part of an endorsement deal. The rapper reaped millions (estimated between $60 and $100 million) when Coca-Cola bought Vitaminwater for $4 billion in 2007.[24]

Retired athletes are another safer alternative to current athletes. We have already discussed the Michael Jordan influence, which continues more than 10 years after his retirement. Steve Rosner, a talent expert, offers this opinion: "What guys do after hours is very much an issue. So it's a little bit safer to go with someone who is 40 years old and credible." Retired athletes are safer, and their credibility and relevance has been nurtured because "all of them grew up in front of us, blossoming at a time when the emergence of ESPN and the investments of a few sneaker companies changed the way consumers view athletes."[25] Obviously, after Dennis Rodman's interesting trip to North Korea in 2013, not all former athletes can be considered risk free.

In a less traditional approach, some clever marketers have hit on another solution to control behavior and hence the image of their endorsers—make sure that they're dead. According to one recent estimate, the size of the market for dead celebrities is about $800 million annually and is growing rapidly.[26] One reason for their popularity, in addition to the safety factor, is that dead celebrities allow advertisers to tap into feelings of nostalgia about times spent gathered around the television watching classic shows—an emotion that reverberates with baby boomers

in particular.[27] Sport marketers have embraced this tactic as well. Jackie Robinson appeared on Wheaties boxes and commemorative Coca-Cola bottles, and famous contemporary athletes thanked him on video in a 1997 Nike commercial. Robinson's estate was projected to earn millions of dollars in endorsement fees, all after he had been dead for more than 25 years.[28]

Will this form of advertising and endorsement become more popular in sport? The question is difficult to answer; most interest in this area appears to be about using dead celebrities with more of a pop culture attraction in the entertainment area. Marilyn Monroe and Elvis Presley have been popular endorsers, in part because of the supply of video from film and television. So although we might want to see Babe Ruth, Ted Williams, or Roberto Clemente, a better prediction is that someday we will see the Beatles, Michael Jackson, or Princess Diana as spokespersons.

Print Media

Print media is the inclusive term used to refer to newspapers, magazines, brochures, posters, programs, point-of-purchase displays, direct mail pieces, and all other forms of printed collateral. Among all forms of print media, newspapers (although the print version is on the decline) have several clear-cut advantages. They are timely because in most cases they are published daily. Day-of-game, membership promotion, or special sales advertising can be placed in a newspaper with short advance notice. The advertising cost is lower than it is for most forms of electronic media such as television. Ads can be placed not only in sports or business sections but also in lifestyle sections, special weekend inserts, and so forth. Although magazines have the advantage of high print quality and color reproduction, they are usually published weekly or monthly. They are also accessible on the Internet. Print circulation (newspapers, magazine, and so on) has been dropping annually over recent years, as seen in figure 10.2.[29] As could be expected, print advertising allocation is declining as a percentage of the advertising budget, and much of that decrease is being reallocated to website advertising and other forms of E-marketing.

Posters are also declining in popularity, but they offer a unique advantage—namely, degree of control—because the organization can determine where and when to distribute them. They can also

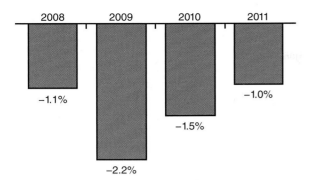

| 2008 | 2009 | 2010 | 2011 |

−1.1%

−2.2%

−1.5%

−1.0%

FIGURE 10.2 All print circulation has declined between 2008 and 2011. Note: Data represent circulation numbers for magazines reported for the last six months audited for each year, ending December 31.

Reprinted, by permission, K.E. Matsa, T. Rosenstiel, and P. Moore, 2011, "Pew Research Center's project for excellence in journalism," *The State of the News Media*. Available: http://www.nacda.com/nacda/nacda-mentoring-institute.html

be self-financing, because the sponsoring organization can sell advertising space on the posters to pay for printing and materials. High schools and collegiate athletics programs (and some minor league sport organizations) are likely to use this form of advertising to list team schedules, upcoming promotions, and special events for their various athletics teams. Although this form of promotion can provide sponsor impressions and drive to retail opportunities, the major limitation is that posters are limited to an immediate area of exposure impact dependent on attraction and flow. Critics might also point out that posters are not green and often contribute to a litter problem.

Game or event programs can be self-liquidating and, depending on the timeliness and uniqueness of the information and the collectible aspect of the publication, can be quite lucrative. The program itself, with its photographs, stories, and statistics, promotes the organization or event and serves as an excellent public relations tool.

Posters and programs may also be part of a point-of-purchase (POP) promotion—a promotional activity that takes place at the moment of purchase. Retailers have relied for years on POP promotions. Retailers must now compete with the Internet for impulse purchases, putting more pressure on the sales environment in their stores and increasing the need for innovative point-of-purchase media, materials, and techniques.[30] For example, a sporting goods store may offer an instant rebate through a couponing activity at the store to encourage the purchase of a particular brand or product, such as athletics footwear,

during the customer's visit. POP promotion is often referred to as reminder advertising. Reminder advertising works in several ways. It can enhance the top-of-mind awareness of the brand, thus increasing the probability that the consumer will include the brand on the shopping list or purchase it as an impulse item. Additionally, it can reinforce the key elements of a national advertising campaign at the point of purchase.[31]

Pocket schedules have been a key print element for sport teams for many years and will continue to be so. The primary function of a pocket schedule is to convey team schedule information—game times, opponents, and dates—in an inexpensive yet convenient format. The pocket schedule also lists promotional events and giveaway-item games in the upcoming season as well as provides contact information and ticket-purchasing instructions. The pocket schedule also serves as a revenue generator because it usually contains the logo of one or more corporate partners (and possibly an offer) who assume the printing and productions costs (and may be charged a licensing fee) for the schedule. In recent times, another print product is the magnetic team schedule, which serves the same purpose as the pocket schedule but is often given away as a premium item on opening day to promote the season.

Direct mail advertising is used widely in the sport industry. Its major advantage is that it reaches only the people whom the organization wants to reach, thus minimizing spending on circulating a message to people who have little interest in the contents. Organizations often promote season tickets, partial ticket plans, and single-game tickets through direct mail. One common approach in selling tickets is to cultivate leads from credit card purchases and to develop a direct mail piece, such as a ticket plan brochure, to mail to cardholders. This results in a highly targeted direct mail campaign because the target audience has already demonstrated a familiarity with and a demonstrated interest in the product. Depending on the information contained in the data records, the direct mail piece could be e-mailed to the target, the target could be called directly without the benefit of the direct mail piece, or the call could take place as a follow-up to the e-mail or direct mail piece.

When designing any print materials or, for that matter, e-campaigns, the sport marketer should consider the following guidelines:

- The headline must flag down the target reader and pull him or her into the text about the product, offering a reward for reading on.

- Because most people reading print ads never read beyond the headline, the headline and the visual component must complement each other and tell the story so clearly that someone who looks only at the headline and the visual can get the message without having to read a word of the body copy.

- The body copy should be detailed and specific, support the headline, and be readable and interesting.[32]

- The reader should know what the next steps are, so a clear call to action should be accompanied by instructions about how to respond.

Research has shown that people recall information better when it is presented both pictorially and verbally.[33] For this reason, sport marketers should use carefully designed images to convey their message. Advertisements describing upcoming promotional items or brochures describing facility renovations, all-you-can-eat seats, premium services, facility rental space, and similar items and concepts should contain photographs, artist's renderings, and links to websites for additional visuals and information whenever possible.

Electronic Media

In this section we consider radio, television, scoreboards, LED signage (previously discussed), and public address systems. All are critical (along with the Internet, discussed later) for reaching today's consumer, whether they are in the venue or watching or listening at home, in their cars, or accessing broadcasts on computers or mobile devices such as tablets or smartphones. Scoreboards and LED signage, although they can represent a significant capital investment, are low in cost in terms of producing messages, and they can incorporate animation, video, and sound to produce a more complete and eye-catching message. They are a cost-effective way of reaching a target market that through its presence in the venue has demonstrated interest in and ability to purchase the product. Scoreboards and public address systems can perform a variety of functions. They can be used to sell inventory such as announcements; provide message spaces and logo display for corporate partners; provide information about upcoming games, other events at the venue, special events, and promotional activities; and even do something as simple as recognizing groups in attendance to encourage them to attend again and make others in the audience aware that opportunities and benefits are available to those attending as part of a group.

Radio

Radio provides an audio message that can be powerful and relatively inexpensive. Major League Baseball teams offer 30-second advertising spots for season-long ad campaigns that are affordable. For example, the Pittsburgh Pirates offer a 30-second spot for $350.[34]

Good copy read by an announcer with a following, backed up by the appropriate action noise or music, can transport us to the game or venue. Radio plays to the imagination and lets us hear the message while letting our minds create a picture that may be based on memories, hopeful expectations, or perhaps just wishful thinking. Because each radio station (and format type) has its own audience, sport organizations can choose a format that is compatible with their target market.

In an ethnically diverse country such as the United States, radio permits sport organizations to offer broadcast and advertising opportunities in languages other than English. Radio enables organizations, particularly those located in New York, Florida, Texas, Arizona, and California, to reach out to their fans in their preferred language. Even a team located as far north as the Minnesota Twins offer a 50-game schedule of Spanish-language broadcast games.[35] The trend to broadcast in Spanish (or other languages, depending on the market) will continue to become a best practice as the population of non-native English speakers continues to grow. A good case example is the Los Angeles Dodgers, who were the first MLB team to do a Spanish-language broadcast. The information provided in figure 10.3 shows that the Dodgers have capitalized on their early entry into Spanish-language broadcasting and that the number of Spanish-speaking fans has grown.

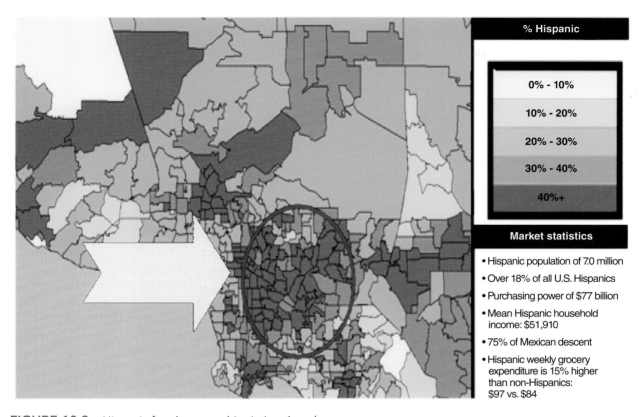

FIGURE 10.3   Hispanic fan demographics in Los Angeles.

From U.S. Census Bureau, *SRC Blue Book 2002*; Geospace International.

- The Dodgers attract more than 1 million Hispanic fans every season.
- Almost half of Dodgers fans (42 percent) in attendance are Hispanic fans.
- Among Hispanic attendees, 40 percent are female.
- Almost half (48 percent) of Hispanic Dodgers fans attend three or more games per year.
- Among Hispanic Dodgers attendees, 55 percent are between 18 and 34 years old.
- The average age of Hispanic Dodgers attendees is 33 (non-Hispanic average age is 43).
- The average household income of Hispanic Dodgers attendees is $61,220, or 21 percent higher than the average L.A. Hispanic ($50,490).
- Of Hispanic Dodgers attendees, 44 percent own their homes.[36]

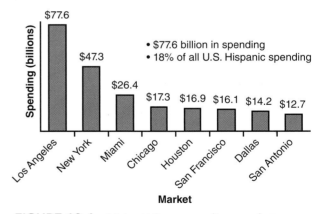

FIGURE 10.4   Major U.S. metropolitan markets.

Strategy Research Corporation's, 2003, *U.S. Hispanic market report.*

Figure 10.4 illustrates the proportion of Hispanic spending in Los Angeles compared with Hispanic spending in other major metropolitan markets.

Internet (streaming) radio and subscription radio is an audio service transmitted on the

Internet. Internet radio involves streaming media, presenting listeners with a continuous stream of audio that cannot be paused or replayed, much like traditional broadcast media. In this respect, it is distinct from on-demand file serving. Internet radio is also distinct from podcasting, which involves downloading rather than streaming. Many Internet radio services are associated with a corresponding traditional (terrestrial) radio station or radio network. Internet-only radio stations are independent of such associations. Currently, more than 300 streaming radio stations have a sport theme or content.[38] Most of this content is free and offers content found in various national (ESPN) and local (The Fan family) stations. Another area is subscription radio (also available through television in many cases), offered by satellite radio provider Sirius/XM. Although these providers provide access to a number of outlets that are available on free Internet radio, they also offer access to paid premium packages offered on radio (and television) by MLB, NASCAR, the NBA, NFL, NHL, and in some cases professional football (soccer) originating outside the United States. The popularity of this type of radio (and television) programming derives from the consumer's ability to listen (and watch) from wherever she or he might be and on a variety of mobile platforms. (See the sidebar "MLB At Bat," which describes both a radio and television product.)

Podcasts

Podcasts are the evolution of radio and can be viewed as complementary, an extension of reach, or a form of competition for attention and listeners or viewers. A podcast is a type of digital media usually consisting of an episodic series of radio, video, PDF, or E-pub files that can be subscribed to and downloaded through web syndication or streamed online to a computer or mobile device. As discussed by Richard Berry, podcasting is both a converged medium bringing together audio, the web, and a portable media player and a disruptive technology that has caused some in the radio business to reconsider established practices and preconceptions about audiences, consumption, production, and distribution. This idea of disruptiveness is largely because no one person owns the technology; it is free to listen to and to create content, which departs from the traditional model of gate-kept media and production tools. Podcasting is a horizontal media form; producers are consumers, and consumers become producers and engage in conversations with each other.[39] Podcasts are not commonly used with live sport programming, but they are used effectively for commentary, sport-themed talk shows, and other types of programming that have a longer shelf life than actual game content.

Television

Although radio has its benefits as compared with television, most notably cost, nothing rivals television in advertising reach and the ability to convey to a mass audience the attributes of an advertiser's product or service. Television has grown in a relatively short time (less than 90 years) from the three national networks (ABC, CBS, and NBC) and the Public Broadcast System (PBS) to four major networks (including FOX) and hundreds of highly segmented channels on cable television and satellite television located

MLB At Bat for iPhone and iPod Touch

The number one source for live baseball, MLB.com At Bat is the official app of Major League Baseball.

New for At Bat 13

- Multiplatform live audio access for At Bat 13 subscribers (portable to Mac or PC with a valid MLB.com account)
- Universal support for At Bat 13 subscribers, accessible on iPhone, iPad, and supported Android phones and tablets
- Redesigned individual team pages
- Updated news section interface
- Classic games library
- Rearchitected navigations
- Additional push notification options
- Closed captioning availability for live video

At Bat 13 Features

- Watch the free MLB.TV Game of the Day or access your MLB.TV premium subscription to watch every out-of-market game
- See key plays and pivotal moments from every game with Live Look-Ins (no blackout restrictions)
- MLB.TV premium subscribers can access and watch archives of every game from the 2013 season on-demand
- Home and away radio broadcasts
- In-progress video highlights
- Enhanced, redesigned Gameday pitch-by-pitch features, including realistic ballpark renderings from all 30 MLB parks
- Condensed games
- Breaking news, standings, schedules, rosters, and stats
- Customize At Bat's home screen to feature a designated favorite team
- Enhanced video library archive, searchable by player, team, or keyword
- Customizable push notifications for game start and end and video highlight availability

At Bat offers several subscription options for access to At Bat 13:

- One-time annual fee of $19.99 for the entire 2013 season
- Monthly recurring fee of $2.99

Requirements: Compatible with iPhone: 3GS, 4, 4S, 5; iPod Touch: 3rd, 4th, 5th generation; and iPad. Requires iOS 5.0 or later.

Based on MLB.com. *At Bat.*

---

throughout the country (and some international programming as well). The NBA was the first professional sport franchise to launch its own network, but it has since been joined by the NFL and Major League Baseball. There is a channel for golf and one for auto racing, and the options will continue to expand. The Mountain West Conference (the first in 2006), Big 10, and Pac-12 all have their own networks, soon to be joined by the SEC. The University of Texas is the sole institution to have its own network.

Television reaches the greatest number of people and conveys both sight and sound. The consumer can watch Albert Pujols hit a mammoth home run, see the fans do the wave, and hear the crack of the bat and the roar of the crowd. High-definition broadcasts, slow-motion replays, a variety of camera angles, and, in limited programming, 3D broadcasts have enhanced the sport-viewing experience. The result has been soaring television ratings and high popularity across the United States, particularly for the NFL. The NBA is probably the most popular of the U.S. sport leagues on a global basis. The NBA has television agreements with 212 countries in 42 languages.[40]

As fewer people watch live television programming because of technology and the freedom not to be tethered, which has led to the decline of appointment viewing, the broadcast networks have come to depend on big events like awards shows, the Olympics, and live sporting events that have a popular following, like the NFL. How popular is the NFL on television?

- Since September 2010, NFL games have broken television records for three consecutive seasons, and they have accounted for 55 percent of the most watched television shows.
- In those three years, of the 247 programs that have reached at least 20 million live viewers, 136 of them have been NFL games.
- Of all TV shows averaging 40 million viewers in that period, 92 percent have been NFL games.[41]

Obviously, premier sporting events and their ability to generate a live audience are important as promotional advertising vehicles for corporations and businesses wanting to use sport to achieve their marketing objectives and ultimately sell their products or services. But as seen in table 10.2, television advertising, because of the high cost related to the events with the largest audiences, may be beyond the budget of many potential advertisers.

TABLE 10.2   2011 Average Prices of a 30-Second Commercial in Selected Live Sport Broadcasts

U.S. sporting events	Price per 30-second message
Super Bowl	$3,100,000
AFC and NFC Championship Games	$1,300,000
NCAA Basketball Championship Game	$1,240,000
College Football BCS Championship Game	$750,000
MLB All-Star Game	$575,000
NBA Finals	$435,000
MLB World Series	$421,000

Data from "Average price of a 30-second TV commercial during major sporting events in the United States in 2011 (in 1,000 U.S. dollars)," *Statistica*.

Just as a story can be told in several ways, audio and visual elements can be combined to produce several types of television commercials. Television commercials can incorporate the following types of structures:

- **Story line**—Telling a story. The message has a beginning, middle, and end.
- **Problem and solution**—Presenting the viewer with a problem to be solved and the sponsor's product as the solution to that problem.
- **Chronology**—Delivering the message through a series of related scenes. Facts and events are presented sequentially as they occurred.
- **Special effects**—Achieving memorability through the use of some striking device, such as an unusual musical sound or pictorial technique.
- **Testimonial**—Advertising by word of mouth. A well-known figure or an unknown man in the street vouches for the value of the product.
- **Satire**—Using sophisticated wit to point out human foibles. This form is generally produced in an exaggerated style, often a parody.
- **Spokesperson**—Using an on-camera announcer who attempts to sell by personal, intimate selling or perhaps by the hard sell.
- **Demonstration**—Using some sort of physical apparatus or experiential element to demonstrate the product's effectiveness, value, and appeal.

Using Your Broadcasts as Sales Tools

Lou DePaoli, EVP/CRO, New York Mets

Over the past 10 to 15 years or so, most professional sport teams have begun airing most, if not all, of their games on television. Previously, many teams believed that airing games on television, specifically home games, would hurt attendance because fans would watch at home rather than buy tickets to the game. Over time teams shifted their philosophy to consider games on TV and radio as three-hour commercials that would generate additional interest in their product, which in turn would cause more games to be broadcast. The shift in philosophy has led organizations to look at their broadcasts as three-hour windows in which to promote their product. Unfortunately, not many teams use that window to its fullest potential to drive additional revenue.

Fortunately, teams that broadcast most of their games have become the norm as opposed to the exception. Many teams, however, stop there and hope that the game itself will lead fans to become more engaged and eventually purchase tickets, merchandise, and so on. My personal philosophy is that if fans are willing to set aside three hours of their time to engage with our product, we need to use that time to market to those fans and get them off the couch and into the ballpark, arena, or stadium. Taking a proactive approach to increasing their level of engagement will lead to additional revenue generation.

One of the biggest concerns that teams and their broadcast rights holders have is being too aggressive and impairing the integrity of the broadcast. A marketer for the team wants to have a quality broadcast but at the same time needs to generate revenue for the organization. Revenue is generated both by selling ads in the broadcast (which can be the domain of the team, rights holder, or shared) and by getting viewers to buy tickets and merchandise, make charitable donations, and so on. Admittedly, it is a fine line to walk, but most organizations are not currently being aggressive enough. Teams need to look at the value of advertising revenues per game compared with the value of generating additional revenues from getting viewers to increase their level of spending with the team through tickets, merchandise, and contributions. A team's broadcast should not be either all media advertising (which currently occurs for some teams) or all focused on team revenue (which doesn't happen currently); rather, a balance between the two must be struck to maximize both sources of revenues.

This discussion leads to the question, What is the proper balance between broadcasting and selling? The answer really depends on a team's current situation in terms of ticket and sponsorship demand, philosophy, and inventory. Regardless of what some organizations might think, inventory is always available to generate revenue whether it is tickets, sponsorship, merchandise, food and beverage, community-based endeavors, ticket wait list, membership clubs, suites, or other items. The key here is to maintain a professional broadcast while not turning it into a three-hour infomercial that will cause viewers to tune out.

Here are just a few ways to use broadcast as a sales tool:

- **Drop-ins**. An essential element to drive revenue in TV and radio broadcasts is drop-ins. Each sport has a different pace of play (e.g., hockey is quick when the puck is in play, but baseball offers frequent breaks during play for foul balls, broken bats, pitching changes, and so on) that will dictate how many and when drop-ins can be used. An example of a drop-in is this: "Hey, fans, don't forget that the New York Mets come to town for a three-game series starting Friday night. You won't want to miss this series against a key NL East rival. Tickets are available by visiting teamwebsite.com or by calling 555-5555." The broadcasters should have a list of these drop-ins at their disposal every game that they can use whenever they have an opportunity to work it into the broadcast.

> continued

- **TV spots**. Running TV spots during broadcasts may sound elementary, but not every team uses their own broadcasts to run their spots. The key here is to make sure that the spots are focused on driving revenue with a strong call to action. Players or the mascot should be used as part of the spot in an effort to (a) provide them exposure outside the playing surface and show that they are regular people just like the viewers and (b) to make the connection between the action at the game and the offer being made.

- **Graphics**. A TV broadcast offers plenty of opportunities to have a graphic appear on the screen highlighting an upcoming game, offer, promotion, or event of interest. The graphic can be a stand-alone at the bottom of the screen, on the score box, or as running text in almost any location. Some of the newer uses of graphics are ghosting a specific social media hashtag in the lower-right corner of the screen and having a full-motion minicommercial there as well while the game is in broadcast. The major TV networks use both of these concepts aggressively to remind viewers of their other programs and upcoming episodes of the current show or to generate social media buzz for the show or the specific episode. Sport teams are now starting to use some of these concepts.

- **In-broadcast-only specials or promotions**. As stated earlier, if viewers have chosen to set aside three hours of their personal time to watch a broadcast, why not market to them? Better yet, why not offer them a special incentive to purchase tickets, merchandise, and so on that is valid only during the broadcast? Or, the team can run a promotion based on what happens in the broadcast, such as offering fans a ticket discount to a future game that has availability based on the number of runs that the team scores or the number of three-pointers that they make. For example, for every run that the Pittsburgh Pirates score in a three-game series versus the Phillies, fans will receive a $1 savings on select seats in the ballpark for a game against the Padres. During the Phillies series every time the Pirates score a run, a graphic of a ticket is shown with the total savings so far. At the end of the series, the total discount is calculated and applied for the Padres series.

- **Strategic use of camera shots**. Having a great relationship with rights holders is important in helping both parties generate revenue. The rights holder is responsible for directing the game, and the team needs to work with the rights holder to develop creative ways to showcase areas within the ballpark, arena, or stadium or provide a behind-the-scenes look at what happens at the event that viewers miss by not being there. Here are two simple examples:

  - The team has a new party area that is shown during the broadcast. Better yet, they have a live read from the new area during the broadcast and show fans having a great time, or they broadcast an entire game from the location. A roaming camera (or possibly preshot footage) could show fans eating some of the great food items, the mascot interacting with fans on the concourse, former players signing autographs for fans, or attendees having a good time with some of the interactive elements at the event. This kind of presentation shows fans why the live experience of attending the game is enjoyable and helps drive some to purchase tickets to attend who might not have otherwise done so.

The preceding are just a few of the concepts that will help turn a broadcast into a sales tool, and more are being developed every day. Teams and their rights holders need to work together to produce a quality broadcast that can generate revenue for both parties.

- **Suspense**—Telling a story, as with the story-line approach, but incorporating a high level of drama into the buildup of curiosity and suspense until the ending.

- **Slice-of-life**—Beginning with a person needing to make a decision or in a situation requiring a solution. This approach then shows how the solution has worked.

- **Analogy**—Instead of presenting a direct message about the product, conveying the message through comparison with something else.

- **Fantasy**—Using caricatures or special effects to create fantasy surrounding the product and product use.

- **Personality**—Relying on an actor rather than an announcer to deliver the message. The actor plays a character who talks about the product, reacts to its use, or demonstrates its use or enjoyment.[42]

Billboards, Blimps, Buses, and 40-Foot-Tall (12 M Tall) Cows

Outdoor ads placed on billboards, on movable billboards, on mobile trailers, on buses, or on other unique promotional platforms can provide a highly visible message, depending on the location and the duration of the placement as well as the uniqueness and appearance of the message. Price varies according to location, the number of placements, and the length of the agreement, but this form of advertising can be relatively inexpensive compared with other forms of advertising like television. Fixed billboards can remain in place over a long time, providing repeated exposure and thus reinforcement of the message.

Billboards mounted on trailers and driven through the marketplace have become commonplace at large special events such as festivals, all-star games, college conference championships, and so forth. The purpose of a movable billboard is twofold. The basic purpose is to draw attention to the event and the message of the advertiser. A second purpose is to expose more people to the message than would ordinarily be the case because a billboard moves throughout a city and within high-traffic locations.

Blimps and small planes trailing advertising banners are also popular forms of outdoor advertising. Companies such as Budweiser, Goodyear, and Fuji have highly visible blimps that travel to sporting events. The concept of blimps has been miniaturized and become a fixture in arenas throughout the United States. A blimp used at Orlando Magic games prior to 2012, sponsored by T.G. Lee Dairy, airdropped coupons, each good for a gallon of milk at participating retailers. In 2012 the blimp was replaced by one that looked like a Southwest Airlines jet because Southwest became a sponsor at the new Amway Center.

But some of the more distinctive forms of outdoor advertising come to us from Chick-fil-A and their agency the Richards Group. According to Stan Richards, principal of the Richards Group, "If any client had asked me years ago whether they could make an impact with a single outdoor billboard, I probably would have said no. That was the conventional thinking at the time. For all my years in advertising, I had heard from media people that you have to have multiple exposures, and if you're going to be on television, people have to see it three times in a two-week period, or whatever the thinking is, to be effective. The Chick-fil-A cows completely changed my view of how advertising works. I know now that if you have one dollar to spend on advertising, spend it doing just one thing one time, and if it's good enough, it will make an impact."[43]

Outdoor advertising can be effective if, in the words of Seth Godin, it has a "purple cow" type of appeal. In other words, does it stand out? Is it unique? Will people remember it and talk about it?

Promotional Concepts and Practices

The remainder of this chapter deals with promotional practices and concepts in the sport industry. Some of the greatest promotions in American history involved sport and entertainment activities. P.T. Barnum, Albert Spalding, C.C. Pyle, Tex Rickard (see the sidebar that follows), Abe Saperstein, Rube Foster, J.W. Wilkinson, Ned Irish, Bill Veeck, Charlie Finley, Walt Disney, Evel Knievel, Don King, Mike Veeck, Madonna, Vince McMahon, Howard Stern, Alice Cooper, Dennis Rodman, Jerry Jones, and Lady Gaga are just a few of the imaginative minds that sought to promote products (or themselves) in imaginative ways. See the sidebar "Sport and Entertainment Promotional Timeline 1858 to 2013" for additional perspective on the development of promotion.

Ari de Wilde, PhD, Assistant Professor of Sport and Leisure Management in the School of Education and Professional Studies at Eastern Connecticut State University, and Chad Seifried, PhD, RAA, Assistant Professor, Sport Management Graduate Program Coordinator, Louisiana State University

George "Tex" Rickard (on the right in the photo) was one of the kings of sport promotion in the early 20th century. His ability to shape perceptions through his promotions campaigns was extraordinary. As the "King of Ballyhoo," Rickard used specific and targeted strategies to generate positive public relations. Ultimately, this allowed Rickard to monetize the social capital that he developed to build a new Madison Square Garden in the mid-1920s. Four examples highlight Rickard's accomplishments.

- **Ringside seats**. Luxury seating did not begin with Tex Rickard, but he did shape the construction and desire for the ringside seat through its location and various amenities. Before Rickard's arrival, boxing rings and stadiums were temporary ad hoc wooden structures, often the domain of underworld hustlers, gamblers, and gangsters. In essence, attending boxing matches, as well as other sporting events, could be dangerous and not like attending a Broadway show. Rickard worked to change the perception and experience at sporting events to make them into a lower-, middle-, and upper-class-integrated night out. At both the old and new Madison Square Garden, Rickard used permanent brick and mortar structures as sport theatres. He hired a chief usher by the name of Willie Stillman, who trained his large, uniformed staff for months. As sportswriter Paul Gallico recalled, "Tickets bore portal, aisle, section, and seat numbers. . . . Special police and guards were on hand for protection and to keep order." After publicizing his staffing, Rickard was able to sell two tickets when before he and others could sell only one.

- **Millionaire**. In his retrospective piece on Rickard, Paul Gallico pointed out the importance of Rickard's construction of athletes as millionaires. Before Tex, the public and the press took an interest in athletics prizes, but Rickard turned this fascination into a national obsession. He steered the press toward the athlete not only as an icon of physical prowess but also as an icon of wealth. In the 1920s no Rickard athletes represented this better than Jack Dempsey and Gene Tunney, who fought in two of the biggest events of the era. Gallico recounted, "Control over a million-dollar asset, the title itself, was at stake and was liable to change hands at any moment and with considerable violence." At the time, everyone knew about millionaires such as John D. Rockefeller and the Carnegies, but athletes were not in the same category until Rickard nudged them there in the eyes of the public. To play on this, his fight tickets were made of paper that felt like money; the backs of the tickets were gold. To publicize the financing of the new Madison Square Garden, Rickard also promoted his investors as the "six hundred millionaires."

- **Good versus evil**. One of the most effective marketing tools Rickard developed was portraying athletics events as good versus evil. In both hockey and boxing, Rickard promoted fighters and teams as battling nationalities, ethnic groups, or races, and he typically spun one as superior to the other. In the famous 1926 Gene Tunney versus Jack Dempsey bout in

Philadelphia, Rickard used this tactic to perfection. Understanding the struggles in which newspapers such as the *New York Herald* and *Times* were engaged, he fed tidbits or seeds of stories that desperate newspapers writers brought to fruition in stories tinted with class or race and good versus evil. As historian Bruce Evensen noted on the Dempsey–Tunney bouts, readers were told that "two 'modern gladiators,' one a 'cave-man' (Dempsey), the other 'a student,' would test the limits of 'brute force' and 'brains.'"

- **Paying the tithe**. Rickard was so concerned with how newspaper reporters portrayed his ventures that he went beyond strong-arming; he developed a slush fund to pay certain reporters. As some contemporaries and historians have suggested, Rickard and other Garden staff had specific sportswriters on the payroll for as much as $4,000. Newspaper publishers barely raised an eyebrow; they were happy that someone else was paying their reporters. Seeing intense growth and competition in the field of sports writing, Rickard seized an opportunity. Furthermore, he effectively used public relations and played off the public's fascination with wealth, class, and social status to realize his goals. In so doing he changed the landscape of big-time sport.[44]

Sport and Entertainment Promotional Timeline 1858 to 2013

Decade	Activity
1850s	Fans paid to attend a baseball game between two teams in the New York City area at Fashion Rack Course in Queens. The game was the first known athletics event that required paid admission from fans (admission was 50 cents). Attendance records varied from 1,500 to 10,000.
	Harvard and Yale competed in the first intercollegiate athletics event (crew). The event, held in New Hampshire, was sponsored by a railroad to promote its line and a new vacation route to prospective fans.
1880s	Albert G. Spalding published the *Spalding Baseball Guide*, an instructional piece that was an attempt to create and expand the market for his products (the historical underpinnings of edu-selling). Spalding's baseball became the "official baseball" of the National League, and promotion of the ball through the Spalding catalog and retailers began.
	Chris von der Ahe, St. Louis magnate, led the creation of the American Association, a rival to the National League. The AA promoted cheaper tickets (25 cents compared with 50 cents in the National League) and beer. National League owners scoffed at the "beer ball league" and at Von der Ahe's use of entertainment features and special promotions.
1900s	Box scores became the doorway that fans were looking for, enabling them to check scores, stats, and details of their favorite players and teams. Now, through advanced technology, fans have 24/7 access to desired information.
	Honus Wagner became the first athlete to lend his name to endorse a product, Louisville Slugger bats, for payment ($75).
	The Doubleday legend (that Abner Doubleday invented baseball) was created to position and promote baseball as a uniquely American game.
	Ty Cobb and Honus Wagner promoted Coca-Cola as "The Great National Drink of the Great National Game."
	Bull Durham (smoking tobacco) began buying outfield signage and offering a prize to any player who hit the sign with a batted ball during a game. As a result, the use of stadium signage to promote products increased.
1910s	The recording of sound on motion picture film was developed.
	Tex Rickard created spectacle in boxing.
	Chalmers Motor Car Company donated a car to the MLB batting champion, the first sport award given for the purpose of product publicity.

> *continued*

Decade	Activity
1920s	The first sporting event was broadcast by radio, a no-decision boxing match on famous Pittsburgh station KDKA. Radio gave sporting fans the ability to witness (by audio) their favorite events from their living rooms. William Veeck began broadcasting Chicago Cubs games on the radio to promote the sport. Gene Sarazen signed an endorsement deal with Wilson Sporting Goods that became the longest running endorsement deal in the history of sport. The original deal was for $6,000 per year and an equal amount for travel expenses. Renewal took place every two years until Sarazen's death in May 1999. Goodyear Tire and Rubber Company built the *Pilgrim*, the first blimp to fly over athletics events. Coke partnered with the Olympics and remains a sponsor to this day. The role of the sport agent as a promoter continued to emerge as Christy Walsh represented Babe Ruth. Red Grange and C.C. ("Cash and Carry") Pyle teamed up to use Grange's superstar status to promote the new NFL and provide credibility.
1930s	Lou Gehrig became the first athlete to appear on a Wheaties Box. The NFL held the first professional sport draft on February 8, 1936. Other major leagues adopted the same strategy in following years. A game between Fordham and Waynesburg (Pennsylvania) College was the first collegiate football game to be televised. The first television was sold. The first televised NFL game happened on October 22, 1939.[45] The game was broadcast to 1,000 homes. The Philadelphia Eagles fell to the Brooklyn Dodgers, 23-14. The Kansas City Monarchs of the Negro Leagues developed a portable lighting system that enabled them not only to play their games at night but also to barnstorm and take their games to various cities through the United States; the concept was so successful that for six years the Monarchs elected not to join the Negro National League, preferring to barnstorm. Night baseball was introduced in the major leagues in Cincinnati. Ned Irish promoted college basketball double-headers at Madison Square Garden, ushering in a golden age of New York City basketball that ended in a gambling scandal in the 1950s.
1940s	The All-American Girls Professional Baseball League was formed because many major league baseball players were serving in the armed forces in World War II. In the first major endorsement by a female, Babe Didrikson Zaharias signed with Wilson Sporting Goods for $100,000 a year. The tobacco industry became more involved in baseball when Chesterfield cigarette signs became a functioning part of the scoreboard in baseball parks; the "h" was lit to signify a hit, and the "e" was lit to signify an error. The World Series was nationally televised for the first time.
1950s	NBC broadcast the first live coast-to-coast sporting event, a football game between Duke University and the University of Pittsburgh. Roderick McMahon (Vince's grandfather, better known as Jess) and Raymond "Toots" Mondt created the Capitol Wrestling Corporation (CWC). The CWC joined the National Wrestling Alliance in 1953 and became the WWF. After losing a lawsuit to the World Wildlife Fund, on May 5, 2002, the company became WWE. *Sports Illustrated* debuted. Disneyland in Anaheim, California, opened. The theme park cost $17 million to build. Bill Veeck introduced bat day, the first of many giveaway days featuring premium items that have become part of the fabric of baseball promotional activities today.
1960s	Six Flags, the first regional theme park, opened in Texas. The Eighth Wonder of the World, the Astrodome, was unveiled, along with Astroturf, the first artificial turf. Phil Knight opened Blue Ribbon Sports. In 1972 the name was changed to Nike. On January 15, 1967, the first Super Bowl game was played between the Green Bay Packers and the Kansas City Chiefs. At the time, the game was called the World Championship Game, but it later took the name Super Bowl. Success of this venture coupled with the Sports Broadcasting Act led to the merger of the NFL and AFL and the emergence and growth of the NFL as America's true national pastime. The International Marketing Group was founded by Mark McCormack, initially as a vehicle to represent Arnold Palmer. IMG became the largest sport marketing agency in the world. The New York Jets and the American Football League signed and marketed Joe Namath, demonstrating again that the credibility and interest in a superstar can promote and solidify the future of an upstart league.

Decade	Activity
1970s	Major League Baseball began experimenting with customized, one-of-a-kind uniform designs. Other sports followed, and now virtually every sport capitalizes on the popularity of uniform variations.
	Walt Disney World Resort opened on October 1, 1971. The Magic Kingdom was its only theme park at first, but Disney has since added Epcot (1982), Disney's Hollywood Studios (1989), and Disney's Animal Kingdom (1998).
	Title IX was enacted, mandating equal access to educational opportunities for men and women.
	Rich Foods paid $60,000 per year for the naming rights to the Buffalo Bills football stadium.
	On October 1, 1975, the Thrilla in Manila, a boxing match between Muhammad Ali and Joe Frazier, became the first pay-per-view athletics event. The bout was broadcast to 276 closed-circuit locations.
	Ball Four, by Jim Bouton, then of the New York Yankees, was published, the first book that portrayed athletes as real people with real problems and behaviors.
	ESPN began broadcasting as the first 24-hour-per-day sports television network.
	Miller Lite embarked on a national advertising campaign using past sport figures (34 of them), the largest quotient in the history of sport advertising.
1980s	Sales of Michael Jackson's *Thriller* reached 20 million.
	The Nintendo home entertainment system was introduced.
	As part of a $2.5 million contract over five years, Nike created Michael Jordan's first shoe, the Air Jordan. This deal paved the way for future endorsements and shoe-centric promotional campaigns by the likes of LeBron James, Derrick Rose, Kobe Bryant, and others. Nike and MJ permanently changed the landscape of athletics shoes.
	John Madden Football was released in 1988. *Madden NFL* has become the premier sports video game and has demonstrated the profitability of sports video game promotion. *Madden NFL* also may be the most widely recognized and accepted curse in sport today.
	The first collegiate football bowl game sold its naming rights—the then USF&G Sugar Bowl.
	The commercial success of the 1984 Los Angeles Olympic Games, organized by Peter Ueberroth, proved that corporate sponsorship could make the Olympic Games a profitable enterprise.
1990s	Live video streaming for sport was introduced. Today, a fan can access favorite sports and teams from almost anywhere. This medium serves as a popular promotional platform.
	After the first UFC event in 1993, mixed martial arts has become a captivating sport around the world. The UFC has industrialized MMA, creating international events and reality TV shows.
	NFL Sunday Ticket was introduced, allowing fans to follow their hometown teams no matter where they are in the country.
	The World League of American Football (which later became NFL Europe) premiered to capitalize on perceived European interest in American sport as well as to provide opportunities for television and merchandising sales.
	Fox became the fourth national broadcast network, using its purchase of NFL television rights and its broadcasting schedule to promote its programming. Fox Sports Net, a syndication of regional sports networks, soon followed.
	In New York City on April 12, ESPN announced that the first Extreme Games would be held in Rhode Island in June 1995. In January the event name Extreme Games was officially changed to the X Games. The reasons for the change were to improve branding opportunities and allow easier translation to international audiences.
	Interleague play in baseball started in 1997 and brought the potential for new and exciting rivalries such as Yankees versus Mets, A's versus Giants, and Cubs versus White Sox.
	Women's professional team sports emerged with basketball (American Basketball League and WNBA) followed by softball and soccer.
	DirecTV home satellite television services were offered along with packages such as the NFL Sunday Ticket, which permitted viewers not only to follow their favorite team regardless of where they lived but also to have access to every team and every game. MLB, NHL, MLS, EPL, and NCAA soon followed.
	With the launch of Commissioner.com and RotoNews.com in January of 1997, the fantasy sports world exploded. Fantasy sports is now a multi-billion-dollar business.
	Grassroots marketing through the creation of interactive fan festivals aimed at fans in markets hosting all-star games and the Super Bowl began. MLB's Fan Fest, NFL Experience, NBA Jam Session, and NCAA Hoop City soon followed.
	Adding to HDTV craze, fans became able to record events (DVR), ensuring that they didn't miss a second of action and setting a new standard for watching games.

> *continued*

Decade	Activity
2000s	Yao Ming became the first international player ever to be selected first overall without having previously played U.S. college basketball. But when the Rockets chose him in 2002, it was his height that had scouts thinking that he could be a Hall of Famer. He connected the NBA with China and a worldwide audience.
	Between 2003 and 2006 came the rise of online poker and ESPN's broadcasts of the World Series of Poker. Americans were captivated with Texas Hold 'Em, creating a buzz.
	Bobbleheads were reintroduced. The dolls helped fill stadiums and arenas across the country.
	Promotions took on a new twist with publications such as a comic book with the Dallas Mavericks. Comic book promotions positioned athletes as superheroes.
	HDTV was introduced on ABC, NBC, CBS, and ESPN. NFL Kickoff Live Free Concerts generated excitement for the upcoming season and paid tribute to the many Americans serving in the U.S. military.
	Steroids and other performance-enhancing drugs cast doubt on the authenticity of records and on athletes as endorsers.
	The NBA played its all-star game in Las Vegas, making the NBA the first major sport league to play in that market.
	Retro merchandise was reintroduced. The NBA Hardwood Classics Collection and MLB's Cooperstown Collection invigorated the online merchandising and retail segments.
	LED signage replaced traditional static signage, allowing sponsors to become visual and animated in messaging.
	Cell phones added portability to sports information and broadcasting.
	NBA premiered the first exclusively dedicated one-sport network, followed by the NFL Network and MLB Network.
	Lance Armstrong and his foundation created the Livestrong campaign in support of cancer research. Through its lifetime the initiative has raised more than $300 million, and people across the globe wear Livestrong wristbands.
	YouTube arrived on the sport scene. Fans could now upload and view sport content around the clock, creating perpetual access to clips and highlights anywhere in the world.
	Facebook became available to users worldwide, and Twitter hit the scene. Both generated unprecedented attention and following for sport and entertainment. Fans followed on Twitter and logged in to Facebook for exclusive photos, leaked news, and updates on games. Social media is perpetually changing sport and promotion.
	StubHub was founded, and the secondary ticket market emerged.
	The first collegiate conference network, the Big Ten Network, debuted.
	The New York Mets and Citigroup agreed to a venue naming-rights deal of $20 million annually, the largest at that time.
2010s	"The Decision" of LeBron James in 2010 set cable records and ushered in a new era of players teaming up during free agency to create a championship team. James became a polarizing figure in sport, changing the NBA forever.
	Linsanity turned into a promoter's dream. Jeremy Lin saw insanity surround him after he led the Knicks to a solid winning streak. He was the first American player in the NBA of Chinese or Taiwanese descent. Linsanity went viral. *Time* named Lin one of the 100 most influential people.
	Possibly the biggest story to rock the sporting world was Lance Armstrong's being banned from cycling for life and stripped of his seven Tour de France titles because of admitted doping.
	The Lion King became the highest grossing Broadway show, overtaking *The Phantom of the Opera*.
	NFL Red Zone Channel debuted and was a great aid to fantasy football participants.
	Walt Disney purchased Lucasfilm Ltd. and its rights for *Star Wars* and *Indiana Jones* for $4.05 billion.
	Wizards center Jason Collins announced on SI.com that he was gay, becoming the first active male athlete in one of the major U.S. pro sports to do so.
	Entertainer Jay-Z joined forces with CAA to create Roc Nation Sports, a sport representation firm.
	MLB At Bat mobile app debuted.
	Longhorn Network, the first network devoted to one collegiate athletics program (University of Texas), debuted.
	Pac-12, Big 12, and SEC Networks began.
	Seven Catholic schools left the Big East Conference but retained the name to form a major collegiate basketball conference with basketball as the primary sport.
	Manchester United received a $559 jersey sponsorship in a seven-year agreement with Chevrolet.

Data from G.E. White, 1996, *Creating the national pastime: Baseball transforms itself 1903-1953* (Princeton, NJ: Princeton University Press); Sugar 1978; and various media sources.

Hallmark Event

A hallmark event, as defined by Ritchie, is a major one-time event (or annually recurring event) of limited duration, developed primarily to enhance the awareness, appeal, and profitability of a tourism destination in the short term, long term, or both. Such events draw their success from uniqueness, status, or timely significance to create interest and attract attention.[46]

Hallmark events promote not only the destination but also the activity and the organization associated with or responsible for the event. Successful hallmark event staging also serves to promote the destination as attractive or the group as qualified or suitable for hosting other similar hallmark events. For the past three decades the city of San Antonio, Texas, hosted hallmark events such as the NBA All-Star Weekend (game and related events occurring Friday through Sunday), the NCAA Final Four (men's and women's), the Alamo Bowl, the Pan American Games, and training camp for the Dallas Cowboys. The success and experience of each event served as an impetus to attract the next event.

In 2012 Dublin, Ireland, hosted the football game between Notre Dame and Navy and four American high school football games leading up to the main event. Overall, 36,000 visitors to Ireland were housed and transported through the country, spreading the impact of the hallmark event. The success of that event will be a key factor in the decision about whether Dublin will host an NFL game in the near future.

Many leagues, teams, and other sport-related organizations create hallmark or special events to promote their sport or activity to interested publics. The NBA, NFL, and NHL have played exhibition games and regular-season games in Europe, and the NBA has also played in Asia. Teams from the English Premier League (EPL) have played matches in the United States to enhance their brands, increase interest in their sport (and television viewership and merchandise sales), and position soccer as a global sport. MLB has played games in Asia and has developed the World Baseball Classic for the same reasons. These events as well as bowl games, conference tournaments, and other types of annual events are done for promotional purposes and are intended to achieve the following:

- Promote the host organization to the public
- Promote the sponsors of the event and their products
- Create unique hospitality opportunities for sponsors and other influencers
- Promote and add to the growth of the particular sport
- Promote the event as a revenue-generating opportunity
- Attract significant media interest and coverage
- Promote the destination as a site not only for future hallmark events but also for tourism and possible economic investment

Internet Sites, Web Pages, Blogs, and More

As technology continues to evolve, particularly in relation to the media, so has the opportunity for fans to follow their favorite sports, leagues, teams, and players. Technological advancements and developments have also given fans who no longer live near their childhood or favorite teams an opportunity to maintain, or perhaps even increase, their affiliation. Internet sites, including websites, chat rooms, blogs, various forms of social media, team-operated and fan-operated team-related websites, online fantasy leagues, and even online gambling sites have met and continue to meet those needs and at the same time serve as promotional vehicles. All the aforementioned Internet sites and opportunities can be used to promote the sport organization by providing information that was not readily available 10 years ago in a content-focused, user-friendly environment that can be accessed by consumers at their convenience and managed to fit their needs. Even more important, consumers can not only manage content but also create and produce content for their own followers. Players or participants can also do this as they seek to create more value for themselves by creating and establishing relationships important to them for one reason or another. So in 2014, anyone with a smartphone can be a content creator and a media provider and thus a promotional catalyst.

Sales Promotions

Sales promotions, which can take the form of price-oriented or non-price-oriented tactics, are an essential part of the marketing strategy of any sport organization. In general, nonprice promotions include special events, giveaway items, and other tangible incentives, whereas price-oriented promotions involved discounting, special pricing, and value-added concepts such as all-you-can-eat seats or other price-related manipulations. Although research suggests that many fans are attracted to price discounts, price promotions may be dangerous if fans become reliant on them. Secondary market sellers such as StubHub and Score Big often provide discounted tickets on a daily basis, and for budget conscious fans they function as the primary market. Thus, many organizations limit their price-related promotions to concepts such as family nights or offer discounts for targeted groups, such as the popular Seats for Soldiers promotion.

In any case, when using any promotional tactics designed to sell tickets for a particular game or event, the best customers—those who have purchased season tickets or other ticket plans and are referred to as season-ticket holders, members, or subscribers—must be protected and not damaged by the promotion. These members or ticket holders should receive something comparable with the discount or item featured in the promotion. Organizations should proactively address these groups before the season either in a letter accompanying their tickets, in an e-mail from their personal account representative, at a fan forum or town meeting, or perhaps all three. The message needs to state that the team will be developing and offering special promotions and discounting during the upcoming season. A rationale, such as trying to increase the fan base, fill the house on certain nights, or ensure that every fan, regardless of household income or size, has an opportunity to attend a game, should be conveyed to the season-ticket holders. One way to address the issue is to provide each season-ticket holder with a specific amount of franchise dollars (scrip) or coupons to use at merchandise or concessions stands during the year to offset the effect of the planned promotional activities. This approach not only serves to minimize the number of potential complaints but also creates a reservoir of goodwill among season-ticket holders, who

can now be ambassadors and spread the word regarding how the organization has treated them. According to Seth Godin, they now have "stories to tell" and can share those stories face to face, through social media, or on blog posts.[47]

Concepts and ideas involving value-added elements can be an effective promotion for increasing ticket sales.

These tactics, however, are becoming less common at the highest levels of professional sports because variable pricing and dynamic pricing can drive the price of those games higher to cover costs or just to maximize revenue opportunities on particular games.

When relying on sponsors to help underwrite the cost of a sales promotion or to provide a revenue stream, the organization must realize that the promotion needs to work for everyone—the fans, the sponsor, and the organization. Table 10.3 depicts the corporate sponsors that were most frequently involved in MLB promotions during the 2012 season.

Unfortunately, organizations can easily be carried away in the spirit of promoting. Markdowns, contests, sponsorships, sweepstakes, holiday sales, special events, open houses, and the like are often initiated with little thought of the desired long-term outcome, especially in sport. Examination of the long list of promotions that baseball teams may offer during the season makes it apparent that sales promotions should be designed with the concept of reverse planning in mind. By reverse planning, we mean that organizations need to determine what it is that they want to happen because of implementing the promotion. In other words, they need to decide what they want to accomplish in the long term and then strategically plan initiatives and activities that will help achieve that specified goal.

Price promotions involve some type of discount, rebate, or other financial incentive in relation to the product or service purchased. According to Donald Ziccardi, "Sales promotion strategies have become the quick fix for companies desperate for customers, fanatically assembled to adjust for economic swings, fashion trends, calendar shifts, and the weather without taking into account the overall marketing plan and its goals and objectives. However, there are long-term effects on the company's image and on customers. For one, sales promotion activities can overshadow the advertising efforts instead of reinforcing them. Second, customers have been conditioned to show only when there is a sales promotion. A price break or a storewide sale could trigger a big sales gain, but then the company could suffer a huge falloff the very next day."[48]

For example, JCPenney tried valiantly to avoid the sale-every-week campaign and promote low everyday prices—and failed miserably. The retailer reverted to the weekly sale platform to bolster their sagging stock price and regain lost customers.[49]

In sport, one negative effect is that attendance traditionally is lower for the event immediately following a promotion. If a promotion does nothing more than induce people to attend one game instead of another, then it is not effective. This pattern indicates that fans are cherry picking—attending games only when a promotion or incentive is offered to choose a particular game. When cherry picking occurs, the value of a sales promotion is minimal unless the promotional item or offer is sponsored by someone other than the sport organization.

As previously mentioned, nonprice promotions include giveaway items or premiums, fireworks nights, concerts, and so on. Table 10.4 lists the top nonprice promotions that teams use. The

TABLE 10.3   Sponsor Involvement in Major League Baseball Promotional Dates, 2012

Rank	Brand	Number of teams	Number of dates
1	Coca-Cola	7	69
2	Chevrolet	11	47
3	Pepsi	9	44
4	MillerCoors	7	38
5	Anheuser Busch	8	28
6 (tie)	AT&T	5	23
6 (tie)	MLB Network	23	23
8 (tie)	KeyBank	2	19
8 (tie)	State Farm	2	19
10 (tie)	Xfinity by Comcast	4	18
10 (tie)	Meijer	2	18

Adapted, by permission, from D. Broughton, 2012, "Everybody loves bobbleheads," *Smith & Street SportsBusiness Journal* 15(3): 9.

TABLE 10.4   Top Nonprice Promotions (Giveaways) in Major League Baseball, 2012

Rank	Category	Number of teams	Number of dates
1	Bobbleheads	26	94
2	T-shirt	24	79
3	Headwear	28	69
4	Backpack or bag	26	50
5	Magnetic schedule	29	46
6	Photo	12	43
7	Toy	22	37
8	Poster	15	33
9 (tie)	Jersey	17	31
9 (tie)	Retail coupon	17	31

Adapted, by permission, from D. Broughton, 2012, "Everybody loves bobbleheads," *Smith & Street SportsBusiness Journal* 15(3): 9.

late Bill Veeck, owner of the Cleveland Indians, St. Louis Browns, and Chicago White Sox (twice), was the master of the nonprice promotion. Veeck, the originator of bat day, recognized the importance of attracting new fans by implementing special theme days such as ladies' days and A-student days. Veeck used fireworks, had roving entertainers, gave away orchids and other premiums, and practiced a promotional philosophy that said, "Every day was Mardi Gras and every fan was king [or queen]."[50] Veeck recognized the need to market something other than the core product, realizing that an organization cannot always field a winning team but must provide an entertaining atmosphere every day. Thus, he pioneered nonprice promotions in sport to placate fans whose team might not be winning and keep them interested in coming out to the park. This idea of promoting something other than the core product is a key to group sales that are often composed of as many nonsport fans as sport fans.

A perceived problem with giveaway days is that, depending on the premium item or promotional concept (e.g., dollar dog night), they may hinder souvenir or concession sales. The marketer must attempt to measure how much sales these giveaways create versus how much they possibly eliminate. Thus, to avoid an adverse effect on souvenir sales, a cap day could involve a cap that does not resemble those sold at the stadium. For example, a number of MLB teams, such as the Kansas City Royals, Pittsburgh Pirates, and Detroit Tigers, honor the Negro League teams that played in their cities during the 1930s into the early 1960s on a promotional day such as Black Heritage or African American Heritage day. During these games both teams wear historically accurate uniforms that honor those Negro League teams, and a commemorative cap similar to those being worn by the players is often the giveaway item for the fans. This promotion is an excellent example of not cannibalizing merchandise sales because these caps are not usually sold in the venue merchandise stores. At the same time, replica uniform jerseys or T-shirts commemorating the occasion could be sold to capitalize on the promotion. For instance, a promotional staple in baseball is dollar dog night (inflationary times and rising costs have elevated this promotion from its earlier position as dime dog night). This promotion (like most nonprice promotional activities) is usually underwritten by a sponsor, in most cases jointly by the stadium concessionaire and its hog dog supplier. Although the club loses out on the sale of hot dogs, the higher attendance, coupled with parking fees and related concessions sales such as soda and beer, more than compensates for the loss.

One reason for the popularity of bobbleheads as a giveaway item is that they are usually not sold as souvenir items. In 2012, 26 MLB teams combined to distribute 2.27 million bobbleheads, a 25 percent increase over the number of bobbleheads distributed in 2011.[51] Table 10.5 shows the most common event-based promotions used by MLB during the 2012 season.

Timing is another key element in the planning of promotions for sport organizations. The

TABLE 10.5 Top Promotions (Events or Themes) in Major League Baseball, 2012

Rank	Category	Number of teams	Number of days
1	Fireworks	22	186
2	Festival and concerts	16	166
3	Ticket discount	9	164
4	Concessions discount	13	127
5	Autographs	6	125
6	Family day	10	103
7	Run the bases	16	100
8	College night	10	76
9	Team history tribute	21	73
10	Kids day	16	67

Adapted, by permission, from D. Brooughton, 2012, "Everybody loves bobbleheads," *Smith & Street SportsBusiness Journal* 15(3): 9.

Scheduling as a Form of Promotion: The Promotional Game-Planning Matrix and the University of South Florida (USF) Football, 2013 Season

Sport marketing professionals in the collegiate ranks are often faced with a dilemma regarding promotional activities for sporting events. On one hand, the coach would like to have every home game promoted; on the other hand, sponsors want to be linked to a promotion that generates the greatest number of impressions and attracts the most media coverage. The promotional game-planning matrix (figure 10.5) can serve as an aid for the sport marketer in identifying games that might benefit from promotional assistance to achieve respectable attendance and other games that might sell out or receive an attendance jump with a promotional boost. The promotional game-planning matrix considers two primary factors. The left column of the matrix presents the first factor—the game date and time during the week when the event is scheduled to take place. The top row of the matrix illustrates the second factor—opponent. These factors are classified as favorable or unfavorable based on the following conditions:

		Opponent	
		Favorable	Unfavorable
Day	Favorable	FF (Miami, Louisville)	FU (McNeese, Florida Atlantic, Cincinnati, Memphis, SMU)
	Unfavorable	UF (None)	UU (None)

Figure 10.5   The promotional game-planning matrix.

• **Game date and time**. Favorable days are identified as those days and game starting times that offer the best chance of attracting potential spectators. Over time, weekends (Friday, Saturday, and Sunday) have proved to be the best time to attract fans in significant numbers; Thursday, Wednesday, Tuesday, and Monday follow in that order. In the case of collegiate sport, the development of television networks and regional sports networks (RSNs), particularly the new collegiate conference networks and their insatiable need for programming, has

> continued

widened the traditional window of collegiate football scheduling from Saturday to encompass almost every day of the week except Sunday and Monday, which have been dominated by the NFL. Unfavorable days are those days that have the least potential to attract spectators, which in this case are Tuesdays followed by Wednesdays and Thursdays. But the opportunity to play at night on television and, in the case of the nonpower conferences, to avoid competing against established teams in their own regions may be seen as more favorable.

- **Opponents**. Identifying an opponent as favorable or unfavorable is not necessarily based on the opponents' win-loss record. A favorable opponent could be a school with a storied tradition that is therefore perceived to be a "name," such as Notre Dame. Local rivalries, teams that have a notable player, a record-setting opponent or player, or a team with a strong following playing in an attractive market are all factors to be considered.

Now that we have identified our classification of days and opponents, we can develop our matrix. Favorable days and favorable opponents will be designated with an F and unfavorable days and opponents will be designated with a U. Consider the 2013 University of South Florida schedule shown in table 10.6.

TABLE 10.6   2013 University of South Florida Football Schedule

Date	Day of the week and time	Opponent
August 31	Saturday 7 p.m.	McNeese State
September 14	Saturday 7 p.m.	Florida Atlantic
September 28	Saturday TBA	Miami
October 5	Saturday TBA	Cincinnati
October 26	Saturday TBA	Louisville
November 16	Saturday TBA	Memphis
November 23	Saturday TBA	SMU

For evaluating favorable versus unfavorable days, this particular schedule offers no differences, although starting times could be influential. None of the days would rate a U—all would be favorable, although some might be more favorable than others. For example, the opening matchup versus McNeese State would be a favorable game for USF because the game is not only the opening game of the season but also the debut of new USF coach Willie Taggart, a coach with local ties who was much heralded and sought after, a factor that would change the expected U rating for a relatively unknown opponent.

When evaluating favorable versus unfavorable opponents, a helpful approach is to weigh the pros and cons of the opponent by analyzing the conditions previously discussed. Thus, opponents with more positives than negatives would receive a positive rating. For example, Miami would receive an F rating based on the following criteria:

- Miami is a recognized national power
- Miami is one of the big three Florida football schools
- Miami has a fan base throughout the state
- Miami has a significant alumni base in the Tampa–St. Petersburg area
- The game positions USF as capable of playing better conference opponents

On the other hand, the University of Memphis would receive a U rating based on the following criteria:

- Memphis is not known as a football school
- Memphis fans do not travel well to support their team on the road
- Memphis is not a team likely to appear on television in the Tampa area
- Memphis is not perceived to be a rival

After the game date and time and the opponents have been classified as favorable or unfavorable, the dates and times and opponents are entered into the appropriate box in the matrix. Games labeled FF, denoting both a favorable day and time and a favorable opponent, may need little promotional assistance, but if the organization is following the peak-on-peak theory (promoting the games with the best chance of attracting a large attendance or selling out games with a favorable day and time and favorable opponent), the best approach may be to secure resources and allocate promotional assets to maximize the opportunity to drive attendance. Likewise, UU games will need the most assistance, although in some cases they will be ignored because the allocation of assets and resources may not produce a favorable ROI. The USF schedule for the 2013 season includes no UU games. The games would rate out as follows:

- FF—Miami (previously analyzed) and Louisville, a nationally recognized and ranked team, defending Big East champion, and featuring Heisman trophy candidate Teddy Bridgewater; may also be scheduled as a Saturday night game.
- FU—all remaining games. Although the games are all on Saturdays, the opponents are generally lackluster. The games could become FF depending on the success of USF.

concept of timing includes day of the week, opponent, starting time, and month of the year (sometimes referred to as time of the season). The sport marketer must determine whether a promotion should be scheduled against a better draw or a weaker draw. A better draw might be defined by a weekend date versus a weekday date, an opponent with a strong tradition of attracting a crowd away from home (New York Yankees, Pittsburgh Steelers, Los Angeles Lakers, Detroit Red Wings), or an opponent with a much talked-about player (Stephen Strasburg and Bryce Harper of the Washington Nationals) who attracts significant media attention and social media buzz.

Promotional Components

The proper way to use sales promotion is to design and conduct balanced and creative sales promotional activities. An effective promotional campaign consists of the right type of activities, conducted at the appropriate time, and appealing to the target market.[52] In this section, we briefly describe and give examples of some program activities.

Theme

In developing the theme or creative component, the marketer needs to ask and answer a number of questions to develop an effective creative strategy. Table 10.7 lists the questions to ask and indicates the reasons for asking them. Although creative strategy development may seem like a function of advertising rather than promotional selling, promotional planning should address this issue annually.

Most effective marketing themes are short, simple, and easily understood. Coca-Cola's "Always the Real Thing" is a simple message. No other product is the real thing. Instead, it is an imitation inferior to the real thing. The aim of the iconic Nike theme "Just Do It" as well as another theme used in the past decade, "I Can," is to fit almost any situation, athletic ability, and target market. With these shoes the consumer can do whatever activity he or she chooses or perhaps do none at all and just make a fashion statement or have comfortable shoes. "Just Do It" does not suggest the value of any sport, activity, or even athlete over another. The message emphasizes participation, without implying serious

TABLE 10.7   Questions to Ask When Formulating a Creative Component

Question	Rationale
What does this customer want?	Identify the target market, understand what they think and why, know what they value, and have documentation of their purchasing habits.
Does our product fit the consumer?	Does the consumer understand the product? How does the perception of the consumer differ from the reality of the product?
How will the competition affect our objectives?	Know and understand the competition, the way that it operates, and its objectives. Whom does the consumer consider a competitor?
What is the competitive consumer benefit?	What is the statement of benefit that the consumer expects from a brand? From an organization? The benefit to the consumer must be clearly stated.
How will marketing communication make the benefit believable to the consumer?	Persuasive communication must gently, subtly, and credibly convince the consumer that the product and its benefits are worthwhile and superior to those of similar products in the marketplace.
What should the personality of the brand be?	The personality must give the brand a life and soul that the consumer can easily identify. It should differentiate the brand from the competition.
How will the consumer define the product?	How is the message positioned in the mind of the consumer? Is it best because it was first? Is it more contemporary? Longer lasting? More fun?
What are the main communication and action objectives?	What action should the consumer take because of the message? Do we expect the consumer to call for information? To go directly to a retailer?
What contact points (mediums) should be used to reach the consumer?	What is the best communication strategy to reach the target market? Direct mail? Television? Telemarketing? Open house? Social media?

Adapted, by permission, D.E Shultz, S.I. Tannenbaum, and A. Allison, 1996, *Essentials of advertising strategy*, 3rd ed. (Lincolnwood IL: NTC Business Books).© The McGraw-Hill Companies, Inc.

competition or belittling low-key recreational activity. The consumer chooses whatever he or she wishes to do by engaging in something personally meaningful and rewarding.

Whenever possible, the theme should capitalize on unique aspects of the product or the marketplace. When moving from Winnipeg to Phoenix in 1997, the NHL Jets changed their name to the Coyotes, an image more in tune with the desert environs surrounding Phoenix. The name and location change provided the new Phoenix franchise with a marketing theme capitalizing on their new home—"Experience the coolest game in the desert."[53] In 2011 the Winnipeg Jets name was revived when the Atlanta NHL franchise was relocated to Winnipeg.

When selecting a theme or a name, the marketer should try to ensure that the theme cannot be turned against the organization in a negative way. Several teams (not mentioned here to prevent embarrassment) have used a creative theme that implied some level of positive performance. Although such themes didn't directly promote winning performance, the perception and implied meaning of a theme such as "We Will" can be easily manipulated, particularly in the realm of social media, which has many fewer restrictions than traditional media forms do. For example, we might see such variations as "We will not meet your expectations," "We will not make the playoffs," or even "We will not be worth the price of admission."

Product Sampling

An effective method for introducing new products and encouraging trial and purchase is to distribute samples to the public. This method is particularly useful in the area of pain relievers, joint medications, and dieting aids, which use websites and media to offer a free two-week sample, many of them featuring retired athletes who promote the health benefits of these products. The beauty of such sampling is the lack of risk to the customer and the opportunity for the manufacturer or supplier to put the product in the hands of a prospect. When no charge is involved (save shipping and handling), people will try almost anything. Gatorade has long emphasized and implemented sampling programs. Gatorade maintains a presence at thousands of sport venues and events throughout the United States and Canada, where it uses sampling to test consumer reaction and response to new flavors, to introduce new products, and to educate (or edu-sell) consumers about why Gatorade is important and beneficial. Gatorade maintains a high presence at marathons, triathlons, the new wave of endurance sports such as Tough Mudder, beach events such as volleyball tournaments, and other settings where the potential consumer is active, building a thirst, and is in need of hydration and replenishment. When combined with couponing (discussed later) sampling can be effective in driving sales and providing a direct ROI or ROE.

Open House

An open house is similar to a free trial offered in product sampling but is geared toward attracting an audience to a facility such as a YMCA or fitness club to encourage people to join activity-based sport and fitness programs or to a professional or collegiate sport venue to show the available seating locations and allow potential customers to view an exhibition game or practice. The sale of ticket packages would be promoted at that time.

Fitness clubs realize that to be interested in a membership, prospective members need to experience the facility and its equipment and classes before deciding whether it is right for them. This experience often takes the form of a free visit or trial membership (usually one week) and comes with an orientation and personal evaluation and consultation. Many YMCAs and fitness clubs periodically schedule a one-day or one-week open house that enables prospective members to sample not only the facilities and equipment but also the programming—yoga classes, personal training, child care, sport leagues, and even social activities. In effect, the open house is the equivalent of the test drive that has been the staple of automotive sales.

On the spectator sport side, professional and collegiate teams hold open houses to give fans and potential fans a peek behind the curtain at what happens during a game. The day's activities might include a guided tour of the locker room, a meeting with former or current players, interaction with the mascot and dance team, an opportunity to participate in a basketball clinic or take batting practice, and, of course, an opportunity to assess the seating inventory and ticket plans available for the upcoming season.

Coupons, Vouchers, and Discount Codes

Coupons, vouchers, and discount codes are a popular and accepted promotional strategy, but they must be appropriate to the image and style of the organization. In some cases, couponing or discount codes may cheapen the organization's image and possibly suggest desperation to generate sales, particularly if the organization has no history of offering coupons or discount codes.

Coupons, also referred to as vouchers, are usually in printed form (many Internet coupons have to be downloaded and presented in making the purchase at a brick and mortar store) and are a staple of the direct mail industry that we discussed in chapter 8. Technology also affords the opportunity for a coupon to be loaded on to a ticket or a membership card. Although coupons are still popular, discount codes, particularly for purchases that can be made online, are becoming more popular because of their ease of use and the ability for the provider to make changes easily and in real time.

A popular newspaper-type coupon or voucher that is also offered online through a price code is a one-price family night promotion. This usually offers four tickets, four soft drinks, four hot dogs (or other concessions item), and possibly parking for one fee, usually between $49 and $99 depending on the level of the organization (major, minor, or collegiate), the cost of the concession items from the concessionaire, and the amount of the sponsorship support. The food portion of this offer may be more easily fulfilled outside the venue, so the food coupon could be redeemed at a sponsoring QSR before or after the game or perhaps sometime during the week of the game. In any case this value-driven promotion is designed to attract families that otherwise might be not be able to attend a game. We have always endorsed this type of value-driven promotion but have also criticized it because it might not be as inclusive as it could be, and hence possibly not as effective. We suggest having the same family target but expanding the focus by stating that the cost is $15 per person, or whatever amount is equal to 25 percent of the promoted cost. We believe that this plan would be better for several reasons:

- The number of single-parent households or households with joint custody continues to grow. By offering this promotion based on four people, the organization inadvertently excludes a single parent and his or her child because they don't fit within the parameters of the four-person family deal.
- The promotion also excludes larger households that may have more than two children or may have extended family like grandparents also living in the home, or possibly outside the home, who would like to be part of family activities. Again, the four-person offer might be perceived as a barrier. At best, it conveys the message that the promotion is not available to many potential customers.

Television has gone to great lengths to provide a vision of the modern family, and sport needs to follow that portrayal, which is a reality, and become more inclusive in program offerings.

Contests and Sweepstakes

Contests and sweepstakes can add glamour, glitz, excitement, fantasy, imagination, and fun to the promotional mix. Although most sport patrons don't expect to win, this interesting promotional strategy offers fans the possibility of winning or watching someone else compete in a contest. This attraction is evident in the success of such reality television shows as *Survivor*, *American Idol*, *The Amazing Race*, and *The Voice*.

Premiums and Giveaways

Organizations use premiums to attract new consumers and encourage greater frequency of purchase among existing consumers. A premium can also be defined as something in addition to the game or event, perhaps a concert, fireworks display, or similar activity. As we discussed in chapter 8, it is becoming more common to add a charge for these premiums to defray costs as well as capitalize on increased demand.

As has been previously mentioned, the MLB Pittsburgh Pirates use both types of premiums. In terms of a premium giveaway item, the Pirates have established T-Shirt Fridays (other MLB teams also use this promotion but may schedule it on other days of the week). The Pirates chose Friday to create a peak-on-peak situation by offering a promotion on a strong day of the week. Initially, the Pirates gave a T-shirt to everyone in attendance, but to reduce cost the organization has reduced the number to the first 25,000 every Friday, which is still a large number of shirts. A different sponsor assumes the costs for the shirts 13 or 14 times per season. According to former Pirates EVP of business operations Lou DePaoli, now EVP/CRO of the New York Mets, "Friday attendance has grown 60.4 percent since we began the promotion in 2009 (from 20,052 to 32,161). While not all of the increase can be attributed to the premiums, our analytics demonstrate that the premium alone is responsible for about 30 percent of the attendance increase."[54]

The Pirates also created a concept called SkyBlast—a Saturday night postgame concert combined with an extraordinary fireworks show. This promotion could be described as peak on peak on peak, and if the game is an interleague game or is against another attractive opponent, the promotion is peak on peak on peak on peak. DePaoli states, "All 14 of these shows since we moved them to Saturday nights and spread them out across three or four months (originally scheduled back to back to back on a Thursday through Saturday) have sold out. Our average for these dates is 37,612 vs. the 25,142 we averaged on those dates prior to the switch."[55]

Demonstrating the clear power of this attractive promotional strategy is the fact that the Pirates did not have a winning season during these periods; no performance factor mitigated the effect of the promotion. (Before the 2013 baseball season, the Pirates had not had a winning season in 20 years.)

Although bat day, pioneered by Bill Veeck, is widely accepted as the first example of a premium item giveaway, a promotion created by the Oakland A's in the early 1980s had a significant influence on giveaways. Organizations began to think thematically and about driving attendance to multiple games. The A's created a promotion called Year of the Uniform, which encouraged consumers to attend multiple (six) games by providing a different clothing item premium (sponsored by Adidas) to members of the target market (those under 14 and their parents or other adults and friends) at each designated game. One game featured a cap, another a jersey, another wristbands, and so on.[56] This promotion was geared to a target market and designed to increase frequency of attendance, an approach related to the frequency escalator described next.

Ultimate Goal: Keeping Consumers on the Escalator and Moving Them Up

The ultimate goal of promotion in sport is to attract consumers, increase awareness and interest, and subsequently raise their consumption of the products or services. When launching a new sport product or offering, marketers have little choice but to expend the majority of their efforts attracting first-time (new) consumers. In such situations, sport marketers in the past have understandably expended most of their efforts and resources on mass media advertising to send their message to a broad market base. After the product was off and gaining momentum, however, many forgot to change their approach and became locked into the new consumer mentality. The Internet has changed the initial approach considerably because it permits a more targeted and cost-effective way to reach the intended audience.

Data consistently show, however, that the more mature a sport organization is, the lower the effect of new consumers is on total attendance or participation figures. This circumstance is true not just in terms of new consumers as a percentage of existing customers but also in terms of attendance frequencies of new consumers versus existing consumers. The effect of new consumers is often minimal and short lived, such as the bandwagon effect that occurs when a team is having a championship season. Although competition for a championship often attracts a number of new fans, the increased attendance of existing consumers or core attendees dictates the long-term viability of the franchise.

The intelligent approach to sport promotion is to attract consumers and bring them progressively up a gradient of involvement and commitment. Bill Giles, former baseball marketing executive and now part owner of the Philadelphia Phillies, called this the staircase approach (figure 10.6); the marketer attempts to move the fan up the stairs so that a light user becomes a medium user and potentially a heavy user.[57]

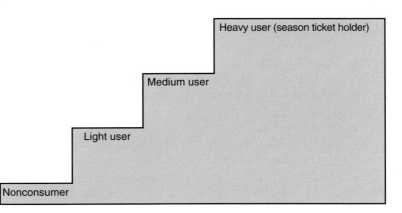

FIGURE 10.6   The staircase approach to sport marketing.

Reprinted, by permission, from B. Mullin, 2000, International marketing: A more effective way to sell sport. In *Successful sports marketing*, 2nd ed. (Durham, NC: Carolina Academic Press), 161.

Staircase Versus Escalator

Although the staircase is similar in concept to the escalator and provides an excellent foundation, it has limitations. First, it assumes that each step in the process entails a distinct and perhaps difficult movement. Second, the staircase implies that all light users are on the same step. Observation of attendance frequency distribution shows that neither assumption is true. Sport consumers are distributed in terms of their attendance or participation frequency across a continuum that runs from 1 through N, where N is the maximum number of events, games, or contests that consumers can attend (or of days in which they can consume the product). The N in professional sport varies greatly. For example, Major League Baseball, which has no exhibition games at home, has 81 regular-season home dates and the potential for more games in the postseason if the team qualifies. The National Basketball Association and the National Hockey League have 41 regular-season games at home, usually 4 preseason or exhibition games, and the opportunity for additional postseason games if the team qualifies. The National Football League has 8 regular-season games at home, usually 2 preseason games, and the opportunity for postseason play. Major League Soccer plays 17 home matches, but clubs can elect to add friendly matches with teams from around the world and exhibition games. They may also participate in national or regional tournament competitions. NCAA football schedules vary from as few as 5 home games to as many as 8, according to the power and influence of the team. The N for other sport industry segments also varies greatly from the typical 200 or more days that a Vermont ski resort could be open, depending on weather, to the 360 days that a YMCA or fitness club could be open. In fact, the frequency distribution is better represented by an escalator, which has many steps that all appear to run into one another. The step between a heavy-light user and a light-medium user is just one extra game or one more visit to the golf course or ski slope.

Before the consumer enters the ranks of existing consumers, she passes through several stages. Bill Giles used the generic term *nonconsumer*, but nonconsumption appears in several forms. Research suggests that as many as 50 percent of all people who consider themselves sports fans have never attended a game.[58] We can therefore construct four levels of nonconsumer hierarchy:

- **Nonaware nonconsumer**—unaware of the existence of the particular sport product and consequently does not attend or participate.

- **Aware nonconsumer**—aware of the sport product but chooses not to attend or participate. Presumably, the product or experience does not offer the benefits that this person is seeking, or the person has no need for this type of product, or the financial considerations involved in attending or participating are outside the means of the consumer.

- **Media consumer**—aware of the sport product, does not consume it directly (by purchasing it from the organization), but does consume it indirectly through the media. This consumption is not limited to spectator sports; it is also seen in participatory sports that receive media exposure. Cable and satellite subscription programming can enhance this experience by providing virtually every game from every team for a fee usually below US$250. Such programming acts as a negative drag on the frequency-of-attending escalator but also creates a frequency escalator for viewership. Because the leagues that provide the programming to the cable and satellite providers are compensated on a per subscriber basis, some may view this as direct consumption.

- **Misinformed nonconsumer**—aware of the product and wishes to consume it directly but does not do so because of misinformation or misperception. The misinformation usually relates to the cost of attending, the availability of tickets or opportunities to attend or participate, or safety concerns. Often, the source of the misinformation is word of mouth from friends or relatives. The misinformed consumer usually consumes the product indirectly through the media.

Figure 10.7 shows the escalator with these lower levels of consumers. The promotional effort and expense to move consumers up the escalator are usually considerably less than those required to move nonconsumers on to the escalator to begin direct consumption. Even more important, response is likely to be considerably greater from existing consumers than from an unaware or uninterested public, unless existing customers are already satiated in terms of interest or demand.

The frequency escalator depicted in figure 10.8 illustrates the attendance levels of consumers. As consumers move up the escalator, total attendance and organizational profitability increase.

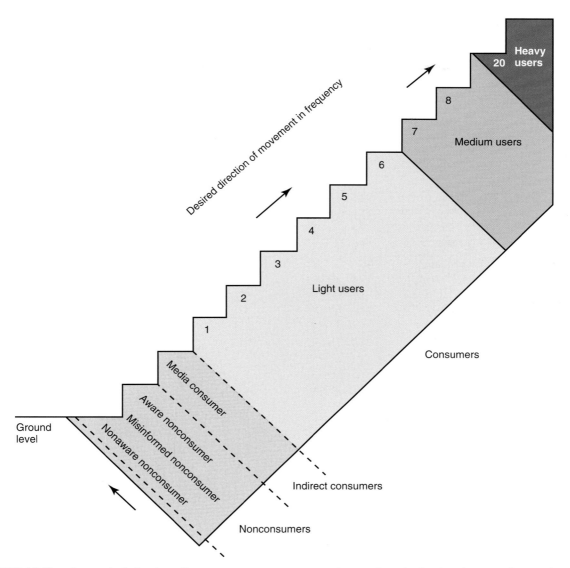

FIGURE 10.7   The goal of all sales efforts is to get consumers on the escalator by having them try the product. The next goal is to move them up the escalator by increasing their frequency of purchase.

The goal is not only to attract new consumers so that they get on the escalator but also to get consumers already on the escalator to move up by increasing their attendance. Figure 10.8 makes it apparent that attendance would increase greatly and financial fortunes would change significantly if each consumer who attended one game per season would increase his attendance to two or more games per season.

Further support for the approach of targeting existing customers comes from the well-known fact that existing satisfied customers are an organization's best sales force. For most segments of the sport industry, referrals from existing customers are excellent sources of leads to be converted. Marketers have a high stake in keeping current customers active and satisfied. Indeed, promotional efforts should focus initially on moving existing customers up the escalator.

Promotional Planning Model

Obviously, marketers of new products or new organizations or those moving into new markets can face situations that have unique challenges or, in some cases, unique advantages. Beyond this, sophisticated campaigns target both existing and potential consumers, concentrating more heavily on current uses. Figure 10.9 shows the promotional progression planning model, a framework for such a campaign.

To be effective, promotions must be arranged and directed. Promotions such as giveaways; all-inclusive one-price nights; discounts; and events such as fireworks shows, concerts, and other forms of entertainment have an audience, but it is a limited audience. Promotional strategies must be developed with the entire range of attendees in mind: first-time attendees, parents who bring children, price-conscious or val-

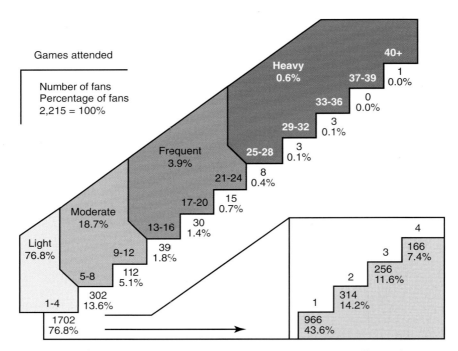

FIGURE 10.8 A frequency escalator showing fan attendance analysis for a playoff-qualifying NBA team. All figures are rounded.

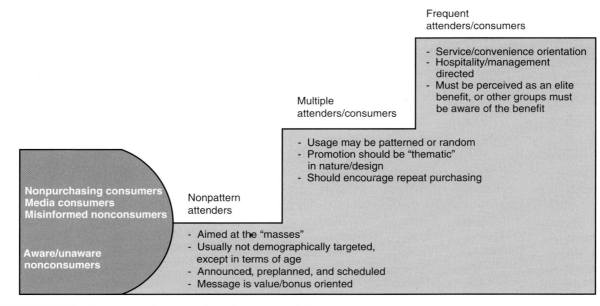

FIGURE 10.9 Promotional progression planning model.

ue-seeking attendees, partial-plan holders and miniplan buyers, group attendees, season-ticket holders (personal and corporate accounts), and attendees who are not participating in any plan or package but perhaps are looking for a social or entertainment experience.

Level 1: Nonpattern Attendees, or Light Users

The consumers on this first level may be classified as having no established attendance pattern (first-time attendees, people with free tickets, sponta-neous attendees, social media followers, bargain hunters, giveaway collectors and eBay traders, people wanting to see the venue because it is an attraction [e.g., Fenway Park], and so on). These people are motivated to attend by a variety of factors including the opponent; the weather; the day of the week; giveaways, special events, and discounts; team performance; and the opportu-nity for social interaction with friends, coworkers, or relatives. Interest in the sport, distance from the stadium, and financial resources may or may not be factors.

These nonpattern attendees, who for the most part are light users, would appear to be the easiest of all consumers to move up the escalator. Given that light users attend or participate at the lowest frequency level (many attend or participate only one to two times annually), they obviously have the greatest room for improvement on frequency. The experiences of organizations that have applied increased frequency programs show that this is true for most light users, although some consumers, regardless of the offers or effort involved, cannot be moved. Activities that succeed in increasing the frequency of light users are also effective in attracting nonconsumers for trial involvement.

Level 2: Multiple Attendees, or Medium Users

Multiple attendees can be categorized as consum-ers who attend between 10 and 30 percent of a team's home games or participate in an activity between 10 and 30 percent of the available dates. Multiple attendees may or may not be purchasers of miniplans or partials plans. Consumers may have various reasons for not owning a ticket plan. Some may be unaware that such plans exist. Some may be aware of the plans but lack understanding of the ownership benefits of such plans. Others

have time commitments or work schedules that are not conducive to plans with set dates. Still others, because of the availability of seats at the ball park, the easy access and affordability of buying tickets on the secondary market without having to make a commitment, or the number of gold courses in the area perceive no advantage to having such a plan. In such situations, some consumers recognize that availability outstrips demand.

Plans offered to those consumers to increase (or stabilize) their attendance or participation frequencies should use a menu approach or membership campaign to attract interest, show value and benefits, and overcome reasons for not purchasing. This approach requires offering several options with different benefits at various price points, offering flex books, or establishing exchange policies for purchasers when other commitments prevent them from attending or participating.

Level 3: Frequent Attendees, or Heavy Users

Frequent attendees include full-season and half-season ticket plan holders, club seat pur-chasers, and the variety of premium seat holders, including loge box and suite owners. In terms of participation, this group includes full golf or tennis members at country and private clubs, fitness center members, season-pass holders at ski resorts, annual pass holders at theme parks, and so on. Promotional strategies aimed at this level must include all benefits and incentives offered to both light and medium users as well as ben-efits exclusive to this level that are perceived as attractive and elite (not available to consumers at lower levels). Such strategies usually emphasize customer service, hospitality, comfort, conve-nience, location, priority, increased communi-cation, interaction, and, most important, access. Access can be defined as access to special events targeted exclusively to this group, access before the public to purchase tickets to shows and events not included in their plan, and access to players and meet-and-greet events involving players or other officials not generally afforded to the lower levels of consumption. This approach not only persuades medium users to become heavy users but also retains heavy users and reduces reasons for defection (decreasing involvement at one level and dropping to a lower level or dropping off the escalator entirely). The benefits of being a heavy user need to be promoted to both light and medium users so that they understand the value and benefit to moving up the escalator. The organization should convey the fact that light and medium users are missing out on unique benefits and opportunities if they remain at their current levels.

Organizations must give careful attention to developing programs to attract customers to the various levels without cannibalizing consumers from higher levels.

Defectors—Descending the Escalator

Regardless of the product or service offered, some consumers overbuy or overcommit to an opportunity. Other reasons that consumers may want to downgrade or even terminate their current level of commitment include team performance, loss of share partners, and the availability of tickets on the secondary market, which can make it difficult for the owner to resell or even give away tickets.

The economic downturn of 2008, a decline in team performance, the increasing sport and entertainment options competing for attention (as well as money and time), and the robust growth of the secondary ticket market have caused us to think about simply maintaining the consumers' current level on the escalator or even just keeping them on the escalator rather than trying to move them upward. Sport is cyclical. Because teams compete at high levels and then undergo rebuilding periods where they are less viable as an entertainment option, are we better off letting consumers downgrade but remain on the escalator in the hopes of moving them back up as performance improves? Are we content to maintain a group of consumers on an escalator that moves neither up nor down? Our explanation of lifetime value (LTV) in chapter 8 suggests that retaining customers at a lower annual spend is better than losing them altogether and trying to recapture them at another time or replace them entirely.

Putting It All Together: An Integrated Promotional Model

Although ticket sales and revenue are obviously a major component of most promotional campaigns, several marketing platforms can boost the value and impact of a fully integrated promotional campaign.

As a marketing platform

- To establish a foundation and brand for future applications
- To create an environment that will build equity or value each year
- To develop a blueprint to emulate in future platforms and campaigns
- To create a market buzz to initiate both on and off the sports pages through grassroots and guerilla marketing activities and extensions
- To create content and conversation on the Internet and through social media channels

As a revenue platform

- To develop a sales platform for increased ticket, sponsorship, and broadcast sales and E-marketing programs and volume
- To build attendance, which in turn affects and increases ancillary revenue streams such as parking, hospitality, facility rentals, food and beverage sales, and merchandising
- To provide a sales base to cross-promote other venue events or create a series of owned events in which the team is the promoter

As an entertainment platform

- To create a memorable experience that brings fans back
- To deliver new broadcast and Internet opportunities and features
- To strengthen the emotional connection and create a bond between the sport product and the fans or purchasers

For those reasons it might be advantageous to consider promotional campaigns as the hub of a wheel. The spokes of the wheel represent the various departmental units of the sport organization that can enhance and build on the promotional concept as well as capitalize on the opportunity through a variety of platforms (figure 10.10).

Starting at the center of the wheel, the promotional concept is the focal point. It should have corresponding goals and objectives, primary and

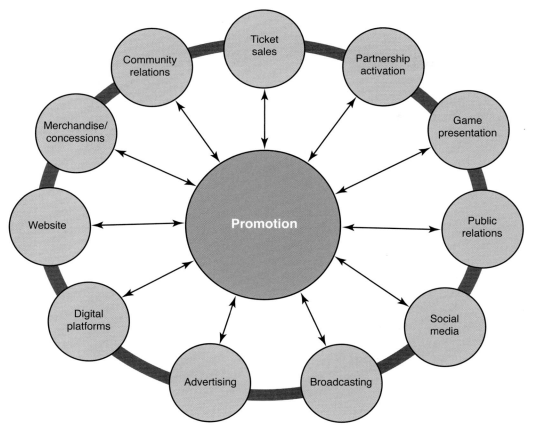

FIGURE 10.10   Promotional wheel.
Original created by Hersh, Mullin, and Sutton 2000; modified by Sutton 2013.

secondary strategies and tactics, and, whenever possible, a hook to draw in the intended audience. For example, beginning with the 2006 NBA Finals (and copied by a number of NBA teams through 2013, such as the Oklahoma City Thunder with blue and the Golden State Warriors with gold), the Miami Heat created a promotional concept for the NBA playoffs that carried into the finals named "White Hot." "White Hot" referred to the way that the team was playing and the game atmosphere—all seats were covered in white, the dance team wore white outfits, and the team launched a line of "White Hot" merchandise.

Addressing each spoke of the wheel provides insight into the successful planning and possibilities of an integrated promotional model.

Wrap-Up

Promotion is a commonly used term in sport marketing. For most, promotion includes advertising, personal selling, publicity, and sales promotion.

At the core of promotion is communication—the attempt by an organization or entity to reach its audience. To be effective, the promotional activity, using all appropriate communication channels, must be able to cut through the clutter of the marketplace, inform and persuade the targeted recipient of the message, and initiate some type of action on the part of the recipient. Advertising through a variety of mediums and channels and by personal selling through endorsements is evolving and changing because of technological advancements and the ineffectiveness of past practices. This evolution has continued and will continue to develop in even more diverse ways through E-marketing, street marketing, and social media, all of which will be evaluated on their effectiveness to deliver the appropriate demographic and their ability to engage that demographic in meaningful ways.

Promotional activities are a valuable strategy to attract new consumers and increase the frequency (participating, purchasing, attending) of current consumers. In determining how to implement such activities, the reverse planning process—knowing what the organization wants to achieve through the promotion (outcome)—is an essential approach.

Promotional activities, which can take the form of price-oriented efforts such as discounting and packaging, or nonprice efforts such as giveaways and special events, are an essential part of attracting consumers and increasing their frequency, spend, or volume. The theory of the consumer escalator suggests that promotions should be a coherent package in which the aim is to ensure a balance among light, medium, and heavy users.

Because the repeat user is the lifeblood of the sport organization, investing extensive time and money in an effort to attract one-time patrons is a questionable strategy. Even if a sponsor underwrites the cost of a giveaway, the marketer must consider the resources (staff, time, and advertising) spent on attracting consumers who may be nothing more than cherry pickers. Obviously, any strategy should include attempts to attract nonusers, but it should not neglect any groups currently on the escalator, who typically provide the bulk of all product consumption. Ultimately, each organization must determine the ideal balance in its promotional strategy. Tactics include some combination of the elements of paid media advertising, personal selling, public relations, and sales promotions. Successful strategies, however, recognize the tendency of consumers to move both up and down the escalator of consumption. The key is to retain them at a place where they are comfortable on the escalator so that they do not need to be replaced and their lifetime value can be maximized.

Promotional concepts that are integrated and have a variety of connecting points and communication channels have a greater likelihood of attracting an interested audience who are likely to act on the promotional offer.

Paid media, depending on the channel employed, is controllable, targeted, cost effective, and productive. Not all organizations have the resources to use a broad paid media approach to promotion, and they may have to rely on other forms of media, which may not be as controllable, to promote their goals and objectives.

Activities

1. Interview 15 to 20 students at your institution to determine the most effective way of reaching them (i.e., communicating a message). After identifying the best methods, determine how your athletics department should attempt to communicate with students (both on and off campus) with regard to attending athletics events.

2. Using the same audience as in activity 1, determine whether price or nonprice promotional activities would be more effective in attracting college students to athletics events. (Note that this point may be moot on your campus if students are admitted free to all athletics events.)

3. When watching television over the next two weeks, keep an advertising journal and classify each advertisement that you see according to the list of structures for television commercials discussed in the chapter. Which commercial type was the most prevalent? Which commercial ad type was the most effective? Why?

4. Give a real-life example of the advertising communication system. Then create your own example of how you would send a message to a desired target.

5. Create a list of promotions that have attracted you to an event. What qualities did these promotions have that made the event attractive?

Your Marketing Plan

In developing your marketing plan, you have generated a list of objectives, strategies, and tactics. Sponsorship can be instrumental in helping you achieve these elements of a marketing plan by providing the resources (not necessarily just financial) needed to be successful. Integrate one or more of the concepts of sponsorship discussed in this chapter into your marketing plan.

Endnotes

1. Compiled from 2013 Major League Baseball team websites and David Broughton, "Everybody Loves Bobbleheads," SSSBJ, 12–18 November 2012, 9.

2. Mike Veeck address at the National Basketball Association Game Presentation Workshop, Seacaucus, NJ, 23 September 2003.

3. R. Batra, J.G. Myers, and D.A. Aaker, *Advertising Management*, 5th ed. (Upper Saddle River, NJ: Prentice Hall, 1996), 47.

4. Ibid., 45.

5. www.mckinsey.com/insights/marketing_sales/a_new_way_to_measure_word-of-mouth_marketing.

6. Ibid.

7. *Media Musing: The Ad That Wasn't There: Is Virtual Advertising Deceptive?* www.smccd.net/accounts/brownm/resources_med.html.

8. D.Stotlar and D. Johnson, "Assessing the Impact and Effectiveness of Stadium Advertising on Sports Spectators, *Journal of Sport Management*, 3 (July 1989): 14–20.

9. N.K. Pope and K.E. Voges, "Sponsorship Evaluation: Does It Match the Motive and the Mechanism?" *SMQ*, 3 (4) (1994): 37–45.

10. D.M. Turco, "The Effects of Courtside Advertising on Product Recognition and Attitude Change," *SMQ*, 5 (4) (1996): 11–15.

11. J. Lombardo, "Toyota Making Most of Unusual Combination," *SSSBJ*, 9–15 January 2006, 5.

12. www.allstatenewsroom.com/channels/News-Releases/releases/allstate-nets-deal-with-college-football-stadiums.

13. C. Brooks and K. Harris, "Celebrity Athlete Endorsement: An Overview of the Key Theoretical Issues," *SMQ*, 7 (2) (1998): 34–44. See also H. Friedman and L. Friedman, "Endorser Effectiveness by Product Type," *Journal of Advertising Research*, 19 (5) (1979): 63–71; and G. McCracken, "Who is the Celebrity Endorser? Cultural Foundations of the Endorsement Process," *Journal of Consumer Research*, 19 (December 1989): 310–321.

14. McCracken, "Who is the Celebrity Endorser?"

15. B. Sugar, *Hit the Sign and Win a Free Suit of Clothes From Harry Finkelstein* (Chicago: Contemporary Books, 1978), 327–329.

16. www.brandextract.com/blog/2012/02/14/jordan-brand-is-losing-its-luster/.

17. www.qscores.com/Web/Sports-Personalities.aspx.

18. http://sports.yahoo.com/news/michael-jordan-still-earns-80-million-175222679--nba.html.

19. www.nypost.com/p/news/business/lance_is_now_at_rear_of_zt2jPAFqtcT8FIewp430ML.

20. http://nikeinc.com/news/nike-statement-on-lance-armstrong.

21. articles.latimes.com/2011/nov/25/entertainment/la-et-hip-hop-drinks-20111125. Also see www.upmc.com/media/newsreleases/2011/pages/pitt-study-finds-us-kids-heavily-exposed-to-alcohol-brands-in-music.aspx.

22. Primack, Nuzzo, Rice, and Sargent, www.primack.net/professional/articles/r039addiction2011.pdf.

23. E. Spanberg, "Athletes Tie Endorsements to Equity Stakes in Upstart Companies," *SSSBJ*, 1–7 October 2012, 19.

24. Ibid.

25. B. King, "Retired but Still in the Game," *SSSBJ*, 9–15 October 2000, 27.

26. S. Kroft, L.F. Devine, and J. MacDonald, "A Living for the Dead," *60 Minutes*, CBS (2009), www.cbsnews.com/stories/2010/06/19/60minutes/main6598800.shtml.

27. D. Gellene, "Outlived by Fame and Fortunes. Dead Celebrities as Pitchmen? Advertisers See Them as 'a Safe Bet,'" *Los Angeles Times*, 11 September 1997, D4.

28. S. Wollenberg, "Jackie Robinson a Celebrity Endorser Again," *Marketing News*, 28 April 1997, 1.

29. http://stateofthemedia.org/2012/magazines-are-hopes-for-tablets-overdone/magazines-by-the-numbers.

30. http://suite101.com/article/pointofpurchase-advertising-trends-a192487.

31. Batra, Meyers, and Aaker, 94–95.

32. Ibid., 425.

33. M.J. Houston, T.L. Childers, and S.E. Heckler, "Picture-Word Consistency and the Elaborative Process of Advertisements," *Journal of Marketing Research*, 24 (December 1987): 359–369.

34. Phone conversation with Lou DePaoli, EVP Pittsburgh Pirates, 28 April 2013.

35. http://minnesota.twins.mlb.com/news/article.jsp?ymd=20130204&content_id=41382892&vkey=pr_min&c_id=min.

36. U.S. Census Bureau, *SRC Blue Book 2002*, Geoscape International.

37. http://losangeles.dodgers.mlb.com/la/sponsorship/hispanic_marketing/index.jsp.

38. http://streamingradioguide.com/streaming-radio.php?format=3.

39. Berry, R., "Will the iPod Kill the Radio Star? Profiling Podcasting as Radio," *Convergence: the International Journal of Research Into New Media Technologies*, 12 (2) (2006): 143–162.

40. www.nba.com/news/international_tv_deals_renewed_021112.html.

41. www.breitbart.com/Breitbart-Sports/2013/01/30/Football-television-ratings.

42. Bara, Meyers, and Aaker, 438.

43. S. Robinson and S. Richards, *The Power of Cow* (Chick-Fil-A published employee book, 2010).

44. B.J. Evensen, *When Dempsey Fought Tunney: Heroes, Hokum, and Storytelling in the Jazz Age* (Knoxville: University of Tennessee Press, 1996), quotation at 83; Paul Gallico, *The Golden People* (Garden City, NY: Doubleday, 1965), quotations at 180, 184, 186, and 191; Bruce Kidd, *The Struggle for Canadian Sport* (Toronto: University of Toronto Press, 1996), quotation at 219; J. Kofoed, "The Master of Ballyhoo," *North American Review*, 227 (March 1929): 282–286; "Madison Square Garden," *Fortune Magazine*, November 1935, 88–108, quotations at 91 and 102; Grantland Rice, "Boxing for a Million Dollars," *American Review of Reviews*, 74 (October 1926), 416–420.

45. http://bleacherreport.com/articles/276454-october-22nd-1939-the-first-nfl-game-is-televised.

46. J.R.B. Ritchie, "Assessing the Impact of Hallmark Events: Conceptual and Research Issues." *Journal of Travel Research*, 3 (1) (1984): 2–11.

47. S. Godin, *All Marketers Are Liars* (*Tell Stories*) (New York: Penguin, 2009).

48. D. Ziccardi, *Masterminding the Store* (New York: Wiley, 1997), 212–235.

49. Brad Tuttle, "JC Penney Reintroduces Fake Prices (and Lots of Coupons too, of Course)," http://business.time.com/2013/05/02/jc-penney-reintroduces-fake-prices-and-lots-of-coupons-too-of-course/.

50. B. Veeck and E. Linn, *Veeck as in Wreck* (New York: Putnam's, 1962), 104–118.

51. D. Broughton, "Everybody Loves Bobbleheads," *SSSBJ*, 12–18 November 2012, 9.

52. Ziccardi, *Masterminding the Store*, 215–235.

53. Phoenix Coyotes 1997 season-ticket brochure.

54. E-mail correspondence with Lou DePaoli, Pittsburgh Pirates, May 17, 2013.

55. Ibid.

56. L. Berling-Manual, "Family Fun Comes to the Forefront," *Ad Age*, 2 August 1984, 11.

57. B. Giles, "Special Effects Needed to Attract New Fans," *Athletic Purchasing and Facilities*, October 1980, 16–18.

58. C. Rees, "Does Sport Marketing Need a New Offense?" *Marketing and Media Decisions*, February 1981, 66–67, 126–132.

Chapter 11
Public Relations

Kathy Connors

OBJECTIVES

- To understand public relations and its role in positioning and in formulation of the marketing mix

- To recognize the importance of effective community relations programming in product positioning and effective marketing efforts

- To understand the role, scope, and influence of the media and how that role can be used in conjunction with public and community relations programming to alter perceptions and influence public opinion and support

How Public Relations, Media Coverage, and Primetime Television Showcased Michael Phelps' Chase for Olympic History

One of the great attractions of watching sport for fans is witnessing athletes and teams reach the pinnacle of their sport, achieve record-breaking performances, and attain historical greatness. A special place is reserved in the sporting landscape for those who etch their names atop the record books and accomplish iconic feats. U.S. swimmer Michael Phelps' record-breaking eight-gold-medal performance at the 2008 Beijing Olympic Games was remarkable and historic. His performance was surrounded by an outstanding public relations campaign.

After winning an impressive eight medals at the 2004 Athens Olympics, including six gold, Phelps emerged from those Games as a teenage Olympic sensation and a household name. In Athens, Phelps fell one gold medal short of tying Mark Spitz's then single-Games record haul of seven gold medals at the 1972 Munich Olympic Games. As the 2008 Beijing Games approached, Phelps stature had grown tremendously because of increased press attention, fascination with his potential historic attempt, and his growing superstar status. The media zoomed in on the storyline of Phelps' second attempt to chase Olympic greatness and match or break Spitz's mark of seven gold medals, which dominated the pre-2008 Beijing Olympics news cycle. Phelps generated headlines worldwide, garnering national and international media attention, including personality profiles and news feature placements in wide-ranging news, lifestyle, and sports outlets such as the *New York Times*, *USA Today*, *Sports Illustrated*, *Men's Journal*, *Vogue*, ESPN's *SportsCenter*, *NBC Nightly News*, NBC's *Today Show*, CCTV, BBC, and EuroSport. The PR and marketing spotlight on Phelps centered not only on his quest to match the seven gold medals but also on the $1 million bonus that he would receive from Speedo, one of his sponsors, if he tied Spitz's record (the Speedo bonus is covered later in this chapter). The Phelps PR blitz before the 2008 Beijing Olympics built anticipation and awareness for his chase at Spitz's medal milestone and provided a rich, compelling storyline that captivated the imagination of sports fans and the public. The Phelps media narrative created expectations and heightened intrigue, raising Olympic interest and driving potential television tune-in to viewers eager to watch the drama unfold.

In mid-2005 Dick Ebersol, then chairman of NBC Sports and Olympics, finalized negotiations with the International Olympic Committee (IOC) to move the swimming and gymnastics competitions for the 2008 Beijing Games to mornings instead of evenings, thus allowing those sports to be broadcast live during the NBC primetime telecasts in the United States.[1]

The change in the Beijing Olympic competition schedule was a brilliant strategic negotiation that proved to be "golden" for Phelps and for NBC. The network's ability to

> continued

Positive public relations has an essential role in promoting the image and ideals of an organization, institution, brand, athlete, or personality in sport. Public relations, or PR as it is often called, is a tool used to amplify a good marketing communications plan. Its value and use should never be underestimated. In today's instant information society, the media and public opinion continue to dominate how we perceive the world around us, including the sport industry. Public relations affects a wide variety of constituents in the marketplace, including the media and the public. In sport, PR applications

can be used to benefit business initiatives, create marketing opportunities, drive television tune-in, sell tickets and merchandise, build an individual athlete or personality's identity and recognition, create brand awareness, and promote community outreach programs. Public relations is an effective mechanism to position a sport organization or athlete in both the local community and the larger sport landscape. Effective public relations efforts and personnel who can proactively promote positive storylines, activities, and initiatives have become critical in the sport setting. These PR practitioners also have to function in times showcase Phelps' nightly swimming feats live in U.S. primetime allowed NBC to reach the largest possible audience available, further amplifying the Olympics coverage and the Phelps storyline. Phelps served as the centerpiece of intense Olympics media attention, commanding the top spot in a rapidly moving multiplatform news cycle during the first week of the Beijing Games, creating water-cooler conversation for the public and fueling even greater interest.

The Olympics are a unique global sporting, cultural, and entertainment spectacle—a television property that the world gathers to watch over the 17 days of the event. The Olympics transcend sport, attracting a diverse audience that includes casual sports fans and viewers who may not typically watch sport. Sport and television at their best are shared experiences, and Phelps' chase for Spitz's record exemplified that concept as viewers worldwide gathered around their televisions, captivated and mesmerized by the dazzling performances. Phelps was not only the story of the Games but also a news figure who dominated headlines worldwide. The Phelps quest played out in U.S. primetime and grew more riveting with each thrilling gold medal victory that took him a step closer to the record. His pursuit was a nightly episodic sport drama filled with dominant races, world records, and split-second photo finishes.

Phelps' epic performance helped catapult NBC's Olympics coverage to become what was, according to Nielsen Media Research, the most watched U.S. television event in history at that time; 215 million viewers tuned in to watch the network's 2008 Olympics coverage. (NBC's 2012 London Games coverage set a new most watched U.S. television event record with 219.4 million viewers according to Nielsen Media Research.)[2] The *New York Times* noted that NBC's Saturday primetime broadcast that aired Phelps' capture of his eighth and final medal of the 2008 Games was the network's best Saturday program ratings performance in 18 years. That Saturday evening, from 11 to 11:30 p.m. when the U.S. medley relay team captured gold, 39.9 million viewers were watching, according to Nielsen Media Research.[3] The unprecedented pre-Games media attention combined with substantial PR, savvy marketing, and a well-developed TV promotional campaign built anticipation, created giant expectations, and aroused curiosity for Phelps' quest in Beijing. Phelps' historic eight-gold-medal performance, delivered under extreme pressure on a grand international stage, received tremendous international press attention, was witnessed by a record television audience, and helped transform Michael Phelps into a sporting celebrity and Olympic icon.

of crisis to help provide reputation management and damage control. The PR department is the conduit through which many communications functions flow, including serving as the chief liaison with the media. The modern 24/7 news cycle moves with speed and intensity. The volume of coverage, rapid rate of reporting, and immediacy of information available make it important for PR professionals to take advantage of opportunities that allow their athletes and organizations to break through and make a meaningful and positive impact. PR personnel must be strong, passionate advocates on behalf of their athletes,

organizations, and brands while promoting them, but they also must be able to respond quickly to negative stories, incorrect reporting, and crises.

Throughout this text we have discussed a variety of ways in which the sport marketer can use advertising and promotions to position the organization and its sport products effectively in the marketplace. Unfortunately, these efforts can be undermined and rendered ineffective if the organization does not also have a good public relations strategy. In this chapter, we examine the role of public relations in the sport context, where it consists primarily of community relations and media relations but can also include social and digital media applications.

ACTIVITY 11.1 Public and Community Relations

In this WSG activity, you're the assistant manager of interactive marketing and community relations for Pocono Raceway. Pocono is a superspeedway located in the Pocono Mountains of Pennsylvania. It is the site of two annual NASCAR Sprint Cup Series races and hosts the IZOD IndyCar Series.

What Is Public Relations?

In 2011–12 the Public Relations Society of America (PRSA) embarked on a campaign to modernize the definition of public relations. The organization's new definition of public relations is "a strategic communication process that builds mutually beneficial relationships between organizations and their publics."[4] According to a corporate definition, offered by Clarke L. Caywood, public relations is "the profitable integration of an organization's new and continuing relationship with stakeholders, including customers, by managing all communications contacts with the organization that create and protect the reputation of the organization."[5] Finally, Govoni, Eng, and Galper emphasized the relationship between the sender and the audience in terms of the credibility of the message. They define public relations as "a multifaceted form of communication, with the intent to foster a positive company or product image in a nonsponsored framework." A key aspect of this definition is its emphasis on nonsponsorship. The authors believe that nonsponsorship "enhances the credibility of the message and cloaks the company with the respectability of the source, which may be viewed by the audience as either the spokesperson or the medium."[6]

For the purposes of sport marketing, we will define public relations as

an interactive marketing communications strategy that seeks to create a variety of media designed to convey the organizational philosophies, goals, and objectives to an identified group of publics for the purpose of establishing a relationship built on comprehension, interest, and support.

This communication strategy, which may take the form of activities as well as formal communication, may also involve players, team management, broadcast personnel, coaching staff, mascots and other product extensions, sponsors, and other key components of the organization.

Public relations is a management function in that it reflects policies and programs developed at the top levels of management. Public relations systematically evaluates attitudes toward the organization and its products and hence depends on an effective and current marketing information system. Public relations identifies the influence of the public interest; this consumer or marketing perspective differentiates public relations from press agentry, a propitiatory agenda, and advertising. Public relations usually involves implementing specific publicity plans and tactics in coordination with the marketing strategy, designed to alter or reinforce consumer perceptions, attitudes, or levels of awareness. The goal of this function is to earn public understanding and acceptance. Finally, the source, or more accurately the perceived source, will in many cases lend credibility to the message or course of action. The following sidebar provides a detailed and functional view of the role, responsibilities, and strategic functions of a PR practitioner in sport.

In sport, public relations is often perceived to be synonymous with publicity or media relations. Many people have developed this perception because public relations directors often deal largely with advocating on behalf of their clients with the press by pitching stories and providing information (biographical, statistical, or promotional) to gain increased media exposure for the sport organization. Effective public relations programs (both media relations and community relations) usually create publicity—news stories, articles, interviews, and other activities. But because this publicity is not paid media, the outcomes are not controllable and there is no guarantee that the stories will be positive. Media relations is a large component of the public relations function and is probably the more important function because of the volume of media coverage available and the influence that media have on sport and society in general. But community relations can be at least equally

Role of a PR Professional

Kathy Connors, Principal and Founder, KMC Consulting, LLC

Public relations is the function of communicating an organization's message externally, including to the press, and a public relations professional is the liaison between those parties. In the modern 24-hour-a-day, 7-day-a-week news cycle world—a culture now fueled by an omnipresent media, blogs, and constant social media conversation—the need for competent public and media relations specialists is expanding. Like their counterparts in other industries, PR professionals in sport need to understand the art of effectively communicating with a wide range of media outlets, external mediums, and contacts on behalf of their organization or clients. The chief role of the public relations professional is to serve as the spokesperson to the media and external constituents on behalf of those they represent. The spokesperson in media interviews or press opportunities can also be an appropriately identified person—an executive, administrator, coach, or athlete.

PR professionals plan and execute media and award campaigns; facilitate interviews for athletes, coaches, and executives; pitch stories to media; respond to media inquiries; and distribute press releases, statistical information, media guides, press kits, photography, and other helpful promotional information and content. PR staffs also determine and schedule media availability sessions with coaches, players, and executives; schedule and facilitate radio and TV media tours; and host media briefings, press conferences, and events for more formal announcements. The ultimate goal for public relations professionals is to cultivate the most positive image possible for those they serve by proactively seeking and accommodating as many favorable opportunities in the press as possible. PR staffs must also manage the difficult or negative press as effectively and professionally as possible.

The most successful organizations fully integrate their public relations efforts with advertising, marketing, sales, sponsorship, community relations, and social media efforts so that the external messages all reflect the same theme. The synergy among these areas of an organization or individual athlete's management team is vital in presenting a unified image through all external communication.

PR professionals should possess the following attributes: credibility and integrity, commitment to serving media outlets in a timely manner, excellent written and spoken communication skills, and ability to work on and with deadlines. Good public relations specialists should adopt the following skills in their practice:

- **Building relationships**. The cornerstone of a successful career in public and media relations is possessing the ability to forge and maintain good working relationships with the press. Even if a reporter or media outlet has done a negative story or is difficult to deal with, the PR professional should seek to manage a working relationship with that reporter or media outlet, always trying to keep the lines of communication open. The need for relationship building should also be important in serving internal organizational constituents and clients as well. Internal colleagues, executives, and clients must be educated to understand the value of publicity and be willing participants in the process. Trust is probably the most important element in building effective working relationships in any realm, including public relations. A skilled public relations person should be a trusted and respected member of the company, organization, or management team and a valued resource for the press.

- **Communication**. Obviously, one of the most important skills in public relations is effective communication. Communications, both internally and externally, should be directed in the most clear, concise, timely, and efficient way. The PR person should produce materials that contain the necessary information in the best and clearest possible way. As mentioned earlier, building and maintaining good interpersonal working relationships is important,

> continued

but when routine and basic information is being exchanged, the PR professional needs to be efficient and considerate of deadlines by using technology and e-mail to their advantage. E-mail is a helpful tool and has become the primary form of communication in business, including between PR professionals and media, but maintaining interpersonal relationships is important as well, so dialogue by phone and occasional in-person conversations are advised. PR spokespersons should keep in mind that in all forms of on-the-record communication, they are speaking as a representative of their organization or client.

• **Creating the public relations plan**. For a large-scale public relations project, a comprehensive plan should be designed to spell out the strategy to promote that message. The plan should detail a chronological outline of how the objective of the campaign will be achieved. When creating the plan, the PR professional should consider the timelines and deadlines of the publications being targeted. Outlets that make sense for the message should be identified, and adequate time should be set aside to meet deadlines, achieve all objectives, and reach the targeted outlets. For instance, if the goal is to increase exposure for the brand, athlete, league, or organization in a certain segment of the population, the PR professional should build a targeted plan around outlets that the demographic group reads, hears, or views. Managing multiple tasks and story placements simultaneously is critical. Opportunities should be maximized in both major outlets and smaller ones. All placements play a role in the overall strategy, especially now because social media has expanded the potential reach of every content platform, media impression, and story placement.

• **Have a balanced and strategic approach**. While evaluating the daily and weekly media requests and the goals and media targets of the PR plan, PR professionals need to use a balanced and strategic approach. They need to evaluate the reactive media requests received and be proactive about securing opportunities that are maximally beneficial. A balance should be struck between stories in traditional and digital outlets and the use of social media. They should consider and include outlets across the full spectrum of media platforms—print newspapers and magazines, TV, radio, digital, websites, blogs, and social media—and recognize the value of securing a range of international, national, regional, and local opportunities.

• **Making the pitches**. After creating a plan or identifying a storyline that is a priority, PR professionals need to be proactive and pitch stories. They should always know who they are pitching to—that they are pitching the right reporters and catering the pitch to the specific publication or outlet. They must be aware of deadlines and be considerate of the time that will be required to cover the story adequately. PR professionals should avoid pitching a reporter a story idea that makes no sense for either the outlet, the subject matter it covers, or the type of stories it typically does.

• **Managing the story**. One of the most important skills in media relations is the ability to manage a story while it is being completed. The routine story and placements usually do not require more than basic interview coordination and postinterview follow-up skills. The art of managing a story is a practice generally reserved for in-depth pieces or pieces in major outlets. The tone or spirit of the piece should always be established at the beginning of the process. By keeping a dialogue going with the reporter as she conducts her interviews (a process in which the public relations professional should be actively involved) and collects her facts, the public relations professional can get an idea of the general direction of the piece. By staying involved in the process, the PR person can correct inaccuracies, make appropriate suggestions, emphasize key points, or learn whether the tone or focus of the story has changed while the piece is being reported.

- **Managing expectations**. Athletes want to be profiled in publications like *Sports Illustrated*, and executives want to be featured in outlets like the *Wall Street Journal*. The role of the PR professional is to make pitches to those outlets and work diligently to create influential media opportunities. Managing the expectation that those proactive pitches will turn into potential placements is also important. PR professionals cannot control or guarantee the success of the pitches or outcomes of the placements if secured, but they can try to forecast the range of opportunities that may be available to their clients in the media marketplace.

- **Media training and talking points**. Being an effective spokesperson and feeling comfortable dealing with media are invaluable skills. Helping athletes and executives achieve success in this area is an important responsibility of the PR professional. Media training and mock interviews are a helpful exercise in preparing people for media interviews and public question-and-answer forums. The public relations professional can provide instruction, suggestions for improvement, and useful techniques during these media training sessions. Providing ongoing feedback on interview performance after media appearances is also recommended. Talking points are a helpful resource in both media training and the public relations practice to help subjects prepare for interviews. Talking points will help people prepare responses to questions, organize thoughts, and stay on the desired message when speaking to the press. The talking points document should include a carefully crafted and clear response to every conceivable question that could be asked on that particular subject. Talking points are recommended especially when dealing with a difficult or complicated matter because they will help the spokesperson stay on message.

- **Crisis management**. Not all public relations is positive, and unfortunately, negative media stories are becoming more common. Managing bad press is a special skill. Obviously, the response required depends on the nature and scope of the issues involved with the negative story or crisis. The first step in this type of reactive situation is formulating a plan for making a media and public response. A quick, effective response will help minimize the damage and ideally will decrease the shelf life of the story—the goal in all crisis or damage control situations. Social media and the ability for media to report quickly on the Internet have made these situations more difficult to handle, because the reporting cycle has now become immediate. PR professionals need to recognize the intensity of the media's desire for a response, but they should not release official statements until they are ready with an appropriate, well thought out, and strategic response.

---

significant in affecting sales, generating positive public sentiment, and building a long-term relationship and connection with the community. Community relations provides the opportunity to make a lasting connection between athletes or sport organizations and the communities where they work and compete. It also provides potential media opportunities in the marketplace and a chance to showcase athletes and the sport organization as good citizens who make a meaningful impact. Sport attracts a large and captive audience, which presents a big platform to promote a powerful message through visible messengers. Sport PR professionals should strive to create media opportunities that amplify an individual or organizational message in the community by using recognizable sport personality messengers.

Media Relations

Public opinion is one of the most powerful forces in society, and media relations is designed to formulate and shape favorable opinion through the mass media. Media relations—communicating with the news media verbally or through other vehicles—must also balance public opinion with business strategy. Depending on its role within the organization, media relations takes one or more of the following approaches: reactive, proactive, or interactive.[7]

Those involved in a reactive media relations situation respond to inquiries. They respond to questions, queries, and requests from the media and other interested parties. In a sport setting, such requests may concern interviews, appearances, autographs, photos, biographies, or profiles of players, coaches, or executives. Besides these simple requests, the reactive function might also relate to requests for statements about or reactions to situations involving organizational policy or business activity.

In proactive media relations, the point of initiation is the organization rather than an external entity. PR professionals contact media outlets with possible story pitches and feature ideas. They distribute player bios, media guides, game notes, highlight films, award flyers, promotional materials, or video pieces to a preselected audience without having been requested to do so. We see an excellent historical example of a proactive approach in a 1907 correspondence between R.J. Hellawell of Spalding & Bros. to James E. Sullivan, the Amateur Athletic Union's driving force, whose real job was president of the American Sports Publishing Company, a firm owned by Spalding. In his letter, Hellawell wrote, "We should have articles in the newspapers praising and telling of the decrease in accidents [in football]. We could have these in the shape of interviews with head Coaches, Trainers and others prominent in Foot Ball. Of course, it would add weight to them. You no doubt will see some way to work out this matter and perhaps you have something in mind that will be better than this suggestion, but I really think that we should do all we could to turn sentiment in favor of Foot Ball."[8]

Although media relations will always have reactive functions, the primary activity should be proactive—to take the initiative in providing information and creating publicity to enhance the perception of the entity. The sidebar, featuring a proactive communications method used by the Boston Celtics, is an excellent illustration of this approach.

ACTIVITY 11.2 Damage Control

In this WSG activity, you will wear many hats as you help Rutgers University control the damage caused by videos showing their men's basketball coach verbally and physically abusing players.

Interactive media relations involves developing mutually beneficial relationships with the media and assisting the media on a variety of issues. This function relates closely to relationship marketing and focuses on building long-term relationships rather than accomplishing short-term public relations objectives. Although these short-term public relations objectives are important, they are just a component of a larger mission designed to facilitate relationships and the essentials of a media relations program. In interactive media relations, either party can initiate the action or activity, hoping that the other will cooperate because doing so is in its best interest.

Community Relations

Once viewed as an afterthought or as an as-funding-permits budget item, community relations has become an integral part of the marketing efforts of sport organizations. Community relations programs and charitable initiatives have emerged as a strategy that sport organizations (particularly those at the professional level) use to deliver outreach programs. The aim of such programs is to achieve corporate public relations objectives related to enhancing public understanding and gaining public approval and acceptance.[10]

Community relations programs are usually implemented in one of three ways. These efforts can be player initiated, team initiated, or league initiated. Within recent years, sport organizations have acknowledged the importance of community relations programs and have added staff to execute these programs or have added community relations responsibilities to the job descriptions of existing staff.

Players are an integral part of community relations initiatives. Almost all community relations programs and most charitable programs have some element of player involvement because the presence of the players and their involvement attracts funding to the program through sponsorship, garners media interest and coverage, and attracts an audience of participants and observers to the program.

Community relations programs complement media relations programs and their goal of raising awareness levels among consumers and the public. Besides raising awareness by being visible in the community, community relations programs attempt to create goodwill. Although the intent of both efforts is to generate publicity for the organization, media relations yields greater immediate results. Community relations

Value of Internal Communications

Internal communications are an effective way to inform, educate, and build relationships with stakeholders. Sponsors and ticket holders are key stakeholders for every sport franchise. The emotional nature of sport dictates that these stakeholders have a strong connection to the organization that can be weakened when they do not support a decision made by the franchise either because they do not have the information or because they are influenced by the media, social media, or other third parties in their interpretations of those decisions. The Celtics have tried to minimize the risk of such occurrences by treating their stakeholders as insiders—the first to know, straight from the organization. The following e-mail was sent to all Celtics e-news subscribers on December 16, 2003, following a trade that was pending at the time.[9]

From: Danny Ainge [dainge@enews.celtics.com]
Sent: 12/16/2003 04:47 PM
To:
Subject: Celtics Beat: Trade Alert

Dear Lou,

As you know, we made a trade yesterday with Cleveland for Ricky Davis, Chris Mihm, Michael Stewart, and a second round draft pick for Eric Williams, Tony Battie, and Kedrick Brown. We hope to have the trade finalized later today pending the completion of physicals.

I think this trade helps us in both the short and the long term. In the short term, it gives us better immediate scoring and rebounding. In the long term, we just got a lot younger and more athletic. Red has always told me you make deals when you are winning. These are two players I tried to get this summer and in the early part of the season, but they were unavailable. I believe the way Tony and Eric have played to start the season made this deal available.

I picked Ricky up at the airport last night and we spent about an hour together. He is thrilled to be a Boston Celtic. We spoke about Celtic tradition, Jim O'Brien's work ethic and expectations, and how things are different here in Boston than they are in most cities. Ricky is a very talented young man. He averaged 20 points, 5 rebounds, and nearly 5 assists per game last season. Even though he is an effective player right now, at only 24 years old I believe he is just starting to come into his prime as a player with all-star caliber upside. I spoke with Paul yesterday regarding the deal. Paul knows Ricky well as they work out together in the summer in Los Angeles and he is very excited to have Ricky as a teammate. He will complement Paul when they are on the court together because he will defend the other team's best offensive wing player.

Chris Mihm is a 24-year-old kid who had some health issues and is now healthy for the first time and playing well. He's 7-feet, 265-pounds, athletic, and he can shoot. He is a better rebounder than anyone we have on our team right now and ranks fifth in the NBA in rebounds on a per minute basis. I believe Chris's future price tag will be much higher than what we had to give up yesterday in the trade to obtain him. I think both Davis and Mihm are at a very good time in their careers where their "stock values" so to speak are at a good purchase price.

Michael Stewart has kind of been the odd man out in a couple of organizations. He is a Mark Blount type of player with great character. He is not offensive minded but can really rebound and block shots.

As I said, the players involved will be going through physicals today, and we hope to get the deal finalized, get them on the court, and begin the process of getting them acclimated to our system. Thank you for your continued interest and support of the Boston Celtics.

Sincerely,
Danny Ainge
Executive Director of Basketball Operations

Courtesy of Danny Ainge.

programs, on the other hand, often have long-term objectives, such as fan development. One of the great benefits of community relations programs and charitable activities is that they allow fans and the community to see athletes and organizations through a different lens and to interact with them in a personal way. These programs provide the opportunity to humanize athletes and sport personalities. Although fans already have an emotional connection to the teams and athletes whom they support and follow, these community events and outreach programs provide an additional perspective and have the potential to make a beneficial human connection. Although the long-term value and effectiveness of community relations programs can be measured in the goodwill and publicity generated, they should also be measured in terms of fan building. Fan building leads to ticket sales, broadcast ratings, merchandise sales, and sponsor interest and value. Fan building through community relations programs is a key ingredient in creating fan identification—the emotional involvement that customers have with a sport organization and the basis for creating relationships with long-term value (e.g., ticket sales, broadcast ratings, merchandise sales, positive word-of-mouth advertising) that we have discussed previously.[11]

For professional sport organizations, community relations may involve designating certain games as community nights so that marketing efforts are directed specifically at a geographic target market. This concept has been so successful that some professional sport teams have defined communities as ethnic groups and have set aside themed days for ethnic celebrations with special food, music, and player appearances (when players from that particular ethnic background are team members).

Community relations can also take the form of corporate philanthropy. Like sales, promotion, advertising, event marketing, and sponsorship activities, corporate philanthropy is intended to position the company in the mind of the stakeholder. But unlike those activities, which are line items in an operating budget, corporate philanthropy activities come from a company's profits.[12] McDonald's and Coca-Cola, for example, use philanthropy to position themselves as good neighbors and to challenge their employees and other businesses to match their efforts and contribute to the selected beneficiaries.

Shortly before the beginning of the 2005–2006 NBA season, Commissioner David Stern announced a new and far-reaching community outreach platform for the NBA called NBA Cares. The initiative positions NBA Cares as the umbrella name for all NBA community efforts, including the following:

Coaches for Kids
NBA and WNBA FIT
NBA Green
Basketball Without Borders
Kia Community Assist

In addition, NBA Cares, the NBA's international community outreach effort, works with myriad internationally recognized youth-serving organizations including UNICEF, Reading Is Fundamental (RIF), Boys and Girls Clubs of America, American Red Cross, Global Business Coalition on HIV/AIDS, KaBOOM!, Habitat for Humanity International, Special Olympics, the Make-A-Wish Foundation, and many others.[13] According to Commissioner Stern, "NBA Cares will be the platform through which players and teams will raise and contribute $100 million dollars for charity, donate more than one million hours of volunteer service to communities worldwide, and build more than 100 educational and athletic facilities where children can learn and play, all over the next five years."[14] Since its launch in October 2005, "The NBA and its teams have raised more than $220 million for charity, provided more than 2.5 million hours of hands-on service, and built more than 810 places where kids and families can live, learn or play" in communities worldwide through the NBA Cares initiative.[15] NBA Cares provides an additional platform for the league's corporate sponsorship partners and broadcast partners to join the NBA in these charitable community and philanthropic programs.

What are the possible outcomes of such a commitment? According to Marc Pollick, president and founder of the Giving Back Fund, a national nonprofit organization that helps athletes and entertainers create and manage high-impact philanthropy, much can be gained. According to Pollick, "Sports possess a loyal and devoted fan base, virtually unlimited access to the media and substantial persuasion with its corporate sponsors. And perhaps the most powerful tool of all: the opportunity, and maybe even the responsibility to *role model* socially conscious behavior in ways that have transformative staying power, in ways that reach across all social strata and boundaries. What other industry in our society has the power in the palm of its hand to make giving back cool? If the NBA says giving is cool, it becomes a self-fulfilling prophecy. Once its fan base is convinced of that notion, imagine the possibilities."[16]

During the 2005 season, the PGA Tour, Champions Tour, and Nationwide Tour participated in the Drive to a Billion, a yearlong campaign focused on reaching the $1 billion milestone in charitable giving—a goal that was achieved later that season.[17] Since its first recorded charitable donation of $10,000 at the 1938 Palm Beach Invitational, tournaments on the PGA Tour, Champions Tour, and Web.com Tour have combined to contribute more than $1.7 billion to local communities.[18] In 2010 the PGA Tour activated an initiative to elevate its charity platform, called Together, Anything's Possible, to "broaden awareness of the outstanding charitable work of the tournaments, sponsors, players and volunteers and to give the Tour's fans and the general public a way to offer their support to these causes."[19] The PGA Tour and its players and tournaments support more than 3,000 charities. The categories of local and national organizations include youth and children, volunteerism, military, health and medical, growth of the game, environment, education and leadership, disaster relief, and community. Some of the organizations supported include Make-A-Wish Foundation of America, Birdies for the Brave, St. Jude Children's Research Hospital, the First Tee, and the Evans Scholars Foundation, among many others.[20] To showcase how important charitable giving is to the PGA Tour, when announcing a new 10-year broadcast contract with its television partners in 2011, Commissioner Tim Finchem pointed out that the new TV agreements provided a decade

Members of the PGA Tour Wives Association prepare items to be given out at a food bank. This is one example of their charitable activities aimed at helping local communities.

to enhance the PGA Tour's ability to grow charitable giving. Finchem stated, "We can now with confidence expect to reach $2 billion in all-time charitable contributions by 2014, and conceivably reach $3 billion by the end of the term. As has been the case over the years, and certainly now, our growth is predicated on the unique partnership of athletes with a very positive image, dedicated sponsors, loyal fans and tournaments, all of which are dedicated to helping people."[21]

The PGA Tour's charitable activities are an excellent example of how sport organizations, athletes, and events can have a meaningful effect on society and contribute to local communities in a positive way by giving back. Bob Lohman, president of the board of trustees at the Ronald McDonald House in Fort Worth, the site of a PGA Tour Wives Association event during the 2012 Crowne Plaza Invitational at Colonial, told *Golf World*, "No other sport gives back like golf does. The charities are so very thankful. We are in a tough economy, and we are thankful for the generosity of golf."[22]

Numerous activities can generate goodwill and revenue for an organization. The key is that both long-term and short-term benefits derive from the development of a balanced, strategically designed community relations or charitable outreach program. The three examples that follow—the Orlando Magic Youth Foundation, KPMG Chip4Charity with Phil Mickelson, and the New York Yankees HOPE Week—show how teams and individual athletes can work together to give back and make positive contributions to the community and charitable organizations.

Orlando Magic Youth Foundation

The Orlando Magic have taken a foundation approach to community relations. The Orlando Magic Youth Foundation (OMYF) was founded in 1988 to raise funds and community awareness to help combat the many physical, emotional, and social challenges facing the children of central Florida. OMYF is part of RDV Sports Team Charities, the nonprofit, private foundations representing the company's three professional sport teams.

In over 22 years of giving, OMYF has had a positive effect on more than 1 million kids. Through private donations, fund-raising events, and contributions, more than $17 million has been raised and distributed to nonprofit organizations that support the mission statement of OMYF. It is truly a team effort by Magic players, coaches, staff, and the DeVos family, in partnership with season-ticket holders, corporate sponsors, fans, and the community.

In addition to receiving a 50-cent match from its funding partner, the Robert R. McCormick Tribune Foundation, 100 percent of every donation to OMYF goes back into the community with an even greater effect. It's a winning combination for everyone.

OMYF fund-raising events and programs include the Black Tie and Tennies Charity Gala and the OMYF Golf Tournament.[23]

KPMG Chip4Charity With Phil Mickelson

PGA Tour star Phil Mickelson participated in the KPMG Chip4Charity, which took place at halftime of the Denver Broncos versus San Diego Chargers Monday Night Football game at Qualcomm Stadium on October 15, 2012. Mickelson, a San Diego native, teamed up with KPMG LLP, his official hat sponsor, to support KPMG's Youth Literacy Initiative. KPMG Chip4Charity provided Mickelson with a chance to make a 100-yard shot to win up to a $1 million KPMG donation for First Book, a nonprofit organization KPMG teams with to provide new books for children in need.[24] Although Mickelson did not hit the $1 million target, KPMG still donated $50,000 to First Book for the purchase of 20,000 new books for children in honor of Mickelson's hitting another 100-yard KPMG Chip4Charity target.[25] The combination of one of the PGA Tour's most popular players, a Monday Night Football game televised on ESPN, and the potential for a donation of up to $1 million for charity was a creative and effective way to cross-promote between NFL and golf media outlets, in addition to promoting to other national and local media to attract attention. KPMG Chip4Charity is an excellent example of a fully integrated corporate sport marketing activation that includes sponsor, PR, charitable, and community relations elements that helped achieve PR goals by drawing attention and awareness for KPMG's partnership with Mickelson, KPMG's youth literacy initiatives, and First Book. The press release announcement provided in the sidebar includes details.

Phil Mickelson Participating in KPMG Chip4Charity at Halftime of Broncos Versus Chargers Game, October 15

PGA Tour Star Trying $1 Million Shot at Monday Night Football Game to Support KPMG's Youth Literacy Initiative

KPMG LLP, official hat sponsor of PGA Tour star Phil Mickelson, announced today that Mickelson will attempt a $1 million KPMG Chip4Charity shot at halftime of the Monday night football game on October 15, when the San Diego Chargers host the Denver Broncos at Qualcomm Stadium. At stake for the 100-yard shot is as much as $1 million for First Book, a nonprofit organization that provides new books for children in need. Mickelson will be located in one end zone, aiming for a target in the other end zone, which will have a green ($50,000 and 20,000 books) and three rings ranging from $100,000 and 40,000 books (outermost ring) to $1 million and 400,000 books (bull's-eye center ring).

KPMG's Family for Literacy teamed with Mickelson and First Book to create KPMG's Blue for Books program in March 2012. The program encourages golf fans to purchase Mickelson's authentic blue KPMG Tour hat at PhilsBlueHat.com.

KPMG donates 100 percent of the net proceeds to First Book, which provides deserving children three books for each hat sold. Mickelson's KPMG Chip4Charity is a marquee component of the Blue for Books campaign.

"This Chip4Charity is very exciting, and has the potential to provide a significant contribution to youth literacy. We created Blue for Books as a way for Phil's fans to wear his hat while also supporting KPMG's Family for Literacy (KFFL)," said John Veihmeyer, chairman and CEO of KPMG LLP, the U.S. audit, tax, and advisory firm. "We understand that the toughest roadblock to children's literacy is access to books. KPMG and Phil share a passion for doing whatever we can to help children in need get off to a good start in life."

Mickelson said, "My wife, Amy, and I feel strongly that literacy and education are critical to the future success of today's youth. I am extremely proud to be part of the Blue for Books campaign and it's just great to know that for every blue hat I see out in the gallery each week, three new books are in the hands of kids who need them most."

Joining Mickelson at the game will be the winner (to be announced October 9) of the Where Is The Blue Hat Taking You? contest, an interactive social media extension of the Blue for Books program. Complete information about the Blue for Books program can be found by following KPMG's Mickelson sponsorship Twitter handle (@MickelsonHat) or by visiting PhilsBlueHat.com.

KPMG's Family for Literacy began five years ago in cooperation with First Book and is led by the spouses of KPMG partners and professionals from across the firm's offices. To date, KPMG has delivered more than two million books to children in local communities throughout the country. In addition to raising money for KPMG's Family for Literacy, KPMG's extended family of volunteers, which includes partners, spouses, employees, interns and alumni, and family and friends, visits classrooms, reads to children, and delivers new books to low-income children. In many cases, these are the first books that their families have owned.

About KPMG LLP

KPMG LLP, the audit, tax, and advisory firm (www.kpmg.com/us), is the U.S. member firm of KPMG International Cooperative ("KPMG International"). KPMG International's member firms have 145,000 people, including more than 8,000 partners, in 152 countries.

Reprinted, by permission, from KPMG. Available: http://www.kpmg.com/US/en/IssuesAndInsights/ArticlesPublications/Press-Releases/Pages/Phil-Mickelson-Participating-In-KPMG-Chip4Charity-At-Halftime-Of-Broncos-Vs-Chargers-Game-Oct-15.aspx.

Saying Goodbye and Showing Appreciation—How Communications Connects Players, Teams, Fans, and the Community

Player departures, either by trade or through free agency, are industry transactions that organizations, executives, and players understand are part of the sport business. Despite the fact that these deals are both routine and expected, they still can be difficult experiences for players, teams, and fans, especially when the player has had a significant influence on the organization's success and the community. Although these situations are often emotional and sometimes bitter, handling the athlete's departure in the best way possible is important.

Some athletes have taken the opportunity to place thank-you advertisements in local newspapers to communicate their appreciation and express thanks to the fans for their support during their time with the team and the city. Organizations have also used newspaper ads to extend thanks to players for their contributions to the organization and community during their time with the franchise. These ads are effective from both a public and community relations perspective. The individual player can express a personalized and positive message reflecting and commemorating his or her time with the team and to fans and the city.

After leaving the Boston Celtics for the Miami Heat during the offseason following the 2011–12 NBA season, Ray Allen placed a full-page advertisement in the *Boston Globe* with the following gracious message:[29]

> Dear Celtics Fans,
> For the past five years, my family and I took great pride in calling Boston home. We have loved living in this city, being members of the Celtics family and being part of your community. These memories will be cherished forever. From my heart, THANK YOU *Boston for this incredible journey.*
>
> Ray Allen #20

When the Boston Celtics traded Paul Pierce and Kevin Garnett to the Brooklyn Nets during the offseason following the 2012–13 NBA campaign, the Celtics organization took out a full-page advertisement in the *Boston Globe* to thank Pierce and Garnett, who helped guide the Celtics to the 2008 NBA championship, the franchise's first NBA title since 1986. The following message was included in the advertisement:[30]

> Thank you
> For your heart
> For your passion
> For your sacrifice
> For playing through the pain
> For bleeding green
> For honoring tradition
> For an amazing ride
> For restoring Celtic pride
> For banner 17

Sharing meaningful and thoughtful social media messages can also be a positive public and community relations outreach tool in these situations. Pierce, who had spent his entire pro career in Boston said goodbye and expressed his thanks by posting a series of photos with the hashtag #THANKYOUBOSTON on Twitter and his newly launched Instagram account. One of the photos included the following message:[31]

> THANKYOUBOSTON. Boston, you've been my home for the last 15 years. Together, we've been through it all. I could not be more grateful for all of your support and Boston will forever be a part of who I am.

Although seeing their favorite players depart for a new team or retire from competition is difficult for fans, players and organizations can make an effort to share a personalized message with the community through traditional or social media platforms to extend well wishes and express feelings of gratitude, appreciation, and farewell.

New York Yankees HOPE Week

In 2009 the New York Yankees introduced HOPE Week, an organization-wide community outreach effort involving Yankees players, coaches, front-office personnel, and sponsors. The spirit of HOPE Week (Helping Others Persevere and Excel) is that "acts of goodwill provide hope and encouragement to more than just the recipient of the gesture."[26] HOPE Week provides an opportunity to garner publicity and attract attention for many worthy causes and to showcase the good works of the individual or organization chosen by the New York Yankees. HOPE Week honorees visit Yankee Stadium on a game day and participate in pregame and on-field activities like batting practice, ceremonial first pitches, and the exchange of team lineup cards after a day of outreach with Yankees players and team personnel designed to showcase the work of the honoree in the community. In 2012 the Yankees made a $10,000 donation to each of the five honorees during the five days of HOPE Week. At the conclusion of the 2010 and 2011 HOPE Week, the Yankees and the Steinbrenner family were honored with the President's Volunteer Service Award, given "in recognition and appreciation of commitment to strengthening the nation and for making a difference through volunteer service." The award was bestowed by the President's Council on Service and Civic Participation in conjunction with the Corporation for National and Community Service.[27] Jason Zillo, the New York Yankees communications director, who helped create HOPE Week commented, "We have a platform and we need to use it. . . . The easy thing in many cases is to open up a checkbook. But for a person to know that another person is giving of themselves is a valuable commodity."[28]

Public Relations in the Sport Marketing Mix

Public relations is a vital part of sport marketing strategy and a critical component of effective sport sponsorship activation plans. One of the objectives of the sport marketing strategy is to develop a brand association between the athlete, team, league, or sport property and their sponsors. Media exposure is a great way to increase awareness of the sponsorship and showcase the connection between the parties in the marketing partnership. Athletes and teams that are capable of capitalizing on PR opportunities to highlight existing marketing relationships illustrate to the sponsor that they are valuable partners. Marketing and PR personnel should work diligently and collaboratively to develop creative and effective PR and media opportunities for sponsor-driven appearances or events to create and extend awareness of the brand association.

Many sponsors are interested and willing to include a community, charitable, or philanthropic element in their marketing partnerships with athletes and sport organizations. Supporting an individual athlete's foundation or a sport organization's charitable initiatives is a great way for a sponsor to extend its charitable activities and develop a more meaningful partnership. The combination of athletes, teams, sponsors, and charitable, philanthropic, or community-driven initiatives can create unique media opportunities locally and nationally.

A good illustration of this concept features Olympic superstar swimmer Michael Phelps, his longtime sponsor Speedo, and the creation of the Michael Phelps Foundation. Phelps won a single-Games record of eight gold medals at the 2008 Beijing Olympic Games and earned a $1 million bonus from Speedo for tying Mark Spitz's seven-gold-medal performance at the 1972 Munich Olympic Games. In a September 2, 2008, appearance on NBC's *Today Show*, Phelps announced that he would start the Michael Phelps Foundation to fund programs for water safety and youth swimming with his bonus money.[32] Phelps was presented with the $1 million bonus by Joseph Gromek, president and CEO of Warnaco, the licensee for Speedo in North America, and Warnaco and Speedo International announced an additional $200,000 donation to the Michael Phelps Foundation in honor of Phelps' eighth gold medal in Beijing.[33] Phelps' quest to break Spitz's record and the chance to earn the $1 million Speedo bonus had generated a great deal of media attention leading up to both the 2004 and 2008 Olympics. Phelps' announcement to use the bonus to create the foundation capitalized on the heavy media interest in the record-setting Phelps after the 2008 Beijing Olympics and attracted additional press attention for Phelps, Speedo, and the launch of the Michael Phelps Foundation.

Sport Public Relations in the Digital Age

The Internet has revolutionized the way that we communicate with each other, and it has transformed the way that people consume media content. Traditional media outlets still are a major source of sports news, but people also turn to social and digital media platforms for information and news updates. Athletes, leagues, teams, and organizations across the global sport industry have embraced social and digital media platforms, including blogs, websites, and social-networking sites like Twitter and Facebook as promotional vehicles to connect with fans and the public (as detailed in chapter 12 on social media). The direct interaction provided on social and digital media platforms is an effective way to stay connected to fans, share information and content, cultivate new followers and fans, and create public interest—an extension of the goals of the PR strategy and job function. Digital and social media have also provided athletes, coaches, teams, leagues, executives, and sponsors their own platforms to break news and a place to share information and opinion, showcase their personalities, describe charitable initiatives, and promote marketing partnerships without having to rely on traditional media outlets to report stories. The sidebar describes how blogs can be used as a PR platform and provides an example of how Dallas Mavericks owner Mark Cuban shares opinions on his blog.

Interactive technology offers many advantages to businesses. The instant and direct communication that these mechanisms provide benefits a variety of constituents including fans, ticket holders, sponsors, and business partners, but organizations must recognize that media outlets and the public follow social and digital media

closely. A Tweet, Facebook post, website message, blog, or video post is an official on-the-record communication from the sender.

Sport PR professionals should be diligent about observing interviews and examining public comments of the athletes, executives, and coaches whom they work with, but the need to monitor and review all comments in the digital age is especially urgent. PR professionals must pay attention to written, photo, or video posts on social media sites and websites of organizations, individual athletes, and executives. Controversial, inappropriate, or negative comments or photos posted or made on social media or blogs or made to traditional media outlets can have an increasingly negative effect on athletes, teams, leagues, or organizations in the digital age because of the speed and intensity with which those messages can be disseminated and shared. PR professionals have to assist in rectifying a negative situation encountered on these platforms and issue a response either on the person's or team's behalf or help the person craft an appropriate reply, just as when an issue rises with a response or comment made to a traditional media outlet.

Public Relations Functions

This section covers public relations functions and outlines a sport application for each. The aim is to clarify the variety of roles that public relations can play and the value of the various roles. To illustrate these roles and their value, we consider the following list of functions:

- Provision of information and general communication (to consumers, shareholders, suppliers, competitors, government agencies, and the public)
- Image shaping or enhancement through organizational publicity
- Community relations (previously discussed)
- Employee relations
- Educational efforts to gain political or popular support for the organizational agenda
- Recruiting and business development
- Launching new products or innovations
- Obtaining feedback and reaction
- Coping with crisis[36]

Shaping and Influencing Opinion: The Role of Blogging

A blog is an online opinion, and it can take any or all of the following forms:

Collection of thoughts

Series of random comments

Reviews or critiques

Recommendations or things to avoid

Blogs have become an essential component of sport and entertainment—two areas where consumers have no shortage of opinions—because they enable the sport organization, athlete, entertainer, or whomever to establish a connection with stakeholders or fans. According to Corey Miller, executive story editor and blogger for *CSI: Miami*, "It's nice for shows to have connections with the fans. It makes you closer and more involved in the product you're watching."[34]

Mark Cuban, owner of the Dallas Mavericks, is one of sport and entertainment's most prolific bloggers. On his site, www.blogmaverick.com, Cuban candidly weighs in on a variety of topics including sport and business. He uses his blog platform for engagement with fans and the public, providing unique access to the opinions, experience, and perspective of a professional sport team owner. In May 2013 Cuban posted a blog announcing a contest for fans to submit ideas for a new uniform design for the Mavericks. This offer was a wonderful mechanism to get fans of the team and the public involved and engaged with the potential new uniform design project. Cuban's blog post follows:[35]

> Help the Mavs Design Our Next Uniform!
>
> May 13, 2013
>
> The Mavs are going to redo our uniforms for the 2015–16 season . . . if we get a unique and original design. What's the best way to come up with creative ideas? You ask for them. So we are going to crowd-source the design and colors of our uniforms.
>
> You know what an NBA uniform looks like. You know what the Mavs colors are for today and the past. We want some new ideas that stay true to our logo and at least close to our current color schemes. Show us what you got!
>
> How do you participate? You post your ideas, pictures, graphics, videos, photos directly on this blog. Yes, we want everyone to see them. Steve Jobs said, "Everything is a remix." Uniforms probably more so than even technology. So we want every post to inspire other ideas and posts.
>
> Who will own your design? The minute you post it, the Mavs will. If you think it's horrible that the Mavs own your design, do not post. If you think it's cool that the Mavs could possibly use your design and you will have eternal bragging rights, then post away.
>
> If we really like your design and you, I may even throw in some tickets. If we don't use your design, it will still be here on this site for now and ever more for you to glance longingly at. If your design is close, if not identical, to other designs, and we pick one of the other designs, for whatever reason, then that's just the way it goes.
>
> If we don't choose any of the designs, including yours, then we don't choose any of the designs. That is life in the big city. Move on.
>
> This is your chance to get bragging rights and put your signature design on the Dallas Mavs and the NBA.
>
> This opportunity will last till the last day in May.
>
> Let's see what you got.

Informing and Communicating

Public relations departments communicate with consumers, shareholders, suppliers, competitors, government agencies, media, and the public. Clearly, this is the aspect of a public relations program that is best understood (by the public) and most frequently used. Informing and communicating is the hallmark of public relations. This function involves the compilation, presentation, and dissemination of product or organizational information to the public or to special segments of the population (alumni, sportswriters, newspapers, electronic media, websites, and blogs). For example, in addition to compiling and providing promotional and statistical information and materials to the media, the department is involved in staffing and assisting the stat crew. The PR department also provides statistical data and player and team background information to television and radio production personnel and on-air broadcasters for game broadcasts. The function of informing and communicating a public relations program also serves to maintain contact with the grassroots support of the organization.

The communications function also involves publishing programs, brochures, sales support materials, and manuals; working with special-interest groups to ensure the accuracy of information (e.g., the Baseball Writers' Association); maintaining and regularly updating websites; developing video and written content for digital media platforms; contributing to social media functions; and answering mail and other inquiries from the public. Although informing and communicating constitute only one of the functions essential to developing and managing an effective public relations program, organizations often allocate resources and energies almost exclusively to this function at the expense of a strategically sound holistic program.

Sport organizations are acutely aware that a good community relations program can result in positive perceptions and, ultimately, financial or other benefits. For example, in intercollegiate athletics, community relations often take the form of stories about hometown heroes that are pitched by media relations staffers at the university to local media outlets. According to a former sports information director and award winner, Howard Davis, the hometown feature is one of the most important functions of a sports information office.[37] This information is important for several reasons: (1) It provides a common denominator for residents of the athlete's hometown and the university; (2) it may prompt residents of the area to attend an athletics contest at the university or to apply for admission; and (3) it may assist the athletics department in recruiting future athletes from that town or region. The hometown feature is a valuable mechanism that achieves both a media relations function and a community relations function. The hometown connection is an important one to reinforce and maintain, not just for college athletics PR staffers but also for media relations personnel in all facets of sport.

Figure 11.1 illustrates the variety of publics with which a collegiate media relations director must correspond and interact.

Shaping and Enhancing Image

Image shaping and enhancement constitute a complex function through which the organization attempts to demonstrate to the public that its products are well made, that its services are first-rate and vital to the industry, and that the organization itself is a responsible citizen and contributor to the community. Corporations, institutions, teams, leagues, and people may engage in this function. Image shaping and enhancement make up a function closely associated with marketing, because public relations personnel work jointly with marketing personnel to introduce new programs, themes, campaigns, sales approaches, and promotional efforts.

McDonald's relationship with the Olympic Games is a good example of the way that a brand can use sport to help corporate image shaping and enhancement. McDonald's has had a long-standing relationship with the Olympic Games that dates back to 1968, when the company airlifted hamburgers to U.S. athletes in Grenoble, France, after they reported being homesick for American food. In 1996 McDonald's became a Centennial Olympic Games Partner, and the company operated the first-ever branded restaurant in the Olympic Village in Atlanta. McDonald's has served as the official restaurant of the Olympic Games since 1996. The 1998 Nagano Games marked this first time McDonald's served as a TOP sponsor (the Olympic Partner TOP Program), which enabled the company to activate the sponsorship on a global level.[38]

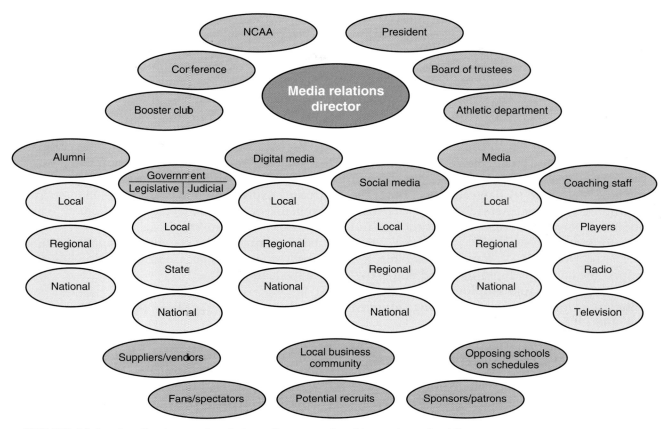

FIGURE 11.1   An effective media relations director works with a variety of publics.

Although some criticize the McDonald's Olympics sponsorship and the Olympic movement's association with fast food, McDonald's has worked hard to combat negative perceptions and media attention by creating a variety of healthy eating and active lifestyle education programs. Ahead of the 2012 London Games, Stuart Elliott of *New York Times* described that McDonald's "will use its coming sponsorship of the 2012 Summer Olympics to bolster efforts to present itself as a nutritionally responsible marketer, particularly when it comes to children. . . . In addition to trying to burnish its nutritional credentials, McDonald's also intends to use the Olympic sponsorship to talk up its efforts in areas like the environment and sustainability."[39]

The 2012 London Games included some unique global activation strategies for the company to promote their brand and employees and encourage healthy eating and lifestyles for children, including the McDonald's Olympic Champion Crew and McDonald's Champions of Play for the Olympic Games. The McDonald's

Olympic Champion Crew program debuted at the 2002 Salt Lake City Games. At the 2012 London Olympics it featured 2,000 of the best managers and crew—the largest crew to serve the global audience assembled at the Games, including athletes, media, coaches, and fans.[40] The McDonald's Champions of Play for the Olympic Games provided an opportunity for kids from participating McDonald's countries throughout the world to be selected through a local process to travel to London to attend the Games. Kevin Newell, McDonald's global chief brand officer, said of the program, "For the first time ever, McDonald's Champions of Play for the Olympic Games will tour and play with athletes at the actual Olympic venues. This will be an unforgettable, inspiring moment for our champions, along with attending the Games, seeing McDonald's chef demonstrations, taking an exclusive tour of the Olympic Village dining area, visiting London's cultural sites, and making new friends."[41]

The Olympic sponsorship has allowed the company to create partnerships with recognizable

Olympic athletes who have promoted the McDonald's brand, its products, and its ideals throughout the world. U.S. Swimmer Dara Torres, a five-time Olympian, served as the global ambassador for the London 2012 McDonald's Champions of Play for the Olympic Games program. Torres commented in a news release, "I want to make a positive difference in the lives of children and families, so it's a natural fit for me to join McDonald's today, and in the years ahead, as we inspire happy and active kids. Together, through the new McDonald's Champions of Play for the Olympic Games, we can reach millions of people about the benefits of balanced food choices and play for kids everywhere."[42]

The McDonald's Olympic sponsorship has helped the company build its brand and showcase its products and employees globally and enhance its image through marketing, advertising, and PR activities.

Promoting Employee Relations

Most corporations recognize that an open flow between management and employees is essential—not only for purposes of morale but also so that employees, who are often the public's first line of contact and communication with the organization, are capable of positive and favorable interaction. Because of the widespread public interest and involvement in sport, which has been documented by the Miller Lite Report on American Attitudes Toward Sport, *Sports Illustrated Sports Poll '86*, all employees of a sport organization should understand management's position on a variety of issues.[43] Players fall into this category of employees, and most universities and professional organizations provide formal training for these player–employees in the areas of public speaking and dealing with the media.

For nonplayer employees, organizations can use a number of effective vehicles to disseminate information from management to employees and vice versa. These tools include employee newsletters, brochures, and documents explaining organizational policies; an ongoing employee-orientation program; in-service training programs and seminars; and regularly scheduled e-mail updates, staff meetings, and special-topic luncheons that work like the town meeting in political election campaigns. Pat Williams, senior executive vice president of the Orlando Magic and a talented

author and motivational speaker, is part of an Orlando Magic initiative called Magic University. This ongoing program is designed to educate and inform all employees with regard to the goals, objectives, and functioning of the Orlando Magic. According to Williams, "Sharing and openness erase barriers and distinctions within the team so that there is no perception of an inner circle or an outer circle. Nobody's in, nobody's out, everyone's together. If people feel that they are in the outer circle, that they are benchwarmers, they soon begin feeling expendable and powerless—and you lose valuable contributors to the team effort."[44]

Lack of information can turn players into benchwarmers; thus, the sport organization must ensure that everyone is informed and feeling part of the team.

Gaining Political or Popular Support

Clearly, a critical function of public relations is to educate as well as inform. Providing information is not necessarily the same as educating. Education, as defined in public relations, includes developing comprehension, understanding information, and applying information in the appropriate context.

Faced with a series of negative stories in the press; increased pressure from media, fans, and former players; the scrutiny of Congressional hearings in October 2009; and litigation brought by former NFL players, the NFL has sharpened and elevated their focus on the issue of player health and safety. The effect of concussions, football-related head trauma, and brain injuries on both former players and on the future health of current NFL players has been moved to the forefront of the league's priorities. In response to the criticism, the NFL has been increasingly proactive in improving its policies and methods of diagnosing and treating concussions and more diligent in its attempts to raise awareness of its players and the public of the issues related to player safety. The NFL and NFLPA agreed in the 2011 collective bargaining agreement (CBA) that the two entities would commit more than $100 million over the duration of the 10-year CBA to medical research, primarily on research of brain injuries.[45]

The NFL released the *Fall 2012 Health and Safety Report*, its first such report, detailing the league's efforts in regard to football health and safety. The report outlined the key pillars of the NFL Player Health and Safety Program:

- Health and safety culture
- Advocacy
- Safety rules
- Research
- Equipment[46]

Besides promoting a culture in the sport that promotes health and safety and making rule changes to increase safety, the NFL has launched a variety of partnerships, research initiatives, education platforms, and communications outreach efforts that provide regular updates on developments on player safety initiatives and progress.

The NFL recognizes its influence on the sport landscape and on all levels of football, especially youth football. The NFL has been proactive in improving safety for its current and future players, and it has exerted its leadership to help improve safety for sport in general. The NFL has taken a proactive leadership position in research and education on the issue of concussions and head trauma. In September 2012 the Foundation for the National Institutes of Health (FNIH) announced that the NFL agreed to donate $30 million, the largest philanthropic gift in the 92-year history of the league "in support of research on serious medical conditions prominent in athletes and relevant to the general population."[47] "Our goal is to aggressively partner with the best scientists to understand more about the brain and brain injuries, to make things safer for our athletes and for others," NFL commissioner Roger Goodell said. "If we can learn more about the brain, we can not only make football safer, but make things safer for other sports and other walks of life."[48]

Recruiting and Developing Business

Because of their unrelenting need to recruit new athletes, intercollegiate athletics programs, particularly high-profile Division I programs, provide fertile opportunities for public relations personnel to apply their skills. Public relations in this context essentially involves image construction (and reconstruction) and refinement. College life must be effectively portrayed to a variety of potential recruits, who are looking to ensure that their vision of college, in terms of the educational and athletics experience, is compatible with the image presented during the recruiting visit. The function of public relations, then, is to ensure that questions are answered; that facilities are portrayed in their best light; that coaches and faculty are prepared to respond to questions and provide needed information; that the image presented is within conference and NCAA rules and regulations; that well-meaning alums and boosters comprehend what they can and cannot do; and that the recruit becomes aware of the entertainment, cultural, and growth opportunities as well as the educational benefits and athletics promises.

The public relations staff (media relations personnel, recruiting coordinator, institutional public relations officer) can accomplish all this by using a variety of platforms. The primary medium is personal selling (chapter 8), which involves one-on-one discussions between the recruit and the recruiter and takes place at the recruit's home and high school and later on the campus itself.

Before this visit to campus, and in many cases again during or after the visit, the recruit may receive a variety of brochures and printed material describing the college, the athletics program, and the opportunities available. This printed material is often augmented by video and other multimedia presentations designed to help the recruit visualize the realities and the possibilities. Since the mid-1970s these multimedia presentations have sometimes taken a fantasy, or what-if, approach that is often emotionally charged. For example, the recruit may sit in the field house or stadium and watch or listen to a scripted hypothetical broadcast of her future exploits and contributions at State University. Another approach is to use films that depict the tradition and stature of the university and its storied athletics program. These films usually feature famous alumni and past athletes endorsing the program and urging the recruit to make the right decision.

The term recruiting is not limited to intercollegiate athletics. It can refer to any of the following:

- At the professional level, convincing draft choices and free agents to sign with a team, promoting the community, and offering various incentives in addition to the financial package. In a similar professional sport context, recruiting would entail describing the activities of agents, financial advisors, and marketing and PR representatives who seek to enter into representation agreements with future and current professional athletes, coaches, executives, and broadcast personalities.

- The efforts by cities and sport commissions to attract professional franchises, amateur sporting events, and special events.
- The efforts of sport marketing agencies to secure sponsorship and corporate involvement for products, concepts, athletes, and events.

In terms of soliciting business opportunities, public relations programs help the organization attract corporate sponsorships by informing the potential corporate partner of the history and tradition of the product, event, or athlete and by helping to build a case for the pending financial agreement. A little research can identify the most influential information. This process may involve generating a basis of comparison with other teams by examining demographic factors or calculating numbers of impressions and the value of those impressions. PR and media outreach that support business initiatives can help drive and create new business opportunities and bring additional value by increasing brand awareness and loyalty, donations, enrollment and merchandise sales, or by attracting new clients.

Launching New Products or Innovations

If new products (or services) or product innovations are going to attract interest and gain market share, an effective public relations campaign is necessary to ensure that the people in the target market are aware of the product, understand the benefits of the product, and, most important, understand why the product is important to them and how it can become part of their lifestyle. The public relations campaign to introduce and launch the WNBA is an excellent example.

According to marketing consultants Al Ries and Jack Trout, the easiest way to get into a person's mind is to be first, and if an organization can't be first, it must find some way to position itself against the product that did get there first.[49] The now-defunct American Basketball League preceded the WNBA into women's professional

basketball by one full season and signed significantly more star players than the WNBA did during that first year. The WNBA was not first, so why was it perceived to be the more successful of the two leagues and generally considered more likely to endure (a belief that proved to be correct)? The explanation is simple. The NBA preceded the American Basketball League, and the WNBA was able to capitalize on the recognition and brand equity of the NBA to introduce itself and launch its marketing initiatives. The NBA brand provided an entree to television and print sources to publicize and promote the league, and to owners and sponsors to help sell it. According to then NBA marketing chief Rick Welts, "Even before it had signed up all 80 players to do the passing and shooting, the WNBA brought in a host of ringers—three television networks (NBC, ESPN, and Lifetime) and a mighty roster of corporate sponsors, to do the selling. No other league in the history of American sport has made its debut with huge, glossy advertising spreads in *Glamour* and *Self* magazines."[50]

The WNBA launch and ultimate success provide a case study in using existing platforms (arenas, teams, owners, television contracts, sponsorships, and broadcasts) to launch a new product; the case also illustrates how to use media and public relations to capture the imagination of the public even if an organization didn't introduce the product first.

Generating and Collecting Feedback

Feedback is essential in the strategic planning process and critical to determining the acceptance and effectiveness of organizational policies and procedures. Public relations personnel play an integral role in monitoring the pulse of the public with regard to their interest in and acceptance and rejection of organizational products, concepts, and practices. Public relations people gather data on public attitudes, economic indicators, consumer preferences and behavior, and political and societal events with which the organization is involved. Feedback may be generated by request (survey or poll) or simply through past action or inaction, without an official request (unsolicited and uninitiated letters or phone calls).

For example, consider developments with regard to the NCAA. In recent years, the NCAA has solicited feedback on recruitment, retention, academic performance, and graduation rates of athletes; on issues relating to Title IX and gender equity; and on a variety of other issues. For the most part, the NCAA has used this feedback to monitor progress and assess public perception, and in some cases to initiate reforms or modify regulations. Although most feedback has been positive, some has been negative and critical. As a result, the NCAA began to alter the structure of intercollegiate athletics. The most notable changes are the formation of a presidents' council and a shift of power to those presidents; higher standards for student-athletes' academic performance; fewer scholarships; increased opportunities for women; fewer coaches (full- and part-time) in some sports; a football national championship; equipment redesign (baseball); and the right of student-athletes to be employed during the academic year. Some of the changes have elicited a positive response, some have aroused criticism, and still others have resulted in litigation. Although some of this feedback was solicited, a portion was generated because of a lack of attentiveness and control in practices within the system. When the outcry and interest reached critical mass, the feedback spurred reform.

Coping With Crisis

One of the most visible roles that a public relations professional performs is coping with crisis and providing damage control. Because most of these cases elicit media interest and often receive intense coverage and scrutiny from the press and the public, the words and actions of the public relations department and its professionals are often in the news and sometimes engender as much interest as the incident that precipitated

Ryan Braun of the Milwaukee Brewers was one of many Major League Baseball players caught up in the Biogenesis PED scandal of 2013.

the crisis. In some cases the effect of these negative situations is short term, but a crisis can have substantial long-term effects. The PR personnel involved in handling the crisis must aim to develop a strategic response that maximizes the effectiveness of the response to alleviate the crisis and that minimizes the lasting damage caused by the crisis. During a crisis or damage control situation, PR professionals must work closely and collaboratively with the appropriate team of people (executives, administration, and legal counsel) to coordinate media strategy and public response.

Sport is not immune to problems. A number of crisis or scandal situations have occurred in recent years. The following are some examples:

- **Biogenesis performance enhancing drug (PED) scandal 2013**: Major League Baseball was rocked again by a PED scandal when a report appeared in the *Miami New Times* in January 2013 alleging that a number of current MLB players may have been provided banned substances by Biogenesis, a Miami clinic run by Anthony (Tony) Bosch.[51] The breaking news report prompted a heavy cycle of negative media stories and created another PED-related public relations crisis for MLB, a league still bruised by the damage associated with admissions of steroid use by All-Stars such as Mark McGwire, revelations of widespread PED use detailed in the 2007 Mitchell Report, and the 2005 Congressional hearings (mentioned below). As a result of these and other incidents, MLB had been working diligently to combat the perception of rampant steroid and PED use in their sport by promoting and showcasing that the stringent mandatory steroid and PED testing program, which began in 2004, was effective in curbing PED use in baseball. MLB launched an investigation into Biogenesis, which resulted in the league handing out lengthy suspensions during the summer of 2013 to a number of players for violating the Joint Drug Prevention and Treatment Program. The most embarrassing element of the scandal was that among the players suspended were two former Most Valuable Players; 2011 National League MVP Ryan Braun of the Milwaukee Brewers, who was suspended for the remainder of the 2013 season, and 3-time American League MVP Alex Rodriguez of the New York Yankees, who was suspended for a whopping 211 regular season games (including

the 2013 postseason and the entire 2014 season).[52] Braun, who had successfully appealed a 50 game PED suspension in 2011, accepted and served a 65 game suspension in 2013. Rodriguez appealed his harsh penalty through arbitration and also pursued legal action (which was withdrawn after the arbitration ruling). Arbitrator Fredric Horowitz ruled to suspend Rodriguez for the entire 2014 season, including the postseason, but also reduced Rodriguez's original ban of 211 games to 162. The Rodriguez suspension is the longest penalty ever for a baseball player using illegal PEDs.[53]

- **Penn State child sex abuse scandal in 2011–2012**. Jerry Sandusky, the former defensive coordinator for the Penn State University football program, was arrested and arraigned on 40 criminal counts on November 5, 2011. The scandal led to the firing of iconic Nittany Lions football coach Joe Paterno. Sandusky was found guilty on 45 of 48 counts of child sex abuse on June 22, 2012, and was sentenced to 30 to 60 years in prison on October 9, 2012. The NCAA announced harsh sanctions against Penn State on July 23, 2012, which included a $60 million fine, a four-year bowl ban, and scholarship reductions. The scandal is widely considered one of the worst in the history of college athletics. Moreover, it transcended the scope of sport and garnered intense national media coverage and scrutiny across all mediums.[54] In September 2013, the NCAA announced that it would gradually restore football scholarships to Penn State starting in 2014-15 in recognition of the University's effort to implement the reforms recommended in former FBI director Louis Freeh's report. Five initial scholarships will be restored per year starting in 2014-15 and the full complement of 85 football scholarships will be restored at Penn State in 2016-17.[55]

- **The steroid scandals in baseball in 2005–2006**. Primarily related to the sanctity of baseball's records and the issue of fair competition, the steroids issue has been examined by the electronic and print media, which have spent countless hours and resources covering congressional hearings, debating new negotiated penalties including a lifetime ban for repeat offenders, and examining the personas of certain suspected violators, notably Jose Canseco (who wrote *Juiced*), Barry Bonds, Mark McGwire, Sammy Sosa, and Rafael Palmeiro. A tradition-rich sport such as baseball is in large part measured by historical accomplishment and records. If the records are viewed as suspect, fans can no longer rely on milestones to judge outstanding performance.

- **Reebok International Limited and the resultant furor in 1997 surrounding a women's running shoe named the Incubus.** In doing its due diligence, the marketing team concentrated on a name that did not exist in the marketplace and did not infringe on any existing trademarks. The shoe was named Incubus, which the dictionary defines as an "evil spirit that has sexual intercourse with women while they are sleeping." Damage control became essential for obvious reasons and because the mistake was large enough to merit coverage on the front page of the *Boston Globe* as well as a mention in *USA Today* and numerous newspapers throughout the country. Reebok vice president of public relations Dave Fogelson acknowledged that a mistake had been made and that steps had been implemented to ensure that such a gaffe didn't happen again.[56]

- **Remarks about women golfers by CBS golf commentator Ben Wright at the McDonald's LPGA Championship in 1995.** Wright commented, "Lesbians in the sport hurt women's golf" and "Women golfers are handicapped by having breasts because their boobs get in the way of their swing."[57] Both the quotations and the attempts by Wright and others to attack the credibility and integrity of the reporter, Valerie Helmbreck, kept the story in the news for an extended period. Ultimately, Wright admitted that he had made the remarks. He received a suspension and underwent counseling. The Wright incident was even more infamous because it was not the first time that callous and flip opinions and remarks had damaged a segment of society and hurt the reputations and careers of notable sport personages, such as Al Campanis and Jimmy "the Greek" Snyder.

- **The NFL's New England Patriots' drafting and termination of Christian Peter.** Peter, who had a checkered past at the University of Nebraska (with eight arrests for charges ranging from trespassing and disturbing the peace to third-degree sexual assault), was drafted by the Patriots in the fifth round of the 1996 NFL draft. After criticism in the media and through phone calls from fans protesting his presence on the Patriots' roster, Peter was dumped by the team, who claimed that they had not investigated his background thoroughly—a contention that Peter disputed.[58]

Sport, Television, and Entertainment Influence on Sport Public Relations

In an earlier time, athletes and sport personalities were seen primarily through the prism of competition. Stories typically focused on athletics accomplishments, on-field sporting heroics and exploits, and game recaps. The pieces were reported primarily by sports media in sports outlets. The late James Michener stated, "Sport, and in particular baseball (during its professional infancy), prospered, because it received, at no cost, reams of publicity in daily and Sunday papers."[59] Michener explained that this coverage, which any other business would have had to pay for, was given freely because of its entertainment value and because a newspaper that contained information about sport would sell more copies, creating both higher circulation and higher advertising rates.

As sport became more popular and more mainstream, and as media coverage grew from newspapers and radio to television and now the Internet, it commanded larger audiences and became increasingly viewed as an entertainment spectacle. As the sporting enterprise expanded, the focus and attention of the media moved beyond the sports press, which presented both great benefits and big challenges to sport PR professionals.

Television coverage has played a transformational role in the tremendous growth of the modern sport industry. TV has fueled the increased media attention that sport received and has helped propel sport, the athletes who competed, and the broadcasters who televised the events into the entertainment business. The creation of ABC's *Monday Night Football* in 1970 and the groundbreaking launch of ESPN, the first all-sports TV network in 1979, both played significant roles in propelling the growth of the sport industry and driving an increase in media attention for sport. *Monday Night Football* and ESPN both helped provide sport with a new cultural relevance and popularity in society, influencing the continued emergence and evolution of sport as an entertainment vehicle.

Monday Night Football moved NFL games into prime time and helped drive the league to a new level of popularity. Bill Gunther and Marc Carter chronicled the development of *Monday Night Football* through the vision of its executive producer, Roone Arledge, and his belief that the program would be as much entertainment as football. It would be a spectacle that people would watch whether or not they cared about the game, and it would appeal to women as well as men.[60] As then NBC Sports chairman Dick Ebersol said about Arledge after Arledge's death in 2002, "'Roone was surely the only television executive of his time who would have dared to put sports in prime time." The effect, according to Ebersol, was that the move to prime time helped transform the business of sport: "All of the money the athletes are making, all the big money in sports, none of that would be happening if not for Roone."[61] (*Monday Night Football* aired on ABC from 1970 to 2005; beginning in the 2006 season, it moved to ESPN. Both ABC and ESPN are owned by the Walt Disney Company.)

The combination of the successful and increased presence of sport in the prime-time television lineup and Arledge's hallmark "up close and personal" philosophy, which introduced U.S. television audiences to relatively unknown Olympic athletes and transformed them into household names, had a lasting influence on future media and TV coverage. Television not only made stars out of the athletes who played the games but also made sportscasters like Howard Cosell, Jim McKay, Al Michaels, Bob Costas, Joe Buck, and Chris Berman famous as they broadcast sports news and events to large audiences. Personalities started to emerge in detail in the media, and the public's appetite to know more about the off-field lives of their favorite athletes and sport personalities grew as well. Storytelling has become an essential tool used by media and PR professionals alike to publicize athletes and cultivate the public's attention, particularly in the effort to attract casual fans who don't follow sport as closely as die-hard sports fan do. This added dimension of information has proved to be an effective mechanism for growing the sport audience by developing a rooting interest and connection to sport, beyond an individual

athlete's playing accomplishments, popularity, stardom, or championship victories.

Created in 1979, ESPN became the first all-sports TV network to broadcast sport 24 hours a day, seven days a week. ESPN's remarkable success showed that an all-sports network could not only survive but thrive. ESPN has revolutionized the sports television landscape and has made the network, as *Bloomberg Businessweek* stated, "among the most profitable television networks in American history."[62] *SportsCenter*, ESPN's flagship news program, transformed the way that people consumed sport because it provided a daily national TV platform for sports highlights and news. *USA Today* reported, "Through multiple airings of *SportsCenter* news shows and seemingly never-ending live events, ESPN has changed how people receive sports." As longtime ESPN anchor Bob Ley stated, "Before ESPN you watched sports two days a week."[63] ESPN has grown into a television powerhouse, as described by *Bloomberg Businessweek* in 2012: "The company broadcasts more than half of all the live sports seen in the U.S. Through dozens of ESPN-branded TV, web, and mobile platforms, it also shapes the ways in which leagues, teams, and athletes are packaged, promoted, marketed, and consumed by the public."[64]

Besides broadcasting sporting events, ESPN offers a full slate of programming and content across various TV networks, a radio network, and ESPN.com for news, discussion, and debate of the issues of the day in sport. TV shows like *SportsCenter*, *First Take*, *Around the Horn*, *Pardon the Interruption* (PTI), and *Outside the Lines* (OTL); radio programs like *Mike and Mike*; and many other programs and content delivered across the network's platforms should be on the daily radar of the PR professional.

After ESPN proved the viability and appetite for this kind of dedicated sport programming, the NBC Sports Network, CBS Sports Network, FOX Sports1, and other national, regional, and local outlets launched sports talk shows and news programming. HBO's *Real Sports*, ESPN's *E:60*, and Showtime's recently debuted *60 Minutes Sports* are shows that air sports news, features, and investigative reports. National and local sports talk radio provides constant discussion, commentary, opinion, and criticism while their hosts debate current sports headlines and issues.

These shows collectively provide an ample range of opportunities for PR personnel to secure interviews for athletes, coaches, executives, and broadcasters to promote their teams, accomplishments, upcoming events, marketing partnerships, and charitable initiatives and to showcase their personalities to gain exposure. The discussion and commentary on ESPN and the other national, regional, and local TV and radio networks' programs influence the views of sports fans and shape public opinion on sport. Engagement and interaction with these and all other media outlets are important.

Today's sport entertainment landscape presents a wide array of opportunities and challenges for sport PR professionals because of the interest level generated by sport. Stories featuring athletes and sport appear in the full spectrum of media across all print, electronic, and digital platforms, spanning topics from general news to sport, business, and lifestyle outlets. Topics include business interests and marketing partnerships, philanthropic and community relations initiatives, athletes' opinions on politics and social issues, and details of the personal lives of sport personalities. You are as likely now to see stories about athletes in *People* and on *Access Hollywood* as you are to see them in *Sports Illustrated* and on *SportsCenter*.

The proliferation of coverage that athletes and sport personalities receive in the media has increased their opportunities to appear on popular prime-time reality TV shows like ABC's *Dancing With the Stars*; to appear in prime-time, daytime, or late-night TV entertainment programs or talk shows; or even to star in their own reality shows. These entertainment TV programs may create positive media exposure and increased marketing, commercial, and business opportunities, which is certainly beneficial. But the exposure can bring additional media scrutiny, which may require attention from PR professionals.

Fans and media want behind-the-scenes access and detailed information—a demand now compounded by the immediacy of the volume of information available on the Internet and social media. The media spotlight that has catapulted sport into entertainment—bringing fame, fortune, and celebrity to athletes—has also brought trouble and controversy. Historic and remarkable athletics achievements and success on the field are documented by the press, but so too are the off-field personal issues and shortcomings (e.g., character issues, substance abuse, performance-enhancing drug use, financial problems). Today's media landscape has the ability both to amplify and celebrate the positive news and, on the other end of the spectrum, to expose and magnify the negative stories. The trend toward sensational and negative media storylines and the increased attention paid to off-field topics and personal lives has caused some athletes, organizations, and PR staffs to be more guarded in their approach to dealing with the press and granting media access.

PR professionals play a significant role in providing strategic counsel to help athletes and organizations navigate the diverse media landscape that requires interaction and access to remain relevant but can be harsh in a time of difficulty and crisis. The ultimate goal for the sport PR professional is to balance the expansive range of media opportunities available by striving to create the maximum amount of positive exposure while avoiding potential pitfalls that the intense scrutiny and media coverage in the digital age can present.

ACTIVITY 11.3 Why Is Communication Important?

In this WSG activity, you're the public relations manager for Lance Armstrong and his Livestrong Foundation. He won the Tour de France seven consecutive times, a record, from 1999 to 2005. Then, in 2012, the United States Anti-Doping Agency disqualified Armstrong from those races (and wins) and banned him from cycling for life for doping offenses. In this activity, you'll consider how to handle Armstrong's situation.

ACTIVITY 11.4 Signing an LGBT Athlete

In this WSG activity, you're the director of public relations and the director of marketing and sponsorship for a team that signed Jason Collins, or another (openly) LGBT athlete. You'll consider the opportunities and challenges that may arise.

Wrap-Up

Public relations is an important part of the marketing equation and the primary vehicle through which an organization interacts with the media and various publics. The media landscape continues to change, and technology will influence the future evolution of the media industry. Although the mediums and platforms may change, the core responsibilities of the PR department and its practitioners continue to revolve around positioning and promoting a favorable image of the sport entity in the marketplace. For public relations to be effective, the PR specialist must react and respond to requests and situations, and actively initiate and develop media relations and community relations efforts in an integrated, proactive methodology. This methodology should focus on short-term and long-term objectives with attention to building and fostering relationships. These activities and the public relations functions in general must play an integral role in both the strategic planning process for the organization and the implementation and management of the strategic plan.

Public relations programs fulfill a variety of roles, including image shaping and enhancement, educational efforts, business development, content development, recruiting, coping with crisis, and community relations. Community relations efforts can take many forms; they can be initiated by players, can be related to teams or institutions, and can be initiated by leagues or governing bodies. These programs must have reasonable organizational resources or receive corporate or philanthropic support to ensure their longevity and the credibility of the sponsoring organization.

In the sport setting, players have an integral role in the success of community relations programs because they can attract media interest and coverage, corporate or philanthropic support, and participants and beneficiaries.

Finally, although media may be receptive to story pitches and can be influenced to consider different perspectives or opinions, they are never controlled by the PR department. Thus, public relations professionals must build mutually beneficial relationships with the various publics related to their particular sport industry segment. Again, these publics are best served if the public relations program is not only reactive but also proactive, creative, and well integrated.

Activities

1. Set up an informational interview and visit the sports information or media relations entity on your campus. During your interview, discuss the concepts of reactive, proactive, and integrated media relations and the amount of time that the entity spends on each approach. Identify an example of each function in that media relations setting.

2. Begin a journal that you will keep for 30 days. The focus of the journal is to identify through sport-related media outlets (e.g., *USA Today*, ESPN.com, *Sports Illustrated*) crises in sport that have required PR response or damage control efforts. Do some issues seem to come up more frequently than others? Do some organizations seem to be more adept than others at dealing with a crisis? Do you think that the strategy used to deal with the crisis was effective?

3. In reading sport-related media outlets and trade publications, identify an example of a fully integrated PR placement that includes sponsors, marketing partners, community relations, or philanthropic storylines. Evaluate the piece and the way in which the marketing, sponsor, or charitable elements are presented.

4. Among the roles of a public relations professional in sport, what roles and functions are the most common (present almost every day)? Which activities occur only occasionally?

5. Assume that you are a community relations director for the WNBA's Phoenix Mercury. Identify the various publics with whom you should communicate on a regular basis.

Your Marketing Plan

In any marketing plan (even those developed primarily for an internal audience), public relations is a critical function. Effective public relations can garner support for your concepts. A solid media relations component can ensure awareness and comprehension of your ideas and intent, and attention to community relations may generate acceptance of your ideas and programs. Review your marketing plan to determine how each of these elements should be addressed to achieve acceptance and support of your objectives internally, externally, or both.

Endnotes

1. Bill Carter, "On TV, Timing Is Everything at the Olympics," *New York Times*, 24 August 2008, www.nytimes.com/2008/08/25/sports/olympics/25nbc.html.

2. "London Olympics on NBC Is Most-Watched Television Event in U.S History," NBC Sports Group press release, 13 August 2012, http://nbcsportsgrouppressbox.com/2012/08/14/ondon-olympics-on-nbc-is-most-watched-television-event-in-u-s-history.

3. Bill Carter and Richard Sandomir, "A Surprise Winner at the Olympics in Beijing: NBC," *New York Times*, 17 August 2008, www.nytimes.com/2008/08/18/sports/olympics/18nbc.html.

4. *Public Relations Defined: A Modern Definition for the New Era of Public Relations*, Public Relations Society of America website, 11 April 2012, http://prdefinition.prsa.org/.

5. C.L. Caywood, "Twenty-First Century Public Relations," in *The Handbook of Strategic Public Relations and Integrated Communications*, ed. C.L. Caywood (New York: McGraw-Hill, 1997), ix.

6. M. Govoni, R. Eng, and M. Galper, *Promotional Management* (Upper Saddle River, NJ: Prentice Hall, 1986), 15–16.

7. M.P. Gonring, "Global and Local Media Relations," in Caywood, *The Handbook of Strategic Public Relations*, 63.

8. R.J. Hellawell, letter to J.E. Sullivan, 14 February 1907, c/o American Sports Publishing.

9. D. Ainge, *Celtics Beat: Trade Alert*, 23 December 2003, dainge@enews.celtics.com.

10. R.L. Irwin and W.A. Sutton, Roles, *Responsibilities and Effectiveness of Urban Community Relations Programs Within Professional Sport Franchises*, presented at Sport in the City: An International Symposium on Cultural, Economic, and Political Considerations, Memphis, TN, 10 November 1996.

11. W.A. Sutton, M.A. McDonald, G.R. Milne, and J. Cimperman, "Creating and Fostering Fan Identification in Professional Sports," *SMQ*, 6 (1) (1997): 15.

12. J.A. Koten, "The Strategic Uses of Corporate Philanthropy," in Caywood, *The Handbook of Strategic Public Relations*, 150.

13. *NBA Cares—Community Programs/Partners*, National Basketball Association website, www.nba.com/cares/.

14. *2005–2006 NBA Community Report*, 2006, New York, 2.

15. *NBA Cares—Mission*, National Basketball Association website, www.nba.com/cares/.

16. M. Pollick, "Stern, NBA Make Doing Well by Doing Good Contagious," *SSSBJ*, 6–12 March 2006, 29.

17. "PGA Tour Reaches $1 Billion Milestone in Charitable Giving as Tournaments Benefit Charities and Communities Across the Country; Goal Set to Reach Next Billion in 10 Years," Wyndham Championship press release, 31 October 2005, www.wyndhamchampionship.com/pga-tour-reaches-1-billion-milestone-in-charitable-giving-as-tournaments-benefit-charities-and-communities-across-the-country-goal-set-to-reach-next-billion-in-10-years.

18. "CBS Sports Special to Highlight Charity on Tour," PGA Tour press release, 27 July 2012, www.pgatour.com/company/2012/07/27/barclays.html.

19. "PGA Tour Announces 2009 Charity Total," PGA Tour press release, 25 January 2010, http://together.pgatour.com/stories/pga-tours-final-charity.html.

20. *Causes We Support*, PGA Tour website, http://together.pgatour.com/causes.

21. "PGA Tour Broadcast Rights Secured Over Next Decade," PGA Tour press release, 1 September 2011, www.pgatour.com/company/2011/09/01/Broadcastannouncement.html.

22. Ron Sirak, "These Gals Are Good," *Golf World*, 10 Sept 2012, www.golfdigest.com/golf-tours-news/2012-09/gwar-pga-tour-wives-charity#ixzz2HhWitljF.

23. *The Magic Touch*, Orlando Magic Youth Foundation brochure, Orlando Magic, 1997, and OMYF Community Spotlight: Orlando Health Foundation, 4 June 2012, www.nba.com/magic/news/cohen_omyf_060412.html.

24. "Phil Mickelson Participating in KPMG Chip-4Charity at Halftime of Broncos vs. Chargers Game on Oct. 15," KPMG press release, 4 October 2012 www.kpmg.com/US/en/IssuesAndInsights/ArticlesPublications/Press-Releases/Pages/

Phil-Mickelson-Participating-In-KPMG-Chip-4Charity-At-Halftime-Of-Broncos-Vs-Chargers-Game-Oct-15.aspx.

25. *Phil Mickelson's KPMG Chip4Charity During Chargers-Broncos Game Nets $50,000 for Charity*, PGA Tour website, 16 October 2012, http://together.pgatour.com/stories/2012-stories/october/phil-mickelsons-kpmg-chip4charity.html.

26. New York Yankees website, *Yankees in the Community*, http://newyork.yankees.mlb.com/nyy/community/hope_index.jsp.

27. Ibid.

28. Kevin Baxter, "Major League Baseball Teams Step Up to Give Back," *Los Angeles Times*, 13 August 2011, http://articles.latimes.com/2011/aug/13/sports/la-sp-0814-baxter-20110814.

29. Matt Pepin, "Ray Allen Thanks Celtics Fans With Ad in Boston Globe," *Boston.com*, 15 July 2012, http://www.boston.com/sports/basketball/celtics/extras/celtics_blog/2012/07/ray_allen_thank.html.

30. Matt Pepin, "Celtics Thanks Paul Pierce, KG With Full-Page Ad in Globe," *Boston.com*, 12 July 2013, www.boston.com/sports/basketball/celtics/extras/celtics_blog/2013/07/celtics_thank_paul_pierce_kg_with_full-page_ad_in_globe.html.

31. Instagram.com, Paul Pierce Instagram account, 16 July 2013, http://instagram.com/p/b11/TObwOgU/#

32. Bob Considine, "Phelps to Use $1 Million Bonus to Start Charity," *Today.com*, 2 Sept 2008 http://today.msnbc.msn.com/id/26506320/ns/today-today_news/t/phelps-use-million-bonus-start-charity/#.UOT6c3dP-NY.

33. "Michael Phelps Launches Foundation, Donates Speedo $1 Million Bonus to Charity, Olympic Gold Medalist Embarks on Eight-City Tour," Speedo/Michael Phelps Foundation press release, 2 September 2008, www.warnaco.com/content/speedousa.com/20080902/20080902_mp.html.

34. A. Oldenburg, "TV Goes to Blogs," *USA Today* (5 April 2006), 1D.

35. M. Cuban, *Help the Mavs Design Our Next Uniform!* www.blogmaverick.com, 13 May 2013, http://blogmaverick.com/2013/05/13/help-the-mavs-design-our-next-uniform/.

36. Compiled from D. Ziccardi, *Masterminding the Store* (New York: Wiley, 1997), 254–259; and D. Wilcox, P. Ault, and W. Agee, *Public Relations: Strategies and Tactics* (Philadelphia: Random House, 1986).

37. H.M. Davis, *Basic Concepts of Sports Information*, 2nd ed. (East Longmeadow, MA: Jeste, 1996), 15.

38. *McDonald's Olympic Games Fact Sheet*, McDonald's corporate website www.aboutmcdonalds.com/

mcd/newsroom/electronic_press_kits/mcdonalds_olympic_sponsorship_renewal/fact_sheets.html.

39. Stuart Elliott, "McDonald's Uses Olympics for Its Own Balancing Act," *New York Times*, 20 July 2011, http://mediadecoder.blogs.nytimes.com/2011/07/20/mcdonalds-uses-olympics-for-its-own-balancing-act/.

40. *McDonald's Olympic Games Fact Sheet*, McDonald's corporate website, www.aboutmcdonalds.com/content/dam/AboutMcDonalds/Newsroom/Electronic%20Press%20Kits/Olympic%20Renewal/McDonalds%20Olympic%20History%20Fact%20Sheet%20-%20_1-6-12_FINAL.pdf.

41. "McDonald's Unveils Sponsorship Plans for London 2012 Olympic Games," McDonald's press release, 20 July 2011, www.aboutmcdonalds.com/mcd/newsroom/electronic_press_kits/mcdonalds_london_2012_olympic_summer_games.html?page=1#.

42. Ibid.

43. For an examination of America's interest in both participation and spectatorship, see Research and Forecasts, Inc., *Miller Lite Report on American Attitudes Toward Sport* (New York: Miller Brewing Co., 1983); and Lieberman Research Inc., *Sports Illustrated Sports Poll '86* (New York: Sports Illustrated, 1986). Proprietary studies such as those published by American Sports Demographics of Dallas, TX, can be obtained for a fee.

44. P. Williams, *The Magic of Teamwork* (Nashville, TN: Thomas Nelson, 1997), 159.

45. Mark Maske, "NFL Donating $30 Million to NIH for Brain Injury Research," *Washington Post*, 5 Sept 2012, www.washingtonpost.com/blogs/football-insider/wp/2012/09/05/nfl-donating-30-million-to-nih-for-brain-injury-research/.

46. *NFL Releases First Report on Football Health and Safety Issues*, NFL Evolution.com, 16 October 2012, www.nflevolution.com/wordpress/wp-content/uploads/2012/10/FINAL-NFL-Fall-2012-Health-Safety-Report.pdf.

47. *NIH Applauds $30 Million Donation From NFL*, NFL Evolution.com, 5 September 2012, www.nflevolution.com/article/NIH-applauds-30-million-donation-from-NFL?ref=1354.

48. Mark Maske, "NFL Donating $30 Million to NIH for Brain Injury Research," *Washington Post*, 5 Sept 2012, www.washingtonpost.com/blogs/football-insider/wp/2012/09/05/nfl-donating-30-million-to-nih-for-brain-injury-research/.

49. A. Ries and J. Trout, *Positioning: The Battle for Your Mind* (New York: McGraw-Hill, 1986), 19–27.

50. R. Thurow, "Full Court Press: Women's NBA Pins Hopes on Clean Play and Hard Marketing," *Wall Street Journal*, 12 June 1997, A1, A8.

51. "Tony Bosch and Biogenesis: MLB Steroid Scandal," Miami New Times.com, Special Reports http://www.miaminewtimes.com/specialReports/tony-bosch-and-biogenesis-mlb-steroid-scandal-3698782/.

52. Paul Hagen, "A-Rod gets ban through 2014; 12 get 50 games," MLB.com, 6, August, 2013, http://mlb.mlb.com/news/article.jsp?ymd=20130805&content_id=55953176&vkey=news_mlb&c_id=mlb

53. Ken Davidoff, "A-Rod suspended for the entire 2014 season," NYPost.com, 11 January 2014, http://nypost.com/2014/01/11/a-rod-slammed-with-162-game-suspension/

54. "Timeline of Jerry Sandusky Sex Abuse Case: State Files Suit Over Related NCAA Sanctions," www.Pennlive.com, 2 January 2013, www.pennlive.com/midstate/index.ssf/2013/01/timeline_of_sandusky_sex_abuse.html.

55. "Executive Committee to gradually restore Penn State scholarships," National Collegiate Athletic Association (NCAA) Website, 24, September, 2013, http://www.ncaa.org/wps/wcm/connect/public/NCAA/Resources/Latest+News/2013/September/Executive+Committee+to+gradually+restore+Penn+State-scholarships.

56. C. Reidy, "Reebok Kicks Itself Over Name With Bad Fit," *Boston Globe*, 20 February 1997, A-1, A-16.

57. R. Martzke, "Wright: 'Lesbians Hurt Women's Golf,' " *USA Today*, 12 May 1995, C1.

58. P. King, "Patriot Games: New England Fumbled When It Drafted Christian Peter and Tried to Recover by Cutting Him Loose," *Sports Illustrated*, 6 May 1996, 32–33.

59. J.A. Michener, *Sports in America* (New York: Random House, 1976), 355.

60. M. Gunther and M. Carter, *Monday Night Mayhem* (New York: Morrow, 1988), 34.

61. Bill Carter, "Roone Arledge, 71, a Force in TV Sports and News, Dies," *New York Times*, 6 December 2002, www.nytimes.com/2002/12/06/business/roone-arledge-71-a-force-in-tv-sports-and-news-dies.html?pagewanted=all&src=pm.

62. Karl Taro Greenfeld, "ESPN: Everywhere Sports Profit Network," *Bloomberg Businessweek.com*, 30 August 2012, www.businessweek.com/articles/2012-08-30/espn-everywhere-sports-profit-network.

63. Rudy Martzke and Reid Cherner, "After 25 Years, ESPN Still Channels How to View Sports," *USA Today*, 17 August 2004, http://usatoday30.usatoday.com/sports/2004-08-17-espn-25-years_x.htm.

64. Karl Taro Greenfeld, "ESPN: Everywhere Sports Profit Network," *Bloomberg Businessweek.com*, 30 August 2012, www.businessweek.com/articles/2012-08-30/espn-everywhere-sports-profit-network.

Chapter 12
Social Media in Sport

Kirsten Corio

OBJECTIVES

- To examine the types of social media content and tactics commonly used in sport marketing

- To understand the necessity to integrate social media programming and initiatives into the marketing communications mix

- To recognize how to generate followers and ROI from sport organization social media content such as Facebook

- To comprehend the role of traditional marketing concepts such as reach, breadth, segmentation, and impressions as they are applied in a social media context

- To understand how to design sales campaigns and track results using social media techniques

- To explore the role of sponsorship and the types and limitations of sponsorship opportunities available through social media

We're Not Sure Why They Call It a Cave Because It Is Anything But . . .

It all started with the MLB Fan Cave, which launched in time for the 2011 season in New York City. The MLB Fan Cave was a first-of-its-kind space mixing baseball with music, popular culture, media, interactive technology, and art. The MLB Fan Cave has expanded and evolved so that it can host fan events, concerts, MLB player and celebrity appearances, as well as the Cave Dwellers, who have watched every game of the MLB season while chronicling their experiences online through videos, blogs, and social media. Hardly sounds like a cave, right? Maybe it is more of an information hub or, as it has been developed for fans of the NHL's New Jersey Devils, Mission Control.

The Devils' Mission Control was designed in 2011 to increase social media following through Facebook and Twitter. This goal would be accomplished by offering Devils fans a forum for voicing their opinions, stories, and ideas around the Devils brand. A group of dedicated fans reposted and managed fan content.

The University of Oregon became the first collegiate sport program to create its own social media command center. Named the Quack Cave, the site is manned by socially savvy (are there really those who are not?) students who monitor and manage fan content from Twitter and Instagram based on hashtags. The Quackers (our name, not theirs) can then manage the content, disseminate it, and engage with fans to create new content.

Among these cave-type endeavors, perhaps the largest fan cave is the newly renamed AT&T Stadium—formerly Cowboys Stadium but also nicknamed Jerry's World and even Death Star. The naming-rights deal was estimated to be worth as much as $18 million per year to the Dallas Cowboys. AT&T global marketing officer Cathy Coughlin said that the company as part of the deal has "doubled its 4G LTE network capacity to benefit its customers inside the stadium, in the plazas and in the parking lots—and is working to nearly double the Wi-Fi capacity for all mobile technology users at the stadium." She added that AT&T also is "enhancing the Cowboys' mobile app with maps and way-finding information to improve the fan experience on game days."

What is the significance of these activities and what does it mean going forward?

- The role of the fan in helping create and manage content has been accepted as a vehicle to build stronger relationships between sport organizations and their fans.

- Fans have a strong desire, perhaps even a need, to stay connected to the team, each other, and the outside world for a large majority of the time.

- This connection comes at a cost but also with an opportunity that marketers are only beginning to learn how to monetize.[1]

The rapid growth of social media has delivered a bounty of fans and followers to sport properties. People proudly declare their fan allegiance and essentially ask their favorite teams to communicate directly with them. This development represents a major shift in communication between teams and fans that may not be obvious to a social native (i.e., one who has grown up with digital and social media).

Before mass adoption of Facebook, teams worked hard to build up e-mail opt-in databases to enable what, at the time, was considered a one-to-one, interactive channel of communication. Teams employed multiple, full-time e-mail marketing managers, designed ad units and registration forms for optimal conversion to an opt-in, and deployed grassroots marketers armed with surveys designed to catch an opt-in. Then they scrubbed those opt-ins against the existing database, created personalized e-mails full of valuable offers, and did whatever they could to ensure that they wouldn't trigger an unsubscribe action. Yet with all those efforts, in 2012 the average team's e-mail opt-in database stood at about 200,000.[2] Compare that to the average Facebook following of a professional team, which is well over a million.[3]

ACTIVITY 12.1 Social Media Introduction

In this WSG activity, you're the director of marketing for your school's athletic department and you realize you've got a lot to learn about social media.

Although sport properties have a relatively easy time attracting fans and followers compared with other brands, building an engaging presence is both an art and a science. Those that had an early presence on the major American-based platforms Facebook and Twitter earned an edge over their competitors. Those that integrate social media into all their marketing attract more of a following than those that don't. And those that have a true, dedicated focus on social media are more effective at engaging fans than those that don't.

Unsurprisingly, these big numbers are attracting big attention from both senior management and marketers of all stripes who would like access to these fans. But a careful balance must be struck. Although social media makes it easy for fans to like, follow, and keep up with their favorite teams, it also makes it easy for them to dislike, unfollow, or perhaps worse, tune out. And social media has yet to deliver results akin to other digital direct marketing strategies. A recent NBA study found that e-mail was 40 times more effective than social media at driving ticket sales.[4]

Although it has yet to prove equal to e-mail as a direct marketing channel, social media is valuable in sport for many reasons:

- It builds an audience of fans to interact with in real time.
- It engages fans in ways that they want to be engaged. Fans get more access, real-time information, breaking news, special offers, and fun stuff. Sport properties and athletes can drive more consumption of brand and content: website page views, video views, articles, photos, sweepstakes, contests, games, and more. Ultimately, it can create more lifetime fans.
- It's viral: Sport teams used to craft strategic plans and incentives to get people to forward an e-mail to their friends. Now, shares, likes, and commenting occur on everything posted.
- It drives behavior that drives business, including tune-in, ticket sales, game attendance, increased brand consumption, merchandise sales, and more interaction with partner brands.
- People not only want to interact with brands on social media but also want to buy from brands. Consider the following stats:
  - More than half (52 percent) of Americans spend at least one hour per week on Facebook.[5]
  - Of those under 35, 56 percent interact with their favorite brands on Facebook.
  - People "like" a brand on Facebook because they are customers (58 percent) or they want to receive discounts and promotions (57 percent).
  - A majority of consumers (56 percent) said that they are more likely to recommend a brand to a friend after becoming a fan on Facebook.

Social sport marketing is an evolving discipline that touches all areas of sport business and requires a sophisticated approach. This chapter explores the most effective techniques in social media management.

How the Celtics Glean Data and Generate ROI from Facebook

Peter Stringer, Senior Director, Digital Marketing, Boston Celtics

In the social media game, the first metric that anyone looks at is the number of likes that a fan page has accumulated. Brands that enjoy followings in the millions are often lauded for being good at social media. But there's more to mastering Facebook than simply building a large fan base.

What do you actually know about your Facebook fan base beyond the basic "insights" analytics that Facebook provides? Not much? More likely, nothing at all.

The good news? You're not alone. Overwhelmingly, marketers know that they need to spend time and energy on Facebook, but they don't have the first idea where to start and aren't willing to make a financial investment either. A million different (read: similar) Facebook companies are trying to get rich in the social media gold rush, but you can't just drop $30,000 with a generic vendor and expect to start kicking butt and taking names.

Few marketers are kicking butt on Facebook. But you should be taking names, along with cities, states, zip codes, phone numbers, and birthdays. A mountain of marketing data is hidden inside Facebook. All you have to do is ask for it and give your fans a compelling reason to agree to give it to you.

Here's the reality: It's great for the Boston Celtics to have 6.7 million fans in 2012—that's the second-largest Facebook audience in North American team sport—but if we didn't know anything about any of them, then they're not really worth much to us.

You have no shot at generating ROI on Facebook if you can't collect any meaningful data about your fans. Facebook commerce, or F-commerce, is still a nascent art at best, and let's face it: Your brand probably doesn't even have a product that you can effectively sell through Facebook, especially if you're a team with a sold-out or prohibitively priced ticket inventory. So how do you monetize your Facebook audience? There are a few ways to do it, but the most direct way involves gathering data from your fans and then contacting them outside the confines of Facebook.

Despite all of the hype around social media, targeted e-mail is still the undisputed champion of digital marketing. And that's where a Facebook application, along with an integrated marketing plan, comes into play. For the Boston Celtics, our Facebook application Celtics 3-Point Play has been a slam dunk. When it launched in October 2009, Celtics 3-Point Play was a first-of-its-kind application in the NBA and pro sport marketing. Since its debut, the concept has been imitated by a handful of other teams that recognized the value of mining Facebook data from their fan pages.

The premise of 3-Point Play is simple. Fans pick three of their favorite Celtics players and predict a statistic for each player's performance in the upcoming game. Points are awarded to fans based on the accuracy and risk of their picks, and the top-scoring player wins tickets to an upcoming Celtics home game. The top player for the entire season wins a pair of playoff strips—tickets to all Celtics home playoff games.

Making picks takes about a minute, so fans can play the game quickly. That's all part of the strategy, because we aimed to identify casual fans who may not have been previous ticket buyers, representing true upside in terms of customer acquisition. Every time fans play, they have a chance to win, but they only need to play once for us to collect their data.

Sounds easy, right? Don't be fooled. Although the game is easy for a casual fan to play, it proves challenging for the same fan to win more than once, even for the hardcore hoop heads who have a distinct competitive advantage by knowing substitution patterns and rebounding averages.

The game appears simple on the surface, but it's far more complicated under the hood. 3-Point Play is a complex, custom-built database application, and you can't develop this type of game by simply buying something generic off the cyber shelf from that vendor who's

346

been harassing you for the last few months. You need to seek out a legitimate technology partner and put in the time and effort to do it right. We spent an entire off-season planning and developing the game, digging into details like the scoring system, the way in which fans challenged their friends, and other important functionality logistics.

Work continued all the way up until opening night of the NBA season, and even then minor bugs popped up after launch. Isobar North America, our partner in developing the game, brought detailed technical expertise to the table throughout the process. Most company marketing departments simply don't have that asset in house, so you'll need to outsource. Make no mistake—you'll need that level of expertise to execute a similar project. These days, every marketing project is a technology project. And technology projects are expensive. You're going to have to spend some significant cash in the short term to chase long-term Facebook ROI.

Speaking of ROI, what exactly is the value of a Facebook fan? Here's the real question: What's the lifetime value of a fan in your database? How much will he spend on tickets and merchandise? I think those are far more informative and important ROI metrics. By promoting 3-Point Play across all our digital marketing channels, we added more than 85,000 Facebook fans to our database over the course of the game's first two seasons. Additionally, we sold over $130,000 of tickets to Facebook fans who played the game in one season alone. Some of those customers were known in our database before they played the game, but it proved an important point: Our Facebook fans were customers, most of whom were yet to be identified. How's that for ROI?

One more important point: Facebook applications don't work like Field of Dreams. If you build it, they won't come—unless you promote it, and promote it heavily. It's well documented that Facebook fans rarely return to your actual Facebook page after liking your page. Here's one of Facebook's dirty little secrets: More likely, they've never even been to your page at all; they just found your logo on a friend's profile or a shared post in their News Feed. So if you want your fans to engage with your application (which lives on your Facebook page), you'll need to promote and link to it everywhere you can, using Facebook status updates, your website, your e-mail newsletter, and your Twitter feed. Also, make sure that your game includes basic viral functionality that allows players to challenge their friends and invite them to play as well.

Facebook is a massive opportunity, but at the end of the day, it's just one of your many marketing channels. It's probably the largest channel you have, but it's still a spoke on the wheel. All of those channels revolve around your database. Facebook, your website, Twitter, contest entry forms, and any other digital marketing platform you control should all be feeding your fans back home where they belong—into your centralized marketing database.

Even after this success story, I can't claim we've completely mastered Facebook. Zuckerberg and friends are constantly changing the rules. What's true today may not be true tomorrow, and every brand has different needs. But by applying a basic yet well-conceived strategy to our Facebook practice, we've been able to solve one of social media's biggest riddles.

Note: A version of this case study was published in the *SportsBusiness Journal* in spring 2012. Peter revised and added additional detail for this publication.

Contact:

Peter Stringer
Senior Director, Digital Marketing, Boston Celtics
@peterstringer
www.peterstringer.com

Reprinted, in part, by permission of P. Stringer, 2012, "Moving beyond like: How one team monetized Facebook base," *Street & Smith's SportBusiness Journal*, Feb. 27. Additional text written by Peter Stringer.

What Is Social Media?

Social media are platforms that enable users to interact digitally with friends, fans, athletes, celebrities, media, and brands in real time. Although Facebook and Twitter are the most well-known social media platforms, other platforms are growing (Pinterest, Instagram, Vine, Tumblr, Google+) and new ones are appearing every day.

> **ACTIVITY 12.2 Social Media Night at the Ballpark**
>
> In this WSG activity, assume you've just announced a Social Media Night at the ballpark. This activity should help you consider and explain the positive and negative outcomes of this event.

Building an Audience

Sport properties organically attract many fans, but they're working hard to acquire others. Winning helps, but it isn't the only way to build an audience. Getting out early on new platforms helps a property gain an advantage over late-comers.

The NBA was the first major league on Facebook and Twitter and counts 27.5 million fans and followers.[6] The NFL, which began later, has 14.1 million. The Orlando Magic was one of the first NBA teams on Twitter and now has 1.1 million followers, whereas the Miami Dolphins began later and have 277,000.[7]

Beyond being a popular and winning brand, organizations need to use tried-and-true direct and brand-marketing techniques to build the maximum audience.

In-Game and In-Event

Fans are naturally social during events. They interact with fellow fans and (usually) root for a common team. Prompts around the venue help remind fans to like or follow the property. Teams can use PA reads, LED boards, jumbotrons, signage, ticket backs, and many other assets in-venue to drive more fans and followers.

Some teams have become more aggressive. The Boston Celtics were the first team in the NBA to place their Twitter handle on the playing court next to their website address, Celtics.com. At Mississippi State University, the #HAILSTATE hashtag has been painted in the end zone. The University of Michigan built on this concept by painting the hashtag #GOBLUE on their field, which was tied to a sweepstakes that was teased by Twitter leading up to the game. The New Jersey Devils have an interactive Digital Zone that rents out iPads, encourages people to stop by during the game, log in to their Facebook or Twitter pages, and enter sweepstakes (see the sidebar that follows). Many teams, including the New York Jets and Washington Redskins, have Twitter boards throughout the public areas of their venues that show tweets related to the team as the event progresses.

In-Broadcast

Professional sport teams can often take advantage of various assets within their game broadcasts to promote team initiatives, including social media participation.

- **During the game.** In-game broadcast reads by the announcer, enter-to-win contests and sweepstakes, and interactive games are the most commonly used in-broadcast tactics to drive fans to engage through social media channels. The Miami Heat were able to achieve a significant lift in their local broadcast ratings by focusing on driving fans to tune in to the broadcast from their social channels (see the case study later in this chapter on leveraging social media to drive television ratings).

- **Postgame.** Postgame press conferences and analysis shows are a great place to encourage conversation about the game on social media. Analysts and announcers can encourage viewers to follow the team on Facebook and Twitter and use specific hashtags while tweeting.

- **Enabling the game to live on.** Several sport events have captured a moment on the field with a massive 360-degree photo that enables fans who were at the event to tag themselves, tell their friends on Facebook, or tweet about it, enabling the event to live on in the digital world. The NCAA Final Four, University of Michigan, University of Wisconsin, AFL, New York Knicks, and New York Rangers are among several organizations that have created these images, some

Mississippi State University's #HAILSTATE signage throughout the stadium reminds fans of the Bulldogs' Twitter account.

of which have driven as many as 37,000 social taggings, shares, and e-mail addresses entered.[8]

Online, Direct, and Digital Marketing

Reminders and calls to action throughout websites and direct marketing, including e-mail newsletters, mobile apps, mobile SMS (short message service) updates, and tags on direct mail pieces, help build social audience among people who are already within the sport team's or property's database. Simplifying logins for contests, sweepstakes, e-mail newsletters, and SMS platforms through Facebook login can drive higher conversion rates. After the Portland Trail Blazers revised their e-mail newsletter opt-in to allow people to sign up by Facebook, nearly 40 percent of registrants chose that option.[9]

Advertising

Although not yet as widely used as other tactics, paid or institutional advertising can drive a greater audience and more engagement on Facebook and Twitter. Paid advertising can take the form of paid ads on Facebook alongside timelines, in promoted tweets, on external websites, or on outdoor media (e.g., billboards). Institutional advertising includes banner ads on the website, courtside signage in-game, broadcast drops, and in-game reads. In one case study, the New York Knicks increased their Facebook page following by over 40,000 in one month. They tested strategies to deploy unique video content, draw more interaction and engagement through apps on their Facebook page, and drive more sharing and likes by paid ads on Facebook. Because this activity occurred in the off-season,

New Jersey Devils Digital Zone

William Carafello, Former Marketing Director, New Jersey Devils

The Digital Zone is a unique way for the New Jersey Devils and Prudential Center to engage people digitally and collect data at games. It's a physical space located on the main concourse of the Prudential Center where fans can interact with the Devils brand through interactive games and sweepstakes, rent iPads, or log in to their social media accounts during games. The primary goal of the Digital Zone is to engage fans with unique content that enables the team to improve its in-event data collection.

Engagement

- **Internet access**. Using one of a number of computers, fans are encouraged to check their fantasy hockey teams, post something on social media, or like the team on Facebook.
- **Radio show**. Before the game starts, fans can listen as the pregame radio show goes live from the Digital Zone, allowing them to interact with the radio voices of the team.
- **Tweet-ups and meet and greets**. During intermissions, the Digital Zone offers many diversions to keep fans' attention. The Devils' social media volunteers, the Devils Army Generals, organize Tweet Up events that include networking opportunities, discussion about the game thus far, and group photo sessions. During select games live interviews are conducted with alumni players, celebrities, charity personnel, or other distinguished guests.
- **Charging station**. The Digital Zone contains a location with multiple plugs that allow fans to charge up during intermissions so that they can continue to engage in social media during the game.
- **iPad rentals**. Fans can rent iPads that contain a number of games and apps, including the Fire and Ice app (a direct link to the Devils' beat reporter) and NHL GameCenter.

Data Collection

- **First-Game Certificate**. Fans attending a game for the first time can receive a First-Game Certificate that commemorates their first hockey game at Prudential Center. The full-color certificate includes a facsimile autograph of legendary goaltender Martin Brodeur. To receive the certificate, fans must provide an e-mail address.
- **Fan photos**. Fans can take a photo in oversized hockey gear and sit in a faux penalty box with friends. Photos are e-mailed to fans, so they must provide an e-mail address.
- **Giveaways and contests**. Fans can spin a prize wheel in exchange for providing some basic personal information. The prize wheel awards items like stickers, T-shirts, and hats. Fans can also enter contests for larger prizes like tickets to an upcoming game, a Zamboni ride, or a luxury suite.

---

during free agency, the team was pleased with the outcome and decided to focus more resources on Facebook optimization. Today, the Knicks stand at 4 million fans on Facebook, putting them fifth in the NBA.[10]

Share-Optimized Content

When great content is shared among friends, a subset of those friends will then like or follow the property. This method is known in direct marketing as tell a friend (TAF) marketing, and social media is made for TAF sharing. Using Facebook's open graph plug-ins makes content viral. When people like, share, or comment on a story or video in the moment, whether on a website or Facebook, the content is validated to their network of friends. Most content websites today include prominent icons that encourage users to comment on or share the article with their social audience, and sport properties should take advantage of such tools. Because Facebook frequently updates their plug-ins and APIs, marketers need to visit their site at http://developers.facebook.com for updated directions on how to leverage their latest and greatest opportunities.

Identifying, incentivizing, and rewarding influencers among team social followings is gaining traction. Not all fans are created equal; a few will have disproportionately large networks of their own. Getting those fans to share content can improve reach exponentially.

The Sacramento Kings worked with Klout, a company that rates social media users based on their influence on specific topics, to identify 25 influencers in the Sacramento area and invite them to come out to a game. Each influencer had followings in the thousands and tweeted frequently about the Kings. The Kings provided them with extra access through a player meet and greet pregame, lower-bowl seats, and the opportunity to sit courtside for a portion of the game or to participate in on-court contests. The reward for the team was more than 5 million impressions, 99 percent of which were positive, gaining a true reach of over 260,000 people.[11] Teams can identify their own influencers with the largest reach by regularly monitoring Twitter activity, particularly the activity of their season-ticket holders.

Leveraging influencers in sport isn't a new concept; teams with season tickets to sell have learned that holding small influencer events at a key influencer's (season-ticket holder's) home can drive tremendous ROI.

Segmenting Audience

A valid question in the area of social media is whether the organization should have different Facebook pages and Twitter accounts to target different segments of the audience. Some teams have tested this method by having Facebook pages and Twitter accounts for season-ticket holders only to provide more customized content to specialized audiences. The Charlotte Bobcats created a "Rookies"-only Facebook account. Targeted accounts can be effective, but they do require extra time, resources, content, access, and interaction. Teams without large staffs should devote their resources to their largest audiences on the largest platforms.

Engaging Fans

Engaging the audience in social media requires an artful balance. Viral audience growth is directly correlated with how engaged the existing audi-

ence is with the content. If fans and followers love what they read, see, and watch, they will share it and won't tune out. A carefully calibrated approach focused on authenticity of voice, listening, learning, optimizing, and delivering is required.

Authenticity of Voice

The voice of social media should sound like a real person, not a website. The voice should have a conversational tone and some personality, but not too much (see the section "Avoiding Pitfalls" later in this chapter). A lack of authenticity of the voice of social media will cause people to tune out.

Different platforms can have different fan bases, each of which expects to hear a unique voice. By surveying fans of different platforms, sport properties can learn quickly what fans expect.

Listening

Social media have enabled brands and sport properties to understand brand perception and reactions to events or news in real-time like never before. A multitude of tools is available to organize and aggregate fan and follower sentiment on specific topics. Are people talking about the pending trade? Did they love the game last night? Do they love the food vendors in the arena? Do they hate the beer? Social media listening enables real-time reaction, correction, and amplification. Organizations do not have to wait for the (also valuable) fan surveys to go out midseason to know how people feel about the team, ticket prices, or the experience at the game.

Learning

The real-time nature of social media enables real-time learning of what works and what doesn't. Are 10 status updates a day too many? Does a status update with a photo get more engagement than one without? Does a tweet with a link get more clicks and retweets than one without? By using Facebook Insights, Twitter Analytics, Bit.ly, Hootsuite, and similar tools, teams can learn on a quantitative basis, iterate, and optimize rapidly. Simple, quick surveys of the digital audience will qualitatively answer many of these questions.

The NBA's Washington Wizards and Boston Celtics have surveyed their Twitter followers and Facebook fans to find out more about what type of content people want to see, when, and how frequently. The findings led to changes including more frequent posting during game days and regularly linking to player and league accounts. Posts that include a photo, video, poll, question, or true breaking news seem to garner the most engagement. In one major league study that analyzed 3,200 Facebook posts across all teams, 2 of the 3 most commented on posts included a link or a visual (photo or video).[12] More interaction and engagement with posts means that such posts from a given page are more likely to get through the ever-changing Facebook news feed algorithm. The level of interaction with specific types of posts can vary by property and personality, and a robust testing plan will quickly reveal what fans most engage with.

Optimizing

Testing is the magic word behind optimization. Many elements can be tested, including the following:

- Time of post
- Audience targeted (on Facebook)
- Type of content
- Surveys
- Polls
- Questions
- Links

What works in one market, for one sport, for one club, and even for one platform may not necessarily work for all. The NBA has found that including a link, a question, and a photo on a Facebook post drives more engagement. The dynamism of social media is also important; Facebook news feed algorithms change, audiences shift, and content can ebb and flow in sport, further underscoring the need for a rigorous commitment to testing.

Delivering

The most progressive teams in social media not only deliver what their fans want but also go the extra distance to provide unique experiences and access. For example, the San Francisco Giants worked with Twitter and partner Virgin America to create an in-game Twitter scavenger hunt. The scavenger hunt included tweets with the hashtag #FlyTheBeard (in honor of pitcher Brian Wilson's beard) throughout the game that gave fans clues to where they could find Virgin America flight attendants in the ballpark (who were bearded, of course). Those who found the attendants were awarded prizes and the chance to win a free flight.

The top brands that deliver in social media, whether in sport or not, demonstrate an organizational commitment to it. They recognize the importance of social media, starting at the executive level, invest in people and software tools, are early adopters and pioneers on new platforms, and convert social sentiment into actions that drive brand loyalty. Consider the top corporate brands in social media:[13]

1. Starbucks
2. Coca-Cola
3. Dell
4. Zappos
5. Ford

Over 77 million people "like" Coca-Cola on Facebook. Nearly a million people are "talking about it."[14] The company encourages its employees to engage in it publicly and represent the brand responsibly. Consider this excerpt from their web page:[15]

> We recognize the vital importance of participating in these online conversations and are committed to ensuring that we participate in online social media the right way. These Online Social Media Principles have been developed to help empower our associates to participate in this new frontier of marketing and communications, represent our Company, and share the optimistic and positive spirits of our brands.

Dell has six official Twitter accounts that are used to answer customer service questions, address issues, and deliver breaking news. Ford may be the most committed of all auto brands to leveraging social media. They launched the Fiesta movement, in which they invited 100 people to drive a Ford Fiesta around (free) while talking about it on their own social accounts, which Ford featured on their accounts without filtering. They unveiled the 2011 Explorer on Facebook.[16] And their head of social media has over 102,000 followers on Twitter. Zappos is widely known for their culture that starts from the CEO, Tony Hsieh, best-selling author of *Delivering Happiness*. Tony has 2.8 million followers on Twitter, and roughly half of all Zappos employees are on Twitter as well. All staffers are encouraged to provide authentic, creative service in real time.

So are executive teams of sport properties thinking about social media in the same way that the mangers of these companies are? Although many have been slow to adopt and conservative (perhaps rightfully; see "Avoiding Pitfalls" later in this chapter) in their approach, several have been aggressive early adopters who have invested in staff and time to understand and leverage social media.

The Miami Heat created the first dedicated, full-time social media group in the NBA in 2010. Their approach was to (1) create a committee of interested people across the organization to study the social media space and brainstorm ideas on the best way for the Heat to leverage, (2) identify the best candidates from within that committee to fill the new full-time social media positions, and (3) have the new social media group report to the president. The high profile of this group enabled them to execute creative strategies that rewarded fans with unprecedented access and exclusive opportunities.

The Miami Heat's social media team has become so well integrated with the basketball operations side of the business that they are given relevant news to break though social channels. They've been able to be the first to break signings, injuries, lineups, and the like, which gives them real credibility to their Twitter followers. Even their beat writers now know that the Heat will break the news first—and they know to follow them!

The Heat are constantly listening to their fans, learning what content drives the most engagement, and adapting accordingly. They learned that fans love to see what players are saying after practice, so they now capture video after every practice and post it quickly, driving incredible numbers in the range of 10,000 to 20,000 views per video.

Driving Behavior

An engaged audience that already loves a team, club, or league is a tantalizing proposition. How can the organization sell them tickets? Get them to come to more games? Drive the sponsors' business? Get them to tell their friends? Get their feedback on the event experience? Have them spend more time on the property's websites and watch more videos? A balanced approach that delivers unique content, breaking news, authentic insider information, and a sense of community can indeed drive those behaviors. The Miami Heat have shown that a focus on driving tune-in through social media is effective. They measured ratings points before and after activation tactics were put into place and saw a measured improvement (see leveraging social media sidebar). The University of Michigan delivered real value to its Facebook followers by offering a ticket presale and was rewarded with big increases in tickets sold for the same period year over year (see Michigan football ticket sidebar). And the New Zealand Rugby World Cup balanced its goals of building a large social community to sell tickets to with valuable content that created a win–win situation for fans and the organizing committee (see Rugby World Cup sidebar).

Sponsors are hungry to get exposure to the followings of sport properties. Unique, creative content, sweepstakes, or experiences that are sponsored can be perceived positively by social media fans. Driving sponsors' own social following is a common objective. The Cleveland Cavaliers were able to drive an 86 percent increase in followers for their partner, Sugardale Hot Dogs, by promoting the opportunity to win tickets to a game through ad banners on Cavaliers.com and in Facebook posts. This type of promotion is win–win: Fans get the opportunity to see a game free, and Sugardale gets more exposure and more fans.

The Washington Redskins are one of the most innovative sport properties in the space where digital content and sponsorship intersect. In late 2010 the Redskins launched a major sweepstakes that integrated Redskins.com, Foursquare, and their partner, Geico. Geico was interested in building their social presence and in being associated with something new and innovative; Foursquare, despite having a relatively small number of users at the time, fit well as the possible next big thing. The Redskins rewarded fans who "checked in" to FedExField or at participating establishments by automatically entering them into a sweepstakes to win game tickets or prizes. The promotion generated a few thousand check-ins per game, providing fans with more engagement and Geico

Jennifer Tobias, former Director of Interactive Marketing and New Media, Miami Heat

Approaching the 2011–2012 season, we faced the challenge of converting Miami Heat Facebook and Twitter followers into television game broadcast viewers. Unlike most other NBA teams, the Heat had a local broadcast, through Sun Sports, that often went head to head with a national broadcast on ESPN or TNT. Out of the 66-game lockout-shortened season, Sun Sports had 54 game broadcasts, including numerous head-to-head matchups against a national broadcast (table 12.1). Reviewing the previous year's ratings demonstrates the disparity when matched up against a national broadcast.

TABLE 12.1   Ratings From Head-to-Head Games With ESPN or TNT During the 2010–2011 Season

Game	ESPN or TNT	Sun Sports
Oct. 29 vs. Orlando	9.28 ESPN	3.47
Nov. 17 vs. Phoenix	4.39 ESPN	3.30
Nov. 24 at Orlando	5.23 ESPN	2.16
Dec. 10 at Golden State	6.49 ESPN	2.73
Dec. 17 at NY Knicks	4.85 ESPN	3.93
Jan. 13 at Denver	3.01 TNT	2.65
Feb. 27 vs. NY Knicks	6.83 ESPN	3.21
Mar. 4 at San Antonio	3.04 ESPN	2.89
Mar. 14 vs. San Antonio	4.65 ESPN	4.66
Mar. 16 vs. Oklahoma City	4.00 ESPN	3.72
Apr. 6 vs. Milwaukee	2.28 ESPN	3.16

Going into the season we saw a tremendous opportunity to leverage our Facebook and Twitter fan base to grow our local game broadcast ratings. We wanted to give our fans and viewers a new reason to tune in. Working with the executive director and producer of our television game broadcasts, we developed a multipronged approach for the integration of social media. This approach involved creating a game broadcast-specific Twitter hashtag, developing a weekly broadcast activation called Sun Sports Facebook Fridays, and using Twitter to host weekly polls.

The Twitter hashtag chosen, #HEATLive (see photo), was built on the branding Sun Sports had already established with their pregame and postgame shows. Our specific goal was to get more people to talk about and engage with the broadcast in a way that ultimately generated greater interest. The hashtag sent a subtle, yet effective, message to viewers and fans that we were both aware and appreciative of their interest, and it provided them with opportunities to engage with the broadcast. Using a hashtag also provided a measurable tool to gauge the success of the promotion.

Each Friday game day, we hosted Sun Sports Facebook Fridays. The day was dedicated to promoting our broadcast and engaging our viewers through a variety of interactive activities, contests, and unique content. Capitalizing on our on-air talent's personalities, we developed specific programming to help our fans build an affinity for them and the broadcast. We introduced a fun

video series on YouTube hosted by Heat sideline reporter Jason Jackson titled "What's Up, (City Name)?" to give a man-on-the-street perspective for our road games. For those fans looking for more straightforward basketball discussions, we used Heat broadcasters Eric Reid and Tony Fiorentino to host live chats on the Heat Facebook page. Building those personal relationships between our fans and the broadcast was important. We also conducted various watch-and-win promotions, giving fans the opportunity to respond on Facebook to a specific cue given in the broadcast for a chance to win tickets, Heat gear, and autographed memorabilia. The unique content and activities were integrated into both the game broadcast and the Heat Facebook page. The goal was to take advantage of our already well-established popularity to drive people to the broadcasts, not just to increase the number of likes on the Heat Facebook page. Quite simply, if fans thought that they had a chance to win something, or perhaps have their question answered on the air, they were more likely to tune in.

Hosting weekly polls on Twitter seemed like a natural fit for Sun Sports. Having hosted polls in prior seasons via text message and achieving disappointing results, we knew that Twitter gave us an opportunity to reinvent the Sun Sports poll. The Twitter polls would be part of the larger scale social integration into the Friday broadcasts. Asking the poll question during the broadcast and through the @MiamiHEAT Twitter account drove more Twitter followers to participate and tune in to the local broadcast to see the results.

After the season-long social media initiative, launched on January 27, we found that our efforts had paid off. The Twitter hashtag #HEATLive was used over 35,000 times over the course of the season, and over 6 million accounts were reached by its use. The weekly Twitter poll also proved a success. During the 2010–2011 season, using text messaging as the medium, Sun Sports saw an average of 150 poll participants per question. During the 2011–2012 season, using Twitter, Sun Sports averaged 400 poll participants per question. Our Facebook Fridays were also successful in engaging followers on Facebook while promoting the broadcasts. The Caption Contests, hosted on the Heat Facebook page, averaged over 2,500 entries, and our social-specific five-part video series "What's Up, (City Name)?" accrued more than 16,000 views over the course of the season.

We also saw impressive results in the head-to-head telecasts with the national broadcast. Sun Sports finished the season with ratings victories in 9 of the 10 last head-to-head matchups with national networks (table 12.2).

TABLE 12.2 Ratings From Head-to-Head Games With ESPN or TNT During the 2011–2012 Season

Game	ESPN or TNT	Sun Sports
Jan. 11 at LA Clippers	3.70 ESPN	3.56
Jan. 12 at Denver	4.36 ESPN	2.88
Jan. 27 vs. NY Knicks	3.80 ESPN	6.07 (Friday telecast)
Feb. 12 at Atlanta	3.10 ESPN	5.07
Mar. 1 at Portland	4.84 TNT	3.63
Mar. 14 at Chicago	4.80 ESPN	5.63
Mar. 16 at Philadelphia	1.97 ESPN	4.27 (Friday telecast)
Mar. 18 vs. Orlando	3.23 ESPN	6.09
Mar. 25 at Oklahoma City	5.59 ESPN	5.86
Apr. 4 vs. Oklahoma City	3.71 ESPN2	8.52
Apr. 10 vs. Boston	4.09 ESPN	6.54
Apr. 12 at Chicago	5.45 TNT	6.51
Apr. 24 at Boston	2.93 TNT	5.00

> continued

Not by coincidence, the tide began to shift on the night we began our season-long social media initiatives on January 27. That game was our first Facebook Friday, and those specific broadcasts have been highly successful in engaging our fans on many levels. Our ratings victories were not insignificant in size either, because in some cases we doubled the national rating. Although many of these broadcast side-by-sides did not fall on Fridays, the Friday telecasts allowed us to engage the fans in a way that made us more relevant than ever before. Fans wanted to follow us and our announcers because we made ourselves interactive and accessible. When given a choice, they chose us over the national alternative.

We concluded our 54-game 2011–2012 regular season with a 32 percent ratings increase over the previous season, as seen in table 12.3. The pregame shows, which aired for all games in the 2011–2012 season (previous seasons featured only home games), were up a collective 29 percent. Even the postgame shows showed a modest improvement of 8 percent.

TABLE 12.3 Sun Sports Television Ratings During 2010–11 and 2011–12 NBA Seasons

	Pregame	Game	Postgame
2011–2012 NBA season averages (54 games):	1.23	6.50	2.47
2010–2011 NBA season averages (70 games):	0.95	4.92	2.26

Considering the results of our 2011–2012 social media initiative, we are going to continue using our social media assets to support our local game broadcasts. As we move forward, we will monitor the results and integrate new activations based on our successes.

Michigan Football Ticket Facebook Presale Builds Audience and Drives ROI

Jordan Maleh, Director, Digital Marketing, Michigan Athletics Department

Before the start of the 2011 Michigan football season, the Michigan Athletics Department, for the first time, offered all fans of the Michigan football Facebook page (facebook.com/michiganfball) priority access to purchase ticket packs and individual tickets before the general public. During the 2011 Facebook presale campaign, home games offered included Western Michigan, Eastern Michigan, San Diego State, Minnesota, Purdue, and Nebraska (excluding games versus Notre Dame and Ohio State). The 2012 presale campaign included the Michigan Football Family Pack (four tickets, four season shirts, four hot dogs, four small fountain drinks, and four game programs) for games against Air Force, Massachusetts, Illinois, Northwestern, and Iowa (excluding Michigan State).

To activate each respective presale, Michigan Athletics implemented the Pac Social Media Platform (through Paciolan) powered by Buddy Media. The platform is a content system that allows users to build applications and tabs for Facebook pages

through a series of application templates. As subscribers to the platform, Michigan Athletics can use it to customize the Michigan football Facebook page with sweepstakes, contests, polls, and games. The Michigan football Facebook presale instituted the notion of "fan-gating," requiring a fan to "like" a Facebook page to unlock content. Michigan football fans landing on the Michigan football Facebook page who had not "liked" the page were greeted with an image inviting them to do so and offering exclusive access to the presale. After the "like" button was clicked, the page refreshed to reveal an image outlining the offer (see the following image) that, when clicked, took fans directly to the presale promotion, where tickets were sold at full price ($75 to $85).

The results of this Facebook campaign are clear:

2011 Season

- 723 tickets sold; $53,805 in revenue
- Acquired "likes": about 7,000; time stamp: Monday, July 11–Monday, July 18

2012 Season

- 1,901 tickets sold; $142,575 in revenue
- Acquired "likes": 7,535; time stamp: Monday, July 16–Tuesday, July 31

Using Facebook to Attract Rugby World Cup 2011 Fans

Shane Harmon, former General Manager, Marketing and Communications, Rugby New Zealand 2011

This sidebar looks at how Rugby World Cup 2011 used Facebook to engage a "stadium of 4 million" Kiwis and attract over 130,000 rugby fans from around the world. Rugby World Cup is Rugby Union's global showpiece, held every four years. The event has grown exponentially since its inception in 1987. New Zealand, home of the legendary All Blacks, was chosen by the International Rugby Board (IRB) as the host for the 2011 tournament. Rugby New Zealand 2011 (RNZ 2011) was appointed as the local organizing committee (LOC). Ticketing was the LOC's only source of revenue (the IRB retained all broadcast, sponsorship, and other commercial revenue streams).

By international standards, Rugby World Cup is a large event. By New Zealand standards, it was off the radar. The LOC's target was over US$200 million in ticket sales (from 48 matches). Reaching this goal would require an attendance of 1.5 million fans. (Bear in mind the New Zealand's population is only 4 million!) The budget was 11 times larger than any event ever held in the country. Given that the New Zealand government was a part owner of the LOC and was contributing significant funding toward stadium upgrades and a range of festival and legacy initiatives, the LOC had a strong imperative to attract international fans to the event. Furthermore, with a limited marketing budget, the LOC was unable to run traditional above-the-line campaigns in international markets.

In 2009 Shane Harmon, GM marketing and communications, and Clare Wolfensohn, online and communications projects manager, turned to social media to address these multiple challenges by establishing a presence on Facebook, Twitter, YouTube, and Flickr. There were two key drivers.

The first was to create vibrant, engaged, and lasting community. "There was very little marketing legacy from tournament to tournament," said Harmon. "We wanted to first and foremost build a community for our tournament, but also to create a core audience that would follow Rugby World Cup into the future." The LOC looked at the terrific work that Vancouver did for the Winter Olympics. "Vancouver were certainly pioneers in the major event space for social media, Harmon said. "However, their Facebook presence was built

> continued

around the Vancouver brand and the 2010 event. There are still over a million fans on their Facebook page, but at little legacy to future hosts such a Sochi."

The LOC made the deliberate decision early on to brand all its social platforms "Rugby World Cup" rather than dating them by adding "2011." This decision was significant, because it allowed the LOC to pass management of its 1.7-million-strong Facebook community on to future host England for 2015.

The second key driver was to leverage social platforms to sell tickets. "Our marketing budgets really only allowed us to run print, TV, and radio domestically" said Harmon. "But for Rugby World Cup to be a true success, both economically and emotionally, we had to attract thousands of fans from around the world." In September 2009, two years out from the tournament, the RWC team launched a Facebook marketing push that included creating a Facebook page, several custom applications, and a number of Facebook ad campaigns. The ad campaigns focused on rugby keywords in target countries of the United Kingdom, Ireland, Australia, France, South Africa, and the United States. Friends of Connections targeting was used, which helped reach the 125 million friends of people who were already fans of the Rugby World Cup page. And then, specifically targeting New Zealand fans, RNZ 2011 ran numerous Facebook Reach Blocks, a premium media buy on the Facebook home page that guaranteed a reach of all Kiwis on Facebook over a 24-hour period. The objective for the Reach Block was to help build a solid fan base in New Zealand itself. Kiwis would ultimately purchase 70 percent of all tickets. After the initial advertising campaign built up a solid fan base, RNZ 2011 relied on generic growth using rich, varied content, including videos, photos, and polls on the Rugby World Cup page. For example, the IRB opened up its extensive video archive to give fans access to historical RWC footage.

In March 2010 (a full 18 months from the start of RWC 2011), the team turned to selling tickets. It had an active and engaged base of some 400,000 Facebook fans. The Rugby World Cup ticketing campaign took place over four phases: (1) venue and team packs, (2) individual tickets, (3) ballots for the semifinals and the final, and (4) the last push in the two months leading into the tournament. At each stage RNZ 2011 bolstered its Facebook presence by creating apps that, although fun and engaging in their own right, carried a strong ticketing call to action. Apps such as the World's Biggest Scrum, Fan Personality Test, and Spot the Ball all had a ticketing call to action built into them at a time when each sales phase was open. Tens of thousands of fans played the games. Each game linked directly to the ticketing website. Through these apps, RNZ 2011 effectively created its own media vehicles from which it could advertise its commercial messages. RNZ 2011 witnessed further growth in "likes" numbers, but more significantly gained substantial traffic to its ticketing website directly from Facebook.

By the end of Rugby World Cup 2011, the team had set a new standard in using social media to drive commercial outcomes. The results included the following:

- A 1.5-million-strong Facebook community, the largest for any standalone event anywhere in the world
- NZ$269 million (US$600 million) in ticket sales, surpassing the budget with three days to spare
- Facebook was the number 2 driver of traffic to the ticketing website after Google
- Attracted 133,000 international visitors to New Zealand against an initial target of 60,000, contributing significantly to the NZ$750 million economic impact from the tournament
- Rugby World Cup 2011 won the prestigious best event accolade in the *SportBusiness* Ultimate Digital Sports Awards 2011

For more information, view the Facebook Case Study on the Rugby World Cup 2011 here: www.scribd.com/doc/97475056/Rugby-World-Cup-Facebook-Ad-Case-Study.

with both a greater presence on the fledgling platform and a positioning that identified it as a forward-looking company.[17]

Social Media Platforms

How many platforms do we need to be on? This question is commonly asked by social media coordinators across sport. Other questions soon follow: How do we balance our content and focus across these platforms? Which take priority? Most teams focus efforts where the greatest numbers of active people are—Facebook and Twitter. The long tail of others includes Google+, Instagram, Foursquare, Tumblr, Pinterest, Socialcam, and a raft of new ones almost daily (figure 12.1).

Facebook is the 800-pound gorilla in the space, having more than 1.15 billion active users on June 30, 2013.[18] Nearly every major sport property has a Facebook presence. Twitter does not publicly disclose its total number of users, but it was reported in March 2012 that they had 140 million active users.[19] Nearly all sport properties have a presence there as well.

Google+ has a user base of 170 million people but has yet to deliver the engaged numbers that both Facebook and Twitter boast. Although three-quarters of the top brands have Google+ pages, their following and related engagement lag far behind those of Facebook and Twitter.[20] Consider that an identical Lady Gaga post on Facebook and Google+ delivered 133,539 "likes" compared with 570 "+1s"! Having a brand presence on Google+ does have positive effects on searches. Brands on Google+ show up in search results more frequently than those that aren't.[21] Improved search engine optimization (SEO) is always desirable for websites. Google+'s Hangout is a unique offering that delivers a point of differentiation from the other platforms. Hangout enables a group video chat of up to 10 people. Live events can also be streamed through Hangout. The Minnesota Timberwolves held a live Google+ Hangout chat event with Brandon Roy in which fans asked various questions. The NFL recently teamed up with Google+ to bring Hangout video chats to their fantasy football platform, enabling virtual drafts and chats throughout the season.

FIGURE 12.1   A look at the multitude of social media platforms and related companies.

Reprinted, by permission, from LUMA Partners LLC, 2012.

Instagram, the photo-editing and sharing app acquired by Facebook for $1 billion in April 2012, has more than 100 million monthly active users.[22] Sport properties like the Boston Celtics (492,000 followers) are increasingly using the platform to share behind-the-scenes photos, giving the fan an inside look at the day-to-day life of a professional athlete. Foursquare, known as a location-based check-in app, is evolving its offering to its 40 million users.[23] It's no longer just about telling people where you are; it's now about discovery and enriching your experience wherever you may be. People love to tell their friends when they're at sports events, so Foursquare should be a natural fit to activate fans, despite not having as large a following as some of the other platforms. Tumblr, with 130 million users, offers a hybrid of the other platforms, but it may be best at featuring rich, timeless content that holds interest beyond just the news of the day.[24] The SI Photo blog, Boston Bruins, Los Angeles Kings, and the NBA have beautiful Tumblr blogs that feature the depth of content and access that only they can provide. Pinterest, with its 25 million users, offers a heavily female audience. It's too early to say definitively what its niche will be, but early indicators are that it may be a strong referrer of e-commerce sales and will be one to watch.

There are literally hundreds of other platforms that are beautifully illustrated by infographics created by sites like Mashable, MediaNeedle, and Social Media Today, and we haven't even discussed the Chinese juggernauts Weibo and Tencent. But because many American sport properties are unable to activate on Chinese networks, we will limit our discussion to the platforms mentioned earlier. Besides the major social media networks, an entire cottage industry that offers ancillary or integrated solutions with social media has sprouted up. Sport properties must carefully evaluate opportunities for both platforms and tangential offerings (see the sidebar that follows).

Management of multiple platforms is difficult. Can the organization be an octopus? How many people are needed to cover all platforms? Is the same thing posted on each one? How can the organization ensure that it is telling the most important, best stories across all media in

Evaluating New Platforms

Melissa Rosenthal Brenner, SVP Marketing, NBA

The NBA, with the largest number of fans and followers among major sport leagues, gets pitched by new technology companies perhaps more than any other type of company. We've simplified our review process to focus on three major areas: design, utility, and terms.

- **Design**. When evaluating new platforms, we look for simplicity, beautiful design, ease of use, and low barriers to adoption. A beautifully designed experience captures your attention and draws you in—until you realize that you have spent more time on the platform than you had thought possible.

- **Utility**. The NBA seeks a clear understanding of how a new platform would be used, how it would fit in with what's already being done, how it would extend the NBA's reach, and how it could build new and distinct audiences.

- **Terms**. Many platforms contain standard terms and conditions ("click-through agreements") that the user is required to click on and agree to before registering for a profile or user account. Such agreements generally don't grant any protections regarding content or intellectual property, and they may fall outside relevant league rules or guidelines. Sport properties should refer platform terms to legal counsel, because they may be signing away valuable rights to sponsorship opportunities, use of IP, and so on just by creating an account. Adding sport content to an emerging platform in many cases provides more value and benefits for the platform than for the sport property. Platform developers are often willing to accommodate properties with separate agreements that supersede the click-through agreement terms.

the right way? Major brands have social media teams consisting of 10 or more personnel devising overall strategy, content mix, and customer service. Zappos employs a team of 10 to manage social customer service alone.[25] Sport leagues typically have much smaller groups, and sport teams even smaller ones; on average, teams have fewer than two full-time employees dedicated to social media.[26]

Many major brands have turned to social media management (SMM) platforms such as Buddy Media, Wildfire, and Vitrue to help manage their social media publishing and content development. These platforms enable content scheduling, rich content and application development, and advanced analytics. The NFL has worked with Buddy Media since 2010, offering its platform to all teams in the league.

Whether teams use SMM tools or not, managing multiple platforms requires balance of content and strong understanding of the distinct qualities of each platform's followers. To ensure consistency of content, storylines, and offers, daily content meetings are recommended. In these meetings, all those responsible for publishing content across various platforms (e.g., e-mail, website, social media, SMS, TV, radio) quickly discuss the news of the previous day (e.g., trades, game results, and highlights) and develop a common narrative. Ideas for unique content for individual platforms can be vetted and approved in this forum. Then, those responsible for publishing to the various platforms apply the right voice and timing to derive the most engagement per platform.

Avoiding Pitfalls

How does an organization keep track of all people with access to their accounts? How do they avoid being hacked? Should they let people comment on everything on Facebook and say whatever they want? Misuse of social media by individuals has on many occasions led to suspensions or even firings. For example, Gilbert Gottfried was fired from Aflac because he tweeted jokes about the Japanese tsunami of 2011, Roland Martin was suspended by CNN for homophobic tweets about a 2012 Super Bowl ad, and Greek athlete Paraskevi Papachristou was barred from participating in the London 2012 Olympic Games after tweeting an offensive comment about African immigrants.

Sport properties must have a strategy to ensure brand protection within social media and to prevent gaffes.

> ### ACTIVITY 12.3 Pros and Cons of Using Social Media in Sports
> Almost everyone talks about how social media can help a team market itself to consumers. In this WSG activity, you will consider and explain some of the pros and cons of social media.

To avoid major social media pitfalls, sport properties, athletes, and celebrities should heed some basic guidelines.

- **Manage access to accounts**. Usually, more than one person has access to post across social networks from the official handle representing the team, league, or person. Follow the advice in the sidebar "Avoiding Social Media Pitfalls: Three Simple Tips from the NBA" for more information on managing account access.

- **Keep personal and official accounts separate**. Many SMM tools enable toggling between multiple accounts, and many a mistake has occurred when a staffer believed that he was posting from his personal account but was actually posting from an official one. For example, Microsoft's Twitter account appeared to insult the conservative political pundit Ann Coulter. Robert Reich, former Clinton administration secretary of labor and current professor of public policy at the University of California of Berkeley, tweeted: "To NY to visit my 4-yr-old granddaughter. Also on ABC's 'This Week' panel w/ Ann Coulter, among others. I'd rather be w/ my granddaughter." Microsoft's Twitter account responded: "@RBReich your granddaughter's level of discourse and policy > those of Ann Coulter." Microsoft deleted the tweet, and the website Politico reported that they said in a statement that the tweet "obviously is not an official statement by the company." A Microsoft spokesperson told Politico, "One of the people who manages our corporate Twitter account thought he was tweeting from their personal Twitter account on Saturday morning but tweeted from our corporate account by mistake. That person immediately realized his mistake and deleted the tweet from our corporate account. We have taken steps to help ensure that this kind

Avoiding Social Media Pitfalls: Three Simple Tips from the NBA

Melissa Rosenthal Brenner, NBA SVP of Marketing

1. **Know who has access to accounts.** In a large organization with a wide range of platforms, dozens of people may have access to post to accounts. Social media managers must know exactly who has access to which accounts.

2. **Change passwords frequently and make them complex.** Positions in social media today are frequently filled with young social media and digital natives. Often they're junior employees or interns, and tenure isn't deep. Passwords must be changed frequently and be of such complex nature that they can't be guessed.

3. **Have clear, written rules on what can and cannot be discussed.** The old advice about e-mail also holds for social media: If you wouldn't say it in a press conference, don't e-mail or post it. Of course, fans don't follow teams or leagues because they want to read press releases and preapproved statements all day; they want authentic, behind-the-scenes content and news and offers that they can't access anywhere else. But clear guidelines, including what types of current events can (and cannot) be commented on and what types of news can be broken through social media, should be put in writing and posted at the desk of every person who ever posts content.

of mistake doesn't happen again."[27] This is one of just many examples of personal and official account mix-ups. Sport properties must provide clear expectations for all who have the ability to post on social media.

- **Reserve the right to delete but do so with caution.** Content or status updates that have already been published can be easily deleted, but often not before someone has taken a screen grab and republished it elsewhere. A gaffe is embarrassing, but being caught trying to hide a gaffe can be more damaging. Many athletes have deleted tweets that they realized were inappropriate, but not before websites like Mashable, Deadspin, and Funny Athlete Tweets had made a story out of them.

- **Own your mistakes.** An organization or individual who makes a mistake must address it head-on with fans and followers. When an employee from the Red Cross accidentally tweeted from the official account instead of her personal account (another reminder to have clear guidelines for personal and official account management) about drinking beer, the Red Cross owned up to it rapidly (figure 12.2). Impressed by the way that the Red Cross handled the gaffe, Dogfish Head Beer then encouraged their fans and followers to donate to the Red Cross, resulting in incremental donations on that day.[28]

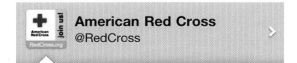

Ryan found two more 4 bottle packs of Dogfish Head's Midas Touch beer.... when we drink we do it right #gettngslizzerd

a HootSuite · 2/15/11 11:24 PM

We've deleted the rogue tweet but rest assured the Red Cross is sober and we've confiscated the keys.

about 11 hours ago via UberTwitter
Retweeted by 86 people

b RedCross
American Red Cross

FIGURE 12.2 (*a*) The accidental Red Cross tweet and (*b*) the Red Cross' response to the accidental (and deleted) tweet.

Reprinted, by permission, from the American Red Cross.

Leveraging Players and Talent

Social media offers fans an incredible opportunity to hear directly from players and talent. Fans no

mcuban Mark Cuban
still some $5 single tickets available 4 2nite vs Hornets. at the AAC box office 30 mins before gm. Also great deals on Plat. seats !

15 Nov

Owners and players can help sell tickets through their own social media followings.

longer have to wait for official interviews, press conferences, or blog posts. Some players have even more followers on social media than the teams that they play for. This circumstance can be both a blessing and a curse for sport teams. If the players are engaged with the team's broader priorities and don't embarrass themselves, their team, or their teammates in social media, they can become tremendous assets in furthering the brand's following.

Social media also offers individual athletes the opportunity to further their own brands, make them more appealing to prospective sponsors, and improve their career outlook after their playing days end. Consider the effect that the 2012 Summer Olympic Games had on the followings of individual athletes. Gymnastics all-around gold medalist Gabby Douglas added more than 550,000 Facebook fans and over 600,000 Twitter followers, and Michael Phelps added over 1 million Twitter followers during the Games. Those numbers, of course, are appealing to brands looking to gain more recognition and consideration. The Ultimate Fighting Championship (UFC) believes that athletes' social participation is so important to furthering fandom of the sport that they've created a bonus structure that awards the most active and effective fighters (see the following sidebar).

properties. When Mark Cuban tweets that inexpensive single tickets remain for select games, he helps sell up to 50 tickets in half an hour. Some NFL clubs have been able to get players' help in selling tickets to games through their own personal Twitter feeds, in some cases helping to prevent broadcast blackouts.

Because people want to hear directly from talent, athletes, and celebrities, integrating sport property social media efforts with talent is crucial. The Golden State Warriors have run Tweedia Day for the last three years as an extension of their annual media day. During Tweedia Day, players have the opportunity to sit down and log in to their respective social accounts, post on the Warriors' official accounts, and have a real dialogue with fans in addition to the media. The team benefits by being able to provide authentic value to fans, and they demonstrate to the players that they can help build their personal following as well.

ACTIVITY 12.5 Social Media Creates Global 'Olympic Village'

In this WSG activity, you will consider and explain the strengths and weaknesses of using PlayUp and social media for the 2012 Summer Olympics Games.

ACTIVITY 12.4 Teams Using Social Media

Sport organizations and athletes have had to adapt their marketing campaigns to take advantage of social media. In this WSG activity, you will learn more about real-time coverage, fan forums, pregame sneak-peeks, and offline tweetups. You will also learn how five teams use social media effectively.

Players, owners, and talent can help drive business objectives for their teams and media

Wrap-Up

Social media is well on its way to becoming an integral part of sport marketing. It can influence all aspects of the business—ticket sales, marketing, sponsorship, digital, community relations, game presentation, broadcast operations, and customer service. The sport properties that understand and harness their power correctly will have an edge over those that don't. People who possess the skills that can help sport properties achieve social media fluency are in high demand; their challenge will be to translate that fluency into true business results.

UFC Awards Winners of Quarterly Twitter Incentive Program

Amy Jo Martin, Digital Royalty

UFC president Dana White and the UFC have long been proponents of fighters taking advantage of social media platforms. White famously instructed his athletes, "Tweet your asses off," believing that the platform is ideal for engaging fans and building fighters' presence. The UFC Twitter incentive campaign, launched in May 2011 at the UFC Fighter Summit, awards 12 bonuses per quarter for creative and successful uses of Twitter. Fighters were placed into one of four categories based on number of followers as of June 1, 2011, the beginning of the quarter. Four prizes were given out within each of these categories: most total followers at the end of the quarter, biggest percentage increase in followers over the quarter, and most creative use of Twitter. Statistics on number of followers were tracked by Digital Royalty, a social media brand management company. Nominees in the most creative category were submitted by fighters, fans, UFC staff, and Digital Royalty; White selected the winners. Twelve bonuses of $5,000 each went to the following nine fighters:

Most followers

- Anderson Silva, UFC middleweight champion: 604,511
- Minotauro Nogueira: 176,852
- Demian Maia: 69,792
- Cris Cyborg, Strikeforce women's featherweight champion: 12,252

Biggest percent increase in followers

- Paulo Thiago: 301 percent
- Minotauro Nogueira: 290 percent
- Demian Maia: 157 percent
- Anderson Silva: 106.5 percent

Most creative

- Forrest Griffin: From the dawn of TUF through his best-selling books, Griffin has been revered for his unique and comic voice. On Twitter, his messages are sporadic but unmistakably Forrest. Notified of his win, he wrote: "Irony: found out on twitter I won a prize for tweeting" and "When the @ufc says most creative what they obviously mean is incoherent ramblings."
- Joe Lauzon: Lauzon used a multiplatform approach to scoop the MMA media and break the news of his UFC 136 fight against Melvin Guillard—with the blessing of the UFC, of course (no leaks!). He wrote a post on his own site with his reasons for taking the fight and his (ultimately correct) prediction about how it would play out. He then tweeted a link.
- Benson Henderson: Henderson live tweeted during the UFC 133 prefight conference call, giving fans access to what is usually a media-only affair. He also took questions from fans during the call, fully incorporating them into the event.
- Joseph Benavidez: Benavidez held a Twitter contest asking fans to suggest and then vote on a new nickname, which was to be announced by Bruce Buffer inside the Octagon at Benavidez's August fight. The contest received over 1,000 mentions and 250 nominations.

Brazilian fighters in particular benefited from a surge in popularity because of August's UFC Rio event. All the fighters who nabbed the awards for most followers and largest percentage growth were Brazilian.

Activities

1. What are some of the reasons that social media is becoming valuable to sport marketing?

2. Has social media ever inspired you to make a purchase that you would not have otherwise made? What aspects of the social media platform drove your buying decision?

3. Visit the social media pages of one of the top five corporate brands in social media previously mentioned in the text. What elements set them apart from other corporate brands that you have seen on social media?

4. What guidelines should teams keep in mind when posting on the team's social media sites? What guidelines should pertain to athletes?

5. You've just been hired as the social media coordinator for a professional team. Your first task is to create a promotion through the team's social media platforms to drive season-ticket sales for next season. Create and describe your promotion and explain how it will increase season-ticket sales.

Your Marketing Plan

In developing your marketing plan, you have developed a list of objectives, strategies, and tactics. Social media can be instrumental in helping you achieve these elements of a marketing plan by providing content through an interactive, organic communication vehicle that, like publicity, can only be guided and shaped, not controlled. Integrate an effective use of Facebook or Twitter to help achieve your sales-related objectives, strategies, and tactics.

Endnotes

1. Material assembled from: http://mlb.mlb.com/fancave/about.jsp#fbid=UOaZOUA_6Md

   http://www.postano.com/blog/how-social-media-is-changing-sports-marketing

   http://www.sportsbusinessdaily.com/Daily/Issues/2013/07/26/Facilities/ATT-Stadium.aspx

2. 2012 NBA Team Digital Report, published to NBA teams by the NBA's Team Marketing and Business Operations.

3. www.sportsfangraph.com; North American professional sports teams only.

4. 2012 NBA Team Digital Report, published to NBA teams by the NBA's Team Marketing and Business Operations.

5. 2011 Chadwick Martin Bailey Consumer Pulse.

6. Facebook.com., NBA's number of likes as of June 27, 2013.

7. Twitter.com., Orlando Magic and Miami Dolphins number of followers as of June 27, 2013.

8. Jordan Maleh, director, digital marketing, Michigan Athletics Department.

9. Stat from Portland Trailblazers' then senior director of digital, Dan Harbison.

10. Facebook. The New York Knicks had 3.7 million likes as of June 27, 2013.

11. Sacramento Kings, Mitch Germann, former VP of marketing and communications.

12. NBA study, December 2010.

13. State of Corporate Social Media, Useful social media, www.usefulsocialmedia.com.

14. Facebook's "Talking about" metric measures user-initiated activity related to a Facebook page, including posting to a page's wall, "liking," commenting, sharing a page post or content on the page, answering a question posed to fans, mentioning a page, "liking" or sharing a deal, or checking in at the page's place.

15. www.thecoca-colacompany.com/socialmedia/.

16. www.forbes.com/sites/shelisrael/2012/05/29/social-media-thought-leader-fords-scott-monty-part-1.

17. www.socialmediaexaminer.com/washington-redskins-kick-off-foursquare-to-reward-loyal-fans/.

18. Facebook, *Facebook Reports Second Quarter 2013 Results*, 24 July 2013, http://investor.fb.com/releasedetail.cfm?ReleaseID=780093.

19. http://blog.twitter.com/2012/03/twitter-turns-six.html.

20. Bright Edge SocialShare, *Tracking Social Adoption and Trends*, February 2012, http://info.brightedge.com/rs/brightedge/images/BrightEdge_SocialShare_February_2012.pdf.

21. Ibid.

22. Instagram, http://blog.instagram.com/post/44078783561/100-million.

23. Foursquare, https://foursquare.com/about/.

24. Mashable, Tumblr cofounder Kevin Systrom, http://mashable.com/2013/06/20/instagram-130-million-users/.

25. Social Media for Customer Service Summit 2011; Scott Klein and Marlene Kanagusuku.

26. Major league 2012 digital staff survey.

27. Read more at www.politico.com/news/stories/0912/81577.html.

28. www.buzzfeed.com/mjs538/red-cross-employee-accidentally-tweets-from-the-of.

Chapter 13

Delivering and Distributing Core Products and Extensions

OBJECTIVES

- To understand distribution as it relates to the marketing process and the place application of the five Ps
- To understand the theory of place as it relates to sport
- To recognize the importance of the venue and facility in sport marketing
- To understand the elements of marketing channels and their application to tickets and retail products

The Big-Time Hockey Experience Has Moved Outdoors

In February 2012 the NHL and the University of Michigan announced a deal in which the league would pay $3 million to lease the Big House (Michigan Stadium) for roughly six weeks around the January 2013 date of the Winter Classic between the Detroit Red Wings and the Toronto Maple Leafs. The university would receive a handsome sum for a cavernous venue that would otherwise sit empty during the winter months. For its money, the NHL counted on selling over 110,000 tickets at a premium to fans who would happily pay for the privilege of freezing while they watched a game that, for many, would be impossible to follow on the ice. And that was assuming that the fans would be sober—alcohol sales had been part of the deal. What the NHL hoped to sell, and what fans hoped to buy, was a special, possibly unique experience—pro hockey in an unusual place.[1]

The 2013 Winter Classic was a victim of the labor lockout, but hockey in the Big House will occur in the future, as long as there is demand. The NHL had begun its outdoor placements in 2008 with a game in Buffalo's NFL stadium. The league was hardly a trendsetter in this venture; hockey had been played in famous football stadiums before. Harvard had done it in 1910. European clubs had played in football stadiums before and after World War II. More recently, Michigan State had played Michigan at Spartan Stadium in 2001, claiming a hockey attendance record of 74,544. This record was broken in 2010 when an IIHF World Championship Tournament game played in a German football stadium drew 77,803 fans. The two Michigan schools responded the next December with hockey's first stop at Michigan Stadium, setting an announced record of 113,411.

Ticket sales were just part of these arrangements. All the hockey properties were experimenting in product distribution, finding bigger platforms for the game experience. The larger strategy was to maximize product exposure across venues and across media—one of the most crucial games in sport. ESPN, which began in 1979 as a cable television network, has moved its brand across a variety of mediums, including radio, restaurants, websites, cell phone apps, magazine, and video games. In 2009 the corporation (which is owned by Disney) took over Disney's Wide World of Sports complex in Orlando, Florida, a venue that has facilities for multiple sport events. The WWS had been host to spring training for the Atlanta Braves, national soccer championships for youth and college teams, the Harlem Globetrotters, and other groups. Disney's senior VP for global sports noted that the name change from the Disney Wide World of Sports to the ESPN Wide World of Sports made simple sense. The new name brought the ESPN brand to the 220-acre (90 ha) facility, which has attracted millions of young athletes who make up "the pipeline for tomorrow for ESPN." ESPN was not waiting for that demographic to come to the brand; the brand was coming to them.[2]

Chapters 10, 11, and 12 examined the use of print, broadcast, social media, and Internet platforms as key elements in marketing strategy. In this chapter, we discuss some other facets related to the effective distribution of the sport product—both the core event and its extensions. We begin with a look at the facility, its location, its layout, and its image. Next, we consider other types of distribution channels related to sport, including retail distribution of merchandise and apparel. Finally, after outlining some features

of effective ticket distribution, we discuss some elements for the analysis of product distribution.

Placing Core Products and Their Extensions

In the previous examples, the NHL and ESPN were engaging in strategy that should be elementary to any sport organization, at any level. They were expanding the distribution of their product or brand to as many outlets as practical and effective, through as many channels as possible. The director of a youth football club or a high school athletics program must think along the same lines, whether it means running clinics and camps in elementary schools, developing electronic newsletters, or using local cable community access television channels to convey information about team tryouts. Effective marketing requires a careful and deliberate strategy for distribution.

In many respects, place (or distribution) decisions may be the most important choices a marketer makes because they have long-range implications and are often harder to change than product, price, promotion, and public relations decisions. Think briefly about the range of product elements that require distribution by a typical sport team:

- The live event itself
- Postgame statistics
- Players and coaches through personal appearances
- Tickets to the live event
- Concessions
- Merchandise, apparel, and memorabilia

These elements require an integrated strategy and long-term commitments of assets. Take the game form itself. In a competitive marketplace, most sport governing bodies, like the NHL, are looking to grow their game by introducing it into new markets. But such strategies are not limited to big-time leagues and big-time budgets. High schools, small colleges, and clubs can also use the following tactics.

- **Scheduling competitions in new markets**. Major League Baseball, the NFL, the NHL, NASCAR, and the NBA have scheduled international exhibitions and tours for years. English Premier League and other world football teams have toured North America with regularity in the last decade. In 2012, for instance, Chelsea, Liverpool, and Tottenham were among the EPL sides that filled their off-season with matches in MLS venues across the continent. Many U.S. college teams play annual or biennial "home" games in outlying areas—sometimes known as outer-rim markets. In the 1880s Yale and Princeton began

playing some football games in Manhattan to attract a bigger paying crowd and expand the fan base. The tradition has continued in college sports. University of New Hampshire men's hockey, for instance, plays one or two "home" games in Manchester's new Verizon Center, some 30 miles (50 km) from its campus arena, in an effort to develop and satisfy a broader consumer market. On November 11, 2011, Veteran's Day in the United States, Michigan State and North Carolina opened their men's basketball seasons on the flight deck of the aircraft carrier USS Carl Vinson. The top fan among the 8,111 attendees was President Barack Obama. Such scheduling of activities away from home need not be for major events. In 2012 Larry Fedora, head coach of the North Carolina Tar Heels football team, decided to hold a spring practice at a high school across the state in Charlotte. Despite having to negotiate the labyrinth of NCAA rules and a lightning strike that ended practice early, the move was a success. Said associate AD Corey Holliday, a different fan base "got to see the Heels, took home some autographs, and had a good time." As long-time sports executive Andy Dolich recently wrote, the variable-venue venture is a hot idea in the industry. Holding events away from home has many attractions. But several cautions arise, including issues of security, services, weather, and fan habits.[3]

- **Reaching out and touching somebody**. In an age of instant global images and datasets, most sport action and information can be consumed just about anywhere. But nothing sells like a real human being. Tours of star players have spurred fan frenzy for at least 150 years. In the 19th century, boxers, cricket clubs, and baseball teams made well-publicized circuits on rail and steamer, taking their skills to distant markets. And new markets need not be distant. Many teams have run off-season or preseason "caravans" of players, coaches, and other staff in circuits that extend to a radius of a few hundred miles. What sets apart these market-making tours is the extra touch of special appearances, clinics, or autograph sessions, where heroes can mingle with their audience. It is one thing to watch a star; it is another to shake his hand or go home with her personalized autograph. Over the last decade, a number of professional teams have staged fan conventions. In July 2008, for instance, the Chicago Blackhawks held one in the Hilton Chicago. More than 10,000 fans attended over one weekend, enjoying seminars and autograph sessions with players, broadcasters, and front-office staff. It was an old-fashioned boosters meeting on steroids.[4]

Any sound marketing plan considers the careful distribution of all critical components of the sport product, from basic game knowledge to specialized team merchandise.

Theory of Sport and Place

We could argue that sport is no different from fast food—it's all location, location, location. Because the core sport product is a game form, simultaneously produced and consumed, the venue of that game form should maximize exposure. In 1995 the Professional Squash Association (PSA) held its New York Tournament of Champions in the middle of Grand Central Station. An estimated 20,000 commuters caught a glimpse of the action. In the words of one top player, that crowd included "more people than had ever before seen it live." Talk about maximizing exposure! Setting up a one-way glass squash court in a major travel center took some work, but the effort paid off. Many sports, however, require less controllable topographic or geographic factors, such as a mountain, beach, or white-water river, where high levels of exposure cannot be guaranteed. McDonald's or Safeway does not operate under such constraints. As we discussed in chapter 6, however, the core experience of the game or the event can be extended in many creative ways, through media distribution, DVDs or online streaming video, merchandise, and apparel—which is exactly the approach that the PSA and other properties are taking to grow their games.[5]

Location is critical to the experience of every sport consumer, whether participant or spectator. At the University of Massachusetts, the lacrosse field is located near the middle of campus. The men's lacrosse team has enjoyed tremendous student support. Crowds number in the thousands for big games. By contrast, the baseball team plays in an out-of-the-way location where crowds have rarely exceeded a few hundred, even for a team with a future Cy Young Award winner on the roster! But the difference goes beyond sheer proximity to the campus center. The lacrosse field is bounded in part by a long bank of grass that is perfectly sloped for students seeking a spot in the warm spring sun, where they can relax, kibitz, root for the home team, and maybe even crack open a book. The grassy embankment is part of an ensemble of elements that make this lacrosse field a special place in the campus life.

The notion of the place *ensemble*—a term developed by geographers—is important for sport marketers who work with core events. They must recognize the elements that enhance or diminish the attractiveness of their venue and surroundings. Take Boston's historic Fenway Park, one of the few North American sport venues that are truly cherished. Fenway's ensemble includes the following elements:

- **Landscape.** Fenway Park's surrounding landscape includes both the urban rhythm of Kenmore Square and the rural serenity of the nearby Back Bay Fens, the first park in Frederick Law Olmsted's Emerald Necklace.

- **Artifacts.** Fenway Park enjoys two noteworthy artifacts: the Green Monster (the left-field wall) inside the park and the giant neon CITGO sign outside.

- **History and memories**. A statue of Ted Williams welcomes fans to the park, one of many such figures at MLB parks. Although Fenway Park is full of memories like Ted Williams' .406 batting average in 1941, none stands out more than Carlton Fisk's game-winning home run in the 1975 World Series.

- **Ideologies.** Fenway Park may not conjure up serious political or social ideologies, but it does evoke notions (true or not) that baseball was somehow a better game when ballparks were simple and quaint, like Fenway.

- **Experiences.** As baseball's premier writer, Peter Gammons, put it, "Fans know the soul of baseball is its atmosphere—the sights, smells, sounds, the very feel of the game."

- **Aesthetics.** Besides the Green Monster, Fenway Park has irregular dimensions around the outfield. The various nooks and crannies not only look interesting but also create havoc for visiting fielders and delight the home fans.

- **Problems.** Fenway has plenty of problems, including traffic jams, limited and outrageously expensive parking, and all too many seats with views obstructed by support columns.

Fenway Park is an iconic "place" in American sports.

The ballpark's capacity—37,496 as of 2012—is the fourth smallest in Major League Baseball. Although this intimacy may add to its charm, it is a serious liability in the highly competitive—and salary-cap-less—world of Major League Baseball, especially when the "Evil Empire" can fill the new Yankee Stadium with 50,291 fans. The current Red Sox owners, who paid $660 million for the team in 2001, needed either to squeeze more revenues from Fenway or build a new park (something the previous owners had announced their intention to do). They chose the path of renovation, and they have done so with care and imagination, largely under the leadership of Janet Marie Smith, who has also worked her magic in Baltimore, Atlanta, and Los Angeles. In Boston, Smith built carefully on the core place elements described previously. The enhancements included the statue of Ted Williams as well as new seats atop the Green Monster and above right field, the latter including a concourse and concessions area. The Red Sox have aggressively brought more than

baseball to the park's sacred turf, including a regular stream of rock concerts, youth activities, and ice hockey games. All of this will alter Fenway's ensemble of place elements, but the Red Sox and their neighbors are cautiously optimistic that the venue's future will be even brighter than its past. Every venue and every place includes a similar ensemble. For this reason, the staging of major events like the Olympics is controversial and interesting. Avoiding some intrusion on someone's sense of place is impossible.[6]

Facility

The facility is the central element of any sport place ensemble. An essential part of the marketing mix, it includes a number of ingredients that influence the attractiveness of the events held within—from accessibility and other transportation-related issues to design and layout, amenities, and personnel.[7]

ACTIVITY 13.1 Orlando Magic's Location

Just as in real estate, in marketing, it's all about location, location, location. In this WSG activity, you will explain how the Orlando Magic can use their location to better market the team, and you will consider whether location really has an impact on team marketing.

External Accessibility and Drawing Radius

Most sport marketers and consultants believe in the "location, location, location" school of thought. For the majority of sport products, the high level of visibility gained through media coverage can often overcome a less accessible site as long as the product is in demand and is getting good media coverage. Nonetheless, a high percentage of a sport facility's customers can be expected to live within an hour's traveling time. This drive-time number will go up as the frequency of events goes down. Football and NASCAR fans have higher drive-time expectations than do baseball season-ticket holders who have 81 games on the menu. Along these lines, venue placement on the periphery of a market area leaves the door open for competition and results in inconvenience for the consumer.

Accessibility influences the size of a facility's drawing radius. Facility directors in the past simply drew concentric circles to define the drawing radius, usually at 5-mile (8 km) intervals, as if distance alone dictated a market. Figure 13.1 illustrates the modern methodology of drawing radii based on drive or traveling time. At multipurpose facilities, the drawing radii change markedly for different events. Note that the drawing radius becomes elongated along major arterial streets and transit systems, providing a more accurate reflection of equal traveling-time segments.

Although the specific dynamics of the sport drawing radius demand much more rigorous consumer research, the following factors appear to be critical:

- **Demographics**. Discretionary time varies with income, occupation, and stage in the life cycle.
- **Duration and frequency of the event**. As noted earlier, most people will travel much longer for an infrequent event (a concert by a favorite artist) than they will for a twice-weekly activity (a game of tennis).
- **Emotional commitment**. Parents will travel hours to watch their children play; casual high school fans may never leave town.
- **Perception of quality**. The big game or the big star will typically expand the drawing radius.

When locating a new facility and performing market feasibility studies, organizations sometimes make assessments of facility drawing power in the various market segments. A new perception of drive time has been the key to opening markets in the American South. For instance, Max Muhleman sold the NBA on a Charlotte, North Carolina, franchise by demonstrating that 5 million people lived within a two-hour drive of a proposed facility—two hours being a perceived maximum for events of NBA quality and frequency. Likewise, "Big Bill" France expanded NASCAR by building facilities with expansive drive-time markets. Jim Foster, France's longtime assistant, recalled the trips to Alabama when France was negotiating to build a track in Talladega: "Alabama might seem in the middle of nowhere, but if you draw a 300-mile [500 km] circle around Talladega—that is the distance race fans come from—they can drive down, see the race, and drive home in one day. There were 28 million people inside the circle." By overlaying radii for competing facilities, it is also possible to determine areas of competition and even probabilities of facility success.[8]

By analyzing how drawing radii change for various events offered at a multipurpose facility, marketers can make adjustments in the event mix to satisfy all market segments. They can also segment the promotional media in direct response to the drawing radii. At the Springfield Civic Center in Springfield, Massachusetts, the analysis of drawing radii revealed a far different pattern for the Ice Capades than for professional wrestling, yet remarkably similar media had been used to promote both events.

The analysis of drawing radii will change when events are scheduled at different times and on different days. Many sport marketers have scheduled their events at the same time every day. When setting starting times, however, a facility manager should account for traveling lead time. Is the market composed primarily of suburbanites who work in the city and stay in town up to the starting time? Or do these people

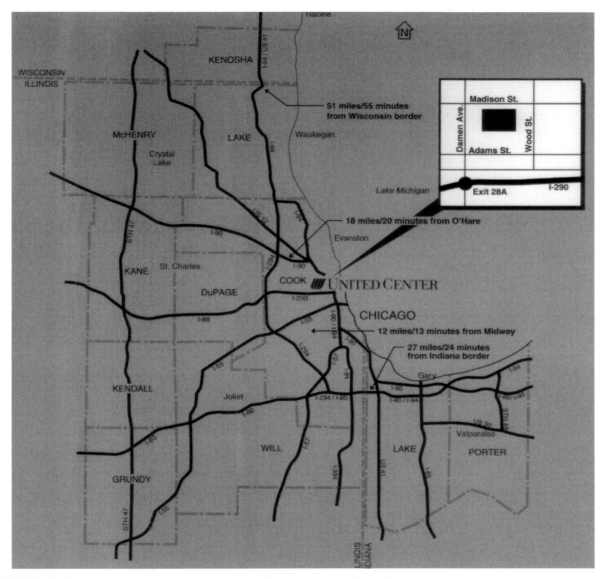

FIGURE 13.1   United Center area map showing drive time as well as mileage.
Courtesy of United Center.

attempt to commute home and then return to the event? Is the market primarily city dwellers? Or is it a mix of the two?

Parking

The facility should offer ample parking. A rule of thumb for stadiums and arenas is one parking space for every four seats in environments where mass transit is available. In 1998, for instance, the San Francisco Giants decided to schedule only 13 weekday games at what was then the new Pac Bell Park (now AT&T Park), largely because of limited parking. The Giants estimated that they needed 12,000 to 13,000 parking spaces for each game at the 42,000-seat facility. This corresponded to about a 1 to 3.3 space-to-seat ratio. With only 5,000 off-street spaces, the Giants had a greater-than-normal dependence on mass transit.[10]

Parking is one of the most vexing aspects of the fan experience. As one old hand explained, fans "want easy ingress, easy egress and they want to tailgate. And they don't like paying for it." For this reason, the sport property should control parking if possible, which permits control of pricing (and revenue) and of parking personnel, who are a crucial part of the overall facility image-building process. A Turnkey fan poll in

The Phoenix Coyotes came to America's Southwest in 1996 as part of an NHL strategy to grow the game in new markets. The other side of the story was a franchise that had a proud history as the Winnipeg Jets, was one of the original members of the World Hockey Association (1972), and had become a member of the NHL in 1979. By the early 1990s, however, the Jets (who had made the NHL playoffs 11 times in 15 years) were seen to be suffering in a weak market, especially for television. And so the move came to the robust demographics of Phoenix. In the same general period the NHL added or relocated teams to Anaheim, Dallas, Tampa, and Raleigh—a series of actions collectively called the Southern strategy.

The Coyotes' first home was in the downtown America West Arena (home of the Phoenix Suns), which dated to an earlier NBA expansion plan. As one later story put it, the Coyotes were "mildly successful" as they made the playoffs and earned fair attendance "despite poor sight lines" in the arena. In 2003, however, the franchise was lured 20 miles (32 km) west to Glendale and a new, supposedly fan-friendly arena. Unfortunately, this move and the arena were based on projections of rosy times in housing and commercial construction. The 2007–08 bust hit Glendale hard. By January 2012 the city's bond ratings were lowered by the major rating agencies. Worse yet, the team hit the skids, finishing out of the playoffs for its first five seasons after the move. Attendance spiraled downward, averaging fewer than 12,000, just two-thirds of capacity.

Many pundits believed that the team's desert days were over; they predicted a move to Quebec. Sport management professor Jordan Kobritz echoed the sentiment of many: "The team was doomed the day they signed on to move to Glendale. . . . The Coyotes have had two strikes against them from the time they arrived." In 2012 the Coyotes rebounded on the ice, winning a division crown and advancing to the conference finals. They lapsed in 2013 and did not qualify for the playoffs. Despite new ownership, their future place seems still in doubt.[9]

2010 found that the biggest parking gripes were (in order) time to leave after an event, cost, lack of availability near the venue, and lack of organization. Worse yet, 65 percent of respondents said that bad traffic and delays on ingress would cause them to avoid future events.[11]

The industry has responded in several ways:

- Online reservation and pay systems like Click and Park or Standard Parking that handle stadium managed lots.

- Reservation aggregators like ParkWhiz in Chicago that work with independent lots.

- Speedier ingress by the use of wireless barcode readers that read the reservation code in a handheld device that the consumer swipes at a gate.

- Wayfinding signage to assist patrons from lots to the venue itself. As one executive put it: "If you can't see the facility from where you parked, the minute you step out of your car, even if it's only 10 min-

utes away, suddenly, psychologically, it's a 6-hour walk." He continued, "You start thinking about all the things that could happen along the way."

- Branded parking lots such as the Lexus lot at the BankAtlantic Center, home of the Miami Marlins, has 250 spots reserved solely for Lexus owners.

Many parking issues seem insurmountable; some can be remedied with ingenuity.[12]

Surrounding Area

A facility links to its surroundings in several ways beyond parking.

- **Design**. New or renovated facilities must fit with local landscape aesthetics. As the author of one study of urban ballpark design concluded, "Ballparks must build upon the character of surrounding structures. Otherwise, they appear as intrusions in the urban fabric." New ballparks in Baltimore, Dayton, Cleveland, Pittsburgh, and Louisville have integrated seamlessly with each city's overall development plans. Whether the facilities yield the economic impact that boosters anticipated, they will contribute to the aesthetics of their communities—no mean accomplishment and nothing to take for granted. Baltimore's Oriole Park at Camden Yards led the way in blending ultramodern features inside the park with old buildings and alleys outside. Pittsburgh's ballpark is built with an eye on blending with nearby bridges and buildings.[13]

- **Politics**. Sport facilities have never been welcomed by everyone, especially nearby residents, who care less about their own easy access to games than they do about the regular infusion of hordes of fans, their cars, and their often unruly behavior. No sport organization should develop its venue without clear dialogue with its neighbors. In the early 1990s Boston College ran into a maelstrom of protest when it announced plans for expanding the football stadium. Local residents claimed that the school had broken a promised moratorium on facilities expansion. In little time, BC faced new legislative and regulatory hurdles, as well as enormous ill will that it might have avoided with clear, early dialogue.[14]

- **Sense of safety**. The immediate environment surrounding a sport facility is an extremely important factor in determining attendance frequency. When a facility is located in an area that customers believe is unsafe, sales will suffer. The environment can also determine the pattern of attendance.

ACTIVITY 13.2 Rupp Arena

Rupp Arena is an arena located in downtown Lexington, Kentucky. It serves as home court to the University of Kentucky men's basketball program, and it is named after legendary former Kentucky coach, Adolph Rupp. In this WSG activity, you will learn more about Rupp Arena and about the facility of your school or favorite team.

Design and Layout

Design and layout are crucial to consumer satisfaction. Several aspects of facility design are important:

ACTIVITY 13.3 Facility Layout and Design

Daytona International Speedway is a race-track in Daytona Beach, Florida. Since opening in 1959, it has been the home of the Daytona 500, the most prestigious race in NASCAR. In this WSG activity, you will consider the importance of the speedway's layout and design.

- **Ease of access, exit, and internal movement to minimize length of lines anywhere**. As noted earlier about parking, few things upset today's consumers more than waiting in long lines, especially if their intent had been to get away from it all. What's worse than waiting to park and then waiting to get into a facility? Maybe it's a long line to get out! In all venues, a key objective is to minimize bottlenecks and maximize crowd flow. Research on queuing (waiting in lines) suggests that people on average inflate their actual time in line by one-third. And as one story reported, "All else being equal, people who wait less than they anticipated leave happier than those who wait longer than expected." The best designs consider consumer flow from the point where they arrive (and even their travel to the venue) to the point where they depart and head safely home. A good design has good flow for humans as well as cars. The location of any concourse is critical to this equation. As noted by one authority, "Today, architects, team owners, and vendors think the concourse is as vital to any venue as the circulatory system is to the human body." A science applies to the queuing experience, and sport marketers would do well to follow it.[15]

- **Access and sight lines for consumers with physical disabilities**. Providing access to those with physical disabilities includes conforming to legal requirements such as the Americans with Disabilities Act (ADA). Some of the key applications of the ADA in stadium design include the following:

  ○ Half of all entrances must be wheelchair accessible.

  ○ One percent of total seating must be for wheelchairs; accessible seating must be integrated and not isolated; companion seats must be provided.

○ One percent of wheelchair seats must be aisle seats without armrests.

○ Lines of sight must be comparable to those of surrounding seats.

Some older stadiums have been slow to change. The University of Michigan, for instance, was sued by the Department of Justice and the Paralyzed Veterans of America for having only 90 wheelchair seats in a stadium that seated over 108,000 people. A 2007 settlement upped the number to 900. Accessibility is more than a legal or ethical issue. Because of an aging population and the advent of technologies that facilitate a more active lifestyle for all people with physical disabilities, facility designs should incorporate the needs of this growing and important market.[16]

ACTIVITY 13.4 Red Bull Arena

The New York Red Bulls is an American professional soccer team based in Harrison, NJ. The team always works on improving its brand image, including using tools to deliver colorful commentary to fans with vision impairments. In this WSG activity, you will learn more about the Red Bulls' approach and consider its effectiveness.

• **Location and design of food services, bars, concession stands, and bathrooms and a sufficient number of these amenities to reduce lines.** Given the rising tide of female fans, sport venues will have to provide additional facilities for women. A study used by the designers of Seattle's Safeco Field found that women spent an average of 3 minutes in a restroom; men spent about 82 seconds. Long waits for both men and women have led to the development of fixture ratios in stadium design. For instance, the International Plumbing Code includes the following guidelines for stadiums:

○ Female toilets—1:40 for first 1,500 female occupants and 1:60 for the remainder exceeding 1,500.

○ Male toilets—1:75 for first 1,500 male occupants and 1:120 for remainder exceeding 1,500.

Overall numbers may vary depending on local codes, fan demographics of the sports in the venue, numbers of intermissions, and section of

the venue (VIPs get more fixtures). These facilities should be clean and well maintained and should be as close as possible to where the consumer participates or watches.[17]

• **Flexible versus dedicated usage.** In the last decade, professional sport teams have moved away from multipurpose venues toward single-use facilities. A main reason has been to maximize sight lines and intimacy for fans. Many people believe that baseball simply doesn't "play" well in a cavernous stadium meant for 70,000 football fans. The same point applies to world football. Major League Soccer has fostered new dedicated facilities in most franchise cities. On the other hand, few schools or colleges can afford specialized venues; flexibility is dictated by budgets and often by space. Further, such facilities must anticipate changes in consumer interest.

• **Aesthetics.** As with any piece of architecture, the sport facility design requires an appealing blend of form, scale, color, and light. The media focus attention on the multimillion-dollar venues such as Brooklyn's new Barclays Center, home of the NBA Nets. In many cases, sponsors are pouring millions into the creation of attractive and interactive "entitlement zones." But even small-budget venues can enhance their attractiveness with concepts used at the big time. For instance, a number of schools and colleges have been imaginative with the use of colorful new logos and marks in otherwise drab entrances, concourses, and gymnasiums. The University of New Hampshire revitalized the atmosphere in its gym, its football field, and its field house with a lot of paint, signs, posters, and images, as well as a gallery of team photos along all hallway walls. Collectively, a small investment has drastically changed the aesthetic experience not only for fans but also, and more important, for the athletes and coaches who call the place home. Marketers should keep abreast of the facility design literature, at all levels, by tracking the Architectural Showcase Awards presented annually by *Athletic Business*, one of the industry's most widely read trade magazines (www.athleticbusiness.com).[18]

Game, Spectacle, and Festival: Framing the Steak and the Sizzle

For as far back as historical sources take us, humans have tended to frame sporting contests with layers of spectacle and festival (figure 13.2).

Long concession lines are a pet peeve of fans everywhere.

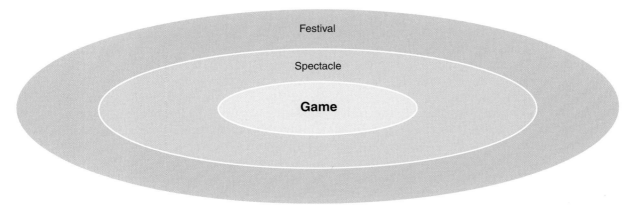

FIGURE 13.2 The standard frames of sport.

People have been motivated to watch sporting contests throughout history. In boxing, they formed a ring around the combatants—hence, the term *boxing ring*. Formal venues defined in wood, stone, or concrete created the threshold that separated the game from the spectacle. But more than just watching always occurred. A festival frame developed outside the layer of spectators. At ancient venues such as Olympia, people mingled, ate, enjoyed musical performances, and listened to poets—all outside the spectacle frame. Modern venues reflect these ancient practices in the forms of special tailgating areas, large concourses, and atriums where vendors hawk their wares. In some arenas, the concourse and festival frame lie outside the frame of seats. In Boston's TD Garden, fans who have milled around between periods buying concessions and mingling in groups must reenter the spectacle through tunnels. In other venues, concourses offer direct sight lines to the action. Camden Yards is a case in point. Similarly, Hadlock Field in Portland, Maine, offers a group picnic area along the right-field line. Here festival and spectacle are combined inside the park.[19]

Designers have worked hard to create concourse areas that merge spectacle and festival. One of the more ingenious developments is slated for the renovated Madison Square Garden. A set of skybridges will span the arena and give fans not only space to walk and mingle but also fabulous sight lines down on the rink or court. As noted in a *New York Post* story, the bridges were a response to several fan complaints, including lack of concourse space and poor sightlines at the higher seat levels.[20]

American football has a long tradition of fusing the three frames into a single experience. As early as the 1890s, Manhattan hosted "big games" between Yale and Princeton, closely covered in national magazines by feature writers like Richard Harding Davis. Manhattan Field would be packed with 30,000 spectators singing songs and chanting cheers in ways now largely lost in North America (but alive in the world's great soccer venues). The bigger show, however, was before the game, outside the field, in the long parade of partisans marching and riding down Fifth Avenue hours before game time, in what Davis called a "circus procession many miles long"—coaches festooned in yellow or blue, filled with young men and women "smothered in furs; and the flags, as they jerk them about, fill the air with color," cheered on by crowds four deep along the sidewalks. As Davis concluded, "Today the sporting character of the event has been overwhelmed by the social interest." Nowhere is this notion more alive than at the University of Mississippi in the pregame tailgating on the Grove—among the magnolias, tents of red and blue, mint juleps in silver mugs, and elegantly dressed fans of all ages. As they say in Oxford: "Ole Miss may not win the game, but we will always win the party." Some Seattleites feel the same way about Husky Harbor, where tailgaters arrive on boats of all kinds in a flotilla that docks on the shore of Lake Washington, at the edge of Husky Stadium. The University of Washington assists this process with a staff member who has a singular title in college athletics—boat moorage manager. One of the latest trends in festival has been the sponsored tailgate promotion, such as the Food City Tailgater of the Game contest outside Neyland Stadium at the University of Tennessee. Winners receive free shopping sprees and SEC championship tickets.[21]

Over a century ago, Richard Harding Davis captured a phenomenon that is now an essential part of marketing—managing the three frames, balancing the sizzle with the steak, the festival and the spectacle with the game itself. Doing this is not always easy. People want food and drink—festival elements—in the spectacle frame. But they don't want vendors blocking their view. And they don't want drunks dowsing them in beer. Leagues want to enhance spectacle, but they don't want players running into the stands, and they limit celebrations that detract from the game.

Sometimes, however, it makes sense to scramble the frames. In the NHL, the Columbus Blue Jackets placed a game in the lobby. Called Big Hockey, it was the old push-and-pull table game, in which tiny plastic players were controlled by levers. But this game was huge—so large that each fan controlled one only lever. Even during games, fans lined up for a chance to play. And when fans were waiting to play, the Blue Jackets hoped that they were also paying attention to the real hockey game on television monitors. Pulling fans away from the live action is always a gamble, but this scrambling of the frames makes sense. "They're connecting with young people," said Phoenix Coyotes' president Shawn Hunter. "In that arena, fans are going wild about Big Hockey. And fan development is on the top of everyone's list." There are many other examples of effective frame management. Giant scoreboards now provide separate spectacles (e.g., league or team highlights) during breaks in live game action. Or they create games within games, such as the interactive, on-screen tug of war developed by Flying Spot, Inc. In this game, fan sections "tugged" with their cheering, and the screen moved accordingly.[22]

Amenities: Convergence Toward the Sports Mall

In a 2012 article about the new Miami Marlins Park, *Sports Illustrated* writer Tom Verducci wrote of its two "bulletproof, polycarbonate aquariums," lime 'n' lobster rolls, retractable lid, and its "$2.5 million neon-colored, fish-and-flamingo-studded piece of performance art beyond the center-field wall." It was, he claimed, a long way from the simplicity that opened a century earlier in Boston. "Fenway's architects didn't sweat amusements," he claimed. "The game was enough in 1912. Not so today. The ballpark is a theme park, an art gallery, a TV studio, a shopping mall, a small city unto itself." Of course, Verducci omitted comparisons that Bostonians made a century earlier between the old Huntington Avenue Grounds and the new Fenway Park. The shift from wood to concrete, steel, and brick was monumental. Local press trumpeted the upgrade. Among the "commodious" and opulent attractions in 1912 were the 95 private boxes in the front row, each seating four people, sold for $250 per season. Venues change with the times.[23]

But it is not just professional or top-level college programs that have felt the urgency to build newer, bigger, and more fan-friendly facilities. In 2012 the north-Dallas suburb of Allen, Texas (population 87,000), opened a spanking new $60 million high school football stadium that *USA Today* reported "covers 72 acres and includes a high-definition video screen and free Wi-Fi for the more than 18,000 in attendance." To be sure, Allen is an affluent city. But its residents sounded like ordinary fans everywhere. They were not satisfied with the old stadium built in 1976 that held 7,000 permanent seats and 7,000 temporary bleachers. Among other things, fans "complained about long lines for concession stands and restrooms." Many small colleges have felt the same pressure to renovate or build anew. Bowdoin College, long a Division III hockey power, opened the new Sidney J. Watson Arena in 2009, named after their Hall of Fame coach. Like the rink at competitor Middlebury College, the "Sid" had 3,000 seats encircled by a wide concourse that

allowed easy fan flow before, during, and after competition.[24]

Today's sport consumers, who pay hundreds of dollars to attend one event with their families, expect a range of amenities that enhance their spectacle and festival experience. Bench seats, boiled hot dogs, a mimeographed program, and a scoreboard that displays only the score—none of this will do. So the big-time venues have responded with a range of amenities. Many of them are designed to provide what is called technological wow. Following are some examples.

- **Connectivity**. Generation Ys, or millennials, now entering prime years as breadwinners and as fans, have grown of age alongside breakthroughs in communications technology. They expect to see the latest connectivity in hotels, resorts, and sport venues. In the late 1990s, the next rage was going to be smart seats wired with small computer screens from which fans (for a premium price) could request replays from various camera angles, check a rule, call up stats, and order food or merchandise. But the costs were extremely high, so few smart seats were developed. Today's fans want wireless connections. As one executive promised, "We're not going to have 80 hot spots or 111 hot spots (for wireless connectivity). We're having one. It's called the whole arena." Nothing less will do.[25]

- **Ever more expensive big screens, electronic message centers, and sound systems**. When arena managers think about fan comfort these days, their concerns go well beyond the older notions of sight lines, seat backs, and warm fannies. St. Paul's Xcel Energy Center seats 18,064 for National Hockey League games and has four seating levels, four separate concourses, and a press level. As described on the arena's website, the center scoreboard supports four 9-foot-by-16-foot (2.7 by 4.9 m) video boards, animated by full-color LED (light-emitting diode) displays. Some of the zanier displays are on the ribbon board signage that wraps around both the suite level and the two upper levels. These provide continuous animation, graphics, and cropped video in almost unlimited colors. At times, focusing on the actual game action must be hard.[26]

- **Upscale food and drink**. Luxury-suite patrons have been munching on shrimp and caviar for years. Suite patrons pay over four times what the typical fan pays per game on food and beverages; in arena jargon, this is the per cap. But if the highbrows demand their Alsatian noodles with kangaroo fillets, that doesn't mean that the hoi polloi will settle for the same old stale hot dogs. Around the American market, stadiums and arenas are typically expanding their offerings at stands, kiosks, and food courts to include items unheard of less than a generation ago—Philly cheesesteak, jalapeno poppers, pierogies, chef salads, chicken fajitas, North Carolina–style barbecue, low-calorie wraps, microbrews, sweet tea, Bacardi breezers, Krispy Kreme donuts, homemade sopapillas, and hand-dipped ice cream. Of course, after paying the bill, some parents might prefer to go back to the old days.

• **High-touch amenities.** Technology cannot solve all problems, especially for families that need child care. The Florida Panthers and other teams have fashioned venue space to provide child care, inking contacts with sponsors like the Learning Experience, which paid for the creation of the Club House for Kids. Grassroots programs lack the leverage of an NHL team, but they can adapt space for similar services.[27]

Reconfigurations: From Suites to Inclusive Club Seats to Special Zones

Two decades ago, club seats became a standard component of big venues. The club-seat concept was clearly designed to offer the upscale consumer something between the luxury suite and the best box or loge season seat. Like the loges, club seats were both segregated from the crowd and standalone; you could buy just one seat for the season. Like the suites, they offered exclusive amenities such as the following:

• Special parking privileges
• Membership in a club that included a restaurant
• Wait service during a game (allowing the patron to call a special number or go online to place an order)
• Invitations to special events

Today, venues have even merged the suites with the club seats. In many markets, luxury suites and their long-term leases lost their 1980s luster as soon as the economy hit the skids, as it did in 2000 and 2008. Rather than agonize over empty suites, some teams and venues became creative. Among the first were the Tampa Bay Lightning and the Ice Palace Arena (now the St. Pete Times Forum), who ripped out a section of suites, renovated it, and created a special B to B networking zone called the XO Club. The plan allowed businesses to purchase individual club seats tied to membership in the adjoining section of dining areas, lounges, and even a cigar room—all with perfect lines of sight on the action. The club's website invited prospects to "be a part of the only membership club in the entertainment industry offering an all-inclusive buffet, beer, wine and VIP parking." Why limit the corporate experience to 12 people in a single suite? The XO Club expanded the networking to hundreds of people and was a smash hit from its beginning. Other teams and venues have since created similar mergers of suites and club seats.[28]

Other sponsored and branded spaces, also known as entitlement zones, have also emerged. The XO Club was no outlier. In the last two decades many other sponsors and venues have given new meaning to the term *zoning*. They have renovated or built new space that ties special experiences or special groups with a particular sponsor. In most of these areas the sponsor has rights to control the fan experience in that zone—hence, the name *entitlement zone*. The TXU Power Zone in Dallas's American Airlines Center was a good example. There, kids (and parents) could play an interactive game that combined a slap shot with information about energy use. Miller Lite developed its Party Zone at the Chicagoland Speedway and other NASCAR venues. Coca-Cola has long been a leader in the notion of controlling space. Its Coca-Cola Corner in Fenway Park was an example. College football programs have developed and used special fan, kid, and family zones for years, often using end zone space that was in light demand. The new twist was matching space with a sponsor.[29]

Vic Gregovits, senior VP of the Cleveland Indians, offered the bottom line on the creative use of space: "We want to keep it active and also add value to our customers." Just about every sport venue, at any level, has space that can be reconfigured or "rezoned." It is often less a matter of money and more a matter of a little vision and hard work.[30]

Event staff are a crucial part of any game presentation.

Personnel

The people who work in a facility may be the major force in projecting a facility's image and in its ultimate success. The attitudes of operations personnel directly affect consumer satisfaction because these workers are the primary (and in many cases, only) personnel whom consumers contact. Yet such non-management personnel are often the least trained among a facility's staff. Event staff are almost all part-timers. How often do patrons face an uncaring or even surly usher? Too often. All this is unnecessary, especially when professional trade associations such as the International Association of Venue Managers (IAVM) offer training programs—in class, online, and in video—on a range of topics including crowd management, food services, and emergency management. Clubs, schools, colleges, and youth programs all run events in venues. Some of the events draw tens of thousands patrons. Staff

training for such events is no longer a luxury; it is a necessity. Stanford University developed extensive staff training, beginning each August, with a four-hour program for all full- and part-time guest services employees, who were paid to attend the program. Equally important, Stanford created an extensive guest services manual that helped ensure consistency in the way that staff members interacted with consumers.[31]

Marketing Channels

Although the facility is the primary element in distributing the core sport product, the concept of place includes other aspects involving the various channels by which marketers can deliver the product, in this case beyond the facility. Channels are simply sets or configurations of organizations linked together to deliver a product to consumers. Channel systems often vary by product line or sales territory within a company's distribution network. Channel systems can be complex; they may shift and share functions, as is often the case in sport marketing. Standard product channels have included the following:

- Manufacturers (M)
- Wholesalers (W) and jobbers (J)
- Retailers (R)
- Consumers (C)

A traditional channel for hard goods would look like this:

$$M \rightarrow W \rightarrow J \rightarrow R \rightarrow C$$

The Internet and direct mail have reconstructed traditional channels of equipment and apparel sales. Consumers can surf the web to find manufacturers' sites, check the online catalog, and order by direct mail, all without using wholesalers or retailers. In the increasingly complex world of sport marketing channels, the two types of systems often operate in parallel, sometimes to reach the same consumer. Take a professional sport team. It has a traditional channel of on-site box offices and kiosks for event tickets:

$$M \leftrightarrow C$$

But it also may televise the event and distribute it by television to a wider audience, so that the channel looks like this:

$$M \leftrightarrow C = Event \rightarrow Media \rightarrow C$$

If the on-site consumer recorded the game on a home DVR, she would be part of both the beginning and the end of the channel! As teams use websites, social media, and wireless connectivity for the redistribution of broadcast highlights and for direct sale of team merchandise and tickets, the channel loops become more complicated.

As any sport organization considers channels for product distribution, it must weigh at least four factors in tandem:

- Expertise
- Cost
- Control
- Adaptability

Marketers must continually monitor the value of their marketing channels. For instance, the Internet is a double-edged sword. Although Internet sales certainly offer consumers more access and control, retailers are realizing that cost savings are not always as high as expected. Although the Internet may reduce the payroll for a sales force, it also forces a retailer to expand distribution warehouses (with all the associated labor costs). Putting any live event on a media platform has similar pros and cons. In summary, no simple formula can be used to determine the best marketing channels. It is a constant balancing act.[32]

Retail Operations

Despite the rise of the Internet, traditional retail outlets remain important elements for sport marketing channels. Specialized outlets for sport products grew rapidly in the 19th century as entrepreneurs recognized, and promoted, an interest in fishing, cricket, baseball, hunting, and other activities among urban populations who could support their businesses. Today's big-box firms such as Sports Authority have a long list of ancestors that include hardware stores and retail chains such as Sears and Montgomery Ward. But today's sport marketplace has seen some new twists as well, especially the channel movement by teams, clubs, and governing bodies forward into the retail business.[33]

To some degree, college programs led the way. The University of Michigan was one of the first to realize the value of merchandizing. Offering a wide array of novelties, Michigan developed a range of retail outlets in the 1970s, including souvenir stands at Michigan Stadium, Crisler Arena, Yost Ice Arena, the tennis and track building, the golf course, and the ticket office. Michigan also had partnerships with high school booster clubs and cheerleader organizations, which sold Michigan novelties as part of their own fund-raising efforts. Finally, Michigan effectively used direct-mail sales to season-ticket holders and other targeted customers on mailing lists that the athletics department purchased. Those practices are now standard.[34]

Professional teams had long operated pro shops in arena lobbies, but the presence of these outlets was often not part of a broader branding and distribution strategy. By contrast, the NBA opened a retail store in Manhattan that was more than a place to buy NBA goods. As described

Team Merchandise: It Takes a Team to Have a Sellout

Dave Perricone, Assistant Professor of Sports Management, Centenary College; Senior Director of Merchandise, New Jersey Devils, 1990–2011

Sport is a different business. A New York Mets VP who spent 13 years with a nonsport company put it this way: "Before, I had control of the product, I could design it the way I wanted it to be. Here the product changes every day and you have to adapt quickly to the changes." This statement is also true in the world of sport merchandise. As we know, times have changed, and we must learn to adapt. Merchandise has changed in the last few years. From bobbleheads to Pillow Pets, merchandise managers must look to see what the new trend is going to be and try to ride it. Working for the New Jersey Devils, an organization that has won two Stanley Cups in the last decade, doesn't solve all merchandise sales problems. But it does teach one thing: To have a successful department in any organization, you need to function as a team. Here are some aspects that helped make us a successful merchandise department.

Think Like the Team's General Manager

One thing I have learned is that you can compare the job of a merchandise manager to that of the GM of a professional team. But in this case, your products (hats, jerseys, T-shirts, and so on) are your players. The merchandise manager wants to get the best performance out of each item. For example, if your product is selling well when it is introduced into the market, you may want to reorder the item and ride the wave. Eventually, however, you have a decision to make that is similar to the choice you must make when an aging player coming off a good year wants to be rewarded with a raise. Do you reinvest, or let the old player go? Similar issues arise with the overall lineup. As the end of the season approaches, you may be selling out on the first order of various items. Now it's time to think ahead, like a good GM. Which items do you reorder (sign again), which do you drop (put on waivers), and which do you buy (sign free agents)—all with an eye on getting the best lineup for next year.

Products

The manager must review every item. Everyone has a different opinion about what products are good and what are bad. In the end, the only opinions that matter are the consumers'. In the end, even if the merchandise manager likes a particular product, the decision must be made based on what is best for the organization. Some of the Devils' research techniques include the following:

- Reviewing what our league's teams as well as other leagues are selling
- Contacting all approved licensees that sell products in our league
- Visiting local shopping malls and seeing what the stores are selling and what the shoppers are buying

Employees

Employees are the key to the success of any organization. Although our team on the ice has wingers and center men, we break down our staff by customer service and pickers and packers. Customer service duties include taking phone orders and putting the orders into the computers. The pickers and packers pick the merchandise off the shelves, pack the orders, and input the shipping information into our shipping computers.

The customer service employees must have knowledge of our products and be familiar with our computer software program. We do not want someone taking an order who keeps putting the customer on hold to figure out how to use the program. The way that the

> continued

employee talks to a customer can determine whether that customer will place an order. We don't want our employees to rush the customer off the phone or be rude to the customer in any way. A disrespectful approach may cause the customer not to place an order and, more important, word of mouth will suggest that our operation is not professional. As with all aspects of Devils' marketing, we don't want to make promises that the company can't keep.

Product Delivery

Not long ago, most teams offered a catalog as a way to market their merchandise. Catalogs were the alternative to going to the store and purchasing a product. In October 2007 the New Jersey Devils moved into the Prudential Center in Newark, New Jersey. The transfer to a new building brought changes to merchandising because the arena contains a team shop adjacent to the main box office. This location creates awareness to fans who are walking by the store.

Fans attending the game may make impulse-buying decisions while viewing the merchandise in the store. One of the major advantages of the team store is that the customer can have a jersey customized in about an hour compared with ordering from a catalog, which would take four weeks.

Most teams have eliminated producing catalogs for several reasons. The cost to produce a catalog, which includes layout, printing, and mailing, is substantial, and the time to complete it can be several months. Using the Internet or a team store will save those expenses.

The NHL controls the teams merchandise site, but each team is allowed to put items on its team store page. The Internet has brought many benefits to sport merchandising. First, the convenience of the Internet makes it easier for fans to buy merchandise if they cannot get to the arena. Second, if an item sells out or becomes unavailable, another product can quickly replace it. Having the ability to change products frequently will help prevent fans from complaining that no product is available. This is another major reason why teams have stopped producing catalogs. Imagine placing a mail order and waiting anxiously for the product to arrive only to receive a letter stating that the order couldn't be completed because the product was unavailable. The Internet helps keeps fans happy. Third, if a product isn't selling, the team can reduce the price or remove it from the online store. Finally, the team can create specials such as product of the week, ticket-holder exclusives, and holiday items.

Evaluate

Like any GM, the merchandise manager must constantly evaluate product and performance. Here are some of the questions to ask, especially if you end up with too much inventory:

- Were the products correct for the target market?
- Was the price too high?
- How much were other retailers selling the same product for?
- Did only a few sizes of a certain product sell?

Think Outside the Box

A GM must think about how to improve the team. Some ways of thinking outside the box and trying to create new ideas are the following:

- **The vending machine**. The first NFL-branded vending machine in the country will sell various forms of Vikings paraphernalia, including Vikings minifootballs and T-shirts. As Vikings chief marketing officer Steve LaCroix put it, "With vending machines becoming more and more commonplace, especially in airports and in other countries, we thought we would test the concept with our fans with a location at Mall of America."

- **Membership**. The New York Red Bulls have come up with a Members Card that can be used to buy product merchandise at games. Cardholders have the benefit of having their own merchandise stands, which accept only the Members Card. Cardholders feel important because the team is doing something special for them.

- **Special events**. Special events such as a draft party are a perfect way to reduce your old inventory. The merchandise manager should go through the stock that will not be carried into next season and offer items at a lower price. The team must remember that a product sitting on the shelf will not bring in any revenue.

Whether we are selling a $1 item or a high-priced item, effective management of a merchandise store requires tight teamwork among people both inside and outside our organization. When customers are happy and we turn our inventory well, for us it's like winning the Stanley Cup.

---

on its website, the NBA Store was a "two-level basketball extravaganza that provides a unique backdrop for corporate functions, cocktail receptions, sit-down dinner parties, and more." The NBA Store was clearly part of a broad distribution strategy that included branded television shows, branded merchandise, and branded fan experiences. In the last decade, dozens of professional teams have opened off-site retail outlets, although failures have been as numerous as successes. Internet stores are the current outlet of choice (see the sidebar on the New Jersey Devils' store). At the same time, many teams have reinvented the notion of the store. The San Diego Chargers, for instance, set up a series of portable kiosks in various areas around Qualcomm Stadium. The kiosks were themed, as one article explained, "to carve the Chargers' fan base into distinct niches and product lines," including kids, women, players, and coaches.[35]

The New England Patriots took the entire retail concept to a new level with the 2007 opening of Patriot Place, a 700-acre (280 ha) shopping and entertainment complex adjacent to Gillette Stadium. Besides the retail stores and restaurants that would be expected at a high-end mall or gallery, Patriot Place houses a health care facility; a cinema; CBS Scene, a restaurant–sports bar–nightclub; and the Hall at Patriot Place, a combination hall of fame and retail outlet. The latter two establishments are located closest to the stadium, following the long tradition of building frames that flow from festival to spectacle to the game itself.[36]

The brilliance of Patriot Place is its fusion of branded and licensed goods with the fan experience of a big game. It can be replicated anywhere, albeit at smaller scales. When all goes well, the consumer does not simply buy a shirt, a cap, or a pair of shoes, or eat a nice meal. The consumer learns more about the team or the league, picks up a playing or coaching tip, sees a game, and returns home with more than a hat—with greater commitment and involvement. A high school athletics director or a soccer club manager can think along similar lines. Network and cable television have not eliminated the need for grassroots education and grassroots heroes.

Ticket Distribution

In August 2012 the NBA and Ticketmaster announced a deal in which Ticketmaster would create a "centralized online portal for fans that is intended to serve as a one-stop shopping site for all NBA tickets." Fans visiting their home team site would be directed to the Ticketmaster–NBA portal that would show all available ticket options for each team, including both primary and secondary ticket markets. The portal should make life easier for fans, and it will bring significant added value to the NBA, because it should provide expansive aggregated data on ticket buyers. The NBA has joined other top-tier leagues in developing new systems to sell and distribute tickets.[37]

Ticket distribution is a good example of the fast-changing environment of sport marketing channels. For some time, consumers have moved away from buying tickets at the gate, at least for the big-league teams with high demand from suburban (or more distant) fans. Within the last decade, many clubs have seen huge swings away from box office sales toward Internet sales. Some box-office-to-Internet-sales ratios have gone from 90:10 to 20:80 or higher. In 2008, 46 percent of Division I college football season-ticket holders renewed their tickets online. In 2011, the number was up to 51.5 percent. New electronic technologies expanded the possibilities of ticket distribution, largely because computerized ticketing eliminated the problems of duplicate tickets, excess stock, and limited choice—all of which had plagued earlier efforts to go beyond the single box office. For those who preferred to walk up for sales or pickup, new ticket kiosks (like those at airports) allowed easy selection and on-site printing, permitting teams and venues to shift payrolls to other areas like security and concessions. Internet sites have also been crucial in managing the secondary market (i.e., initial buyers reselling their tickets). And the age of wireless smartphones has brought new apps that deliver paperless tickets. Every consumer can be a virtual box office.[38]

Technology has also expanded the objectives of ticket distribution. In 2005, for instance, the University of Maryland began using ticket distribution to drive student commitment to its football and basketball teams. Any fully enrolled (and athletics-fee-paying) student could request and print tickets for football and men's basketball on a secure website. In both sports the number of tickets was often insufficient to meet student demand, so tickets were distributed by lotteries weighted by several variables, including loyalty points gained from past attendance (determined by a gate-based scanning system). The students' personal accounts allowed them to do several tasks online, including the following:

- Track their attendance history
- View their loyalty point total
- Print tickets that become available
- Cancel a previously claimed ticket

The last function was crucial, because if students did not cancel tickets at least a day ahead of a game, they lost loyalty points. But a late cancellation was still better than a no-show. More than two no-shows in a football season (or five in a career) or three in a basketball season (or eight in a career) meant no tickets at all, ever![39]

As with any decision on marketing channels, a balance needs to be struck among the factors of expertise, cost, control, and adaptability. The last decades have seen a variety of distribution programs beyond the box office. We now take a brief look at these systems.

- **Partnerships with other consumer retail outlets.** Ticket distribution often goes hand in hand with new sponsors and new promotions. In the late 1990s, for instance, MLB's San Francisco Giants created a 10-year partnership with Chevron, whose corporate headquarters were local. Part of the estimated $15 to $20 million deal included the prospect of Chevron gas stations selling Giants tickets. A few years earlier, the Cleveland Lumberjacks had worked out a deal with northeastern Ohio Burger King stores in which BK purchased 15,000 tickets for each of two Burger King Buyout Nights. Fans who wanted tickets to either game had to get them at a Burger King outlet, which enabled BK to create a number of promotional packages to drive store traffic. Many of these deals included ticket kiosks at targeted retail outlets such as grocery stores, which could provide leverage for other forms of sponsorship. In 1998, for example, the Texas Rangers established electronic kiosks, provided by ETM Entertainment Network, at 60 Kroger supermarkets in north Texas. Ranger fans could use a credit card to buy the best tickets available for the games of their choice. Hard tickets were printed on the spot. In 2004 the New Orleans Saints worked a ticket distribution deal with minor league baseball teams in Jackson, Tennessee, and Mobile, Alabama. In 2009 the Miami Dolphins opened a partnership with Duffy's, the team's "official sports grill." At Duffy's 24 locations, fans could buy a package deal that included a meal, a ticket, and a bus trip. By 2011 the team hoped to sell 10,000 to 12,000 packages. High school and small college programs can profitably use this avenue, especially if most or all of their tickets are general admission. Partnering with local or outer-market retailers, especially in sporting goods or clothing, is a good way to drive sales. Such programs may be particularly effective ways to help promote holiday or postseason tournament sales. In some sports like baseball, retail outlets are still a key component of ticket distribution. As one executive put it, "So many people still want that experience of buying a ticket from a person, and retail sales is like that. It is a good way to support your overall ticket operation." Human touch still has a place in a high-tech world.[40]

• **Partnerships with ticket firms**. A decision to move ticket sales beyond a simple box office typically meant a partnership with a ticketing company. In 1968 Ticketron used electronic networking to open new worlds of ticket distribution for all kinds of events. The American ticket market was eventually dominated by Ticketmaster (which bought Ticketron in 1991 and absorbed ETM in 2000), Tickets.com (which absorbed BASS Tickets), Paciolan, CyberSeats, Choice Ticketing Systems, and a few others. StubHub rose to prominence with the secondary ticket market in America. Viagogo (started by StubHub cofounder Eric Baker) won contracts in the English Premier League and in Europe. Firms have varied in the scope of their services, the degree to which their systems were integrated into those of the client team or venue, and the associated costs. Some of the issues to be addressed in any partnership have included consumers' ability to print tickets on their own computers or at a kiosk or automated teller and ticket machine (ATTM), wireless transmission for paperless tickets by special apps to smartphones, transaction fees, and consumers' ability to return or resell tickets.[41]

• **Telephone systems**. In the late 1990s the Boston Red Sox began using the NEXT ticketing system, which was an automated, credit card, phone-order system designed as an alternative to Ticketmaster. Unlike Ticketmaster, the NEXT system did not brand its own tickets. In the case of the Red Sox, for example, the consumer appeared to be dealing directly with a Red Sox operation (even though it was all automated), and the tickets were issued on Red Sox stock. Better yet, there was no $6 surcharge. The NEXT system handled 400 calls at a time and could sell 75,000 tickets in an hour—a task that was impossible for humans.[42]

• **Payroll deductions with selected companies**. Colleges have for some time offered direct payroll deductions for employees who were also season-ticket holders, maximizing ease of access and payment. With the expansion of electronic banking systems, this possibility has extended to employees of any company that uses electronic

payrolls. In the early 1990s the Hamilton Canucks of the American Hockey League worked with the City of Hamilton to offer the city's 6,000 public employees season tickets through payroll deduction. The city had an interest because the Canucks played in a city-owned rink, and a portion of ticket and concession revenues were returned to the city.[43]

• **Roving box office**. In 2009 the Los Angeles Dodgers began employing a roving Dodgertown van that looked like one of the countless food trucks that roamed the streets of many Los Angeles neighborhoods. But this van sold tickets, not burgers or tacos. As Terry Lefton reported, the van was "intended to give the Dodgers a presence at shopping areas, parks and festivals, and provide an easier way to position Dodgers tickets as an impulse buy." The high-tech truck was equipped with satellite and wireless connections, computers, and printers. Despite their annual sale of over three million tickets over the prior five years, the Dodgers were not resting, especially in a soft economy. In addition, the van was expected to increase the team's presence in Asian and Hispanic markets, which the Dodgers hoped to grow.[44]

• **Home delivery**. Sometimes computers can't solve a problem. In the fall of 2004 Ball State University football faced serious pressure to sell tickets. An NCAA rule (since loosened) required all Division IA programs to average 15,000 fans in home game attendance. To reach that goal for the home opener, associate athletics director Matt Wolfert came up with a novel ticket distribution system to faculty and staff. On Terrific Ticket Tuesday, he hand-delivered tickets, within 30 minutes of any telephone order, or the tickets would be free. As Wolfert chased around campus in his SUV—what he called a traveling ticket window—he felt energized: "If I can't be excited about it and I'm in charge of selling it, how can I expect anyone else to be excited about it?" His home delivery program paid off in additional sales of over 250 tickets.[45]

Secondary Ticket Market

Chapter 8 describes secondary market sales in detail, but here we remind readers that managing secondary sales is a crucial function for any sport property that has controlled gates, venues with reserved seats, and full-season or partial-season ticket plans. The stakes are high at the big time. For a variety of reasons, some people with tickets want or need to unload them. The Internet was a logical place to do so, whether on eBay, Craigslist, or some other site.

In 2000 the San Francisco Giants were among the first teams to unveil an electronic ticket exchange for season-ticket holders. By using the Giants' Double Play Ticket Window (at www.sfgiants.com), season-ticket holders could sell tickets "at any price above the face value of the ticket." The price was determined by the season-ticket holder. A convenience fee of 10 percent was added to the ticket price. Fans bought the tickets by credit cards and received them either by mail or at the park. The system worked because the Giants used electronic turnstiles. When a season-ticket holder gave up a ticket, the original bar code was invalidated, and a new one was allotted to the new ticket. In a way, this system was legalized scalping, but it allowed the Giants to control transactions. More tickets were available online to the public well in advance of games. And more than anything, it kept season-ticket holders happy. Giants COO Larry Baer was optimistic about the new system: "We think we'll be looking at something like a 90 percent renewal next year because of this program."[46]

StubHub moved quickly into this domain, and fans embraced the opportunity. The market has grown. During the five days before a July 2011 Atlanta Braves game, for instance, over 500 people used StubHub to sell some 2,000 tickets for a total of $48,801. As *SportsBusiness Journal* noted, "Nine out of 10 tickets cost less than they would have at Braves.com." Ticketmaster and the NBA developed a system described earlier. StubHub and Paciolan have developed similar systems for some American colleges and universities. Viagogo has websites (with local languages) in 25 European countries. As Paciolan CEO Dave Butler put it, "I tell presidents and ADs all the time that the secondary market is going to happen with you or without you." In the end, as one associate athletic director said, "It's not about revenue. It's about customer service." Viagogo executive Edward Parkinson put it more graphically: "Where previously you had to take your chances on Ebay, or Gumtree, or a tout on the corner, if you buy a ticket with Viagogo you're guaranteed to get the ticket you paid for and get it on time for the event." Sellers and buyers have benefited in this new world of distribution.[47]

Staying Creative

As the previous examples suggest, the marketer must use creativity in planning and implementing new channels of distribution. Keeping abreast of the latest technologies and keeping an open mind are critical to success. For instance, the notion of a smartphone was relatively new when we published the last edition of this book (2007). The term had been hatched only a decade before by the manufacturer Ericsson. In 2008 only 20 percent of the phone market was "smart" enough to surf the web. That number is rising, and its effect has been huge, as noted in this and earlier chapters. Marketers must constantly think ahead and stay nimble. As Brian Rolapp, senior vice president of digital media for the NFL, put it: "Anyone who says they know where the world is going on this is lying to you. So you need to be flexible." Consumers can now use smartphones to search for tickets, buy tickets, navigate to a venue, find a reserved parking spot, enter a special turnstile, find a seat, order food, check player and team statistics, and view replays. And that may be just a start.[48]

Marc Andreesen, the founder of Netscape, wrote a 2011 *Wall Street Journal* piece on how specialized software and apps were altering and disrupting whole industries—finance, publishing, photography, automobiles. Old leaders like Kodak had failed to keep up and thereby had met their doom. Andreesen predicted that health care and education were next up for "fundamental software-based transformation." He might have added sport. A marketer can distribute sport product elements in endless ways across multiple platforms and channels. In the case of wireless transmission to smartphone apps, the key issues include the following:

- What kind of apps and product elements? Audio, video, live gamecasts, highlights, stadium maps, fantasy game, interviews, stats?
- What platforms? iPhone, Android?
- What carriers: Exclusive with Verizon? Across all carriers?

- Price?
- Sponsors?

Little downtime occurs with technological change, its effects, and its role in product distribution.[49]

Sometimes moving forward means thinking backward. A number of Major League Baseball teams, including the Boston Red Sox, have experimented with showing games at area cinemas. The Red Sox recognized a need to extend the communal baseball experience beyond the ever-sold-out Fenway Park. Television and radio were doing an excellent job for most fans, but some wanted to share the game with others in a large venue. In 2004 the Red Sox answered that need by partnering with selected area movie theaters for live, high-definition video screenings of several games. At some theaters, vendors hawked beer and hot dogs, some fans sang "Take Me Out to the Ballgame" during the seventh-inning stretch, and others did the wave. Tickets cost between $5 and $10. Said one fan: "If you want to take your family, you have to take out a minimortgage to go to Fenway Park. But this gives you a chance to feel as close as you can to being in the ball park." Sounds like a good deal.[50]

Ironically, this approach replicated distribution efforts over a century earlier when entrepreneurs used telegraph reports to fashion "live" theater events of away games. Fans paid to attend a theater where a stage manager would announce play-by-play telegraph reports and move figures around a big board that conveyed a crude sense of a ball field. But whether the game was conveyed by telegraphy or HD video signals, the theater experience was a collective one. It nurtured fan community. Some scientific evidence supports this notion, as reported in the *Journal of Sport Management*. Researchers collected survey and focus group data from 188 such theater baseball fans at one event. They concluded that fans believed that "the cinema offers an authentic environment," and that for some attendees "the cinema experience was preferred over that of the ballpark."[51]

The following are some simple questions that marketers need to ponder continually:

- Who are my consumers and what are their needs?
- Where are my consumers?

- What are my products and their extensions?
- What vehicles, especially using new technologies, are available for distribution?

Product-Place Matrix

Ultimately, the marketer wants to ensure effective and efficient use of all available distribution channels. New technologies are not restricted to top-tier professional teams and leagues. Schools, colleges, and clubs have successfully used public access cable channels and webcasts to deliver their events to a wider audience. New media, wireless, and digital products also create opportunities at all levels. Big-leagues organizations need not be the only ones that expand distribution in the digital and wireless age. Of course, not many teams have the draw and power of the Red Sox. But anyone can be thoughtful and imaginative. A valuable analytical tool is the product-place matrix (table 13.1), which helps conceptualize both the array of products and the distribution channels. A simple start to a matrix for a collegiate sport program might look like this. Each row represents a product element (event, players, coach), and each column represents a distribution outlet (venues, media).

The matrix simply provides a graphic representation of current or planned product distribution. In this example, the players and coaches are "distributed" in many ways beyond the game itself. They have autograph sessions after games; they offer clinics and talks to Greek houses and civic groups nearby or in outer markets. The coaches also are "distributed" by coach's corner shows on radio and television, on Internet chat rooms, or on podcasts. Marketers can consider how best to fill each part of such a grid, using their imagination and creativity.

ACTIVITY 13.5 Thunder from Seattle to Oklahoma City

In this WSG activity, you will consider whether a team move is good or bad, and you will learn what the Oklahoma Thunder has meant to its home city.

TABLE 13.1   Product-Place Matrix

Product	Place					
	Field house, fields	Old media	New media	Retail outlets	Greeks, civic groups	Outer markets
Events	Games	Releases, TV, radiocasts, Internet	Gamecast app for cell phone, tablets; tags of user-created content on YouTube	Game highlights on video kiosks in mall	Highlight films, pep rallies	Home game scheduled in a remote city; gamecasts on big screens
Players, coaches	Autograph sessions	Coach's corner on radio, TV, Internet blog	Podcasts on iTunes; miniclinics on YouTube	Clinics, autographs	Speeches on substance-free living	Clinics, press meetings
Tickets	Box office	Trade-outs with media, Internet	Facebook, Twitter promotions	Schedule cards, posters, electronic kiosks	Group sales	Group sales
Merchandise	Concourse	Local cable, direct mail, Internet	Facebook, Twitter promotions	Licensed outlets	Fund-raisers	Licensed outlets

Wrap-Up

Although the place function in sport marketing bears remote resemblance to the distribution function in consumer product marketing, its importance among the five Ps of sport marketing should not be minimized. The place in sport begins with the ensemble of elements, comprising the venue or facility and its surroundings. The facility location is critical to the success of most sport businesses. Of equal importance are the facility image and operation, which are influenced by physical design, amenities, and the attitudes of facility personnel. The core event and its extensions must then be distributed by way of marketing channels that include retail outlets and the media. The marketing channels for sport products are limited only by budgets and imaginations, but the possibilities can be graphically illustrated by use of a product-place matrix.

Activities

1. Apply the theory of place to your favorite sport venue, as we did to Fenway Park. What are the most important elements of the ensemble? What elements of the place ensemble could be accentuated in the design or in promotions?

2. Analyze a local facility in terms of its accessibility, flow, drawing radius, parking, aesthetics, staffing, security, surroundings, design and layout, and amenities. How would you improve these areas?

Your Marketing Plan

1. Outline a ticket distribution plan for your organization that makes use of some new technologies mentioned in this chapter.

2. Create a product-place matrix for your organization. Think carefully about alternative channels for distributing your various products.

Endnotes

1. "NHL to Pay Michigan $3M," *SSSBJ*, 13–19 February 2012, 8; http://en.wikipedia.org/wiki/The_Big_Chill_at_the_Big_House.

2. Reuters, "Disney to Rebrand Sports Complex as ESPN," www.sports-city.org/news_details.php?news_id=9925&idCategory=146.

3. Greg Bishop, "Playing Games Out of Place," *New York Times*, 25 July 2011, D1; Greg Bishop, "Season Tips Off in Location Unlike Any Other," *New York Times*, 12 November 2011, D3. UNC story in Mike Phelps, "New Paths Ahead," *Athletic Management* (August-September 2012, 30–32.

4. Tripp Mickle, "NHL Teams Flock to Convention," *SSSBJ*, 31 August 2009, 8; Andy Dolich, "How Valuable is a Variable-Venue Venture?" *SSSBJ*, 16 January 2012, 24

5. J. Fraiberg, "A Racket at Rush Hour," *Sports Illustrated*, 9 October 1995, 16.

6. For an excellent analysis of place, space, and the Beijing Olympics, see X. Ren, "Olympic Beijing: Reflections on Urban Space and Global Connectivity," *International Journal of History of Sport*, 26 (8) (July 2008): 1011–1039. For the London Olympics, see Sarah Lyall, "A Buoyant Bedlam at the Olympic Park," *New York Times*, 4 August 2012, D1, www.nytimes.com/2012/08/04/sports/olympics/at-the-olympic-park-a-buoyant-bedlam.html?ref=todayspaper. For world football venues, see Benjamin Flowers, "Stadiums: Architecture and Iconography of the Beautiful Game," *International Journal of the History of Sport*, 28 (8–9) (2011), 1174–85. The notion of ensemble is developed in J. Bale, *Sport, Space and the City* (London: Routledge, 1993); J. Bale, *Landscapes of Modern Sport* (Leicester, UK: University of Leicester, 1994); J. Raitz, ed., *The Theater of Sport* (Baltimore: Johns Hopkins University Press, 1995). For Fenway, see P. Gammons, "The Place Is the Thing," *Boston Globe*, 25 April 1995, 76; Megan Tench, "Making Fenway Bright," *Boston Globe*, 24 November 2004, B-1, B-6; Mike Tierney, "In Baseball's Bronze Age: Statues are Becoming Bigger Part of Landscape," *New York Times*, 21 September 2011, B15.

7. For a solid survey see Gil Fried, *Managing Sport Facilities* (Champaign, IL: Human Kinetics, 2010).

8. E. Cohen, "Miles, Minutes, and Custom Markets," *Marketing Tools*, July–August 1996, 18–21; M.

Levine, "Know Your Facility's Drawing Radius," *Sports Management Review*, Spring 1977, 1. P. Gollenback, *American Zoom* (New York: Macmillan, 1993), 87. On Charlotte, see E. Hinton, "Long Way to Go," *Sports Illustrated*, 18 December 1995, 59–62.

9. Ken Belson, "Coyotes' Time in Arizona May Be Nearing an End," *New York Times*, 11 February 2012, D5.

10. "Will There Be a Giant Parking Problem at Pac Bell Ballpark?" *SBD*, 20 August 1998, 13. See also the parking ratio issue related to the L.A. Coliseum in L. Mullen, "Coliseum Parking Could Add $100M to Cost," *SSSBJ*, 26 April–2 May 1999, 5.

11. Dave Broughton, "Park It," *SSSBJ*, 11 October 2010, 1, 17–22, quotation at 1, poll at 17.

12. Broughton, "Park It," 22; Don Muret, "Branded Parking Lots Have Room for Perks," *SSSBJ*, 11 October 2010, 20.

13. M. DiNitto, "Fields of Vision," *Athletic Business*, January 1999, 38–45.

14. Z. Dowdy, "BC Told to Redo Plan for Parking," *Boston Globe*, 2 September 1993, 25, 30.

15. Alex Stone, "Why Waiting Is Torture," *New York Times*, August 19, 2012, SR12. For a classic account of changes in flow made at Stanford Stadium in anticipation of the 1985 Super Bowl, see J. Anderson, "Management by Design," *Athletic Business*, August 1985, 28–34; Steve Cameron, "Traffic Flow Inside Venue as Important as Outside," *SSSBJ*, 30 July–5 August 2001, 22; A. Goldfisher, "Concourses Designed to Serve Up Profits," *SSSBJ*, 24–30 August 1998, 22.

16. Bill King, "Equal Access?" *SSSBJ*, 9 July 2007, 1, 17–22.

17. "Head Count," *SBD*, 22 June 1999, 15; Don Muret, "Will We Ever See the End of the Line?" *SSSBJ*, 25 July 2011, 1, 20–22.

18. Paul Steinbach, "Venue Visuals," *Athletic Business*, August 2005, 63–70.

19. The seminal work on framing in sport is John MacAloon, "Olympic Games and the Theory of Spectacle in Modern Societies," in *Rite, Drama, Festival, Spectacle: Rehearsals Toward a Theory of Cultural Performance*, ed. John J. MacAloon (Philadelphia: Institute for the Study of Human Issues, 1984), 241–280.

20. Jeremy Olshan, "MSG Going Above and Beyond," *New York Post*, 24 May 2010, www.nypost.com/p/news/local/manhattan/msg_going_00laBbpLH-bjuaH2F2uDK0O.

21. Richard Harding Davis, "The Thanksgiving Day Game," *Harper's Weekly* 37 (December 1893, 1170–1171) in *Major Problems in American Sport History*, ed. Steven Riess (Boston: Houghton Mifflin, 1997), 116–118. For Ole Miss, see Dwight Garner, "Of Parties, Prose and Football," *New York Times*, 16 October 2011, TR1. For Husky Harbor, see Greg Bishop, "Tailgating Crowd's Unlikely Roar, Ahoy," *New York Times*, 14 October 2011, B11. Don Muret, "Sponsors Become Part of Tailgate Experience," *SSSBJ*, 11 October 2011, 21

22. Dan Bickley, "Pro Sports May Be Pricing Fans Out of Stadiums," *Arizona Republic*, 24 June 2001.

23. Tom Verducci, "The Age of Aquariums," *Sports Illustrated*, 9 April 2012, 58–59. On Marlins Park, see also Michael Kimmelman, "A Ballpark That May Be Louder Than the Fans," *New York Times*, April 28, 2012, A1. For Fenway, see Richard Johnson, *Field of Our Fathers: An Illustrated History of Fenway Park* (Chicago: Triumph Books, 2011), 2–3.

24. Eric Prisbell, "$60 Million for a High School Stadium With Free Wi-Fi," *USA Today*, 29 August 2012, www.usatodayhss.com/news/article/60-million-for-a-high-school-stadium-with-free-wi-fi--57419910.

25. Janet Morrissey, "The Millennials Check In," *New York Times*, 13 March 2012, B6; Bill King, "Keeping Fans Connected," *SSSBJ*, 1–7 November 2004, 15–17.

26. "Arena Features," www.xcelenergycenter.com/about-us/arena-features.

27. Don Muret, "Sponsor Starts In-Arena Child Care," *SSSBJ*, 18 January 2010, 4

28. http://hockey.ballparks.com/NHL/TampaBay-Lightning/index.htm Note that the XO Club still exists but in a different venue location and context. See also John Lombardo and Don Muret, "Pistons Look at Cutting Half of Arena's Suites," *SSSBJ*, 30 January 2012, 1, 6.

29. Michael Smith, " 'Miller Lite Party Deck' All About Having Fun," *SSSBJ*, 23 July 2007, 23.

30. Don Muret, "Fan Cave Catches on Quickly With Tribe Fans," *SSSBJ*, 1 November 2010, 22.

31. See the IAVM website at www.iavm.org. The Stanford training program is described in Roy Purpur and Betsy Alden, "The Guests Are Here," *Athletic Management*, 13 (2) (February–March 2001): 6–11.

32. For an interesting approach to evaluating channel values, see Irving Rein, Philip Kotler, and Ben Shields, *The Elusive Fan: Reinventing Sports in a Crowded Marketplace* (New York: McGraw-Hill, 2006), 245–6

33. S. Hardy, "Adopted by All the Leading Clubs: Sporting Goods and the Shaping of Leisure," in *For Fun and Profit*, ed. R. Butsch (Philadelphia: Temple University Press, 1990), 71–101.

34. M. Palmisano, "Merchandising Can Mean Added Revenue for You," *Athletic Purchasing and Facilities*, October 1980, 22–24.

35. Don Muret, "Chargers Find Niche in Retail Sales, *SSSBJ*, 15 January 2007, 8.

36. Bruce Schoenfeld, "Shopping in Stadium's Shadow," *SSSBJ*, 19 November 2007, 1, 28–30. www.patriot-place.com.

37. John Lombardo and Eric Fisher, "Deal Will Create NBA Portal on Ticketmaster," *SSSBJ*, 20 August 2012, 1, 31. For another view of Ticketmaster (in the concert arena) see Chuck Salter, "Ticketmaster: Rocking the Most Hated Brand in America," *Fast Company*, July–August 2011, 90–97, 118.

38. Jay Weiner, "Are the Days Numbered for the Paper Ticket?" *SSSBJ*, 18 June 2007, 17–21; Jay Weiner, "Walk Up Sales Stumble as Technology Advances," *SSSBJ*, 18 June 2007, 20; Eric Fisher, "MLB Fanpass to Make Paperless Ticketing Push, *SSSBJ*, 19 March 2012, 1, 45; Michael Smith, "Colleges's Season-Ticket Delivery Shifts Online," *SSSBJ*, 24 October 2011, 5.

39. For current policy see: www.umterps.com/fls/29700/pdf/tickets/13-14StudentTicketPolicy.pdf?DB_OEM_/D=29700

40. Quotation in Don Muret, "Teams Still Making Sales in Retail Outlets," *SSSBJ*, 23 May 2011, 18; "Chevron Inks Reported $15–20M Pact With MLB Grants," *SBD*, 4 December 1997, 3; "Burger King Sells Tickets Their Way—Lots of Them," *Team Marketing Report* (January 1994): 4, 7; "ETM Remote Locations and Kiosks," *SBD*, 9 February 1998, 10; *Migala Report*, 1 July 2004, www.migalareport.com; Don Muret, " 'Dolphins Express' Finds More Riders," *SSSBJ*, 23 May 2011, 18.

41. L. Miller and L. Fielding, "Ticket Distribution Agencies and Professional Sports Franchises: The Successful Partnership," *SMQ*, 6 (March 1997): 47–55; Andrew Cohen, "Ticket to the Future," *Athletic Business*, September 2001, 55–61. Adam Fraser, "Just the Ticket," *SportsPro Magazine*, October 2010, 98–101.

42. W. Suggs, "Sox Ticket System Target Ticketmaster," *SSSBJ*, 18–24 May 1998, 7.

43. "Payroll Deductions Add Up to Hamilton Season Tickets," *Team Marketing Report* (October 1992), 5.

44. Terry Lefton, "Tickets Served Up From Roving Dodgers Truck," *SSSBJ*, 25 May 2009, 6.

45. Kevin O'Connor, "Football Tickets Delivered in 30 Minutes, or Less," *NewsLink Indiana*, 31 August 2004, www.newslinkindiana.com.

46. "Giants Offer Web Ticket Exchange for Season-Ticket Holders," *SBD*, 14 June 2000, 15.

47. Quotation in Michael Smith, "Colleges Jump on Secondary Bandwagon," *SSSBJ*, 24 October 2011, 23; Bill King and Eric Fisher, "Second Thoughts: Teams Face a Secondary Market That Has Redefined the Ticket Business," *SSSBJ*, 24 October 2011, 15; and Adam Fraser, "Just the Ticket," *SportsPro Magazine*, October 2010, 98–101. See also John Lombardo, "ScoreBig," *SSSBJ*, 27 September 2010, 5.

48. Bill King, "What's the Right Call on Wireless?" *SSSBJ*, 22 February 2010, 1, 13–19, quotation at 13.

49. Marc Andreessen, "Why Software Is Eating the World," *Wall Street Journal*, August 20, 2011, C-2.

50. Jenn Abelson, "High-Definition Heroes," *Boston Globe,* 9 June 2004, B-1, B-7; Jenn Abelson, "New Season for 'Game Night' Screenings," *Boston Globe,* 8 April 2005, C-1, C-3.

51. Sheranne Fairley, B. David Tyler, "Bringing Baseball to the Big Screen: Building Sense of Community Outside of the Ballpark," *Journal of Sport Management*, 26 (3) (2012): 258–270. On 1890s telegraph theater, see Stephen Hardy, *How Boston Played: Sport, Recreation, and Community, 1865–1915* (Boston: Northeastern University Press, 1982), x.

Chapter 14

Legal Aspects of Sport Marketing

Steve McKelvey
John Grady

OBJECTIVES

- To introduce the key legal concepts and issues that affect the marketing of the sport product

- To inform sport marketers about the need, and the methods used, to protect intellectual property associated with the creation of a sport product or event, or with ideas developed out of sport sponsorship and licensing programs

- To examine the legal limits of sport marketing and promotion so that sport marketers can better manage risks and avoid legal liability

Despite all the muscle flexing of the London Summer Olympic Games brand police, the jury remains out on the topic of ambush marketing simply because the jury was never called in. What promised to be a full-scale siege in the battle against ambush marketing ended with a fizzle.

With each successive Olympic Games, event organizers have implemented stricter (and arguably overprotective) measures to ensure that official sponsors are protected from ambush marketing, a controversial practice whereby businesses that are not official sponsors conduct advertising and promotional activities that seek to capitalize on the event's good will, reputation, and popularity. From a strictly legal standpoint, ambush marketers rarely infringe on the trademarks of the sport organization or event that they are allegedly ambushing, making brand-protection efforts difficult.

As a bid requirement to hosting the London Games, special legislation was enacted by the British government to provide the Olympic Movement with additional ambush-marketing protection for the period of time surrounding London's hosting of the Games. This legislation created the London Olympic Association Right, an unprecedented approach to protecting Olympic intellectual property that future host countries are likely to emulate. This right of association specified that implying a commercial or contractual association with the Olympics would violate the LOAR (albeit the legislation did provide a safe harbor for honest business practices).

Before the Games, the aggressive ways in which the International Olympic Committee (IOC) and the London Organizing Committee for the Olympic Games (LOCOG) enforced the legislation left many crying foul. For example, in May, the Olympics' brand police were successful in halting a window display simulating the Olympic rings made from plastic gym ropes and Olympic torches crafted from old "For Sale" signs at a real estate agency. The display was witnessed by LOCOG officials during the Olympic torch relay. LOCOG demanded that the trademark-infringing display be removed or else face formal legal action: "Whilst we appreciate your enthusiasm and support, use of the Olympic rings in the window of a commercial office inevitably creates an association between [the real estate chain] and the Games and allows the [real estate] brand to benefit from the goodwill and excitement of the Olympic Torch Relay."

Remarked a branch manager of the real estate agency: "We thought this is a once-in-a-lifetime thing. This is not about the Olympics for people. This is about the Olympics for [official sponsors] Lloyds Bank, Samsung and Coca-Cola." It was later acknowledged that two LOCOG lawyers accompanied the entire torch relay to address any other potential incidents of ambush marketing.

Other small businesses, such as the owner of a lingerie shop and a butcher who displayed sausages in the shape of the Olympic rings, were also ensnared in LOCOG's ambush-marketing crackdown. Although this type of aggressive enforcement is called lunacy by those affected, industry observers and critics questioned why LOCOG was choosing to go after small businesses seeking to share in the celebration of their country's hosting the Games. Moreover, from a strategic perspective, these local businesses posed no real commercial threat to global Olympic sponsors like Coca-Cola, Samsung, and Adidas.

> *continued*

This chapter addresses the issues that arise at the intersection of sport marketing and the law. Without a working knowledge of the legal aspects of sport marketing, those who market the sport product (ranging from teams to players to events), as well as corporations that market their products and services through sport, risk a host of legal consequences. Hence, this chapter provides an overview of the general concepts and practical issues that are most relevant to sport marketers,

After the Games began and the incidents of true ambush marketing revved up, enforcement efforts seemingly kept a much lower profile. For example, Nike, no stranger to the Olympic ambush game, used its high-profile campaign "Find your greatness" to showcase ordinary athletes finding greatness in cities around the world named London (talk about clever!). With the start of the campaign timed to occur just a few days before the opening ceremony, Nike's actions initially raised the ire of LOCOG's brand enforcement team. But it relented, promising only to "monitor the situation," and ultimately determined that a lawsuit was unwarranted. Nike's performance managed to achieve a high level of global consumer awareness among Olympic visitors, television, and online audiences.

Another high-profile ambush incident was launched by Irish online betting site Paddy Power, whose billboard ad featured a fictitious egg and spoon race in London, France. The billboards claimed Paddy Power was the "Official sponsor of the largest athletics event in London this year! There you go, we said it (ahem, London, France that is)." LOCOG directed the outdoor advertising space provider to remove the billboards as a violation of the Olympic special legislation but was forced to retreat when Paddy Power sought a court order blocking removal of the billboards. Paddy Power argued that the content did not contravene the special legislation. Media outlets suggested that LOCOG's reversal was strategic in order to avoid negative publicity during the height of the Games. In hindsight, Paddy Power's cheeky billboards may be notorious for their typically irreverent creativity but also noteworthy for the response they provoked by LOCOG.

A third well-publicized example of alleged ambush marketing was Beats Electronics' recognizable headphones, Beats by Dre, worn prominently by American and British Olympic athletes on the pool deck and before athletics events at Olympic Stadium, thus providing international TV exposure. Others implementing well-publicized marketing campaigns conducted without legal recourse included, but were not limited to, Tetley Tea, Red Bull, Virgin Media, Puma, and Mizuno.

Undoubtedly, the legislation deterred many smaller and risk-averse companies from engaging in ambush marketing or simply showing their local pride and excitement about hosting the Games. But the legislation proved ineffective in thwarting companies who were both clever and intent on associating with the Games. It's indeed ironic that the legislation and the threats of legal action stopped so many companies that were not intent on ambush marketing, but were unable to stop all those companies that were blatantly seeking to ambush. Furthermore, the overzealous approach to its brand protection efforts arguably served to tarnish the Olympic brand, given the amount of negative publicity that surrounded those efforts.

It will be interesting to see, when the United States next hosts an Olympic Games, whether Congress and local legislators will be willing to enact special legislation that provides the IOC and the local organizing committee with ambush-marketing protection as broad as that afforded the IOC and LOCOG for the London Games.

Reprinted, by permission, from A. Madkour, 2013, "Ambush marketing lessons from the London Olympic Games," *Street & Smith's SportBusiness Journal*, pg. 25.

including intellectual property law, right of publicity law, promotions law, and ambush marketing. At the outset, we must recognize that these legal issues are complex and require assistance from attorneys who specialize in these areas.

Intellectual Property

After many decades, Jill B. Fan's favorite hometown team, the Aces, has finally reached the World Series. As both a die-hard fan and an entrepreneur, Jill is eager to put to use all the marketing ideas that she has been dreaming up to take advantage of this momentous event. For instance, she has come up with a catchy slogan to emblazon on T-shirts, above a logo that is remarkably similar to that of the Aces, and she plans to sell the shirts outside the stadium. She's also developed her own special logo to commemorate the event: two interlocking baseballs that prominently feature the colors of her hometown team, with the words *"World Champs"* superimposed across the baseballs. She has already visited GoDaddy.com and secured the URL www.WorldChampAces.com, where she plans to blog regularly about her love for her hometown team, write features on Aces players that include their photographs, and sell her wares. She can't wait to begin cashing in.

The primary goal of intellectual property law is to reward invention, ingenuity, and creativity to maintain an open and competitive marketplace. To encourage this type of progress in science and the arts, the framers of the U.S. Constitution delegated to Congress the power to protect the intellectual property rights of artists, authors, and inventors by granting them "the exclusive right to their writings and discoveries."[1] Thus, property rights are granted to protect the products of one's intellect. If Jill B. Fan has a unique idea, she should be entitled to capitalize on it—as long as she is not infringing on the prior rights of others. Although people often see the symbols identifying intellectual property rights (© [copyright], ™ [trademark], and ® [patent]), most do not realize the exact nature of the legal protection provided to a trademark, copyright, or patent owner. The first section of this chapter focuses primary attention on the area of trademark law, the area of greatest relevance to sport marketers. Copyright and patent law, as well as a form of intellectual property recognized as the right of publicity, is also discussed in terms of its relevance to sport marketers.

To decide the type of legal protection that people should use to protect new ideas or products, we must first examine the character of the intellectual property. For example, trademarks protect unique words, names, symbols, and slogans; copyrights protect original works of authorship; and patents protect inventions (new designs and novel processes). Ownership rights to trademarks may last forever, whereas rights to copyrights and patents have time limits. A trademark, copyright, or patent owner may grant permission for its use to others for a fee, an arrangement known as *licensing*. When another person does not have permission or licensed rights to use the copyright, trademark, or patent, that person is said to be infringing on the intellectual property owner's rights.

A single product can conceivably receive intellectual property protection across all three intellectual property categories. Take, for example, Spalding's line of Infusion basketballs. The manufacturer has a patent on the technology that enables consumers to inflate the ball with a micropump that is built into the ball, a copyright on the information conveyed on the packaging, and a trademark for the unique name of the product ("Infusion").

Overview of Trademark Law

Trademarks serve five important purposes. A consumer's decision to purchase a T-shirt featuring the logo of his or her favorite team, the Blue Sox (a fictional sport team), provides a good illustration. First, trademarks serve to *identify the source or origin* of the product (or service) and to distinguish it from others. Based on the logo on the T-shirt, the consumer knows that the Blue Sox team is the source of this product. Second, trademarks *protect consumers* from confusion and deception. In other words, the law allows the Blue Sox to sue any other person (individual or company) who seeks to confuse or deceive the consumer into believing that the Blue Sox were the source of the product purchased, when they weren't. Third, a trademark is used to designate a *consistent level of quality* of a product (or service). Thus, the consumer knows that when she buys a T-shirt with the Blue Sox logo, the product has been confirmed for quality and won't fall apart in the washer. Fourth, a trademark represents the *goodwill* of the owner's products (or services). In other words, the consumer has chosen to buy a Blue Sox T-shirt because he or she has good feelings about the Blue Sox. Fifth, trademarks signify a *substantial advertising investment*. The Blue Sox have invested tremendous time and financial resources in building the value and goodwill of their name and trademarks, and the law is designed to discourage other companies from trading off this goodwill or diminishing this value by using similar marks on their competitive products (or services).

Trademarks are protected on the national level by the Federal Trademark Act of 1946, commonly referred to as the Lanham Act.[2] The Lanham Act, which has become increasingly important for sport marketers involved in the marketing of sport products, teams, players and events, protects three primary types of marks: trademarks, service marks, and collective marks.

A *trademark* is a word, name, symbol, or device used by a person, generally a manufacturer or merchant, to identify and distinguish its goods from those manufactured and sold by others, and to indicate the source of the goods.[3] This section also includes trade dress, a particular type of trademark that provides protection for the packaging of a product. In the sport setting, it typically involves the product's shape, color, or color scheme, a concept that will be discussed later in this chapter.[4]

A *service* mark is a word, name, symbol, or device used to identify and distinguish a company's services, including a unique service, from those of another service provider.[5] Service marks are typically used in the sale or advertising of an intangible service, such as the entertainment value of a sport event. For example, the *World Series* and the *NCAA Final Four* are service marks, in that they are events (services provided to fans), as opposed to tangible products (you can't go out and buy a World Series, although some fans would argue otherwise!).

A *collective* mark is defined in the Lanham Act as a trademark or service mark used by the members of a cooperative, an association, or other group or organization, and serves to indicate membership in a union, an association, or other organization.[6] Good examples of collective marks are the logos used by the players associations in

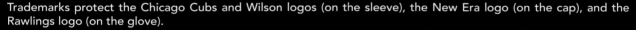

Trademarks protect the Chicago Cubs and Wilson logos (on the sleeve), the New Era logo (on the cap), and the Rawlings logo (on the glove).

the professional sport industry, as well as the logos of the leagues themselves.

To gain national trademark protection under the Lanham Act, the trademark must be registered with the United States Patent and Trademark Office (USPTO), which also resolves any disputes related to trademark registration. For the trademarks of local, community-based sport events and properties, in which federal trademark protection may be deemed not necessary, protection is still afforded under various state statutes that provide their own protections similar to those provided by the Lanham Act but which typically fall under the theory of unfair competition (discussed later). Although federal registration of a mark is not required to establish ownership rights in a mark, it does provide several important benefits, including the following:

- The ability of the trademark owner to sue in federal court

- The ability to obtain trademark registration in foreign countries

- The opportunity to file the trademark with the U.S. Customs Service to prevent the importation of infringing foreign goods

- The acknowledgment and protection of the goodwill of the trademark holder

- The provision of public notice throughout the nation of trademark ownership, thus creating an easier burden of proof in trademark infringement lawsuits[7]

Ownership of a trademark generally requires the holder to appropriate the mark and to use it for commercial purposes.[8] Since 1988, however, the Lanham Act has allowed an individual to apply for registration to the USPTO if the applicant can establish "a bona fide intention" to use a trademark in commerce within a reasonable period.[9] Unlike copyrights and patents, which have expirations, trademarks can last indefinitely as long as the trademark owner continues to use the trademark in commerce.[10] When creating a new trademark, sport marketers are advised to hire intellectual property counsel to conduct a trademark search to determine whether any conflicting marks already exist (this can typically be done for several hundred dollars). Furthermore, although the USPTO does not conduct searches for the public, it does provide a public library of marks as well as an electronic searchable database (available at www.uspto.gov).

What Marks Can Be Protected?

The USPTO classifies marks on different levels. Simply put, the more distinctive the mark is, the more likely it is that it will be considered for federal registration and thus afforded protection under the Lanham Act. The issue of distinctiveness will typically come up during the registration process, raised either by the USPTO or by a competitor seeking to challenge the registration of a proposed mark (legal counsel for sport properties regularly review trademark application lists to ensure that a person is not seeking to register a mark that the sport property would find objectionable).

Trademarks that are inherently distinctive and completely distinguishable are characterized as *fanciful* or *arbitrary*.[11] Sport marketers challenged with creating a trademark (for instance, the name of a team, an event, or product) should endeavor to create a mark that is fanciful or arbitrary. Such marks are invented for the sole purpose of functioning as a trademark. In the past several years, minor league baseball teams have led the way in creating fanciful names, such as the Wisconsin Timber Rattlers, the Cedar Rapids Kernels, and the West Tennessee Diamond Jaxx (such fanciful names and corresponding logos have also proven a boon to merchandise sales). Other common examples of fanciful trade names within the sport world include Speedo and event names such as MotoX and Hoop-D-Do.

Arbitrary marks, although not as distinctive as fanciful marks, are words, names, symbols, or devices that are commonly known words but have become associated with a particular product or service through the advertising and marketing efforts of the owner. Examples in the sport world include the Gravity Games, Field Turf, and Arena Football League.

The last category of inherently distinctive marks is *suggestive* marks. Although weaker than fanciful or arbitrary marks, a suggestive mark subtly connotes something about the product or service but does not actually describe any specific ingredient, quality, or characteristic of the product or service. With suggestive marks, the consumer must use her imagination to draw an association. The more suggestive the mark, the more consumer imagination is required to make the association. Examples include Powerade, a word that suggests certain characteristics that the isotonic beverage provides to sweating consumers, and Nike (a Greek goddess who was the personification of victory).

On the opposite end of the spectrum are trademarks that, on their face, do not distinguish one product or service from another and typically use common words in their ordinary spelling and meanings. Such marks are referred to in trademark law as being either *descriptive* (which are difficult, although not impossible, to protect) and *generic* (which are never entitled to trademark protection). Thus, sport marketers are advised to refrain from creating marks that would be deemed either descriptive or generic.

Besides deeming a mark descriptive, the USPTO will refuse to grant trademark registrations on several other grounds. These include instances in which the proposed trademark possesses immoral, deceptive, or scandalous matter; disparages or falsely suggests a connection with persons (dead or alive), beliefs, institutions, or national symbols; possesses any insignia of the United States, any state or municipality, or a foreign nation; consists of a name, portrait, or signature of any living person without the person's consent, or consists of the name, portrait, or signature of a deceased president during the life of his widow without her consent; or is merely a surname.[12]

The issue of disparaging or slanderous trademarks arose in the 1990s when a group of Native Americans requested that the Trial and Trademark Appeal Board cancel the trademarks of the Washington Redskins.[13] Although the Native American group initially won the case, the Redskins appealed and ultimately prevailed, based in part of the court's determination that there was a lack of evidence that the trademarks were disparaging to a substantial group of Native Americans.[14] The loss of trademark protection would not have meant that the Redskins could not have continued to use the team name and logo. But the loss of its registration would have made enforcing its rights in the unregistered marks, under either federal or state law, much more difficult and might have allowed others to make and sell products bearing the previously registered logos.[15]

Meaning of Secondary Meaning

Descriptive logos and marks can gain trademark protection if they are deemed by the courts to have acquired secondary meaning, defined as "a mental recognition in buyers' and potential buyers' minds that products connected with the symbol or device emanate from or are associated with the same source."[16] One of the most hotly contested areas of sport litigation over the past few years has focused on whether color schemes of college and professional teams are subject to trademark protection. This determination is based on the extent to which the team color schemes have acquired secondary meaning. One of the earliest such cases involved a lawsuit filed by the Seattle Seahawks against an apparel manufacturer who was producing football-style jerseys in Seahawks colors, albeit without the Seahawks logo. The court held that the Seahawks' color scheme on a football jersey had acquired secondary meaning, entitling the Seahawks to trademark protection over this particular use of its color scheme on football jerseys.[17]

The collegiate sport industry has provided the latest legal forum for debating the concept of secondary meaning with regard to school color schemes. In *Board of Supervisors of LSU v. Smack Apparel, Inc.*, the defendant sold apparel using LSU's team colors (purple and gold), although without any other official university logos or insignias.[18] The apparel contained expressions that obliquely referred to the university and that were calculated to appeal to LSU fans. For example, one T-shirt bearing the phrase "Sweet as Sugar!" was sold after LSU won the Sugar Bowl. The university claimed trademark rights in the team colors. The court, although acknowledging that colors were not inherently distinctive, held that the secondary meaning requirement was met because consumers identified the colors with LSU and were likely to associate the goods with the university. Note that this particular case also turned on the First Amendment free speech rights of the defendant Smack Apparel. Hence, although the court ruled in favor of the university with regard to apparel that included team colors with laudatory phrases, it held in favor of Smack Apparel on the majority of T-shirts that, although using team colors, included nonlaudatory phrases and imagery that were deemed to fall into the category of parody, a type of speech afforded the highest level of First Amendment protection.

The case involving Alabama sport artist Daniel Moore has also heightened the debate between trademark law and First Amendment freedom of expression. In 2005 the University of Alabama sued Moore for selling paintings depicting Alabama football players.[19] The particular painting that triggered the action depicted an Alabama defender, in a crimson and white uniform, sacking the Notre Dame quarterback. The university name and logos did not appear in the painting, but the university claimed that its color scheme of crimson and white (referred to in legal terms as trade dress) was widely recognized as a symbol of the university, thus creating a likelihood of confusion as to the source of Moore's painting. In 2012 the 11th Circuit Court of Appeals ruled that Moore had a First Amendment right to include the crimson and white uniforms in his paintings and that this right trumped the university's trademark rights in its color scheme.[20] Hailed as a significant victory for sport artists, the ruling means that Moore can continue including Alabama's team colors in his paintings and commercial art prints without the university's permission. In September 2013, a federal judge brought final closure to this eight-year legal saga, ruling that the transfer of Moore's artwork onto "mundane products" including T-shirts and mugs was also permissible.

Trademark Infringement

The licensing of trademarks has become a billion-dollar business across both professional and collegiate sports. To preserve these revenue streams, sport marketers have become increasingly vigilant in protecting against trademark

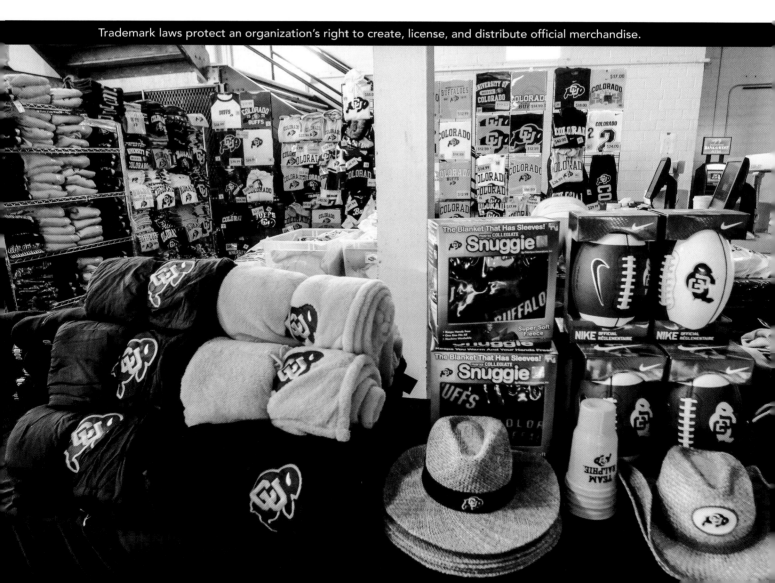

Trademark laws protect an organization's right to create, license, and distribute official merchandise.

infringement, sometimes even at the risk of generating negative public relations. For instance, Major League Baseball has in the past threatened legal action against teams in the Cape Cod League, a college baseball summer league, for using team names trademarked by MLB.[21] Major college football teams have also threatened legal action against high schools using their marks.[22] The Lanham Act provides three primary legal claims that are often jointly incorporated into a lawsuit: (1) *trademark infringement*, which protects against uses of a trademark that are likely to cause confusion or mistake, or to deceive; (2) *false designation of origin*, which is designed to prevent uses of another's trademark that cause confusion as to affiliation or sponsorship; and (3) *dilution* of a famous mark's distinctive quality.[23] The burden of proving these Lanham Act violations is on the trademark owner.

Traditional Trademark Infringement

The Lanham Act defines infringement as "any reproduction, counterfeit, copy, or colorable imitation of a registered mark in connection with the sale, offering for sale, distribution, or advertising of any goods or services on or in connection with which such use is likely to cause confusion, or to cause mistake, or to deceive" without the consent of the trademark holder.[24]

Remember that the purpose of trademark law is, first and foremost, to protect consumers. Hence, the linchpin of a trademark infringement case is the likelihood of consumer confusion, which plaintiffs typically attempt to prove with consumer surveys. The factors used by the courts in determining likelihood of confusion were first developed in the seminal case *Polaroid Corp. v. Polarad, Inc.*[25] Although other federal courts have enunciated their own "likelihood of confusion" factor test, they all generally adhere to the eight factors initially set forth in the so-called Polaroid Test.[26]

Assume that the Aces sue Jill B. Fan, alleging that creating and selling her T-shirts (sporting her catchy slogan above a logo remarkably similar to that of the Aces) constitutes trademark infringement. The Aces' ability to prove likelihood of confusion will be based on the court's evaluation of the following eight factors, or a combination of them:

- The *strength of the Aces' trademark*. (Is the Aces' trademark fanciful, arbitrary, suggestive, descriptive with secondary meaning, or generic?)
- The *degree of similarity* between the Aces' trademark and Jill B. Fan's alleged infringing trademark.
- The *similarity of the products* involved.
- The *market channels involved*. (Do the Aces offer their product to a group of consumers that is similar to that which Jill B. Fan seeks to target?)
- The *distribution channels involved*. (Do the Aces sell their product in the same places as Jill B. Fan is offering her product?)
- The *intent of the defendant* in adopting the trademark. (Does evidence show that Jill B. Fan is trying to confuse consumers into believing that her product is somehow sponsored by or affiliated with the Aces?)
- The *sophistication of the potential consumers*. (Are buying consumers sophisticated enough to understand that the Aces are not the source of Jill B. Fan's product?)
- The *evidence of actual confusion*. (Can the Aces provide evidence, typically through consumer surveys, that consumers are confused about the source of Jill B. Fan's product?)

False Designation of Origin

A second claim under which a trademark owner may sue is termed *false designation of origin*. The Lanham Act protects trademark owners by prohibiting a competitor's false designation of origin when it "is likely to cause confusion . . . or to deceive as to the affiliation, connection, or association of such person with another person, or as to the origin, sponsorship, or approval of his or her goods, services, or commercial activities by another person."[27] Under this theory, the owner of the trademark must establish that the public recognizes that the trademark identifies the owner's goods and services and distinguishes its goods or services from others. After such public recognition is established, the plaintiff must then prove that the defendant's use of the trademark is likely to confuse or deceive the public into thinking that the plaintiff was the origin or source of the product or service. Oftentimes, this is discussed as the alleged infringer confusing the public that it has a sponsorship affiliation with the organization that owns the trademark.

One of the leading sport-related cases is *Dallas Cowboys Cheerleaders, Inc. v. Pussycat Cinema, Ltd.*[28] In this case, the defendant owned and operated an X-rated cinema in which it showed a pornographic film titled *Debbie Does Dallas*. In the film, an actor was shown wearing a uniform strikingly similar to that of the Dallas Cowboys Cheerleaders. The marquee posters advertising the film depicted the woman in a Dallas Cowboys Cheerleader uniform and referred to Dallas and the Dallas Cowboys Cheerleaders. The court, in ruling for the Cowboys cheerleaders and barring distribution of the film, ruled that the plaintiff had a valid trademark (based on the concept of secondary meaning) in their uniform's white boots, white shorts, blue blouse, and star-studded white vest and belt. The court found it likely that the public would associate the Cowboys cheerleaders with the movie and would be confused into believing that the plaintiffs had sponsored the movie.[29] Although the defendants argued that no reasonable person would ever believe that the Cowboys Cheerleaders would be associated with an X-rated film, the court challenged such a reading of consumer confusion as too narrow. Instead, the court stated that to evoke consumer confusion, the uniform depicted in the film need only bring to mind the Dallas Cowboys Cheerleaders, which the court stated it unquestionably did.[30]

Dilution

A third potential claim is for dilution of a famous trademark through what is known as blurring or tarnishment. Two recent sport-related decisions have served to illuminate the application of the doctrine to sport-related trademarks through interpretation of the 2006 amendments to the Federal Trademark Dilution Act of 1995 (FTDA).[31] Both decisions provide guidance to sport-related brands and sport teams that seek to bring dilution claims (typically brought in conjunction with trademark infringement and unfair competition claims). Dilution can occur by blurring (whereby the defendant's use of an identical or similar mark or trade name impairs the distinctiveness of the plaintiff's famous mark) or by tarnishment

(whereby the defendant's use of a similar mark or trade name harms the reputation of the plaintiff's famous mark).[32]

The FTDA was enacted in 1995 to protect the owner's investment in his mark and consists of the "lessening of the capacity of a famous mark to identify and distinguish goods and services of the owner of the famous mark such that the strong identification value of the owner's trademark whittles away or is gradually attenuated as a result of its use by another."[33] Although the seminal 2003 Supreme Court case on dilution, *Moseley v. V Secret Catalogue, Inc.* held that the FTDA "unambiguously require[d] a showing of actual dilution, rather than a likelihood of dilution,"[34] the 2006 Dilution Amendments established that the plaintiff need only show that the defendant's mark is likely to cause dilution by blurring or tarnishment, regardless of the presence or absence of actual or likely confusion, of competition, or of actual economic injury.[35] The 2006 Dilution Amendments included a reconfiguration of the factors used to determine whether a mark is famous for dilution purposes and stated that dilution claims were not applicable to trademarks that had acquired only "niche fame."

To state a dilution claim under the 2006 Dilution Amendments, a plaintiff must first show (1) that he or she owns a famous mark that is distinctive, (2) that the defendant has commenced using a mark in commerce that allegedly is diluting the famous mark, (3) that a similarity between the defendant's mark and the famous mark gives rise to an association between the marks, and (4) that the association is likely to impair the distinctiveness of the famous mark or likely to harm the reputation of the famous mark.[36]

The linchpin of a dilution claim is the premise that the trademark be famous. Perhaps the most significant clarification of the 2006 Dilution Amendments is the requirement that the mark "be widely recognized by the general consuming public of the United States as a designation of source of the goods or services of the mark's owner."[37]

Two recent sport-related cases illustrate that this requirement is more easily met by international household brands that distribute their products on a national basis. Conversely, it can pose a more significant hurdle for sport organizations whose market for consumers is locally or regionally based.[38]

In *Adidas America, Inc. v. Payless Shoesource, Inc.*, the court found Adidas' three-stripe mark to be famous since as early as 1970.[39] The court held that a reasonable fact finder could conclude that Payless' two-stripe mark was nearly identical or essentially the same, and that "a significant segment of the consuming public would likely focus on that element as an identifier essentially the same as the [Adidas] mark."[40] A jury subsequently returned a decisive verdict in favor of Adidas on the trademark infringement and unfair competition claims, awarding $304 million.[41]

Contrary to the decision in *Adidas*, which involved a widely recognized, global sport brand, the 2007 decision in *Board of Regents, The University of Texas System v. KST Electric, Ltd.* (hereinafter *UT*) suggests a much higher hurdle for sport organizations such as college and university athletics programs in surviving summary judgment motions based on federal dilution claims.[42] KST Electric, a local company owned by avid UT fans, designed a company logo that consisted of a longhorn silhouette with a "K" on the left cheek area of the longhorn, an "S" on the right cheek area, a "lightning bolt T" in the face of the silhouette, and the words "ELECTRIC, LTD" in the space between the horns (referred to by the court as the "Longhorn Lightning Bolt Logo") (hereinafter, "LLB Logo"). The university sued KST Electric for trademark dilution, among other claims. The court applied the likelihood of dilution factors as enumerated in the 2006 Dilution Amendments, most notably the requirement that the mark be "widely recognized by the general consuming public of the United States."[43] To support its claim, the university included the fact that (1) its football games were regularly televised on ABC and ESPN and its longhorn mark was prominently featured in those broadcasts, (2) its men's basketball team had been nationally televised 97 times in the previous five seasons, (3) its football team had appeared in the national championship game, (4) UT football players had been featured solely or as part of the cover of *Sports Illustrated* 10 times from 1963 through 2006, and (5) UT held the record for most royalties earned in a single year on the sale of officially licensed merchandise.

The judge ruled the university's "circumstantial evidence" to be "largely evidence of niche market fame."[44] Of much greater weight to the court was survey evidence provided by KST. In arguing that UT's mark was not sufficiently recognized on a national level to rise above the level of "niche fame," KST presented a national survey that demonstrated that only 5.8 percent of respondents in the United States associated the UT registered longhorn logo with UT alone and only 21.1 percent of respondents in Texas associated the UT registered longhorn logo with UT alone. The court ultimately held that the survey evidence presented by KST indicated that UT had achieved only niche market fame for the purposes of trademark dilution.

Based on the courts' decisions in the *Adidas* and *UT* cases, we are left to speculate about what collegiate or professional sport organization trademarks would meet the 2006 Dilution Amendments standard to sustain a federal dilution claim. For instance, although we would think that the Dallas Cowboys or Notre Dame Fighting Irish marks would indeed be famous, the court's decision in *UT* raises the specter that they might instead rise only to the level of niche fame; the general consuming public of the United States might not widely recognize those marks, especially if they are not fans of those particular sports.

Taking Action Against Alleged Infringers

What should a sport property or manufacturer do when it discovers a case of alleged trademark infringement? The property owner typically drafts a letter to the alleged infringer asking the person to cease and desist (i.e., stop) the alleged infringing activity. If the alleged infringer refuses to cooperate, the Lanham Act (as well as applicable state laws) entitles the trademark owner to bring suit for injunctive relief—a court order to stop the infringing activities before and during the trial. To be granted an injunction, the intellectual property owner has to demonstrate three elements to the court: (1) that the trademark owner will be irreparably harmed by the infringing activities, (2) that the trademark owner will be more harmed if the injunction is not granted than the defendant will be harmed if the injunction is granted, and (3) that the trademark owner can demonstrate a strong likelihood of winning the infringement case. After the injunction is received, the owner seeks a trial on the merits of the case to receive a financial remedy for the infringement.

Defenses to Trademark Infringement

When a trademark infringement claim is brought, the defendant may raise a number of defenses, including abandonment, fair use, that the trademark is or has become generic, or that the trademark is merely functional (the functionality test).

Abandonment

Unlike copyrights and patents, which expire, trademarks can last indefinitely, provided the holder continues to use the trademark in commerce. Under the Lanham Act, however, a trademark can be deemed abandoned when the trademark owner discontinues its use *and* does not intend to resume using the mark within a reasonable length of time.[45] Thus, when a sport property changes its name or logo but wishes to retain ownership of previous marks, it must take precautionary steps to prevent abandonment of these marks. Typically, these steps include maintaining the marks' registration at the appropriate renewal periods and periodically using the old marks in some manner. Sport marketers should note that marks can also be deemed to be abandoned as a result of excessive licensing, lack of supervision over other parties' licensed use of the marks, or both. Because trademarks are valuable, courts do require substantial proof of abandonment.[46] One interesting case, *Abdul-Jabbar v. General Motors Corp.*, raised the issue of abandonment of a birth name.[47] During the time leading up to the 1993 NCAA men's Final Four, General Motors ran an advertisement that used trivia regarding Kareem Abdul-Jabbar's UCLA and NCAA records. When Abdul-Jabbar had set the records, his name was Lew Alcindor. Besides citing the trivia question, Abdul-Jabbar alleged that the advertisement compared the car to him. General Motors responded that when he converted to Islam he abandoned the name Lew Alcindor and thus infringement did not occur. In finding for Abdul-Jabbar, the judge stated, "One's birth name is an integral part of one's identity . . . it is not "kept alive" through commercial use. . . . An individual's decision to use a name other than the birth name . . . does not therefore imply intent to set aside the birth name, or the identity associated with that name."[48]

Fair Use Defense

Trademark rights are not absolute, and the law allows the use of another's trademarks on or in connection with the sale of one's own goods or services as long as the use is not deceptive.[49] Thus, a fair use defense allows, for instance, a company such as Adidas to use the Nike trademark in its ads to compare the two products. The fair use defense has been successfully used by a company that sold refurbished discounted golf balls manufactured by another company.[50] The fair use defense has also been found applicable under the constitutional protections of commercial speech. For example, in a case involving the United States Olympic Committee, a court found that a publisher who produced a magazine titled *OLYMPICS USA* did not infringe on the USOC's rights to the word *Olympics*.[51] The court held that to restrict a publisher's use of the word *Olympics* would raise serious issues regarding the First Amendment protection afforded news media organizations.

Genericness

As discussed earlier, one cannot obtain trademark protection for generic terms, even through the acquisition of secondary meaning. Thus, an alleged infringer can argue that the trademark in question is generic. Because of this, leagues cannot claim to own terms such as *championships* or *the big game*. Moreover, a well-known trademark can become generic over time if it is not aggressively protected by the trademark holder. Well-known examples include aspirin, cellophane, and trampoline, all of which were at one time registered trademarks and have since fallen into the public domain. The possibility that a trademark will become generic points out the need for companies to protect and promote their trademarks aggressively.

Functionality

A final defense involves marks that do not describe or distinguish the product or service but are necessary for the product to exist. The functionality defense was unsuccessfully raised in the Dallas Cowboys Cheerleaders case discussed previously, whereby the defendant claimed that its depiction of an actress in a cheerleading uniform similar to those worn by the Dallas Cowboys

Cheerleaders was not trademark infringement because the uniform design was not a trademark but rather a functionality of performing. The court disagreed, holding that the uniform was not just a function of performing as a cheerleader. Thus, the fact that the item serves or performs a function does not mean that it may not be at the same time capable of indicating sponsorship or origin.

Additional Trademark Protection Issues

Legal issues for sport marketers continue to emerge from the use of the Internet for commerce, communication, public relations, and advertising. The advent of the Internet has led to a wild, wild, west of trademark issues, most notably cybersquatting, whereby individuals registered domain names solely for the purposes of trying to sell the name back to the rightful trademark owner. Both the courts and the U.S. legislature have addressed this earliest form of trademark infringement on the Internet. Numerous cases have held that use of another's trademark in a domain name can constitute trademark infringement in violation of the Lanham Act.[52] Before 1999 a trademark owner's sole remedy for the use of its trademark in a domain name was limited under the Lanham Act to infringement or dilution claims. But in 1999 Congress passed the Anticybersquatting Consumer Protection Act (ACPA).[53] Under the ACPA, a person is liable if that person "has a bad faith intent to profit from that mark" and registers, traffics in, or uses a domain name that "in the case of a mark that is distinctive at the time of registration of the domain name, is identical or confusingly similar to that mark" or "in the case of a famous mark that is famous at the time of registration of the domain name, is identical or confusingly similar to or dilutive of that mark."[54] Under the ACPA, several remedies are available, including forfeiture or cancellation of the domain name, transfer of the domain name, and recovery of monetary damages. Practitioners need to remain diligent in the registration of new team names and slogans that are used in domain names.

As we move toward a global economy in which more companies seek to do business abroad, more information is carried on the Internet, and more commerce is transacted through the Internet, owners of intellectual property must consider registering copyrights, trademarks, and patents in foreign countries. To provide better protection to trademark owners operating in international commerce, the Madrid Protocol went into effect in 2003. Under the Protocol, a U.S. trademark applicant is now able to file a single application with the USPTO to obtain protection in all protocol member countries. Over 60 countries are signatories to the protocol. Thus, U.S. trademark applicants no longer need to endure the costly and time-consuming process of filing separate registrations in each country in which they seek protection. After an application is filed in the United States, the USPTO forwards it to the International Register of the World Intellectual Property Organization (WIPO) for processing.

The sale of licensed products and the staging of sporting events in foreign countries have become increasingly important revenue streams for U.S.-based sport properties. Furthermore, tremendous growth is occurring in sport industries in China, Korea, and the nations of Europe, particularly for sports such as baseball, basketball, American football, and action sports. U.S.-based sport marketers need to be cognizant of the importance of ensuring that the trademarks that identify their products, services, and events are protected in these countries.

Copyright Law and Sport Marketing

In her excitement over the Aces' pending World Series victory, Jill B. Fan has written a clever song titled "The Aces Clear the Bases" that she intends to market. Using her entrepreneurial spirit, she also plans to record the World Series games, edit the clips herself, and sell copies of the video, called *The Road to the Title*, over the Internet.

An understanding of copyright law is also important for sport marketers. Copyrights, for instance, protect the music that is played during games and require sport marketers to seek approval through ASCAP, which protects musicians' copyrights of their works. Sport marketers who are responsible for creating advertising or promotional campaigns that use written works, music, pictures or graphic designs, or audiovisual works, including broadcasts of sporting events, need to be aware of copyright laws.

At the outset, an important point to understand is that, in the context of copyright law, a person cannot copyright a mere *idea*. This concept was illustrated in the case of *Hoopla Sports and Entertainment, Inc. v. Nike, Inc.*, in which the plaintiff unsuccessfully sued Nike for allegedly stealing its idea for a high school basketball all-star game.[55] Although the plaintiff alleged copyright infringement, the court, in granting Nike's motion to dismiss, held that the idea for the game was not copyrightable.

Copyright law is primarily governed by the Copyright Act of 1976, which protects original works of authorship appearing in any tangible medium of expression.[56] In addition, the Digital Millennium Copyright Act provides copyright laws regarding digital creations and the Internet.[57]

A copyright can be for something currently in existence or something to be developed later; but the work must be something that can be perceived, reproduced, or otherwise communicated. Works of authorship include the following:

- Literary works, such as books and stories
- Musical works, including any accompanying words
- Dramatic works, including any accompanying music
- Pantomimes and choreographic works
- Pictorial, graphic, and sculptural works
- Motion pictures and other audiovisual works
- Sound recordings
- Architectural works[58]

Because of the large number of advances in technology, these protected works are defined in broad terms. Copyright protection for an original work of authorship, however, does not extend to any idea, procedure, process, system, method of operation, concept, principle, or discovery, regardless of the form in which it is described, explained, or illustrated.[59]

The Copyright Act grants a copyright owner the right to do the following:

- Reproduce or distribute copies or sound recordings of the copyrighted work to the public by sale, rental, lease, or lending
- Prepare derivative works based on the copyrighted work
- Perform the copyrighted work publicly (literary, musical, dramatic, and choreographic works; pantomimes; motion pictures; and the like)
- Display the copyrighted work publicly (literary, musical, dramatic, and choreographic works; pantomimes; and pictorial, graphic, or sculptural works, including individual images of a motion picture or other audiovisual work)
- Perform the copyrighted work publicly by means of digital audio transmission (sound recordings)[60]

Under common law, copyright protection begins at the time that the work originates and is fixed in a tangible form. But registering a copyright with the U.S. Copyright Office, like registering a trademark, provides several benefits to the copyright owner in the event of its unauthorized use. For instance, registering a copyright allows the copyright owner to sue immediately for infringement (otherwise, if the copyright is infringed, the owner must first register the copyright). Also, if a copyright is not registered before alleged infringement, the amount of recoverable damages is limited. In the event that a person does not choose to register her work with the U.S. Copyright Office, she should at least be sure to keep excellent records of her work as she is creating it and place a copyright symbol, or write out the word *copyright*, along with the origination date and her name, on the work. Another good idea is to notarize the ideas expressed to prove that the date listed on the copyrighted work has been accurately reported.

The U.S. Copyright Office also accepts registration for online works. Again, the key factor in determining whether the online site is copyrightable is whether it possesses original authorship.[61] Copyright protection for works created on or after January 1, 1978, exists for a term consisting of the life of the author and 70 years after the author's death, after which time the work of authorship falls into the public domain.[62] If the work was created by more than one person, the protection endures for the term consisting of the life of the last surviving author and another 70 years after the last surviving author's death. An employer holds the copyright on works created for an employer. For works made for an employer, the duration of the employer's copyright protection is 75 years from the time of publication or 100 years from the time of creation, whichever expires first.[63]

Copyright Infringement

Copyright infringement occurs when someone makes an unauthorized use of a copyrighted work. Courts consider four factors when determining whether copyright infringement has occurred:

- The purpose of the use, including whether such use is of a commercial nature or is for nonprofit educational purposes

- The nature (character) of the copyrighted work

- The amount and substantiality of the portion used in relation to the copyrighted work as a whole

- The effect of the use on the potential market for, or value of, the copyrighted work[64]

Defenses to Copyright Infringement

In a copyright infringement case, a defendant may challenge the authenticity of the copyright. But as is more commonly the case, a defendant may claim the defense of the fair use doctrine, which was originally created by the courts as a

Although the actual broadcast of the Super Bowl is protected by copyright law, news organizations that photograph the game own the copyright to their photographs.

means of ensuring that creativity was not stifled through rigid enforcement of copyright law. The fair use doctrine, as first enunciated by the courts, has since been incorporated into the Copyright Act.[65] As such, it allows for the fair use of a copyrighted work when the use is "for purposes such as criticism, comment, news reporting, teaching (including multiple copies for classroom use), scholarship, or research."[66] The courts use the four factors stated earlier to determine whether the use made of the work falls within the fair use defense.

In a leading sport-related case, film clips of Muhammad Ali fights appeared in the documentary *When We Were Kings* despite an attempted preliminary injunction by the copyright owner of the clips to bar their use.[67] The court found that the defendant was likely to succeed on the fair use defense, thus allowing the film clips (between 9 and 14 clips, amounting to a total duration of 41 seconds to 2 minutes) to be used.[68] The key factors appeared to be that the work was a documentary and, although clearly commercial, was a combination of comment, criticism, scholarship, and research. In addition, public interest favored the production of Ali's biography, the use was quantitatively small, the clips were not the focus of the work, and use of the clips would have little or no effect on the market for the plaintiff's copyrighted fights.[69]

Copyrights and Sporting Events

You hear it during every game and no doubt know it by heart: "This telecast is a copyright of the National Football League. Any rebroadcast, retransmission or any other use or description or accounts of this telecast without the express written consent of the National Football League is prohibited." But what does it really mean?

The question of whether sport events are copyrightable has yet to be fully answered. Currently, only broadcast or cable transmissions of sport events are copyrightable.[70] In 1976 Congress amended the Copyright Act expressly to ensure that simultaneously recorded broadcasts of live performances and sport events would be protected by copyright law.[71] Congress found authorship in the creative labor of the camera operators, director, and producer. On the other hand, it would appear that the actual sporting events are not copyrightable because no authorship exists. In an event-related case, *Prod. Contractors, Inc. v.*

WGN Continental Broad. Co., the District Court for the Northern District of Illinois determined that a Christmas parade was not a work of authorship entitled to copyright protection.[72]

As technology has progressed, the issue of who owns what intellectual property has expanded. A seminal case in determining ownership of statistics and scores of games while in progress arose in 1996 when the NBA sued Motorola and STATS, Inc. for copyright infringement.[73] Motorola's SportsTrax pager system displayed the information on NBA games in progress including the running play by play, the team in possession of the ball, whether the team was in the free-throw bonus, the quarter of the game, and the time remaining. The information was updated every two to three minutes, and more frequent updates were made near the end of the first half and the end of the game. A lag of approximately two to three minutes occurred between events in the game and the appearance of the information on the pager screen. SportsTrax's operation relied on a data feed supplied by STATS reporters, who watched games on television or listened to them on the radio. Using personal computers, the reporters keyed in changes in the score and other information such as successful and missed shots, fouls, and clock updates. The information was then relayed by modem to STATS' host computer, which compiled, analyzed, and formatted the data for retransmission. The information was then sent to various FM radio networks that in turn emitted a signal received by the individual SportsTrax pagers. STATS also provided slightly more comprehensive and detailed real-time game information on its website. There, game scores were updated at 15-second to 1-minute intervals, and player and team statistics were updated each minute.

In deciding whether the NBA owned the statistics and scores of its games while they were in progress, the court determined that Congress intended to protect the league's interest only in the recorded broadcasts of games, not in the real-time data (scores, key plays, and so on) acquired by Motorola's employees and then broadcast on Motorola pagers. Thus, the court found that Motorola and STATS did not unlawfully misappropriate NBA's property by transmitting near-real-time NBA game scores and statistics taken from television and radio broadcasts of games in progress.

Although the athletics competition itself may not be copyrightable, event organizers can take steps to protect their proprietary interest in an event.[74] For instance, ESPN used a trademark symbol for the name *Extreme Games* and for the *X* symbol in securing trademark protection. A copyright notice was also affixed on all of ESPN's X Games promotional materials. Although these steps cannot protect ESPN and other event organizers from competitors who hold an event similar to the X Games (witness the subsequent emergence of the Gravity Games, Dew Tour, and StreetGames), it does protect ESPN from another's use of the name *Extreme Games* and the *X* symbol.[75] Choosing a distinctive trademark, establishing long-term contracts with participants, and prohibiting sponsors from creating or sponsoring similar competitive events can further protect event ideas.[76]

Technological advancements in broadcasting over the Internet continue to raise challenging intellectual property issues for sport events and properties, many of which have involved the application of copyright law. In the early days of these emerging technologies, the distribution of near-real-time scores to consumers with special devices (such as pagers) was upheld by the court under First Amendment principles. The most notable sport case was *NBA v. Motorola* (cited earlier), which held that although the NBA owned the copyright in the broadcast itself, it did not have ownership of the facts of the game after they were in the public domain. Of particular significance in this case was the fact that the defendant Motorola did all the work to obtain and transmit the game scores. This case was distinguished by a subsequent sport case, *Morris Communication Corp v. PGA Tour, Inc.*, in which a U.S. Circuit Court of Appeals found that the PGA Tour was justified in denying Morris Communication, a Georgia publisher of print and electronic newspapers, the right to sell real-time tournament data that had been collected and produced by the PGA Tour through a system called ShotLink.[77] Although the case was brought and decided strictly on antitrust grounds (and not a copyright claim), the court's decision was swayed by its reasoning that compiling scores in golf is more difficult than in other sports because of the simultaneous action of numerous players, and that the PGA Tour had spent millions of dollars building the only system that does it.

Patents

Jill B. Fan is also exploring, through an overseas manufacturer, the production of what she believes is a novel contraption—a plastic baseball that, with the push of a button, releases a banner that says "World Series Champs" and plays "Take Me Out to the Ballgame." (Jill has, to her credit, researched and determined that the copyright to this song has expired.) She has been advised to procure a patent on this product, which she intends to sell on the Internet. Again, she can't wait to cash in.

Sport marketers will typically have the least involvement with the area of patent law. For those involved in the manufacturer's side of the sport industry, however, an understanding of patent law is especially important. Companies invest tremendous amounts of money in developing new technologies for everything from athletics shoes and playing products (witness the Spalding Infusion micropump technology discussed earlier) to novel scoring apparatuses and technological enhancements such as the yellow first-down line that is commonly used in football telecasts. The ability of inventors to profit from their ingenuity is grounded in the protections under patent law.

A patent may be granted to anyone who invents or discovers any new and useful process, machine, manufacture, or composition of matter, or any new and useful improvement.[78] A patent cannot be granted for a mere idea; it can be granted only for the actual invention or a complete description of it. Like a copyright, a patent has a limited duration. Currently, its duration is 20 years from the date on which the application was filed with the U.S. Patent and Trademark Office.[79] During those 20 years, a patent owner must not violate antitrust laws by virtue of having a patent, such as by unreasonably limiting the licensing of the patent or by using the patent to fix prices or restrain trade. After the 20 years expire, anyone may make, use, sell, or import the invention without the permission of the patent owner.

New methods or processes for playing sport have also been deemed patentable. For example, the Arena Football League (AFL) and its parent company, Gridiron Enterprises, Inc., have been issued patents in the United States and Mexico for Arena Football's game system and method of play.[80] Debate, primarily academic in nature, has also arisen as to whether athletes can patent their moves (as processes).[81] For instance, could Jim Fosbury, inventor of the Fosbury flop technique, have secured a patent on his revolutionary way of clearing the high bar (bended, back first), thus preventing his competitors from using the technique? Could U.S. Olympian Evan Lysacek create and subsequently patent a revolutionary figure-skating jump that would stifle his competitors? Although some have argued persuasively that such athletic moves fall squarely within the definitions of what is patentable, courts and commentators have suggested that, from a practical standpoint, the enforcement of such patent rights, as well as the chilling effect it would have on competition, makes this a moot point. But perhaps it's only a matter of time.

In summary, patent law is the most complex of the three areas of intellectual property. As a result, this area is the one in which people or organizations will most likely need legal guidance for the registration process and protection.

Sport Marketing Communications Issues

The process of communicating marketing messages to sport consumers raises a number of legal issues for marketers of sport organizations, teams, and product manufacturers. Although relatively few cases involving the sport industry have been litigated, sport marketers need to be careful not to run afoul of federal laws against false advertising and deceptive consumer practices, as well as the state laws (adopted by all 50 states) enacted for the protection of consumers and businesses from unfair, false, or deceptive advertising and consumer practices.

Commercial communications typically implicate the First Amendment guarantee of free speech because commercial speech is entitled to some level of constitutional protection from governmental restraints. A balancing act is required between the sport organization's constitutional right to engage in commercial speech and the government's interest in protecting consumers from fraudulent or deceptive business practices. Commercial speech, of which advertising is the most common form, has been defined as speech that does not do more than propose a commercial transaction. Furthermore, nonsport cases have held that speech does not lose its

First Amendment protection "because money is spent to project it."[82] The seminal 1980 Supreme Court case, *Central Hudson Gas & Electric Corp. v. New York Public Service Commission*, provided a four-factor test to determine whether a state's (government's) restrictions on commercial speech are constitutional: (1) the commercial speech must concern a lawful activity and not be misleading, (2) the state must have a substantial interest in the restriction of the speech, (3) the regulation must directly advance the state's interest, and (4) the regulation must be no more extensive than necessary to meet the state's interest.[83] Put another way, the governmental purpose or objective of the rule or regulation that prohibits the speech must be sufficiently important to allow a governmental entity to restrict a person's First Amendment rights, and the restrictions must be directly connected to achieving the government's stated objectives.

One notable sport case involved an effort by the Kentucky Racing Commission (a governmental entity) to enforce rules prohibiting jockeys from wearing advertising (commercial speech) on their uniforms during a race, in particular the 2003 Kentucky Derby.[84] As the 2004 Kentucky Derby approached, a number of jockeys filed a lawsuit to prevent enforcement of the commission's advertising ban. The commission argued that the rule was in place to protect the integrity of horse racing; the restriction on sponsor logos would ensure an unobstructed view of the jockey if misconduct was alleged and would foster confidence in the betting public by preventing collusion among jockeys sponsored by the same advertiser. The court found that although the commission's objectives were laudable, the ban on commercial speech was not directly connected to achieving the commission's objectives.

Occasionally, the issue of whether commercial speech is present it is not clear. The *Nike, Inc. v. Kasky* case, decided in 2002, provides a key lesson for the public relations department in any sport organization.[85] To determine whether speech is commercial or noncommercial, the court will look at three elements: the speaker, the intended audience, and the content of the message. The Nike case revolved around whether statements made by Nike as part of a public relations campaign rose to the level of commercial speech. Nike had sent written statements to newspapers and letters to university presidents and athletics directors defending itself against allegations of violating human rights in its treatment of workers in Asian countries. The plaintiff, Marc Kasky, sued Nike on behalf of the public under California business laws alleging that Nike's statements were false and misleading. The court had to determine whether Nike's statements, made as part of a public relations campaign, were commercial or noncommercial speech. The court held that Nike's allegedly false and misleading statements were properly characterized as commercial speech. The distinction is important in the context of sport marketers because most states' statutes dealing with deceptive trade practices such as false advertising apply only to commercial speech. Sport organizations must therefore be cognizant that even in distributing communications by press releases and letters to stakeholders such as season-ticket holders and the media, courts are likely to deem these communications to be a form of commercial speech and thus susceptible to claims of deceptive business practices.

Ambush Marketing

One of the largest sources of revenue for sport properties comes from the sale of "official sponsor" rights. Corporations often invest significant amounts of money to secure the rights, typically exclusive within a product or service category, to use the sport property's trademarks in their advertising and promotional campaigns as a means of associating with the sport property's positive goodwill. But marketers working on the property side of the sport industry face challenges from a method of marketing called ambush marketing. Ambush marketing occurs when a company capitalizes on the goodwill of a sport event by using a variety of advertising

The clever advertising campaign conducted by online gambling company Paddy Power during the 2012 London Olympic Games illustrates the many challenges of trying to stop the practice of ambush marketing.

and promotional tactics to *imply* an official association with that sport event. The ambusher's tactics weaken a competitor's official association with the event acquired through the payment of sponsorship monies.[86]

Over the past decade, perceptions of and perspectives on ambush marketing have evolved as a result of dialogue among both scholars and practitioners. From the earliest definitions of ambush marketing as a pejorative term, which described it as an "immoral" practice, has emerged not only an acknowledgment of the considerable vagueness that surrounds the concept but also a conceptual framework of ambush marketing that more accurately reflects the balancing of sponsors' contractual rights against the rights of nonsponsors to maintain a market presence during an event through legal and competitive business activities.[87] Hence, although at one extreme end of the ambush marketing conceptual debate is what the Olympics Movement publicly refers to as "parasite marketing,"[88] at the other end are much more neutral terms such as "parallel marketing."[89] Historically, the term *ambush marketing* has been defined from the perspective of the sport property. The review of the academic literature illustrates the challenges in conceptualizing ambush marketing, the term that was coined during the 1984 Los Angeles Olympic Games to describe the marketing activities of nonsponsors such as Kodak, which used a variety of tactics to "ambush" official sponsor Fuji.[90] The earliest definitions of ambush marketing were pejorative, implying unethical business conduct laden with evil intent (thus supporting the perspective of event organizers and official sponsors). For instance, the term was initially defined as "a company's intentional efforts to weaken—or ambush—its competitor's "official sponsorship." It does this by engaging in promotions and advertising that trade off the event or property's goodwill and reputation, and that seek to confuse the buying public as to which companies really hold official sponsorship rights."[91]

Townley, Harrington, and Couchman later stressed the concept of unauthorized association in defining ambush marketing, stating that the practice "consists in the sports context of the unauthorised association by businesses of their names, brands, products or services with a sports event or competition through any one of a wide range of marketing activities; unauthorised in the sense that the controller of the commercial rights in such events, usually the relevant governing body, has neither sanctioned nor licensed the association, either itself or through commercial agents."[92]

In this context, ambush marketing has been viewed as not only those activities aimed specifically at undermining a competitor's official sponsorship of an event but also those activities that seek to associate a nonsponsor with the sporting event itself. Additional literature on ambush marketing has suggested that, in contrast to the pejorative definition, ambush marketing can be more broadly defined to describe "a whole variety of wholly legitimate and morally correct methods of intruding upon public consciousness surrounding an event."[93] Although the practice of ambush marketing has been widely debated, the answer as to whether it is an "immoral or imaginative practice . . . may well lie in the eye of the beholder."[94] For instance, event organizers and their official sponsors typically denounce as ambush marketing any activity by a nonsponsor that wittingly or unwittingly intrudes on the property's or official sponsors' rights, thus potentially detracting from the sponsor's exclusive association with the sport property. Using this definition, for instance, even a company that purchases advertising within the telecast of a sports event could be construed by the event organizer and official sponsor as an ambush marketer regardless of that company's business motives, ethical perspective, or legal rights. On the other hand, such activity engaged in by nonsponsors can also be perceived and defended as nothing more than a part of the normal "cut and thrust" of business activity based on a strong economic justification.[95] Further illustrating the ambiguities surrounding the concept of ambush marketing, researchers have argued that it is unrealistic to expect nonsponsors to make decisions regarding sponsorship differently than they would with regard to other promotional techniques designed to compete in the marketplace.[96] Perspectives on and attitudes toward the practice of ambush marketing are largely influenced by the marketer's role in the sponsorship equation. Sport properties and official sponsors will typically hold a viewpoint far different from that of nonsponsors. Although unilaterally labeling ambush marketing as illegal, immoral, or unethical is improper, we should recognize that sport properties may have legitimate concerns if they are unable to prevent unfettered ambush marketing.

Companies may engage in ambush marketing for a variety of reasons. First, the company may view the official sponsorship rights as being too expensive to afford. Second, the company may be excluded from becoming an official sponsor because of a sport organization's restrictions on the number of sponsors or specific product or service categories. Third, the company may be blocked from becoming an official sponsor because of a sport organization's preexisting exclusive deal with a competing company. Event organizers and official sponsors typically consider such tactics unethical, without acknowledging that they are not illegal. The following ambush marketing tactics, provided in the context of marathon running, are by no means exhaustive, but they serve to illuminate the wide range of tactics typically used in combination by ambush marketers.[97]

• **Use of generic phrases**. Although event organizers have become increasingly vigilant in protecting their intellectual property through the registration of marks and symbols associated with their events, ambush marketers often create generic phrases that refer to the event. For example, although the New York Road Runners Club owns the phrase "New York City Marathon" and other phrases related to the event, ambush marketers can create generic phrases such as "The Big Race" or "The Race Through the Boroughs," which, when accompanied by relevant artwork (such as a drawing of the New York City skyline or a map of the five boroughs), can create an implied association between the ambush marketer and the event.

• **Purchase of advertising time within the event broadcast**. The purchase of advertising within a sporting event telecast is one of the most common and popular tactics of ambush marketing. Because the New York Road Runners organization sells its broadcast rights to a third-party broadcaster, it relinquishes a certain measure of control over the advertisers. Although event organizers typically negotiate contractual language that provides their official sponsors with the right of first refusal to purchase advertising within the event telecast, they are rarely in a bar-

gaining position to prohibit their broadcast rights holders from selling advertising to nonsponsors or even competitors of official sponsors. Hence, nonsponsors can purchase advertising within the event telecast that even features creative elements tied to a running theme.

• **Presence in and around the event venue**. In the early days of ambush marketing, companies employed blimps and airplanes with trailing banners to ambush a major sporting event. Although event organizers have closed this ambush opportunity by working closely with the Federal Aviation Administration and with host cities to enact air traffic restrictions during such events, clever ambush marketers have continued to use other tactics for on-site presence, including strategically placed billboards, tents and inflatables in high-traffic locations, distribution of literature and samples to consumers attending the event, and temporary spray painting of corporate logos along the course route. Ambush marketers of marathon events have even resorted to paying college students to distribute temporary forehead tattoos, as Reebok did at the 2003 Boston Marathon as a means of ambushing Adidas.[98]

• **Conducting consumer promotions**. Such promotions typically are offered at retail locations and are supported by point-of-sale displays that feature visuals themed to the particular sporting event and words that refer generically to the sporting event. For instance, a company intent on associating itself with the New York City Marathon might, in the weeks leading up to the marathon, conduct an in-store running-themed promotion offering consumers discounts on the purchase of running shoes in exchange for proofs of purchase. Or, a company could conduct a sweepstakes that offers winners the chance to meet the marathon champions (assuming that the ambush marketing company could arrange this). Although purposely avoiding the use of any registered trademarks, such promotions are intended to lure consumers through an implied association with the marathon.

• **Congratulatory messages**. Companies often create advertisements offering congratulations to winning teams or athletes. For instance, the day after the New York City Marathon, a nonsponsor could run an advertisement in the local newspaper congratulating the winners by name. Such a tactic is typically legal under the First Amendment, particularly as long as the advertiser refrains from using the ad to convey explicit selling messages or sales offers.[99]

The more popular and global the event is, the more often ambush marketing arises. Historically, one of the most fertile grounds has been the Olympic Games. Generally, the United States Olympic Committee (USOC), when confronted with alleged ambush marketing activity, has been successful in negotiating business settlements with infringers who, more often than not, are simply unaware that their activities are in violation of the USOC's broad trademark rights afforded through the Ted Stevens Olympic and Amateur Sports Act of 1998 (OASA).[100]

But when alleged ambush marketers are not amenable to settlement, the USOC has been vigilant in resorting to the courts. For example, a federal judge granted the USOC's request for a permanent injunction preventing a camp organizer from producing a children's summer camp called Camp Olympik.[101] The USOC also threatened to sue to halt an event called the Redneck Olympics, claiming trademark infringement, unfair competition, and trademark dilution.[102]

Although ambush marketing is difficult to eradicate, sport properties can limit its occurrence in several ways. For instance, to prevent nonsponsors from purchasing advertising within the broadcast of an event, a sport property typically negotiates a clause in its agreement that requires its broadcast rights holders to provide official sponsors the right of first refusal to purchase advertising within the broadcasts, as well as a clause requiring the rights holders to monitor potential trademark infringements by nonsponsors. Sport properties can also negotiate with host cities to ban marketing activity that competes directly with official sponsors. For instance, the NFL requires the host city to create a "clean zone" during its annual Super Bowl week, imposing a ban on nonsponsor advertising and promotional activities in the area surrounding the facility that hosts the event.

A sport property seeking to protect itself against ambush marketers must be proactive. The property should consider using advertising to explain potential negative effects of ambush marketing to consumers and the media. When faced with ambush marketing activity, the property might also consider launching a public relations campaign accusing the ambusher of unfair business tactics (typically called a name-and-shame campaign). Sport properties remain reticent, however, to bring lawsuits involving ambush marketing, in part for fear of an adverse court decision. As a result, settled case law on the specific issue of ambush marketing is limited. In the only decided North American case specifically addressing ambush marketing, a Canadian court upheld Pepsi-Cola Canada's ambush marketing activities, much to the chagrin of the NHL.[103]

> ### ACTIVITY 14.1 Ambush Marketing
> In this WSG activity, you're the director of marketing for a company that spent over six figures to make its product an official sponsor. However, through ambush marketing, your competitors are getting their products promoted as well.

Right of Publicity and Invasion of Privacy

Jill B. Fan has decided that, during the World Series games, she is going to stand outside the stadium and sell a poster bearing illustrations of a few Aces players. She has asked a friend of hers in art school to provide renderings of the players. The poster is going to read "Good Luck Aces Stars." She has secured a local hardware store to underwrite the printing costs of the posters in exchange for displaying the store logo on the posters.

Those employed as marketers for sport teams, sporting goods manufacturers, or individual athletes need to be aware of the intersection of right of publicity and invasion of privacy. Although these claims fall within the area of tort law rather than intellectual property law, these areas at the intersection of sport marketing and the law are extremely important.

The right of publicity was originally intertwined with invasion of privacy, but courts have since separated the right to be let alone from the commercial right to control the use of one's likeness or identity.[104] Invasion of privacy arises out of the common law of torts or state statutes. Among other things, the right of privacy protects against intrusion on a person's seclusion, the misappropriation of a person's name or likeness, unreasonable publicity, and placing a person in a false light. One of the landmark sport-related cases dealing with invasion of privacy was *Spahn v. Julian Messner, Inc.*, in which Hall of Fame pitcher Warren Spahn sued the publishers of an unauthorized fictional biography, *The Warren Spahn Story.*[105] The book, the whole tenor of which projected a false intimacy with Spahn, was fraught with inaccuracies and fabricated events dealing with Spahn's marriage, family life, and relationship with his father, among other things. Although the book was laudatory of Spahn, the court held that "the offending characteristics of the book comprehend a nonfactual novelization of plaintiff's alleged life story and an unauthorized intrusion into the private realms of the baseball pitcher's life—all to Spahn's humiliation and mental anguish."[106]

The right of publicity, on the other hand, prevents the unauthorized commercial use of a person's name, likeness, or other recognizable aspects of his or her persona. It gives people the exclusive right to license the use of their identity for commercial purposes. More than half of all jurisdictions in the United States recognize the right of publicity, although nine states, including New York and Illinois, have rejected the right of publicity after death. In a legal action arising from the misappropriation of a person's name or likeness for a product, an advertisement, or any other commercial use, a plaintiff may choose to sue under invasion of privacy, the right of publicity, or both.

Cases often arise on both of these legal theories in the sport setting when a sport celebrity attempts to stop the misappropriation of his or her name and likeness. Athletes have discovered the commercial value in their names and likenesses, and thus enforcing the right of publicity is crucial in this age of the branding of athletes. The first such case in sport, *Haelan Laboratories v. Topps Chewing Gum*, involved a dispute over the right to market trading cards of professional baseball players.[107] In that case, the court established a property right in a person's identity, naming it the right of publicity.[108] The court recognized the right of the players to grant a license (or exclusive privilege) to merchandisers to use their likenesses for the manufacture and sale of the cards. This case opened the door for athletes and celebrities to enforce a right of publicity against those misappropriating their names and like-

nesses. In a similar case, *Uhlaender v. Henricksen*, a court enjoined the maker of a table game from using MLB players' names without their consent because the players had a proprietary interest in their names, likenesses, and accomplishments.[109]

Because of the strength of the First Amendment protection of free speech or expression, permission is not needed to use a celebrity's name or likeness in a book, newspaper, magazine, television news show or documentary, or other news media outlet. Courts have also upheld the use of the name or likeness of an athlete to advertise or promote media publications in which the athlete or entertainer once appeared. In both *Namath v. Sports Illustrated*[110] and *Montana v. San Jose Mercury News, Inc.*,[111] courts allowed media entities to use the plaintiffs' photos from prior editions of their publications in advertisements to sell their publications. The courts held that the photographs represented newsworthy events and that a newspaper had a constitutional right to promote itself by reproducing its news stories. These cases differ from the previously discussed *Abdul-Jabbar v. General Motors*, in which Alcindor's name and likeness were misappropriated in an advertisement for the Olds 88 automobile. Although Alcindor's record is in fact newsworthy, its use was to advertise an Oldsmobile and thus was not protected by the First Amendment.[112]

The First Amendment may also play a role in the appropriation of a person's name or likeness in parodies. In a lead case on this issue, *Cardtoons, L.C. v. Major League Baseball Players Association*, the Court of Appeals for the 10th Circuit granted full protection to the parody cards created by the plaintiff based on its First Amendment rights.[113] The court determined that the parody cards provided social commentary on public figures, MLB players, who were involved in a significant commercial enterprise, Major League Baseball. The court stated that the cards were no less protected because they provided humorous rather than serious commentary. Thus, the plaintiff's First Amendment right to create the parody trading cards outweighed the MLB Players Association's right of publicity in their members' names and likenesses.[114]

Courts have also recognized a right of publicity and trademark protection for nicknames. In *Hirsch v. S.C. Johnson & Son, Inc.*, the plaintiff, Elroy "Crazylegs" Hirsch, alleged that the nickname belonged to him, that it had commercial

Companies often run advertisements congratulating the achievements of players and teams. Typically, the players and teams saluted in these one-time advertisements appreciate the positive publicity. Occasionally, however, the subject of the congratulatory message can take offense, believing that the use of his or her likeness stretches beyond the bounds of the First Amendment and is instead an unauthorized commercial use.

Such was the case for NBA legend Michael Jordan. To celebrate Jordan's induction into the Basketball Hall of Fame in September 2009, *Sports Illustrated* published a commemorative issue to acknowledge Jordan's contribution to the game. One of the advertisers that appeared in the commemorative issue was Jewel–Osco Food Stores, which operates about 175 grocery stores in the greater Chicago area. Jewel–Osco's advertisement featured a pair of basketball shoes spotlighted on the hardwood floor of a basketball court. The number 23 (Jordan's longtime uniform number) appeared on the tongue of each shoe, and the following message was positioned above the photo of the shoes:

> A Shoe In! After six NBA championships, scores of rewritten record books and numerous buzzer beaters, Michael Jordan's elevation in the Basketball Hall of Fame was never in doubt! Jewel–Osco salutes #23 on his many accomplishments as we honor a fellow Chicagoan who was "just around the corner" for so many years.

Beneath this message was Jewel–Osco's trademark logo with the slogan "Good things are just around the corner."

Jordan sued the grocery store for using his image and likeness in the advertisement without his permission, claiming a violation of his right of publicity (*Jordan v. Jewel Food Stores, Inc.*, 2012 WL 512584 at 1 [N.D. Ill. Feb. 15, 2012]). A district court judge in Illinois was faced with deciding whether Jewel Food made commercial use of Jordan's identity for a profit without his permission. These types of claims often turn on whether the advertiser is engaged in commercial versus noncommercial speech. In simplest terms, if Jewel–Osco's advertisement was deemed not commercial in nature, then the company would not be liable. The factors weighed by the court involved whether the speech was an advertisement, whether the speech referred to a specific product or service, and whether the speech had an economic or for-profit motivation.

Ultimately, the judge concluded that Jewel–Osco's advertisement was noncommercial speech entitled to full First Amendment protection. The judge found that the ad's focal message recounted Jordan's accomplishments and congratulated him on his career and induction into the Hall of Fame. The judge pointed out that the shoes, the number 23, and the hardwood floor evoke Jordan and the sport and team for which he enjoyed his success. The judge further held that the advertisement did not propose any kind of commercial message, because readers would be at a loss to explain what they have been invited to buy. The judge reasoned that the advertisement was a "tribute by an established Chicago business to Chicago's most accomplished athlete" (p. 7). Finally, the judge ruled that Jewel–Osco had no profit motive to exploit the Jordan brand commercially because Jewel–Osco was not compensated for having created the ad.

The court's decision raises several questions. First instance, does Jewel–Osco not stand to benefit commercially in the eyes of the public by associating itself with one of the most valuable sport brands in the world? Is it not promoting its own brand in the process of displaying an iconic visual of Jordan? After all, it displayed its "Good things are just around the corner" slogan and trademark logo right beneath its statement that Jordan was "just around the corner for so many years." Does Jewel–Osco not stand to enhance its reputation by associating itself with Jordan's goodwill and fame? Indeed, it would have been interesting to see whether a jury would have thought that Jewel–Osco's advertisement misled the public into thinking that Jewel–Osco and Jordan were associated in some way. But as it stands, this decision reinforces the First Amendment protections that are typically afforded to congratulatory advertisements.

value, and that knowing this the defendants marketed a shaving gel for women called Crazylegs.[115] In an action against S.C. Johnson & Son, Inc., Hirsch sought a remedy under two legal theories. Hirsch argued that the defendant violated his right to privacy by misappropriating his name and likeness for commercial use and infringed on his trademark rights to the nickname "*Crazylegs.*" The court determined that a celebrity's nickname had value and that Johnson could not use the name "*Crazylegs*" without permission from or payment to Hirsch for its use. The court found that all that is required to protect a nickname is that the nickname clearly identifies the wronged person.[116]

Debate continues as to where to draw the lines between athletes' right of publicity and First Amendment freedoms.[117] One of the seminal sport cases involved Tiger Woods. In *ETW Corp. v. Jireh Publishing,* noted sport artist Rick Rush created and distributed prints titled *The Masters of Augusta* that prominently featured Woods.[118] Notwithstanding the fact that Rush profited by selling lithographs of his artwork, the U.S. Court of Appeals held in favor of the artist, ruling that such creative works of art are protected under the First Amendment and thus trump an athlete's right of publicity. Interestingly, the court reasoned, among other things, that Woods was earning more than enough money from his tournament winnings and other commercial endorsement deals. Subsequent cases, such as the Missouri court decision upholding a $15 million judgment for former NHL player Tony Twist for the unauthorized use of his name and likeness in a comic book series and the athletes' cases against EA Sports (see "Emerging Issues" later in this chapter) have served only to blur the legal lines between the right of publicity and the First Amendment.[119]

Legal debate has also been waged over who owns player statistics and the corresponding player names in the context of online fantasy games.[120] In 2006 a federal court held that although the Major League Baseball Players Association (MLBPA) and its players had a valid claim under right of publicity law, the protections afforded the dissemination of public information under the First Amendment outweighed the players' right of publicity.[121] This decision spurred a similar lawsuit in which CBS Interactive claimed it should not have to pay licensing fees to the NFLPA and Players Inc. in exchange for operating its fantasy football games.[122] Because of these decisions, companies selling online fantasy sport leagues are free to do so without obtaining licenses from the appropriate sport leagues. Many online fantasy game providers, however, continue to secure league licenses because of the "official" status, authenticity, and incremental marketing benefits that the respective league can provide as a point of differentiation from nonlicensed online fantasy games.

Contractual Issues Involving Consumers

Given the increasing levels of financial commitment involving tickets to sporting events, both sport organizations and fans today often resort to the courts. Most of these cases are decided using contract law. For instance, the Washington Redskins and New England Patriots are among professional sport teams that have sued season-ticket holders who were in default on their payments.[123] The practice of teams' suing their own season-ticket holders has been criticized because it is unclear whether the teams have sustained any damages because of the season-ticket holders' breach of contract. A party to a contract has a general duty to mitigate damages. Given that both of these teams have lengthy waiting lists for season tickets, it would appear obvious that they could easily resell the season-ticket packages. The money received from the resale of the tickets would reduce the amount of damages owed from the defaulting consumers.

But both the Redskins' and Patriots' season-ticket agreements included a liquidated damages clause arguably giving the teams a right to payment for every year of the multiyear agreement regardless of whether or when they resold the tickets. The liquidated damages clause in the Patriots' personal seat license (PSL) agreement was upheld by a Massachusetts court in the 2008 case of *NPS, LLC. v. Minihane*,[124] although the court struck down an accelerated payment provision as "grossly disproportionate to a reasonable estimate of actual damages made at the time of contract formation."[125] Although teams reserve the right to include such liquidated damages clauses in their agreements, and the law supports the right to enter into contracts, teams should be careful of the negative publicity that arises in the process of suing season-ticket holders.

Ticket holders have also sued teams for a variety of reasons. For instance, season-ticket holders sued the New York Giants and New York Jets, claiming that their PSL agreements were illegal restraints of trade in violation of antitrust laws and a violation of the New Jersey Consumer Fraud Act.[126] The suit alleged that 45,000 season-ticket holders were forced to purchase PSLs for a one-time payment of between $1,000 and $25,000 to renew or purchase season tickets in the new stadium.[127] This class-action implied right to purchase tickets without paying for the PSL ultimately failed.

Sport marketers also need to be careful in how they package and sell season tickets. For instance, in 2012 a group of University of Pittsburgh basketball season-ticket holders filed a class action lawsuit against the university seeking to overturn the university's new season-ticket plan for the men's basketball team.[128] The plaintiffs alleged that Pitt's new ticket plan was a breach of an expressed guarantee that Pitt had made with its season-ticket holders. Before the opening of the Petersen Events Center in 2002, Pitt created and promoted a season-ticket plan that promised in writing that season-ticket holders would be able to keep their same seats every year if they maintained or increased their contributions to the Department of Athletics' fund-raising program Team Pittsburgh (currently called the Panther Club). Pitt subsequently announced a new plan that reassigned nonclub season-ticket seats every year based on a number of factors, including the size of contributions to the Department of Athletics' new fund-raising drive. The lawsuit alleged that Pitt was in breach of contract and had violated consumer protection laws. The class-action lawsuit was eventually settled, and the affected season-ticket holders were allowed to retain their seats for the next five seasons if they met specified donor levels.[129] Similarly, in 2012 a class-action lawsuit was brought against Comcast-Spectacor, owner of the Philadelphia Flyers, alleging that the team had excluded the 2012 Winter Classic regular-season game against the New York Rangers from the season-ticket package only after season-ticket holders had prepaid for each of the 44 preseason and regular-season games for the Flyers' 2011–2012 season.[130] Comcast-Spectacor then offered to resell the Winter Classic tickets back to the season-ticket holders but only if they also paid for tickets to two unrelated games—an exhibition featuring Flyers and Rangers alumni and a minor league hockey game. The lawsuit claimed that Comcast-Spectator also charged season-ticket holders, who already paid a $10 processing fee for the original season tickets, excessive and unearned processing charges for all three tickets. Although these lawsuits were eventually dismissed or settled, they illustrate the types of issues that sport marketers need to be cognizant of in their relationships with customers in seeking to avoid not only unnecessary litigation costs but also the negative publicity that results from such customer relations practices.

Promotion Law Issues

Sweepstakes and contests are popular tactics for sport organizations and corporations to engage consumers and generate brand awareness and sales. If handled improperly, however, they can have expensive and embarrassing consequences, including negative publicity and legal liability. Hence, sport marketers need to understand the distinction between sweepstakes, contests, and lotteries.

Lotteries are promotions in which the elements of prize, chance, and consideration are present. Technically, lotteries also include raffle promotions in which the consumer pays for a raffle ticket (although in practice local raffle promotions are common and rarely investigated by authorities). As a rule, only states themselves have the legal right to conduct lotteries. By eliminating any one element (i.e., the prize, the chance, or the consideration), an organization can legally sponsor a promotional game without violating state lottery laws.[131]

Sweepstakes and instant-win games are popular promotional tactics designed to encourage product or service sales. But to eliminate the consideration element, their rules must clearly state that no purchase is necessary. This requirement is most commonly achieved by providing an alternative method of entry (AMOE). Although the consideration element is most often in the form of a payment for a purchase, the consideration element may also be found in nonmonetary methods of entry if the participant is required to exert substantial effort,[132] such as completing a lengthy survey, making multiple trips to a retail location, referring a friend, or otherwise devoting substantial time to participate in the sweepstakes.[133] Conversely, requiring participants to use the Internet (a paid service) or a 900-number phone service to enter the sweepstakes has been deemed, through Congressional bills and settled lawsuits, not to constitute the consideration element.[134] Regardless of whether the sweepstakes entry comes by purchase of a product or service or the AMOE, each method of entry must be given equal treatment and a sponsor of the sweepstakes may not directly or indirectly encourage participants to enter by the purchase-based method.

Contests are typically structured to eliminate the element of chance by requiring some level of skill or expertise. Typical examples include coloring contests, create-an-ad contests, and competitions to throw a ball through a target. Most states use the dominant element test to evaluate whether skill or chance dominates in determining the contest winner.[135] In other words, in a consumer promotion based on skill, the participants' skills or effort must govern the result and not be just part of a larger scheme. Hence, for example, a marketer can't have consumers enter a coloring contest and then ultimately select the winner at random. This requirement necessitates a careful enunciation of the rules of the contest and the judging criteria on which the winners will be selected. Most courts have held that contests that require participants to predict winners of events do not rise to the level of skill required to make the promotion legally a contest (legally, these would be deemed to be sweepstakes).

Promotional games often involve an issue as to whether it represents some form of illegal gambling. Courts generally distinguish between bona fide entry fees (which typically include proof of product purchase) and bets or wagers. Generally, entry fees do not constitute bets or wagers when they are paid unconditionally for the privilege of participating in a sweepstakes or contest and the prize is for a specified amount that is guaranteed to be awarded to one of the participants. When the entry fees and prizes are unconditional and guaranteed, the element of risk necessary to constitute betting or wagering is absent.

Gambling, on the other hand, represents an activity in which parties voluntarily make a bet or wager. The legality of online fantasy sports contests was upheld in 2007 in the case of *Humphreys v. Viacom*.[136] The plaintiff challenged the industry as a form of illegal gambling under New Jersey law. The district court, however, dismissed the case and stated that courts throughout the country have long recognized that it would be "patently absurd" to hold that "the combination of an entry fee and a prize equals gambling."[137] The court reasoned that to decide otherwise would result in countless popular contests being construed as illegal gambling, including everything from golf tournaments to essay competitions. The court interpreted the fee paid by online sport fantasy gamers as part of a contractual agreement between the online provider and the participant, not a wager or bet.

One increasingly popular form of promotional games is insured-prize promotions tied to specific performances of a team. Typically, these promotions require a consumer to make a purchase before the start of the season. Then, if a particular event occurs (e.g., the team wins the World Series), the consumer's cost of the purchase is reimbursed. This scenario was the subject of litigation in 2007 when the Massachusetts attorney general sued Jordan's Furniture claiming that its Monster Deal promotion constituted an illegal gambling scheme.[138] This promotion enticed consumers to purchase furniture before the start of the 2007 season on the condition that if the Red Sox won the 2007 World Series, the furniture would be free. The court determined that this promotion did not constitute an illegal lottery because it could not determine whether consumers were buying furniture purely for the purposes of entering the promotion or simply because they needed or wanted furniture.[139] Ultimately, to eliminate any legal issues, Jordan's Furniture, in its similar future promotions, provided all participants with a rebate on future furniture purchases (regardless of whether the Red Sox won the World Series), to eliminate the chance element. Notwithstanding this court decision, sport marketers need to make sure that similar insured-prize promotions conditioned on some future event meet legal muster.

For sport marketers, the most important advice with regard to promotion law is that each state has its own set of laws and regulations defining the elements of prizing, chance, and consideration. Hence, sport marketers seeking to conduct a sweepstakes or a contest must consult promotion law experts in the planning stages.

Emerging Issues

In this section, we consider several emerging issues at the intersection of the law and sport marketing.

Athletes' Use of Social Media

In 2012 Nike became the first company in the United Kingdom to have a Twitter campaign banned after the UK's Advertising Standards Authority (ASA) decided that its use of the personal accounts of soccer star Wayne Rooney violated rules for clearly communicating to the public that his tweets were advertisements.[140] Nike, who had an endorsement deal with Rooney, ran the Twitter campaign as part of its wider Make It Count advertising campaign. Rooney's tweet, which went out to his 4.37 million followers, said: "My resolution—to start the year as a champion, and finish it as a champion . . . #makeitcount gonike.me/make it count." As stated by the ASA, "We considered that the Nike reference was not prominent and could be missed. We considered there was nothing obvious in the tweets to indicate they were Nike marketing communications."[141]

For sport marketers, ranging from sport organizations to athlete representation firms to sponsors, the regulations that govern the commercial use of social media are an area of growing concern. The Rooney example illustrates the effect of the UK's ASA. The corresponding authority in the United States is the Federal Trade Commission (FTC), and it too has focused increasing attention on the issue of athletes' use of social media when used to promote endorsement deals.

In 2010 the FTC published new guidelines for companies and athletes seeking to leverage social media to promote products and services with the enactment of its *Guides Concerning the Use of Endorsements and Testimonials in Advertising*.[142] The new *Guides* clarify that celebrities, including athletes, have a duty to disclose their relationships with companies when making endorsements outside the context of traditional advertising in which the audience would not otherwise reasonably expect that a financial connection exists between the athlete and the advertiser. As examples, the *Guides* include (illustrated here in the context of athletes) whether the athlete is compensated, whether the company provided the product or service to the athlete for free, the length of the relationship between the company and the athlete, the extent of the athlete's previous receipt of products or services from the company or the likelihood of future receipt of such products or services, and the value of the items or services received by the athlete.

The new *Guides* also offer additional guidance by listing nine hypothetical examples. The third hypothetical presented in the *Guides* is relevant to sport figures, because it discusses an appearance by a well-known professional tennis player on a television talk show. In the hypothetical example, the show host compliments the player on her recent solid play. The player responds by crediting her improved play to her improved vision, the result of laser vision correction surgery done at a clinic that she identifies by name. The player raves about the ease of the procedure, the kindness of the eye doctor, and other benefits, such as the ease of driving at night. The player does not reveal that she has a contractual relationship with the eye doctor to speak positively about the eye company in public settings, but she does not appear in any broadcast commercials for the company. This hypothetical states that the weight and credibility of the player's endorsement is adversely affected because consumers are unaware of the contractual relationship that the player has with the eye doctor. The *Guides* thus direct that an athlete in this situation must disclose the relationship.

The hypothetical continues but alters the facts to analyze the player's discussion of the eye doctor on a social media site. Assume that instead of speaking about the clinic in a television interview, the tennis player touts the results of her surgery, mentioning the clinic by name, on a social networking site that allows her fans to read in real time what is happening in her life. Given the nature of the medium in which her endorsement is disseminated, consumers might not realize that she is a paid endorser. Because that information might affect the weight that consumers give to her endorsement, her relationship with the clinic should be disclosed.[143]

Companies using athletes as an endorsement vehicle need to remember the underlying rationale of the *Guides*—that consumers have a right to know when they are being subjected to a sales pitch. Although the *Guides* do not address every potential scenario involving companies' use of athletes, endorsements, and social media, they provide a framework for recommendations that these companies, as well as sport organizations, athletes, and their agents, should be aware of before engaging in marketing campaigns using social media.

Among other measures, companies should provide training and guidance to their athlete endorsers about how to use social media in a manner that adheres to the *Guides*. Such measures will best address the joint liability to both parties that may arise under the act. For instance, with respect to Twitter, it is recommended that endorsers end their tweets with, depending on the situation, #ad, #spon (short for "sponsored by"), or #samp (short for "free samples provided") so as to inform consumers truthfully.[144]

Athletes Trademarking Names and Slogans

A growing trend among professional and high-profile amateur (Olympic) athletes is seeking trademark protection of their names, slogans, or catch phrases associated with them.[145] Players use the benefits of trademark law not only to assert ownership and control over their trademarked names and slogans but also to generate ancillary revenues by licensing the use of these

Tim Tebow trademarked the action known as "Tebowing," illustrating a growing trend of athletes seeking trademark protection for their names as well as the actions that become synonymous with their identity.

marks on all types of commercial products and services. Noted examples include the NBA's Jeremy Lin's trademarking of the word "Linsanity"; Terrell Owens' trademarking of the phrase "Getcha popcorn ready," a phrase that he coined when he was acquired by the Dallas Cowboys in 2006; American Olympic swimmer Ryan Lochte's trademarking of his odd catchphrase "Jeah," which he explained as having been ripped from rapper Young Jeezy's often-used expression "Chea!"; and Tim Tebow's trademark registration for the image of "Tebowing," whereby he kneels with his fist to his forehead as though in prayer.[146] Lawyers who handle intellectual property matters for athletes say that the practice of trademarking names and phrases has accelerated recently as athletes seek to extend their brands into the entertainment world.[147] Furthermore, with the explosive growth of social media, trademarking an athlete's name gives the athlete and his or her legal team greater ability to control how the trademark is used and on what products or services, as well as monitor for unauthorized uses, ultimately enhancing the overall value of the athlete's brand.

Use of Current and Former Student-Athletes Likenesses in Video Games

One of the most hotly contested legal issues facing marketers of college sports, the NCAA, and the manufacturers of sport video games has been the use of likenesses of current and former student-athletes, notably in EA Sports video games, which the athletes have alleged is a violation of their right of publicity. In 2009 Sam Keller, a former student-athlete and quarterback for Arizona State University and the University of Nebraska, filed a class-action lawsuit against Electronic Arts, the NCAA, and the Collegiate Licensing Company (CLC) in the United States District Court Northern District of California. He sued EA for using his likeness without his consent and the NCAA and CLC for facilitating that use.[148] Keller also claimed that the use of his likeness and the likenesses of other student-athletes violated NCAA bylaw 12.5, which prohibits the commercial licensing of the "name, picture or likeness" of athletes at NCAA-member institutions.[149] Keller's proposed class consisted of all student-athletes whose likenesses had been used without their consent in the *NCAA Football* and *NCAA Basketball* video games. The complaint alleged that EA's unauthorized use of his likeness deprived the college football athletes of their statutory and common law right of publicity.[150] In December 2010 the Keller class action was consolidated with another class action brought against EA and the NCAA by former UCLA student-athlete and basketball player Ed O'Bannon.[151] The O'Bannon complaint, asserting the legal rights of former collegiate players, included antitrust claims against the NCAA that were dismissed, but Keller's right of publicity claims against EA survived. EA has argued that it does not use student-athlete likeness or, alternatively, that any use of athlete likenesses are protected expression under the First Amendment. In September 2013, EA Sports agreed to pay a reported $40 million to settle the O'Bannon/Keller right of publicity lawsuit.[152] The settlement was undoubtedly spurred by an earlier 3rd Circuit Court of Appeals decision in the *Hart vs. Electronic Arts* Sports case discussed below. The O'Bannon/Keller right of publicity lawsuit against the NCAA is still pending.

The use of collegiate player names and stats has also now expanded to include fantasy sports. In 2008 CBSSports.com announced plans to host a fantasy college football game using the names and statistics of current student-athletes.[153] Although the move raised eyebrows in the college sports community because it was the first fantasy game to use actual player names, the NCAA decided not to intervene to stop the game "because of the added exposure fantasy sports can bring the student-athlete," and, according to the NCAA president at the time, Myles Brand, because "the right of publicity is held by the student-athletes, not the NCAA."[154] The NCAA's decision not to seek to protect the intellectual property rights of current student-athletes raised concerns about the marketing and legal implications resulting from the rapid evolution of licensing the images of amateur athletes for use in commercial purposes. In 2009 the NCAA Task Force on Commercial Activities responded to the growing problem and recommended that member institutions address commercial activity on a campus-by-campus basis. The case also raised the lingering issue of whether the names of amateur athletes and their statistics are already in the public domain and therefore do not need a license to be used in fantasy sports.

Balancing the Right of Publicity and the First Amendment in Video Games

With increasing demand for sport video games as well as advances in technology that have enhanced the quality of virtual players in such games, it was inevitable that digital representations of current and former college athletes would eventually be featured in the games. With the creation of a series of video games focused on NCAA sports, the manufacturer of these games, Electronic Arts (EA), has added to an already confusing area of law with an emerging and complex legal issue: When do the publicity rights of NCAA athletes featured in sport video games trump the First Amendment?

The First Amendment allows video game manufacturers the right to make creative works, whereas the right of publicity allows athletes to protect the commercial rights in their images and control how their images are used. A high-profile former college athlete, Ryan Hart, a star quarterback from Rutgers from 2002 through 2005, sued Electronic Arts (EA), the video game manufacturer, over his virtual depiction and the virtual depictions of a class of athletes like him in EA's *NCAA Football* video game series. Hart claimed that the inclusion of his virtual likeness in the form of a digital avatar without his permission violated his right of publicity. Specifically, Hart cited the fact that in *NCAA Football 2006*, the Rutgers quarterback, player number 13, is 6 feet 2 inches tall (188 cm), weighs 197 pounds (89 kg), and resembles Hart. EA's defense to Hart's legal claims centered on First Amendment protections, which allow video game manufacturers to make creative works, and relied on previous court decisions that have protected the expressive content found in video games.

In balancing Hart's right of publicity against EA's First Amendment right to create video games featuring athletes such as Hart, the Third Circuit Court of Appeals in May 2013 applied the transformative use test. Under this test, the court must determine "whether the celebrity likeness is one of the "raw materials" from which an original work is synthesized, or whether the depiction or imitation of the celebrity is the very sum and substance of the work in question . . . whether the product containing a celebrity's likeness is so transformed that it has become primarily the defendant's own expression rather than the celebrity's likeness." In applying the test to the video game at issue, the court noted that "the digital Ryan Hart does what the actual Ryan Hart did while at Rutgers: he plays college football, in digital recreations of college football stadiums, filled with all the trappings of a college football game. This is not transformative; the various digitized sights and sounds in the video game do not alter or transform [Hart's] identity in a significant way."

Furthermore, the court dismissed EA's arguments that the ability of gamers to make changes in Hart's digital avatar was creative enough to satisfy the test, noting that "[i]f the mere presence of this feature were enough, video game companies could commit the most blatant acts of misappropriation only to absolve themselves by including a feature that allows users to modify the digital likenesses." The court also rejected EA's argument that including other creative elements of the game, such as realistic college stadiums, satisfied the test: "It cannot be that content creators escape liability for a work that uses a celebrity's unaltered identity in one section but that contains a wholly fanciful creation in the other, larger section." Reflecting the competing interests at stake, the court concluded by stating, "In finding that *NCAA Football* failed to satisfy the transformative use test, we do not hold that the game loses First Amendment protection. We merely hold that the interest protected by the right of publicity in this case outweighs the constitutional shield."

The decision in *Hart v. Electronic Arts* confirms that athletes, including current and former college athletes who have historically been unable to enforce their publicity rights, are now able to mount successful legal challenges to video games that include digital representations of them in their games.

The case is *Ryan Hart v. Electronic Arts*, Case No. 11-3570 (3rd Circuit Court of Appeals, decided May 21, 2013).

Wrap-Up

Intellectual property law is not only complex but also, as seen in the areas discussed earlier, in flux in terms of the law. In cases ranging from *NBA v. Motorola* to *Keller v. EA Sports*, rapid advancements in technology have significantly altered the legal landscape. As new technologies emerge, questions such as what constitutes an athlete's persona will continue to raise legal issues. Additionally, some commentators have expressed concerns that trademark law has been too broadly extended beyond its primary purpose—to protect consumer confusion. As sport marketers seek to protect their own creativity and avoid infringing on the creativity of others, they would do well to have a basic understanding of copyright, trademark, and patent law, as well as the torts of invasion of privacy and the right of publicity. When complex legal issues confront sport marketers, a good rule of thumb is to rely on legal counsel with specific expertise to handle the situation.

Activities

1. The introduction of this chapter presents a fictional fan (Jill B. Fan) who is preparing to capitalize on her favorite team's trip to the World Series. Applying the trademark law concepts discussed in this chapter, do you think that she will be on the right side of the law with regard to the T-shirt logos that she is creating? Why or why not? If you were deciding the issue of likelihood of confusion in this case, what additional information might you need? With regard to the website that she envisions, do you think that she will be able to retain the website name? Why or why not? Finally, advise Jill on the right of publicity issues that she needs to be aware of regarding her plans to blog about the Aces players and use their photos in her blogs.

2. You are the in-house legal counsel for a start-up energy drink company. You have been asked to review the plans for a marketing campaign timed to coincide with the start of the Y Games, an extreme sports competition. The energy drink company is not an official sponsor of the Y Games, but a well-known official sponsor is in the energy drink category. The company wants to use imagery with an action sports theme, including snowboarding, and plans to activate the campaign primarily using social media. The company does not plan to use any of the Y Games' registered trademarks but does plan to have a well-known snowboarder who will be competing in this year's Y Games serve as a highly visible spokesman and contribute unique content, including comments immediately after competition, on the company's Facebook page. Discuss how you will approach determining the legal issues raised by the campaign as well as the possible threat of legal action over ambush marketing. Then, based on the examples and cases discussed throughout the chapter, suggest alternatives that could be used in the campaign to resolve the legal issues that you have identified.

3. Watch or attend a major sporting event and identify all aspects of the event that could be protected using the various intellectual property laws discussed in this chapter. How would you use these laws to create a comprehensive plan for protecting the event's intellectual property? Discuss who owns each type of intellectual property that you have identified.

Your Marketing Plan

Assume that you are the head of marketing for Koka-Kola, a national soft-drink company. Your leading competitor is the official sponsor of the upcoming Major League Baseball World Series. Devise an ambush marketing plan that outlines the tactics that you will recommend your company use to capitalize on the excitement of this upcoming event—without violating trademark laws.

Endnotes

1. U.S. Constitution, art. 1, § 8, states, "Congress shall have the power to promote the progress of science and useful arts, by securing for limited times to authors and inventors the exclusive right to their own writings and discoveries."

2. 15 U.S.C. §§ 1051–1127 (2009).

3. 15 U.S.C. § 1127 (2009).

4. *Two Pesos Inc. v. Taco Cabana, Inc.* 505 U.S. 763, 765 (1992), citing *John H. Harland Co. v. Clarke Checks, Inc.*, 711 F. 2d 966 (11th Cir. 1983).

5. 15 U.S.C. § 1127 (2009).

6. Ibid.

7. See, U.S. Patent and Trademark Office, "Basic Facts About Trademarks," www.uspto.gov/trademarks/basics/BasicFacts.pdf.

8. See, *Blue Bell, Inc. v. Farah Manufacturing Co. Inc.*, 508 F. 2d 1260 (5th Cir. 1975), citing *United Drug Co. v. Theodore Rectanus Co.*, 248 U.S. 90 (1918).

9. 15 U.S.C. § 1051 (b) (1) (2009).

10. F. Foster and R. Shook, *Patents, Copyrights, and Trademarks: The Total Guide to Protecting the Rights to Your Invention, Product or Trademark . . . Now Better Than Ever*, 2nd ed. (New York: Wiley, 1993), 185.

11. See *AMF, Inc. v. Sleekcraft Boats*, 599 F. 2d 341, 349 (9th Cir. 1979).

12. 15 U.S.C. § 1052 (2009).

13. *Harjo v. Pro-Football, Inc.*, 50 U.S.P.Q. 2d 1705 (P.T.O. 1999).

14. *Pro-Football, Inc. v. Harjo*, 284 F. Supp. 2d 96 (D.D.C. 2003).

15. Carol Leonnig, "Redskins can keep trademark, judge rules." *The Washington Post*, Oct. 2, 2003, p. 1.

16. *National Football League Properties, Inc. v. Wichita Falls Sportswear, Inc.*, 532 F. Supp. 651, 658 (1982), citing *Levi Strauss & Co. v. Blue Bell, Inc.*, 632 F. 2d 817 (9th Cir. 1980).

17. Ibid.

18. *Board of Supervisors for La. State University, et al. v. Smack Apparel Co.*, 550 F. 3d 465 (5th Cir. 2008), *cert. denied*, 556 U.S. 1268; 129 S. Ct. 2759 (2009).

19. *University of Alabama Board of Trustees v. New Life Art, Inc.*, No. 09-16412 (11th Cir. 2012). See also J. Grady, "University of Alabama Case to Test Limits of Trademark Licensing in Sport Art Cases," *Sport Marketing Quarterly*, 14 (4) (2005): 251–252.

20. Ibid.

21. Rob Duca, "Major League Baseball Plays Hardball With Cape League," *Cape Cod Times*, 7 March 2008, www.capecodonline.com/apps/pbcs.dll/article?AID=/20080307/NEWS/803070339.

22. See Dennis Read, "Is Your Logo Safe?" *Athletic Management*, 17 (5) (August/September 2005), www.momentummedia.com/articles/am/am1705/logo.htm; Larissa Chinwah, "Colleges to High Schools: Stop Using Our Logos," *Daily Herald*, 30 November 2010, www.dailyherald.com/article/20101130/news/712019831/.

23. Trademark Dilution Act of 1995, 15 U.S.C. § 1125 (c) (amended Oct. 6, 2006).

24. 15 U.S.C. § 1114 (1) (2009).

25. 319 F. 2d 830 (7th Cir. 1963).

26. See, generally, Richard Kirkpatrick, "Likelihood of Confusion Issues: The Federal Circuit's Standard of Review," *American University Law Review*, 40 (1990): 1221–1236.

27. 15 U.S.C. 1125 (2009).

28. 604 F. Supp. 2d 200 (2d Cir. 1979).

29. Ibid., 205.

30. Ibid.

31. Trademark Dilution Revision Act of 2006, Public Law 109-312 (109th Cong.).

32. 15 U.S.C. § 1125 (c) (1) (2009).

33. *Horphag Research Ltd. v. Garcia*, 328 F. 3d 1108 (9th Cir. 2003).

34. 537 U.S. 418 (2003): 433.

35. 15 U.S.C. § 1125 (c) (1).

36. Ibid.

37. 15 U.S.C. § 1125 (c) (2) (A).

38. See Steve McKelvey, "Recent Trademark Dilution Cases Redefine Concept of 'Fame,' " *Sport Marketing Quarterly*, 17(3) (2008): 173–177.

39. *Adidas America, Inc. v. Payless Shoesource, Inc.*, 529 F.Supp.2d 1215 (2007). *Cert. denied*, 549 U.S. 881; 127 S. Ct. 188 (2006).

40. Ibid., 1246.

41. Nate Raymond, "Adidas Awarded $304 Mil. in Trademark Suit," 8 May 2008, www.law.com/jsp/pa/PubArticlePA.jsp?id=1202421215504&Adidas_Awarded_304_Mil_in_Trademark_Suit&slreturn=20121012105638.

42. *Board of Regents, the University of Texas System v. KST Electric, Ltd.*, No. A-06-CA-950LY, 2008 U.S. Dist. LEXIS 8883 (W.D. Tex. 2008).

43. 15 U.S.C. § 1125 (c) (2) (2009).

44. *Board of Regents, the University of Texas System v. KST Electric, Ltd.*, No. A-06-CA-950LY, 2008 U.S. Dist. LEXIS 8883 (W.D. Tex. 2008): 49.

45. 15 U.S.C. § 1127 (2009).

46. See *Indianapolis Colts, Inc. v. Metropolitan Baltimore Football Club, L.P.*, 34 F. 3d 410 (7th Cir. 1994).

47. 85 F. 3d 407 (9th Cir. 1996).

48. Ibid., 410.

49. 15 U.S.C. § 1127 (2004).

50. *Nitro Leisure Products, L.L.C. v. Acushnet Co.*, 341 F.3d 1356; 2003 U.S. App. LEXIS 17822 (2003).

51. *United States Olympic Committee v. American Media, Inc.*, 156 F. Supp. 2d 1200 (D. Colo. 2001).

52. See "Protecting Your Trademark on the Internet: Courts Limit Free Riding on the Information Superhighway," *Newsletter, Intellectual Property Law Section of the ABA*, 2 (3): 1–12.

53. 15 U.S.C. § 1125 (D) (2009).

54. 15 U.S.C. § 1125 (d) (1) (A) (2009).

55. 947 F. Supp. 347 (N.D. Ill. 1996).

56. 17 U.S.C. §§ 101 et. seq. (2009).

57. 17 U.S.C. §1201-1205 (2009).

58. 17 U.S.C. § 102 (2009).

59. 17 U.S.C. § 102 (2009).

60. 17 U.S.C. § 106 (2009).

61. See, N.E. Garrote and K.C. Maher, "Protecting Website's Look and Feel via Copyright and Trademark Law," *New York Law Journal*, 9 June 1998, www.nylj.com.

62. 17 U.S.C. § 303 (Sonny Bono Copyright Term Extension Act of 1998).

63. Foster and Shook, *Patents, Copyrights, and Trademarks*, 154.

64. 17 U.S.C. § 107 (2009).

65. Ibid.

66. Ibid.

67. See, *Monster Communications, Inc. v. Turner Broadcasting System, Inc.*, 935 F. Supp. 490 (S.D.N.Y. 1996).

68. Ibid., 495.

69. Ibid., 496.

70. *National Basketball Ass'n. v. Motorola, Inc.*, 105 F.3d 841 (2nd Cir. 1997).

71. 17 U.S.C. § 101 et. seq. (2009).

72. 622 F. Supp. 1500 (N.D. Ill. 1985).

73. *National Basketball Ass'n. v. Motorola, Inc.*, 105 F.3d 841 (2nd Cir. 1997).

74. Anne M. Wall, "Sports Marketing and the Law: Protecting Proprietary Interests in Sports Entertainment Events," *Marquette Sports Law Journal*, 7 (1996): 77.

75. Ibid., 77.

76. M.H. Reed, *IEG Legal Guide to Sponsorship* (Chicago: International Events Group, 1989): 180–182.

77. 364 F. 3d 1288 (2004).

78. 35 U.S.C. § 101 (2009).

79. 35 U.S.C. § 154 (a) (2) (2009).

80. Liz Mullen, "Arena Football Asks Court to Crack Back on Rival," *SportsBusiness Journal*, 1 (7) (June 1998): 13.

81. See Jeffrey A. Smith, "It's Your Move—No It's Not! The Application of Patent Law to Sports Moves," *University of Colorado Law Review*, 70 (1999): 1051–1065.

82. *Virginia State Board of Pharmacy v. Virginia Citizens Consumer Council*, 425 U.S. 748 (1976): 761.

83. 447 U.S. 557, 100 S. Ct. 2343 (1980).

84. *Bailey v. Kentucky Racing Commission*, 496 F. Supp. 2d 795 (W.D Ky. 2004).

85. Cal. 4th 939, 45 P.3d 24 (Cal. 2004).

86. Steve McKelvey, "Atlanta '96: Olympic Countdown to Ambush Armageddon?" *Seton Hall Journal of Sport Law*, 4 (2) (1994): 397–445.

87. Dean Crow and Janet Hoek, "Ambush Marketing: A Critical Review and Some Practical Advice," *Marketing Bulletin*, 14 (1) (2003): 1–14.

88. Michael Payne, "Ambush Marketing: The Undeserved Advantage," *Psychology and Marketing*, 14 (4) (1998): 323–331.

89. J. Glengarry, 2007. Let's Not Ambush Civil Rights. Buddle Findlay, New Zealand.

90. Dennis Sandler and David Shani, "Olympic Sponsorship vs. Ambush Marketing: Who Gets the Gold?" *Journal of Advertising Research*, 29 (1989): 9–14.

91. McKelvey, 20.

92. Stephen Townley, Dan Harrington, and Nicholas Couchman, "The Legal and Practical Prevention of Ambush Marketing in Sports," *Psychology and Marketing*, 15 (4) (1998): 333–348.

93. Tony Meenaghan, "Point of View: Ambush Marketing: Immoral or Imaginative Practice?" *Journal of Advertising Research*, 38(1) (1994): 77–88.

94. Ibid., 85.

95. Ibid., 85.

96. David Shani and Dennis Sandler, "Ambush Marketing: Is Confusion to Blame for the Flickering of the Flame?" *Psychology and Marketing*, 4 (1/2) (1998): 62–84.

97. The discussion of ambush marketing and the New York Marathon is reprinted with permission from FIT Technology, from Steve McKelvey, Dennis Sandler, and Kevin Snyder, "Sport Participant Attitudes Toward Ambush Marketing: An Exploratory Study of ING New York City Marathon Runners," *Sport Marketing Quarterly*, 21(2) (2011): 7–18.

98. Noah Liberman, "Marathon Ambush a Real Head-Scratcher," *SportsBusiness Journal*, 28 April 2003, 4.

99. Steve McKelvey and John Grady, "Sponsorship Program Protection Strategies for Special Sport Events: Are Event Organizers Outmaneuvering Ambush Marketers? *Journal of Sport Management,* 22(5) (2008): 397–445.

100. 36 U.S.C. § 220501 et. seq. (2000).

101. *United States Olympic Committee v. Tobyhanna Camp Corporation d/b/a Camp Olympik, et al.;* M.D. Pa.; Civil Action No. 3:10-CV-162, 2010 U.S. Dist. LEXIS 117650; 11/4/10.

102. Matt Brooks, "Redneck Olympics Under Fire from U.S. Olympic Committee," *Washington Post* (10 August 2011), www.washingtonpost.com/blogs/early-lead/post/redneck-olympics-under-fire-from-us-olympic-committee/2011/08/10/gIQAnfS16I_blog.html.

103. 42 C.P.R. 3d 390 (B.C. 1992).

104. *Cardtoons v. Major League Baseball Players Association,* 95 F.3d 959, 967 (10th Cir. 1996), citing Vol. 1, J. Thomas McCarthy, The Rights of Publicity and Privacy, § 1.1[A] [1] (1996).

105. 43 Misc. 2d 219, 250 N.Y.S. 2d 529 (1964).

106. Ibid., 232.

107. 202 F.2d 866 (2d Cir. 1953), cert. denied, 346 U.S. 816 (1953).

108. Ibid.

109. 316 F. Supp 1277 (D. Minn. 1970).

110. 363 N.Y.S. 2d 276 (1975).

111. 34 Cal. App. 4th 790, 40 Cal. Rptr.2d 639 (1995).

112. 85 F. 3d 407 (9th Cir. 1996).

113. 95 F. 3d 959 (10th Cir. 1996).

114. Ibid.

115. 280 N.W. 2d 129 (1979).

116. Ibid.

117. See D.E. Wanat, "Entertainment Law: An Analysis of Judicial Decision-Making in Case Where a Celebrity's Publicity Right Is in Conflict With a User's First Amendment Right," *Albany Law Review,* 67 (1) (2003): 251–277.

118. 332 F.3d 915 (6th Cir. 2003).

119. *Doe, a/k/a Tony Twist v. TCI Communications, et al.,* 2002, Mo. App. LEXIS 1577 (Mo. Ct. App., 23 July 2002), aff'd in part, rev'd in part & remanded, 110 S.W.3d 363 (Mo. 2003), cert. denied, 2004 U.S. LEXIS 76 (U.S. 2004). See also John Grady, Steve McKelvey, and Annie Clement, "A New 'Twist' for 'The Home Run Guys': An Analysis of the Right of Publicity Versus Parody, *Journal of Legal Aspects of Sport,* 15(2) (2005): 267–294.

120. See Teresa Baldas, "Pro Sports: Technology Changes Rules of the Game," www.law.com/jsp/article.jsp?id=1109128216973.

121. *C.B.C. Distributing and Marketing, Inc. v. Major League Baseball Advanced Media,* 505 F.3d 818 (8th Cir. 2007). Cert. denied, 128 S. Ct. 2872, 171 L. Ed. 2d 831 (2008).

122. *CBS Interactive Inc. v. National Football League Players Association, Inc. and National Football League Players Inc.;* D. Minn.; Civil No. 08-5097 ADM/SRN, 2009 U.S. Dist. LEXIS 368; 4/298/09.

123. James Grimaldi, "Washington Redskins React to Fans' Tough Luck With Tough Love," *Washington Post,* 3 September 2009, www.washingtonpost.com/wp-dyn/content/article/2009/09/02/AR2009090203887.html.

124. 451 Mass. 417 (2008).

125. Ibid., 421.

126. Ken Belson, "Judge's Ruling Keeps Alive Lawsuit Over Seat Licenses," *New York Times,* 20 November 2009, www.nytimes.com/2009/11/21/sports/football/21seats.html?_r=0.

127. *Oshinky v. New York Football Giants, Inc. et al.,* Case No. 2:2009cv01186 (N.J. Dist. Ct. 2009).

128. "Pitt Season Ticket Holders File Class Action Suit Against University," 29 March 2005, www.prnewswire.com/news-releases/pitt-season-ticket-holders-file-class-action-suit-against-university-54367592.html.

129. "Accord Reached in Athletic Ticket Suit," 9 June 2005, www.utimes.pitt.edu/?p=944.

130. "Flyers Sued Over Classic Tickets," 7 May 2012, http://espn.go.com/nhl/story/_/id/7901813/fans-sue-philadelphia-flyers-winter-classic-ticket-policy.

131. Tywanda Lord and Laura Miller, "Playing the Game by the Rules: A Practical Guide to Sweepstakes and Contest Promotions," *Franchise Law Journal,* 29 (2009): 3–8.

132. Ibid.

133. Ibid.

134. Ibid.

135. Ibid.

136. *Humphrey v. Viacom Inc., et al.,* Case No. 06-2768 (D.N.J. 2007).

137. Ibid.

138. Eli Bortman, "The Jordan's Furniture 'Monster Deal': Illegal Gambling? Taxable Income? *Business Law Review,* 41 (Spring 2008): 31–43.

139. Alan Burke, "Salem Lawyer Takes a Swing at Jordan's 'Monster Sweep,' " *Gloucester (MA) Times,* 6 November 2008, www.gloucestertimes.com/local/x645313948/Salem-lawyer-takes-a-swing-at-Jordans-Monster-Sweep.

140. Hannah Furness, "Wayne Rooney Reprimanded for Advertising Nike on Twitter," 20 June

2012, www.telegraph.co.uk/technology/twitter/9343349/Wayne-Rooney-reprimanded-for-advertising-Nike-on-Twitter.html.

141. Ibid.

142. *Guides Concerning Use of Endorsements and Testimonials in Advertising*, 16 C. F. R. § 255.0 to § 255.5 (2010). See also, Steve McKelvey & James Masteralexis (2011). "This Tweet Sponsored by . . : The Application of the New FTC Guides to the Social Media World of Professional Athletes," *Virginia Sport & Entertainment Law Journal*, 11: 222–248.

143. Ibid.

144. Christina Rexrode, "Twitter Changes Business of Celebrity Endorsements," *USA Today*, 3 November 2011, www.usatoday.com/tech/news/story/2011-11-03/celebrity-twitter-endorsements/51058228/1.

145. Brett Harris Pavony and Jaia Thomas, "For the Love of the Name: Professional Athletes Seek Trademark Protection," *Pace Intellectual Property Sports and Entertainment Law Forum*, 2 (1) (Spring 2012): 153–166.

146. Dough Williams, "Athletes Trademarking the Phrase That Pays," 13 July 2012, ESPN.com., http://espn.go.com/blog/playbook/fandom/post/_/id/6108/athlete-trademarks-becoming-commonplace; "Lochte Trademarks 'Jeah!' His Odd Catchphrase," *New York Daily News*, http://articles.nydailynews.com/2012-08-17/news/33252446_1_lochte-plans-jeah-trademarks.

147. Pavony and Thomas, 2012.

148. *Keller v. Electronic Arts, Inc.*, 2010 U.S. Dist. LEXIS 10719 (N.D. Cal., 2010).

149. *Keller*, Complaint: 13.

150. Baker, Grady, and Rappole, 2012.

151. In re Student-Athlete Name & Likeness Licensing Litigation, 2010 U.S. Dist. LEXIS 139724 (N.D. Cal. 2010).

152. Players to Receive $40 Million. ESPN.com (Sept. 28, 2013). http://espn.go.com/college-football/story/_/id/9731696/ea-sports-clc-settle-lawsuits-40-million-source].

153. Nando Di Fino, "College Football Fantasy Game to Name Names," *Wall Street Journal*, 31 July 2008, http://online.wsj.com/article/SB121733679819593215.html.

154. Ibid.

Chapter 15

Putting It All Together

OBJECTIVES

- To be able to compare and contrast the interaction and effect of the five Ps on one another

- To understand how organizational structure, job descriptions, and staff training affect organizational control of the marketing function

- To understand the need for analytics and accountability in achieving control and marketing effectiveness

- To recognize some standard benchmarks of marketing performance in sport

Singing From the Same Song Sheet

Nowhere is having an orchestrated ticket marketing, sales, and service, or TiMSS plan as the Aspire Group calls it, more important than in intercollegiate athletics.[1] In most athletics departments, the various functions that are responsible for each of the areas involved or that directly affect the success of the property's ticket revenue and attendance generation do not work in concert with one another, and they often have different bosses, who do not collaborate well. In most athletics departments, these functions include ticket sales, ticket or box office, marketing partnership and sponsorship sales, development, and communications and sports information. Many universities really have no ticket sales function. About 20 BCS and 35 FCS schools have outsourced the function to third parties such as Aspire, IMG, Learfield, or one of a handful of other smaller outsourcers, and another 25 or so schools have developed an in-house ticket sales operation. Most of the 124 BCS schools and many FCS schools have outsourced their marketing partnership and media rights to third parties such as IMG, Learfield, CBS Sportsline, and Nelligan. In few cases, except for the Aspire–Nelligan partnership, do these outsourced sponsorship sales vendors ever fully integrate ticket marketing into their partnership agreements, to the detriment of the collegiate property. Most ticket or box office staff report to the athletics CFO, and the emphasis is on inventory and financial control, not sales and service. The marketing functions at most universities are focused on PR and sports information, these days on electronic, digital, and social media platforms. Again, this function does not focus on sales and service. Finally, most athletics development and university development functions (fund-raising) are protective of their domains and not targeting ticket sales per se.

Because these functions report up through different bosses and are not fully integrated at the athletics director level, gross underperformance occurs in ticket sales and attendance. This practice is understandable given that most ADs spend most of their time being politicians, keeping the university president, board of trustees, major donors, and senior university administrators happy, to say nothing of monitoring the coaches of the major revenue-producing sports. At the same time, most ADs are busy acting as the chief fund-raising officer, raising as much money as they can to retain their Olympic sport programs that might otherwise be cut. This thankless task has led to many of the country's top ADs to choose to leave the profession early. "This job is not fun anymore," said Joel Maturi, then the athletics director at the University of Minnesota. "I spend more and more of my time involved with politics and money and less and less of it with coaches and the student-athletes, which is where I want to be spending my time, and should be spending the majority of my time."[2]

In this chapter, we examine the range of cross-effects among the five Ps—the sport marketing mix. We also consider some principles necessary for the effective control of these elements and their related functions in the sport organization. As we noted in chapter 2, strategic marketing management, with its integration of product, price, place, promotion, and public relations, must be managed in a way that moves the organization toward its overall objectives.

Cross-Effects Among the Five Ps

So far we have treated each element of the marketing mix mainly in an isolated fashion, yet clearly these elements have a simultaneous cross-effect on the consumer. A potential buyer of a sport product does not view the price of a product in isolation from the promotional mix, the place function (the venue), or the nature of the product and product extensions. This effect can be assessed using a cross-effect matrix (figure 15.1). The figure summarizes the degree to which each element interacts with the others. In this section, we provide a more complete assessment of these interactions.

Effect of Product and Price

The effect of product and price is more truly the effect of price on product. Price, as we have discussed previously, is the most visible and most readily communicated variable of the marketing mix. Price influences perceptions of quality and value, and thereby directly affects product image. More often than not, consumers are balancing product and price in their minds as they consider purchasing a sport product. But the consensus choice is based primarily on perceived value. People are willing to pay twice as much for a Starbucks coffee as they do for a Dunkin' Donuts or McDonald's coffee. But as the latter two quick-serve retailers have improved their branding, in

the case of Dunkin' Donuts, and rebranded, in the case of McCafe, their coffee prices and sales volume have both risen. An ESPN/Chilton poll surveyed 800 people aged 12 to 44 who had purchased logoed sport merchandise within the past three months. The results (see tables 15.1 and 15.2), broken down by age group, suggest that all age cohorts viewed quality and price as important purchase criteria, but that consumers under age 25 viewed product quality (in this case, brand name) as slightly more important than did their elders, whereas consumers aged 25 to 44 viewed price as slightly more important than did their juniors.

The National Sporting Goods Association (NSGA) released a report in March 2010 stating that Americans spent $8 billion in 2009 on sport logo apparel, a staggering amount that illustrates the high demand for sport apparel.[3] Further evidence of this phenomenon is the rapid growth of Under Armour, the company started by Kevin Plank, a football player at the University of

	Product	Price	Place	Promotion	Public relations
Product		Price = value	Images	Product position	Consumer receptivity
Price			Images interact	Choice of media	Sincerity of public relations
Place				Images interact	Images interact
Promotion					Completely interdependent
Public relations					

FIGURE 15.1   Cross-effect matrix for the five Ps of sport marketing.

TABLE 15.1   Results of ESPN/Chilton Poll Asking, How Important Is the Brand Name on the Item When Purchasing Sports Logo Clothing?

Importance	Age			
	12–17	18–24	25–34	35–44
Not at all or not so important	19.4%	25.0%	36.0%	29.9%
Somewhat or very important	80.5%	75.0%	63.9%	70.1%

Reprinted, by permission, from ESPN, 1998, "ESPN Chilton sports poll: Are purchasing discussions based on brand?" *Street & Smith's Sports-Business Daily,* pg. 16.

TABLE 15.2   Results of ESPN/Chilton Poll Asking, How Important Is the Price of the Item When Purchasing Sports Logo Clothing?

Importance	Age			
	12–17	18–24	25–34	35–44
Not at all or not so important	17.3%	24.4%	16.3%	12.0%
Somewhat or very important	82.7%	75.6%	83.8%	88.0%

Reprinted, by permission, from ESPN, 1998, "ESPN Chilton sports poll: Are purchasing discussion based on brand?" *Street & Smith's Sports-Business Daily,* pg. 16.

Maryland who was frustrated with clothing that absorbed sweat and became heavy and uncomfortable. In less than 10 years, his company has grown to $1 billion in sales per annum by fully realizing its mission to "Make All Athletes Better" and being the most innovative sport clothing supplier in this space.[4]

Consumers often view low-priced products as being low-quality products and high-priced products as being high-quality or prestigious products. Price–product strategies based on such perceptions depend on supply, demand, the demographic level of the consumer who has adopted the product (whether people drive Jaguar, Lexus, or Mercedes), and market elasticity. This can also be a tricky business. Nike was burned badly when it misread the market for its new Tiger Woods line of apparel. The style and the supporting ads had Nike's usual hard-edged, "in-your-face," antiestablishment look and feel. As *Sports Illustrated* reported, however, such products did not appeal to the core of golf's consumers. They appealed to kids, who could not afford the $75 shirts or the $225 shoes. Said one Oregon golf shop operator: "Young kids like it, but young kids don't have the money to buy it." Or, as another golf executive put it, "Nike tries to use the different-is-cool theme that works well in sports. But in golf that formula doesn't work." Parents might part with $120 for a pair of Air Jordans, but will they do so for a polo shirt or golf shoes? Tiger Woods went on to develop his own line of apparel with his "TW" logo brandings. His venture had great success despite his off-course indiscretions that led to a diminished image among traditional golf fans, the media, and many in the public, particularly women.[5]

Marketers of women's athletics have faced the related conundrum of increasing the cost of their products at the same time that they seek increased attendance. They have hoped that fans perceive higher value in higher prices. For instance, in the late 1980s, as women's basketball began to draw a larger fan base, the Ohio State women's program recognized the need to charge admission to a formerly free event but knew that the move would be a gamble. Their answer was to develop a promotion with local Big Bear supermarkets that focused on key games. Television, radio, and newspaper ads detailed the availability of coupons with any Big Bear purchase—coupons were redeemable, with $1, for a ticket with a face value of $2 or $3. This approach created a sense of value for the product and helped raise the team's average attendance by 1,500.[6]

Effect of Product and Place (Venue)

Consumers develop a product image based on their perceptions of the product's attributes. Similarly, sport consumers develop perceptions of the place in which an event occurs, namely, a facility image. These two images are interactive. When the New York Stars of the old Women's Professional Basketball League (WBL) played their home games in the Iona College gymnasium in White Plains, New York, the small, remote college gym hurt the image of the product. The

Stars could not convince fans that their sport was big time when it was played in a minor facility. A move to Madison Square Garden helped, but the increased overhead could not be borne by the severely underfinanced team. The Stars, who had been champions in 1980, folded, and a year later, so did the WBL. Consumers are convinced of one thing in sport: Big-league products demand big-league places—a sentiment played out again in the WNBA's success at the expense of the American Basketball League. As we noted in chapters 6 and 13, the sport venue is part of the product. That immutable law helps drive the move to "techtainment" venues and sports malls that have multiple screens and speakers, and games that assault all senses simultaneously.

The smartest marketers, however, recognize that sport consumers seek multiple places for their product consumption. Michael Eisner once described Disney's strategy as "operating on two tracks . . . yin and yang, the paradoxical pull of the opposites." Eisner continued, "We're convinced that people will seek more diverse entertainment in their homes, but also that they'll take advantage of familiar outdoor gathering spots and seek out new ones." In retrospect, Eisner's plan was clear—the careful placing of Disney's branded products in multiple strategic locations. Take ESPN. The ESPN consumer can stay home to watch *SportsCenter,* read ESPN's magazine, or surf through ESPN.com. When she tires of home, she can travel to the nearest ESPN Zone restaurant to mingle with like-minded ESPNies, trading "Boomer" Berman imitations with a well-schooled wait staff. In the 1990s and the first decade of the new millennium, the adage taken from the movie *Field of Dreams*—"If you build it they will come"—seems to apply to just about every new stadium and arena. In today's wirelessly connected world, considerably more digital and social media savvy is required to create sellouts, even if the new venue is perceived to be a palace.[7]

Effect of Product and Promotion

Products define appropriate formats and media for promotions. For instance, Nike is unlikely to promote its Tiger Woods line through classified ads in the local paper, which is not the place to advertise high-priced golf apparel. Full-color ads in a golf magazine and classy electronic e-mails and YouTube video postings would make much more sense. Similarly, the promotional mix defines the product position. As we saw earlier, Nike appeared to miss the mark in its first attempt to position the Woods line. The ad campaign influenced consumers who were not in a position to buy the product. We can see a more successful blend of promotion and position in the efforts of the then New Jersey Nets to attract fans. Before the 2009 season, the team launched a strategy aimed at all fans, not just Nets fans. The strategy aimed to attract ticket buyers with the offer of a free reversible jersey from each of the 5 marquee games within a 10-game package. Such notable opponents would include the Los Angeles Lakers and Cleveland Cavaliers. Essentially, one side of the jersey would display the name of a key player for the Nets and the other side would feature the name of a popular opposing player, like Kobe Bryant or LeBron James. These superstar rosters help fuel the hype attached to these leading matchups, thus enhancing the appeal for audiences. With the additional incentive of a free Kobe or LeBron jersey, fans of the opposing teams may be more inclined to purchase tickets to those games. Clearly, the Nets organization hoped that this promotion would put more fans, of either team, in the seats come game time.[8]

Sometimes, efforts to enhance the fan experience do just the opposite. Although fan songs and chants have defined many venues (and still do in the world of soccer), the art form has never really taken hold in North America, as evidenced by the frequent fan prompts from video boards to "Make some noise" and PA announcers' calls to "Get on your feet!" No such prompting is needed around the world where the fans spontaneously react to game situations with either clever creations or old favorites. Too many teams have abdicated responsibility to control fan behavior. Instead, they have simply cranked up contemporary rock music and resorted to Animal House videos. Rick Church, president of the Information Display and Entertainment Association (a trade group for big-screen producers), wondered if louder was better: "If it's 150 decibels, are you really having fun?" Professional teams should take a cue from college sport teams that have marching bands or pep bands that celebrate the team and its community. Some teams just don't seem to understand the linkage of promos and product position. In 2000, for instance, Arena Football's Albany Firebirds announced that they would put microphones on four or five players. Fans could then hear "close up and personal" by renting a headset for $12. The headsets included a warning about profanity, a point recognized by the Firebirds' running back, Eddie Brown. "I wouldn't wear it because of the language I use," he said. Although Brown worried about young fans picking up bad language, the Firebirds seemed oblivious. Perhaps it's not surprising that with judgment like that, the franchise is now defunct.[9]

Effect of Product and Public Relations

Public relations, a special part of promotions in sport, has an obvious effect on product image and position. But public relations efforts rely on the whim of the media to a much greater extent than do promotional efforts such as advertising or direct marketing and electronic media channels, which the marketer controls. This is a tricky business. Although marketers hope to cultivate the media, they cannot expect a reporter to be a shill. When franchises exercise contractual rights to fire radio or television announcers whom they handpicked, the press and the public are usually outraged. Consumers expect announcers to be homers (those who clearly favor the home team) to some degree and to engage in some spin control, but they have a sense of limits.

At a national level, leagues and corporations play the game with greater stakes on the table. For instance, Nike earned a well-deserved reputation in the late 1980s and early 1990s for its innovative advertisements and promotions, which created such high brand equity that most people didn't need a name to know what a swoosh or "Just Do It" stood for. But the same aggressive, cocksure, antiestablishment image may have fueled a backlash in public relations. As Nike became the 800-pound gorilla of sport, the media focused on troubling aspects of Nike's labor practices in the Asian factories where its products were made. No matter what data Nike offered about the relative value of its wage scale, no matter how many celebrities returned satisfied from inspection tours, Nike could not seem to win on its own turf of media images. To make matters worse, Nike was further burned by distribution of a new Nike Air model that outraged Muslims, who saw a resemblance between the flame-shaped image on the shoe and the Arabic word for Allah. In 1999 Nike joined the World Bank, the Gap, the International Youth Foundation (IYF), and other organizations to form the Global Alliance for Workers and Communities. The alliance interviewed thousands of workers in an effort to improve labor conditions. As one might expect, Nike was aggressive in its PR about the work of the alliance. But the controversy continued, as a quick Google search of "Nike and labor" reveals.[10]

If preventing public relations gaffes in developing athletics shoes is difficult, it is nearly impossible to develop a foolproof athlete who conforms to a sport's chosen image both in the venue and out. For most consumers, players are the game. When they misbehave in their personal lives, the whole product suffers. For every David Robinson or Tim Duncan, there are seemingly two Terrell Owenses. Rafael Palmeiro can be a hero one day and a bum the next. NBA commissioner David Stern admitted, "We have to consider, in an honest way, what impact we have on society. We have to let our players know that we like their contributions but also that they have to behave themselves on and off the court." Amid the seamless components of the sport product, including players, venues, equipment, apparel, rules, and so on, any small action may have massive implications for public relations. As we outline in chapter 11, knowing how to properly handle a crisis is critical for handling the fires that continually flare up. In today's Twitter world that has simultaneous communication going global within seconds, the foolish utterances of certain players and sport celebrities can create instantaneous crises.[11]

Effect of Price and Place

The interaction of price and place has two major effects. First, sport consumers expect to pay higher prices for better facilities. This phenomenon has existed for some time. Witness the growth in racquetball and fitness clubs in the 1970s. YMCAs and YWCAs had offered such programs for years, yet the newer clubs with their sleek decor and sophisticated facilities charged higher prices but still captured the bigger share of the market. During the 1980s Ys responded by building upscale facilities to capture the yuppie market; the private clubs then attacked the tax-exempt status of the Ys. The controversy focused on the interaction of price and place, because both sides recognized that in sophisticated markets consumers would pay a higher price for a more prestigious facility. The same principle applies to spectators who line up to pay higher prices for the benefits of premium-seating amenities such as clubs and suites, especially when they offer all-inclusive food and beverages, reserved close-in parking, personal or permanent seat licenses, and luxury suites. Perhaps the best example of this factor is the willingness by fans of the NFL's New York Giants to buy every seat in the new MetLife Stadium through an expensive personal seat license (PSL). The converse is also true, as the Boston Bruins discovered when their overpriced upper-bowl seats at TD Garden arena did not sell. Lower prices were a prerequisite to ticket sales in those remote locations.[12]

Another place–price principle is that consumers tend to pay more for convenience (which is a benefit). Most people still expect to pay a surcharge for tickets that they purchase over the phone, online, or at a grocery or music store. They save time (another important benefit) if they don't have to drive to a central box office, and for the most part they accept the additional convenience fee. Attitudes are changing, however, in that more people expect instant, online, downloadable ticket and parking-pass printing. Similarly, consumers were traditionally willing to pay more for sporting goods that they purchased at local sporting goods stores. Although the larger discount houses stocked the same product, the convenience (and more personal service) of the local store compensated for the additional cost of the drive time to the big-box store. But today, more people buy their products online, saving large sums despite shipping fees and overnight delivery. In summary, sport consumers will pay more to view a sport in a more attractive or convenient location, to play a sport at a more attractive (or more challenging, as in golf) facility, or to purchase sporting goods in a local store. The concept of place includes manifold benefits (or costs) that influence the consumer's perception of a fair price.

Effect of Price and Promotion

In the past, the price of a product dictated the media for advertising the product, for several reasons. First, the price determines the profit margin on the product and hence the promotional budget and in turn the media choice. Second, the price of a product reflects not only its nature and cost but also the market to which the product is targeted. In both cost-plus and market-based pricing, the price reflects the target market's demographics and its media choices. Even a casual look at newspapers or television reveals this pattern. Whereas the maker of a new "foolproof" fishing lure might run a 30-second spot during a cable television fishing show (whose viewers match the product's target audience), a large chain like MVP or Dick's Sporting Goods still prefers a multipage, multicolor insert for regional newspapers whose readers cross a wide range of demographics. The lower cost of Internet advertising, e-mailing, and texting, of course, has changed this element considerably.

The last example suggests that size and scope might influence price and promotion. During the first decade of the millennium as many media and large companies purchased less mass media for their advertising and shifted over to digital media, social media, and targeted direct marketing, which have much lower costs, smaller companies and products with lower price points could now market and promote by electronic, digital, and social media vehicles.[13]

Effect of Price and Public Relations

Any ticket promotion is promoted based on value. Sport consumers keep value front and center when they make purchase decisions. In that respect, pricing strategies can have a strong effect on public relations, for better or worse. College and university athletics programs learned this lesson, sometimes the hard way, as they moved in the last two decades to required "donations" for the right to buy football or basketball tickets in preferred locations. This system was the forerunner of the personal seat license (PSL), and some schools didn't handle the process well. Alabama, for instance, could not keep ahead of one maelstrom of criticism, as word spread about a surcharge. One administrator admitted, in words that have since echoed across the industry, "We didn't handle it right. We should have called a press conference and explained everything in great detail." What they should have done is hired a customer service or fan relationship

The Pittsburgh Pirates' Sunday Kids Day is an example of the cross effect of price and promotion. Parents could be more willing to spend money on additional tickets knowing there's an added benefit.

management center (FRMC) staff to talk personally to all affected season-ticket account holders.

University of Northern Colorado athletics was likewise under media attack in the fall of 2005 when Director Jay Hinrichs announced a first-ever parking fee for home football games. UNC was moving up from Division II to Division IAA, so revenue was a greater issue. Hinrichs further argued that the $5 fee would support additional customer service. This plan didn't sit well with Matt Schuman of the *Greeley Tribune,* who responded that most of the 4,500 or so regular fans cared little about customer service. The team was coming off a 2-9 season. The program needed a way to attract more fans to the newly expanded 8,500-seat Nottingham Field. In Schuman's opinion, "An additional $5 may give them just another reason to stay away."[14]

In 1987, the Pittsburgh Penguins earned lots of positive PR with their Playoff or Payoff ticket campaign, where season ticket holders received a $1 per game refund if the Penguins did not make the playoffs. The idea was alive and well in 2003, when the Nashville Predators, Atlanta Hawks, and Florida Panthers ran similar promotions for season-ticket sales. But the Predators knew that they would receive a payoff for their coffers even if they had to give money back to their fans. A survey indicated that without a playoff or payoff pledge, season-ticket renewals would have been 70 percent. With the pledge, renewals were 83 percent, close to the figure of the year before, despite a price hike. Although these teams gambled with revenues, they had a sure bet on positive PR. The promotion did not fare so well for the Hawks, who failed to make the playoffs and had to refund millions of dollars in their playoffs-guaranteed pledge.[15]

In the late 1990s Coca-Cola walked away from its long-term sponsor relationship with the NFL, in part because it feared negative publicity from the deep-well pricing of concessions at NFL stadiums. Coke correctly believed that it did not need high-priced stadium signage to gain brand recognition. More important, exclusive pouring rights were backfiring. Consumer research showed Coke that 4 out of 10 people blamed Coke, at least partially, for the overpriced, watered-down stadium beverages. The question was simple for then Coke executive, now Turner Broadcasting president Steve Koonin: "I'm going to pay for the privilege to upset people?"[16]

Some player agents, to many the epitome of venality, have shown similar concern about image. In this case, the issue was high-priced autographs. Autograph-show promoters, recognizing the players' myopic greed, started contacting players directly rather than working through their agents, who might suggest to their clients that gouging an owner is one thing but gouging a young fan is another. Wade Arnot, whose firm represented several Detroit Red Wings players, was blunt about autograph shows: "It's not something we support."[17] The debacle in NCAA FBS football involving the 2012 season Heisman Trophy winner Johnny Manziel of Texas A&M University, who had signed a large amount of memorabilia that found its way on to online sites for sale, only further illustrates this point.

Effect of Place and Promotion

The ability to promote the interior design or layout of an old, dilapidated facility parallels a tailor's ability to make silk purses out of sows' ears. In other words, it is almost impossible. One of the biggest problems facing University of Alabama at Birmingham athletics director Brian Mackin is trying to grow UAB's football brand and revenues. Home games are played in historic but ancient Legion Field, which has old amenities, is located in a low-income neighborhood, and typically has 60,000 or more empty seats. The sport facility image is a strong one, and it directly influences the product image, as we discussed in chapter 13. Take Oakland Coliseum. The cold, windy, wet environment may not have affected Raiders ticket sales much when season-ticket holders make only a 10-game commitment for a franchise epitomized by fans who wear spiked dog collars. A great record in the 1970s and '80s didn't hurt either. Not so with A's fans, whose sport (baseball) evokes images of lazy, sunny summer days. The A's tried valiantly to overcome their location's liabilities, particularly the large blocks of seats with bad angles and located a considerable distance from the field.[18]

Some organizations have promoted special components of their venues. Take, for instance, the penalty box of ice hockey—a place that conjures up images of tough guys cooling off in the "sin bin." The San Antonio Dragons (International Hockey League, 1996–1999) developed a clever promotion playing off this special place. Once per period, the Dragons' mascot, Freddy the Fanatic, moved into the stands and hauled an unsuspecting attendee (for being too quiet, for wearing the opponent's colors, for whatever Freddy thought inappropriate) off to a "fan penalty box" (sponsored by Miller Brewing) behind one of the goals. Besides a close-up view, the fan got a small prize as part of the sentence. Fans seemed to love the promotion, cheering wildly whenever Freddy neared their sections. The Dragons even planned to make an inflatable version of the box for outside events.[19]

Effect of Place and Public Relations

A new facility has implications for all the other Ps. For instance, a new seat configuration requires a rescaling of ticket prices, which must be done with care to protect the overall franchise image.

Excessive jumps in price usually backfire into images of gouging and greed, which can take years to overcome. Likewise, new policies can upset fans, as the New England Patriots discovered when they moved to Gillette Stadium in 2002 on the heels of their first Super Bowl championship. Hoping to open more tickets to the thousands of fans on their season-ticket waiting list, the Patriots invoked a new policy that prohibited existing ticket holders from transferring their seats to anyone else—by deed, contract, will, or any other means. Many longtime holders were upset, among them Tom Maguire. When he learned that he and his brothers could not inherit their father's tickets, he said, "It felt like a slap in the face." The Boston Globe ran a bold headline: "Pass Interference: The Patriots Prohibition on the Transfer of Season Tickets Has Some Fans Crying Foul." But the Patriots argued that they built Gillette Stadium without the use of seat licenses. In their opinion, allowing the transfer of tickets would amount to recognizing de facto licenses, which would unfairly deny others access to tickets. Fans on the waiting list agreed, but the Patriots had learned a hard lesson.[20]

To maximize the positives in their move to the new PNC Park, the Pittsburgh Pirates commissioned the local PR firm of Burson-Marsteller to manage a 14-month campaign leading up to the grand opening in April 2001. The campaign included direct mail, a series of press conferences, special events, news releases, newspaper inserts, and a website. The program paid off in positive images, a 2-month sellout of luxury boxes, and record-breaking season-ticket sales. With a small market and a small revenue base, the Pirates knew that they had one chance for a place-based spike in image and sales. They made the most of it.[21]

Effect of Promotion and Public Relations

Publicity is one of the four elements traditionally identified under the promotion umbrella; therefore, the two are interdependent. As stated previously, the effect of a favorable or unfavorable public relations image cannot be underestimated. Conceivably, the public relations image can totally negate immense promotional efforts. The source credibility and high level of exposure from media coverage cannot be duplicated by promotional efforts. Similarly, a promotional bomb can return savage mockery from press and public alike. Arena Football's Orlando Predators found their franchise the subject of unflattering attention in *Sports Illustrated* when the league fined them $10,000 for scheduling a promotion that would have awarded a keg of beer and $500 to the fan who brought the "best" inflatable doll. Apparently, the Predators were slow learners. A year before they had paid for a billboard that "featured scantily clad women bent over to snap a football with the catchphrase 'Get Behind Your Team.'"[22]

Controlling the Marketing Function

We have seen that each element of the marketing mix is interdependent, some to a larger extent than others. Because each has the ability to influence the others, the only way to ensure marketing effectiveness is to control all parts of the marketing effort. In this section, we outline a comprehensive plan for measuring the appropriate analytics to ensure that the return on objectives (ROO), return on investment (ROI), and cost of sale (COS) are where they should be. Only with these accountability measures in place can marketing and managerial control be effective. This plan has as its ultimate goal ensuring the creation and delivery of products that satisfy consumer wants and needs.

A sound control system can nurture and preserve the credibility of the image that consumers hold of both the product and the organization. The notion of control spans all levels of the industry—from the NFL's dictating specifications on player uniforms (shirts tucked in, socks pulled up and taped) to a local YMCA's training its staff to react courteously to member complaints. Control is a central feature in successful marketing. Even the smallest item can create negative images that seriously undermine the overall organizational image. A small flaw may not affect all consumers or publics that interact with an organization, its personnel, products, services, or facilities, but it can affect enough people to cause damage. An athletics club stupid enough to have cigarette machines in the lobby would communicate inconsistency, insincerity, and a stronger adherence to the profit motive than to the health motive. Coaches who repeatedly violate NCAA recruiting rules send a subtle but powerful message that their other promises cannot be believed. Maintaining consistency is important in a marketer's ability to communicate a clear and precise position. Inconsistencies blur images and project incoherent product positions.

The key to controlling the marketing mix lies in setting a clear direction for all units and personnel and ensuring that all functions work from the same playbook. In college athletics, marketing, ticket sales, the outsourced media rights partner, athletics development (fund-raising), and the box office (ticket service) all need to be on the same page. Employees need a road map to tell them where to go and how to get there. They need to know how they will be evaluated and how their efforts relate to those of other departments or functions in the organization. An effective marketing control system, then, must be part of an

Controlling the effect of the various marketing functions is especially important during a time of crisis, such as the child abuse scandal that rocked Penn State, which, among other fallouts, resulted in the removal of a beloved statue.

ongoing planning system that has at least four components:

- Mission statements and objectives that have been established in light of current market position regarding desired position
- An organizational structure that marshals resources to meet objectives
- Employee performance standards and criteria that logically link performance to specific marketing and sales objectives
- Methods to adjust strategy, structure, and personnel in light of performance

In short, marketing control must be incorporated into an overall strategic plan.[23]

Mission Statements and Objectives

Mission statements and objectives link strategic planning (an organization's assessment of its relationship to its wider environment) with operational planning (tactics that move the organization toward its goals). One type of planning cannot succeed without the other. In other words, every piece of the marketing mix should be framed within a broader strategic vision. All too often, a sport organization's annual strategic plan is just a budget devoid of strategy and tactics. A good example of a broad strategic mission statement comes from Middlebury College, a highly competitive Division III program in Vermont:

Athletics are an essential part of the overall educational experience at Middlebury College. The College endeavors to provide athletic programs that are comprehensive and varied, offering athletic opportunities to all students. The Athletic Department is committed to the following:

- A physical education/wellness program that stresses good health, physical fitness and life-time activities.

- A vigorous intercollegiate sports program that strives for achievement and excellence.

- An intramural program that encourages students of varied abilities and skills to participate in a wide range of recreational athletic activities.

- A club sports program that offers opportunity for intercollegiate competition in a less structured environment.

This statement makes it clear that, unlike its athletics department counterpart at the University of Texas at Austin, Middlebury's athletics department must support a broad base of activities, such as recreation and wellness, not just intercollegiate competition. This perspective is typical in Division III. Middlebury's coaches and athletes want to win as much as anyone, but the department stands for something more than victories, which will influence decisions on budgets, staffing, facilities, and marketing. The same principles apply to the high school, the multinational equipment company, or the local fitness club: The mission statement is the touchstone for all strategy and tactics.[24]

Clear, realistic, measurable objectives are the next step in setting the marketing course. Later in the chapter, we will consider some standard indexes of performance, or what are now called performance analytics (e.g., not just overall attendance levels, but season-ticket holder retention levels broken down by first-year [new] purchases, premium seat holders, partial and miniplan holders, and so on) that must be used in setting objectives. Leaders, however, should not wait until after the fact to consider objectives. Objectives must always be viewed as part of a continuous chain of ends and means, targets along the road to success. Vague or unrealistic objectives can be problematic, as Major League Soccer (MLS) has found. In the league's second season, the commissioner publicly set an attendance objective of 20,000 fans per game—a target that would bring owners close to the break-even point but a good 30 percent increase over the attendance average of the year before. Unfortunately for MLS, the final attendance average was 14,616 per game, nearly a 10 percent decrease from the first season. Did this mean that MLS was in serious trouble? Not necessarily. But the drop in attendance required a reassessment and realignment of goals and strategies from short-term to long-term outlooks. As the commissioner put it, "A lot of people want to instantly assess you as a breakthrough or as a lack of a breakthrough." It was clear to him and the league owners that MLS could no longer think in specific terms.[25]

Linking Organizational Structure to Strategy

In many organizations, marketing functions are not centralized, and this arrangement has caused problems. For instance, in professional and collegiate sport, linkages between the marketing, sales development, and public relations functions are often minimal. Specifically, in professional sport, the VP of public relations and the director of marketing often report to different people. Likewise, in collegiate athletics, the sports information director (SID), who usually has a journalism background, and the director of marketing often report to different people. At times, the units are antagonistic, vying for scarce resources or the ear of a higher executive. Such organizational conflict, usually the result of historical development, is illogical, given that public relations and marketing and promotion should be part of an integrated marketing plan. A comprehensive marketing structure is needed to direct the efforts of marketing personnel, to align those efforts with organizational goals and policies, and to ensure that they complement and do not duplicate one another. This mistake is perhaps best exemplified in game presentation and entertainment. If PR is in charge, the video and hustle boards and PA systems focus on stats, replays, and public announcements. These elements are important, but they are not the entirety of the desired fan experience. If marketing is in charge, fan entertainment, sponsor exposure elements, and ticket sales for future games are likely featured much more extensively.

As we noted in chapter 2, structure should evolve from organizational strategy. When the Atlanta Braves realized the need to juice the fan experience in 2004, they reorganized their marketing department to include a stadium group that focused on in-game presentation. Likewise, in the late 1990s, the then Dallas Burn of MLS realized that their objective of building a stronger base of Hispanic fans required a change in their marketing structure. At the time they had only one person working on this objective—a Hispanic media liaison who also worked in community relations. The Burn made him director of the new Department of Hispanic Marketing and Community Development that had a staff of two account executives and a community liaison. From a single person trying to do several jobs, the Burn now had four people with a single mission. The Burn had reconfigured structure to follow strategy. On the other hand, the Women's United Soccer Association failed to align structure with strategy. A start-up league that required strong ticket sales to survive, the WUSA was top-heavy with senior executives and hollow at the level of sales staff. No wonder the league folded so quickly.[26]

We offer a sample design for a sport marketing function in figure 15.2. Although the sample is geared to high-performance spectator sport, the framework can be adjusted to the needs, resources, and products of other sport organizations. After outlining some of the basic positions, we discuss indexes and measures for evaluating performance.

- Chief Revenue Officer, Chief Marketing Officer, or Senior Associate Athletics Director– External Affairs

– Responsible for all marketing, sales, and communication efforts, reporting directly to the organization's chief executive or athletics director

– Oversees all other marketing, sales, service, and communication directors

– Responsible for developing an annual strategic plan; outlining all marketing goals and objectives, strategies and tactics, and program activities; and controlling their effectiveness

– Determines budgets and resource allocations

- Executive Assistant of Marketing and Communications

– Supports the CRO, CMO, or senior associate athletics director

– Supports all marketing, sales, service, and communication directors and staff

- VP or Director of Marketing or Customer Experience*

– Responsible for the design, layout, and media selection of all advertising and collateral materials (electronic and print)

- Manager of Advertising and Promotions

– Responsible for all creative copy and illustrations in all print media published by the organization (an in-house function in larger sport organizations, particularly those with two teams or responsibility for managing the venue;

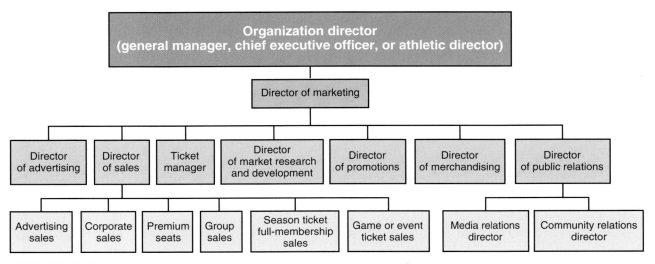

FIGURE 15.2 An optimal organizational chart for the sport marketing function.

may be contracted out to an advertising agency in smaller organizations and in most collegiate environments)

– Responsible for working with the creative department or outside advertising agency in generating, planning, and implementing all paid media initiatives (TV, radio, print, outdoor, and electronic digital and social media programs)

– Responsible for developing the promotional calendar and the execution of all sales promotions, give-away items, and all pregame and postgame events

– Coordinated with the role of the director or manager of in-game entertainment, the director or manager of public relations, and the director or manager of community relations

• Manager of Creative and Graphic Design

– Responsible for design, layout, and production of all electronic and print collateral and advertising

– Frequently tasked with design and layout of all print publications such as game program, media guides, yearbook, season-ticket and group-ticket brochures, pocket schedules, and so on

• Manager of Market Research and Consumer Knowledge

– Responsible for providing primary and secondary market data; identifies and creates preliminary penetration plans for new markets

– Provides service support to sales and public relations staff in terms of market research, intelligence, and fan demographic data and match to potential marketing partner consumers

• Manager of Database Marketing

– Responsible for overseeing database marketing for the organization and executing the organization's fan contact data capture plan

– Responsible for all data collection efforts (sales entry, enter-to-win ballots, texts, website visitors, and so on)

– Responsible for overseeing data entry, maintenance, and hygiene (cleaning, de-duplicating, and data appending)

– Production of all lists and segmented targets for campaigns and outbound sales efforts

– Responsible for producing reports on database demographics and trends, such as geotargeting based on sales patterns (heat mapping)

• Manager of In-Game Entertainment

– Responsible for producing all in-game and fan experience programs in venue, consisting of all of the following elements:

– Game experience script for each game or event and coordination of all entertainment and experience elements
  ○ Video production, execution, and timing
  ○ PA announcer
  ○ Band and music
  ○ Dance team
  ○ In-venue spirit squad
  ○ Promotional and sponsor elements, contests, and other entertainment features

• Manager of Electronic Media

– Responsible for developing and executing the mobile marketing strategy, coordinating and supporting with the director or manager of advertising and promotions in all sales efforts and marketing campaigns delivered electronically through the Internet, e-mail, mobile, digital, and social platforms

• Mobile Marketing Coordinator

– In larger sport organizations, in coordination with the manager of creative and graphic design, this position produces the mobile electronic media campaign creative, oversees execution and analysis of return on objectives (ROO) and return on investment (ROI)

– In collegiate environments, manages the student volunteer staff, one per each sport, that produces daily blogs, photographs, and video postings for the sport, which are shared through relevant platforms to insiders, season-ticket holders, parents and friends of student-athletes, and other relevant constituencies

- E-Marketing Coordinator
  - In larger sport organizations, performs the same role as the mobile marketing coordinator for all Internet and e-mail campaigns
- Web Master
  - Responsible for managing the website—design, layout, positioning, and content
  - Ensures freshness and relevance and meets the organization's needs in brand imaging, communication, information, entertainment, engagement, and driving commercial revenues (ticket sales and sponsor partner activations)
  - Supports the many interests that the website serves and supports (e.g., the sport coaches and players, marketing, sales, marketing partnership, venue operations, public relations and communications, community relations, and promotions)
- Social Media Coordinator
  - In larger organizations, works closely with the e-marketing coordinator and mobile marketing coordinator to execute programs through the appropriate social network channels
- VP or Director of Corporate Marketing Partnerships*
  - Responsible for all corporate marketing partnerships and sponsorships
  - Oversees all sales, service, and activation staff
  - Develops the annual partnership sales and service plan
  - Evaluates and prices inventory and packaging and exclusivity strategy
- Manager of Partnership Sales
  - Responsible for overseeing all sales staff and all efforts in meeting revenue goals
- Manager of Partnership Service
  - Responsible for overseeing all partnership service staff and all sponsor activation and service elements and programs
- VP or Director of Ticket Sales and Service*
  - Manager of premium seating sales and service. Responsible for sales of luxury boxes or suites and club or premium seating that combines suite amenities but has fewer seat purchase requirements
  - Manager of new season-ticket sales. Responsible for overseeing the sales of all full, partial, and miniticket plan sales
  - Manager of group ticket sales. Responsible for overseeing the sales of all group ticket programs, including the effective execution of all fan experience package (FEP) elements
  - Manager of season-ticket service and retention. Responsible for the service and retention of all existing season-ticket accounts, whether full plan or partial or miniplan holders; achieves annual renewal goals plus add-on (additional seats) and up-sell (move to better and more expensive seat locations) targets
  - Manager of ticket service. Directs the efforts of the ticket office or box office staff (and window sales staff on game day); responsible for managing the ticket inventory, account management, control of all tickets, fulfillment, and distribution; produces all sales, financial, and inventory reports; allocates tickets to various constituencies and ticket outlets (distribution network); allocates press or guest passes and media credentials
- VP of Communications or Sports Information Director
  - Responsible for all relations with the media
  - Disseminates information, distributes press releases, creates media guides, has input into website content, and organizes press conferences
  - Coordinates with the ticket manager on press credentials and the assignment of media to the press box
  - Controls the press box and develops game-day statistics
- Manager of Public Relations
  - Directs the media relations and publications functions
  - In larger organizations, has an assistant

- Manager of Customer Relations
  - Develops, coordinates, and executes all community relations activities
  - Responsible for activity development in the community and at the facility, including sport camps or clinics, community nights, athlete and personnel appearances, and relationships with general consumers other than the media; also responds to all fan mail
- VP of Broadcasting*
  - Manages the broadcast function; if rights are maintained in-house, manages production and on-air talent and coordinates with marketing partnership sales and service staff to ensure delivery of all sponsor and advertiser obligations; ensures quality broadcasts and manages spot inventory and trafficking team and program advertising to drive ticket sales
- Director of Athletics Development**
  - Oversees the athletics development function and staff and ensures accomplishment of revenue goals through the annual fund, major gifts, and all capital campaigns

Notes

*In intercollegiate athletics, these functions may be outsourced.

**Intercollegiate athletics only.

Each of these functions is essential to an effective marketing effort. The failure to perform any one of the functions substantially reduces marketing efficiency. Small organizations typically combine these functions because of resource limitations. But depending on the skill set of the employee, critical responsibilities are invariably not performed at all or are executed at a less than satisfactory level. Another approach is to subcontract these functions to sport marketing firms or advertising agencies. When necessary, the directors of various functions can carry out the operational activities as well as maintain their primary responsibilities for planning and control. A small organizational structure, however, can have a collapsing effect. The necessity of combining roles can have the following counterproductive results:

- Lack of specialization results in lack of expertise. A manager hires either a person who is an expert in one task and not good in the other or someone who has general ability but no expertise in either task. This circumstance is common in colleges that hire one person to direct both marketing and communications.
- The emphasis turns to operations (getting the job done) rather than planning or control. Accomplishing the operational tasks precludes planning or reflecting on performance or strategies. The ability to analyze staff performance and provide training diminishes rapidly.

This latter effect can be visualized from figure 15.2. In small structures, the higher levels of management activity are lost and the degree of specialization is severely reduced; planning and control ceases completely or is limited to budget preparation. Some might claim that the structure in figure 15.2 is unwieldy and too expensive. Obviously, size and scope vary with the organization's objectives and resources, but invariably organizations get what they pay for. In revenue generation, organizations need to invest in people and resources to generate revenues and attendance.

Performance Measures for the Marketing Units

As noted earlier, the entire marketing unit needs clear objectives that move it closer to the organization's overall goals. A large college athletics department, for instance, may have marketing goals that include (1) improving the brand or program image, (2) increasing ticket revenues, and (3) obtaining a larger share of the entertainment market locally or regionally.

Such organizational goals can be translated into specific marketing objectives that clarify, for instance,

- the number of favorable stories that the public relations staff should nurture in print or electronic media;
- improved results in fan satisfaction surveys;
- the amount of revenue to be generated through various ticket packages, licensing agreements, or television contracts; or
- relative increases in television or radio ratings in comparison with those of competitors (e.g., regional professional teams).

Marketers must recognize and employ standard units of measurement to determine whether they are reaching their goals. In the club industry, trade associations like the International Health, Racquet & Sportsclub Association (IHRSA) have prepared standard industry data reports that provide essential benchmarking data such as club averages on items like revenue per member, revenue per square foot, and membership turnover.

Historically, the spectator sport industry lacked regular, rigorous surveys that established such benchmarks of performance. Leagues commissioned occasional surveys, but these did little to grab the attention of managers and marketers. In the last decade, however, trade publications such as *Team Marketing Report, SportsBusiness Daily*, and *Street & Smith's SportsBusiness Journal* have created indexes of performance, such as *TMR*'s fan cost index (discussed in chapter 8). But clearly the most effective effort was the NBA's Team Marketing and Business Operations (TMBO), which was funded to the highest level by commissioner David Stern. TMBO developed numerous best practices that have been widely adopted by the entire sport business industry. Following are some other recent attempts to develop performance ratios and indexes:[27]

- Alan Friedman (*Team Marketing Report* founder) and Paul Much also created a penetration index to analyze the performance of professional sport teams. The penetration index simply took a team's total attendance for the most recent season divided by the total population of the team's metropolitan statistical area. Of course, the penetration index must be analyzed with other data such as the number of competing professional franchises and collegiate sport teams in the market (given the spillover of seasons), but it offers a starting place for analysis.

- The rise of Internet commerce has resulted in greater efforts to measure success. The industry no longer accepts hits as an index of popularity, because the number of hits is a technical measure of the number of files served. The industry standards are unique visitors, the average time that a visitor spends at a given site (typically per month), and website visits. For e-mailing messages and campaigns, the essential measures are open rates, click-through rates, page views, and length of time on the site.

- *Street & Smith's SportsBusiness Journal* offers regular features that analyze marketing performance. These include attendance variations as a function of special promotions such as bobblehead giveaways, mascot birthday parties, and fireworks; Internet popularity; television ratings; and radio penetration.

- Likewise, academic journals such as *Sport Marketing Quarterly* and the *Journal of Sport Management* have fostered public dialogue on the strengths and weaknesses of measurements such as signage exposure, consumer recall and recognition, and economic impact studies.

- Consulting firms such as J.D. Power and Associates have provided teams with in-depth assessments of customer service satisfaction.

Of course, indexes are always subject to debate. But they must be developed before they can be debated and tested in the marketplace, so the trends noted earlier are all to the good—for the industry, its marketers, and its consumers.

As you'll see in the upcoming sidebar on the Brevard County Manatees, general objectives must be refined for the people working in each unit. The Manatees built their checklist based on a general objective—to attract additional casual customers and families and move them up the escalator. The following are some sample measures that can be adjusted for any overall plan.

Some sample analytics for each area of marketing are as follows:

Sales

- Sales dollar volume measured by number of units sold (tickets, signs, advertisements, and so on) and revenue
- Market share or increase in sales volume measured from year to year
- Percentage of prospects contacted from salesperson's contact records
- New business developed, measured from actual sales records by unit and dollars

Public Relations (each component of the public relations function can be monitored using appropriate criteria)

Media Relations

- Amount of media coverage (e.g., column inches, airtime) as evidenced by records such as clippings files

- Quality of coverage and media receptivity to the sport organization
- Quantity of legitimate media complaints received
- Number of unique visitors to the organization's website

Community Relations

- Number of community groups contacted
- Number of community projects held in the community or at the facility
- Sales revenues (e.g., merchandising) that result from the community relations effort
- Number of positive and negative letters received from the public
- Number of children who participate in special programs (summer reading, student achievers)

- Measurable outcomes of community projects (e.g., reading level improvement among children who participated in a team-sponsored reading program; total land area of new fields built for a community)

Ticket Service (Box Office) Manager

- Accuracy of financial records
- Minimization of errors, losses, or unaccountables
- Development of a ticket distribution network and innovations in distribution policies

Promotions and Advertising

- Number of promotions generated
- Sales response to each specific promotion

Screening Marketing Programs, Initiatives, Campaigns, and Promotions Against Objectives

Minor league baseball is known for its constant stream of promotions. Almost every inning of every game seems to be filled with some attraction beyond the game itself. As reported by Dan Migala in the *Migala Report,* the Brevard County (Florida) Manatees, a single A ballclub, developed a set of criteria against which to screen all proposed promotions. The Manatees saw families, especially moms, as their principal targets for promotions. They wanted to move casual fans up the escalator. Some of the promotions might flop, but they wanted above all to avoid negative press or negative word of mouth because of an offensive program. Here is the Brevard County Manatees promotional idea checklist:[28]

Is it fun?

Is it feasible?

Is it affordable?

Will it add to the fan experience?

Will it be a $2 bill? (i.e., unwanted or avoided)

Is the timing right?

Is it suffering from the 8-ball syndrome? (dead in the corner)

Has the remainder of the staff approved?

Is it marketable?

Will we have to apologize tomorrow?

Will it promote the team or sponsor positively?

Will it pass the family test? (If your immediate family came to the game, would Mom be proud or ashamed?)

What will happen if we don't seize the moment?

And last of all, when in doubt, WWVD (what would Veeck do)?

- Overall image developed from promotional activities, as measured by brand strength and brand awareness or message awareness research; number of opens and click-throughs on an e-mail campaign and actual sales results determined from embedded promotional codes

Marketing and Sponsorships
- Media exposure of sponsor images (e.g., minutes of television time)
- Sponsor renewal rate

Merchandise and Team Store or Pro Shop
- Revenue per square foot
- Stock turn

Market Research and Development
- Timeliness and accuracy of data collected (primary)
- Recentness of secondary data supplied
- Ability of data-based marketing system to stimulate sales and marketing effectiveness
- Number of new markets developed and direct sales from those leads

This last function is perhaps one of the hardest to control because the output is the least subject to quantitative performance appraisal. Some relationships, however, can be computed.

Research and development is surely a creative process; a good data-based marketing system processes and analyzes consumer complaints as carefully as it does ticket sales. Likewise, the chief marketing officer or chief revenue officer must be creative in fashioning a system of appraisal criteria that is both fair and challenging. The effective manager is aware of all industry standards—from concession per caps to sponsor recognition rates, unique visitors, and attendance as a percentage of venue capacity. The manager is limited only by imagination and data availability.

Linking Personnel Performance to Strategy

The marketing effort may be conceptualized as a series of goals and objectives, followed by specific strategies and tactics designed to accomplish those goals, but nothing happens without a dedicated and competent staff. Someone or some group, then, must also lead and manage. We discussed sales staff training in chapter 8, but we reiterate here some simple steps to follow to enhance staff performance across the marketing functions.

- **Step 1.** The manager or director sits down with the staff, using a participative approach to setting performance goals and objectives. The manager or director clearly communicates expectations, performance goals, methods of evaluation, probable rewards for success, and negative reinforcements for failure.

- **Step 2.** Performance is evaluated, initially at monthly intervals for most staff (with intervals lengthening over time). For the first-time sales staff in inside sales of the fan relationship management center (FRMC), these evaluations are daily for the first week and then generally weekly for the next few months until best practice has become a habit. After satisfactory performance occurs, most marketing staff members are evaluated only once every 12 months. Again, sales staff are measured against weekly goals for call volume, call duration and quality, the number of referrals and in-venue appointments set (the root), and sales volume by units and dollars (the fruit).

- **Step 3.** When the staff member has areas of weakness or areas that need improvement, the director or manager should outline the course for training, development, or corrective action.

- **Step 4.** At each annual review, a new "contract" is developed that builds on the experience of the previous evaluation period and provides a joint commitment to achieving goals.

Dr. Roland Smith, who has consulted with major league teams on their human resources strategies, has a series of useful questions to ask about any performance evaluation system:

- Does it encourage the behavior that results in higher levels of performance?
- Is it fair?
- Does it equitably reward top performers for their efforts?
- Does it clearly represent a roadmap to success for average performers? (Compensation and performance management guide behavior.)

- Does it identify poor performers in a real-time manner (for corrective action)?
- Is it easily administered?
- Are the performance metrics clearly identified and easily understood?

Through a systematic approach to managing the marketing function, the director can directly influence the organization's success. Each function is crucial to the marketing effort, whether performed by specialists or by people who perform two or more activities. To make a simple sport analogy, the marketing staff are the athletes out on the field, in the trenches, day after day. To ensure a coordinated, successful effort, they need a genuine plan (the marketing and sales plan) and intelligent, hands-on, face-to-face, constructive coaching.[29]

Numbers Versus Core Values

Jack Welch, a longtime CEO of General Electric, told the authors of *Built to Last* that GE boiled down its personnel evaluation to two sets of items: core values and numbers. Although one could argue that numbers should always reflect core values, Welch understood that too often the most easily measurable numbers crowded out equally important but sometimes unquantifiable criteria. Welch's description conjures the image of a small table that provides a simple, preliminary screening tool (table 15.3).

The table reinforces the firm's belief that core values count more than numbers. Someone who advances core values always gets another chance; someone who makes the numbers but does not embody values gets a hard, long look. As Welch put it, "The problem is with those who make the numbers but don't share the values. . . . We try to persuade them; we wrestle with them; we

TABLE 15.3 Core Values and Numbers

| | | Embodies core values | |
		Yes	No
Numbers performance	Yes	Promote onward and upward	Take a hard, long look
	No	Give another chance	Fire them

agonize over these people." Welch's attitude is an important one for sport managers to remember. Numbers should never trump values in personnel evaluation, but values alone are not sufficient to maintain long-term employment.[30]

ACTIVITY 15.1 The Five Ps
In this WSG activity you will compare and contrast the interaction and impact of the five Ps on one another, and you will consider how sport organizations use the five Ps to market their products.

Wrap-Up

The notion of control moves the sport marketer from a land of wishful thinking to a realm of meaningful management. We have emphasized the need to control the marketing function, from research on potential consumers and their needs, to market segmentation, to product position, to the marketing mix, to sponsorships, and finally to an evaluation of success. In today's sport marketplace, marketers must be managers and managers must be marketers.

As we have illustrated with countless examples throughout this textbook, the sport industry is evolving rapidly. Going forward, the pressures will only increase to develop effective, innovative, and creative sport marketing techniques. The simple selling-of-sport approach—a giveaway here, some fireworks here and there—will not suffice. The market is more crowded and consumers are more complex than was the case in 1928, when sport promoter Tex Rickard told a reporter, "By merely reading the newspapers, most anybody can tell what the public wants to see." The future Tex Rickard will be part scientist, armed with the latest techniques for research and development, and part artist, reshaping the product with creative inspiration that evokes passion and inspires colleagues and consumers alike. And in today's digitally connected world, the successful sport marketer will have a firm grasp of technology, social media, and the rapidity with which tastes and attention change. Whatever the game, the technique will be the same. A comprehensive, controlled, and strong marketing effort, coupled with listening and observing skills and creative ideas, will be the winning formula.

Activities

1. As a simple review, find at least two examples of each cross-effect among the five Ps, either in this book or in some other resource.

2. Using an example from a current sport organization, illustrate the effects of price on the remaining four Ps. Describe scenarios that demonstrate both positive and negative effects.

3. In your estimation, does one of the five Ps have greater cross-effect than the others? Price perhaps? Find examples to defend your position.

Your Marketing Plan

Lay out a clear diagram of the marketing structure for your organization. Be sure that the structure logically follows the direction and requirements of your overall strategy and its related plans. Include job descriptions and performance criteria for each position. Outline a process for evaluating each staff member, each unit, and the marketing unit as a whole.

Endnotes

1. The notion of ticket marketing, sales, and service as a coordinated function and the service mark concept of the TiMSS plan were developed in 2011 by the principal author of this text, Dr Bernie Mullin, in his role as chairman and CEO of the Aspire Sport Marketing Group LLC.

2. Presentation by Joel Maturi, then athletics director at the University of Minnesota at the Annual Collegiate Athletics Forum presented by *SportsBusiness Journal*, Marriott Hotel, New York in December 2010.

3. Presentation by Kevin Plank, owner and CEO, to the Leaders in Performance Conference, held at Chelsea Football Club's Stamford Bridge Stadium, London, England, in October 2010.

4. Ibid.

5. "SI Says Nike Made 'Vast Miscalculation' on Tiger Woods Line," *SBD*, 19 August 1997, 3.

6. L. Zepp, "Supermarket Promo Lifts Attendance for Ohio State Lady Buckeyes Games," *Amusement Business*, 6 February 1988, 13, 15.

7. Michael Eisner with Tony Schwartz, "Running the Mouse House," *Newsweek*, 28 September 1998, 58.

8. "Jazz and Hostess Offer Fans a Colorful Snackfood," *Team Marketing Report* (March 1994): 6.

9. Stuart Miller, "New Technology Is Transforming Games Into Multimedia Events," *SSSBJ*, 10–16 March 2003, 33; Russell Adams, "Before Game and After, Razzle-Dazzle Reigns," *SSSBJ*, 10–16 March 2003, 32; "Full Immersion: AFL Offers Fans a Wired Experience," *SBD*, 19 April 2000.

10. For scholarly assaults on Nike, see Steven Jackson and David Andrews, *Sport, Culture and Advertising: Identities, Commodities, and the Politics of Represen-tation* (New York: Routledge, 2005); "Nike Pulls Shoe Offensive to Muslims," *Boston Globe*, 25 June 1997, C-2.

11. "Stern Says League Needs to Address Player Behavior Issues," *SBD*, 2 June 1997, 13.

12. P. Amend and W. Tobin, "Tax Exempts: A Snake in the Grass?" *Club Business*, November 1988, 34–38, 64–67.

13. "New Texas Twister: Rangers/Stars Combine Ticket Packages," *SBD*, 6 March 1998, 17; D. Kaplan, "Tom Hicks Eyes Profits—and Wins—in His Sports Ventures," *SSSBJ*, 8–14 February 1999, 1, 46.

14. Matt Schuman, "Paying the Price: Parking Fees Will Hurt UNC Fans," *Greeley Tribune*, 8 September 2005, www.greeleytrib.com; B. Lumpkin and P. Finebaum, "Alabama Weathers Storm Over Priority Ticket Plan," *NCAA News*, 10 June 1987, 9.

15. Tom Weir, "Promise of Refund Paying Off in PR," *USA Today*, 19 March 2003, 3C.

16. A. Bernstein, "NFL's Soft-Drink, Fast-Food Deals Slow in Coming," *SSSBJ*, 15–21 June 1998, 9.

17. "Are Autograph and Collectible Shows Worth It for Athletes?" *SBD*, 1 September 1998, 5.

18. L. Berling-Manuel, "Giants Weathering Bay City Blues," *Advertising Age*, 2 August 1984, 10–11.

19. "IHL Dragons Increase in-Arena Interaction by Putting Partisans in Penalty Box," *Team Marketing Report*, 9 (January 1997): 9.

20. Bruce Mohl, "Pass Interference," *Boston Sunday Globe*, 3 October 2004, E-1, E-8.

21. Wayne Henninger, "Road to New Home Smoother With Fine-Tuned Campaign, Pirates Find," *SSSBJ*, 11–17 June 2001, 12.

22. "For the Record," *Sports Illustrated,* 26 April 2004, 24.

23. For excellent insight into strategy and control in sport organizations, see T. Slack, *Understanding Sport Organizations: The Application of Organizational Theory* (Champaign, IL: Human Kinetics, 1997); D. Howard and J. Crompton, *Financing Sport,* 2nd ed. (Morgantown, WV: Fitness Information Technology, 2003).

24. Middlebury College Athletics website, http://www.middlebury.edu/about/handbook/athletics.

25. A. Bernstein, "Without a Breakaway Threat, MLS Aims for Steady, Long-Term Growth," *SSSBJ,* 13–19 July 1998, 14.

26. Russell Adams, "Braves New World: Gains at Tate, on TV," *SSSBJ,* 10–16 May 2004, 6; *SBD,* 27 November 1997, 8. On the WUSA, see Richard Southall, Mark Nagel, and Deborah LeGrande, "Build It and They Will Come? The Women's United Soccer Association: Collision of Exchange Theory and Strategic Philanthropy," *SMQ,* 14 (3) (2005): 158–167.

27. A. Friedman and P. Much, *Inside the Ownership of Professional Team Sports* (Chicago: Team Marketing Report, 1997); "Top Sports Radio Stations," *SSSBJ,* 14–20 August 2000, 30; "Web World: NBA Scores With Playoffs," *SSSBJ,* 28 June–4 July 2004, 14; Langdon Borckington, "Texans Bring in J.D. Power to Gauge Service," *SSSBJ,* 29 July–4 August 2002, 8; "Giveaways That Paid Off at the Gate," *SSSBJ,* 18–24 October 2004, 18; Mark McDonald and Daniel Rascher, "Does Bat Day Make Cents? The Effect of Promotions on the Demand for Major League Baseball," *Journal of Sport Management,* 14 (2000): 8–27. For a different look at community relations, see Stephen Hardy et al., "Image Isn't Everything," *Athletic Business,* May 2006, 50–56.

28. *Migala Report,* 1 August 2004, www.migalareport.com; Official website of Brevard County Manatees, www.manateesbaseball.com, 2005.

29. Roland Smith questions in the *Migala Report* 1, 1 March 2004, www.migalareport.com.

30. James C. Collins and Jerry I. Porras, *Built to Last: Successful Habits of Visionary Companies* (New York: HarperCollins, 1999), 72.

Chapter 16
The Shape of Things to Come

In developing this chapter, we jokingly referred to it as the Nostradamus chapter. Our intent was to provide our thoughts on what the future, the next five years or so, might hold for sport marketing. What follows is our humble attempt to look beyond the veil and see what *may* be. We gratefully acknowledge the contributions of our contribution visionaries.

From Our Crystal Ball

Before looking forward, let's review what we said in 2007, predicting what we would see by 2013. The original prediction is in italics, exactly as it appeared in the third edition of *Sport Marketing*, which was released in 2007.

- *The portability of sport viewership will provide true connectivity and on-demand information.* If anything, we underestimated how widespread and critical portability turned out to be by 2013, and it is only going to become more prevalent as a source for up-to-the-minute content as well as for watching sporting events and possibly, in the near future, concerts and other forms of live entertainment.

- *Sport facilities in Europe and Asia will take on a decidedly American look as American interest, the potential of media dollars, affiliation with American professional leagues, as well as investment have a major influence.* Again, largely because of the growth and influence of AEG, we were accurate on this prediction. The O2 in London, Shanghai's Mercedes-Benz Arena, London's Wembley and Emirates Stadiums, and Allianz Arena in Munch are just a few of the venues that now rival or exceed the best facilities in North America.

- *Small-market baseball owners will pressure MLB to find a solution to the lack of competitiveness that plagues the league.* Some definite fiscal change has occurred through increased revenue sharing and the revenue produced by MLBAM. Teams such as the Pittsburgh Pirates have invested that money into the player draft and building their farm systems to be able to compete, at least periodically. I would rate our grade on this prediction as incomplete; more change is coming but not to the extent that we predicted would occur by 2012.

- *Corporate sponsors' names, logos, or both will appear on the uniforms of at least one professional league in the United States.* Again we were close—the WNBA has some teams with sponsor names, and a majority of teams in MLS have sponsor identification on the uniforms. But our prediction was targeting MLB, the NBA, NFL, and NHL, and we thought that the NBA would be first. So where do we stand, and why has it not moved further along? A significant number of professional teams in all leagues have sold sponsorships on their practice uniforms, but none of the big four leagues has taken the plunge and sold the game uniform. The NBA and its teams have come out in favor (not unanimously) of selling sponsorship identification, initially in the form of a patch, and have been discussing not only how to implement the sales process but also, and more important, how to share the revenue, which at this point appears to be the main obstacle.

- *Collegiate athletics programs will figure out that they are also in the sport entertainment business and need to sell tickets. Ticket sales departments in major universities will become more prevalent.* We were spot-on with this prediction as the Aspire Group (created by coauthor Dr. Bernie Mullin) and others have emerged as major providers of this service and have grown exponentially in the past four years. Although some schools, particularly nationally ranked programs with historically high attendance, have taken this operation in house, outsourcing has become the model for several reasons. First, outsourcing media and sponsorship sales has produced greater financial returns. Second, college athletics departments face difficulty when trying to implement standard sales compensation programs such as commissions and performance bonuses, which are not common forms of compensation in colleges and universities.

- *Women's professional sport leagues will show little "real" growth.* We felt uncomfortable about making this prediction and even worse about being accurate. The WNBA has entered its 17th season, and women's professional soccer has been resurrected from the ashes of the WUSA, but neither has shown a consistent pattern of growth. The WNBA has welcomed three major stars from the college ranks and is buoyed by a new relationship with ESPN that may attract viewers and drive attendance. On the nonteam side of women's professional sport, the WTA and LPGA are healthy and experiencing international growth. These results demonstrate one of our abiding principles: Markets cannot be assumed or taken for granted. Girls and women are playing basketball and soccer in huge numbers, but this does not automatically translate into a market of consumers willing to pay to watch the games.

• *Cell phones and PDAs will become the ticket and credit card accepted at all major sport venues while continuing to be a valued source of interactive marketing and participation opportunities.* Look around you. Thanks to Apple, who really drove home the importance of portability and being connected without being tethered, we are consuming sport where and when we please, and we are the program and content managers. We have not quite reached the point where we can use our cell phones as wallets. We are close, but our sport teams and venues have not invested sufficiently to make this as commonly practiced as it will be by 2015.

• *At least one more major U.S sport league will follow the lead of the NFL and hold its championship game at a neutral site. In addition, more All-Star Games will be located in major entertainment and tourism destinations both in the United States and abroad.* We completely missed on the first half of this prediction. MLB, the NBA, and the NHL all play a best-of-seven series. Taking the seventh game and moving it to a neutral site penalizes both the players and the fans. On the second half of the prediction, the NBA has chosen a major tourism destination site (Las Vegas) as well as other tourism destinations that are also NBA cities for its all-star games. It is becoming apparent that the NBA is less concerned with rotating games to every NBA city and more concerned with creating a week of memorable events and activities that promote the league and its players in markets that are attractive and accessible nationally and internationally. In that same vein, look for the NBA to be the first of the four major U.S.-based leagues to hold its all-star game outside the United States.

• *The availability of national media outlets (i.e., regional sports television channels) and the lure of quick cash infusions will begin having a noticeable effect on top-tier high school athletics programs, which will schedule athletics contests on a national scale and "rent" athletes for one- or two-year terms to become attractions.* Although this has occurred, additional reasons have been in play. The power and influence of the AAU is reshaping high school basketball. High schools are chosen because of their history of producing elite athletes, their relationship with influential AAU coaches, past rankings, and

their history of traveling to televised out-of-state games. Sadly, the neighborhood in which a player resides is not necessarily a critical factor for elite high school athletes.

Overall, I would give us a grade of A minus. We could have done better, but given the time when we made these predictions, we believe that we have lived up to our self-proclaimed abilities as prognosticators.

From Our Crystal Ball Redux: By the Year 2020

Therefore, we offer our predictions for things that we think we will see by 2020, along with four things that we would like to see happen, although we may be engaging in wishful thinking.

• *Corporate sponsorship names and logos will be placed on game uniforms.* We are taking no real risk here; it almost happened in the NBA, and we have no reason to think that it won't happen in the next six years. The size of the revenue stream and the limited associated costs make it a certainty; how to share and fairly distribute the revenue is the only major question that remains to be answered. We believe that the NBA will be first. The real question is who will be second; we predict the NHL. One consequence of this development could be cannibalization of venue naming rights.

• *We will stop referring to the big four professional leagues in the United States and will have a big five.* The growth of the MLS geographically and in terms of attendance and viewership will force the conversation. Among the contributing factors are the success of the MLS in markets such as Seattle, Kansas City, and Portland; the global involvement and influence of the EPL and other international leagues; and the reach and power of ESPN and NBC in making the sport available on their families of networks. Competition and interest among other networks has resulted in multiple broadcasting opportunities for soccer programming in the United States.

• *The success (in terms of attendance, ratings, and financial payments to NCAA schools) of the four-team playoff for the national championship in college football will result in another round of conversation to expand the playoff format.* We see expansion to six or eight teams after the agreement is renewed and expanded. This change will result largely from reorganization of the NCAA by establishing a premier or superdivision comprised of the following six conferences:

Big 10

Big 12

Pac-12

Atlantic Coast Conference (ACC)

Southeastern Conference (SEC)

American Athletic Conference

Although the names might not be geographically or numerically accurate, the economic and media power clearly lies with those conferences. Establishing a distinct division of these schools will prevent them from leaving the NCAA to create their own organization (at least for now). At the same time, clear-cut divisional lines may help other divisions become more defined in terms of identity and financial solvency.

- *The success of the secondary market will force teams to reconsider the definition of the term season ticket, leading to the death of the original season-ticket concept (every game) in some but not all markets.*

- *Emphasis on the game-day experience at the venue will undergo a major transformation based on technology, emotional connectivity, and benefits to the attendee.* Getting people to attend and leave their home theaters and connectivity will continue to be a crucial challenge for sport teams and leagues. The concern is how the concept of enhanced fan experience will evolve. Much of the current emphasis revolves around apps that provide fans readily accessible sport content that may or may not enhance the in-stadium or in-arena experience and frequently fails to have the desired effect of driving more people to attend in person. Nonetheless, we see content providers in this space growing rapidly by helping fund bandwidth growth and increased connectivity within sport venues to satisfy a younger generation that desires to be always connected.

- *Despite rule changes, fear of long-term brain damage, and other health and safety concerns, we see little if any measurable decline in the popularity of football at any level in the next six years or so.* After that, anything is possible, depending on lawsuits and the willingness of soccer moms and even the president of the United States to encourage and support their sons in playing America's national pastime. The possibility is also becoming a real

concern in ice hockey. If these concerns continue to increase, look for lacrosse to become a boom sport.

- *Corporate partnership opportunities and benefits will extend dramatically to a corporate partner family that includes other businesses as well as the consumer base of each of those businesses, resulting in a B to B+C approach.* The partners will be seeking less signage and more engagement through activation and long-term equity in community involvement programs.

- *Fans will become more involved in decision making regarding how the sport is played, packaged, or presented.* The 2013 PGA Championship, in which fans voted on the location of pin placements, along with recent development of having fans vote on uniforms, promotions such as giveaway items, and concessions menus are going to become commonplace. Whether the experiment of permitting fans to vote on the contracts and renewal of a GM (MLS' Seattle Sounders in 2012 retained GM Adrian Hanauer, who is also an owner, with a 96 percent approval rating) is extended to other sports is beyond the view in our crystal ball.

- *Globalization in terms of competition and broadcasting will continue to increase at a high rate.* The race to be the first league with an international presence in a meaningful championship-focused competition and experience will be clearly an area of emphasis. We believe that the first will most likely be UEFA's European Champions League or the Barclays Premier League ahead of the NBA, which could also emerge.

Here are four things that we would like to see happen:

1. That the massive increase in TV rights payments and the greater inside access provided to rights holders (i.e., to coaches, players, or athletes on the sidelines and in dressing rooms) does not diminish in-person attendance

2. Commercially successful women's professional sports

3. Extended global competition in North American sports and a true world champion in the traditional major league sports—baseball, hockey, and basketball

4. More support and interest in the long-term welfare of the student-athlete and sharing the wealth with those who produce it

Again, we have solicited the thoughts and efforts of some of our respected colleagues in the field, both nationally and internationally. We now share their thoughts with you.

Abraham D. Madkour

Executive Editor
SportsBusiness Journal, Daily, and Global

Over my 20 years of working in the sport business, I don't recall a more bullish environment around the industry. Frankly, July 2013, as I write this, is as good a time as any to be in the sport business. Sport is clearly proving to be the most valuable entertainment offering in the world, with constant and growing demand. Although many argue that all elements of society are cyclical, I believe that the sport industry will be an economic and social force well into the next six years, when I'm targeting this column to be revisited. But keep things in perspective. Although a lot can happen in six years—Apple didn't unveil its first mobile app until July 2008, and see how much that has changed the consumer experience—progressive change is often slow. So, keeping that in mind, here are a few predictions on where I think the industry is headed in 2020.

- **Some things will never change**. Sports media in 2020 will be far more customized and personalized, but overall it's going to look a lot like it does now. People will be able to watch in more ways than ever, especially with the growth of mobile devices and tablets, and personalization will certainly be enhanced in that the consumer will be able to direct replays, angles, access, and footage. But here's what won't change: Television will still reign supreme for sport, and ESPN will still be battling Fox, which will still be battling NBC Sports and CBS Sports. Most of the big media rights deals run up until the early 2020s, so expect the current landscape to remain the same. People are waiting for big, nontraditional companies like Google, Apple, and Microsoft to make a major investment in sports media.

But I don't see anything on the horizon, and if they do, it wouldn't come until around 2025, which is when they can pick up the rights. My bet is that Google, Apple, and Microsoft will work with ESPN and Fox to share the rights, rather than compete with them for rights.

- **Click, buy, get it now**! Look for more of an Amazonification of the sport experience. I antic-

ipate a better screen experience for fans, which will result in the immediate click, purchase, and delivery discipline that has been at the core of the success of Amazon. The ability for consumers to purchase everything that they potentially see on the screen should significantly increase commerce across merchandise and various forms of products.

- **Games without frontiers**. The globalization of sport will increase. I am not ready to say that by 2020 a major league will have an international franchise rooted outside North America, but we will see more progress toward that eventuality. Buildings and arenas still need to improve throughout the world, but we could see the NHL with a stake in a major European hockey league with multiple games in Europe; the NBA's foray into China, India, and even the United Kingdom will result in some sort of starter or developmental league in those markets; and MLB could build on its World Cup of Baseball with sponsored leagues in various parts of the world. The league that draws the biggest debate over its international growth is the NFL. Well, for one, I expect the league to maintain its series of regular-season games outside the United States. And because of its schedule and frequency of games and its emphasis on growth, I could see the league placing a franchise in the UK or elsewhere in Europe. I don't believe that they will go the route of a startup developmental or affiliated leagues based on their experience with the World League. Outside the big four, Formula 1 will look to have two races in the United States, and NASCAR will look to export some of its events to Mexico and South America. And the big question is just how big the EPL can become. The league certainly will be playing regular-season games in New York and Los Angeles, and you could see it eclipse MLS in the United States.

- **On campus**. I have two thoughts on college sports. The new football playoff will become one of the seminal holidays on the sport calendar and be a complete success—from commercial support to ratings, to media, to public discussion and coverage. The semifinals and then finals in early January set the table nicely for the NFL playoffs and deliver a healthy start of the year in the sport business. Also, watch the development of the new college football playoff's operation, currently in Dallas. Some say that it could grow so powerful in its resources and executive ranks that it could pose a threat to the NCAA's Division

I management, or at least as an alternative if the grousing about the NCAA's management and leadership continues. On that subject, I believe that another division will be formed within the NCAA Division I made up of between 50 and 75 schools, because there currently seems to be too much angst and bifurcation between the haves and the have-nots. But even with these changes, I don't expect all the issues in college sports to be resolved. As the astute Georgetown AD Lee Reed said at a panel recently when asked to predict where intercollegiate athletics will be 10 years from now, "You'll have four people sitting here talking about very similar issues. I think we're going to be talking about, discussing, and trying to solve the same issues that we have today."

- **The real estate play**. With ticket revenue close to hitting a ceiling for many organizations, there is constant pressure to grow revenue and build out the developmental footprint. I expect more sport organizations to study the real estate development models used in certain markets, such as L.A. Live and Patriot Place in Foxboro, Massachusetts, and look to partner on such ancillary projects. Such ventures are not a fit for every market, but we will see them done by successful organizations that need to diversify their businesses and aim to be players in the development around their own facilities rather than leave the prize to third parties. These projects may also serve as conduits for greater community and civic involvement.

Here are some other predictions: After more than 22 years, MLB will see a new commissioner when Bud Selig steps down after 2014. The NBA will finally approve a 2 1/2-by-2 1/2-inch (6-by-6 cm) advertising patch to be placed on players' jerseys after the revenue-sharing model is agreed on before the 2016 season. We will see a more developed sport business scene in Asia and Africa. And finally, I offer one unfortunate prediction and one total cop-out. First, the unfortunate one is that women's sport leagues in the United States will continue to struggle economically and in terms of mainstream media coverage. The cop-out is that I have no idea what effect social media will have on the fan experience, the fans' relationship with players and teams, or the ramifications for traditional media.

Susan Schroeder

VP Global Marketing Partnerships
National Basketball Association

One of the most fascinating aspects of sport business, in particular sponsorship, is that no two days are alike, no two months are alike, and even no two seasons are ever the same. New ideas, new deals, and new people keep it riveting and keep us pushing the envelope. What's clear is that the pace of change in our space is rapidly accelerating like never before—thanks to technology, the increasing empowerment of consumers, and the proliferation of outlets for consuming sport content and promoting brands. As we head toward 2020 and beyond, this cycle of change will continue to accelerate and create countless exciting new opportunities for fans, brands, properties, and professionals in our space.

What all this likely change ahead makes equally clear is that managing the web of relationships between brands and properties and agencies and media partners will also become increasingly complex, requiring ever greater multidisciplinary skills, knowledge, and vision. As the days of signage and ticket deals recede further into the rearview mirror (hooray), the person who can sell, manage, and retain successful sponsorships will resemble a cross between a marketing All-American and a UN ambassador.

The story of sponsorship in 2020 will be about how the fan experience has been revolutionized in venue, through media, and by everything in between. It will be about the increasingly sophisticated art and science of defining how all the innovations represent opportunities that deliver tangible value to all stakeholders. Reaching this goal will take people who can integrate, solve, create, and advocate for even more change (to current partnerships or new ones) at an even higher level than we see today. Like never before, innovation is going to make sponsorships obsolete the moment that the ink is dry. The next shiny object will have brands looking to properties and media partners to put them there, contract or not. Relationship managers will have to be savvy and sophisticated to make it all work, to keep partnerships thriving, and to maintain a semaphore of success in a cluttered marketplace.

Properties and agencies that build a structure to recruit, nurture, and motivate top-shelf relationship managers, that keep their business units consultative and accountable to partners, that provide ongoing training, and that reward retention and growth (as much as new business) will be at a distinct advantage.

In a future of constant change, the one constant will be the human factor in making partnerships, technology, and brands succeed. Organizations that have the talent, and the will, to grow their people will be the big winners.

Professor Luca Petruzzellis

Department of Business and Law Studies
University of Bari Aldo Moro
Bari, Italia

The world of sport is constantly changing because of the varied challenges posed not only by the industry but also by daily life. Experience is the paradigm and the value to which any league, team, sport center, or event must tend to. When people watch for, shop for, and practice sport, they are exposed to various specific stimuli, such as physical, mental, and social benefits; team-identifying colors; typefaces; slogans; mascots; and characters. These stimuli appear as part of a sport or team's identity (e.g., name, logo, signage, athletes or players), marketing communications (e.g., advertisements, brochures, celebrities), and in environments in which the sport is experienced or marketed (e.g., arenas, streets, events). These stimuli constitute the major source of subjective internal responses, which can be a cognitive, affective, and behavioral experience.

Because sport is synonymous with a healthy and balanced lifestyle, nutrition is strongly linked to sport performances and plays an important role in achieving remarkable results, whether at the professional or amateur level. Unfortunately, the growing use of performance-enhancing drugs (PEDs) because of the huge commercial interest in sport has turned talent, passion, and sacrifice into unevenness, eagerness, and shortcuts, thus undermining the real significance of sport.

Therefore, the growing importance of financial and marketing aspects call for greater professional management that should consider the social and ethical aspects of the sport industry. The emphasis should be on transmitting the right message and creating a healthier environment in which this message can flow.

Market rules, however, have overturned the spirit of sport, especially in the Olympic Games. For example, the U.S. basketball teams may have a sponsor name on their jerseys next year. Barcelona Football Club had not had a sponsor name or logo on the uniform for many years, but they decided to join a social cause with UNICEF and are now sponsored by Qatar Sports Investments. After two years of having a nonprofit sponsor on the uniform, they now carry the Qatar Airways name on the jersey.

The constant push given by financial and marketing aspects and the quest for excellence and astonishing results have also created "designer athletes," who go from being a hero to an icon, from being a role model to a celebrity. Athletes feel pressure to gain notoriety rather than be the best athlete they can be.

Above all, technology is increasing the level of sport performances by pushing the limits of physical performance and creating expectations for sensational results. For example, the world records in the FINA World Championship in Rome 2009 benefited from innovative swimming wear, diminishing the importance of talent and physical performance. Changes in the materials of tennis rackets and the ball in volleyball have affected the way that the sport is played and experienced.

Globalization of teams has accelerated in the cross-leagues or superleagues (like rugby in Europe or the NBA in Europe), which has created cross-border teams and, in a negative sense, rootless teams (e.g., the Nets from New Jersey to Brooklyn, the New Orleans Jazz becoming the Utah Jazz, the Charlotte Hornets becoming the New Orleans Hornets and then the New Orleans Pelicans).

All that said, the main challenge for the sport industry is fan disengagement. Their attachments loosen because of both negative events (e.g., doping, bad results) and social changes (e.g., economic crisis, television competition). The relationship between sport and fans is constantly changing. On the one hand, the fan is looking for an engaging experience while watching the match live. It is a matter not only of technical performance but also of experiential involvement. On the other hand, the contact between the spectator and the team is closer in TV than it is live because of technology that discloses the very moment and aspect of the game and the experience.

In conclusion, innovation, technology, and new emerging sports are the variables that are reshaping the future of sport. These variables characterize our future society.

Professor Alan Seymour

Northampton Business School
University of Northampton
Northampton, England

Sport marketing in the UK is alive and well. A vibrant perspective is illuminating the blue skies of a bourgeoning discipline, in both academia and, more important, the applied and practitioning sectors.

In the business of sport and the growth of fan engagement with all aspects of sporting pursuits, marketing associations with all these contexts will clearly develop substantially in the 21st century. The movement and momentum has been exponential within UK markets but additionally has been contextualized around major, iconic sporting events. The recent successful backdrop of the London Olympic Games and the continuing successes of major sporting events like Wimbledon, the FA Cup Final, and Open Golf Championships have only added to this status. A major focus on these classic settings has provided relevant options for sales and sponsors.

The significant academic and practitioner focus in research and sporting engagements with fans suggests a growing necessity for sport properties and organizations to develop new platforms of association with their publics, audiences, and loyal fan bases.[1] Fans' voices and new media in particular are not only being voiced more but also need to be heeded more!

The growing consideration and response among sport marketers is to understand the motivations that bring people to consume sporting events and related goods and services. Sport and sport marketing are essentially about consumption and engagement whereby the ethos and relevance to marketers lie in the effect that this has on their goods, services, and reputations.[2]

The landscape of sport business is changing, has changed, and will need to change ever more dramatically to meet the persuaders' challenge in the dawning of the new business age that we are all entering. As Philip Kotler so eloquently but practically put it: "In the coming decade marketing will be re-engineered from A–Z. There is little doubt that markets and marketing will operate on quite different principles in the early years of the 21st century."[3]

Sport as a construct within academic research and a consideration for conceptual thinking has not truly registered fully in the UK. Sport marketing needs to address this, and the author and many other sport marketing academics in the UK are leading the way by offering new degrees at UK universities as well as conference opportunities for sport marketers.[4]

The authors and theorists with sporting frameworks and practicing marketers would most likely take a fallback position along traditional and well-versed marketing models, theories, and paradigms. The view should be taken, therefore, that this contributes a new strand of thinking of distinctiveness and separation. The debate needs to recognize this and consider the effect and information channels that are consequently created. The continued commentary that sport has become a significant driver of leisure tourism, for example, and consequently a vital component in place marketing only adds to the catalyst perspective of sport as a marketing tool.[5] Sporting events, and the marketing of them, reside in the locations and settings surrounding them. Consequently, events, sport brands, and sport properties are significant marketing drivers.

The attention within the UK given to sport, its place in our lives, and its contribution to language and culture make it a major influence on attitudes, behavior, and community. The marketer who ignores sport as an influence on the consumer, especially the male consumer, makes a major mistake. Although much of this overview commentary on sport marketing needs to focus on the practical issues of sponsorship, promoting sport teams, and sport and advertising, we can also acknowledge that research in marketing and consumer behavior has tended to ignore sport.

Future Research Frameworks and Discussions

The sporting canvas is a cornucopia of engagements and partnerships that the marketing world would be wise to respect. In appreciation of this theme, it is useful to appraise some models and frameworks of marketing participation, patronage, and association. Schwartz and Hunter suggest the development of what they term the "sport marketing decision support system" (DSS) whereby the importance of research is "to collect the various data available in one place for use in making efficient and effective sports marketing decisions."[6] Recent sport marketing opportunities emanating out of the success of the Olympic Games will certainly lead to extended association with sponsors, together with legacies and increased sport participation. Audiences and publics alike will evolve to give further opportunities for sales and commercial benefits and rewards. The resultant new fan engagements and partnerships will give sport marketers more meaningful prosperity because these connections are being fuelled by social media, thus enhancing this development. The association dispensed and connected to sport teams and events could and should be registered as a mechanism for marketing segmentation and reference. Behaviors, motivations, practice, and patronage are key constructs to be considered in any sport marketing planning. The insight and intensity that this patronage brings by sport enquiry should lead to greater understanding and appreciation of how sport marketers can benefit from a study of this nature. As Rein, Kotler, and Shields remark, "The challenge for the sports industry is to find other avenues and paths to create committed fans."[7]

Reawakening Marketing Myths and Legends

Sport marketing has contributed to a revitalization of marketing activities and trends. Wherever the author ventures and delivers lectures, seminars, and workshops, the conversation always returns to the belief that sport is the oxygen of the masses and that audiences respond with vibrancy and commitment. These are now the vital tools of fan response and the voice for sport marketers. Commit to the fans, engage with their requests, and listen to their growing experiences and expertise. A 2007 article in the *Observer* suggests the new philosophy of games without frontiers whereby 21st century sport spawns a new era of explosive globalization in the marketing of sporting events and associations.[8] Retaining old fans and attracting the new world fan will become an accepted norm of marketing practice within the contexts of sporting domains. A comparison of

the last 20 years of growth indicates the pace at which sport offers the new marketer a completely different type of audience. This snapshot captures the essence of this changing landscape of sport marketing in the UK:[9]

- 14—the number of live league football matches shown on TV in 1986–87; today Sky and Setanta (now ESPN) show 184 matches.
- £3 million—sum paid by BBC and ITV for football rights per season; the latest deal with digital TV is worth £1.7 billion (£567 million for the next three seasons).

The sport marketing dynamic will prosper in creating platforms of marketing equity only by connecting with their audiences and publics. This connection should develop exponentially and transformationally. This play may be evident not only through the elusive fan concept as depicted by Rein et al. but more significantly for marketing practice through the new captivated fan.[10] Given the increasing capacity of sporting events to grow exponentially, fan base marketing and evaluation is critical in sport marketing. As Mahony and Howard suggest, sport marketers need to develop loyalty among both existing and new sport fans to ensure their competitive edge in expanding their economic potential through these loyal fans and potential new fan bases.[11]

The UK markets are plentiful because sport tends to be both front- and back-page news. This commentary attempts to raise the metaphorical sporting bar in this essential new debate.

Tom Hoof
Vice President–Marketing
Tampa Bay Rays

In MLB, the at-home TV and in-ballpark experiences will have merged. Ballparks will be featuring 10G speed. You'll see plays before they happen. OK—that's not possible, but ballparks will provide tablets for rent. These tablets will provide the game from all sorts of angles, replays, and deals on merchandise and food. Fans will be able to order from their seats and interact with the between-inning entertainment. Video replay for home runs and close plays will become routine. To save time, umpires will have access to tablets and will be able to see instant replays from several different angles almost immediately. No longer will they go to the secret room somewhere under the ballpark. Balls and strikes and most plays will remain the same and will still be part of the game. Requests for a replay will be limited.

Replays of close plays, currently banned on the ballpark big screen, will be allowed. Pitchers will be wearing a harder cap to help prevent brain injuries. MLB will expand to additional cities and include 32 teams. Cities like Charlotte and Nashville will have baseball.

Baseball will regain its status as America's number one pastime. RSN deals will provide huge profits for teams. The quality of the broadcasts will become even better because fans will be able to watch the game from a variety of different angles, with or without announcers. Content will be king for TV. NBC will get back into baseball after a 30-year hiatus. At least five teams will enter into broadcast deals with companies like Google and Netflix.

Curt Gowdy will be reincarnated along with Mel Allen, Harry Caray, and Ted Williams.

Eric Woolworth

President, Business Operations
Miami Heat

Putting on my Nostradamus hat and looking down the road to the years 2020–2025, what do I see for NBA teams? In a word, mobile. By 2020 I would expect that the league, its teams, their RSNs, and the cable operators will have figured out how to deliver mobile content to consumers effectively and profitably, including live NBA game action. But beyond the obvious content play, mobile technology holds the key for enhancing the consumer experience. Existing consumer data paints a clear picture of people increasingly relying on their mobile devices to purchase goods, to travel, to receive information, and to deliver information. Although our industry has not been on the cutting edge, I expect that by 2020 we will have caught up. Ticketing technology is on the verge of being able to deliver reliable venue access in a consumer-friendly way. Imagine having your game ticket pop up on your mobile screen when you get within 100 yards of the venue; that possibility is a lot closer than many people believe. Right behind access will come the ability to create cashless environments in our arenas without

having to rely on fan loyalty cards; everything a fan needs to buy hot dogs, jerseys, and the like will be on their phones. And the best part is that, although teams will provide a more consumer-friendly experience, they will use this mobile technology to achieve the holy grail of getting a true 360-degree view of their fans. The technological backbone of the mobile platform will allow teams to track consumer spending in venue like never before, which in turn will allow teams to craft more direct plans and benefits tailored to its different kinds of fans. By the years 2020–2025 I expect that we will have moved beyond the phase of early adopters and into widespread use of mobile technology to create a dynamic new mobile NBA world.

Hunter Lochmann

Chief Marketing Officer
University of Michigan Athletics

In my two and a half years of working in college athletics, I've seen many differences in how professional sports are run and operated. Many reasons account for these variations, and, of course, there are pros and cons to each. But at the end of the day, the passion that resides within college athletics cannot be topped. This passion positions college athletics as the sport property most likely to emerge with the highest growth between its fan and corporate metrics (ratings, revenue, sponsorship, and so on). But this prospect of rapid growth comes with its share of questions as to what the future will look like. So what could the college athletics landscape look like in 2020?

- **Governing body**. Will the NCAA exist in the same form as it does today, or will a new governing body oversee the schools that have elite football programs? As of this writing, the call for NCAA reform is at a fever pitch because of the realization that the same set of rules and guidelines cannot work for all schools and all sports. Unless the NCAA can change this rigid one-size-fits-all mentality, we may see a new acronym governing the largest athletics schools across the nation.

- **Paying student-athletes**. Speaking of the NCAA, all eyes are on the Ed O'Bannon vs. NCAA lawsuit, which challenges the NCAA's use of student-athletes' images for the organization's commercial purposes. Recently, additional student-athletes have joined this class-action suit. The ultimate decision could have profound implications for compensation for student-athletes. Space limitations preclude extensive discussion of this debate, but if college athletics departments ultimately have to pay student-athletes, the money will need to come from somewhere, most likely at the expense of something else like fielding certain sports.

- **Conference realignment**. I'm lucky. I work for a school that is a member of a strong conference in the Big 10. I didn't realize this when I got here, but I do now because a strong conference is paramount for revenue growth, brand building, and brand consistency. We've seen some changes to the Big 10, but that is only through adding schools (Rutgers, Maryland) rather than either disbanding or becoming less recognizable (e.g., Big East). Without lucrative TV packages, will these smaller conferences survive, or will we have a handful of megaconferences consisting of 16 to 20 or more schools?

- **Nonprofit in a profit-seeking world**. If college athletics departments were listed on a stock exchange and you were a savvy investor, you would do your research and invest elsewhere. Only 22 Division I colleges operated in the black last year (out of approximately 120 schools playing Division I football), and those that made money work on the slimmest of operating surpluses (a margin no investor would be comfortable with). Unfortunately, most fans read and hear about all the money that athletics departments receive from the networks, ticket sales, sponsors, and so on, but they don't realize the significant expenses it takes to run an athletics department. For instance, at Michigan, one small (yet significant) example is the cost of athletics scholarships. This past calendar season, we paid the university $18 million to fund the athletics scholarships that exist across the 31 sports and more than 900 student-athletes. Out-of-state annual tuition costs close to $60,000, and no parameters are placed on coaches about where to recruit. Thus, in sparing no expense, these are real dollars spent to obtain the best student-athletes from around the world. If you were to look at another school's ledger, you'd see that the university either funds all of its athletics scholarships or pays a good portion of it. Along the lines of obtaining the best student-athletes

comes the need for top-notch facilities. In the world of college recruiting, an arms race has developed regarding who has the biggest, most comfortable, and most impressive facilities (stadium, practice facility, academic center, strength and conditioning, and so on). In this area, no funds are coming from an owner's deep pocket, a government-funded tax program, or any other tactic normally derived at the professional level. In college, stadiums are built through athletics department funds. So what does all this mean? College athletics departments need to raise more money than ever, and one of the more important levers we control is ticket pricing and the associated seat donations. When creating football pricing for future years, we need to walk a fine line between raising prices and donations and outpricing our fan base because Michigan athletics cannot be successful without a full Michigan Stadium.

- **At-game versus at-home experience**. Even in 2013, we focused hard on keeping Michigan Stadium (and all venues) full and making sure that fans continue to enjoy the at-game experience in comparison with the at-home experience. When ticket prices increase, fans expect more and they should—better customer service, better food, better merchandise, a great home schedule, and a great atmosphere. These concerns are not unique to college athletics; all entertainment options fight the same battle. We chip away at improving each of these aspects with a strong emphasis on the experience and atmosphere of attending events at Michigan. Football Saturdays are entrenched in the plans and memories of hundreds of thousands of Michigan alumni. The event includes not just a three-hour football game but also a weekend of plans, tailgating, watching the band march in pregame, and singing "The Victors" at the end of a great win. This advantage held by colleges cannot be replicated, but we need to supplement it during the three-hour window of the game through event presentation elements that create "wow" experiences. What are the things that fans will remember after each game that they would have missed had they stayed at home? Flyovers always get a "wow," but what will the innovations be in 2020? Connected to the at-game experience is the use of technology. Fans expect that their technology experiences will include all the amenities that they are accustomed to at home—fast Wi-Fi and cell service to ensure that the second-screen experience is available, quick and easy points of sale when purchasing food and merchandise, and, of course, innovations in engaging fans in attendance through technology. Michigan in 2013 had none of these for a number of reasons (but we are working on it). Michigan in 2020 needs to have these elements or we risk losing fans to their home TVs.

These are just some of the things that I think about as the chief marketing officer when looking into the future. These issues don't take into account the myriad of other subjects that cross the athletics director's plate (student-athlete academics, student-athlete welfare, compliance, and so on). Although we don't know what the future holds, we do know that college athletics will continue to grow in fans, opportunities, and innovations.

Mike Boykin

EVP Sports Marketing
GMR Marketing

- **Global economic shifts**. As sponsors continue to grow globally, every major U.S.-based sport league has a Euro division to provide brands the global platform that they demand. In addition, Latin America and its growing number of billionaires become a new focal point of global growth as the increased market value of water creates wealth on par with that of Middle East oil sheiks in the 1990s and 2000s. As a result, South American football leagues grow to rival the Premier League.

- **Safety**. Research on concussions and the tragic first on-field death of a professional athlete because of head trauma result in mass changes to every league's safety policy. The NFL expands its ban on hits to include velocity, and linemen no longer begin plays in a crouched position. In baseball, pitchers and corner infielders wear helmets, and heading the ball is no longer allowed in soccer. Boxing and MMA fighters wear padded Olympic-style headgear. Fighting is outlawed in hockey. Despite these changes, TV ratings in all properties continue on their six-year growth curve after the stock market crash of 2019. Technology advances change the equipment in major sports annually as teams get real-time information on head and joint injuries.

- **College**. The 10-year anniversary of the College Football Championship is celebrated with a new $100 billion multimedia and content deal with NBC Sports Group. The 32-team playoff has exceeded all expectations and has surpassed the NFL playoffs and Super Bowl as America's premier sporting event. NBC Sports' deal further cements the network as the clear leader in sport in North America and continues ESPN's recent slide in the broadcasting and content world.

- **2024 Philly Olympics**. The return of the Summer Games to the United States for the first time in 28 years creates unprecedented fan, media, and corporate interest. It also marks the first major sporting event for which NBC will roll out its virtual ticket, which allows fans to purchase access to live video feeds from various viewing areas in the stadiums and arenas for varying prices. When used with Google Glass 9.0, the service promises to revolutionize the out-of-arena experience for fans.

- **The new generation**. After half a decade of transition regarding the succession of many of the professional teams owned by one family for generations, a new breed of younger owners has replaced legendary names like Jones, Steinbrenner, Hendrick, and Wirtz after their families opted to divest ownership because of the new laws governing estate taxes. This new collection of owners, who made their fortunes in the post–Great Recession resurgence of the banking industry, are redefining franchise finances as teams cope with the death of public stadium and arena financing.

Stacey Allaster

Chairman and CEO
Women's Tennis Association

In 2023 the WTA will celebrate 50 years since its founding by Billie Jean King—five decades of achievement and business growth that transcended sport, sending a strong message about the potential of women in any modern, progressive society. The WTA's role as a global force for empowerment and equality will remain at the heart of the WTA's competitive differentiator. Over the next 10 years we envision transforming ourselves from the number one premier sport and entertainment property for women to the most inspirational and exciting sport entertainment experience on Earth.

Ongoing globalization and digital content distribution will be central to the WTA's growth strategy in the next 10 years. Opportunities in Asia and the Pacific will be key, building on the boom experienced by women's tennis in the region after the WTA opened headquarters in Beijing in 2008, which was followed by Singapore's spectacular hosting of the season-ending WTA Championships from 2014 through 2018, coinciding with the opening of a Singapore regional office at the end of 2013 that optimized business development and fan growth in Southeast Asia. Other emerging markets, notably India and Latin and South America, will be increasingly important for the globalization of our fan base.

Indeed, women's professional tennis will be more internationally diverse than ever. By 2011, 10 nations were represented in the top 10 of the world rankings, and the emergence of talent from nontraditional markets could mean that as many as 50 countries will be represented in the top 100. Whether global superstars or local heroes, the very best will continue to be the world's highest paid female athletes. WTA prize money began at $1 million in 1973 and reached $100 million in 2012. We expect that it will near $250 million by 2023.

As we look to product presentation, the traditional tennis powers will remain a force with the four Grand Slam tournaments. These events will continue being more traditional, while WTA tournaments will have evolved from sporting events to true sport entertainment experiences—more intense, epic moments; increased fan participation; and more combined women's and men's events, a winning format according to fans and sponsors. As in recent decades, the number of WTA events is likely to remain in the 55 to 60 range, and by 2023 the WTA will have grown an entry-level professional event into a regional or global series. Today, 5 WTA 125s are being staged in the emerging markets, and by 2023 it can evolve into its own development tour with up to 25 events.

Fan engagement will continue to evolve as the fight for the consumer's limited time and discretionary income will be at all all-time high. Thanks to digital technology and social media, by 2023, fans will be getting even closer to the sport and their favorite athletes. Interactive TV broadcasts will blend live game action with social media and gaming consoles, immersing fans into sport like never before. Gone is the differentiation between cable and terrestrial TV, as cross-platform broadcasts become the industry standard.

Giorgio Gandolfi

Principal
GG Sport Marketing and Communication Services
Cremona, Italy

The economic crisis that began in 2010, and is still continuing in Italy, has badly damaged Italian professional basketball. Many teams have ceased operations, even those with a rich tradition and history of success, such as Benetton Treviso. To predict the scenario in the next 15 years is not easy, but let me concentrate on my crystal ball. I visualize that these Italian professional teams will realize that instituting sport marketing business practices and not just relying on team performance will be an accepted way to operate. After years of trying to be the drop that excavates the rock, a new generation of sport marketers will be seen as a real asset for the clubs. As key members of the front office, they will have much more power and an efficient staff under them, realizing a dream for the sport marketers of past generations. I also see a new generation of club executives—people with open minds, no longer focused only on the team, the players, and the wins and losses. They will consider and run the franchise as a company.

I see the Italian Division I League becoming a real league—with a commissioner a la David Stern who has power to fine teams and executives if they do not follow the rules, a staff of more than five people, and an effective marketing and communication department. In the crystal ball I see also a federation that really takes care of basketball and promotes it to increase interest and participation among children who do not know basketball, a federation not tied, for political reasons, to regional officials who have little interest in basketball but have only, as we say in Italy, interest in their "chair" and privileges.

I see a new generation of people who work in basketball—team and federation executives, coaches, and referees—who have reached the top positions thanks to their skills and based on meritocracy, not because they are sons, relatives, or friends of politicians or of important current or former sport VIPs or executives.

Wait a second, let me see, a final fantastic prediction: I see the teams, the league, and the federation working jointly so that Italian basketball can be an unbelievable example for other sports in this country—new modern arenas, basketball played in all the schools, sold-out crowds, children dribbling in the streets and not playing soccer. Wait! What is that annoying sound? It's the alarm clock. Too bad . . . It was only a dream. An impossible dream? Who knows? Sometimes the miracle happens.

Ward Bullard

Google

Current Situation

Historically, monetization of sport properties was based on ticket sales, but now professional sport depends on media and marketing rights for additional sources of revenue. Despite fans' greater access to content (TV, web, social) from their favorite sport, team, or athlete, the conversation is rarely two-way, and fans feel increasingly on the fringe as their attendance takes a backseat to media partners, sponsorships, and luxury-suite holders.

The 2011 PricewaterhouseCoopers *Changing the Game* report indicated that growth in ticket revenues had slowed dramatically. Attendance at events was taking a greater percentage of fans' discretionary income (as ticket prices increased). Besides the fact that the current core fan base is feeling financial pain, the emerging next generation of fans (called Generation C by YouTube and others) is not likely to devote the same type of discretionary spend on sport. Instead, they are likely to seek quality participatory experiences and to prefer exercise or playing sport to watching sport passively.

Bruce Baillie, PWC New Zealand's markets managing partner behind the report, says, "The over 40s are getting older and over time will diminish, so there is a generational gap developing (where) you have to satisfy the people who are going to games now as well as entertaining the kids or you will lose them and in 10 years' time nobody will be going to the game." Stadiums are a big part of the equation. The strong attendance reported during the first 10 or more years of San Francisco's AT&T Park has been tied directly not only to the Giants' success on the field but also to the successful creation of a compelling entertainment experience that is as much an outdoor cocktail party as it is a baseball stadium.

Moving to a Fan-Centric Model

Just as consumer Internet companies such as Facebook and Google have put concerted effort into knowing their users across devices (from computer to tablet to mobile phone) to drive magical product experiences (and provide additional value to their advertising clients), the sport industry will need to be similarly oriented by 2020 by investing in technology that allows leagues and teams to know a lot more about their fans, thereby creating deeper and more meaningful relationships for fans with the sports that they love.

So how will this work? Fans will expect a much more homelike experience while at stadiums. And we are not talking only about high-speed wireless connectivity. I'm talking about the ability to have your favorite hot dog, beer, and snack ordered automatically on arrival at the stadium, delivered just between the second and third innings as you prefer. Furthermore, when you cannot make that critical game (home or away), you'll have a way of turning your living room (or man cave, if so lucky) into a virtual extension of the stadium, integrating the sights, sounds, and even possibly smells (no, I'm not just talking about Google Nose). You'll also be part game director and part instant replay supervisor. You'll have the ability to control camera angles and replays, and even to mute your least favorite announcer (I promise it's not personal, Joe Buck) while automatically synchronizing your favorite local radio broadcast team (Jon Miller and Dave Flemming).

The folks at South Korea's SK Telecom showcased some of this fan-centric vision at the Mobile World Conference in Barcelona in 2012. They recognized that baseball stadiums in Seoul are microcosms of the future, providing a look into the challenges that will be faced by wireless operators and hardware device manufactures over the next 5 to 10 years. Their NFC-enabled experience brought the fans to the heart of the action, from the moment that they arrived in the parking lot to their arrival in the stadium all the way to the food and merchandise experience.

Fan Fickleness and Flight to Quality

Although it is tough to argue that March Madness is suffering from lack of interest, the same cannot be said for the other four months of the college basketball season. Even though the NCAA Division I men's basketball per-game attendance average was down only slightly during the 2012 season, a *Chronicle of Higher Education analysis* published in March 2012 found that about one in five hoops programs saw an attendance drop of 20 percent or more over the past four seasons. "We are aware that there are regular-season attendance issues in certain places," said then Xavier University athletics director Mike Bobinski, the NCAA Division I Men's Basketball Committee chair for 2012–13.

Of the 10 men's basketball teams that witnessed the most fan attrition over the past four seasons, five are members of the Pac-12, where average crowds dropped from 7,808 in 2010–11 to 7,143 last season. "The product on the floor wasn't up to our performance expectations this year, and that didn't warrant the ticket sales that we're used to. We only had two teams in the NCAA tournament," said conference spokesperson Dave Hirsch. As a season-ticket holder of Stanford men's basketball, I've watched a steady decline in attendance at all levels, from student groups to big boosters. Large chunks of seats are left unoccupied throughout Maples Pavilion as the team has struggled. What was once a hard ticket (only five years ago) is now a hard ticket to give away (judging by my many friends' rejection of my courtside seats). Given the competitive landscape across sport, Stanford is not alone in suffering significant declines.

Furthermore, the growth in sport properties on cable and satellite make new global sports, such as soccer and cricket, more accessible. Sports fans and broadcasters alike have become increasingly attracted to the international soccer leagues (England, Mexico, Germany, and so on) over recent years. As a result, NBC Sports has decided to go all in on the English Premier League, largely accepted as the best league of the world's most popular sport, spending $250 million to show all 380 EPL games live on U.S. television.

Assuming no significant negative externalities (for example, another major labor stoppage or massive concussion backlash), I expect that in 2020 the sport landscape will be organized similarly to today's setup. Although the leagues will have benefited significantly from the wealth creation of the prior decade, the prospects for the decade ahead (the 2020s) will seem less certain. Sponsors and luxury-suite holders will demand more perks and more access (high-roller treatment) if they are to maintain their current spend levels. Because of shortening attention spans and increasingly fractured interest, the sport industry will be challenged to generate the same volume of mind share with the next generation. Although people will still have enthusiasm for attending live sporting events, leagues and teams will need to reflect the evolving fan preferences. It will be less about the game on the field and more about the overall entertainment value. The fan in 2020 will be even more fickle and will spend less time and money on sport products of inferior quality. To remain competitive, the industry must adopt a fan-centric, technology-first model and provide unique, memorable, and highly shareable experiences.

ACTIVITY 16.1 The Future of Sport Marketing

In this WSG activity, you will hear two recent graduates just starting in the sport industry discuss how sport marketing can help an organization and where they see sport marketing in the next five or so years.

Wrap-Up

Although no prognosticator is ever 100 percent accurate, we hope that we have shed some light on issues that the reader should be aware of and then can monitor over the next several years. As the old proverb says, to be forewarned is to be forearmed, so consider yourselves armed with some thoughts from those of us involved in the world of sport marketing on a daily basis. We hope that our thoughts and insights can help you make the types of informed decisions that are essential for success now, in 2020, and beyond.

Endnotes

1. Seymour, A. 2010. *A game of two halves*. Academy of Marketing Conference; Hall, J. et al. 2010. An empirical model of attendance factors at major sporting events, *International Journal of Hospitality Management*, 29(2); Rein, I., Kotler, P., Shields, B. 2006. *The Elusive Fan*. McGraw-Hill, New York: NY.

2. Seymour, A. 2010. *A game of two halves*. Academy of Marketing Conference.

3. Kotler, P. 2003. *Marketing Insights*. John Wiley, New Jersey.

4. www.northampton.ac.uk/downloads/7467-NBS_Future_of_Sport.pdf

5. Kahle, K.A., and Riley, C. 2004. *Sports Marketing and the Psychology of Marketing Communication*. Laurence Erlbaum Associations, New Jersey.

6. Schwartz, E.C., and Hunter, J.D. 2008. *Advanced Theory and Practice in Sport Marketing*. Elsevier, San Diego: CA.

7. Rein, I., Kotler, P., Shields, B. 2006. *The Elusive Fan*. McGraw-Hill, New York: NY, p. 43.

8. *The Observer*, UK, October 28, 2007.

9. Ibid.

10. Rein, I., Kotler, P., Shields, B. 2006. *The Elusive Fan*. McGraw-Hill, New York: NY.

11. Mahoney, D.F., and Howard, D.R. 2001. Sport business in the next decade: A general overview of expected trends, *Journal of Sport Management*, 15(4): 275-296.

Index

Note: The italicized *f* and *t* following page numbers refer to figures and tables, respectively.

Courtesy of Bernard Mullin

Bernard J. Mullin, PhD, is chairman and CEO of the Aspire Group, a leading global management and marketing consulting business focusing on the sport and entertainment industry. He previously served as president and chief executive officer of Atlanta Spirit, LLC, where he was responsible for overseeing all team and business operations for the NBA's Hawks and NHL's Thrashers and management of the world-class Philips Arena.

Mullin has more than 30 years of experience in the sport management industry involving executive positions with professional teams and leagues, where he specializes in start-ups and turnarounds, breaking numerous all-time league ticket sales and attendance records. In addition to his position in Atlanta, Mullin served as the NBA's senior vice president of marketing and team business operations, president and general manager of the IHL's Denver Grizzlies, senior vice president of business operations for the Colorado Rockies, and senior vice president of business for the Pittsburgh Pirates. He has also acted as the owner's representative on major design and construction projects, including Coors Field and University of Denver's award-winning athletic facilities.

Before and during his career in professional sports, Mullin spent several years in intercollegiate athletics and higher education. He served as vice chancellor of athletics for the University of Denver and as professor of sport management at the University of Massachusetts. Mullin holds a PhD in business, an MBA, and an MS in marketing from the University of Kansas, where he coached the varsity soccer program. He holds a BA in business studies from Coventry University in England, where he played soccer semiprofessionally for the Oxford City Football Club.

Courtesy of Stephen Hardy

Stephen Hardy, PhD, was a professor of kinesiology and affiliate professor of history at the University of New Hampshire until his retirement in 2014. In 2003-2004, he served as interim vice provost for undergraduate studies. Hardy has also taught at the University of Massachusetts (where he earned his PhD), the University of Washington, Robert Morris College, and Carnegie Mellon University. Over three decades, he taught courses in sport marketing, athletic administration, and sport history as well as a popular introduction to the sport industry. Besides *Sport Marketing*, his publications include *How Boston Played* (1982, 2003) and numerous articles, book chapters, and reviews in academic presses. He is completing a coauthored history of ice hockey. His reviews and opinions have appeared in popular outlets such as the *Boston Globe*, *New York Times*, and *SportsBusiness Journal*. From 1995 to 1999, he was coeditor of *Sport Marketing Quarterly*. In 1997, he was elected a fellow of the American Academy of Kinesiology and Physical Education. He has won college and university awards for excellence in research and teaching.

Hardy has extensive experience in college athletics. He played hockey for Bowdoin College in the late 1960s and cocaptained the 1969-70 team with his twin brother, Earl. After coaching stints at Vermont Academy and Amherst College, he joined the Eastern College Athletic Conference in 1976, where he served as assistant commissioner and hockey supervisor until 1979. During that time, he supervised collegiate championships in venues such as the Boston Garden and Madison Square Garden, and he worked closely with the NCAA Ice Hockey Committee and its affiliated championships. He served on the board of directors of the America East Athletic Conference from 2000 to 2002. In 2003, he was selected by the Hockey East Association as one of 20 special friends to celebrate the league's 20th anniversary. At UNH he served as faculty representative to the NCAA and chaired the president's Athletics Advisory Committee from 1996 to 2011. He is a founder of the Charles E. Holt Archives of American Hockey, which are located at UNH's Dimond Library. He lives with his wife, Donna, in Durham, New Hampshire.

Courtesy of Bill Sutton

William A. Sutton, EdD, is the founding director and professor at the sport and entertainment business management graduate program in the management department at the University of South Florida. He is the founder and principal of Bill Sutton & Associates, a consulting firm specializing in strategic marketing and revenue enhancement. Sutton has gained national recognition for his ability to meld practical experience in professional sports with academic analysis and interpretation.

His consulting clients cover a who's who of professional athletics: the NBA, WNBA, NHL, Orlando Magic, Phoenix Suns, MSG Sports, and New York Mets. Sutton frequently serves as an expert on the sport business industry. His insights and commentary have appeared in *USA Today, New York Times,* CNBC.com, *Washington Times, Fox Business, Orlando Sentinel, South Florida Sun-Sentinel, Advertising Age,* and *Brand Week.* On the international front, Sutton is a contributor to the Italian publications *Basketball Gigante* and *FIBA Assist.*

Sutton served as vice president of team marketing and business operations for the National Basketball Association. In addition to working at the NBA, Sutton was past president of the North American Society for Sport Management (NASSM), a founding member and past president of the Sport Marketing Association (SMA), president of the Southern Sport Management Association, a special events coordinator for the City of Pittsburgh, a YMCA director, vice president of information services for an international sport marketing firm, and commissioner of the Mid-Ohio Conference. He was inducted into the College of Education Hall of Fame at Oklahoma State University (2003) and as an inaugural member of the Robert Morris University Sport Management Hall of Fame (2006), and received lifetime achievement awards from the Southern Sport Management Association (2012) and the Sport Entertainment & Venues Tomorrow conference at the University of South Carolina. He lives with his wife, Shana, in Tampa and Clearwater Beach, Florida.